# SEATTLE
# BEST PLACES

The most discriminating guide to Seattle's
restaurants, shops, hotels, nightlife,
arts, sights, and outings

Edited by
Nancy Leson and Stephanie Irving

SASQUATCH BOOKS
SEATTLE

Seventh edition

Library of Congress Cataloging in Publication Data
Seattle best places: the most discriminating guide to Seattle's restaurants, shops, hotels, nightlife, arts, sights, and outings/edited by Nancy Leson and Stephanie Irving. — 7th ed.
    p. cm.
    Includes Index.
    ISBN 1-57061-055-X
1. Seattle (Wash.) — Guidebooks. 2. Seattle Region (Wash.) — Guidebooks.I. Leson, Nancy, 1959-.
II. Irving, Stephanie, 1962-.
F899.S43S396 1996
917.97'7720443 — dc20

Copy Editor: Don Roberts
Proofreader: Marni Keogh
Cover Design: Karen Schober
Cover illustration: Don Baker
Interior design: Lynne Faulk
Interior illustrations: Jerry Nelson
Fold-out maps: David Berger
Interior maps: Vikki Leib and Charles Reidy
Composition: Kate Basart

The Best Places guidebooks have been published continuously since 1975. Evaluations are based on numerous reports from locals and traveling inspectors. Final judgments are made by the editors. Our inspectors never identify themselves (except over the phone) and never accept free meals, lodgings, or other services. Readers are advised that places listed in previous editions may have closed or changed management, or are no longer recommended by this series. Reviews in this edition are based on information available at press time and are subject to change. The editors welcome information conveyed by users of this book, as long as they have no financial connection with the establishment concerned. All Best Places guides are available at bulk discounts for corporate gifts, conventions, and fund-raising sales for clubs and organizations.

Sasquatch Books
615 Second Avenue, Suite 260
Seattle, Washington 98104
(206)467-4300
email:     books@sasquatchbooks.com
website:   http://www.sasquatchbooks.com

# CONTENTS

**ACKNOWLEDGMENTS** *iv*

**INTRODUCTION** *v*

**HOW TO USE THIS BOOK** *vii*

**RESTAURANTS** *1*

**NIGHTLIFE** *97*

**THE ARTS** *137*

**EXPLORING** *161*

**SHOPPING** *225*

**LODGINGS** *321*

**DAY TRIPS** *341*

**RECREATION** *371*

**ESSENTIALS** *399*

**CALENDAR OF EVENTS** *417*

**INDEX** *430*

# Acknowledgments

Thanks to the many writers and reviewers who helped bring this seventh edition up to date: Anne Abrams, Katherine Alberg, Rachel Bard, Bruce Barnhart, Knute Berger, Peter Blackstock, Mary Anne Christy, Celia Congdon, Connie Cooper, Claire Dederer, Roger Downey, Sheri Doyle, Mark Eleison, Sheila Farr, Jim Goldsmith, Sumi Hahn, Emily Hall, Tom Keogh, Pippa Kiraly, Alicia Comstock Litwin, Paul Litwin, Ann Lovejoy, Erikka Martin, Mac McCarthy, Fred Moody, Cynthia Nims, Ann Paulson, J. Kingston Pierce, Sherrie Saint John, Gary Sarozek, Eric Scigliano, Barbara Spear, and Melissa Trainer.

Special thanks are extended to eagle-eyed copy editor Don Roberts and proofreader Marni Keogh, and to editorial assistants Meghan Heffernan and Jennifer O'Neal.

# Introduction

Seattle is a charming metropolis grown up in the middle of an evergreen forest. It's a city famous for its enduring relationships with Boeing and Bill Gates, Pearl Jam and Pike Place Market, and coffee, always coffee, available in steaming cups from mobile espresso carts that sprout on street corners like mushrooms after a good rain.

It rains here. A lot. At least that's what we tell folks from everywhere else who come to our corner of the Northwest to eye the real estate. But you won't find the denizens of the Emerald City hiding under umbrellas or wasting away indoors. This is a town where cops ride bikes, farmers and fishmongers hawk their wares at open-air markets, gardeners putter be it January or July, and early-morning kayakers paddle in the wake of log booms and container ships.

Situated between sparkling Puget Sound and Lake Washington, and dotted with lakes, Seattle is nearly surrounded by water, with mountains just about everywhere you look. On clear days, Mount Rainier's distant snow-capped presence has even been known to halt commuter traffic—which continues to worsen as the population grows and the city's bedroom communities spread farther afield.

Ours is a food-lover's paradise. The flavors of the Northwest are on display to extraordinary effect in Seattle's renowned Pike Place Market, at high-end supermarkets that are destinations in their own right, and at a growing number of restaurants that are carving a permanent niche in the collective culinary consciousness of visitors from around the nation and the world. Here you'll sample fresh Alaska spot prawns bursting with edible roe; sweet Penn Cove mussels and briny Willapa Bay oysters; Dungeness crab, Copper River salmon, and Hoh River sturgeon. The season's farm-fresh bounty comes to the table in the form of perfect red raspberries, plump Rainier cherries, multicolored peppers of every conceivable shape, Walla Walla sweet onions, and an enticing array of musky-scented wild mushrooms gathered in the secret places few are willing to reveal. The city's artisan bakers have risen to the occasion, producing breads to rival those of their European counterparts. And exotic spices and unusual ingredients that would be hard to find in other cities are as readily available in the neighborhood grocery as they are in Seattle's many ethnic markets and specialty food shops.

When it comes to entertainment, Seattle has a firm place in the spotlight. The "Seattle Sound" continues to be imitated by young musicians everywhere, although the word "grunge" was expunged from the local vocabulary long before the layered, ripped-flannel "look" had its debut on the catwalks in New York. When singer Kurt Cobain bid a final farewell at his Lake Washington home, the city made headlines the world over; and we're proud to say that our Grammy-toting homegrown band, Soundgarden, got its name from a Seattle public art installation. Jazz, too, has strong roots here, and world-class vocalists like Diane Schuur and Ernestine Anderson—who call the city home—sometimes play in surprisingly small venues. Where better to indulge eclectic musical tastes than in Pioneer Square, where numerous clubs offer blues, jazz, R&B, funk, Cajun, and more for a single cover charge.

As for classical music, the Seattle scene is getting surprisingly broad and satisfying. If you can get a ticket, any production by Seattle Opera—which mounts scenically ambitious programs notable for singers who act well—is a rare treat. The Seattle Symphony is full of excellent musicians, and music director Gerard Schwarz does well with modern composers and late Romantics.

Live theater draws audiences whose tastes are as eclectic as the companies that don the greasepaint. From classic drama to full-scale Broadway musicals, high camp to far-out fringe, venues throughout the city provide the stages for a broad spectrum of productions featuring local and national talent.

This is also a movie town: first-run and art-house theaters abound, the annual Seattle International Film Festival is the hottest ticket in town, and Hollywood film crews seem to be setting up klieglights everywhere.

But there's nothing Hollywood about Seattle. We'd just as soon be sprawled out in Victor Steinbrueck Park, watching the ferries with a messy sandwich in hand, than "doing lunch" in some fussy restaurant; we're as likely to be climbing Mount Rainier as climbing Microsoft's corporate ladder; and while the rest of the world sits home drinking instant Nescafé, we're grinding our own fresh-roasted coffee beans and drinking a cup on the fly.

—*The Editors*

# How to Use This Book

This is a rare city guidebook, as candid and frank as it is informative and trustworthy. It is written by and for locals, but visitors will find it just as valuable. Best Places reviewers do not identify themselves when they review an establishment, and they accept no free meals, accommodations, or any other services. These books have no sponsors or advertisers.

**Star Rating System** Every place featured in this book is recommended. We rate restaurants and lodgings on a scale of zero to four stars (with half stars in between), based on uniqueness, enjoyability, loyalty of local clientele, excellence of cooking, performance measured against the place's goals, cleanliness, and professionalism of service. *All listings are recommended, even those with no stars.*

| ★★★★ | The very best in the region |
| ★★★ | Distinguished, many outstanding features |
| ★★ | Some wonderful qualities |
| ★ | A good place |
| **(no stars)** | Worth knowing about, if nearby |
| [*unrated*] | Too new to rate or undergoing major changes |

**Price range** When prices range between two categories (for example, moderate to expensive), the lower one is given. Call ahead to verify, as prices are subject to change

| $$$ | Expensive (more than $80 for dinner for two; more than $100 for lodging for two) |
| $$ | Moderate (between expensive and inexpensive) |
| $ | Inexpensive (less than $30 for dinner for two; less than $60 for lodging for two) |

**Addresses** All listings are in Seattle unless otherwise specified. If an establishment has two Seattle-area locations, we list both addresses; if there are more than two, we list the original, downtown, or recommended branch, followed by the words "other branches."

**Phone Numbers** All calls are local from Seattle (area code 206), except where indicated. Telephone numbers preceded by area code (206) or (360) are long distance from Seattle.

**Map Indicators** The letter-and-number code listed after each phone number refers to the coordinates on the fold-out maps included in this book. Single letters (as in F7) refer to the downtown Seattle map; double letters (FF7) refer to the Greater Seattle map on the flip side.

**Checks and Credit Cards** Many establishments that accept checks require a major credit card for identification. American Express is abbreviated as AE, Diners Club as DC, MasterCard as MC, Visa as V.

**Restaurants**  Our reviews are based on information that was accurate at press time. In the inconstant restaurant business, chefs and serving staff may move from one establishment to another, and a restaurant's menu changes are as likely to reflect the season's bounty and the latest dining trend as a change in chef or ownership. These variables (for better or worse) may affect quality and consistency.

**Lodgings**  Many hotels and other lodgings fill up quickly due to the influx of tourists (in summer) and business-folk (year-round). It is wise to make reservations as far in advance as possible. Some B&Bs have two-night minimum-stay requirements and particular cancellation policies. Some do not welcome children or smokers. Most prefer that you leave your pets at home. Ask before making your reservations.

**KIDS and FREE**  We have provided [KIDS] and [FREE] labels throughout the book to indicate attractions and events that are especially suited to children or that are free of charge.

**Reader Reports**  At the end of the book is a report form. We receive hundreds of reports from readers suggesting new places or agreeing or disagreeing with our assessments. They greatly help in our research and help inform our evaluations. We encourage and appreciate your response.

**RESTAURANT INDEX** *3*

Star Rating *3*

Location *4*

Food and Other Features *6*

**TOP 200 RESTAURANTS** *13*

# Restaurant Index

## STAR RATING

★★★★
Campagne
Georgian Room (Four
    Seasons Olympic Hotel)
The Herbfarm
Lampreia

★★★½
Adriatica
Dahlia Lounge
Fullers (Seattle Sheraton
    Hotel and Towers)
Gerard's Relais de Lyon
Rover's

★★★
Al Boccalino
Cafe Campagne
Cafe Juanita
Chez Shea
Etta's Seafood
The Hunt Club
    (Sorrento Hotel)
Il Bistro
Il Terrazzo Carmine
Kaspar's
Le Gourmand
The Painted Table
    (Alexis Hotel)
Pirosmani
Place Pigalle
Ponti Seafood Grill
Queen City Grill
Ray's Boathouse
Saleh al Lago
Shiro's
Sostanza
Szmania's
Tulio (Hotel Vintage
    Park)
Union Bay Cafe
Wild Ginger

★★½
Bistro Provencal
Cafe Flora
Cafe Lago
Canlis
Flying Fish
I Love Sushi
Isabella Ristorante
Marco's Superclub
Nikko (Westin Hotel)

Shanghai Garden
Shea's Lounge

★★
Anthony's Beach Cafe
Anthony's HomePort
Assaggio Ristorante
Azalea's Fountain Court
Bahn Thai
Boca
Cafe Nola
Chandler's Crabhouse and
    Fresh Fish Market
Chanterelle Specialty
    Foods
Chinook's at Salmon Bay
Chutney's
Ciao Italia
Coastal Kitchen
Crêpe de Paris
Cutters Bayhouse
Cyclops
El Greco
F. X. McRory's Steak,
    Chop, and Oyster House
Filiberto's
Firenze
Fremont Noodle House
Hi-Spot Cafe
Il Bacio
Italianissimo
Izumi
Kabul
Kaizuka Teppanyaki and
    Sushi Bar
The Kaleenka
Kikuya
Madison Park Cafe
Maltby Cafe
Manca's
Maple Leaf Grill
McCormick and Schmick's
Metropolitan Grill
Mona's
The New Mikado
    Restaurant
Pandasia
Pasta & Co.
Pegasus Pizza and Pasta
Phoenecia at Alki
The Pink Door
Pleasant Beach Grill

R & L Home of Good
    Barbeque No. 1
Red Mill Burgers
Ristorante Buongusto
Ristorante Machiavelli
Ristorante Paradiso
Ruby's on Bainbridge
Salvatore
Santa Fe Cafe
Sawatdy Thai Cuisine
Sea Garden
Sea Garden of Bellevue
Shamiana
Shamshiri
Shuckers (Four Seasons
    Olympic Hotel)
Snappy Dragon
Still Life in Fremont
Swingside Cafe
TestaRossa
Thai Restaurant
Tommy Thai's
Tosoni's
Un Deux Trois
Yarrow Bay Grill and
    Beach Cafe
Zeek's Pizza

★½
Ayutthaya
Bizzaro Italian Cafe
Bush Garden
Cactus
Cafe Vizcaya
Caveman Kitchens
The Chile Pepper
Ciao Bella Ristorante
DaVinci's Flying Pizza and
    Pasta
El Puerco Lloron
5 Spot Cafe
The Four Swallows
Gravity Bar
Il Paesano
Kamalco
Kells
Koryo Restaurant
La Dolce Vita
Maddox Grill
Maggie Bluffs
Maximilien in the Market
Mediterranean Kitchen

Moghul Palace
Musashi's Sushi & Grill
The New Jake
  O'Shaughnessey's
Nicolino
Palisade
Phad Thai
Piecora's
Provinces Asian Restaurant
  & Bar
Restaurant Shilla
Saigon Bistro
Salute
Serafina
74th Street Ale House
Siam on Broadway
Spazzo
Stage Right Cafe
Tokyo Japanese Restaurant
Two Bells Tavern
Union Square Grill
Yanni's Lakeside Cafe

★
Armadillo Barbecue
Beeliner Diner
Big Time Pizza
Blacksheep Cafe and
  Catering
Broadway New American
  Grill
Burk's Cafe
Burrito Loco
Cafe Illiterati
Cafe Septième
Cafe Veloce

Catfish Corner
Continental Restaurant
  and Pastry Shop
Copacabana
Cucina! Cucina!
Dixie's BBQ
Emmett Watson's Oyster
  Bar
Ezell's Fried Chicken
Fremont Classic Pizza and
  Trattoria
Harbor City Barbecue
  House
Huong Binh
Ivar's Acres of Clams and
  Fish Bar
Ivar's Indian Salmon House
Ivar's Mukilteo Landing
Judkins Barbecue
  Restaurant
Kirkland Roaster & Ale
  House
Lombardi's Cucina
Lombardi's Cucina of
  Issaquah
Luna Park Cafe
Mae's Phinney Ridge Cafe
Mandarin Garden
Neelam's Authentic Indian
  Cuisine
Noble Court
Philadelphia Fevre Steak &
  Hoagie Shop
Pizzeria Pagliacci
Pizzuto's Italian Cafe
Pogacha

Pon Proem
Rikki Rikki
The Roost
The Rose Bakery and
  Bistro
Seoul Olympic Restaurant
Si Senor
Sisters European Snacks
Stone Way Cafe
Streamliner Diner
Sunlight Cafe
Surrogate Hostess
Sushi-Ten
Tandoor
Taqueria Guaymas
Thai Terrace
That's Amore
Third Floor Fish Cafe
Thirteen Coins
Thompson's Point of View
Three Girls Bakery
Trattoria Mitchelli
Triangle Tavern
Viet My
Waters, a Lakeside Bistro
Zula

**[no stars]**
Bakeman's
Gene's Ristorante
Gordo's
Maya's
Pho Bac
Seattle Bagel Bakery
Spud Fish and Chips

## LOCATION

**Bainbridge Island**
Cafe Nola
The Four Swallows
Pleasant Beach Grill
Ruby's on Bainbridge
Sawatdy Thai Cuisine
Streamliner Diner

**Ballard/Shilshole**
Anthony's HomePort
Burk's Cafe
Cafe Illiterati
Gordo's
Le Gourmand
Lombardi's Cucina
Ray's Boathouse

**Bellevue**
Azalea's Fountain Court
Cucina! Cucina!
Dixie's BBQ
Firenze
I Love Sushi
Mediterranean Kitchen
Moghul Palace
The New Jake
  O'Shaughnessey's
Noble Court
Pasta & Co.
Pogacha
Sea Garden of Bellevue
Seoul Olympic Restaurant
Spazzo

Sushi-Ten
Tokyo Japanese Restaurant
Tosoni's

**Belltown**
Cyclops
Flying Fish
Lampreia
Marco's Superclub
Queen City Grill
Shiro's
Two Bells Tavern

**Bothell**
Blacksheep Cafe and
  Catering
Gerard's Relais de Lyon

**Broadway**
(*see also Capitol Hill*)
Broadway New American
  Grill
Cafe Septième
El Greco
Gravity Bar
Pizzeria Pagliacci
Siam on Broadway
TestaRossa

**Burien**
Filiberto's

**Capitol Hill**
(*see also Broadway*)
Ayutthaya
Coastal Kitchen
Kamalco
Piecora's
Ristorante Machiavelli
Surrogate Hostess
Zula

**Central District**
Catfish Corner
Ezell's Fried Chicken
Judkins Barbecue
  Restaurant
R & L Home of Good
  Barbeque No. 1
Thompson's Point of View

**Crown Hill**
Burrito Loco

**Denny Regrade**
Restaurant Shilla

**Des Moines/Redondo**
Anthony's HomePort

**Downtown**
Assaggio Ristorante
Crêpe de Paris
Dahlia Lounge
Fullers (Seattle Sheraton
  Hotel and Towers)
Georgian Room (Four
  Seasons Olympic Hotel)
Gravity Bar
Isabella Ristorante
The Kaleenka
McCormick and Schmick's
Metropolitan Grill
Nikko (Westin Hotel)
The Painted Table
  (Alexis Hotel)
Pasta & Co.
Seattle Bagel Bakery

Shuckers (Four Seasons
  Olympic Hotel)
Tulio (Hotel Vintage Park)
Un Deux Trois
Union Square Grill
Wild Ginger

**Eastlake**
Serafina

**Edmonds**
Anthony's Beach Cafe
Anthony's HomePort
Chanterelle Specialty
  Foods
Ciao Italia
Provinces Asian Restaurant
  & Bar

**Fall City**
The Herbfarm

**First Hill**
The Hunt Club
  (Sorrento Hotel)

**Fisherman's Terminal**
Chinook's at Salmon Bay

**Fremont**
Fremont Classic Pizza and
  Trattoria
Fremont Noodle House
Ponti Seafood Grill
Still Life in Fremont
Swingside Cafe
Triangle Tavern

**Green Lake**
Mona's
Saleh al Lago

**Greenwood/Phinney Ridge**
Mae's Phinney Ridge Cafe
Phad Thai
Red Mill Burgers
Santa Fe Cafe
74th Street Ale House
Yanni's Lakeside Cafe
Zeek's Pizza

**International District**
Bush Garden
Harbor City Barbecue
  House
Huong Binh
Kaizuka Teppanyaki and
  Sushi Bar
The New Mikado
  Restaurant
Pho Bac

Saigon Bistro
Sea Garden
Shanghai Garden

**Issaquah**
Cucina! Cucina!
Lombardi's Cucina of
  Issaquah
Mandarin Garden
Nicolino
The Roost
Stage Right Cafe

**Kent**
Caveman Kitchens

**Kirkland**
Anthony's HomePort
Bistro Provencal
Cafe Juanita
Cafe Veloce
Cucina! Cucina!
DaVinci's Flying Pizza and
  Pasta
Izumi
Kirkland Roaster & Ale
  House
Rikki Rikki
Ristorante Paradiso
The Rose Bakery and
  Bistro
Shamiana
Third Floor Fish Cafe
Tommy Thai's
Waters, a Lakeside Bistro
Yarrow Bay Grill and
  Beach Cafe

**Lake City**
Caveman Kitchens

**Leschi/Madrona**
Hi-Spot Cafe

**Madison Park/Madison Valley**
Cactus
Cafe Flora
Madison Park Cafe
Manca's
Philadelphia Fevre Steak &
  Hoagie Shop
Rover's
Sostanza

**Magnolia/Interbay**
Maggie Bluffs
Palisade
Pandasia
Szmania's

---

**Maltby**
Maltby Cafe

**Mercer Island**
Pon Proem

**Montlake**
Cafe Lago

**Mount Baker/Seward Park**
Maya's
Pizzuto's Italian Cafe
That's Amore

**Mukilteo**
Ivar's Mukilteo Landing

**North End**
Koryo Restaurant

**North Lake Union**
Ivar's Indian Salmon House

**Pike Place Market**
Cafe Campagne
Campagne
Chez Shea
Copacabana
Cutters Bayhouse
El Puerco Lloron
Emmett Watson's Oyster
   Bar
Etta's Seafood
Il Bistro
Kells
Maximilien in the Market
The Pink Door
Place Pigalle
Shea's Lounge
Sisters European Snacks
Three Girls Bakery

**Pioneer Square**
Al Boccalino
Bakeman's
F. X. McRory's Steak,
   Chop, and Oyster House
Il Terrazzo Carmine
Trattoria Mitchelli
Viet My

**Queen Anne/Seattle Center**
Bahn Thai
Canlis
Chutney's
5 Spot Cafe
Kaspar's
Mediterranean Kitchen
Pasta & Co.
Pirosmani
Pizzeria Pagliacci
Restaurant Shilla
Ristorante Buongusto
Thai Restaurant
Zeek's Pizza

**Ravenna/Wedgwood**
Ciao Bella Ristorante
La Dolce Vita
Pandasia
Salute
Santa Fe Cafe

**Redmond**
Big Time Pizza
Il Bacio
Kikuya
Si Senor

**Renton**
Gene's Ristorante

**Richmond Beach/
Mountlake Terrace**
Maddox Grill
Thai Terrace

**Roosevelt/Maple Leaf**
Maple Leaf Grill
Salvatore
Shamshiri
Snappy Dragon
Sunlight Cafe

**Sand Point/Laurelhurst**
Union Bay Cafe

**Sea-Tac**
Thirteen Coins

**South Lake Union**
Chandler's Crabhouse and
   Fresh Fish Market
Cucina! Cucina!
I Love Sushi
Thirteen Coins

**University District**
Continental Restaurant and
   Pastry Shop
Il Paesano
Neelam's Authentic Indian
   Cuisine
Pizzeria Pagliacci
Tandoor

**University Village**
Pasta & Co.

**Wallingford**
Beeliner Diner
Bizzaro Italian Cafe
Cafe Vizcaya
The Chile Pepper
Kabul
Musashi's Sushi & Grill
Stone Way Cafe

**Waterfront (Alaskan Way)**
Ivar's Acres of Clams and
   Fish Bar

**West Seattle/Alki**
Adriatica
Boca
Luna Park Cafe
Pegasus Pizza and Pasta
Phoenecia at Alki
Spud Fish and Chips

**Westlake**
Adriatica

**White Center**
Taqueria Guaymas

**Woodinville**
Armadillo Barbecue
Italianissimo

## FOOD AND OTHER FEATURES

**Afghan**
Kabul

**All Night**
Thirteen Coins

**Bagels**
Seattle Bagel Bakery

**Bakery**
The Rose Bakery and
   Bistro
Surrogate Hostess
Three Girls Bakery

**Barbecue**
Armadillo Barbecue

Caveman Kitchens
Dixie's BBQ
Harbor City Barbecue
   House
Judkins Barbecue
   Restaurant
R & L Home of Good
   Barbeque No. 1

## Breakfast
5 Spot Cafe
Beeliner Diner
Blacksheep Cafe and
  Catering
Broadway New American
  Grill
Cafe Campagne
Cafe Illiterati
Cafe Nola
Cafe Septième
Chanterelle Specialty
  Foods
Coastal Kitchen
Continental Restaurant and
  Pastry Shop
Georgian Room (Four
  Seasons Olympic Hotel)
Hi-Spot Cafe
Luna Park Cafe
Mae's Phinney Ridge Cafe
Maggie Bluffs
Maltby Cafe
Saigon Bistro
Seattle Bagel Bakery
Sisters Cafe
Still Life in Fremont
Stone Way Cafe
Streamliner Diner
Sunlight Cafe
Surrogate Hostess
The Hunt Club (Sorrento
  Hotel)
The Painted Table (Alexis
  Hotel)
Thirteen Coins
Three Girls Bakery
Trattoria Mitchelli
Tulio (Hotel Vintage Park)
Waters, a Lakeside Bistro

## Breakfast All Day
Beeliner Diner
Broadway New American
  Grill
Coastal Kitchen
Continental Restaurant and
  Pastry Shop
5 Spot Cafe
Mae's Phinney Ridge Cafe
Stone Way Cafe
Thirteen Coins

## Brunch
Anthony's HomePort
Boca
Cafe Campagne
Cafe Flora

Cafe Illiterati
Chandler's Crabhouse and
  Fresh Fish Market
Cutters Bayhouse
Cyclops
Ivar's Indian Salmon House
Lombardi's Cucina
Lombardi's Cucina of
  Issaquah
Maddox Grill
Manca's
Marco's Superclub
Maximilien in the Market
Palisade
Ponti Seafood Grill
The Roost
Sunlight Cafe
TestaRossa

## Burgers
Blacksheep Cafe and
  Catering
Broadway New American
  Grill
Gordo's
Maggie Bluffs
Maple Leaf Grill
Red Mill Burgers
Stone Way Cafe
Two Bells Tavern

## Cajun/Creole
Burk's Cafe
Catfish Corner

## Caribbean
Boca

## Chinese
Harbor City Barbecue
  House
Mandarin Garden
Noble Court
Pandasia
Sea Garden
Sea Garden of Bellevue
Shanghai Garden
Snappy Dragon

## Coffee House
Cafe Illiterati
Still Life in Fremont

## Continental
Azalea's Fountain Court
Canlis
Georgian Room (Four
  Seasons Olympic Hotel)
Pleasant Beach Grill
Tosoni's

## Delivery
Pandasia
Piecora's
Pizzeria Pagliacci
Snappy Dragon
Zeek's Pizza

## Desserts Excellent
Adriatica
Azalea's Fountain Court
Cafe Septième
Dahlia Lounge
Etta's Seafood
Il Bacio
Surrogate Hostess
Tulio (Hotel Vintage Park)

## Dim Sum
Noble Court

## Diner
Beeliner Diner
5 Spot Cafe
Mae's Phinney Ridge Cafe
Stone Way Cafe
Streamliner Diner

## Ethiopian/East African
Zula

## Fireplace
Azalea's Fountain Court
Bistro Provencal
Cafe Juanita
Filiberto's
Gerard's Relais de Lyon
The Hunt Club
  (Sorrento Hotel)
Pleasant Beach Grill
Pogacha
Ponti Seafood Grill
The Roost
Sostanza

## Fish 'n' Chips
*(see also Seafood)*
Anthony's Beach Cafe
Chinook's at Salmon Bay
Emmett Watson's Oyster
  Bar
Gordo's
Ivar's Indian Salmon House
Ivar's Mukilteo Landing
Spud Fish and Chips

## French
Bistro Provencal
Cafe Campagne
Campagne
Crêpe de Paris

Gerard's Relais de Lyon
Le Gourmand
Maximilien in the Market
Rover's
Un Deux Trois

## German
Szmania's

## Gourmet Takeout/Deli
Cafe Campagne
Pasta & Co.
Un Deux Trois

## Greek
Continental Restaurant and
    Pastry Shop
Yanni's Lakeside Cafe

## Grill
Broadway New American
    Grill
F. X. McRory's Steak,
    Chop, and Oyster House
Kirkland Roaster & Ale
    House
Maddox Grill
Maple Leaf Grill
McCormick and Schmick's
Metropolitan Grill
The New Jake
    O'Shaughnessey's
Palisade
Pleasant Beach Grill
Ponti Seafood Grill
Queen City Grill
The Roost
Union Square Grill
Yarrow Bay Grill and
    Beach Cafe

## Health-Conscious
Blacksheep Cafe and
    Catering
Cafe Flora
Gravity Bar
Still Life in Fremont
Sunlight Cafe

## Indian (India)
Chutney's
Moghul Palace
Neelam's Authentic Indian
    Cuisine
Shamiana
Tandoor

## Inventive Ethnic
Cafe Nola
Chanterelle Specialty Foods

Coastal Kitchen
Cutters Bayhouse
Cyclops
Dahlia Lounge
Etta's Seafood
Fullers (Seattle Sheraton
    Hotel and Towers)
Hi-Spot Cafe
Maple Leaf Grill
Marco's Superclub
Mona's
Ruby's on Bainbridge
Shea's Lounge
Sostanza
Stage Right Cafe
Swingside Cafe
Szmania's
Triangle Tavern
Union Bay Cafe
Waters, a Lakeside Bistro
Yarrow Bay Grill and
    Beach Cafe

## Irish
Kells

## Italian
Al Boccalino
Assaggio Ristorante
Bizzaro Italian Cafe
Cafe Juanita
Cafe Lago
Cafe Veloce
Ciao Bella Ristorante
Ciao Italia
Cucina! Cucina!
DaVinci's Flying Pizza
    and Pasta
Filiberto's
Firenze
Fremont Classic Pizza and
    Trattoria
Gene's Ristorante
Il Bacio
Il Bistro
Il Paesano
Il Terrazzo Carmine
Isabella Ristorante
Italianissimo
La Dolce Vita
Lombardi's Cucina
Lombardi's Cucina of
    Issaquah
Nicolino
Pasta & Co.
Pegasus Pizza and Pasta
The Pink Door
Pizzuto's Italian Cafe

Ristorante Buongusto
Ristorante Machiavelli
Ristorante Paradiso
Saleh al Lago
Salute
Salvatore
Serafina
Sostanza
Swingside Cafe
TestaRossa
That's Amore
Trattoria Mitchelli
Tulio (Hotel Vintage Park)

## Japanese
Bush Garden
I Love Sushi
Izumi
Kaizuka Teppanyaki and
    Sushi Bar
Kikuya
Musashi's Sushi & Grill
The New Mikado
    Restaurant
Nikko (Westin Hotel)
Restaurant Shilla
Rikki Rikki
Shiro's
Sushi-Ten
Tokyo Japanese Restaurant

## Kid-Friendly
Anthony's Beach Cafe
Anthony's HomePort
Armadillo Barbecue
Blacksheep Cafe and
    Catering
Cafe Flora
Chinook's at Salmon Bay
Cucina! Cucina!
DaVinci's Flying Pizza and
    Pasta
5 Spot
Huong Binh
Ivar's Acres of Clams and
    Fish Bar
Ivar's Indian Salmon House
Ivar's Mukilteo Landing
Madison Park Cafe
Maggie Bluffs
Manca's
Pegasus Pizza and Pasta
Phad Thai
Pizzuto's Italian Cafe
The Roost
Spud Fish and Chips
Surrogate Hostess
Szmania's

**Kitsch**
Armadillo Barbecue
Beeliner Diner
Bizzaro Italian Cafe
Cafe Illiterati
Cyclops
DaVinci's Flying Pizza and
　Pasta
5 Spot Cafe
Luna Park Cafe
Mae's Phinney Ridge Cafe
The Pink Door
Rikki Rikki

**Korean**
Koryo Restaurant
Restaurant Shilla
Seoul Olympic Restaurant

**Late Night**
Broadway New American
　Grill
Campagne
Cafe Septième
Cucina! Cucina!
F. X. McRory's Steak,
　Chop, and Oyster House
Mona's
Queen City Grill
Sea Garden
Spazzo
Thirteen Coins
Trattoria Mitchelli
Two Bells Tavern
Union Square Grill

**Mediterranean**
Adriatica
Cyclops
El Greco
Mona's
Phoenecia at Alki
Pirosmani
Spazzo

**Mexican**
Burrito Loco
The Chile Pepper
El Puerco Lloron
Maya's
Si Senor
Taqueria Guaymas

**Middle Eastern**
Kamalco
Mediterranean Kitchen
Phoenecia at Alki

**Northwest Cuisine**
Azalea's Fountain Court

Chez Shea
Dahlia Lounge
Etta's Seafood
Fullers (Seattle Sheraton
　Hotel and Towers
Georgian Room (Four
　Seasons Olympic Hotel)
Ivar's Indian Salmon House
The Herbfarm
The Hunt Club (Sorrento
　Hotel)
Kaspar's
Lampreia
Le Gourmand
Manca's
The Painted Table (Alexis
　Hotel)
Place Pigalle
Queen City Grill
Rover's
Szmania's
Union Bay Cafe

**Outdoor Dining**
Anthony's Beach Cafe
Anthony's HomePort
Azalea's Fountain Court
Broadway New American
　Grill
Cactus
Campagne
Caveman Kitchens
Chandler's Crabhouse and
　Fresh Fish Market
Copacabana
Cucina! Cucina!
DaVinci's Flying Pizza and
　Pasta
El Puerco Lloron
Emmett Watson's Oyster
　Bar
Filiberto's
Fremont Classic Pizza and
　Trattoria
Gerard's Relais de Lyon
Gordo's
Hi-Spot Cafe
Il Paesano
Il Terrazzo Carmine
Ivar's Acres of Clams and
　Fish Bar
Ivar's Indian Salmon House
Ivar's Mukilteo Landing
Kells
Kirkland Roaster & Ale
　House
Lombardi's Cucina

Madison Park Cafe
Maggie Bluffs
Manca's
Marco's Superclub
The New Jake
　O'Shaughnessey's
The Pink Door
Place Pigalle
Pleasant Beach Grill
Pogacha
Ponti Seafood Grill
The Roost
Rover's
Serafina
Shuckers
Si Senor
Sostanza
Spud Fish and Chips
Still Life in Fremont
Streamliner Diner
Surrogate Hostess
Szmania's
TestaRossa
Triangle Tavern
Un Deux Trois
Waters, a Lakeside Bistro
Yarrow Bay Grill and
　Beach Cafe

**Oyster Bars**
Chinook's at Salmon Bay
Emmett Watson's Oyster
　Bar
F. X. McRory's Steak,
　Chop, and Oyster House
McCormick and Schmick's
Shuckers (Four Seasons
　Olympic Hotel)

**Pan-Asian**
Palisade
Provinces Asian Restaurant
　& Bar
Wild Ginger

**Persian**
Shamshiri

**Pizza**
Assaggio Ristorante
Big Time Pizza
Cafe Lago
Cafe Veloce
Ciao Italia
Cucina! Cucina!
DaVinci's Flying Pizza and
　Pasta
Fremont Classic Pizza
　and Trattoria

---

**Restaurant Index:** *Food and Other Features*　　　9

Gene's Ristorante
Il Paesano
Isabella Ristorante
Lombardi's Cucina
Lombardi's Cucina of
  Issaquah
Maggie Bluffs
Pegasus Pizza and Pasta
Piecora's
Pizzeria Pagliacci
Pizzuto's Italian Cafe
Pogacha
Ristorante Machiavelli
Salute
Salvatore
TestaRossa
That's Amore
Trattoria Mitchelli
Zeek's Pizza

## Private Rooms
Anthony's HomePort
Bistro Provencal
Bush Garden
Cafe Juanita
F. X. McRory's Steak,
  Chop, and Oyster House
Georgian Room (Four
  Seasons Olympic Hotel)
Kaspar's
Kirkland Roaster & Ale
  House
Kaizuka Teppanyaki and
  Sushi Bar
Manca's
Mandarin Garden
McCormick and Schmick's
Metropolitan Grill
The New Mikado
  Restaurant
Nikko (Westin Hotel)
Ponti Seafood Grill
Ray's Boathouse
Sea Garden
Szmania's
Third Floor Fish Cafe
Tulio (Hotel Vintage Park)
Wild Ginger
Yarrow Bay Grill and
  Beach Cafe

## Romantic
Adriatica
Al Boccalino
Azalea's Fountain Court
Campagne
Chez Shea
Dahlia Lounge

Fullers (Seattle Sheraton
  Hotel and Towers
Georgian Room (Four
  Seasons Olympic Hotel)
Il Bistro
Il Terrazzo Carmine
Lampreia
La Dolce Vita
Place Pigalle
Queen City Grill
Rover's
Serafina

## Russian/Georgian
The Kaleenka
Pirosmani

## Satay Bar
Wild Ginger

## Seafood
*(see also Sushi)*
Anthony's Beach Cafe
Anthony's HomePort
Chandler's Crabhouse and
  Fresh Fish Market
Chinook's at Salmon Bay
Cutters Bayhouse
Emmett Watson's Oyster
  Bar
Etta's Seafood
Flying Fish
Ivar's Acres of Clams and
  Fish Bar
Ivar's Indian Salmon House
Ivar's Mukilteo Landing
Maddox Grill
McCormick and Schmick's
The New Jake
  O'Shaughnessey's
Ponti Seafood Grill
Ray's Boathouse
Sea Garden
Sea Garden of Bellevue
Shuckers (Four Seasons
  Olympic Hotel)
Third Floor Fish Cafe
Yarrow Bay Grill and
  Beach Cafe

## Smoking, No
Ayutthaya
Beeliner Diner
Blacksheep Cafe and
  Catering
Burk's Cafe
Cafe Flora
Chanterelle Specialty
  Foods

Chez Shez
The Chile Pepper
Cutters Bayhouse
Dahlia Lounge
Fullers (Seattle Sheraton
  Hotel)
Gravity Bar
The Herbfarm
The Kaleenka
Le Gourmand
Maltby Cafe
Maple Leaf Grill
Musashi's Sushi & Grill
Pandasia
Pasta & Co.
Rover's
Saleh al Lago
Santa Fe Cafe
Seattle Bagel Bakery
Still Life in Fremont
Streamliner Diner
Sunlight Cafe
Swingside Cafe
TestaRossa
Thai Terrace
Three Girls Bakery
Union Bay Cafe

## Soul Food
*(see also Barbecue, Cajun)*
Catfish Corner
Ezell's Fried Chicken
Thompson's Point of View

## Soup/Salad/Sandwich
Bakeman's
Blacksheep Cafe and
  Catering
Cafe Septième
Hi-Spot Cafe
Luna Park Cafe
Madison Park Cafe
Maltby Cafe
Pasta & Co.
Philadelphia Fevre Steak &
  Hoagie Shop
Seattle Bagel Bakery
74th Street Ale House
Sisters European Snacks
Still Life in Fremont
Stone Way Cafe
Streamliner Diner
Sunlight Cafe
Surrogate Hostess
Three Girls Bakery
Two Bells Tavern

## South American
Copacabana
Si Senor

## Southwest
Boca
Cactus
Santa Fe Cafe

## Spanish
Cafe Vizcaya

## Steak
Canlis
F. X. McRory's Steak,
  Chop, and Oyster House
Metropolitan Grill
The Roost
Union Square Grill

## Sushi
*(see also Japanese)*
Bush Garden
I Love Sushi
Izumi
Kaizuka Teppanyaki and
  Sushi Bar
Kikuya
Musashi's Sushi & Grill
Nikko (Westin Hotel)
Rikki Rikki
Shiro's
Sushi-Ten
The New Mikado
  Restaurant
Tokyo Japanese Restaurant

## Takeout Only (or mostly)
Caveman Kitchens
Dixie's BBQ
Ezell's Fried Chicken
Gordo's
Harbor City Barbecue
  House
Judkins Barbecue
  Restaurant
Pasta & Co.
Pizzeria Pagliacci
Red Mill Burgers
Spud Fish and Chips
Surrogate Hostess
Taqueria Guaymas
Three Girls Bakery

## Tapas
Cactus
Cafe Vizcaya
Spazzo

## Tavern
Kells
Maple Leaf Grill
74th Street Ale House
Triangle Tavern
Two Bells Tavern

## Thai
Ayutthaya
Bahn Thai
Fremont Noodle House
Phad Thai
Pon Proem
Sawatdy Thai Cuisine
Siam on Broadway
Thai Restaurant
Thai Terrace
Tommy Thai's

## Vegetarian Options
Blacksheep Cafe and
  Catering
Georgian Room (Four
  Seasons Olympic Hotel)
Shanghai Garden
Sisters Cafe
Still Life in Fremont
Surrogate Hostess

## Vegetarian
Cafe Flora
Gravity Bar
Sunlight Cafe

## Vietnamese
Huong Binh
Pho Bac
Saigon Bistro
Viet My

## View
Anthony's Beach Cafe
Anthony's Homeport
Campagne
Canlis
Chandler's Crabhouse and
  Fresh Fish Market
Chez Shea
Chinook's at Salmon Bay
Copacabana
Cucina! Cucina!
Cutters Bayhouse
Kirkland Roaster & Ale
  House
Maximilien in the Market
Palisade
Pegasus Pizza and Pasta
The Pink Door
Place Pigalle

Ponti Seafood Grill
Ray's Boathouse
Spazzo
Spud Fish and Chips
Third Floor Fish Cafe
Waters, a Lakeside Bistro
Yarrow Bay Grill and
  Beach Cafe

## Wheelchair Accessible
Al Boccalino
Anthony's Beach Cafe
Anthony's HomePort
Armadillo Barbecue
Assaggio Ristorante
Ayutthaya
Azalea's Fountain Court
Bakeman's
Big Time Pizza
Blacksheep Cafe and
  Catering
Broadway New American
  Grill
Burrito Loco
Bush Garden
Cactus
Cafe Campagne
Cafe Flora
Cafe Illiterati
Cafe Juanita
Cafe Lago
Cafe Nola
Cafe Veloce
Cafe Vizcaya
Campagne
Catfish Corner
Chandler's Crabhouse and
  Fresh Fish Market
Chanterelle
Chinook's at Salmon Bay
Chutney's
Ciao Italia
Coastal Kitchen
Continental Restaurant and
  Pastry Shop
Crêpe de Paris
Cucina! Cucina!
Cutters Bayhouse
Dahlia Lounge
Dixie's BBQ
El Greco
Emmett Watson's Oyster
  Bar
Etta's Seafood
F. X. McRory's Steak,
  Chop, and Oyster Hou
Firenze

---

5 Spot Cafe
Flying Fish
Fremont Classic Pizza and
  Trattoria
Fullers (Seattle Sheraton
  Hotel and Towers
Gene's Ristorante
Georgian Room (Four
  Seasons Olympic Hotel)
Gerard's Relais de Lyon
Hi-Spot Cafe
I Love Sushi
Il Bacio
Il Paesano
Il Terrazzo Carmine
Isabella Ristorante
Italianissimo
Ivar's Acres of Clams and
  Fish Bar
Ivar's Indian Salmon House
Ivar's Mukilteo Landing
Izumi
Kamalco
Kaspar's
Kells
Kikuya
Kirkland Roaster & Ale
  House
Koryo Restaurant
La Dolce Vita
Lombardi's Cucina
Lombardi's Cucina of
  Issaquah
Luna Park Cafe
Maddox Grill
Maltby Cafe
Manca's
Mandarin Garden
Maple Leaf Grill
Maximilien in the Market
Maya's
Metropolitan Grill
Moghul Palace
Mona's

Neelam's Authentic Indian
  Cuisine
Nicolino
Nikko (Westin Hotel)
Noble Court
Palisade
Pasta & Co.
Pegasus Pizza and Pasta
Phad Thai
Philadelphia Fevre Steak &
  Hoagie Shop
Phoenecia at Alki
Pizzeria Pagliacci
Pleasant Beach Grill
Pogacha
Pon Proem
Ponti Seafood Grill
Provinces Asian Restaurant
  & Bar
Queen City Grill
Ray's Boathouse
Red Mill Burgers
Restaurant Shilla
Rikki Rikki
Ristorante Machiavelli
Ristorante Paradiso
The Roost
The Rose Bakery
  and Bistro
Saigon Bistro
Saleh al Lago
Salvatore
Santa Fe Cafe
Sawatdy Thai Cuisine
Sea Garden of Bellevue
Seoul Olympic Restaurant
Serafina
74th Street Ale House
Shamiana
Shamshiri
Shiro's
Shuckers (Four Seasons
  Olympic Hotel)
Si Senor

Snappy Dragon
Sostanza
Spazzo
Stage Right Cafe
Still Life in Fremont
Streamliner Diner
Sunlight Cafe
Surrogate Hostess
Sushi-Ten
Swingside Cafe
Szmania's
Taqueria Guaymas
TestaRossa
Thai Restaurant
That's Amore
The Chile Pepper
The Herbfarm
The Hunt Club (Sorrento
  Hotel)
The New Jake
  O'Shaughnessey's
The New Mikado
  Restaurant
The Painted Table (Alexis
  Hotel)
Third Floor Fish Cafe
Thompson's Point of View
Tokyo Japanese Restaurant
Tommy Thai's
Tosoni's
Trattoria Mitchelli
Tulio (Hotel Vintage Park)
Two Bells Tavern
Un Deux Trois
Union Bay Cafe
Union Square Grill
Waters, a Lakeside Bistro
Wild Ginger
Yanni's Lakeside Cafe
Yarrow Bay Grill and
  Beach Cafe
Zeek's Pizza

# Restaurants

**Adriatica** ★★★½ Climbing the two challenging flights of stairs leading to the Adriatica may be the culinary equivalent of reaching the summit of Mount Rainier: always worth the effort. In 1980 Jim Malevitsis opened this handsome tri-level restaurant high above Lake Union where he continues to preside over the comfortably cloistered warren of small dining rooms. Longtime chef Nancy Flume has left her kitchen post in the capable hands of talented young Katherine McKenzie, who continues to turn out Flume's time-tested renderings of herb-kissed grilled meats and other Mediterranean-inspired fare. Start with one of the Greek appetizers; the creamy taramasalata is the best around and the calamari fritti is renowned for the garlic quotient of its skorthallia. If you're inclined to have pasta, the fettuccine with smoked duck is a standout. Only a fool would skip dessert here, and the proof is literally in the pudding of an airy chocolate espresso soufflé and a feathery puff pastry layered with lemon custard. ■ *1107 Dexter Ave N; 285-5000; map:D3; $$$; full bar; AE, DC, MC, V; checks OK; dinner every day.*

**Al Boccalino** ★★★ The rustic Al Boccalino is equally good for a business get-together, a special celebration, or a meaningful dinner for two. Intoxicating drifts of herbs and garlic wafting from the antipasti table greet you when you enter the old brick building just off Pioneer Square. Its chic mottled mustard-and-raw-brick walls are accented with dark wood and stained glass; a skewed shape to the two rooms creates the desired atmosphere of intimacy and intrigue. The menu features the best of southern Italian cuisine with an expanded focus on Italy's other regions. Split for two, any pasta choice would make a great first course. In these times of restraint, the bistecca alla

Fiorentina—a perfectly delicious and perfectly *enormous* aged porterhouse—is not for the faint of heart. It comes simply broiled with olive oil and fresh ground pepper. Seafood shines in this kitchen, where the chefs know a thing or three about timing. Ahi tuna, seared on the outside and pink on the inside, manages to taste at once tart and sweet, thanks to a marinade of red wine vinegar and golden raisins flavored with saffron and rosemary. Succulent sea scallops never see the heat longer than necessary and border on divine. The wine list is solidly Italian, as is the noise level when things get busy. Special kudos to the servers, who show great patience when the rest of your party is a half-hour late. A great place to do lunch, too. ■ *1 Yesler Way; 622-7688; map:N8; $$$; beer and wine; AE, DC, MC, V; checks OK; lunch Mon–Fri, dinner every day.* &

### Anthony's HomePort ★★ ■ Anthony's Beach Cafe ★★ In a
city where most seafood restaurants come in multiples and are based more on marketing concepts than on culinary ideas, Anthony's HomePort stands out. The original on Kirkland's waterfront continues to clone itself onto other nearby shores (Everett, 252-3333; Des Moines, 824-1947; Edmonds, 771-4400; Shilshole Bay, 783-0780), banking hard on the excellent quality of their seafood. Well-deserved raves go to high-profile chef Sally McArthur for overseeing the fishified menu: robust cioppino filled with local mussels and Discovery Bay clams; buttery, crab-packed, Dungeness crab cakes with a ginger plum sauce; a fine rendition of fish 'n' chips; a simple piece of grilled halibut or salmon. Sunday brunch is ordered off a menu—what a refreshing surprise at a waterside restaurant—and Sunday nights draw the blue-hairs and family crowds for all-you-can-eat crabfeeds. Lunches are served at the Everett and Shilshole HomePorts only. The views, of course—over whatever body of water happens to be outside your particular branch's window—are peerless.

**Top 200 Restaurants**

The popular Edmonds extension, **Anthony's Beach Cafe** (771-4400), sells summer year-round: cheeriness, generous drinks, and all-you-can-eat fish 'n' chips on Monday. Tuesday sees the ante upped with all-you-can-eat prawns. Salads, sandwiches, steamed shellfish, pastas, and great fish tacos round out the inexpensive menus both here and at Anthony's Oyster Bar & Grill (downstairs from the Des Moines HomePort). Both are open for lunch and dinner. At press time, a downtown outpost is scheduled to open at the Port of Seattle's Bell Street Pier, with a seafood cafe and a fish 'n' chips bar in addition to a more upscale dining room. ■ *135 Lake St S, Kirkland (and branches); 822-0225; map:EE3; $$; full bar; AE, DC, MC, V; checks OK; dinner every day, brunch Sun.* &

### Armadillo Barbecue ★ Leave refinement in the glove compartment when you enter this West Texas barbecue joint plopped

down in the wilds of Woodinville. "Ya just can't use enough disinfectant on these tables," claim owners Bob and Bruce Gill, wielding a garden sprayer. The brothers serve up their own brand of perverse humor as a regular side dish along with tender, lean pork and extra-moist chicken, both thoroughly and powerfully smoked, served with a rich hot-sauce tang and sides of molasses-heavy beans and cakey corn bread. It all adds up to a fine Texas feast. Sit at the counter and you can jaw with cooks—all schooled in rapid repartee—sip one of 40 beers, and order a "Snake Plate," which gives you "three bucks worth o' stuff," for $4. Salads won't convert anyone to vegetarianism. The massive oven/smoker, right behind the counter, cannot seem to contain all the smoke it produces, so customers usually go home lightly smoked outside as well as in. ▪ *13109 NE 175th St, Woodinville; 481-1417; map:BB2; $; beer and wine; AE, DC, MC, V; checks OK; lunch, dinner every day.* ᕱ

**Assaggio Ristorante** ★★ There's an air of festivity at Assaggio, and we're not sure whether to attribute it to the fact that the high-ceilinged two-room trattoria is always packed with customers (making for an amiable din), whether it has to do with owner Mauro Golmarvi's open-armed welcome at the door (he seems to know half the people walking through it), or whether it's caused by the visual effect of finely chopped parsley strewn like confetti over every antipasti, soup, and entree plate set before you. By the time you order dessert, you'll expect to find the ever-present flecks pinch-hitting for the cocoa on the tiramisu. Whatever it is, Assaggio lends a likable neighborhood Italian restaurant feel to this downtown hotel space. The chef is creative with his appetizers and pastas, cooks a mean Pollo Mattone (a fragrant roasted chicken half), knows how to sauce a veal saltimbocca (with just the right combination of sage, wine, and butter), and bakes a terrific thin-crusted pizza. Meantime, Golmarvi keeps the staff of attentive servers well in hand. ▪ *2010 4th Ave (Claremont Hotel); 441-1399; map:H7; $$; beer and wine; AE, MC, V; checks OK; lunch Mon–Fri, dinner Mon–Sat;* ᕱ

**Ayutthaya** ★½ Soothing pastel colors and clean, smooth lines create a calming antidote to the fiery food, which is prepared carefully and authentically here on Capitol Hill by the Fuangaromya family (members of which also own Thai Restaurant on lower Queen Anne—see review). It's good to make reservations; there's little waiting room. The seafood is excellent—a sizzling platter of shrimp spiked with basil, chiles, and garlic is a show in itself. Local businesspeople crowd the place at lunch for one of the best deals in town, so arrive early. Service is patient, and the only thing smoking here is the food. ▪ *727 E Pike St; 324-8833; map:L1; $; beer and wine; AE, MC, V; no checks; lunch Mon–Fri, dinner Mon–Sat.* ᕱ

▼

**Top 200 Restaurants**

▲

**Azaleas Fountain Court** ★★ There is no more romantic dining spot in Bellevue than Azaleas. On weekends, live jazz accompanies dinner; in summer, the courtyard—complete with small fountain—beckons. Any time, the dining room's country/continental ambience provides a warm backdrop for the chef's seasonal menus. Bites of lamb shank in spring, for instance, zing with tangy capers, artichokes, and tomatoes. Flaws are few and small (a lunchtime chicken sandwich with shiitakes and havarti offered a strenuous jaw workout, due to overzealously toasted bread). Count on sophisticated service and delicious homemade sorbets and ice creams. ■ *22 103rd Ave NE, Bellevue; 451-0426; map:HH3; $$$; full bar; AE, MC, V; local checks only; lunch Tues–Fri, dinner Mon–Sat.* ఉ

**Bahn Thai** ★★ Bahn Thai has long been a good place to initiate novices in Thai cuisine: the atmosphere is safe and pleasant, the service is speedy, and their two-star is not much hotter than most spicy Italian sausages. Curries are usually a good bet, or try the tom kah gai—the classic Thai soup that's tart with aromatic lime leaves, lime juice, and lemongrass. It makes a good foil for chicken satay or mee krob. The sautéed scallops with prik pao are hot without overwhelming the delicate scallop flavor. If you're lucky, the chef will prepare sizzling fish—crisp on the outside, moist within, with a pungent yet sweet sauce. ■ *409 Roy St; 283-0444; map:B5; $; beer and wine; AE, MC, V; no checks; lunch Mon–Fri, dinner every day.*

**Bakeman's** Bakeman's is headquarters for the working-class sandwich, now an institution among Seattle's office workers. No sprouts, just shredded iceberg lettuce; no gherkins or cornichons, just crunchy dills; handmade meat loaf instead of pâté; and real turkey sandwiches made from honest-to-God real, juicy, baked turkey with big hunks of skin still attached. As you move down the counter, be ready with your choices: white or wheat bread; light or dark meat, or mixed; mayo or no mayo; cranberry, double cranberry, or hold the cranberry. If the waiting line is snaking around the room, don't let it scare you off; things move with amazing speed here. Go ahead and order a cup of chili or a bowl of soup to accompany your sandwich (the turkey noodle will remind you of Grandma's), and be sure to say yes when jivemeister Jason tries to fast-talk you into a piece of carrot cake. ■ *122 Cherry St; 622-3375; map:N1; $; beer and wine; no credit cards; checks OK; lunch Mon–Fri.* ఉ

**Beeliner Diner** ★ A genuinely fake, big-as-a-minute diner (which has spawned the popular 5 Spot Cafe on Queen Anne and Capitol Hill's Coastal Kitchen: see reviews), the Beeliner has some of the liveliest ambiance (some would say, "verbal abuse") in town. Those in the mood for free-flowing, back-to-back conversation, grab a booth. From a stool at the counter, observe the classic art of hash slinging, performed here with

**CLOSED**

▼

**Top 200 Restaurants**

▲

the barking narration necessary to add genuine diner zest to a simple cheeseburger and Cobb salad. What's there not to love about the spicy grilled pork chops with potato pancakes and spiced apples, or a roast chicken dinner with real home-style mashed potatoes, skins and all, served up with Parker House buns? The turkey potpie (that's "hen in a pen" in dinerspeak) suits us just fine: lots of vegetables and chunks of tender turkey float in gravy beneath a puffed pastry crust. And every day there's a different Blue Plate Special. Indulge in a root beer float and save room for the coconut cake. ■ *2114 N 45th St; 547-6313; map:FF7; $; beer and wine; MC, V; local checks only; breakfast, lunch, dinner every day.*

**Big Time Pizza** ★ In the face of Big Competition, Big Time maintains its hold on the top spot in byte-land. Even if the pizzas were not so good—built on a rich, flavorful crust from hand-tossed dough, with toppings representing styles from Greece to Mexico to Thailand—we would go there for the 20-some wines offered by the glass. There are plenty of beers on tap as well. Our faves remain the Pesto Plus (with fontina, sun-dried tomatoes, mushrooms, artichoke hearts, and pesto) and the Greek Pizza (feta, kalamata olives, Roma tomatoes, green peppers, and oregano). Best is Big Time's attention to unusually savory toppings: cappocolla, chorizo, blue cheese, Montrachet, and portobello mushrooms. The calzone oozes mozzarella, encased in a deliciously chewy, handmade crust. A few pan-tossed pastas and green salads round out the menu. ■ *7281 W Lake Sammamish Pkwy NE, Redmond; 885-6425; map:EE2; $; beer and wine; MC, V; checks OK; lunch, dinner every day.* &

**Bistro Provencal** ★★½ The most dramatic change since Philippe Gayte opened this place in 1973 has been its name. Le Provencal is now Bistro Provencal, and name change or *non*, you won't find a more reliable restaurant on the Eastside. The cozy, country-inn atmo remains, as does the creaky old dessert tray, which could have served napoleons to Napoleon. You're likely to be waited on by one whose native tongue is French and whose service may prove erratic, lacking some attention to detail, but the food has been, is, and probably always will be well worth a minor inconvenience. The menu emphasis is bistro, and includes a terrific, inexpensive four-course prix-fixe meal. Begin with a full and flavorful onion soup, followed by a good crisp salad with a sprinkling of goat cheese. Among the five main-course selections is the Daube Avignonnaise, a very simple, very good Provençal-style beef stew that chef Gayte has been preparing since the day his restaurant opened. Other options might include rabbit stew, steak au poivre, or duck breast with blackberries. You can also choose from more upscale items on the à la carte menu. Or try the deluxe, five-course, prix-fixe "menu gastronomie." ■ *212 Central Way, Kirkland; 827-3300; map:EE3; $$; full bar; AE, DC, MC, V; local checks only; dinner every day.* 占

**Bizzarro Italian Cafe** ★½ Nestled into a former garage in Wallingford, Bizzarro demonstrates clearly that it deserves its name. When it's good, it's very, very good, but don't be surprised if you encounter a good meal and terrible service, or vice versa. Frequently re-decorated, the cafe can be rife with anything from an upside-down garden—complete with picnic and ants—to a resurrected dinosaur park. The food, too, is varied and imaginative, with ingredients ranging from the sublime to the ridiculous. This is clearly a neighborhood favorite, with servers greeting regulars by name and placing their standard orders without any prompting. Appetizers might include an appealingly simple warm goat cheese with roasted garlic, zesty calamari sautéed with vegetables and fresh herbs, and an overly doughy focaccia. Bread is nothing special. Among the pastas, an outstanding choice is the mix-and-match, where diners choose a pasta shape and marry it with their favorite sauce. Full dinners are a bargain, with soup or salad included. On any given evening, though, salads may be less than fresh, and soups overseasoned. The menu changes seasonally, so watch for the return of the consistently good roast chicken. There is a limited selection of wines by the glass and bottle. ■ *1307 N 46th St; 545-7327; map:FF7; $; beer and wine; MC, V; checks OK; dinner every day.*

**Blacksheep Cafe and Catering** ★ The Blacksheep caters to a certain crowd, the kind that's apt to come off the Burke-Gilman Trail with a bike and a couple of kids. Everything here is carefully considered: there's limited use of saturated fats, oils, sulfites, and preservatives, and nary a trace of Styrofoam in the house. About half of the menu is vegetarian; beef (if you must) comes free of antibiotics and hormones. At lunch, stand at the counter to order salads, sandwiches, or unusual burgers, and they'll be brought to your table. The curry chicken (with grapes and peanuts complementing the curry's twang) is heartily recommended. Burgers appear in many outfits, from the real thing to a marinated tofu number or a baked Sunburger—a vegan mesh of ground sunflower seeds, minced vegetables, and seasonings. Stick to the simple things here. A cioppino special arrived less than hot, loaded with seafood and vegetables, and topped by an overkill of basil aioli better spread on the garlic bread than mixed into the already sweet stew. Dinner service can be sloppy and forgetful. ■ *18132 Bothell Way NE, Bothell; 485-1972; map:AA4; $; no alcohol; MC, V; checks OK; breakfast Sat–Sun, lunch Tues-Sat, dinner Tues–Fri.* 占

**Boca** ★★ Boca fits in nicely with Alki's anywhere-south-of-Seattle mood. Across the street from a beachside volleyball court, Boca brings the feel of the beach inside. A salty, sandy, magical realist mural covers the walls. Margaritas are the house drink; comply when your server suggests a premium tequila—well worth the extra dollar or so. The menu continues the little grass shack theme with a just-right assortment of Caribbean food. An otherwise perfectly choreographed dinner was marred only by an empanada appetizer: heavy, dry pastry dough with uninspired beef and potato fillings. From there on out, expect smooth sailing. Especially good are the Jamaican-style "jerked" baby back ribs, seemingly dry on the outside, but yielding a savory, subtle juiciness within. Kudos for Boca's Bass, a nice piece of fish slathered in fermented black beans, wrapped in banana leaves, and grilled. This best expresses what's good about the food here: traditional, simple, tropical preparation methods transformed by imaginative treatment. All of the food at Boca is prettily presented, making the most of brightly colored ingredients. On weekends, there's an un-abashedly Southwestern brunch. Expect the requisite huevos rancheros and a Texi-Cali version of stuffed French toast among other options. If you're stumbling into Boca after a late night on the beach, you may need the heavy-handed flavors (in turn, overpoweringly spicy, salty, or sweet) to make an impression upon your dulled senses. In that case, forget the food and head straight for the Bloody Marys. ■ *2516 Alki Ave SW; 933-8000; map:II9; $$; full bar; AE, MC, V; local checks only; lunch Mon–Sat, dinner every day, brunch Sun.* &

**Broadway New American Grill** ★ Several awkwardly proportioned rooms—united only by their common commitment to head-scratchingly weird light fixtures—are gathered together under one roof to form this noisy (and hugely popular) restaurant. The food often borders on mediocre, but it's *the* place to go when you've got the munchies and can't decide whether to have eggs, a sandwich, a slab of grilled fish, or a drink and some fries: it's your choice, no matter what time of day or night. The burgers are big and juicy and perfectly grilled. Don't bother with the mostly deep-fried appetizers and choose carefully among the more upscale-sounding entrees (no matter how good the pork tenderloin might sound, it's not). Order your burger and and a bartender's margarita and hunker down. ■ *314 Broadway Ave E; 328-7000; map:HH7; $; full bar; AE, MC, V; local checks only; breakfast, lunch, and dinner every day.* &

**Burk's Cafe** ★ Indolent and tropical are not words one usually associates with Ballard, but at Burk's, an exception must be made. This brightly painted wood-frame building looks as though it belongs on a lazy wharf in Biloxi. The illusion is fostered inside, where ceiling fans whirl and tile floors make for a pleasant racket when the room is full. What Burk's lacks is the down-and-dirty attitude that makes for a real deep-fried

▼

▲

Southern experience; only in Seattle would a Cajun joint ban smoking, even at the bar. It all feels just a little too clean, despite the good-natured attempts of the waitstaff to juice the place up a bit. But the food is fiery and down-home, starting with the crock of pickled okra that graces each table. The appetizers are all dependable, including a wonderful squid with chile butter. For dinner, there's both filé and okra gumbo, homemade sausage (too dry on a recent visit), crawfish in season, and an excellent specials list that sometimes includes various blackened fish, pork in molasses sauce, and fresh catfish (no bargain and not so nice to look at). All the dinners come, classically, with red beans and rice. While the pecan pie is the best in town, other desserts—such as bread pudding with whiskey sauce served chilled and gelatinous—can disappoint.
■ *5411 Ballard Ave NW; 782-0091; map:EE8; $$; beer and wine; MC, V; local checks only; lunch, dinner Tues–Sat.*

**Burrito Loco** ★ Greenwood parents are known to coerce their kids into behaving by bribing them with an afternoon visit to Burrito Loco for a delicious churro—a cinnamony stick of fried dough. But grown-ups come for the wonderfully authentic savory fare, especially the enormous burritos, the perfectly sauced chicken mole, and the carne asada. Burrito Loco also serves something you won't find at competing Mexican eateries: tortas, Mexican sandwiches served on soft white bread with a variety of toppings (try the barbecued pork: the sauce is great). Mini-mall locale and cuisine of the sun notwithstanding, the atmosphere inside—with pine walls and booths—is reminiscent of nothing so much as a comfy ski chalet. ■ *9211 Holman Rd NW; 783-0719; map:DD8; $; beer and wine; MC, V; checks OK; lunch, dinner every day.* ⅃

**Bush Garden** ★½ Bush Garden is one of the most popular among the older Japanese restaurants in town, favored for its extensive menu, long hours, numerous tatami rooms, karaoke cocktail lounge, and free parking. Inside, it's ornate (to the point of excess in the foyer area), with a footbridge over a babbling stream, paper lanterns and umbrellas, and lots of rattan. Upstairs, a banquet room can accommodate busloads of tourists or schoolkids, and often does. The long sushi bar segues into the robata bar, which ends in the open grill area, allowing patrons an opportunity to watch the entire cooking operation at work. As for the food, you might experience excellent sashimi, tasty black cod kasuzuke, wonderful clam soup, and light, amply portioned tempura. On a recent visit, a nearby table of Japanese businessmen were treated to dish after dish of pickled vegetables, creamy fresh tofu, and artful platters of raw and cooked fish. Those watching the parade were green with envy.
■ *614 Maynard Ave S; 682-6830; map:R7; $$; full bar; AE, MC, V; no checks; lunch Mon–Sat, dinner every day.* ⅃

**Cactus** ★½ On many evenings, the crowd at Cactus spills out onto the sidewalk. And it's not only the Madison Park neighbors who have discovered that the sun-drenched cuisines of Mexico and the Southwest are a great antidote to yet another gray Seattle day. Even on a winter weeknight, there always seems to be a lively crowd enjoying the breezy decor of brightly painted tables and hanging dried peppers. Be careful not to overstuff on the freshly made chips and salsa—there are many appealing dishes ahead. Start with tapas and you may not need to go any further. These flavorful tidbits are enough to make a very satisfying light meal, especially the perfectly cooked calamari, tortilla española, and the berengena asada (eggplant with cilantro pesto). Navajo fry-bread or tortillas accompany the main dishes. The familiar Mexican reliables— fajitas, enchiladas, and the like—are well done, but other choices can offer more interesting options. Pollo Relleno, for instance, is a particularly successful multilayered combination of chicken, cheese, and peppers. Cactus may have one of the more interesting beverage lists in town, including Mexican soft drinks and mineral water, but the wine list is limited. There's a no-reservation policy, but loaned beepers let you stroll the charming neighborhood while you cool your heels. Limited dinner seating is also available at the bar, the perfect catbird seat for the open kitchen. ■ *4220 E Madison St; 324-4140; map:GG6; $$; full bar; DC, MC, V; checks OK; lunch Mon–Sat, dinner every day.* &

**Cafe Flora** ★★½ Cafe Flora's meatless, smokeless, boozeless ethic is rooted in a larger vision: multiculturalism, responsible global stewardship, and a fervid righteousness about health. Political and social agendas aside, this very attractive, very '90s place has become a mecca for vegetarians and carnivores alike. Concessions have been made for the regulars who longed to sip something more potent than rosemary-laced lemonade; you may now enjoy a glass of merlot with your Portobello Wellington (a mushroom-pecan pâté and grilled portobellos wrapped in pastry) or drink a beer with your Oaxaca Tacos (a pair of corn tortillas stuffed with spicy mashed potatoes and cheeses, set off by a flavorful black bean stew and sautéed greens). Soups are always silky and luscious, salads sport interesting (and often organic) ingredients, and diners who don't do dairy will always discover something cleverly prepared to suit their dietary needs. Never hesitate when the dessert tray makes the rounds. ■ *2901 E Madison St; 325-9100; map:HH6; $$; beer and wine; MC, V; checks OK; lunch Tues–Fri, dinner Tues–Sat, brunch Sat–Sun.* &

**Cafe Illiterati** ★ After trying several different culinary approaches in this ramshackle old Ballard storefront, Bobby Beeman has found his groove. And a groovy groove it is. Cafe

▼

Top 200
Restaurants

▲

Illiterati has become a clubhouse for the strange soul of Ballard. New Age and unconventional types, local businesspeople, scenesters who've fled Capitol Hill for the Ballard good life—all crowd into the high-ceilinged, junk-store cafe and onto its porch off the back that overlooks the ship canal (across the street and between some buildings). Savory and filling breakfasts and lunches are served every weekday. On weekends, the place is crowded with 25-year-olds who look like they got dressed in the dark. Weekend brunches are benevolently hearty (read: "good hangover food"), featuring a pesto-laden egg strata and the best breakfast burrito going. Espresso drinks are always made to a high standard. ■ *5327 Ballard Ave NW; 782-0191; map:EE8; $; beer and wine; MC, V; local checks only; breakfast, lunch Mon–Fri, brunch Sat–Sun.* &

**Cafe Juanita** ★★★ This converted creekside house hasn't changed much since Peter Dow opened it in 1979. Inside, it's small and unpretentious, with a few etchings and many, many wine bottles by way of decor. There's no printed menu, just dish names on blackboards (spiedini misti, pollo pistacchi, agnello verdure, anitra con arugula, pasta puttanesca), and servers must rattle off detailed explanations to nodding, short-term memory–challenged diners—"Now, what were those first three things you said?" Once over that hurdle, it's an easy, consistently pleasurable glide through dinner. The legion of regulars don't even need help deciding among the country-Italian offerings: about half the menu items have been there off-and-on for a decade and more. Dow's presence has kept this ship sailing calm waters over the years, though these days, there's yet another competent chef handling things in the kitchen, putting *his* new mark on Dow's tried-and-true menu. Meanwhile, Dow keeps busy schmoozing diners, dispensing his own wines (Cavatappi sauvignon blanc, cabernet sauvignon, or Maddalena), and only occasionally stepping into the small, open kitchen. ■ *9702 NE 120th Pl, Kirkland; 823-1505; map:DD3; $$; full bar; MC, V; checks OK; dinner every day.* &

**Cafe Lago** ★★½ Chef/owners Jordi Viladas and Carla Leonardi fuel the fires at this rustic Montlake cafe reminiscent of trattorias that dot the hills of Tuscany. A flaming brick oven, butcher-paper–topped tables nestled together, and prettily stenciled walls entice a loyal neighborhood clientele. The menu, which changes regularly, includes a strong selection of antipasti, a quartet of pastas, and a half-dozen pizzas. When compared to other not-so-fancy Italian restaurants, the offerings may seem somewhat expensive, but rest assured, your money's well-spent here. Start with the astounding antipasto sampler, which might include thick slices of fresh mozzarella, salty Asiago cheese, herby goat cheese nudging up against roasted red peppers, a head of roasted garlic, a selection of cured meats, and crostini swabbed with olive paste. Fruit-wood imparts a smoky flavor to the fabulous thin-crusted pizzas, and the handmade pastas give new meaning to the word ethereal. The lasagne con melanzane—"unlike any lasagne you have ever had," according to the menu—lives up to the billing. The sheets of pasta come rolled thin as a wonton, layered with eggplant, béchamel, and ricotta, with a bright red tomato sauce. Simply extraordinary. Feathery ribbons of fettuccine with coppa, garlic, Parmesan, and cream prove to be magically light. The wine list runs the gamut in prices, with a few Northwest offerings and some rather fine Italian bottlings. The high ceilings make for a noisy room, but, hey, that's Italian. ■ *2305 24th Ave E; 329-8005; map:GG6; $$; beer and wine; MC, V; checks OK; dinner Tues–Sun.* &

**Cafe Nola** ★★ Imagine yourself holding a bowl of café au lait with both hands, indulging in an apple cranberry crisp, and having a heart-to-heart with a friend. Bainbridge Island's Cafe Nola is the perfect setting. Uniting their culinary talents, sisters Melinda Lucas (a former pastry chef at LA's illustrious Spago) and Mary Bugarin (a former caterer) have transformed a Puget Power office into an elegant eatery decorated in soft wheat tones. Breakfasts (baked goods, mostly—with an entree or two for those with bigger appetites) and lunches (panini and outstanding salads composed with, say, marinated portobellos and butternut squash) come carefully prepared. At dinner, served a couple of nights each week, you might encounter spicy agnolotti with tomato sauce or a sublime rack of lamb with parsnip-potato gratin. While the antipasti misti is lovely, the flavors of its colorful elements don't live up to its visual impact. In sum, expect a well-executed dinner that might benefit from a touch more creativity, do have dessert, and consider catching an early ferry for a relaxing daytime repast. ■ *101 Winslow Way, Bainbridge Island; 842-3822; $–$$; beer and wine; MC, V; checks OK; breakfast, lunch Tues–Sun, dinner Fri–Sat.* &

**Cafe Septième** ★ In 1994 Kurt Timmermeister moved his legendary Septième into the former home of the decidedly unchic Andy's Diner. And while the now defunct downtown Septième may be remembered for its intensely cozy European atmosphere, the big, busy, Broadway version is a different scene altogether. Divided into smoking and nonsmoking sections by Andy's original Formica counter, this Septième comes dressed in blood red walls and pretty linen-topped tables with a simple, inexpensive menu even better than that which came before. You can still sip perfect café au lait while eating glorious pastries, but lunch really shines with soups, salads, and sandwiches (including a superb eggplant, red pepper, and olive tapenade number), and dinner includes a mean roast chicken with garlic mashed potatoes. Open till midnight every day. ■

▼

**Top 200
Restaurants**

▲

*214 Broadway Ave E; 322-9909; map:GG7; $; beer and wine; MC, V; local checks only; breakfast, lunch, dinner every day.*

**Cafe Veloce** ★ Amid decor celebrating the golden age of Italian motorcycle racing, Cafe Veloce delivers pasta and pizzas for fledgling connoisseurs on spaghetti-and-meatball budgets. For creativity and quality, it beats its bargain-basement-pasta competitors, like Olive Garden, hands-down. Entrees arrive quickly, thanks to an efficient kitchen, the pastas attractively presented on oversize platters flecked with chopped basil. The Pasta Muffaletta is inspired by the New Orleans sandwich, with a black olive compote and pieces of ham and salami sautéed with penne and olive oil. Pasta Portofino features baby clams and mushrooms, lots of garlic, a little T-sauce, and a couple of fresh basil leaves tossed in for a burst of flavor. Crisp-crusted pizzas include quattro formaggi and clam Victoria. Owner Todd Fell's collection of vintage Italian racing motorcycles is just for looks, not for delivery. ■ *12514 120th Ave NE, Kirkland; 814-2972; map:CC3; $; beer and wine; AE, DC, MC, V; checks OK; lunch and dinner every day, breakfast Sat–Sun.* &

**Cafe Vizcaya** ★½ It's hard to say whether Cafe Vizcaya is so vastly appealing because of the quality of the food or its novelty. Tapas, the oiled finger foods of Spain, are showing up on menus all over town these days, but this dusky Wallingford haunt continues to purvey some of the city's best (read: more authentic) versions. Consider making tapas your whole meal—that way you can try the gambas y vieiras negras (blackened prawns and scallops over a bed of spinach, peppers, carrots, and mushrooms drenched in balsamic vinaigrette), the tamal en Casuela (spicy polenta with chorizo topping), the frituras de Bacalao (cod fritters with Romesco sauce), *and* the boniato (sweet-potato fries with papaya-tomatillo salsa so good you'll be tempted to order a second helping). The entree menu extends the cafe's culinary reach beyond the borders of Spain, including a few pasta dishes held over from the storefront's former incarnation as an Italian restaurant. Cuba, the birthplace of owner Barbara Soltero, is represented in the form of several citrus-steeped meats. Of course, there are those who come strictly for the paella. Here one can assemble a light, inexpensive supper or roll out all the stops, collecting plates all over the table. The bar area up front makes for a romantic retreat, sherry in hand, on a blustery day. ■ *2202 N 45th St; 547-7772; map:FF6; $$; full bar; MC, V; checks OK; dinner Mon–Sat.* &

**Campagne** ★★★★ ■ **Cafe Campagne** ★★★ Linen tablecloths, tiny vases of flowers, and wall space dedicated to wine bottles help set the mood for country French in a very urban setting at Campagne. Located in a courtyard of Pike Place Market, the restaurant takes its cue from the cuisine of southern France. Owner Peter Lewis (one of the city's most gracious hosts) and some of Seattle's finest servers will ensure that you dine with gusto. Campagne offers a deliciously rich cassoulet in addition to other nightly specials reflecting the day's catch, the season's offerings, and the soothing inspirations of chef Tamara Murphy (who won the coveted James Beard award for Best Chef in the Northwest in 1995). There are so many successes here—an inspired, carefully wrought wine list not the least among them. Campagne has a wonderful late-night menu available in the exceptionally romantic (but often smoky) bar. Dining at a courtyard table while sipping a framboise Sauvage is the next best thing to a trip to France.

Lewis's **Cafe Campagne**, which opened in 1994 just below its stylish sibling, often proves too small to accommodate those who throng to this casual bistro-cum-charcuterie. Wherever you sit (at a cherry-wood table or the elegant counter), be sure to utter the most important words spoken here: garlic mashed potatoes. At lunch or dinner, the herby rotisserie chicken or classic steak frites will put you over the edge. Takeout, too. ▪ *Campagne: 86 Pine St; 728-2800; map:I7; $$$; full bar; AE, DC, MC, V; no checks; dinner every day.* ♿ ▪ *Cafe Campagne: 1600 Post Alley; 728-2233; map:I7; $; beer and wine; AE, DC, MC, V; no checks; breakfast, lunch, dinner Mon–Sat, brunch Sun.* ♿

**Canlis** ★★½ Everyone has an opinion about Canlis. Some say it's Seattle's finest celebratory restaurant, others say it's an anachronistic joke. We say, you gotta love a place this dedicated to making the customer feel like visiting royalty; the legendary valet parking *alone* is worth the price of admission (you arrive, step out of your car—no questions asked, no names exchanged—and it's waiting magically at the door when you leave hours later). The host, in his carefully pressed tuxedo, bows graciously. You're shown to a table, or better yet, to a seat at the piano bar where you'll get to hum along with every Burt Bacharach tune ever written. There's a timeless quality about the place, from the twinkling lights around Lake Union below, to the elderly patrons sipping martinis and celebrating the fact that they're still alive and kicking, to the kimono-clad waitresses—some of whom are in their fourth decade here. You won't find the latest in trendy dining at Canlis, but there is no better place for the annual thick steak accompanied by a noble cabernet. There's no shortage of seafood, either, including lobster bisque, Canlis's signature sautéed prawns, salmon (with hollandaise, of course), or scallops, all well-prepared. Some dishes are absurdly expensive ($27 for three deliciously grilled jumbo prawns), others just absurd (soft-shell crab, dusted with Parmesan, flash-fried, and served with tartar sauce). And while much ado has been made about the famous

▼

**Top 200 Restaurants**

▲

Canlis Salad (an overdressed knockoff on a caesar, tossed tableside with prefab dressing), we say skip it and splurge on an after-dinner drink at the piano. The high prices carry over to the wine list, which is so extensive it has a table of contents. ∎ *2576 Aurora Ave N; 283-3313; map:GG7; $$$; full bar; AE, DC, MC, V; checks OK; dinner Mon–Sat.*

**Catfish Corner** ★ Here's a small neighborhood cafe with comfortable booths, a jolly regular clientele, and restorative soul food: sweet Louisiana catfish, deep-fried just right (get extra tartar sauce) and perfect with a few hush puppies and maybe some pie. The potato salad is very good. Great for take-out, too. ∎ *2726 E Cherry St; 323-4330; map:HH6; $; no alcohol; no credit cards; checks OK; lunch, dinner every day.* &

**Caveman Kitchens** ★½ The late Dick Donley was a tinkerer with both machines and food. He spent years experimenting with methods of smoking ribs, chicken, turkey, sausage, ham, and salmon over alder and (when available) apple wood. What he finally achieved was outstanding—especially the moist smoked turkey. Donley's six children carry on after him, and nothing has changed. There is no inside seating, but in warm weather you can eat outside on picnic tables and go across the street to the neighborhood store for beer. Most people take out, loading up on the smoked goods and accompaniments such as beans, potato salad, coleslaw, and a terrific bread pudding with butterscotch whiskey sauce. A second Caveman (11700 Lake City Way NE, 362-8464) is now open in Seattle. ∎ *807 West Valley Hwy, Kent; 854-1210; map:QQ4; $; no alcohol; MC, V; checks OK; lunch, dinner every day.*

**Chandler's Crabhouse and Fresh Fish Market** ★★ Chandler's is quintessential Seattle, due in part to the view of Lake Union with its boats and seaplanes coming and going, the lights of Queen Anne Hill in the distance, and the representative cross-section of Seattle types at the bar or in the dining room. The menu offers a gastronomic geography lesson on Puget Sound with a variety of local oysters, Dungeness crab, clams, and mussels, not to mention the wide selection of fresh fish, all cooked with tender attention. Crab cakes are moist, delicious, and actually taste of crab, and the menu boasts a healthy salmon component. Chandler's recipes often bow to a cross-cultural mix of ingredients with listings such as cherry-smoked Alaskan halibut with apricot ginger glaze, or a wonderful Grays Harbor sturgeon with lemongrass, asparagus, and jasmine rice. Service is attentive, and there's an extensive wine list, heavy on the Northwest labels. Even the desserts have a local tang with fruits in season. ∎ *901 Fairview Ave N; 223-2722; map:D1; $$$; full bar; AE, DC, MC, V; checks OK; lunch Mon–Fri, dinner every day, brunch Sat–Sun.* &

▼

**Top 200 Restaurants**

▲

**Chanterelle Specialty Foods** ★★ Perhaps better known
for breakfast, lunch, and baked goods, casual and kitchen-
confident Chanterelle really shines at dinner, where a list of
nightly specials reflects an ethnically diverse—and surprisingly well executed—range. In addition to a couple of salads
and sandwiches and a killer black-bean burrito, the regular dinner menu features a half dozen pastas (terrific salads included)
in the $10 range. But locals in the know clamor for the spe-
cials—among them handmade seafood pot-stickers, enormous
slabs of sausage-laden lasagne, and artfully sauced lamb
shanks. Breakfast is a delightful affair (waffle-lovers should opt
for the light, orange-flavored cornmeal waffles). Well-meaning
service can prove slow when it's busy—and it usually is, since
this combination of '70s-style fern deli and cozy bistro is clearly
the best restaurant in Edmonds. ■ *316 Main St, Edmonds;*
*774-0650; $; beer and wine; MC, V; checks OK; breakfast ev-*
*ery day, lunch and dinner Tues–Sat. &*

**Chez Shea** ★★★ ■ **Shea's Lounge** ★★½ Chez Shea is one
of Seattle's gems. You might walk through the Pike Place Market a hundred times and not know that Sandy Shea's tiny, romantic hideaway is perched just above, looking out over the
Sound. Dinner at Chez Shea is a prix-fixe affair, with four ▼
courses reflecting the bounty of the season and ingredients
fresh from the market stalls below. A winter meal might begin
with a ricotta and Parmesan-rich soufflé set atop a roasted
tomato sauce, followed by Hubbard squash soup, tangy with
diced cabbage and thickened with pearly riso. The main course ▲
could be a rack of Ellensburg lamb, roasted with herbes de
Provence, or a salt-cured fillet of king salmon, served atop
garlic-infused mashed potatoes. Service is always sure and
gracious.

In celebration of the restaurant's 10th anniversary (in
1994), Sandy Shea opened **Shea's Lounge**, an unpretentious,
sexy little bistro that's wed to Chez Shea by way of a common
door. The menu offers about a dozen dishes, heavily influenced
by the flavors of Spain and Portugal. The perfect place to meet
a friend for a little something before or after. ■ *Corner Mar-*
*ket Building, Suite 34; 467-9990; map:J8; $$$ (Chez Shea);*
*$$ (Shea's Lounge); full bar; AE, MC, V; checks OK; dinner*
*Tues–Sun.*

**The Chile Pepper** ★½ It's an odd eating experience: food that's
sometimes fiery, sometimes subtly distinctive, but always wonderfully complex, is served inside a dining room that's as dull
as any we've seen in Seattle. Maybe the ploy is to throw the brilliance of the food into high relief. The Gonzales family purveys
the regional cuisine of the upland Mexican state of Guanajuato,
where the sauces are rich marriages of flavor, not unlike a good
curry. An outstanding mole poblano sauce served on chicken

is neither the sweet chocolate Oaxacan mole nor the bland, pale, nut sauce other eateries seem to buy by the tub. It's as dark as chocolate, redolent of cinnamon, clove, laurel, sesame, almonds, peanuts, tart tomatillos, black pepper, and several kinds of chiles. The chiles rellenos is the most popular dish here, lightly battered and laden with cheese. Ceviche is served in a tall glass, topped with guacamole; the slight fire of the guac plays nicely against the citrus and cilantro flavor of the fish. ∎ *1427 N 45th St; 545-1790; map:FF7; $; beer and wine; no credit cards; checks OK; lunch, dinner Mon–Sat.* ♿

**Chinook's at Salmon Bay** ★★ It's big, busy, and formulaic, but the Anthony's HomePort folks seem to be using the right bait here at their showplace in the heart of Fishermen's Terminal. The industrial-strength design with very high ceilings, steel countertops, visible beams and ventilation ducts, matched with an appealing collection of action-packed fishing photos, fits well with the bustle around the working marina. The seemingly never-ending menu ranges from broiled, steamed, fried, and sandwiched seafood to Japanese stir-fries and big, juicy burgers. We suggest you nab a few things off the regular menu (tempura onion rings and a half-dozen oysters) and pay close attention to the daily special sheet (say, Copper River salmon chargrilled with sun-dried tomato-basil butter or excellent mahi-mahi tacos with homemade salsa). For dessert, try a big piece of blackberry cobbler—if you haven't already overdosed on the warm focaccia brought to you in basketsful by friendly servers. ∎ *1900 W Nickerson St; 283-4665; map:FF8; $$; full bar; AE, DC, MC, V; checks OK; breakfast Sat–Sun, lunch and dinner every day.* ♿

▼
Top 200
Restaurants
▲

**Chutneys** ★★ Chutneys opened in 1995 with at least one certain advantage: the owners include Bill Khanna, formerly of the Eastside's popular Raga and New York's Bombay Palace. Clearly, Khanna and his partners have left no consideration neglected. The casually elegant Queen Anne dining room is a tranquil oasis, presided over by dozens of carved bas-relief gods and goddesses who appear to be smiling. And who could blame them? If you're not yet familiar with the zesty flavors of the Asian subcontinent, this is an excellent place to begin. Gracious servers are happy to explain dishes and make recommendations. Before you can scan the menu, a basket of pappadum appears with two of the restaurant's namesake chutneys. Among the excellent starters are the onion bhaji—a variation on onion rings—and remarkably light vegetable pakoras. Entrees can be ordered at varying degrees of heat, to be chased with a cocktail, an Indian beer, or a mug of milky, cardamom-infused tea. Though Indian food can be fiery, even the curry vindaloo—synonymous in some restaurants with tongue-searing heat—is spicy without going overboard. Main dish selections offer many delicious options, such as chicken tikka masala (which combines the appeal of the tandoor with a creamy tomato yogurt sauce) and a mixed tandoori grill (with succulent lamb chops, chicken, and fish among the generous offerings). Individual portions of perfectly cooked basmati rice are served in shiny copper pots, and there are many appealing vegetarian options. Don't overlook the breads, especially the garlic nan. For dessert, indulge in a slice of mango cheesecake. The lunchtime buffet is a considerable bargain. ■ *519 1st Ave N; 284-6799; map:GG8; $$; full bar; AE, DC, MC, V; checks OK; lunch, dinner every day.* &

### Ciao Bella Ristorante ★½
Ciao Bella is the second in what is now a trilogy of restaurants opened by native Umbrian Gino Borriello—also to his credit is Edmonds' Ciao Italia (which he sold in 1995 in order to open stylish Isabella in downtown Seattle; see reviews for both). One reviewer was in for a shock upon her first visit to Ciao Bella—recoginizing the Ravenna site as her former preschool. Resisting the impulse to climb up on the table and sing "Frère Jacques" (an Acorn Academy daily ritual), our reviewer constrained herself and merely sat at the table to enjoy some refined and unpretentious food. The seafood appetizers are all good, especially the prawns in a slightly creamy marinara (with plenty of sauce left over for sopping up with bread). There's a sort of triage approach to dinner here: minimal effort is exerted on salads so utmost attention can be paid to well-composed entrees. The specials list shines: from trinette mare e moti (a plentiful collection of clams, mussels, prawns, mushrooms, and peas over pasta) to tender veal in a sauce of artichoke hearts, mushrooms, and cream. Pastas can be uneven—a simple penne with mozzarella, basil, and tomato, which should be light and fresh, can be gummy and leaden. Ciao Bella is neither groundbreaking nor flawless, just simple and charming as a neighborhood Italian place should be. ■ *5133 25th Ave NE; 524-6989; map:FF6; $$; beer and wine; AE, MC, V; local checks only; dinner every day.*

### Ciao Italia ★★
Owner Patrick Girardi, an erstwhile young restaurateur if ever there was one, bought this Edmonds favorite from his former employer, Gino Borriello (who still owns Seattle's Ciao Bella Ristorante and has since opened Isabella Ristorante; see reviews). Ciao Italia's strip-mall location aside, the pleasant atmosphere—at once candlelit and casual—works to fine effect. The menu is full of Italian meat-and-pasta standards done in better-than-standard fashion. Make sure someone at the table orders the simple, elegant pizza margherita, and choose pastas from the specials list, which here always seems to yield the best efforts of the chef. Dinners come with boring-but-complimentary salads; meat dishes include

▼

**Top 200
Restaurants**

▲

outstanding grilled vegetables. ■ *546 5th Ave S, Edmonds; 771-7950; $; beer and wine; MC, V; local checks only; dinner every day.* 🕭

**Coastal Kitchen** ★★ Neighborhood restaurant kingpins Peter Levy and Jeremy Hardy (of Wallingford's Beeliner Diner and Queen Anne's 5 Spot Cafe fame; see reviews) launched their third joint, on the eastern reaches of Capitol Hill, in 1993. We think it's their best effort to date. This is the food of the coast—any coast, tweaked with a Jersey diner/Mom-for-the-'90s sensibility. The regular menu sports some serious winners, like a tender half of roast chicken and a grilled pork chop dinner plate with juicy, spicy chops nudging up against mashed potatoes and gravy so good you'll be begging for seconds. There's fresh fish, simply grilled, and the All Day Long Breakfast, with maple-smoked bacon, hashbrowns, toast, and eggs. The kitchen cooks up quarterly-changing getaways to far-flung coastal locales, and this is where the cooks get rowdy and imaginative. We've scarfed Gulf Coast fried green tomatoes with aioli and crowder peas; epazote- and lime-laced Michoacán seafood stew; and Thai-style spring rolls with a spicy-sweet dipping sauce. Exotic cocktails like the Blue Moon Martini (it's very, very blue) make imbibing more fun than usual. Be fore-warned: the menu is written in such fractured Huck Finnified vernacular (y'all know they're duckin' and dippin' and tryin' to be interestin') that it may get on your nerves as much as the clattery din. ■ *429 15th Ave E; 322-1145; map:HH6; $$; full bar; MC, V; local checks only; breakfast, lunch, dinner every day.* 🕭

▼

**Top 200 Restaurants**

▲

**Continental Restaurant and Pastry Shop** ★ Simple, friendly, and airy, this U District classic has the atmosphere of a Greek storefront cafe, with owners George and Helen Lagos and their son, Demetre, making you feel like part of the family. Breakfast (served all day)—with eggs, wonderful Greek fries, and a souvlaki skewer—is a great bargain. Later in the day try the lentil or avgolemono soup or dolmades, with galatobouriko for dessert. The specials are usually chicken in lemon, garlic, and olive oil (very good); or spanakopita, crisp and buttery, stuffed with spinach and feta. You can buy authentic ingredients from the adjoining deli. ■ *4549 University Way NE; 632-4700; map:FF6; $; beer and wine; MC, V; no checks; breakfast, lunch, dinner every day.* 🕭

**Copacabana** ★ Seattle's only Bolivian restaurant doesn't quite recall the authenticity of Ramon Paleaz's original Pike Place Market dive—the one with the counter that tilted so much that servers had to jam forks beneath the plates to keep them upright—but the splendid sun deck (great for viewing Elliott Bay and Pike Place Market) comes close. The family recipes are still used: the spicy shrimp soup; the heaping paella; salteñas, juicy meat-and-raisin–stuffed pastries; huminta, a piquant corn pie topped with cheeses; poached halibut with sautéed onion and tomato in a mild saffron sauce. Like the Spanish, Bolivians seem to cook everything to death, and everything here is a tad pricier than you'd expect. Visit on a warm day, when lingering over a chilly beer and eating light is on your mind, and sit on the balcony to soak up a bird's-eye view of the Market—some of the best people-watching around. ■ *1520½ Pike Place; 622-6359; map:J8; $; beer and wine; AE, DC, MC, V; no checks; lunch, dinner Mon–Sat (summer); lunch every day, dinner Fri–Sat (winter).*

**Crêpe de Paris** ★★ Annie Agostini's Rainier Square crêperie bustles midday, a fine spot for a business lunch or a break from downtown shopping. Choose from hearty salads, sandwiches, and the namesake crêpes—light and crisp with a variety of fillings, from ratatouille to beef bourguignon. In the evenings crêpes appear only among the desserts and the menu changes to more traditional fare, such as lamb chops and seafoods. But the icing on the cake is the cabaret dinner theater, showcasing local talent in humor and song. The shows generally run Thursday through Saturday, when reservations are advised. There's seldom a crêpe in sight at show dinners, which feature instead a prix-fixe arrangement with soup or salad to start, followed by a choice of six entrees: perhaps salmon with leeks in a lobster sauce, pork tenderloin in apricot sauce, or game hens with juniper berries—all carefully and beautifully prepared, then topped off with a dessert of the chef's choosing. ■ *1333 5th Ave (Rainier Square); 623-4111; map:K6; $$; full bar; AE, MC, V; no checks; lunch Mon–Fri, dinner Mon–Sat.* ⅁

▼

**Top 200 Restaurants**

▲

**Cucina! Cucina!** ★ Cucina! Cucina! is overwhelming! overwhelming! There's the place, a slick Italianate chamber sectioned into parts: the open kitchen, the upper bar, the lower bar, the dining area, the broad deck—with Lake Union shimmering outside the window. There are the patrons, looking like they're going right from here to either the Academy Awards or the Sorority Ball (and making, incidentally, just one hell of a racket). And there's the menu which, with its multitudinous antipasti, zuppe, insalate, pizze, paste, and griglie, makes you tired just looking at it. The waitstaff is a young, enthusiastic bunch—god knows they'd have to be to keep up the pace. Some of the nibbles are quite good: the focaccia, whose aroma perfumes the whole place, is garlicky and delicious; the four-cheese (mozzarella, provolone, Gorgonzola, and Parmesan) pizza, made in the wood-burning oven, is a creamy, smoky delight; and we've even had a very good veal Marsala. Cucina! continues to clone itself throughout the region with branches in Kirkland (822-4000) and Issaquah (391-3800), and farther afield in Tacoma and Spokane. ■ *901 Fairview Ave N (and* branches); 447-2782; map:D1; $$; full bar; AE, DC, MC, V; checks OK; lunch, dinner every day. ⅃

**Cutters Bayhouse** ★★ Overlooking Elliott Bay on the north edge of the Pike Place Market (and overlooking the homeless, the tourists, and the lunchtime crowd at Steinbrueck Park during the day), Cutters is busy morning, noon, afternoon, and night. You can order just about anything from the vast menu—*if* you can only make up your mind. There's Chinese, Japanese, Cajun, Italian, salads, pastas, seafood, and more—and much of it is quite good. We've enjoyed excellent pastas, including Northwest Seafood Fettuccine (with a healthy toss of Dungeness crab among the cream and shellfish) and a terrific black bean soup-of-the-day. Warm housemade focaccia comes gratis, though you shouldn't let that keep you from ordering a romaine salad with creamy Maytag blue cheese. Pasta combos, with choice of soup or salad, are a great buy; unfortunately, the seasonal greens tossed with strawberry vinaigrette may arrive overdressed and sweet enough to be dessert. Service at the door is prompt and friendly, but once seated, you may encounter a slip-up or two. The view from the dining room makes up for it. The bright, crowded bar offers a good selection of wines by the glass, sucked up by the upwardly mobile types congregating after work or a workout at the Seattle Club across the street. ■ *2001 Western Ave; 448-4884; map:J8; $$; full bar; AE, DC, MC, V; checks OK; breakfast Sun, lunch, dinner every day.* ⅃

▼

**Top 200 Restaurants**

▲

**Cyclops** ★★ The neighborhood that Cyclops feeds is not so much one of geography as it is one of temperament—and lots of it. Gina Kaukola opened this Belltown hangout in 1990, and Cyclops has since become a damn good place to eat. The decor is kitschy without being tiresome, the menu eclectic without being far-fetched. Blue doors swing open on a room crowded with old chrome, red vinyl, religious imagery, and funky lamps. The menu will guide you through the Mediterranean and beyond, with a common thread of warm flavors and simple, pretty presentation. The specials board presents a dizzying array of options—a couple of pastas, a couscous or two, a nice pork loin or lamb dish. The empanada verduras is a delicious pastry shell stuffed with vegetables and pumpkin seeds. A couscous stew might arrive laden with figs and prunes. Weekend nights can be a little hectic, but once you've secured a table, you won't be rushed as you sit sipping wine with dinner, then coffee with dessert, watching the strange and beautiful people. ■ *2416 Western Ave; 441-1677; map:F8; $$; beer and wine; MC, V; no checks; lunch Mon–Fri, dinner every day, brunch Sat–Sun.*

**Dahlia Lounge** ★★★½ The Dahlia Lounge is, for many locals and out-of-towners, synonymous with the Seattle food scene. Many of us learned about Northwest foods from kitchen maverick Tom Douglas, and grew accustomed to his clever juxtaposition of cultures within a meal, indeed within a plate. With his star ever rising, Douglas opened Etta's Seafood (see review). He now shuttles between the two very different restaurants and his latest project, a third downtown restaurant at Fifth and Lenora, scheduled to open at press time. Yet even in his absence, the food at the Dahlia is executed with an artist's eye and an epicure's palate. The restaurant's scenic appeal lies in a stylish two-level dining landscape of vermilion and gold and brocade (and papier-mâché fish lamps between the booths)—and the intriguing presentations on your plate. Pan-seared calamari, in a broth fragrant with chiles, Chinese black beans, and Thai basil, comes paired with coconut rice cakes. A Persian play on ravioli marries Middle Eastern flavorings—yogurt, mint, and cumin—with such Asian ingredients as cilantro and ginger. And you'll not find a better version of the salty-sweet Japanese specialty, kasu cod, than that served here. A few disappointments of late—an overcooked roasted duck one night; Tom's signature baby back ribs with a sorry, cakey version of the oft-fabulous Chinese pancakes on another; slight lapses in service on a couple of occasions—have unfortunately cost the Dahlia its four-star-status. As for desserts, we're inclined to say they're the best in town—and we'd consider bestowing our first *fifth* star on the perfect coconut cream pie. ■ *1904 4th Ave; 682-4142; map:I7; $$; full bar; AE, DC, MC, V; local checks only; lunch Mon–Fri, dinner every day.* &

**DaVinci's Flying Pizza and Pasta** ★½ It could be 1969, judging from the trippy Day-Glo and black-light decor, tempered with a touch of modernity—big-screen TVs in the bar, which jumps with young singles looking for excellent pizza, pasta, and perhaps other things as well. DaVinci's fronts two streets, wrapping around the corner of a building, with garage-door–type walls that open in fine weather. The back room is the lake-view restaurant proper, only a little more sedate than the bar. Avoid the heinous barbecue smoked-chicken pizzas. Much better is the Leonardo's pizza with aged salami, Greek olives, chèvre, peppers, and tomatoes saucelessly combined with olive oil on a bready crust in a clean marriage of flavors. Better still are the pastas, including excellent lasagne and divine cannelloni. Sandwiches are unusually satisfying, desserts heavenly. There's a section of meat and fish entrees, but you're better off with the basics. ■ *89 Kirkland Ave, Kirkland; 889-9000; map:EE3; $; full bar; AE, DC, MC, V; checks OK; lunch, dinner every day.*

**Dixie's BBQ** ★ Discovering Dixie's BBQ requires a little faith. Despite the streetside sign, this tan steel building looks for all the world like an automotive repair garage. Guess what? It is. Hours before cracking open a crankcase at Porter's Automotive Service, Gene Porter fires up his smoker, desciptively

▼

**Top 200 Restaurants**

▲

named Dino, in a converted 1,500-gallon tank. It was faith that launched this enterprise: Gene and his wife, Dixie, started barbecuing for the family church. Eventually, they partitioned off 600 square feet of the garage and opened for business. The brief menu lists five dinner options—pork rib, beef rib, chicken or turkey wings, and a combo plate—along with a brisket sandwich, a few sides, and a dessert or two. On a lucky day, you'll find Dixie has baked a lemon cake—if you're even luckier, a sweet potato pie. It's primarily take-out, but with a few tables in the garage/waiting room and outside in the driveway, it's the only place we know where you can get brisket and a brake job at the same time. ■ *11522 Northup Way, Bellevue; 828-2460; map:GG3; $; no alcohol; no credit cards; local checks only; lunch and dinner Mon–Sat.* &

**El Greco** ★★ El Greco is a calm oasis amid the crowded bustle on neon-lit, see-and-be-seen Broadway. Warm wood, linen napkins, fresh flowers, and world-beat music make this Mediterranean-inspired bistro a neighborhood favorite. Hummus and baba ghanouj are to be expected, but such fabulous dishes as creamy, fennel-spiked arborio rice topped with five perfectly cooked prawns and scented with ouzo (we've had risotto half as good at twice the price) and a wild mushroom ragout (an earthy concoction of mushrooms and vegetables served with crisp, smoked-mozzarella potato cakes) are a welcome surprise. Come for a latte served in a big cup and hope for the warm apple-and-rhubarb crisp served à la mode. ■ *219 Broadway E; 328-4604; map:HH6; $; beer and wine; MC, V; checks OK; lunch and dinner Tues–Sat, brunch Sat–Sun.* &

**El Puerco Lloron** ★½ This place transports you back to that cafe in Tijuana, the one with the screaming hot pink and aquamarine walls and the bent, scarred "Cerveza Superior" tables. Remember the wailing jukebox and the cut-tin lamps and the woman quietly making corn tortillas by the door? It's all here. Belly up to the cafeteria line, place your order (dishes run a paltry $4 to $5), and fight for a table—in warm weather those outdoors are as hard to get as parking spots. Try the taquitos plate, three excellent masa corn tortillas rolled around a filling and served with rice, beans, and a scallion. The chiles rellenos, so often bungled by American chefs, are fresh and bright with flavor. At the end of the counter pick up fresh lemonade or a Mexican beer. ■ *1501 Western Ave, Seattle; 624-0541; map:J8; $; beer and wine; AE, MC, V; no checks; lunch, early dinner every day.*

**Emmett Watson's Oyster Bar** ★ Occupying a cheery back-alley cranny in the Soames-Dunn Building, the namesake restaurant of Seattle's most curmudgeonly journalist embodies some of the casual irreverence of this town. The tiny flowered courtyard is nice when warm noontime sunlight drifts down to the tables; when the weather is wet, take refuge inside at one of the booths. Part of the draw is the oysters. Regulars drop in just to slip down one or a half-dozen on the half shell or fried up hot and sandwiched on a French roll. Others love the salmon soup, a clean, clam-based broth with big chunks of the pink fish. Still others come for the chowder and a Guinness (one of many bottled brews and drafts available). Or the fish 'n' chips—true cod dipped in a spicy breading, fried in light cottonseed oil, and drizzled, if you wish, with Cajun garlic sauce. ■ *1916 Pike Pl (Pike Place Market); 448-7721; map:J9; $; beer and wine; no credit cards; checks OK; lunch every day, dinner Mon–Sat.* &

**Etta's Seafood** ★★★ When Tom Douglas opened his second restaurant, Etta's, in early 1995, it was not immediately clear whether history was being repeated or made. The remodeled, '90s-style seafood house—with one small, conversation-friendly dining room and another larger and much noisier noshery complete with a bar and counter seating—occupies the husk of the late Cafe Sport (where Douglas first made his mark a decade ago before achieving culinary fame at his own Dahlia Lounge—see review). Douglas has the chutzpah to list starter courses like fire-grilled tamales with Jack cheese and ancho chiles ($3 each) alongside beluga caviar ($44 an ounce). His lengthy menu dares you to choose between such wonders as a simple wedge of iceberg lettuce topped with an extraordinary blue cheese dressing or a lively octopus and shiitake salad with a tangy citrus marinade. Choosing from almost as many "sides" to go along with the Dungeness crab cakes or a broiled Maine lobster is even more daunting. (Hint: Don't miss the red bliss mashed potatoes.) Start with an ass-kicking Bloody Mary, and save room for dessert. ■ *2020 Western Ave; 443-6000; map:I8; $$$; full bar; AE, DC, MC, V; checks OK; lunch, dinner every day.* &

**Ezell's Fried Chicken** ★ None of this Chicken Littles stuff—this is the real article—the stuff that a thinner Oprah Winfrey dreams of now that she's stopped having it flown from here to Chicago—with fresh, moist meat (your choice of light or dark), beautiful, crackly golden crust, and a tangier crust with a Creole bite on the spicy pieces. Get parts, a whole chicken, or even the livers and gizzards. Dinner includes real mashed potatoes and rather tasteless gravy. Also a remarkably good coleslaw—cabbage chunks and carrot shreds held together by a sweet, peppery sauce. The sweet, cake-textured rolls can be purchased by the dozen. Finish with a fat wedge of sweet-potato pie. Expect long lines during lunch hour—Garfield High's across the street—and don't expect to sit down: this is take-out only. ■ *501 23rd Ave; 324-4141; map:HH6; $; no alcohol; no credit cards; checks OK; lunch, dinner every day.*

▼

**Top 200 Restaurants**

▲

**F. X. McRory's Steak, Chop, and Oyster House** ★★ Seattle's poshest sports bar is, appropriately, just a bounce away from the Kingdome, and it's always jammed on game nights. Seattle singles and sports figures hang out at the Whiskey Bar for some of the high-scores there (choose among 145 different bourbons to knock back with one of 28 microbrews on tap). And it's also one of the few places around where you can smoke a fine cigar while sipping a Cognac. Booze and sports aside, the food here is actually very good. In the oyster bar, slurp a handful on the half shell or tackle a Dungeness crab from the tank. Entree portions are ample and dinners come with a mondo baked potato. The crispy haystack onions we like, the steakhouse mushrooms not so much. Beefeaters snap up the roasting box beef, a near-perfect prime rib with fresh horseradish, the T-bone steaks, and the gigantic Boston Butt pork chop with red sauce. For leafeaters, there are salads. Save room for the luscious bourbon pecan pie. ■ *419 Occidental Ave S; 623-4800; map:P9; $$; full bar; AE, DC, MC, V; local checks only; lunch Mon–Fri (Sat, Sun during Kingdome events), dinner every day.* &

▼

**Top 200 Restaurants**

▲

**Filiberto's** ★★ Recently celebrating its 20th anniversary, Filiberto's is among the most authentic and, on a good day, the best of the local Italian restaurants. The look is cheery and trattoria-perfect (even the dishwashing area in back is finished in imported tile). Service can be erratic, but the food is the primary focus here, with good attention to the basics. The long menu emphasizes Roman and other midregion preparations of pasta (including delicious gnocchi), veal, poultry, and rabbit, right down to the real stracciatelle alla Romana (the Italian version of egg-drop soup). There's a large, well-priced selection of Italian wines in a help-yourself wall display; a real pizza oven which turns out noteworthy pizza and calzone; and a bocce court out back, complete with lighting for nighttime play when weather permits. ■ *14401 Des Moines Memorial Dr, Burien; 248-1944; map:NN7; $$; full bar; AE, MC, V; checks OK; lunch, dinner Tues–Sat.* &

**Firenze** ★★ Owner Salvatore Lembo squeezes considerable Mediterranean atmosphere out of this small mall restaurant just a ravioli toss from Crossroads Cinema: terra-cotta floor, sun yellow stucco walls, one antique sideboard, one old chandelier, and many, many wine bottles. Sinatra knocks out a tune to the crash of dishes dumped in a serving station just outside the kitchen. Expect traditional Italian offerings among the pasta, veal, and chicken dishes. Spaghetti carbonara is dreamily creamy, generously spiced, and loaded with pancetta. A tender chicken breast or veal fillet rests in a lake of Gorgonzola sauce. Skip the veal marsala and move on to a veal piccante, sauced with sun-dried tomatoes, capers, and lemon—simple, elegant, sublime. Nightly specials can include osso bucco, risotto, and the occasional salmon. Servers know their stuff and don't try to force a dessert on you, though you wouldn't mind being forced to eat the dainty little tiramisu. ■ *15600 NE 8th, Bellevue; 957-1077; map:HH3; $$; full bar; AE, DC, MC, V; local checks only; lunch Mon–Fri, dinner every day.* &

**5 Spot Cafe** ★½ Most mornings there's a line under the big neon coffee cup outside this Queen Anne landmark. It's a Big Fun kind of place at the top of the Counterbalance and, in fact, it counterbalances an architecturally pretty cafe with a kitschy menu and calm, pleasant service. That menu brags, "We're all over the map." No kidding. Expect such standard regional American fare as Southern-style tasso ham, red beans, and rice; Northwest salmon cakes; and New England roast chicken supper. A Food Festival Series mixes in a different region (say, Florida or Texas) on a rotational basis, plus a nightly bargain like Shaker meat loaf for $5 ("a five spot") starting at 5pm. We give a "hubba hubba" to the moist coconut-pineapple coffee cake and the updated red flannel hash at breakfast, which may be the best you'll ever eat. A great pair of dinner pork chops comes with rib-sticking mashed potatoes and gravy, though we know folks who can make a meal out of an order of french fries and a Pabst Blue Ribbon in the bar (aka the Counterbalance Room). Burgers are not the forte here, and vegetarians have some good choices. No one should pass up the bread pudding or the chocolate cake. ■ *1502 Queen Anne Ave N; 285-SPOT; map:GG8; $; full bar; MC, V; checks OK; breakfast, lunch, dinner every day.* &

▼

Top 200
Restaurants

▲

**Flying Fish** ★★½ Opened in 1995, this swanky joint, all bustle and clean lines and great aromas, is dead-bang in the middle of Restaurant Row along Belltown's stretch of First Avenue. Chef Christine Keff (late of the Hunt Club and others) has assembled a menu paying lavish homage to seafood, not only with sparkling renditions of the usual Northwest suspects— Dungeness crab in a fiery Sichuan sauce, grilled king salmon— but with exotic imports rarely if ever encountered on local lists. These "flying fish" may include a tender fillet of arctic char served in a rich chanterelle sauce; a moist, snapperlike escolar in a delicious chipotle vinaigrette; or the firm whitefish called opah, cooked to a turn and served in red pepper oil. Most fun is ordering off the by-the-pound section of the menu and sharing great platters of crab, mussels, snapper, and such around the table (watch for swiftly mounting prices), then augmenting with one or two tapas-size noshes of sashimi-grade yellowfin tuna or a fried oyster caesar. It's a jolly, clattering place—too loud for some—but once servers find their footing and hipsters move on to newer haunts, the Flying Fish should be a solid, innovative addition to Seattle's growing seafood scene. ■ *2234 1st Ave; 728-8595; map:G8; $$; full bar; AE, DC, MC, V; checks OK; dinner every day.* ሌ

**The Four Swallows** ★½ The funky pub which once drew so many regulars to Lynwood Center was transplanted in 1993 to a charming house a scenic mile from the ferry dock. Much of the original spirit remains (though the gift shop in the front of the house is a bit confusing). One sits inside at cozy high-backed booths in winter, outside on the breezy deck in summer, and enjoys Italian-inspired dinners like fresh ravioli with roasted plum tomatoes, clam linguine with garlic and shallots, and a rotating list of homemade pizzas. Though performance varies in an affably casual way, you can expect more hits than misses. Don't miss the sprawling antipasto plate, which might feature such nibbles as crostini, goat cheese, roasted garlic, figs, and roasted eggplant. The other end of the meal is similarly commendable, particularly the velvety crème caramel. Service is warm and knowing. ■ *481 Madison Ave, Bainbridge Island; 842-3397; $$; beer and wine; AE, MC, V; checks OK; dinner Mon–Sat.* ሌ

**Fremont Classic Pizza and Trattoria** ★ The tiny, cheery Fremont Classic feels almost like a let's-pretend restaurant; nothing is taken too seriously here. Servers are fun and feisty, as befits a small neighborhood restaurant; decor, neither here nor there, is just plain cozy; and, if you stick to the pizza, you can enjoy an utterly delicious, unpretentious meal. Chef Paul's pizza dough is of the thin, crackly, floury, slightly chewy sort and his sauce is of the refreshing, chopped-up-tomato variety—a perfect combination. You can choose between traditional pizzas (your choice among the usual suspects) or one of chef Paul's inventive concoctions. We tend to prefer the former: the crust and sauce are so good, it's a shame to disguise them with a bunch of goop. The simplest pizza of all, the Margherita—tomatoes, mozzarella, Asiago, extra-virgin olive oil, and basil—is smashing. Pasta dishes are less successful. You get huge piles of chewy pasta, oversauced, relentlessly flavorful, and almost tiring in their robustness. Desserts are fine if you've got room, but you won't miss anything if you haven't. ■ *4307 Fremont Ave N; 548-9411; map:FF7; $; beer and wine; DC, MC, V; local checks only; dinner every day.* ሌ

**Fremont Noodle House** ★★ Finally. A Thai restaurant whose atmosphere can compete with its food for your sensory pleasure. You can't help but be drawn in off Fremont's main drag to inspect this wood-filled temple of Thai good taste, where rice-paper lampshades hang from the ceiling, a curio cabinet displays Thai photos, and mirrors make the oft-crowded room appear much larger than it is. A short menu offers fragrant noodle-based soups and sautés and simple rice dishes spiked with various meats, seafoods, and vegetables. Among the half-dozen appetizers is mieng hahm, a most sensually appealing starter. Arranged on a large wooden platter are tiny individual bowls of colorful, freshly chopped condiments—toasted coconut, ginger, Thai chile, peanuts, red onion, and lime—meant to be folded into the accompanying bai cha plu (dark green leaves), then dipped into a sweet sauce to assuage the heat. At $7.50, it's the most expensive dish on the menu. Service is swift and exceptionally polite. ■ *3411 Fremont Ave N; 547-1550; map:FF8; $; beer and wine; MC, V; checks OK; lunch, dinner Tues–Sun.*

### Fullers (Seattle Sheraton Hotel and Towers) ★★★½ A
hushed elegance complements the stunning display of contemporary Northwest glass and artwork. You sink into a high-backed, almost-private banquette, or into the cushioned comfort of a table next to the calming waterfall of a George Tsutakawa–designed fountain. "Hmmmm," you say. "Nice, in a stuffy, museum-ish way." Prepare for an attitude adjustment. Your taste buds will be spun in all directions by chef Monique Barbeau—third in a line of very young women chef-execs—who has been putting her bold signature on the Fullers menu since 1992. Schooled in the four-star kitchens of New York, Barbeau flouts convention, getting bolder with every local and national award. Bite-size sashimi-grade tuna, flavored with shiso leaf and tossed with wasabe vinaigrette, shows up in an edible potato-parsnip basket; a composed salad of watermelon and feta cheese sports tart red sumac and sage pesto. Some would be better off with a trio of Ellensburg lamb chops in a port demiglace with a luscious potato–goat cheese tart—staid by comparison. We like the casual sophistication of the waitstaff, the fussy press-pot-and-chocolate-straw coffee service, and the chance to prove to ourselves that hotel-restaurant fine dining is *not* a contradiction in terms. ■ *1400 6th Ave; 447-5544; map:K5; $$$; full bar; AE, DC, MC, V; checks OK; lunch Mon–Fri, dinner Mon–Sat.* &

### Gene's Ristorante
Gene's is home to many surprises—some nice and some not so nice. On a recent visit, our first surprise was the straggling line of leather-chapped women who were leaving as we entered. One by one, the women straddled their hogs and rode away. "The Renton Ladies of Harley," our hostess informed us. "They meet here once a month." As to the food, the appetizers and pizza are surprisingly good, and the entrees can be surprisingly, well, bad. Among the appetizers, the torta—with its crispy, chewy crust layered with sun-dried tomatoes, artichoke hearts, ricotta and mozzarella, and accompanied by a little bowl of marinara dipping sauce—wins raves. Pizzas also reflect this crunchy-chewy aesthetic. The salads are excellent, including one that recently harbored what actually tasted like home-grown tomatoes. The entrees are

▼

▲

another story: pastas are slathered in heavy, sweet red sauces; the pork Dijonnaise tastes like a diner pork chop, not warranting its high price tag; and the polenta crumbles in an unappetizing way. The biggest surprise of all is the chocolate mousse, which, all in our party agreed, tasted like a Charleston Chew mashed into a wineglass. We say, stick with pizzas, appetizers, and salads, and enjoy the roar of the hogs. ■ *212 S 3rd St, Renton; 271-7042; map:NN3; $$; beer and wine; AE, DC, MC, V; checks OK; lunch Mon–Fri, dinner Tues–Sat.* &

### Georgian Room (Four Seasons Olympic Hotel) ★★★★ A
grand space for those grand occasions, the Georgian Room, with its high ceilings, ornate chandeliers, and all the accoutrements of fine dining, will take you back in time to a place that—believe it or not—still exists. As you sink back into your banquette-built-for-two, the tuxedoed maître d' pours your martini from an elegant shaker, a staff of smiling, professional waiters dressed in full "Love Boat" regalia tend to your every need, and a pianist tinkles the ivories in the center of the room. And you should come prepared to pay a lot for the experience. Chef Kerry Sear prepares a warm salad of winter cabbage speckled with duck cracklings wearing a perfect slice of foie gras. Feather-light nubbins of potato gnocchi stand up to a mushroom broth enriched with sliced cèpes. Entrees appear as objets d'art—a rack of lamb crowns a plate garnished with garlic-stuffed olives and Swiss chard. Four joints of pheasant sauced with caramelized onions beg for a side of Sear's butter-drenched, garlic-whipped yellow Finn potatoes. Private parties can reserve in the Georgette Petite room. Afterward, step into the Georgian Terrace for a very civilized Cognac and a cigar. ■ *411 University St; 621-7889; map:K6; $$$; full bar; AE, DC, MC, V; no checks; breakfast every day, dinner Mon–Sat.* &

▼
**Top 200
Restaurants**
▲

### Gerard's Relais de Lyon ★★★½ If you do something special
and you do it well, chances are you will endure, and the world will be a better place for having you. If not the world, definitely Bothell. Enter Gerard Parrat, whose outpost and bastion of French cuisine still offers—after 20 years—a last great hope for lovers of fine, formal dining. Choose from the two prix-fixe menus, the découverte ("discovery" menu, six courses) or dégustation ("tasting" menu, seven courses), and you're in for a culinary feast lasting two to three hours. The back room of this multiroom converted house is our choice, since cigarette smoke can drift from the middle to the front room. Better even than the warming gas fireplaces is the lovely courtyard out back. Service is friendly and the food consistently superb. A meal might begin with a thin slice of Cognac pâté brought before the first course. From there the meal proceeds through sublime roast garlic soup, a roulade of marinated vegetables, and a sausage-filled ravioli in duck consomme; onward to duck

in a dark orange sauce and past a palate-freshening salad; heading finally into a Grand Marnier soufflé. One could faint from sheer delight and volume. Fortunately, you *can* order à la carte if you plan to eat again sometime during the coming week. ■ *17121 Bothell Way NE, Bothell; 485-7600; map:AA4; $$$; full bar; AE, DC, MC, V; checks OK; dinner Tues–Sun.* ᓬ

**Gordo's** Gordo's at Shilshole is a sunny-day spot, the type of place that—corn dogs and all—conjures up memories of those childhood summers at the beach that you wish you'd had. They've got a couple of roadside picnic tables set up outside (there's no inside seating), but we recommend grabbing the greasy (hey, that's the point here) goods and heading up to Golden Gardens. Lots of customers swear by Gordo's burgers, but we go for the no-nonsense fish 'n' chips. Save room for one of the scrumptious made-to-order milk shakes. ■ *6226 Seaview Ave NW; 784-7333; map:E8; $; no alcohol; no credit cards; local checks only; lunch, dinner every day (early dinner in winter).*

**Gravity Bar** ★½ Meet George Jetson. His boy Elroy. Daughter Judy. Jane, his wife. Need we say more about Seattle's slickest vegetarian restaurant and juice bar, with its conical tables of galvanized metal and green frosted glass lit from within for the ultimate Jetsons effect. Chic patrons down shots of wheat grass, becoming rejuvenated before your very eyes, but most shy from the dark green sludge and opt instead for a banana-pineapple blend, or carrot-spinach-beet. Entrees are luscious, healthful, and beautifully presented: mounds of brown rice and steamed vegetables with a glistening lemon tahini sauce; chapatis rolled with hummus and fresh vegetables; miso soup with buckwheat noodles; tempeh burgers with barbecue sauce on whole-grain rolls; sun-dried tomatoes and provolone on thick fingers of rye. The freshest of fresh juices can get expensive, but indulge. You'll feel like a million bucks later. ■ *113 Virginia St; 448-8826; map:I8; $$; beer and wine; MC, V; local checks only; lunch, dinner every day, brunch Sat–Sun.* ■ *415 Broadway E; 325-7186; map:HH6; $$; no alcohol; no credit cards; local checks only; breakfast, lunch, dinner every day.*

**Harbor City Barbecue House** ★ Often overlooked, Harbor City had the first *real* Chinese barbecue oven in town—a large, drumlike contraption large enough to roast a whole pig as it hangs vertically and turns slowly. The results are some of the most tender, moist morsels we've found in Seattle. Stop the chef from pouring barbecue sauce all over your portion; it can be a very leaky affair if you take it to go. Besides, meat that good doesn't need to be soaked in sauce. ■ *707 S King St; 621-2228; map:R6; $; beer and wine; DC, MC, V; no checks; lunch, dinner Tues–Sun.* ᓬ

**The Herbfarm** ★★★★ What began as a front-yard wheelbarrow filled with a few extra chives for sale has become a trustworthy haven of gourmandise in the Cascade foothills. (The legendary difficulty in securing reservations has been slightly alleviated since the proprietors began leaving a quarter of their 32-seat dining room unreserved until 1pm Friday of the week before the weekend in question.) What the Herbfarm presents is not simply a meal, but an opportunity for tasting, learning, and talking about what you have eaten. Meals generally begin with a short tour of the 17 herbal theme gardens, and the education continues throughout, as owner Ron Zimmerman and chef Jerry Traunfeld narrate from the open kitchen. Co-owner Carrie Van Dyck brings a stuffed bear named Herb into the act, providing the only oversweetened moments of the whole feast. And a feast it is. A dinner might begin with sparkling wine perfumed with a sweet herbal extract and move to a soufflé of Oregon white truffles baked in a fresh brown eggshell, a risotto rich with wild boletus mushrooms and shavings of Sally Jackson's handcrafted sheep cheese, and a sorbet made from Champagne and Douglas fir needles. The entree? Perhaps an herb-crusted Ellensburg lamb keeping company with wild, locally gathered mushrooms, or a lavender-steamed loin of rabbit wrapped in mustard leaves. Each course comes with a matched wine, including a rare dessert wine such as a 1915 Cossart-Gordon Madeira. Plan on three hours for lunch, four to five for dinner, and plan on paying dearly (though you'll never regret it) for this extraordinary celebration of Northwest bounty. ■ *32804 Issaquah–Fall City Rd, Fall City; 784-2222; $$$; wine only; AE, MC, V; checks OK; lunch or dinner Fri–Sat, occasional meals Thurs and Sun; (closed in March).* &

**Hi-Spot Cafe** ★★ Since Joanne Segura and Michael Walker took the helm in 1994, the Hi-Spot Cafe has finally risen above its Moosewood-with-meat image. This old multilevel Victorian, with its outdoor deck for warm-weather dining, is ever inviting. The bakery is now out of sight, making room up front for a sleek espresso bar and a few cafe tables. Breakfast is still breakfast: same long lines; same baked eggs; same great cinnamon buns. Lunch includes the requisite soups, salads, and groovy '90s sandwiches. But dinner (where chef Segura gets to strut her stuff with a menu that changes monthly) is now the real reason to head here. You'll find appetizers such as a Gorgonzola cheesecake with roasted red pepper sauce, or brandade de morue—a classic rendering of the warm, spreadable mash of potato and salt cod. Spicy Caribbean seafood stew gets its bright coloring from fiery-hot harissa mellowed with coconut milk; a mixed grill comes with an innovative version of dolmades: Swiss chard leaves stuffed with rice and garbanzo beans over a peppery tzatziki sauce. Well-conceived salads and a quartet of pastas are always ready for the less adventuresome. Entrees won't set you back much more than $10 and wine list prices hover in the low end, making it worthwhile to stray from your own neighborhood to this Madrona neighborhood destination. ■ *1410 34th Ave; 325-7905; map:GG7; $; beer and wine; MC, V; checks OK; breakfast every day, lunch Mon–Fri, dinner Tues–Sat.* &

### The Hunt Club (Sorrento Hotel) ★★★ The Hunt Club, along with Fullers and the Georgian Room, remains in the bold forefront of good, even excellent, hotel dining. The clubby bar and carefully partitioned dining room—considered a bit dark and cloistered by some—are warmed with burnished mahogany paneling and deep red brickwork. If the kitchen suffers from a bad case of musical chef-execs, the Powers That Be are quick to ensure that those chefs are worthy of top toque status. In 1994, chef Eric Lenard, a well-schooled young upstart from San Francisco, took over where his two talented predecessors left off. Lenard's contribution to the Hunt Club's menu relies on rich reductions and bold flavorings. We've been impressed with the naturally sweet and artfully spiced butternut squash ravioli, a deep, lavender-stoked sauce on a stellar rack of lamb, the roasted smokiness of a fillet of king salmon, and the solicitous-yet-affable service. After dinner, savvy patrons retire to the lobby bar for coffee and dessert—homemade ices or an exceptional crème brûlée. ■ *900 Madison St; 343-6156; map:L4; $$$; full bar; AE, DC, MC, V; checks OK; breakfast, lunch, tea, dinner every day, brunch Sat–Sun.* &

**Huong Binh** ★ While other less successful eateries come and go, this tidy Vietnamese restaurant, in one of the many strip malls marking the ever-expanding Vietnamese commercial area near the International District, continues to hold its own. We've had feasts here, huge brimming tables-full, for under $20. One such: banh beo (steamed rice cake topped with brilliant orange ground shrimp), cha hue (a steamed pork roll), bahn hoi chao tom (grilled shrimp on sugar cane—hint to novices: you eat the shrimp, then suck the cane), and a couple of dishes starring pork and shrimp skewers with rice. Pork is particularly nicely done: tender, pounded thin, and marinated in garlic and lemongrass. Best of all, these grilled dishes come in traditional Vietnamese fashion with an accompanying fragrant garden of herbs, to allow you to dress your food to your liking. ■ *1207 S Jackson St; 720-4907; map:HH6; $; beer and wine; no credit cards; local checks only; lunch, early dinner every day.*

**I Love Sushi** ★★½ Chef Tadashi Sato has created a pair of premier Japanese restaurants on either side of Lake Washington. Both feature bustling, bright, high-energy sushi bars with exquisitely fresh fish—and a friendly, helpful staff to keep things running smoothly. At the sushi bar, Sato and his minions—in their traditional hajimaki (headbands)—attract many Japanese customers who know a good thing when they eat one. The sushi combinations are a veritable bargain (particularly at lunch), while such traditional Japanese specialties as sea urchin, abalone, and fermented bean paste may raise the stakes somewhat. The hot dishes, including flame-broiled fish cheeks, the ubiquitous tempura, and chawan mushi—a steamed custard egg soup that is the ultimate in Japanese comfort food— are excellent. There's not much of a nonsmoking section at the Lake Union restaurant. In Bellevue, you can sing along nightly in the karaoke bar. ■ *1001 Fairview Ave N; 625-9604; map:GG7; $$; full bar; AE, MC, V; no checks; lunch Mon–Fri, dinner every day.* & ■ *11818 NE 8th St, Bellevue; 454-5706; map:HH3; $$; full bar; AE, MC, V; no checks; lunch Mon–Sat, dinner every day.* &

**Il Bacio** ★★ The skills of chef Rino Baglio—whose list of credentials runs longer than uncut linguine (he helped prepare the wedding feast for Chuck and Di, and cooked for Princess Caroline of Monaco)—deserve a far grander setting and far better seating than this faux-Italian patio in a strip mall. But once you fork into a luscious risotto laden with bits of sausage and porcini mushrooms, or the cappellini all'aragosta (featuring not exactly the advertised lobster tail, but a close crustacean relative, the langoustine) sauced with an intensely flavorful demiglace of lemon, rosemary, and garlic, it won't matter where you are. Baglio's beautifully rendered Italian specialties will create all the ambience you need. The creamy tomato-basil soup starts things right, and you'd be foolish not to leave room for dessert, which comes from Baglio's nifty little adjacent Pasticcerie Il Bacio. ■ *16564 Cleveland St, Redmond; 869-8815; map:EE1; $$; beer and wine; MC, V; checks OK; lunch Mon–Fri, dinner Mon–Sat.* &

**Il Bistro** ★★★ Through the years, Il Bistro has been a cherished refuge down a narrow cobblestone street in Pike Place Market. The low-ceilinged, intimate rooms, rounded arches, and whitewashed walls are a perfect background for enjoying food, wine, and the company of friends. The lower-level bar is a favorite spot to linger over an apertif or share a convivial late-night supper. Current owners Tom Martino and Dale Abrams continue to keep the Bistro going strong as the restaurant continues into its third decade. There are always interesting specials at Il Bistro (say, tiny morel mushrooms playing inspired complement to a tangle of tagliatelle), but this is a place where many patrons know what to order before they leave home. Il Bistro consistently serves one of the best racks of lamb in Seattle—and just the right wines to go along with it (there's a lengthy list of Chiantis). Those who once had a love affair with pasta here may find the offerings hit-or-miss, but the sexy Euro-bistro atmosphere, and the wonderful veal carpaccio and Antipasto Dino, will help you forget the kitchen's occasional flaws. Dessert? The Marquis, a simply deadly piece of chocolate, is divine. ▪ *93-A Pike St (Pike Place Market); 682-3049; map:J8; $$$; full bar; AE, DC, MC, V; no checks; dinner every day.*

**Il Paesano** ★½ As you head north up the Ave, things begin to look a little bleak. Tumbledown houses, going-out-of-business sales, bookstores increasingly marginal in their leftist missions. And then an oasis: Il Paesano. Accordian music spills over the cinderblock patio, luring you into this endearing little box of a trattoria, which features the everyday food of Italy. The menu comprises a list of pastas, a few meat entrees (often oversalted), and excellent pizzas on crackerlike crusts (one serves well as an appetizer for two). The calamari in marinara is delicious, the salads (free with your entree, a practice we thought had been outlawed inside Seattle city limits) uneventful, the rigatoni alla carbonara chewy but well-sauced, the zabaglione stunning, and the bill the biggest delight of all. The wine list is mostly Italian, good, and affordable. ▪ *5628 University Way; 526-0949; map:FF6; $$; beer and wine; MC, V; local checks only; dinner Mon–Sat.* ᕋ

**Il Terrazzo Carmine** ★★★ Be prepared to spend an entire evening at Il Terrazzo, for dining at Carmine Smeraldo's restaurant is an event. Graze through the wonderful antipasti and watch for Seattle's rich and famous, who are likely to be dining beside you in this comfortably airy restaurant or on the outside terrace. Deciding among the pastas is a feat, but it's the sauces on the stunning array of meat entrees here that get the greatest applause. The sweetbreads with prosciutto and peas are lightly smothered in a wonderful wine sauce. And the fork-tender veal piccata, a good test of any Italian restaurant, has an equally good reduction sauce, just slightly zingy from capers. Robust Nebbiolo grapes lend a richness to the Barolo sauce that cloaks the tender fillet of beef. The wine list is extensive and includes some prime Tuscan reds usually found only in tiny hill villages. Prices here are high, but there are tables in the bar where you might share the antipasti and a couple of glasses of wine, and call it dinner. ▪ *411 1st Ave S; 467-7797; map:A8; $$$; full bar; AE, DC, MC, V; checks OK; lunch Mon–Fri, dinner Mon–Sat.* ᕋ

**Isabella Ristorante** ★★½ Gino Borriello took a chance when he made a foray into a downtown dining scene already inundated with Italian restaurants. The former owner of Ciao Italia in Edmonds and present owner of Ciao Bella in Ravenna (see reviews) gambled wisely, and the success of Isabella, which opened in 1995, proves that Seattle always has room for another *good* Italian restaurant. With its slick decor (towering carmine walls, cobalt columns, and uncluttered spaces) and caring service (Gino and his wife, Tama, direct a team of friendly, capable servers) Isabella is chic but not so intimidating that you couldn't bring your grandmother. Chef Peter Levine orchestrates in the kitchen, where a smashing, mint-tinged panzanella salad, succulent grilled meats, exceptional stuffed pastas, toothsome risotto, and pizzas baked in an imported wood-fired oven are among his engaging repertoire. ■ *1909 3rd Ave; 441-8281; map:I7; $$; full bar; AE, MC, V; checks OK; lunch Mon–Fri, dinner every day.* &

**Italianissimo** ★★ By now a Seattle legend, Luciano Bardinelli found fame with Settebello in Seattle, impossible rent at Stresa on the Kirkland waterfront, and perhaps the perfect, lasting niche in this unlikely suburban location. Here, he consistently exceeds expectations in a relaxed, casual atmosphere that attracts more families than it does ultra-discerning foodies. There's a country-kitchen feel here, from the green-and-cream–tiled floors to the greeneried patio. The service tends toward casual and the menu looks familiar to those who know Bardinelli—thin-crust pizzas, simple pastas (paglia e fieno, capellini with tomatoes and basil), and meats (a preponderance of veal, which is not a bad thing, considering the delicate preparation of a barely sweet, spicy Marsala and a powerfully rich osso bucco Milanese). The calamari stew is spicy and satisfying. Antipasti and desserts are temptingly on view as you enter. ■ *17650 140th Ave NE, Woodinville; 485-6888; map:AA1; $$; beer and wine; AE, DC, MC, V; checks OK; lunch Mon–Fri, dinner Mon–Sat.* &

**Ivar's Acres of Clams and Fish Bar** ★ ■ **Ivar's Indian Salmon House** ★ ■ **Ivar's Mukilteo Landing** ★ The late Ivar Haglund was a legend in this town—entrepreneurial dynamo, master of the corny pun ("Keep Clam"), prolific fish fryer. He has passed away (God rest his sole), but his legacy lives on in the form of three waterside restaurants, two take-out fish bars, and fast-food outposts all over the city (not recommended here). The newest is Ivar's Mukilteo. Best loved, however, is Northlake's Indian Salmon House, a replica of an Indian longhouse where salmon and black cod are properly broiled over a smoky alder fire and served with corn bread. Consistent it's not, but Seattleites often take guests here anyway. Acres of Clams is the most centrally located for tourists, the slickest, and therefore the laziest—you might encounter overcooked salmon or flawed service. Kids will love the place. The Salmon House and Acres of Clams both have take-out adjuncts with outdoor seating; wonderful for cod 'n' chips or (excellent) clam nectar, enjoyed in quintessentially Seattle settings. ■ *Pier 54; 624-6852;*

*map:L9; $$; full bar; AE, MC, V; checks OK; lunch, dinner every day.* & ▪ *401 NE Northlake Way; 632-0767; map:FF7; $$; full bar; AE, MC, V; checks OK; lunch Mon–Sat, dinner every day, brunch Sun.* & ▪ *710 Front St, Mukilteo; (206)347-3648; $$; full bar; AE, MC, V; checks OK; breakfast, lunch, dinner every day.* &

**Izumi** ★★ Tucked into taco-and-burger land in a Kirkland shopping center, Izumi is a favorite among the local Japanese community. Part the dark blue half-curtain inside the front door, and suburbia is left behind; you're in the competent care of servers in traditional sea green kimonos. Things move briskly at lunch, when Japanese families sometimes mingle with the business crowd. (Lunch hours are 11:30am to 1:30pm, and they mean it. If you linger past 2pm, you're likely to realize that the background music has just stopped midphrase.) Unagi (broiled freshwater eel) and mirugai (geoduck) sushi are outstanding; roe enthusiasts can sample the eggs of four different sea creatures. Tonkatsu, port cutlet in a light, crisp breading, is juicy, tender, and generously portioned. For those who tread lightly into Japanese cuisine, the tempura crust is exceedingly light and the teriyaki excellent—and not overly sweet. Makunouchi can be had at lunch, or in two sizes at dinner—the larger a feast of sushi, sashimi, tempura, teriyaki, and cooked vegetables presented in a lacquer box. Wash everything down with a big Asahi beer. ▪ *12539 116th Ave NE, Kirkland; 821-1959; map:EE3; $$; beer and wine; AE, MC, V; checks OK; lunch Mon–Fri, dinner every day.* &

**Judkins Barbecue Restaurant** ★ South of Jackson Street and east of 23rd lies Judkins Park, Seattle's barbecue mecca. It's not much to look at—a few tables and vinyl chairs crowded into a plain little room—but the Southern-style food is first-rate and the menu, consisting of various barbecue dinners and sandwiches, fried chicken, and side dishes, is short and sweet. Barbecued ribs are meaty pork with just the right amount of fat, dripping with Judkins's trademark spicy-sweet sauce. Savory chicken comes dusted with herbs and flour that trap a good amount of grease under the skin. Pieces are small, and rightly so: some BBQ joints give you chicken parts of such astonishing size you might suspect the original hen could have moonlighted as Big Bird. Side dishes, including the traditional red beans, runny greens, and macaroni and cheese, might be wonderful: emphasis on the *might*. Service, though somewhat spacey, is warm and welcoming. Dinner is unfashionably early, so be on time. ▪ *2608 S Judkins St; 328-7417; map:HH6; $; no alcohol; no credit cards; no checks; lunch, early dinner every day.*

**Kabul** ★★ In Afghanistan the king's cooks marinated and grilled the finest meats, infusing dishes with mint, cilantro, and dill, and applying the cooling touch of yogurt and the zing of scallions. Recipes were guarded jealously and passed down through the generations. Sultan Malikyar and his family emigrated from Kabul, Afghanistan, in the late '70s to Seattle. Malikyar still cooks from his father's kabob recipe; his chaka (garlic yogurt sauce) and rice come from his mother's side. This is fragrant, elegant food: crisp bolani (scallion-potato turnovers with chaka for dipping); jan-i amma (a sort of Afghan version of tzatziki); ashak (delicate scallion dumplings topped with beef sauce—or a vegetarian tomato sauce—and more chaka); kabobs served on lovely heaps of basmati rice. Service is unfailingly friendly, and the room—with its simple decor, glass-topped tables, and colorful accents—is almost as soothing as the cardamom- and rosewater-flavored custard served as dessert. ■ *2301 N 45th St; 545-9000; map:FF7; $; beer and wine; AE, DC, MC, V; local checks only; dinner Mon–Sat.*

### Kaizuka Teppanyaki and Sushi Bar ★★
Jeff and Lisa Kaizuka got their hands on the shabby, vacant space that once housed the original Nikko and turned it into one of the city's best-kept secrets: a *quiet*, neighborhood, mom-and-pop–run Japanese restaurant. Kaizuka is now beautifully and simply decorated with six teppanyaki tables, four private tatami rooms, and a sushi bar that's comfortingly small. Smiling Jeff Kaizuka entertains at the teppanyaki tables, flashing his knives and flash-searing beef, chicken, and seafood. The generous cuts of maguro, hamachi, and saba folded over lightly seasoned rice are as decidedly less expensive than those purveyed elsewhere. Running between the two rooms, Lisa Kaizuka works the floor, tending tables as well as the door, making sure everyone feels at home. On busy nights, service may be a bit slow, but the wait is always worth it. ■ *1306 S King St; 860-1556; map:II6; $$; beer and wine; AE, DC, MC, V; no checks; lunch Mon–Fri, dinner Mon–Sat.*

### The Kaleenka ★★
You'll rarely find food more comforting than that served in this richly decorated Russian cafe whose menu borrows from many regions of the former Soviet Union. Eastern European accents drift from talk at nearby tables as you sit down to a pot of black currant tea served in a graceful Uzbek teapot. Try a filling plate of vareniky (Ukrainian dumplings stuffed with farmer cheese or spicy potato) or some fragrant samsa (pastries filled with cumin-spiced lamb, served with a sour cream–based dill sauce). The garlicky pilmeny (ravioli-like beef dumplings) float in a huge bowl of beef consommé topped with a dollop of sour cream. Lunch is a bargain. ■ *1933 1st Ave; 728-1278; map:I8; $$; beer and wine; MC, V; checks OK; lunch, dinner Mon–Sat.*

### Kamalco ★½
Kamalco serves its fragrant Middle Eastern food in a whitewashed dining room warmed by a wall the color of

summer buttercups. You may see the matriarch of this family-run enterprise sitting near the door peeling garlic—practically a full-time job, since they use upward of 50 pounds of the stuff a week. Start with zahrah, lightly fried sweet cauliflower dipped in a tangy tahini sauce, or baba ghanouj mashed with lemon juice and tahini and served under a slick of olive oil. Be careful not to overdo it with the appetizers. Dinners are huge. You'll begin with a bowl of robust lentil soup or a salad of nondescript greens dressed with garlic, lemon, and mint. Half a spit-roasted chicken with crisp skin and mega-volts of garlic is sided with pilaf, tahini, and tender white beans stewed in a spicy tomato sauce. Some prefer the shish tawouk—large chunks of white chicken meat marinated in a tangy sauce and grilled on a skewer. Whatever you order, you won't want to be in a rush. The place is often understaffed, the food is truly cooked to order, and you'll need lots of time to finish the gargantuan portions. ■ *414 E Pine St; 323-7565; map:J2; $; beer and wine; AE, MC, V; local checks only; lunch Tues–Fri, dinner every day.* ♿

**Kaspar's** ★★★ Kaspar's by the Bay said goodbye to Belltown and relocated to the elegant, multitiered, remodeled space on lower Queen Anne that once housed the venerable Le Tastevin. We like Kaspar's by the Seattle Center so much better—and so do the pre-theater/opera/ballet crowd who know where to go for a great opening act. Swiss-born and trained, chef Kaspar Donier imaginatively couples classic international cooking styles with fresh Northwest ingredients, and the best of the results can be astonishing. We've had marvelous Muscovy duck breast, garnished with a gingery fruit salsa and escorted by the finest sour cream mashed potatoes imaginable, and perfectly sautéed sea scallops with a spicy bacon sauce over fresh spinach. Desserts consistently reveal the deft hand of a classical pro. Kaspar's wife, Nancy, keeps a watchful eye over a multitude of serving staff, while his brother, Markus, acts as sommelier and catering manager. A cold sampler menu, perfectly executed, is offered in the chic and comfortable wine bar where elegant food is wisely scaled down from the complexity of the dishes served in the restaurant. ■ *19 W Harrison; 298-0123; map:A8; $$$; full bar; MC, V; no checks; dinner Tues–Sat.* ♿

▼

Top 200 Restaurants

▲

**Kells** ★½ The very Irish McAleese family (with strapping young sons galore) run this Irish pub-style restaurant that fits perfectly into the rich ethnic mix of Pike Place Market. The food is straightforward but often surprisingly good: meat pies, leg of lamb, broiled fish, and roasted chicken—hearty, hot, and accompanied by particularly good soda bread. On a blustery day it's a great spot for a comforting lunch of soup and a pastie. The waitstaff and barmen are a friendly band of Irishers. Drop by for a pint of ale in the convivial bar; there's live Irish music in a separate venue in the back Wednesday through Saturday nights. ■ *Post Alley, Pike Place Market; 728-1916; map:H8; $$; full bar; AE, MC, V; no checks; lunch, dinner every day.* &

**Kikuya** ★★ Though it's tucked away in an unprepossessing strip mall, enough people find their way to this small, informal eatery to make a wait at lunchtime likely. No tatami rooms, no kimonos, just good, straightforward fare prepared well and served efficiently. The excellent sushi bar provides visual entertainment. Watch as the cooks turn out reliable tempura, good gyoza, dependable donburi, spicy yakisoba, and fresh sashimi. Meals come with pickled cucumbers, miso, a small salad, and green tea. ■ *8105 161st Ave NE, Redmond; 881-8771; map:EE2; $$; beer and wine; MC, V; no checks; lunch and dinner Tues–Sat.* &

**Kirkland Roaster & Ale House** ★ This was the fifth formula restaurant from the McHugh/Firnstahl dynasty before their final parting. It's just Firnstahl's now, and as formulas go, nobody does it better. Located smack in downtown Kirkland, it's a study in dark wood, green trim, and many windows, some of which look out on a nice deck, others offering a peekaboo view of Lake Washington. Service is generally good: eager, yet casual. The multipage menu has lightened up, now offering a multitude of lower-cal, lower-fat salads, sandwiches, and meat dishes. The name Roaster derives from the 9-foot-high infrared vertical spit-roaster at its heart, slow-roasting chicken and pork, roast beef and turkey, variations of which comprise most of the menu. If you're not a meat eater (or a fan of one of 20 or so beers on tap), you probably don't belong here. A private room holds 40 by arrangement. ■ *111 Central Way, Kirkland; 827-4400; map:EE4; $$; full bar; AE, DC, MC, V; checks OK; lunch, dinner every day.* &

**Koryo Restaurant** ★½ A newcomer on the Korean restaurant front, Koryo, open in 1995, already has a loyal following, and no wonder: it's the brightest, friendliest Korean restaurant out there. There's a tatami alcove for those accustomed to sitting on the floor, a section for those who wish to grill their own dishes, several regular table-and-chairs arrangements, and, best of all, a karaoke bar that's practically in another building. The care and insight that went into the seating arrangement are also evident where it counts the most: in the food. The kalbi come perfectly marinated; the kimchi and vegetable side-dish assortments are fresh and well-seasoned. Although the dwen jang jigae, a thicker, spicier, and stronger version of Japanese miso soup, can be too intense, it shows promise and might satisfy someone with a very high tolerance for salt. No doubt Koryo's best dish is the dolsot bi bim bap—a wonderful assortment of shiitake, fiddlehead ferns, and other vegetables

▼

**Top 200 Restaurants**

▲

served with beef and rice in a hot stone jar. Slather on a spoonful of the accompanying red pepper paste, mix everything together, and savor this "mixed-up rice" with a bottle of the Korean beer OB. Those who aren't familiar with chopsticks may want to order bi bim bap for sheer dining ease; it's one of the few dishes that must be eaten with a spoon. ■ *12020 Aurora Ave N; 362-5009; map:DD7; $$; full bar; AE, MC, V; no checks; lunch, dinner every day.* &

**Lampreia** ★★★★ Likened to the urbane fine-food haunts of New York and San Francisco, Scott Carsberg's sleek restaurant exudes sophistication. While plate as palette—with splashes of color and unexpected combinations of flavor dazzling the eye and the tongue—has become synonymous with the Seattle food scene, chef Carsberg offers a gentle reprieve: a minimalist approach for maximum effect. In his world, simplicity is key—from what's on the walls (a warm-toned paint and little else) to what's on the table (a heavy fork, a knife, a glass, a linen napkin, a candle), to what's on the plate (food so visually understated that the depth of flavor comes as a complete shock). Zealous use of seasonal, regional, and organic ingredients is akin to religion here. The intermezzo course acts as a preview of things to come, or a light meal in itself: perhaps a thick slice of foie gras atop a bed of spicy-sweet red cabbage, or perfectly sautéed razor clams. A choice of four or five entrees might include a tender veal chop tinged with lemon zest and garnished with giant capers, or a fillet of white king salmon swathed with herbed oil and served essentially unadorned over three fat spikes of asparagus. Indulge in an after-dinner cheese fest; an astounding selection of rare and wonderfully stinky cheeses makes a nice alternative to dessert. The wine list is carefully wrought and reasonably priced. Service is as polished as the silver. ■ *2400 1st Ave; 443-3301; map:G8; $$$; full bar; AE, MC, V; no checks; dinner Tues–Sat.*

**Le Gourmand** ★★★ An unprepossessing storefront on the edge of Ballard doesn't seem like much of a destination, and the city's foodies always seem to be buzzing about some more fashionable place. But Bruce Naftaly, one of the founding fathers of Northwest regional cooking, quietly puts out some of the most delectable plates of Northwest bounty in the city, with admirable consistency, in a room as serene as a garden. Seasonal produce and fish arrive daily from Naftaly's carefully chosen list of local suppliers, all to be generously embellished with his forte—sauces—and garnished with edible blossoms from his backyard garden. Dinner here is comprised of appetizer, entree (which carries the price of the meal), and salad. Every dish is carefully considered as to season, taste, and presentation—the entree arrives on its own plate, center stage, with vegetables on a separate dish. Depending on the time of

▼

▲

year, you might begin with an earthy nettle soup or a delicate leek-and-onion tart crowned with juniper berries. A meal might include impossibly tender veal medallions in a sublime chanterelle sauce and a noble rack of lamb followed by a salad of wild greens feathered with calendulas, nasturtiums, and rose petals. The only caveat we have is a longstanding one: service ought to be more polished in a dining room this distinguished.
■ *425 NW Market St; 784-3463; map:FF8; $$$; beer and wine; AE, MC, V; checks OK; dinner Wed–Sat.*

### Lombardi's Cucina ★ ■ Lombardi's Cucina of Issaquah ★ If
you grew up in a big Italian family—or wish you did—you'll feel at home at Lombardi's. From the moment you enter, you're embraced by the friendly, comfortable, slightly boisterous atmosphere. Walk in and you smell the garlic. Walk out and you smell *like* garlic. Their motto, "We eat, therefore we reek": it's impossible to avoid. They even celebrate the stuff each fall with a popular garlic festival held at both locations. The menu is weighted (literally) in the direction of cheese and cream, with a wonderfully rich cannelloni verde, studded with chicken, walnuts, and fresh spinach, and a few pastas on the lighter side. Little pizzas, light but for the weight of cheese, make excellent appetizers, just dotted with tomato sauce and toppings on a thin crust. It's best to forget dietary restrictions here. Once you get past the entrees, a couple of outstanding desserts beckon (try the cannoli or an ultra-rich crema caramellata). The wine list is moderate, with some notable Italian reds. Service is relaxed but professional. ■ *2200 NW Market St; 783-0055; map:FF9; $$; full bar; AE, MC, V; local checks only; lunch Mon–Sat, dinner every day, Sunday brunch.* & ■ *719 NW Gilman Blvd, Issaquah; 391-9097; $$; full bar; AE, MC, V; local checks only; lunch Mon–Fri, dinner every day, Sun brunch.* &

### Luna Park Cafe ★ The charm of West Seattle is its terminal
lack of hipness; it's a neighborhood that doesn't feel the need to *keep up.* The Luna Park Cafe, with its anachronistic hodgepodge of memorabilia, provides the perfect clubhouse for those souls who love to feel cast adrift on the waters of time. The food is, for the most part, as retro as the atmo. Burgers, turkey dinners, and meat loaf are all served with a straight face: no sage stuffing, no imaginative spices, just good old-fashioned cookery. The authenticity stops at the salads, which are 1990s romaine rather than 1950s iceberg. More concessions are made to the health-conscious in the form of spinach salads, tostadas, and the delicious veggie burger, which is a kind of simulacrum for sinful eating. Servings are enormous; when they say jumbo hot fudge sundae, they mean it. There's a solipsistic satisfaction to be found here, whatever you order: sitting at a booth, flipping through the tableside jukebox, you can forget about the world on the other side of the viaduct. ■ *2918 SW Avalon*

▼

**Top 200
Restaurants**

▲

*Way; 935-7250; map:JJ9; $; beer and wine; MC, V; checks OK;* *breakfast, lunch, dinner every day.* &

**Maddox Grill** ★½ North King County residents who want a good meal close to home head for the Maddox Grill, which stands alone in the parking lot of a Richmond Beach mini-shopping center. Inside, wooden latticework creates an airy, almost gazebo-like environment. A recent visit made us consider suggesting a decorative update, though—say, new upholstery and a fresh coat of paint. But it's the food that will bring you back to the Maddox Grill. Fresh fish and steaks, respectfully prepared, and friendly, attentive service continue to be the restaurant's strong suits, while the hollowed-out sourdough round filled with a potato-rich New England–style clam chowder continues to attract the blue-haired ladies-who-lunch. The Grill's Reuben sandwich, surprisingly, can stand up to the best of them. And you may not be able to get enough of the tender oysters—sometimes a special—carefully breaded and deftly pan-fried. The Gorgonzola-and-pear salad has been a hit, the caesar salad a miss. Mesquite-grilled salmon appears on the Sunday brunch menu, as do Belgian waffles, eggs Benedict, and that famous bread-bowl. ■ *638 NW Richmond Beach Rd; 542-4766; map:AA6; $$; full bar; AE, DC, MC, V; checks OK; lunch Mon–Sat, dinner every day, brunch Sun.* &

▼

▲

**Madison Park Cafe** ★★ It's best in summer, when you can sit out in the sun-dappled brick courtyard and enjoy a lovingly crafted breakfast: a well-pulled café au lait, delectable spinach-and-tomato baked eggs, and some of the best hot, buttery, flakey scones in town. At lunch, fresh salads, fancy cream soups, and imaginative pastas and quiches draw a loyal, well-heeled crowd from the surrounding neighborhoods. The servers always seem to remember who you are and are quite patient with children. No dinner, as the cafe caters private parties most evenings. ■ *1807 42nd Ave E; 324-2626; map:GG6; $; beer and wine; MC, V; checks OK; breakfast Tues–Sun, lunch Tues–Sat.*

**Mae's Phinney Ridge Cafe** ★ On weekend mornings, the line outside Mae's is a microcosm of North Seattle—couples in athletic clothes; others in Birkenstocks, looking as if they just crawled out of bed; families with young children; youths with varicolored hair, tattoos, and body piercings. These patrons line up because Mae's offers one of the most dependable breakfasts in the neighborhood. It may look like the wait will be long, but that's rarely a problem since there are four sprawling dining areas. Of particular interest to bovine fans is the Moo Room, where everything is Holstein and milk shakes. Although Mae's serves lunch, breakfast is the specialty and is served all day. No one leaves hungry, thanks to the Paul Bunyan–size portions of breakfast potatoes and toast served with nearly every breakfast variation. Pastry lovers should opt for the coffee cake (the cinnamon rolls tend to be oversized and under-flavored). Spud fans should order the Spud Feast, a mountain of potatoes topped with cheese, sour cream, and salsa. In addition to omelets, pancakes, and the breakfast regulars, there's a selection of egg scramblers, made with everything from veggies to seafood. Service is casual and friendly, though you may need to flag down your server for a coffee refill. An espresso bar offers access from a walk-up window. ▪ *6412 Phinney Ave N; 782-1222; map:FF8; $; no alcohol; AE, MC, V; checks OK; breakfast every day, lunch Mon–Fri.*

**Maltby Cafe** ★★ Upstairs, the 1937 WPA project Maltby School gymnasium remains as it was. Downstairs, in what used to be the school cafeteria, the Maltby Cafe dishes up outstanding country breakfasts and equally satisfying lunches. Finding the place the first time might be tough, but you'll never forget the way. A Saturday morning repast can fill you for the weekend. Unhurried, bountiful breakfasts feature delicious omelets—the Maltby is a huge affair, stuffed with more than a cup of assorted veggies, ham cubes, even pieces of roast beef—good new potatoes, old-fashioned oatmeal, and thick slices of French toast. If you have to wait for a table (which is usually the case on weekends), order one of the legendary, giant cinnamon rolls, then savor it on the steps outside. At lunch, great sandwiches and soups (try a Reuben, made with their own corned beef). ▪ *8809 212th St SE, Maltby Rd, Maltby; 483-3123; $; beer and wine; MC, V; checks OK; breakfast, lunch every day.* &

**Manca's** ★★ The Manca family has been in the restaurant business for over a century, so if you get the feeling that you're dining among family here, don't be surprised. You are. The handsome young Mancas who run this casual-yet-elegant Madison Park dining room have a genetic knack for making everyone feel they're at a wonderful family gathering. The menu offers everything from a burger with fries to an enormous rack of meaty barbecued back ribs to a tender filet mignon. Inspired renderings of chicken, seafood, and pastas round it all out, and there's even a listing of spa entrees (no added fats or oils). On weekend mornings, Mark and Mory Manca take over the kitchen and whip up Dutch babies (their secret family recipe for custardy crêpe-like pancakes that rise to delectable heights) topped with lemon and powdered sugar. ▪ *4000 E Madison St; 323-7686; map:GG6; $$; full bar; DC, MC, V; checks OK; lunch Tues–Fri, dinner Tues–Sun, brunch Sat–Sun.* &

**Mandarin Garden** ★ Locals love this place because its unassuming ambience lures mainly those in the know. Chef Andy Wong, a native of Shanghai, handles equally well the delicate flavors of Mandarin and the heat and spice of Sichuan and

Hunan. But be assured that if you order a starred dish, you're going to get hot and spicy. A recent Hunan chicken lunch, for instance, packed a wallop as well as a mess of delectable chicken, deepfried, then sautéed. Praiseworthy dishes include melt-in-your-mouth kung pao chicken, mixed seafood Sichuan, and variations on bean curd. Two private rooms are available for banquets. Peking duck should be ordered a day in advance.
■ *40 E Sunset Way, Issaquah; 3929476; $; beer and wine; MC, V; local checks only; lunch Mon–Sat, dinner every day.* &

**Maple Leaf Grill** ★★ Don't let the pub atmosphere fool you. And whatever you do, don't belittle the culinary artistry of co-owner/chef "Rip" Ripley by calling his food "pub grub." One look down the long, plate-filled bar or into the big, wooden booths proves that "grub" doesn't even come close to describing the food served here. You're just as likely to fork into a grilled breast of rabbit sauced with cumin, garlic, and olives or a Thai-inspired plate of shrimp and basil ravioli, as a burger with fries (though they serve plenty of the latter). With the blues on the sound system and the convivial customers hoisting a brew, waiting for a seat, and trading gibes with co-owner David Albert, you'll get the feeling that you're at a neighborhood housewarming party. ■ *8909 Roosevelt Way NE, Seattle; 523-8449; map:DD6; $$; beer and wine; MC, V; checks OK; lunch Mon–Fri, dinner every day.* &

▼
Top 200
Restaurants
▲

**Marco's Supperclub** ★★½ A more appropriate name for the place might be Marco's Success Story. When expat Chicagoans Marco Rulff and Donna Moodie opened this groovicidal Belltown bistro, they crossed their fingers in hope that years of tableside experience, an adventurous and capable chef, and a strong staff of friendly yet sophisticated servers would bring business their way. And it was clear from the day the doors opened that the husband-and-wife team had more than luck going for them. Since then, their sexy, noisy, and *busy* restaurant has welcomed hordes of savvy diners who come for the warm, funky atmosphere and the trip-around-the-world menu. Forgo the pastas, but certainly order the fried sage appetizer, pork tenderloin marinated in juniper berries and herbs, subtly spiced Jamaican jerk chicken served up with sautéed greens and mashed sweet potatoes, or cumin- and coriander-spiked Moroccan lamb. A bar running the length of the room is a great perch for those dining alone. In summer, a colorful, plant-filled deck out back practically doubles the seating capacity. ■ *2510 1st Ave; 441-7801; map:F8; $$; full bar; AE, MC, V; checks OK; dinner every day, brunch Sun.*

**Maximilien in the Market** ★½ There is something so undeniably French about François and Julia Kissel's French market cafe, something about the mismatched silverware and the broad Elliott Bay view, about the dark wood antiques and the light reflected off the wood-framed mirrors. All you seem to need here are a crusty loaf of bread and a bottle of wine. Luckily, you don't have to stick to bread and wine when a simple lunch can be assembled out of steamed mussels with wine and herbs, a salade Niçoise, or excellent fish 'n' chips. A four-course dinner is available, including perhaps a fillet of halibut broiled with a basil beurre blanc, a New York steak with sautéed mushrooms, a bowl of shellfish-rich bouillabaisse, or a simple ham and cheese omelet. Sometimes there are flaws: wine served from a bottle that's been open too long, a salty soupe à l'oignon. But here you simply sigh, slather butter on another round of bread, and nod, *c'est la vie.* ▪ *81-A Pike St (Pike Place Market); 682-7270; map:J8; $$; full bar; AE, DC, MC, V; no checks; breakfast, lunch, dinner Mon–Sat, brunch Sun.* ら

**Maya's**  All roads, if taken far enough south, lead to Maya's, the Mexican institution in Rainier Beach. We don't know how they manage to fit the entire neighborhood into one building, but every night they pull it off. Families sit next to necking couples, and you may witness a group of teenagers shrinking in embarrassment as one of their teachers walks in. Everyone's there for the food, which is plentiful, affordable, and good—in a refried beans, rice, and shredded lettuce kinda way. Your meal will arrive mere seconds, it seems, after you order it. As usual, this is a bad omen. Tortillas can be soggy and chewy, enchiladas not heated all the way through, quesadillas not quite crispy. But the price is right, the meat dishes are savory and spicy, and the neighborhood atmosphere is festive and warm. ▪ *9447 Rainier Ave S; 725-5510; map:KK5; $; full bar; AE, DC, MC, V; no checks; lunch, dinner every day.* ら

**McCormick and Schmick's** ★★  No, you're not in New York *or* San Francisco. It just feels that way in this big seafood restaurant that bows to chophouse tradition complete with dark wood paneling, booths, a glitter bar, and waiters with black bow ties. You'd think they'd been grilling lamb chops and salmon steaks since the turn of the century. Don't smirk—they do it well, if not with perfect consistency. Just remember to keep it simple: order seafood (if it swims or clings to rocks, it's probably on the astounding fresh sheet), and stay away from the pasta. Start with fresh oysters; then hope there's steelhead in season. The straightforward work at the grill includes meat, game, and poultry. Suits sit at the lengthy counter, reading *The Wall Street Journal* while knocking back single-malt Scotch and waiting for their double-cut pork chops. At lunch M and S is too busy for its own good—service adopts a hurry-up attitude, and you have to sit in the hall until your whole party assembles—but dinners are more relaxed. A private room holds up to 24 guests. The bar holds a crowd. ▪ *1103 1st Ave; 623-5500; map:L8; $$;*

*full bar; AE, DC, MC, V; local checks only; lunch Mon–Fri, dinner every day.*

**Mediterranean Kitchen ★½** You can practically whiff the garlic from one side of 520 to the other, thanks to these twin versions of the same restaurant. The Middle Eastern fare is powered by the owner's belief in the healthful as well as gustatory properties of this edible bulb. Since the original's 1980 opening, Kamal Aboul Hosn (who works the stoves in Seattle, while his son, Tony, handles the Eastside kitchen) claims to have served over a million of the chicken wings marinated in vinegar and slathered with roasted garlic, just like his grandfather first made in Lebanon. The shawarma (chicken or beef) come balanced by the flavors and textures of grilled onions, green peppers, and tomatoes, served with tahini sauce. Vegetarians can trust the hummus, baba ghanouj, Lebanese labnie, and tabbouleh. Enormous quantities (even with the appetizers) at very low prices have earned the Mediterranean Kitchen institution status. ▪ *4 W Roy St; 285-6713; map:GG7; $; beer and wine; AE, DC, MC, V; no checks; lunch Tues–Fri, dinner every day.* ᠂ ▪ *103 Bellevue Way NE, Bellevue; 462-9422; map:HH3; $; beer and wine; AE, DC, MC, V; no checks; lunch, dinner every day.* ᠂

**Metropolitan Grill ★★** This handsome, money-colored haunt in the heart of the financial district does a booming business among the stockbrokers and Asian tourists. The bovine is divine here at Suit Central, so you'd do well to stick with the steaks. Pastas and appetizers are less well executed, but a list of large, appealing salads, sandwiches, and a daily fish special present good alternatives to beef for the lunch crowd. Waiters are of the no-nonsense school, which suits the table-hopping power brokers just fine. Financiers count on the Met's 30-person private room as a dependable dinner venue. ▪ *820 2nd Ave; 624-3287; map:M7; $$$; full bar; AE, DC, MC, V; local checks only; lunch Mon–Fri, dinner every day.* ᠂

▼

**Top 200 Restaurants**

▲

**Moghul Palace ★½** You've gotta like a place that makes its own mango ice cream, all fruity and chunked up with pistachios and almonds. It's a fine way to top off a beautifully spiced meal that comes rich in saffron, exotic as Marco Polo, and warming to the core with clove, cumin, and coriander. Owner Shah Kahn added this second Eastside Indian eatery following the success of Indiagate in nearby Eastgate. The servers here may not know much about the food, but don't worry: chef Salah Uddin certainly does. Mussels swim in a barely hot sweet-kissed curry, for which an order of naan—particularly the onion-cilantro version—is a must for dipping. Among the dinner entrees, the kormas are particularly good and the tandoori specialties quite adequate. You can't go wrong with curry. You can, however, go wrong with mango ribs—nice sauce, paltry bones. The lunch buffet offers an opportunity for sampling the old favorites and some spicy salads. ■ *10303 NE 10th St, Bellevue; 451-1909; map:HH3; $$; full bar; AE, DC, MC, V; checks OK; lunch Mon–Sat, dinner every day.* &

**Mona's** ★★ Tito Class and Annette Serrano's restaurant—named with Mona Lisa in mind, and decorated (so it seems) by the ghost of Frida Kahlo—is a warm addition to the Green Lake neighborhood. Thirteen votive-lit tables—each set with one eye-catching, cobalt-blue pint glass—draw your attention away from the handsome wine bar at the back of the large, high-ceilinged room and from Serrano's original artwork, which adorns the stippled green walls. The small menu ranges from Spain to Greece to Tunisia to Italy. Appetizers (marinated bites of squid, perhaps, served atop a bed of herby orzo in a sherry-spiked tomato sauce) are artful, salads pungent with innovative dressings, and entrees—from a hefty paella to a simple, pan-seared salmon, to pork chops marinated in Caribbean spices—delicious and modestly priced. Dinner is served till midnight on Friday and Saturday. ■ *6421 Latona Ave NE; 526-1188; map:EE7; $$; beer and wine; AE, MC, V; checks OK; dinner only, Tues–Sat.* &

▼

**Top 200 Restaurants**

▲

**Musashi's Sushi & Grill** ★½ It's a small, stylish Wallingford restaurant that's easy to find: it's the one with the line stretching out onto the sidewalk. The menu is limited to a few well chosen items, plus sushi—smoked salmon and yellowtail, octopus, great California rolls—that doesn't cost half a week's wages for a few ethereal bites. Consequently, Musashi's enjoys a devoted following. Some come for the good curries, others for the chicken teriyaki, and others for the inexpensive bento boxes that include skewers of roasted vegetables and chicken, rice, sweet omelet slices, kami kamaboko (fish cake), and a generous sampler of sashimi, all beautifully presented in black lacquer boxes. As praiseworthy as the food is the congenial atmosphere, which seems to spring from the magic between the proprietors and their customers. When you leave, you'll feel that you have been in the secure company of kindred souls. No smoking. ■ *1400 N 45th St; 633-0212; map:FF7; $; beer and wine; no credit cards; local checks only; lunch Tues–Fri, dinner Tues–Sat.*

**Neelam's Authentic Indian Cuisine** ★ Up on the Ave—a strip chock-a-block with ethnic restaurants vying for the dining dollars of starving students—delightfully officious and prettily costumed Neelam Jain is not above rushing to the doorway of her dimly lit East Indian restaurant to convince hesitant passersby to come in and try her bargain-priced dinner specials. And we're convinced. Those specials include, among other offerings, 14 chicken- or lamb-based curries, and for a 10-spot you'll get a hubcap-size plate with a choice of entree, cooling raita, fragrant dal, cumin-scented basmati rice, feathery-light naan, an appetizer (potato samosas or chicken pakoras), a beverage, *and* dessert. Forget the à la carte stuff. And show restraint when asked how hot you like your curry, or youuuu'll be sorrrrry. ▪ *4735 University Way NE; 523-5275; map:FF6; $; beer and wine; AE, DC, MC, V; checks OK; lunch, dinner every day.* &

**The New Jake O'Shaughnessey's** ★½ For many years it was only Jake's, unique and excellent, its reputation built on beef and lamb. Then came the shift toward lighter fare. Another major menu change has shifted the emphasis again—with the likes of prime rib, salmon, and caesar salads in various guises. Fortunately, you can still get a pot of clams simmered lightly in cream with vermouth and butter (excellent for dipping, requiring seconds on the sourdough bread). A couple dozen microbrews wash it all down. Special desserts include a bourbon pecan pie and the trademark Snicker's pie, a concoction of praline ice cream, roasted peanuts and caramel sauce, topped with whipped cream and served on a cookie-crumb crust. ▪ *401 Bellevue Square, Bellevue; 455-5559; map:HH3; $$; full bar; AE, DC, MC, V; checks OK; lunch, dinner every day.* &

**The New Mikado Restaurant** ★★ In 1994, the fading Mikado, the oldest and once the most venerated Japanese restaurant in Seattle, was bought by the Moriguchi family, owners of the Northwest's finest Asian supermarket, Uwajimaya. Rejoice. The New Mikado is now living up to old expectations. Tatami rooms (one will seat 35!) look absolutely inviting, prices have plummeted—and best of all, the quality of food is high and service is again professional, courteous, and timely. You may choose from a vast menu with nearly 20 tsumami (appetizers), a world of udon, soba, and donburi, and the usual assortment of Japanese dinner specialties (broiled beef, teriyaki chicken and salmon, tempura, and sukiyaki among them). The sushi bar has been spruced up with comfortable new seats where you may savor exceptional nigiri sushi—such as the sockeye salmon and buttery yellowtail we've swooned over and the biggest tamago (egg omelet) we've ever laid eyes on. The Mikado house roll (six assorted fish sliced into four big disks) is supreme. ▪ *514 S Jackson St; 622-5206; map:P7; $$; full bar; AE, MC, V; local checks only; lunch Mon–Fri, dinner Mon–Sat.* &

**Nicolino** ★½ On warm days, the sunny brick courtyard is the place to be. On cold or rainy days, head for the cheerful little dining room, pleasantly cluttered with wine bottles and family pictures, maps and mandolins, for a steaming plate of soul-warming pasta. Though they've been known to heavyhand the prawns and chicken, Nicolino's past (and the low prices) fuel its reputation and crowd-attracting popularity. You won't find

▼

Top 200
Restaurants

▲

showy dishes, yet a simple pasta can be stunningly executed, while the fork-tender veal shank in the osso bucco Milanese comes atop fettuccine so buttery the taste comes right through the tomato sauce and orange zest. Hearty slices of peasant bread are meant to be dredged in herb, garlic, and chile-spiked olive oil, and accompanied by a soothing glass of Chianti. ■ *317 NW Gilman Blvd, Issaquah; 391-8077; $$; beer and wine; MC, V; checks OK; lunch, dinner every day.* &

### Nikko (Westin Hotel) ★★½

When the first Nikko moved from its inconspicuous International District location to the Westin, a flashy, highly decorated, $1.5 million remodeled restaurant awaited. Nikko's second incarnation offers one of the most attractive Japanese dining rooms in the city, and the enormous sushi bar is a great place to enjoy impeccable raw fish, including the astounding Nikko Roll (seven different pieces of fish rolled with avocado and rice). Perennial non-sushi favorites include black cod marinated in sake lees and then broiled to flaky perfection, or crisp soft-shell crab. One of the most satisfying rainy-day dishes is the much maligned sukiyaki, a soulful one-pot meal. And you can always enjoy a plate of grilled thises and thats from the robata bar. ■ *1900 5th Ave; 322-4641; map:I6; $$$; full bar; AE, DC, MC, V; no checks; dinner Mon–Sat.* &

▼

### Noble Court ★

During the week, when it's not so crowded, request one of the tables lining the windows looking out on the small creek—and you're less likely to notice the worn interior and slightly uncomfortable seating. The menu ranges from standard kung pao and fried rice to the more exotic shark-fin soup, stewed abalone, and bird's nest with crabmeat soup. Live tanks at the entrance display fish and crustaceans ready for a little black bean sauce. The restaurant is a favorite with the Eastside's growing Chinese population, who show up on weekends for what many consider to be the best dim sum on either side of the Lake Washington bridges. Expect to wait up to an hour. Noble Court now does dim sum during the week as well, though the range of selections is somewhat limited and the ambience can't match those weekend feeding frenzies. ■ *1644 140th NE, Bellevue; 641-6011; map:HH2; $$; full bar; AE, MC, V; no checks; lunch, dinner every day.* &

### The Painted Table (Alexis Hotel) ★★★

Chef Tim Kelley honed his craft in NYC at the estimable Vong and Bouley before heading to Seattle. Here in the colorful, contemporary, two-tiered dining room of one of Seattle's finest boutique hotels, Kelley has made his mark in clever, tasteful, artistic fashion. His signature appetizer, a layered goat cheese and vegetable "salad," is a textured tower of grilled eggplant, creamy goat cheese, and oven-dried tomatoes with an onion confit and a spray of fresh greens. A stunning rack of baby lamb chops is encrusted with herbs and stacked tall above a glossy reduction sauce; tamarind-basted Long Island duck slices lie on a nest of egg noodles in a Thai-spiced broth. Well-meaning service is often far less polished than the glossy digs might lead you to expect. ■ *92 Madison; 624-3646; map:M8; $$$; full bar; AE, DC, MC, V; checks OK; breakfast every day, lunch Mon–Fri, dinner every day.* ᕲ

**Palisade** ★½ ■ **Maggie Bluffs** ★ Inside, with a waterfall and seawater tidal pool (complete with marine life), tropical-looking plants and trees, chandeliers festooned with glass balls, and a player piano perched on a ledge *over* the bar, Palisade might be mistaken for the Hyatt Regency in Maui. Outside, beyond the Elliott Bay Marina to the grandstand view of the city and Sound, it's definitely Seattle. Step over the cobblestone bridge into the expansive dining area where there's not a bad seat in the house. The menu, too, is vast and highlights contemporary grilling, searing, and rotisserie cooking styles for a variety of fish, meat, and poultry. Order the pupu platter and you'll sample most of the appetizers; try the shellfish chowder and you'll be rewarded with a velvety broth crowded with veggies and bites of crab and shrimp. Imaginative entree preparations favor sweet-and-sour glazes and Polynesian-inspired creations. A stand-out combination is the spit-roasted prime rib paired with grilled hazelnut prawns. Consider a simple fish preparation—perhaps an apple wood–grilled escolar, a mild, moist Fijian whitefish both succulent and sweet. Finish with a trio of burnt cream custards flavored in turn with classic vanilla, rich chocolate, and Grand Marnier.

Downstairs is the burger bar, **Maggie Bluffs**, whose simple, straightforward atmosphere—with food to match (big burgers with shoestring fries, pizzas, and salads)—offers respite from the South Pacific schmaltz. ■ *Palisade: 2601 W Marina Pl (Elliott Bay Marina); 285-1000; $$$; full bar; AE, DC, MC, V; checks OK; lunch Mon–Sat, dinner every day, brunch Sun.* ᕲ ■ *Maggie Bluffs: 2601 W Marina Pl (Elliott Bay Marina); 283-8322; map:GG7; $; full bar; AE, DC, MC, V; checks OK; breakfast Sat–Sun; lunch Mon–Fri, dinner every day.* ᕲ

**Pandasia** ★★ What was once Panda's is now Pandasia. But that's the only change you'll find at this neighborhood Chinese hot spot. The sight of steaming pot-stickers, plates of rich orange beef, and sautéed eggplant in a spicy sauce has been known to tempt customers into ordering too much. It's hard to go wrong with the extensive menu, and even harder to find a time when the line of waiting customers isn't spilling out the door. Somehow Pandasia handles a busy take-out and delivery service as well. The same terrific specialties are at both locations: mu-shu pork with homemade pancakes; perfectly cooked, dry-sautéed green beans with almonds; a stand-out General Tso's chicken, which quietly explodes inside the mouth with tender meat and vibrant seasoning. There are almost 100 dishes from which to choose. ■ *7347 35th Ave NE; 526-5115; map:EE6; $; beer and wine; AE, MC, V; local checks only; lunch Mon–Sat, dinner every day.* ⅃ ■ *1625 W Dravus; 283-9030; map:FF8; $; beer and wine; AE, MC, V; local checks only; lunch Mon–Sat, dinner every day.*

**Pasta & Co.** ★★ The leading fresh-pasta emporium in Seattle features pasta made to absorb sauces a shade thinner than usual, and fine deli foodstuffs (sun-dried tomatoes, European and domestic olive oils, exotic sauces and spices, the makings of antipasto plates) to be purchased and enjoyed at home. Though both the Bellevue Square (10218 NE Eighth Street, 453-8760) and original University Village (2640 NE University Village Mall, 523-8594) branches do a healthy business in ready-to-eat take-out items, the only stores that offer seating are the central downtown deli, with its counter stools and stylish glass walls, and the new Queen Anne location (2109 Queen Anne Avenue N, 283-1182), with only a handful of seats for dining-in. Owner Marcella Rosene's vast repertoire includes Chinese vermicelli salad; beefy lasagne, judiciously seasoned; hazelnut tortellini in a velvet cream sauce; a simple toss of spirelli pasta and fresh basil; black bean soup. Order it up at the deli line, then pray for a seat. ■ *1001 4th Ave (and branches); 624-3008; map:M6; $; beer and wine; MC, V; checks OK; breakfast, lunch, early dinner Mon–Fri.* ⅃

**Pegasus Pizza and Pasta** ★★ Alki dwellers are the first to tell you that the best reason to venture to West Seattle is still the Greek pizza at Pegasus. It's feta and mozzarella, olives, onions, fresh spinach, ground beef, and sunflower seeds, all mounded on a buttery, gritty-textured (like good homemade anadama bread) crust, and served on a cake plate. Toppings, including the dense, potent tomato sauce, are applied with epicurean restraint. Pasta, by comparison, is an afterthought. The setting is very Seattle: a lot of windows, great views of Puget Sound, and friendly waiters. They do a brisk take-out business, too. ■ *2758 Alki Ave SW; 932-4849; map:II9; $; beer and wine; MC, V; checks OK; dinner every day.* ⅃

**Phad Thai** ★½ The Greenwood crosswalk is not where you'd expect to find a reliably good Thai restaurant, but it would be a mistake to overlook Phad Thai. Although the amiable service can sometimes slow to a crawl when it's busy, Phad Thai is a real find—a comfortable, family-friendly, neighborhood establishment. An added attraction: Phad Thai uses no MSG. To call this unassuming place family-friendly would be an understatement: waiters are quick to tend to hungry children (and their parents). Among the appetizers, vegetarian spring rolls

▼

**Top 200 Restaurants**

▲

arrive piping hot and crisp from the fryer and the satay is moist with a well-textured peanut sauce. The namesake dish, phad Thai, offers a perfect balance of tofu, peanuts, and egg to season the rice noodles. Curries are delicate yet full-flavored, and the chicken in peanut sauce is inspired. Colorful seafood dishes, including the spicy scallops with bamboo shoots and other vegetables, are consistently fresh. ■ *8530 Greenwood Ave N; 784-1830; map:DD8; $; beer and wine; MC, V; checks OK; lunch Mon–Tues, Thurs–Fri, dinner every day.* &

### Philadelphia Fevre Steak & Hoagie Shop ★

Ask any expat Philadelphian and they'll tell you: it's not Pat's Steaks, but, as they say in the City of Brotherly Love, "What's it to yez?" Still, the cheesesteaks and hoagies at this Madison Valley luncheonette are the closest thing to the real McCoy around here. And if you sit at the counter listening to wisecracking grillmeister Renee LeFevre's David Brenneresque accent while reading *Philadelphia Magazine*, you'll get more Philly flavor than you bargained for. Renee will grill up a pile of thinly sliced rib-eye steak with onions, add some white American cheese and hot cherry peppers if you like, and serve it up on an Italian roll. Eat it as you should, with a basket of french fries and a TastyKake, and you'll learn the real reason Rocky Balboa had to run up and down the steps at the Philadelphia Art Museum. ■ *2332 E Madison St; 323-1000; map:GG6; $; beer only; AE, MC, V; no checks; lunch Mon–Sat, dinner Mon–Fri.* &

▼

▲

### Pho Bac

This oversize shack, smack in the middle of a busy intersection, is crowded and funky, serving nothing but pho—the classic everyday dish of Vietnam. You won't need a menu, and you won't have to wait long for a bowl of the fragrant, herb-infused beef stock topped with paper-thin slices of raw beef that cook through as you slurp up the rice noodles nesting in the bottom. Order either a large ($4.50) or small ($4) portion, and garnish it from a plate of fresh basil, bean sprouts, jalapeño, and lime that arrives alongside the steaming bowls. Customize your soup to suit your fancy with fish sauce, chile sauce, and hoisin kept in squeeze bottles on the table. ■ *1314 S Jackson St; 323-4387; map:HH7; $; no alcohol; no credit cards; no checks; lunch, dinner every day.*

### Phoenecia at Alki ★★

Hussein Khazaal's fans (whose devotion verges on the cultish) have followed him from one off-the-track location to another. Finally he and they have a site worthy of his talents. At this, Phoenicia's third incarnation, the ocher-sponged walls seem to glow with Mediterranean sunshine. The standard hummus and baba ghanouj are here, but then it's off on pan-Mediterranean explorations: saffron and pine-nut risotto with shellfish; Moroccan eggplant with penne and tomatoes; excellent, inventive thin-crust pizza; several versions of the most fragrant marinated lamb you've ever tasted; and a mariner's ransom of exquisite seafood. To round it all off you may choose, appropriately, between espresso and Turkish coffee, tiramisu and baklava. ■ *2716 Alki Ave SW; 935-6550; map:II9; $$; beer and wine; MC, V; local checks only; lunch Tues–Fri, dinner Tues–Sun.* ⅃

**Piecora's** ★½ We know people who drive across town just to sit down to one of Piecora's oversize thin-crust pies and dream of New York. You'll know you've come to the right place when you see that damsel of the dispossessed, Lady Liberty, dressed in neon and hoisting a pizza above a crowded storefront. At this busy neighborhood joint decorated with New York subway maps and other Big Apple kitsch, delivery drivers run in and out, the din can reach epic proportions, and pizza tossing is a fine art. Some 20 toppings are available on pizzas sold by the pie, the half pie, and the slice. Pastas, sandwiches, and generous salads, too. Pizza's served until midnight on weekends. ■ *1401 Madison St; 322-9411; map:M1; $; full bar; MC, V; checks OK; lunch, dinner every day.*

**The Pink Door** ★★ The low-profile entrance (just a pink door off Post Alley) to this Italian trattoria hidden away in Pike Place Market belies the busy scene within. In the winter, the dining room grows noisy around a burbling fountain, but come warmer weather, everyone vies desperately for a spot on the trellis-covered terrace with its breathtakingly romantic view of the Sound. Owner Jackie Roberts finally did away with her long-standing prix-fixe menu and now serves dinner à la carte, offering hefty plates of pasta and a few fish/meat/poultry dishes. Or you can construct a fine meal from the limited bar menu (the antipasto misto is a Tuscan feast, and the aglio al forno—roasted garlic with a scoop of ricotta-Gorgonzola cheese spread—is a most slatherable nosh). The Pink Door overflows with Italian kitsch, which is not lost on the arty, under-30 set that call the place home. There's often live music at night. ■ *1919 Post Alley; 443-3241; map:J8; $$; full bar; AE, MC, V; no checks; lunch, dinner Tues–Sat.*

▼

**Top 200 Restaurants**

▲

**Pirosmani** ★★★ In a city grown jaded to the wildest of world cuisines, Pirosmani—offering the foods of the Republic of Georgia, nestled between the Black and Caspian Seas—takes you around the world in the time it takes to navigate Queen Anne Hill. From the polished and refined surroundings—the linen and candlelight, the serene professionalism of the staff, the well-heeled patrons—you might never guess the exotic tastes to come. Then dinner arrives, and you suddenly notice how very red the walls are. Chef Laura Dewell offers a gentle education in the foods of Georgia; her small menu is split between those and dishes from the Mediterranean, which are every bit as alluring. Appetizers with the strangest names yield the loveliest results: khachapuri and spinach pkhali is a spinach pâté tweaked with walnuts, cilantro, and garlic scooped up with a gooey cheese bread. You can gussy up your food still further with a trio of Georgian condiments brought to each table in little pots. Don't hesitate where fish is concerned: a Near Eastern preparation of rare tuna—rubbed with Syrian spices and wrapped in grape leaves—is served over a Turkish sauce of pomegranates, walnuts, and red peppers. Braised duck Satsivi, a classic Georgian creation, comes bone-in, smothered in a thick walnut sauce with the nuances of coriander, cinnamon, cayenne, paprika, and fenugreek. ■ *2220 Queen Anne Ave N; 285-3360; map:GG8; $$; beer and wine; AE, DC, MC, V; local checks only; dinner Tues–Sat.*

**Pizzeria Pagliacci** ★ It's human nature: we tend to take our institutions for granted. When it comes to pizzerias, this is a mistake. We get distracted by the herbed dough at one new pizza joint; by the whacky toppings (barbecue sauce and dried apricots?) at another; by the elaborate piercings on the staff at a third. Meanwhile, Pagliacci waits for us like a faithful old dog, thumping its tail on its Formica floor when we come crawling back. All Pagliacci locations offer the same simple yet eternal lure: thin-and-tangy cheese pizzas. Their tasty crusts are the result of thorough research by the owners, who ultimately settled on Philadelphia-style. The true test of this exceptional crust is the original cheese pizza, which is unadorned except for a light, fresh tomato sauce and mozzarella. Served hot from the oven, it's hard to beat. Skip the salads (salty and blah, one and all), and go straight to the cheesy tomato source. This place is about pizza, and that's it. You can take out from all Pagliacci locations, or eat in at the Capitol Hill, lower Queen Anne, and University District branches. Comfortable, echoing, and sometimes hectic, they're all fine places for a solo meal. A phone call to Pagliacci's central delivery service (726-1717) will get you delivery from the closest outlet. ■ *426 Broadway (and branches); 324-0730; map:HH7; $; beer and wine; MC, V; checks OK; lunch, dinner every day.* ⟁

▼

Top 200
Restaurants

▲

**Pizzuto's Italian Cafe** ★ It's the Seward Park version of the neighborhood Italian restaurant: red-and-white–checked tablecloths, red linen napkins, Pavarotti in the background, and acoustics that make it possible to converse without raising your voice. Food is piping hot, service friendly and fast. Pastas, made fresh and topped with rich sauces, are excellent (this is not a place for the cholesterol- or weight-conscious). A plate of meat-filled tortellini alla Romano with marinated artichoke hearts and wild mushrooms is enough for two meals, and you can expect the highly seasoned veal piccata to disappear from your plate at astonishing speed. Best is the superb pizza. A crisp-but-still-chewy crust covered with the freshest ingredients— tomatoes seemingly just out of the garden—is light enough to make this a fine appetizer for two. ■ *5032 Wilson Ave S; 722-6395; map:JJ5; $; beer and wine; MC, V; local checks only; dinner Mon–Sat.*

**Place Pigalle** ★★★ Long on charm, short on space, this classic Seattle bistro with a Puget Sound view is everything a stylish Northwest restaurant should be, and more. Small wonder, then, that locals find owner Bill Frank's hideaway in Pike Place Market the perfect spot to sip an eau-de-vie, lunch with a friend, or engage in a romantic dinner à deux. A range of intriguing dishes combines the freshness of Northwest ingredients with recipes that speak here of France and Italy, there of New Mexico and New Orleans, all filtered through the imagination of a crew of young chefs. Ask for a table by the window, and sample something as simple as onion soup gratinée (with its beefy broth, silky onions, and chewy Gruyère), or as sophisticated as roulade of duck confit (a pasta sheet rolled with preserved duck, goat cheese, and butternut squash). On sunny days, a small crowded skyway is used by those anxious to catch every daylight ray, but the inside tables have the advantage of being in the sight line of your waiter. ■ *81 Pike St; 624-1756; map:J8; $$$; full bar; MC, V; local checks only; lunch, dinner Mon–Sat.*

**Pleasant Beach Grill** ★★ Bainbridge Island's only white-linen restaurant is quietly tucked away in a large Tudor house on the island's southwest corner. Islanders have always favored the pine-paneled bar, warmed by a fireplace and with couches for sinking into with a drink or dessert. Under the direction of chef Hussein Ramadan, the grill has found a pleasant consistency much appreciated by the locals. His menu includes a sauté of prawns, scallops, and whitefish (in a Thai-style sauce of curry, lemongrass, and coconut milk) and an excellent 10-ounce slab of New York pepper steak, with specials inspired by fresh seasonal ingredients. Stick with the simpler grills and seafoods and enjoy the ample portions and skilled service. In warm weather, dine outdoors on the terrace. In winter reserve a table in the appealing fireside lounge. ■ *4738 Lynwood Center NE, Bainbridge Island; 842-4347; $$; full bar; AE, DC, MC, V; checks OK; dinner every day.* &

**Pogacha** ★ Properly speaking, a pogacha is a chewy Croatian dinner roll baked in a wood-fired oven. Here at this rather stark little eatery, they stretch the dough to make what looks, to the uninitiated, like pizza. The pogachas are thin, flavorful, and topped with ingredients that only a few years ago sounded darned exotic (a simple mix of garlic oil, feta, and red onion makes a zingy, zesty pie). Order the Four Seasons for a sampling of four pogachas topped, individually, with artichokes; mushrooms and pesto; five cheeses; and tomato and basil (red sauce upon request). There are usually a half dozen pasta dishes, such as the Croatian Cousins, a dish of calamari and shrimp served over cappellini and dressed with a light, garlicky tomato sauce. There's no compelling reason to go beyond basic pasta and pogacha, though a couple of serviceable meat dishes—especially the skewered marinated lamb—aren't bad. ■ *119 106th Ave NE, Bellevue; 455-5670; map:HH3; $; beer and wine; AE, MC, V; no checks; lunch Mon–Fri, dinner Tues–Sat.* ঙ

**Pon Proem** ★ Sheer, unadulterated capsicum is not the story at Mercer Island's nifty little Thai joint, though the seasoning is there in a no-nonsense star scale ("chok dee" next to five stars means "good luck"). While the red curry chicken lacks a certain oomph, everything else sampled here displays balance and a deft touch at the wok. Three kinds of soy sauce, plus chile paste, give the chicken dish called gai pahd met ma muang better balance than a gymnastics team. Vegetarian phad Thai is freshened by red cabbage, carrots, and sprouts. Deep-fried dishes are consistently pleasing, especially the gai Pon Proem—chewy, mildly spicy chunks of meat for finger-dipping (call it Chicken McNuggets for grownups). Modest digs in a strip-mall setting are warmed by the owner's hand-sewn seat-cushion covers and window treatments. ■ *3039 78th Ave SE, Mercer Island; 236-8424; map:II4; $; beer and wine; AE, MC, V; no checks; lunch Mon–Fri, dinner every day.* ঙ

**Ponti Seafood Grill** ★★★ Ponti, tucked almost under the Fremont Bridge, might inspire dreams of the Mediterranean, with its canalside perch, stucco walls, red-tiled roof, and elegantly understated dining rooms. But its true inspiration is defined by its food, not its mood. Call it pan-Asian, call it fusion cuisine, but give credit where it is due: to chef Alvin Binuya. Borrowing from an array of ethnic flavors (with more than a passing nod to Asia), Binuya performs cross-cultural magic with such signature dishes as black pepper tuna carpaccio (drizzled with soy vinaigrette) and Thai curry penne (with broiled scallops, Dungeness crabmeat, spicy ginger-tomato chutney, and basil chiffonade). Dine outdoors in warm weather, or take advantage of the view during a leisurely Sunday brunch. ■ *3014 3rd Ave N; 284-3000; map:FF8; $$$; full bar; AE, DC, MC, V; local checks only; lunch, dinner every day, brunch Sun.* ঙ

**Provinces Asian Restaurant & Bar** ★½ Years ago, the thought of a pan-Asian restaurant was too much for many monoethnic eaters. But today, the idea is accepted even in the suburban town of Edmonds—where a serene and decidedly older crowd enjoy a range of Asian cuisine in an attractive, dimly lit dining room set in a quaint shopping mall. We like the friendly, efficient service, the occasional dish of sweet-and-spicy broccoli stems brought to the table gratis, and the

▼

▲

Bangkok Hot and Sour Soup—served in a clay pot brimming with large prawns, bay shrimp, fresh scallops, and straw mushrooms, fragrant with lemongrass and large enough to feed four. The Cantonese-style seafood lobster sauce is dense with shellfish and vegetables and flavored with salty Chinese black beans. A huge portion of Mongolian ginger beef is a touch sweet but pleasantly potent with ginger and garlic. The abbreviated lunch menu, including humongous bowls of udon noodle soup, is a bargain and a half. The adjoining cocktail lounge—where folks meet to bend an elbow, smoke a cigarette, and make merry—is decidedly more boisterous, though that doesn't seem to bother the teetotalers sipping their green tea in the dining room. ■ *201 5th Ave S, Edmonds; 744-0288; $$; full bar; AE, DC, MC, V; local checks only; lunch Mon–Sat, dinner every day.* ⅙

**Queen City Grill** ★★★ You slide into a high-backed wooden booth and schmooze with friends. Fashionably chic people perch at the bar with cigarettes and cocktails. Queen City is a restaurant where the menu is pared down to a short list of dishes done really, really well, offset by a couple of specials— a nice ethic in this era of multiethnic, pan-continental eateries. The disbelieving should sample the melting tuna carpaccio appetizer (tinged with peppercorns and wasabe). Or a genuine caesar salad, done as Cardini envisioned: whole-leaf hearts of romaine, simply dressed in olive oil, lemon, and Worcestershire. The entrees, too, are simply prepared, mostly on the grill— from seared, fresh ahi tuna to a perfect New York steak to Jamaican jerk chicken (spicy and charred on the outside, but fall-off-the-bone tender inside). The mixed grills (meat or fish), served on surfboard-size platters, are a great demonstration of the kitchen staff's abilities. Service is impeccable; reservations are recommended. ■ *2201 1st Ave; 443-0975; map:G8; $$$; full bar; AE, DC, MC, V; checks OK; lunch Mon–Fri, dinner every day.* ⅙

▼

**Top 200
Restaurants**

▲

**R & L Home of Good Barbeque No. 1** ★★ The family-run R & L, here for nearly half a century, offers up the whole she-bang—a sociable, comfortable barbecue meal with what might be the tastiest Louisiana-style ribs and hot links in the city. Owner Mary Collins Davis alder-smokes her meats, then adds a rich, tangy sauce (choose your fire quotient). Best picks are the meaty ribs, the tender brisket, and the hot links, in sandwiches or on dinner platters. Try the four-way platter (three meats plus chicken for two people) with white bread and potato salad or beans. The sweet, hand-squeezed lemonade is heaven, and the peach cobbler and sweet-potato pie aren't half bad. The atmosphere is nothing fancy, but the place is clean as a whistle. ■ *1816 E Yesler Way; 322-0271; map:HH6; $; beer only; no credit cards; no checks; lunch, dinner Tues–Sat.*

**Ray's Boathouse** ★★★ With its peerless, unabashedly romantic view of Shilshole Bay and the Olympics beyond, Ray's is *the* place for waterfront dining. It's a rare pick—one favored by tourists and locals alike—where the food is superior and the service ever efficient and helpful. Ray's is a good place to educate yourself about seafood—about different kinds of oysters, perhaps—and what wines go well with them. In composing your meal, take advantage of the fresh fish that Ray's is famous for, and pay particular attention to the daily fresh sheet. We've had our socks knocked off by grilled white king salmon smeared with a nutty arugula pesto, and an exceptional steamed smoked black cod fillet. The superb wine list is organized by country and varietal, with a page devoted to splits. If the reservation wait for the dining room proves weeks long (and in summer, it well may), try the moderately priced upstairs cafe, especially popular at happy hour. The view (and the deck seating) helps you forget that the cafe service is less than it should be. ▪ *6049 Seaview Ave NW; 789-3770; map:EE9; $$$; full bar; AE, DC, MC, V; local checks only; lunch, dinner every day.* ☐

**Red Mill Burgers** ★★ When Babe and John Shepherd were school kids, they often hung out at the Red Mill—an old diner-style restaurant. Thirty years after the Red Mill served its last meal, the brother-and-sister team opened their tiny, namesake Red Mill Burgers in a corner of an old brick building on Phinney Ridge. Within weeks they were attracting crowds of burger worshippers who came for one of their 18 varieties of the all-American favorite. Within months, they expanded into an adjoining space to accommodate the hordes. This is not a fast-food joint, but the wait is worth it, as you'll see when you sink your teeth into a burger topped with thick slices of pepper bacon, anointed with a smoky housemade mayo, and sandwiched between a big, warm bun with the freshest of lettuce and tomatoes. Those who eschew things that "moo" will be pleased by the array of vegetarian and chicken offerings (try the verde chicken burger with roasted Anaheim peppers and Jack cheese). Everyone will love Babe's killer onion rings dipped in a cornmeal batter laced with thyme, cumin, and cayenne pepper. Top it all off with a Creamsicle-flavored malt or a milk shake. ▪ *312 N 67th St; 783-6362; map:EE8; $; no alcohol; no credit cards; checks OK; lunch, dinner Tues–Sun.* ☐

**Restaurant Shilla** ★½ After more than a decade in business, Shilla has settled comfortably into its enviable—if somewhat drab—location near Seattle Center. A steady stream of locals and tourists are rewarded with solid renditions of such classic Korean dishes as kalbi (barbecued short ribs), bulkogi (barbecued rib-eye), and jap chae (glass noodles tossed with sautéed vegetables). The requisite side dishes (gratis with certain entrees) vary in type and quality with every visit. Sometimes the cabbage kimchi is at its pickled prime; other times the pickled daikon radish and marinated soybean sprouts are better. But with at least half a dozen to choose from, there's always enough of these savory, salty palate stimulants to inspire you to finish your rice. Stray from the beaten path: forgo the hibachi for some of Shilla's hearty soups. Particularly satisfying examples are kalbi tang, made with beef short ribs, and yuk hae jang, with spicy shredded beef. Be prepared to smell like your dinner after you leave; although the hibachi tables have exhaust hoods, smoke from the barbecue will linger in your clothing. Shilla also serves Japanese fare, including sushi, but stick with the Korean menu—among the best in the city. ■ *2300 8th Ave; 623-9996; map:F5; $$; full bar; AE, DC, MC, V; no checks; lunch, dinner every day.* &

**Rikki Rikki** ★ They should call this place Kicky Kicky for its casual, up-to-date Japanese decor; no kimonos here, just weird, hoopy chairs and walls plastered with a sort of kitschy decoupage of blown-up Japanese comics and advertising. Overhead, monster-size rice-paper fans hang as sort of a suspended ceiling. The small menu offers the Japanese standards—noodles, teriyaki, and such, plus the lovingly prepared and artfully constructed sashimi and makimono (try the Kirkland roll with yellowtail, cucumber, and masago). In season there's delicious bonita or red clam—a great, spiky-looking affair. Specials often overmatch the kitchen, so stick to the regular menu (legions of lunchtime noodle slurpers can vouch for the udon). Dealing with service can be a challenge, as evidenced by the customer who ordered maguro to go, double-checked with the server to ensure it wouldn't be mackerel, then arrived home to unwrap a package of California rolls. ■ *442 Park Place Center, Kirkland; 828-0707; map:EE3; $$; beer and wine; AE, MC, V; local checks only; lunch Mon–Sat, dinner every day.* &

**Ristorante Buongusto** ★★ You've got to hand it to the tireless trio of Varchettas who own and operate Queen Anne Hill's friendly, neighborhood Italian dining room. Roberto (in the kitchen) and his brother and sister-in-law, Salvio and Anna (who run the floor), are a nonstop, homey Italian tour de force. Theirs is a bright, active place with tiled floors and graceful archways that evoke the warmth of an Italian terrazzo. The large remodeled house hums with the voices of a casual crowd that return again and again for the consistently good southern Italian fare. The menu features some of the most reliable pastas in town—rigatoni alla Buongusto, chunks of sausage and eggplant in a perfect ragu; and rotolo di Mamma Flora, medallions of pasta stuffed with bubbling veal, ricotta, and spinach. ■ *2232 Queen Anne Ave N; 284-9040; map:GG7; $$; full bar; AE, DC, MC, V; no checks; lunch Tues–Fri, dinner every day.*

▼

**Top 200 Restaurants**

▲

**Ristorante Machiavelli** ★★ There seems to be an Italian restaurant on every corner in town, but few corners attract as many happy campers as Capitol Hill's 12th and Pine. Machiavelli isn't big on decor, and the menu may look slightly standard at first glance—reminiscent of the old family-style Italian-American spots—but on closer inspection, this is the real thing, at pleasingly moderate prices. The use of chicken liver in the lasagne and in the bolognese sauce signals a chef with true Italian roots. The carbonara's not overwhelming, but rather a skilled toss of pasta, Parmesan, cream, and pancetta, and the gnocchi has a sterling reputation. The pizza here is a skinflint's dream: plate-size with a thin, breakaway crust and enhanced with a couple of good ingredients. The staff is skilled in keeping customers happy and keeping food on the table, striking the right balance between unobtrusive and affable to keep your meal upbeat. ■ *1215 Pine St; 621-7941; map:HH7; $$; full bar; MC, V; no checks; dinner Mon–Sat.* &

**Ristorante Paradiso** ★★ Owner/chef Fabrizio Loi's labor of love, just off Kirkland's main drag, is a surprisingly sophisticated culinary treat in unpretentious digs. Much of the menu remains constant from the 1991 debut. Openers include a beautifully arranged plate of grilled vegetables for two, or a generous bowl of fresh, perfectly cooked mussels and clams in a wine-based broth so good you'll scoop up every drop. There's a range of meat dishes, including a delicate saltimbocca, and a long list of pastas. We like the cannelloni gratinati—lovely pasta crêpes stuffed with a delicate mix of ground veal, chicken, and mozzarella served with two sauces (one red, one white). A great selection of wines, featuring many Italian labels, priced from the mid-teens and up. ■ *120 A Park Lane, Kirkland; 889-8601; map:EE3; $$; beer and wine; AE, DC, MC, V; local checks only; lunch Mon–Sat, dinner every day.* &

**The Roost** ★ The Roost—the abbreviated name of Issaquah's first saloon, Cooper's Roost—celebrates the sporting life of hunters and fishers, as well as the pleasures of a mainstream American menu (customers are welcome to post pictures of their Big Catch on the wall by the restrooms). The steaks, which range from large to enormous, are owner Mick McHugh's pride, cut and aged to exacting specifications. And if it's not cooked right, the server may, as we have experienced, jerk it off your plate and return shortly with an entire new platter. Big, fresh, green salads and real mashed potatoes are added pluses. The Roost caters to families (up to three kids per adult are fed absolutely free on Wednesdays) and offers nightly specials such as prime rib on Sundays and fried chicken on Mondays. The front room is a lively, high-beamed bar. ■ *120 NW Gilman Blvd, Issaquah; 392-5550; $; full bar; AE, DC, MC, V; checks OK; lunch, dinner every day, brunch Sun.* &

▼

Top 200
Restaurants

▲

**The Rose Bakery and Bistro** ★ On a given night, one regular customer might momentarily man the cash register, another bus tables; there's an orthopedic surgeon who's been known to help with dishes. Otherwise, everything that gets done at this homey little spot with the sloped floors set among achingly humble digs gets done by Al and Suzanne Jacobs. It's a neighborhood restaurant in the truest sense, where customers might bring in a flat of homegrown berries for the day's pie making. What started as a bakery has since expanded to add a little lunch and a little dinner, with fresh pasta, dirt cheap. If sauces are sometimes a little thin, they are thick with garlic, and there's nothing anemic about the huge slices of fresh pie. You can't miss the place; the sign's as big as the dining room. ■ *9827 NE 120th Pl, Kirkland; 820-6862; map:DD3; $; beer and wine; no credit cards; local checks only; lunch Tues–Sat, dinner Mon–Sat.* &

**Rover's** ★★★½ Chef Thierry Rautureau, who began his culinary apprenticeship in the French countryside at age 13, is Seattle's answer to Jacques Pepin—a handsome elf with a warm wit, a world of personality, and an inspired hand in the kitchen. His restaurant, a small house tucked into a garden courtyard in Madison Valley, underwent a remodel in 1995, expanding both the seating area and the kitchen. Best of all, Rover's once-stark dining room has been warmly redecorated. Dinners here are marvelously sauced, classically French-inspired treatments of not strictly Northwest fare. Rautureau's forte is seafood, and he's adept at finding the best-quality ingredients. It may feel a tad fussy and expensive, but portions— with, perhaps, the exception of the precious five-course *menu degustation*—are served with a generous hand. A whole Maine lobster, out of the shell, steamed and served with a Perigord truffle sauce, is savored with each mouthful. Tender pink slices of venison in a dark green peppercorn sauce taste surprisingly delicate. Expect ever-professional service, and expect sticker shock when perusing the carefully chosen wine list. Dining in the courtyard, weather permitting, is an enchanting experience. ■ *2808 E Madison St; 325-7442; map:GG5; $$$; beer and wine; AE, DC, MC, V; checks OK; dinner Tues–Sat.*

**Ruby's on Bainbridge** ★★ Maura and Aaron Crisp have turned this location next door to the island's only movie theater into a mini-destination restaurant. It's a steamy, garlicky little place a hobbit might love—just casual enough for the locals, just sumptuous enough for weekend guests and day trippers. The menu changes often, but you'll encounter such entrees as fettuccine tossed with wild mushrooms, swordfish dressed in soy and ginger, and pork tenderloin with a raspberry reduction. Salads are standouts. ■ *4569 Lynwood Center Rd, Bainbridge Island; 780-9303; $$; beer and wine; MC, V; checks OK; lunch Tues–Sun, dinner every day, brunch Sat–Sun.*

**Saigon Bistro** ★½ Light, airy Saigon Bistro is a cut above the many other cafes found along Jackson Street's Little Saigon. The open kitchen lends the room life, and this may be Seattle's only Vietnamese restaurant with a view—albeit one of the Duwamish corridor. The menu's many options reflect the Southern Vietnamese style of cookery, and everything here is prepared with care. A signature dish is bun mang vit, the apotheosis of soup and salad: a light soup of noodles in duck stock on one side, and a duck and cabbage salad with sweet, pungent ginger sauce on the other. Eggplant hot pot and oc (snail) soup are also stand-outs. Many dishes can be ordered in cold- and hot-weather versions: with dry noodles, fragrant broth, or roll-your-own rice pancakes served with an array of fresh herbs. ■ *1032 S Jackson St; 329-4939; map:HH6; $; beer and wine; MC, V; no checks; breakfast, lunch, and dinner every day.* &

**Saleh al Lago** ★★★ Saleh Joudeh is a native of the Middle East who left his heart in central Italy 20-some years ago. Self-taught and earnest about his restaurant, Joudeh has put out some of the most consistently good central Italian food in Seattle here at Green Lake since 1982. The two-tiered, pink-hued destination dining place is more popular with Seattle's money-eyed muck-a-mucks than with the city's youthful trend-seekers (who may find the room too bright, the menu too traditional). But what Saleh al Lago might lack in excitement, it makes up for in execution: the menu is steadfast and true—as is the staff. You're not likely to find a better plate of calamari than this lightly floured version sautéed with lemon, garlic, and parsley. Risotto is done to chewy perfection here, perhaps with a rich red sauce and bits of filet mignon or with chicken, arugula, and Gorgonzola. Try the sautéed Provimi veal with its delicate quattro formaggi sauce or the nutmeg-tinged housemade spinach-and-cheese ravioli. Bored with tiramisu? Think again before you pass up Saleh's. ■ *6804 E Green Lake Way N; 524-4044; map:EE7; $$$; full bar; AE, MC, V; local checks only; lunch Tues–Fri, dinner Tues–Sat.* &

▼

**Top 200 Restaurants**

▲

**Salute** ★½ ■ **La Dolce Vita** ★½ A shift in ownership hasn't affected the charming trattoria atmosphere, the food, or the prices at Salute. Even the waiters are still dark and handsome (though their Italian counterparts are gone, and their replacements have Laurelhurst accents). But not to worry. Italian pop music favorites like "Volare" and "That's Amore" lend that certain warmth. Everything here is made fresh, and the kitchen holds off on the garlic, letting the food's flavors sing their own song. The homemade gnocchi with a lush tomato sauce is superb, while the veal marsala with porcini mushrooms can use a little oomph. A simple spaghetti al burro, however, proves remarkable, causing one to pause and wonder how anything can taste so good with so few ingredients. Still no reservations, but then waiting in the chummy little bar isn't so bad.

Next door is the pretty sister, **La Dolce Vita**, a comely ristorante with a different (but equally good) menu and live opera on Saturday nights. Cordon Bleu–trained Ali Chalel commands the kitchen amiably, turning out really wonderful veal cannelloni with three sauces, lamb scalloppine, and some good gnocchi. The wine list is decidedly Italian. For the antiques-and-flowers atmosphere, excellent food, and classical entertainment (there's also romantic violin and piano music on Fridays), you pay only a few dollars more than you would next door; and La Dolce Vita *even* takes reservations. ■ *(Salute) 3410 NE 55th St; 527-8600; map:EE6; $$; beer and wine; AE, MC, V; local checks only; dinner Tues–Sun.* ■ *(La Dolce Vita) 3426 NE 55th St; 523-3313; map:EE6; $$; full bar; AE, MC, V; local checks only; lunch Mon–Fri, dinner Mon–Sat.* &

**Salvatore** ★★ What with so many Italian restaurants going upscale and every other restaurant in town going Italian, this neighborhood dinner spot continues to impress by getting all the essentials right—the old-fashioned Italian way. Much of the warmth here stems from Salvatore Anania himself, who brings his amore for the southern Italian food of Basilicata to his North End landing. Service is friendly and more than helpful (you might *need* help choosing from among the many Italian wines offered). We suggest starting with one of the thin-crusted pizzas but passing on the lackluster salads. Take your waiter's cue when it comes to specials, or order the spicy, satisfying penne puttanesca. Even though they've moved the entranceway and added a few cafe tables, on busy nights Salvatore's no-reservations policy may still leave wannabe diners crowded and waiting in a tight space. ■ *6100 Roosevelt; 527-9301; map:EE6; $$; beer and wine; MC, V; checks OK; dinner Mon–Sat.* &

**Santa Fe Cafe** ★★ In a city that still has little to show in the way of Southwestern cuisine, Santa Fe's menu offers a particularly welcome respite from the "Mexican" fare we've grown accustomed to in these parts. The overall dining experience at these sibling cafes (there's one in Ravenna, another on Phinney Ridge) is consistently good, thanks to genuinely friendly and able service, and a great menu. Start with the silky garlic custard and the creamy artichoke ramekin and marry that with a red chile beer (Full Sail Amber Ale spiked with chile peppers). And those are just for teasers. Entrees run the gamut from pork tamales to spicy enchiladas or chicken-filled crêpes. If your meal doesn't come with posole—flavorful Southwestern hominy—ask for some on the side. Desserts include such stand-outs as banana flan, tequila sherbet, and bread pudding. ■ *2255 NE 65th St; 524-7736; map:EE6; $$; full bar; AE, MC, V; checks OK; lunch Tues–Fri, dinner every day.* ■ *5910 Phinney Ave*

▼

**Top 200 Restaurants**

▲

*N; 783-9755; map:EE7; $$; full bar; AE, MC, V; local checks only; lunch Sat–Sun, dinner every day.* &

**Sawatdy Thai Cuisine** ★★ Now that islanders have had Sawatdy to themselves for a while, perhaps it's time they let Seattle in on their secret: some of the best Thai food in the Seattle area can be found on Bainbridge Island. Island life is a trade-off, with residents often settling for mediocre dining experiences in exchange for convenience. Not so at this modest mid-island restaurant (no view, and next door to a gas station). The place runs like clockwork, and you can rest assured that every fragrant dish is well executed and every customer well cared-for. Reservations are a good idea. ■ *8780 Fletcher Bay Rd, Bainbridge Island; 780-2429; $; beer and wine; MC, V; checks OK; lunch Tues–Fri, dinner Tues–Sun.* &

**Sea Garden** ★★ ■ **Sea Garden of Bellevue** ★★ The name says it all: the best efforts are put into anything that comes from the sea—particularly if it spent its last minutes in the live tank up front. The place is nothing fancy, but we've always been enamored of Sea Garden's ability to keep such consistently excellent seafood so reasonably priced. Expect subtle Cantonese fare, the tamely spiced stuff we all enjoyed before we developed our culinary crush on fiery Sichuan or Hunan food. Choose lobster or crab and they'll bring it snapping mad in a bucket to your table for inspection. Minutes later it arrives, perfectly turned out, chopped into tender pieces and served with a consistently finger-lickin'-good black bean sauce, or a refreshing ginger and green onion sauce. Big, succulent sea scallops populate a plate with honey-glazed walnuts. Naturally sweet spot prawns on wooden skewers burst with flavor. The extensive menu offers plenty of vegetarian options, plus exotics like jellyfish, sea cucumber, or fish maw. Larger parties fill the somewhat dreary upstairs room. Open late every day.

▼

**Top 200 Restaurants**

▲

In 1994 the Sea Garden moved east in a big way. Rather than move into used digs—as do many of the Seattle eateries branching into Bellevue and the Eastside—the owners, an extended family, built from the ground up. It's not a grand place, but it is smart and bright. Service (at both restaurants) ranges from adequate to exasperating. ■ *(Seattle) 509 7th Ave S; 623-2100; map:R6; $; full bar; AE, MC, V; no checks; lunch, dinner every day.* ■ *(Bellevue) 200 106th Ave NE, Bellevue; 450-8833; map:HH3; $$; full bar; AE, DC, MC, V; no checks; lunch, dinner every day.* &

**Seattle Bagel Bakery** Seattleites rarely match Manhattanites in their lust for the doughy rings, but this spot next to the Harbor Steps (take a bagel-to-go and eat by the fountains) comes close to inspiring the same passion. The only way it differs from what you might find in New York is that it's clean, airy, nonsmoking, and full of sunlight. Sometimes warm, always fresh, these little wonders of raisins, cheese, garlic (gotta be a garlic lover, for the cooks are generous), or poppyseed can be eaten alone or split open and heaped with cream cheese and lox— or *Oy!*—turkey and sprouts, without smothering the taste of the bagel. ■ *1302 Western Ave, Seattle; 624-2187; map:L8; $; no alcohol; no credit cards; local checks only; breakfast, lunch every day.*

**Seoul Olympic Restaurant** ★ Some of the best Korean food in the Seattle area is in a nondescript office complex in Bellevue. There are plenty of choices only a Korean would love, which might explain why they don't even bother to translate some of these on the menu. If you ask, the server might short-circuit your interest, dismissing an entry as "too hot," "not cooked," or simply, "You won't like that one." But if you're the adventuresome type, go for it and check out a plate of steaming tubular animal innards. Or try the Korean barbecued beef (steeped in a simple marinade of soy sauce, sugar, and wine), or crispy dumplings, or even the salad bar selections, which include a pungent kimchi. ■ *1200 112th Ave NE, Bellevue; 455-9305; map:HH3; $$; full bar; AE, MC, V; local checks only; lunch, dinner every day.* &

▼

**Top 200
Restaurants**

▲

**Serafina** ★½ Moody Serafina—sometimes it's a dish of creamy pasta in the dark, sexy dining room, sometimes a couple of shared appetizers in the leafy courtyard. You feel you haven't so much walked into a restaurant as into a setting— forest green ceilings, Pompeii red walls, cloth wall sconces, a table tucked romantically behind a column or half-walls. There's a definite feeling of lushness here, and the menu doesn't deny it. Sensuous, serious ingredients abound—herbs, fragrant cheeses, roasted meats—and indeed it's possible to overdo it at Serafina, since some of the dishes are so *over* herbed and *over* creamed they're hard to finish. The handful of appetizers (mezza) are meant to be an Italian round of tapas: calamari fritti, bruschetta with tomato and arugula, baked eggplant. Pastas include such zingers as carciofi e spinaci (artichokes and spinach) in leek and Gorgonzola cream; if the specialties della campagna include the spiedini di agnello (lamb) with smoked pancetta, don't hesitate to try it. There's a faintly overly self-conscious feel here, somehow inappropriate to the rustic feel Serafina is trying to convey, of too much effort put into foods that should be simple. There's live jazz every night. ■ *2043 Eastlake Ave E; 323-0807; map:GG7; $$; full bar; DC, MC, V; checks OK; lunch Mon–Fri, dinner every day.* &

**74th Street Ale House** ★½ The 74th Street Ale House is the embodiment of truth in packaging. The main business of this establishment is beer, and the ambience is uncompromisingly tailored to suit: bar, bar stools, noisy regulars, and TV ever tuned to the game. You can also eat—plainly, cheaply, and well. Sandwiches are the standard order here: a bulging, steaming, piping-hot grilled pastrami on rye with sauerkraut and Swiss cheese—a royal Reuben in all but name. An Italian sausage sandwich or beefburger, both with fragrant oily peppers and onions bursting out of a crisp split baguette. The chicken sandwich—a breaded breast cutlet topped with melted mozzarella on rye toast slathered with cream cheese—has been voted Seattle's best so many times it should run for mayor. There's an innovative vegetarian sandwich, a traditional caesar, and special pastas that are far beyond pub quality. The soup of the day may be a hearty lamb stew. Nobody will purse their lips if you linger; lingering's what this place is all about. Oh, and 17 draft beers and ales on tap. ■ *7401 Greenwood Ave N; 784-2955; map:DD8; $; beer and wine; MC, V; checks OK; lunch, dinner every day.* &

**Shamiana** ★★ Shamiana stands out among ethnic restaurants on the Eastside, often winning "best of" polls. Brother-and-sister team Eric and Tracy Larson grew up as foreign service kids in East Pakistan (now Bangladesh), and after their return to the United States found themselves hankering for the food they remembered. Now Eric's in the kitchen, Tracy runs the front of the house, and their mother, Nancy (Memsahib) Larson, oversees the operation. Eastern cooking meets Western chefs here in the happiest of ways: stunning creations include a velvet butter chicken wallowing in cumin-scented butter, tomato, and cream sauce. A Pakistani barbecue turns out flame-broiled meats and some mouthwatering (and mouth-igniting) versions of traditional Indian curries. Vegetarians can select from crisp samosas stuffed with crunchy potatoes or aloo dum Kashmiri, potatoes simmered in spicy yogurt sauce. The menu notes which dishes are made without dairy products and gives a heat guide to ordering curries. Dinner may top $20, but lunch is bargain city, with a buffet that changes daily. ■ *10724 NE 68th St, Kirkland; 827-4902; map:EE3; $; beer and wine; AE, DC, MC, V; checks OK; lunch Mon–Fri, dinner every day.* &

**Shamshiri** ★★ When you visit Bob Behmanesh's pretty, diminutive Persian restaurant—a magnet for Iranians and culinary adventurers alike—you'll learn by tasting why the foods of Persia (now Iran) are so highly regarded in the world of sophisticated cuisines. Start with the aphrodisiacal eggplant borany—a meld of roasted eggplant, onions, and garlic served with pita. The Ash-e-reshteh, a vegetable soup, comes drizzled with kashk (Persian buttermilk), and zereshk polo (chicken and rice with tart barberries and saffron) is often listed among the daily specials. Bareh kabob, a marinated lamb skewer, garners special praise, as does the fesenjon—a rich purée of walnuts in a pomegranate sauce served over baked chicken.

▼

Top 200
Restaurants

▲

Ghormeh sabzi, a beef-based stew fragrant with dried herbs you never knew existed, is just fine, while the dal adas, a vegetarian red lentil stew billed as "spicy," leaves much to be desired in the flavor department. Do order dessert. Silky Persian ice cream, scented with rosewater, has jewels of pistachio and frozen cream tucked here and there. Most intriguing is the faloudeh, rice noodles suspended in a firm rosewater granita. Surely, this is the food of aristocrats. ■ *6409 Roosevelt Way NE; 525-3950; map:DD6; $; beer and wine; DC, MC, V; checks OK; lunch, dinner every day.* &

**Shanghai Garden** ★★½ Owner/chef Hua Te Su caters to a largely Chinese clientele in this very pink restaurant in the International District. Mr. Su (as he is respectfully known) attracts diners from every Chinese province with regional dishes that change seasonally. The menu is vast and filled with exotica such as black-moss-and-bamboo-fungus soup, sautéed hog maw, and fish-head casserole. Come prepared to be wowed by anything made with pea vines or with the chef's special hand-shaven noodles. The vivid tendrils of the sugar pea plant resemble sautéed spinach, and you'd never imagine they'd cook up this tender and clean-tasting, never more so than when paired with plump shrimp. The noodles, shaved off a block of dough, are the main ingredient in a dozen different dishes. Try them in what we're sure will be the best chow mein you'll ever eat. This might be the only Chinese restaurant in town where desserts should not be missed. ■ *524 6th Ave S; 625-1689; map:R7; $; beer and wine; MC, V; no checks; lunch, dinner every day.*

**Shiro's** ★★★ Seattle's best-known sushi chef, Shiro Kashiba, sold his legendary Nikko Restaurant after 20 years, moved it to fancy digs in the Westin Hotel, presided there for a year, then retired. Briefly. In 1995, to the delight of legions of fans, he opened Shiro's. Graced with a blond hardwood sushi bar, linen-draped tables, and the presence of the master, this immaculate, simply decorated Belltown storefront was an immediate hit. While the small menu offers full-course dinner entrees as well (tempura, sukiyaki, and teriyaki with accompanying rice, salad, and miso soup), it's the sushi that commands full sensual attention: this is the most lustrously gleaming fish you'll see in this town, and you'd do best to heed the call. At lunch, the bento box gives you an opportunity for serious sampling, and sushi is decidedly more affordable. ■ *2401 2nd Ave; 443-9844; map:F8; $$$; full bar; AE, MC, V; no checks; lunch Mon–Fri, dinner Mon–Sat.* &

**Shuckers (Four Seasons Olympic Hotel)** ★★ There's an oddly mixed clientele at handsome Shuckers: lots of power-lunching suits, families from the hotel eating with their kids, and people dining peacefully alone. The helpful staff caters to all, with generally swift, businesslike service for the first; crayons, orange juice, and a plate of maraschino cherries for the second; and a friendly word and plenty of attention to the last. The seafood here (as it should be) is fine, with a few solid favorites: honey-roasted salmon, a slightly sweet geoduck stew, a creamy-dressed caesar salad with plump crab or shrimp. If you're in the mood for a whole crab, fine—you can have it roasted or steamed. If you want oysters, this is the place. And if you like your fish grilled rare, tell them, and it will be so. Quality notwithstanding, we'll lodge a small complaint over slightly inflated prices. ■ *Four Seasons Olympic Hotel: 411 University St; 621-1984; map:L7; $$–$$$; full bar; AE, DC, MC, V; no checks; lunch Mon–Sat, dinner every day.* &

**Si Senor** ★ The influences of the cuisines of Peru and the area of northeastern Mexico centering on the city of Monterrey help account for much of the originality on this menu. And while you can order the usual south-of-the-border standbys, why miss out on exotica? Lomo de almendra is marinated pork loin in a deliciously dark and almond-flavored sauce; seco, a Peruvian lamb dish, comes sauced with a blend of cilantro and onions. Devilishly hot and spicy camarones à la diabla are prawns sautéed with mushrooms in a complex, deep red sauce. A dinner-size appetizer, anticuchos, will astound those frustrated by skimpy little sticks of Thai satay; here you get a platter with baked potatoes flanking skewers laden with flat slabs of tender, marinated, charred beef heart (don't balk: if you didn't know it, you'd never guess). The staff is lively and lighthearted, occasionally barreling into the dining room with a platter and hollering, "Cheeseburger!" Live Andean music accompanies dinner on weekends. ■ *2115 Bellevue–Redmond Rd, Redmond; 865-8938; map:EE1; $; full bar; AE, DC, MC, V; checks OK; lunch, dinner every day.* &

**Siam on Broadway** ★½ Among Seattle's multitude of Thai restaurants, tiny Siam wins the popularity contest, hands down. Working the woks and burners in a tiny open kitchen fronted by counter seating, a quartet of women move with utmost grace, portioning meats and vegetables, dipping into salty potions. They produce, among other flavorful dishes, what might be the city's best tom kah gai—the chicken soup spicy with chiles, sour with lemongrass, and soothed with coconut milk. The menu doesn't stray far from the Bangkok standards, but the dishes created by the deft hands in the kitchen are distinctive. Sit at the counter and enjoy the show or wait for one of only 15 tables in the back. You won't have to wait at **Siam on Lake Union** (1880 Fairview Avenue E, 323-8101), a newer, larger outpost. Nor will you have to search for a parking space (they've got a private lot). Though good, the food here doesn't quite live up to its Broadway sibling's. ■ *616 Broadway E;*

324-0892; map:GG7; $; beer and wine; AE, MC, V; checks
OK; lunch Mon–Fri, dinner every day.

**Sisters European Snacks** ★ Show up early in the morning for
a kaiser waffle or a German pastry and you'll see sisters Aruna,
Mariam, and Nirala Jacobi chopping, stirring, and simmering
ingredients in preparation for what will inevitably be a busy
day. Their colorful shop, with a counter facing out on busy Post
Alley, occupies what may be the brightest corner of Pike Place
Market. It's a very pretty, very girly place, with the amiable sib-
lings chattering back and forth in their native German and legions of lunchers arriving for sandwiches and for soups that
originate from all over the globe—from silky African peanut to
hearty cabbage potato with sausage to exotic Indian dal. The
Jacobis create focaccia sandwiches with such integral ingredients as Roma tomatoes, baked eggplant, Black Forest ham, and
assorted cheeses (fontina, feta, mozzarella, and cream). The focaccia is stuffed in a variety of combinations, grilled to crisp,
melting perfection, and served with a small salad. ■ *1530 Post
Alley, Pike Place Market; 623-6723; map:I8; $; no alcohol; no
credit cards; local checks only; breakfast, lunch every day.*

▼

**Top 200
Restaurants**

▲

**Snappy Dragon** ★★ Judy Fu is a one-woman Chinese noodle
factory and wokmeister extraordinaire whose quiet, competent
elegance lends a note of grandeur to the kitchen at this quaint
North End house-turned-restaurant. Fu cooked professionally
for others for over 25 years before opening her own restaurant
in 1993; those of you who frequented Panda's before it became
Pandasia will remember her as the stately flour-smudged head
chef, ever rolling out handmade noodles at the open kitchen
there. Here, with the help of her son and daughter-in-law—who
manage the phone, the floor, and a line of cooks, and help her
keep pace with a busy take-out and delivery trade—Fu turns
out those famous homemade noodles, rolled and cooked to
order; a sampling of authentic clay hot pots and well-executed
versions of the standard wokked-up chicken, pork, beef, and
vegetable dishes; and some of the city's finest mu-shu. Outstanding appetizers include jiao-zi (boiled meat-filled dumplings
with a fragrant dipping sauce) and a delicate green onion pancake (think: Chinese focaccia). Big bowls of comforting soups
star Fu's thick, tender noodles. ■ *8917 Roosevelt Way NE;
528-5575; map:DD6; $; full bar; AE, DC, MC, V; checks OK;
lunch Mon–Sat, dinner every day.* ⅃

**Sostanza** ★★★ Erin Rosella's Sostanza, with its papaya-
colored walls, exposed wood beams, brick fireplace, tiny outdoor terrace, and decidedly Tuscan mood, rests quietly on the
farthest end of Madison Park's tony commercial strip. The
menu's focus (and the restaurant's management) has seen a
number of changes since Rosella—then a serious 23-year-old
chef—first opened the doors in 1991. Sostanza has finally

found its stride, maturing into a casually elegant neighborhood
restaurant with friendly, unpretentious service and a deliciously overindulgent and frequently changing menu. The
menu offers a three-course prix fixe of country-Italian origins
with a nod toward country-French: goat-cheese–stuffed grilled
radicchio and Belgian endive, an intense shrimp and tomato
bisque, housemade pappardelle with porcini and portobello
mushrooms, and grilled lamb chops with a garlic herb jus are
examples of offerings whose quality, quantity, and price (dependent on your entree choice) add up to perhaps one of the
best higher-end bargains in town. Lunch is a smaller, à la carte
version on the dinner-fare theme. ▪ *1927 43rd St; 324-9701;
map:GG6; $$; beer and wine; AE, MC, V; checks OK; lunch
Mon–Fri, dinner Mon–Sat.* ૬

**Spazzo** ★½ The top floor of a glass-and-steel bank building is
about as unlikely a place as you'll find for a rustic Mediterranean restaurant. Yet that is the pervasive theme at oddly
named Spazzo (an unfortunate corruption of *spasso*—"fun" in
Italian). A showy creation of the Schwartz Brothers dynasty,
Spazzo features a menu that supposedly draws from everywhere the olive tree grows, though these days (judging by dinner entrees) it seems to grow mostly in Italy. Other regions are
represented mostly in the tapas menu, the restaurant's best feature. You can make a meal of these appetizer-size delights,
each of your party ordering two or three, then swapping
around. The Med spreads—including baba ghanouj, hummus,
whipped feta, taramasalata, and tapanade—are outstanding.
Entrees can be adventuresome or just plain tiresome (like the
Moroccan lamb couscous—overdone lamb, artichoke hearts
warring with cilantro, plus mouthfuls of annoying little unpitted olives). ▪ *10655 NE 4th St, Bellevue; 454-8255; map:HH3;
$$; full bar; AE, DC, MC, V; checks OK; lunch Mon–Fri, dinner every day.* ૬

**Spud Fish and Chips** After 50 years, Spud is still a swell
family fish-frying enterprise. It has spawned locations in
summertime's highest-density neighborhoods—Green Lake's
northeast shore (6860 Green Lake Way N, 524-0565) and
Juanita Drive in Kirkland (9700 NE Juanita Drive, 823-0607)—
but only the original Alki Beach outpost gets our vote for consistency and quality control. Fresh, large pieces of lingcod are
coated with a crispy cornmeal blend, lightly deep-fried in
canola oil (Spud's nod to modern health concerns), and served
atop a pile of those namesake spuds peeled, cut, and fried fresh
every day. Some people go for the prawns and chips, clams and
chips, or oysters and chips, but many are satisfied to stick with
the fish. Eat inside, outside, or across the street by the water.
▪ *2666 Alki Ave SW; 938-0606; map:II9; $; no alcohol; no
credit cards; no checks; lunch, dinner every day.*

**Stage Right Cafe** ★½ That's not wainscoting and brick—it's scenery paint. Red velvet curtains drape not in front of the stage, but in front of a kitchen that turns out food attractive and tasty enough to warrant the spotlights aimed at tabletops. On nights when a show plays the adjacent Village Theater, Stage Right's kitchen groans and strains to accommodate the on- slaught. Other nights, or mornings or afternoons, things are more relaxed—a better time to sip a bowl of spicy curry lentil or zesty orange carrot soup. A woodsy wild mushroom ragout—one of the many boldly flavored vegetarian dishes— comes chockablock with shiitakes and porcinis. Harvest Chicken stars a very large, tender, pan-fried breast nesting on a bed of fettuccine, the whole dish flavored by a sweet-kissed cider-cream sauce graced with slices of sautéed apple. Many dinner entrees can be had at lunchtime, along with good sand- wiches. After-theater options include sherry or port, along with delightful apple pandowdy. ■ *301 Front St N, Issaquah; 392- 0109; $$; beer and wine; MC, V; checks OK; lunch, dinner ev- ery day, brunch Sat–Sun.* &

▼

Top 200
Restaurants

▲

**Still Life in Fremont** ★★ Fremont's favorite coffeehouse is a Seattle classic: a big, steamy, well-lit space with a wall of win- dows, mismatched wooden dining tables and chairs, a big '40s radio, and Dick Powell and June Allyson's old coffee table. Add to these good art, good weekend entertainment, and— remember these?—good vibes. Still Life smacks of the '60s, when all hanging out required was a good book and a bowl of soup. Indeed, the soups are stunning: thick purée of curried split pea and sweet potato, or perhaps parsnip and celery root. The short sandwich menu is now overshadowed by the grow- ing list of specials: a wild-rice rosemary salad studded with smoked turkey, green beans, mushrooms, crunchy carrots, and hazelnuts; a hefty square of polenta topped with tomato, red pepper, olives, and pepper Jack; a pie packed with arti- chokes, red peppers, and smoked mozzarella. There's a heavy, but not strict, emphasis on vegetarian choices here. Or you may choose to sip a good beer, a cup of steaming chai, and nosh on a sweet. You'll leave reflecting on your good fortune that there is, in fact, still life in Fremont. Service is your own. ■ *705 N 35th St; 547-9850; map:FF7; $; beer and wine; no credit cards; local checks only; breakfast, lunch, dinner every day.* &

**Stone Way Cafe** ★ Does anyone eat weekend breakfast at home anymore? Breakfastophiles (of which there must be mil- lions in this town) rate the homey Stone Way high on several counts: best Portuguese sausage, fastest-moving weekend line, most mediocre coffee (a kind of perverse distinction in Latte- town). Favorites include corned-beef hash, biscuits and gravy, and a wide variety of omelets (some surprisingly inventive).

There's also lunch, when the burgers are homemade and grilled to order and the soups are wonderful (chicken, vegetable, beef noodle—nothing too threatening). Owner Charlene Iverson will tell you what to order for your kids, then recite your check from memory. Don't miss the blackberry pie—hot and sweet, not cloying, and topped with vanilla ice cream. ■ *3620 Stone Way N; 547-9958; map:FF7; $; no alcohol; no credit cards; checks OK; breakfast every day, lunch Mon–Fri.*

**Streamliner Diner** ★ A Bainbridge Island clubhouse where locals swill coffee for hours on end, chasing morning into afternoon. Do these people have jobs? How can they afford their expensive sneakers? However they pull it off, the lackadaisical vibes generated by these relaxed islanders make the Streamliner a great ferry-ride destination. The harried Seattleite can sail to Bainbridge, stroll a few minutes to the Streamliner, sink into a chair, and fully exhale. The room is pretty and light, with a few hippified diner-ish touches like the long, curving, wooden counter and the 1940s tablecloths. The breakfast menu is extensive, featuring a funky mixture that fits right in with the decor: hearty omelets, lots of fresh baked goods, perfect waffles, a veggie tofu scramble, a fabulous fried-egg sandwich. An almost ridiculously rich quiche-of-the-day is served, it seems, by the quarter-pie. The potatoes are old-fashioned and delicious—no Shake 'n' Bake coating of seasonings here. Sausage, bacon, and meat loaf are all of an uncommonly high quality. Lunch features homemade soups, salads, and sandwiches, plus one hot entree a day, perhaps an excellent pesto calzone with scallops, bacon, and green onions. ■ *397 Winslow Way, Bainbridge Island; 842-8595; $; no alcohol; no credit cards; checks OK; breakfast every day, lunch Mon–Sat.* ♿

**Sunlight Cafe** ★ With an ambience perhaps associated more with the '60s than with the '90s, the Sunlight continues to thrive because what it does, it does well. The owners are dedicated to vegetarian food. Come for a weekend brunch of a crunchy eggless sesame waffle and a plate of hot potatoes with sautéed onions. Also worth a try are blueberry-yogurt hotcakes, French toast (even a vegan version), and a wonderful fruit salad with big chunks of ripe fruit and nuts with a drizzling of yogurt-honey-tahini dressing. Breakfast generally features waffles, eggs with home-fries, and huevos rancheros, in addition to freshly baked goods. Later in the day choose salads (lemon-tahini is the best dressing), vegetarian soups, and huge entrees (a great nutburger). The Sunlight has achieved institution status, due in equal parts to good, solid food and a shamelessly mellow character (with a shamelessly mellow staff). ■ *6403 Roosevelt Way NE; 522-9060; map:DD6; $; beer and wine; no credit cards; checks OK; breakfast and lunch Mon–Fri, dinner every day, brunch Sat–Sun.* ♿

**Surrogate Hostess** ★ Every happy bourgeois dream of a cafeteria is fulfilled here at Capitol Hill's neighborhood dining room, though not every dream every day. Folks sit with other folks at big collective tables, meeting friends, reading books, watching their kids (this is a good place for them), and enjoying good, inventive, home-style food. The place's reputation as something of a repository of yuppie angst—those who don't have jobs, those who have jobs but are disenchanted with them, those who have kids and can't decide whether to send them to private schools or not, and on and on—is as strong as ever. As for the food, there are usually several good salad choices—along with a pasta or potato dish, an excellent quiche, a pâté, and soup. Breakfast at the Surrogate is a big Seattle tradition—unique egg dishes; beautiful coffee cakes made with seasonal fruits; great hot cereal; sensational, light cinnamon rolls. The bakery is, in fact, the Surrogate's primary strength. ■ *746 19th Ave E; 324-1944; map:GG6; $; beer and wine; MC, V; local checks only; breakfast, lunch, dinner every day.* ᕕ

**Sushi-Ten** ★ There's only one good reason to come to this tired-looking little restaurant, but it's a very good reason. Every night of the week, plunk down a twenty and enjoy all-you-can-eat sushi. Sushi chef Masashi Seki rolls up and slices and arranges your favorites (tuna, yellowtail, the ubiquitous California roll) and they'll come until you drop. Weekends can get a little rambunctious. The rest of the small dining room (where you can order plump gyoza, light-batter tempura, and sparingly doused teriyaki chicken or salmon) is more conducive to leisurely conversation. ■ *2217 140th Ave NE, Bellevue; 643-6637; map:CC6; $$; beer and wine; MC, V; no checks; lunch Mon–Fri, dinner every day.* ᕕ

**Swingside Cafe** ★★ Owner/chef Brad Inserra (he's the guy working his buns off in the Swingside's absurdly small kitchen) produces a world of big flavors and an always inventive menu. There are hearty stews and sautés and pasta dishes of his Pittsburgh-Sicilian provenance spiced with unpredictable North African, Creole, and nouvelle-American accents. The brown Moroccan sauce melts in the mouth; tangy seafood dishes sing of the sea. Everything's rich, delicious, and amply portioned; don't overorder or you may have to be carried home. Desserts are a sometime thing, depending on who's supplying. As for atmosphere, you've probably forgotten eating out could be as simple, casual, and friendly as this. ■ *4212 Fremont Ave N; 633-4057; map:FF8; $$; beer and wine; MC, V; local checks only; lunch Tues–Fri, dinner Tues–Sat.* ᕕ

**Szmania's** ★★★ The pretty neighborhood village of Magnolia may be hard to find, but Szmania's makes it worth the trouble. Ludgar and Julie Szmania (pronounced *Smahn-ya*) opened

▼

**Top 200 Restaurants**

▲

their comfortably modern restaurant in 1990; it is now one of the city's most sought-out dining spots. The open kitchen provides a stage set where German-born Ludger uses Northwest ingredients to create such wide-ranging dishes as Jäegerschnitzel with spaetzle and roasted monkfish with a chanterelle cream sauce. Sit at the bright kitchen counter space and watch him work, or retreat to the far recesses of the dining room. Servings are generous, and the Szmanias know it; many entrees are offered in half-portions. Expect strong flavors that work well together—such as a paillard of beef coated with onion and mustard in a rich cabernet sauce—and occasionally some that don't, like an ill-conceived lamb saltimbocca. And take note of the loveliest array of vegetables ever to garnish a plate. For dessert: the signature pots de crème trio. ▪ *3321 W McGraw St; 284-7305; map:FF8; $$; full bar; AE, DC, MC, V; local checks only; dinner Tues–Sun.* ⅙

**Tandoor** ★ This little room on the Ave is so bare, one suspects the owners are conducting a sensory deprivation experiment. Then the food arrives. Tandoor serves exquisite and reliable Indian food, with an emphasis on tandoori-style cooking. Meat or fish is marinated overnight in yogurt spiced with chili powder, turmeric, ginger, and garlic. The next day the chicken is sprinkled with saffron and chili powder before being roasted in a charcoal-fired clay oven. The result is moist, smoky, and wonderful. A good introduction is the chicken tikka masala, tender and delicious. Also recommended is the eggplant bhatta. Eggplant is roasted, mashed, then sautéed with onions—it's like a dish from a fantasy Thanksgiving dinner. The side dishes here are tasty as well: basil and garlic naan is chewy with a hint of oil; raita is cool and soothing, not too salty; and the rice pulao is fragrant and perfectly prepared. ▪ *5024 University Way; 523-7477; map:FF6; $; beer and wine; AE, DC, MC, V; no checks; lunch, dinner every day.*

▼

Top 200
Restaurants

▲

**Taqueria Guaymas** ★ Ethnic oases such as these are usually found near gritty industrial centers (in this case White Center south of Harbor Island's once-thriving steel and flour mills—a 15-minute drive from downtown, but a world away from the city's less authentic *yupperias*). The fare is as simple and working class as the decor: a small lunch counter and picnic tables for those who aren't ordering to go; a fridge full of beer and a TV blaring Spanish soap operas. Tacos, burritos, and other reliables come jazzed up with options like tongue, tripe, or brains, as well as the usual chicken, beef, and pork for the less adventuresome. Huge prawns are featured in dishes such as coctel de camarones, a spicy, gazpacho-style blend of prawns, avocado, tomatoes, and cilantro; or in platters of camarones al mojo de ajo, where the wondrous crustaceans swim in melted butter and chopped garlic (order by the half-pound). On weekends, try the hangover special, menudo (tripe soup). Sample the daily thirst quenchers ladled from big glass jugs: melon juice, rice water, or a sweet hibiscus drink. A trio of outposts can be found in West Seattle, Lynnwood, and Renton—but this is the real McCoy. ■ *1622 Roxbury St SW; 767-4026; map:II8; $; beer and wine; no credit cards; checks OK; lunch, dinner every day.* &

**TestaRossa** ★★ The main event at this sparkling, bright Broadway eatery is stuffed pizza—the closest analogy we can draw being four-and-20 blackbirds baked in a pie. These rich creations ooze all manner of blue-ribbon treats: San Remo sun-dried tomatoes, roasted eggplant and red peppers, lamb sausage, Poblano chiles, pesto, caramelized onions, kalamata olives. All this bounty is laced together with milky domestic mozzarella and reggianito cheese from Argentina, then bathed in a robust tomato sauce. The basic stuffed pizza (which takes a while to cook) easily serves three, particularly if those three have, through the wait, nibbled on focaccia or bruschetta with pesto, herbed Montrachet, and roasted garlic. We're consistently impressed with the finesse evident in lighter fare also, as in a splendid salad with red-leaf and butter lettuces, soy-honey marinated mushrooms, and pistachios in a mandarin orange vinaigrette; or a lemony toss of cappellini pasta, sautéed shrimp, peppers, broccoli, and peas. TestaRossa is run by pros who aim to please: take-out, delivery, and catering are available, and service is efficient. The smokeless atmosphere buzzes cheerfully—till midnight on weekends. ■ *210 Broadway E; 328-0878; map:HH7; $; beer and wine; AE, MC, V; local checks only; lunch, dinner every day, brunch Sat–Sun.* &

**Thai Restaurant** ★★ One of Seattle's first noteworthy Thai restaurants remains a local favorite. The staff are incredibly efficient; they swirl by in their cool, bright shirts, trailing essences of coconut, peanut, and orange. Start with the mee krob, a nest of crunchy noodles fried with a tangy citrus flavor and topped with red pepper, a sweet plum sauce, bean sprouts, shreds of red cabbage, and tofu. The spring rolls are wrapped in a tender rice pancake, filled with lettuce and surimi; they're good dipped in plum sauce and dabbed in chopped peanuts. The tender squid sautéed with garlic and pepper sauce is outstanding. Hotness is not quite dependable here: someone in the kitchen likes playing with fire. ■ *101 John St; 285-9000; map:B8; $; full bar; AE, MC, V; local checks only; lunch Mon–Fri, dinner every day.* &

**Thai Terrace** ★ Mountlake Terrace Mall is an unlikely place to find good food, much less good Thai food. Thai Terrace is, happily for diners, an anomaly. Everything is unquestionably fresh. The vegetables glisten with their original colors. The subtle vegetarian spring rolls and the crisp Pinky in the

▼

**Top 200 Restaurants**

▲

Blanket (shrimps wrapped in wonton skin and fried) are nice antidotes to the fiery ricochet from the tender squid in chile sauce or the excellent phad Thai when spiced with anything more than one star. In Thai tradition, end the meal with home-made coconut ice cream and sticky black rice in coconut milk—an especially light version. ■ *21919 66th Ave W, Mountlake Terrace; 774-4556; $; beer and wine; AE, MC, V; no checks; lunch Mon–Fri, dinner Mon–Sat.*

**That's Amore** ★ The neighbors flock to this cheery, urbane cafe on the Mount Baker/Leschi ridge, almost as if it's their private club. The cooking style reflects owners Celester and Salina Gray's take on Italian, and portions are certainly decent. Neighbors show up for plates of creamy lemon fettuccine or a nicely crusted pizza with artichokes and what-have-you. A very fresh, very thin focaccia, crisp and warm, arrives with a wedge of creamy, blue-veined cambozola cheese to spread like butter over each slice: heaven. The chef uses red pepper without temerity, so, if you must, ask him to put on the brakes. The off-hand, city cafe atmosphere is great for families (there's a children's menu), with plenty of selections for the vegetarian in the group, too. Jockey for a seat that faces the back window, as the view of Seattle is *va-va-vavoom!* ■ *1425 31st Ave S; 322-3677; map:HH6; $; beer and wine; DC, MC, V; local checks only; lunch, dinner every day.* &

**Third Floor Fish Cafe** ★ For either casual or occasion dining, the Third Floor is a handsome spot, with varnished dark woods and accents in shades of vermilion, orange, aqua, and yellow. The room is laid out to take advantage of the panoramic view of Lake Washington and Seattle. Too bad the kitchen has long been inconsistent—one minute turning out yummy little crab cakes with a complex corn relish, artfully served on a fish-pattern plate, the next minute slinging a tender piece of mahi-mahi with the clumpiest of rice and blandest of veggies. Then the kitchen again soars, executing a superb daily special of mild, sweet monkfish in a flavorful lobster sauce. The best plan is to stick to the basics and trust that the fish will be delicious. The bar is great for grazing, and there's a small banquet room with a bit of a view. ■ *205 Lake St S, Kirkland; 822-3553; map:EE3; $$$; full bar; AE, MC, V; checks OK; lunch Mon–Fri, dinner Mon–Sat.* &

**Thirteen Coins** ★ It'll take a lot more than 13 coins to pay for the privilege of sinking into one of the humongous booths or sitting in one of the high-backed leather counter seats watching chefs work the grill at this Seattle dining institution. But who can resist the opportunity to choose from a menu so varied (with breakfast, sandwiches, pasta, fish, and meat dishes) and so perfectly dated (with eggs Benedict, fettuccine alfredo, and a complimentary antipasto plate)? Especially when it's all

Restaurants

▼
Top 200
Restaurants
▲

87

available any time of the day or night every day of the week. Around-the-clock dining and short-order food have made these twin restaurants popular for many years (helped by the fact that they occupy neighborhoods—by the *Seattle Times* building and the airport, respectively—with little competition). ▪ *125 Boren Ave N; 682-2513; map:F2; $$; full bar; AE, DC, MC, V; checks OK; breakfast, lunch, dinner every day (all day).* ▪ *18000 Pacific Hwy S; 243-9500; map:OO6; $$; full bar; AE, DC, MC, V; checks OK; breakfast, lunch, dinner every day (all day).* ⅍

**Thompson's Point of View** ★ By the time you finish your meal, a glow of satisfaction will transform your view of this rather plain room. The star entree, lightly breaded catfish, is moist with a crisp skin and accompanied by excellent long-simmered red beans and rice. In fact, the side dishes are often the best part of the meal. Thompson's gives you two with each dinner, and you may find yourself in an agony of indecision over the potato salad, black-eyed peas, sweetened yams, creamy baked macaroni and cheese, green beans with ham hocks, and Southern-style greens that set you down in a Georgia diner with your first bite. Corn bread—shaped like a pancake, crispy around the edges, and bathed in butter—arrives on its own plate. You might feel challenged by the sheer size of these meals: the Thompson Burger is a massive soul-food sandwich with sliced hot links, crisp bacon, a grilled beef patty, cheese, and condiments on an egg bun (and, yes, you *can* hear your arteries slamming shut); meat loaf comes in two hearty slabs. Our advice: Gobble up the side dishes, make a dent in the entree, and take the rest home. ▪ *2308 E Union St; 329-2512; map:HH6; $; full bar; MC, V; local checks only; lunch, dinner every day.* ⅍

**Three Girls Bakery** ★ Stop by any day around noon, and the crowd around Three Girl's L-shaped lunch counter will likely be three hungry locals and a couple of displaced New Yorkers deep. Sandwiches don't get a whole lot better than this, and *whole* is the operative word here, 'cause there ain't no halves, as the hard-working, wisecracking architects of meat-and-cheese will gladly tell you. There's soup—nothing fancy, but filling and hot—and a meat loaf sandwich like Mother used to make. On those depressing gray days, a trip to the Market for a bowl of spicy chili and a slice of pie—served up with a fat squirt of whipped cream by one of the most efficient counter staffs in town—will surely cure what ails you. Order bakery fixings at the take-out window—a loaf of pumpernickel or Russian rye, an apple fritter, perhaps a rugalach or three, and the best cheese croissants in the state, according to some. The restaurant closes at 5:30pm; the bakery at 6pm. ▪ *Pike Place Market; 622-1045; map:J8; $; no alcohol; no credit cards; checks*

*OK; breakfast, lunch every day.*

**Tokyo Japanese Restaurant** ★½ Presided over by Taka Saito, former sushi chef at Kirkland's Kikuya, Tokyo offers what may be the broadest selection of sushi and sashimi—albeit distinctly *Americanized* sushi and sashimi—on the Eastside. Popular with families, the dining room looks out on Loehmann Plaza's parking lot. Couples should opt to eat at the sushi bar, where creative rolls—like the Popeye (with spinach), the Evergreen (with a stand of green-leafed sprouts shading the roll), or the Kamikaze (the kitchen sink of rolls)—are ably prepared. The tonkatsu's deep-fried crust is bone dry, but unfortunately so is the pork. You can't go wrong with big bowls of ropy udon, and the deluxe makanouchi bento packs in enough sushi, sashimi, tempura, teriyaki, and such to feed two. An excellent selection of sake lists representatives from virtually every prefecture of Japan. ■ *3500 128th Ave SE, Bellevue; 641-5691; map:II2; $$; full bar; MC, V; no checks; lunch Mon–Fri, dinner every day.* &

**Tommy Thai's** ★★ Dish for dish, this is one of the best Thai restaurants in the region, even if it is tucked away in the middle of a Rose Hill shopping strip. The interior is typically spare, with an aquarium set into the back wall. Though the original owner sold out and moved back to Thailand, new owners have curried—oops, *carried* on and increased the popularity. Vegetarian spring rolls are served with homemade plum sauce. Lunch specials include one of these, along with a delicious bowl of hot and sour Thai soup flavored with galangal, lemongrass, and lime leaf. Be careful with the stars: everything is served on the hot side of "hot," including a superb gai-yuang (barbecued chicken) accented by sweet strips of pepper and fresh basil. Best of all is the Siam Ocean, a glistening sautéed dish of shrimp, scallops, squid, salmon, and clams, served in a chile-paste sauce with fresh basil and lemongrass. A slightly gummy phad Thai is the only unhappy surprise we've encountered here. ■ *8516 122nd Ave NE, Kirkland; 889-2447; map:DD3; $; beer and wine; MC, V; local checks only; lunch Mon–Fri, dinner every day.* &

▼

**Top 200 Restaurants**

▲

**Tosoni's** ★★ To its many loyal regulars, it's known as Walter's place. They know that the humble, strip-mall exterior belies the Old World delights awaiting inside, where chef Walter Walcher and a sous chef work the open kitchen, presiding over a small booth-lined room filled with antique cabinets and armoires. Vegetarians appreciate the porcini risotto and the goat cheese–stuffed morels. Meat eaters have kept the garlic lamb—tender strips sautéed in olive oil, heavily garlicked, and smartly peppered—on the menu for 12 years. While generously portioned main courses are often spectacularly good, side dishes have been known to arrive cool (garlic mashed potatoes) or soggy (beans). ■ *14320 NE 20th St, Bellevue; 644-1668; map:HH2;*

$$; beer and wine; MC, V; checks OK; dinner Tues–Sat. &

**Trattoria Mitchelli** ★ Good enough, they say, is never good enough. Well, guess what, they're wrong again. Dany Mitchell has earnestly built himself an empire of restaurants that serve good enough Italian food: Angelina's Trattoria, Bella Luna, Stella's Trattoria. Mitchell alone has provided Seattle with places where you can host a lively impromptu party in the bar or restaurant at almost any time of night. Yes, the food is usually mediocre, but that's not really the point. Think of it instead as dependable food, some of it quite good, such as the ravioli in butter and garlic, the pizzas, anything made with veal (usually fresh and tender), and breakfasts of Italian frittatas and cheesy omelets. Besides, mediocrity never had a more appealing bohemian backdrop than the original trattoria in Pioneer Square. ■ *84 Yesler Way; 623-3885; map:EE8; $; full bar; AE, MC, V; checks OK; breakfast, lunch, dinner every day.* &

**Triangle Tavern** ★ Hip remodels of skanky old taverns are the thing in Seattle these days. The Triangle (born in the '30s as the Classic Tavern) is one of the most impressively stylish, and the menu's swell. The decor is (naturally) triangular, the service flaky (admittedly hungover), but with the food we have little complaint nor do any of the legion of fans who stand drinking a brew while waiting for a table. Expansive appetizers include roasted garlic with goat cheese, nicely sided with roasted red peppers, olives, and bread; and a Middle Eastern plate heaped with hummus, baba ghanouj, and tabbouleh. When your dinners arrive, there's hardly room on the tiny table (or in the stomach) for what may be set before you: angel hair pasta in a smooth Gorgonzola-spinach sauce, a dependable Creole seafood gumbo, or a spinach lasagne stacked with three cheeses. Sandwiches are fine for dinner as well; a Philadelphia-style cheesesteak sided up with a caesar salad is cheap at twice the price. The small space is noisy and smoky and the desserts do not inspire; but generally the food is inventive and well prepared, and there are windows on three sides and outdoor tables from which to gaze upon prettified Fremont. ■ *3507 Fremont Pl N; 632-0880; map:FF8; $; beer and wine; MC, V; local checks only; lunch and dinner every day.*

**Tulio (Hotel Vintage Park)** ★★★ Tulio's neighborhood Italian charm belies its busy downtown hotel location. Downstairs, where most of the action takes place, tables with red-checkered cloths are packed in tightly, the sweet scent of roasted garlic hangs in the air, and a wood-burning oven and open kitchen make the ever lively room even livelier. The addition of an upstairs dining room allows space for larger parties. Service is swift, knowledgeable, and attentive, and with chef Walter Pisano in charge, your meal is always in good hands. His bruschetta mista (a mix of breads, marinated mushrooms, goat cheese, tapenade, and tomatoes tossed with pine nuts and currants) and the calamari fritti (enough spicy fried squid to feed a navy) will start things off right. The artful and very fresh "primi" courses, such as the smoked salmon ravioli tart with a lemon cream sauce, pique the palate. Roasted and grilled cuts of meat and fish round out the dinner menu, while thin-crusted pizzas and cheesy calzones add a casual note to the lunch offerings. Breakfast is a welcome respite from typical hotel fare. ▪ *Hotel Vintage Park: 1100 5th Ave; 624-5500; map:L6; $$; full bar; AE, DC, MC, V; local checks only; breakfast, lunch, dinner every day.* ♿

**Two Bells Tavern** ★½ Belltown's starving artists tried not to tell anyone about the excellent, cheap burgers on sourdough at the funky Two Bells, but word got out and now the tavern is packed all the time with an eclectic crowd, joining in common worship of the burger. It's big and juicy, smothered in onions and cheese, served on a sourdough roll with your choice of side orders, including a rich, chunky potato salad. Another favorite with the Bells crowd is the hot beer-sausage sandwich. Satisfying isn't the half of it—this food is so full of flavor and freshness and goes so well with the beer that you don't care about getting mustard all over your face. Food is served till 11pm (midnight on weekends), but the tavern stays open till 2am. ▪ *2313 4th Ave; 441-3050; map:F7; $; beer and wine; MC, V; no checks; lunch, dinner every day, breakfast Sat–Sun.* ♿

▼

**Top 200
Restaurants**

▲

**Un Deux Trois** ★★ Owner Judy Schocken presides over this warm splash of Southern France on the rue de First Avenue. The small, white-linen and blond-wood dining room kitty-corner from the Seattle Art Museum is popular with the lunchtime saumon-et-sauvignon-blanc crowd, office-workers stopping at the gourmet take-out counter for a soupçon of this or that, and the (too few) dinner patrons who stay for the French bistro fare. You'll find the delicacies of the Dordogne here—from cassoulet to onion soufflé to rabbit en croute—with butterfats as punctuation, not foundation, lending a lighter note than would be expected from such classically hearty fare. A robust, elegant roast chicken—its crackling skin comes encrusted with herbes de Provence and lined with pancetta—is a staple of the restaurant's lunch, dinner, and take-out trade. Wall-size windows let in the whole sweep of this busy, somewhat gritty South-of-the-Market corner, lending Un Deux Trois its urban character. ▪ *1329 1st Ave; 233-0123; map:K8; $$; beer and wine; AE, MC, V; checks OK; lunch, dinner every day.* ♿

**Union Bay Cafe** ★★★ In this softly lit Laurelhurst storefront, folks are as likely to be celebrating a birthday or anniversary as stopping in for a relaxing dinner after a hard day's work.

Chef/owner Mark Manley often leaves his kitchen to welcome guests and discuss dishes. His ever-changing menu is small and trenchant; performance never wavers. Keep a watchful eye for any appetizer made with mushrooms. A starter of Penn Cove mussels, scented with basil and ginger and smoothed with a touch of cream, proves that while his menu leans toward Italian, Manley can do Asian, too. Meats are handled with particular care, as evidenced by slices of venison sauced with chanterelles and huckleberries. Fresh fish and seasonal produce are well respected in this kitchen. You'll find vegetarian options at every meal; a reasonable wine list offers first-rate choices by the glass. For dessert—anything, from the bread pudding to a crisp made with apples and bourbon-soaked cherries. The bill is the final pleasure. Manley has plans to move next door to a new, expanded space (3513 NE 45th) that is still under construction at press time. A small courtyard will allow room for outdoor seating. ■ *3505 NE 45th St; 527-8364; map:FF6; $$; beer and wine; AE, DC, MC, V; checks OK; dinner Tues–Sun.* &

**Union Square Grill** ★½ The Union Square Grill has run through a lot of schticks: first as a French brasserie, then as a steak house, then as a clubby steak house complete with the maître d' you were supposed to have known for years. Today, it's simply a perfectly dependable steak house. There is an undeniably hearty, masculine, somehow glitzy feel to the handsome dining room, with its dark wood, yellow light, and oversize antique advertising posters. At lunchtime, the place is a sea of businessfolk, all of whom seem to be negotiating that last detail of a very important deal. In the evening, the crowd varies, and usually includes theatergoers taking advantage of a well-executed pretheater menu. As for the standard menu, only a curmudgeonly vegetarian could feel disappointed. Beef, in its many guises, inevitably makes a fine choice; the kitchen is less successful when venturing into grilled-halibut-over-wilted-spinach territory. For those nostalgic for the tableside histrionics of the '70s, a caesar salad is a must. Unrelentingly well intentioned service is sometimes less sophisticated than you'd expect. For dessert, the cheesecake is surprisingly light, with a delicate graham cracker crust (skip the overly sweet fruit topping). The bar is a favorite downtown watering hole, thanks to a flashy selection of martinis and full-menu availability. ■ *621 Union St; 224-4321; map:K6; $$$; full bar; AE, DC, MC, V; local checks only; lunch Mon–Fri, dinner every day.* &

**Viet My** ★ At lunchtime, this bright, busy spot is standing room only. Owner Chau Tran is a whirlwind of energy: she's either vigorously scraping the grill, doling out menus, or directing the kitchen, which turns out food that is always exact and delicious. Start with the rice-paper rolls, generously stuffed with shrimp, pork, vermicelli, cilantro, and mint. The pho—a fragrant beef broth layered with herbs, scads of noodles, tender beef, and fresh sprouts for dunking—gets better the farther down you go in the bowl, as the herbs infuse and flavors assert themselves. Chau also offers several curries, a half dozen chow meins, and eight or so soups. Even for such generous exotica as beef wrap, you won't pay more than $6, and usually much less. ■ *129 Prefontaine Pl S; 382-9923; map:Q6; $; no alcohol; no credit cards; local checks only; lunch, dinner Mon–Fri.*

### Waters, a Lakeside Bistro ★  A bistro it ain't. Lakeside, it is—

best visited on a warm day when you can relax by the lawn and watch the progress of sailboats and shoreline joggers while seated on beautifully crafted wooden deck furniture (indoors, the atmosphere is just shy of dreary). In 1995 the Woodmark Hotel made a bold move, scrapping the staid, stuffy, continental approach of the former Carillon Room, and re-creating a hotel restaurant whose menu offers, if not exactly *bistro* fare, then kicky fusion stuff with local ingredients and Asian flair. Here you'll find the likes of Japanese miso grilled vegetables with jasmine rice and ponzu dipping sauce listed along with the meat loaf. You'll meet up here and there with remoulade and aioli, pear wasabe and mizuna slaw, and chipotle cream. King salmon stuffed with wild mushrooms proves to be delightful, despite heavy salt content. The lunch and dinner menus are virtually identical, with an equal number of entrees, a couple of sandwiches (try the crab cake version), and the requisite salads. ■ *1200 Carillon Point, Kirkland; 803-5595; map:EE3; $$$; full bar; AE, DC, MC, V; checks OK; breakfast, lunch, dinner every day.* と

▼

**Top 200
Restaurants**

▲

### Wild Ginger ★★★  The Wild Ginger is wildly popular. Bask-

ing in the glow of much national attention are owners Rick and Ann Yoder, whose culinary vision—inspired by much time spent in Southeast Asia—has left a lasting impression on the Seattle restaurant scene. Just as the restaurants and markets of Bangkok, Singapore, Saigon, and Djakarta offer a wide range of multiethnic foods, so does the Wild Ginger, which brings together some of the best dishes from these Southeast Asian cities. At the mahogany satay bar, order from a wide array of sizzling skewered selections: simple seared slices of sweet onion and Chinese eggplant, or tender Bangkok boar basted with coconut milk. Wherever you sit, indulge in the succulent Singapore-style stir-fried crab, fresh from live tanks and redolent with ginger and garlic; mildly hot, slightly sweet beef curry from Thailand; and laksa, a spicy Malaysian seafood soup whose soft, crunchy, slippery textures and hot and salty flavors encompass everything good about Southeast Asian cookery.

Great live jazz makes the Ginger the city's most happening scene on Monday nights. ■ *1400 Western Ave; 623-4450; map:J8; $$; full bar; AE, DC, MC, V; no checks; lunch Mon–Sat, dinner every day.* &

**Yanni's Lakeside Cafe** ★½ One of the brightest spots in Seattle's neighborhood ethnic dining scene is one of its best Greek restaurants. The place exudes the humble comforts of a Greek taverna. The deep-fried calamari appetizer is meal-size, with tender, perfectly fried squid and a side of pungent skordalia for dipping. That and a horiatiki salad—a heaping mound of tomatoes, cucumbers, kalamata olives, peppers, romaine, and feta cheese—can make a complete dinner for two, along with the good pita. The moussaka is especially good, each layer distinct, yet the whole a pillow of richly blended flavors, and we know people who swear by the spit-roasted chicken (which is also available for take-out). The music is appropriately manic. ■ *7419 Greenwood Ave N; 783-6945; map:EE8; $; beer and wine; MC, V; checks OK; dinner only Mon–Sat.* &

**Yarrow Bay Grill and Beach Cafe** ★★ There are two restaurants here, one on top of another, each with a gorgeous Lake Washington view. Originally intended to be an Eastside version of Ray's Boathouse in Shilshole (three of the four Ray's owners started Yarrow Bay), these siblings have evolved over the years into fine, unique dining spots. Chefs have come and gone, quality has dropped and soared. Most recently, with the return of chef Vicki McCaffree, the upstairs grill is better than ever. A piece of fresh Atlantic salmon could not be more perfectly done, steamed in sake and ginger, and topped with a sesame-kissed shiitake-ginger-butter sauce. Half the entree menu comes from the sea, with such Pacific Rim touches as an appetizer of tea-smoked duck with kimchi, or a Thai-style crab cake. All this is complemented by a deep wine list and plenty of wines by the glass.

▼

**Top 200 Restaurants**

▲

Downstairs, the Beach Cafe is lively. Knock a few bucks off the upstairs prices and sample a jazzed-up United Nations menu, with Moroccan chicken, Cajun-fried rock shrimp, or selections from the country of the month. Competition from neighboring Cucina! Cucina! hasn't hurt the "scene" here the least bit. ■ *1270 Carillon Point, Kirkland; 889-9052 (Yarrow Bay Grill) or 889-0303 (Beach Cafe); map:EE3; $$$; full bar; AE, DC, MC, V; checks OK; lunch, dinner every day, brunch Sun (cafe only).* &

**Zeek's Pizza** ★★ The original Zeek's—known for its absurd pizza toppings and too-nice-to-be-for-real staff of pizza-throwers, salad-makers, and money-takers—is tucked into an ugly strip mall between Seattle Pacific University and the Fremont Bridge. In 1995, young pizza impresarios Doug McClure and Tom Vial's busy pizza parlor gave rise to a second (much

bigger) Zeek's on Phinney Ridge. At either, you should not
hesitate to order the Thai-One-On, a pizza doused with the
makings of phad Thai: chunks of chicken, slivers of carrot,
crunchy mung bean sprouts, and fresh cilantro atop a spicy hot
peanut sauce that'd do a satay proud. Purists might lean toward
the Frog Belly Green, with basil pesto, Roma tomatoes, and
whole-milk mozzarella layered over a very white, slightly
doughy crust with an olive oil glaze. Then there's the weird-but-
wonderful Texas Leaguer (with barbecued chicken, red onion,
and cilantro), and the El Nuevo Hombre (with salsa, refried
beans, and fat slices of jalapeño). Order by the slice or the pie,
to eat in or take out. Good, huge, inexpensive salads, too. ■ *41
Dravus St; 285-6046; map:FF8; $; beer only; MC, V; checks
OK; lunch, dinner every day.* ⅙ ■ *6000 Phinney Ave N; 789-
1778; map:EE7; $; beer and wine; MC, V; checks OK; lunch
Mon–Fri, dinner every day.* ⅙

**Zula** ★ Mixing and toasting his 14 secret spices in this homey
East African restaurant just steps away from Broadway, De-
abesai Yemane has created a culinary niche popular with both
native Ethiopians and the Broadway set. Everything arrives on
a sharing platter, to be plucked up with ingera—the soft, sour
flatbread that serves as spoon and fork. Try the spicy chicken
with greens (bearing in mind that "spicy" as described on this
menu does not refer to the heat quotient). This complex dish
is served with lettuces and alitcha—a tender, tasty cabbage and
potato dish. Zegnie—a stew featuring your choice of beef,
lamb, or chicken—is one hot little number, so ask for a side of
soothing homemade cottage cheese. Vegetarians will appreciate the vegetarian platter with spicy lentils, alitcha, carrots,
greens, and yellow split peas; *everyone* will appreciate the
warm, accommodating service. ■ *916 E John St; 322-0852;
map:GG6; $; full bar; MC, V; local checks only; dinner
Mon–Sat.*

# NIGHTLIFE

## NIGHTLIFE INDEX  *99*

**Bars, Pubs, and Taverns: Type**  *99*

**Bars, Pubs, and Taverns: Location**  *100*

**Entertainment: Music/Type**  *101*

**Entertainment: Location**  *101*


## NIGHTLIFE  *103*

**Bars, Pubs, and Taverns**  *103*

**Entertainment**  *120*

**Desserts, Coffees, and Teas**  *129*

# Nightlife Index

## BARS, PUBS, AND TAVERNS: TYPE

*(See also Entertainment in this chapter)*

**Bargain/Free Happy Hour Hors d'oeuvres**
Anthony's HomePort
Arnie's Northshore
Benjamin's
The Brooklyn
Louie's Cuisine of China
Nickerson Street Saloon
Nikko
Ray's Cafe

**Dance Floors**
Garden Court (Four
 Seasons Olympic Hotel)

**Drinks with a View**
Adriatica
Anthony's HomePort
Arnie's Northshore
Athenian Inn
Benjamin's
Canlis
Cucina! Cucina!
Cutters Bayhouse
Daniel's Broiler
Ernie's Bar and Grill
 (The Edgewater)
Leo Melina (deck only)
Leschi Lakecafe
The Pink Door (deck only)
Place Pigalle
Ray's Cafe
Roanoke Inn (deck only)
Salty's on Alki/Salty's at
 Redondo
Shea's Lounge
Space Needle

**Gay/Lesbian Bars**
The Easy
Thumpers
The Wild Rose

**Happy Hours**
Alki Tavern
Anthony's HomePort
Arnie's Northshore
Athenian Inn
Belltown Billiards
Benjamin's
The Brooklyn
Duke's Bar and Grill

New Jake
 O'Shaughnessey's
Nickerson Street Saloon
Old Pequliar
Paragon Bar & Grill
Roanoke Inn

**Piano Bars**
Canlis
Cloud Room (WestCoast
 Camlin Hotel)
Ernie's Bar and Grill
 (The Edgewater)
Garden Court (Four
 Seasons Olympic Hotel)

**Pool Tables**
Alki Tavern
Belltown Billards
The Blue Moon
College Inn Pub
Comet Tavern
The Duchess Tavern
Eastlake Zoo
The Fabulous Buckaroo
Grady's Montlake Pub and
 Eatery
Linda's Tavern
Nickerson Street Saloon
The Old Pequliar
The Red Onion Tavern
Roanoke Inn
The Sloop
Temple Billiards
211 Club

**Outdoor Seating**
Adriatica
Anthony's HomePort
Arnie's Northshore
Belltown Pub
Benjamin's
The Bookstore...A Bar
 (Alexis Hotel)
The Brooklyn
Campagne
Cucina! Cucina!
Deluxe Bar and Grill
Duke's Bar and Grill
Harbour Public House
Kells

Kirkland Roaster & Ale
 House
Leo Melina
Leschi Lakecafe
Linda's Tavern
Morgan's Lakeplace Bistro
Nickerson Street Saloon
Pacific Northwest Brewing
 Company
Pescatore
Pioneer Square Saloon
Place Pigalle
Pleasant Beach Grill
Ray's Cafe
Red Door Alehouse
Roanoke Inn
Salty's on Alki/Salty's on
 Redondo
Triangle Tavern
Wedgwood Alehouse

**Romantic**
Adriatica
Campagne
Daniel's Broiler
The Fireside Room
 (Sorrento Hotel)
Il Bistro
Il Terrazzo Carmine
Kaspar's
Shea's Lounge

**Smoke Free**
Belltown Pub
Fiddler's Inn
Hilltop Alehouse
Kaspar's
McMenamin's Pub
Nickerson Street Saloon
Old Town Alehouse
Pescatore
The Trolleyman
Virginia Inn

**Sports Bars**
Big Time Brewery and
 Alehouse
The Duchess Tavern
Sneakers

---

**Nightlife:** *Bars, Pubs, Taverns*

**Bainbridge Island**
Harbour Public House
Pleasant Beach Grill

**Ballard/Shilshole**
Anthony's HomePort
Conor Byrne's Public
  House
Hattie's Hat
Louie's Cuisine of China
The Old Pequliar
Old Town Alehouse
Pescatore
Ray's Cafe
The Sloop

**Bellevue**
Duke's Bar and Grill
Morgan's Lakeplace Bistro
The New Jake
  O'Shaughnessey's
The Pumphouse

**Belltown/Denny Regrade**
Belltown Billiards
Belltown Pub
Casa U-Betcha
Cyclops
Ditto Tavern
Five Point Cafe
Frontier Room
Queen City Grill
Two Bells Tavern
211 Club

**Capitol Hill**
Comet Tavern
Deluxe Bar and Grill
The Easy
Linda's Tavern
Roanoke Park Place Tavern
Thumpers
The Wild Rose

**Des Moines/Redondo**
Anthony's HomePort
Salty's at Redondo

**Downtown**
The Bookstore...A Bar
  (Alexis Hotel)
The Brooklyn
Cloud Room (WestCoast
  Camlin)
The Fireside Room
  (Sorrento Hotel)

Garden Court (Four
  Seasons Olympic Hotel)
Leo Melina
McCormick & Schmick's
McCormick's Fish House
  and Bar
Palomino
Shuckers (Four Seasons
  Olympic Hotel)
Union Square Bar & Grill
Virginia Inn
Wild Ginger

**Eastlake**
Eastlake Zoo

**Edmonds**
Anthony's HomePort
Arnie's Northshore

**Fremont**
The Fabulous Buckaroo
Red Door Alehouse
Triangle Tavern
The Trolleyman

**Green Lake**
Latona by Green Lake

**Greenwood/Phinney Ridge**
74th Street Alehouse

**Kirkland**
Anthony's HomePort
Kirkland Roaster & Ale
  House
Smokie Jo's Tavern

**Issaquah**
Issaquah Brewhouse
The Roost

**Lake Union**
Adriatica
Arnie's Northshore
Benjamin's
Canlis
Cucina! Cucina!
Franco's Hidden Harbor
Red Robin

**Leschi**
Daniel's Broiler
Leschi Lakecafe

**Madison Park/Montlake**
The Attic
Grady's Montlake Pub and

Eatery
The Red Onion Tavern

**Mercer Island**
Roanoke Inn

**North End**
Cooper's Northwest Ale
  House
Fiddler's Inn
Wedgwood Alehouse

**Pike Place Market**
Athenian Inn
Campagne
Cutters Bayhouse
Il Bistro
Kells
The Pink Door
Place Pigalle
Shea's Lounge

**Pioneer Square**
F.X. McRory's Steak, Chop,
  and Oyster House
Hart Brewery and Pub
Il Terrazzo Carmine
J & M Cafe
Owl 'N Thistle
Pacific Northwest Brewing
  Company
Pioneer Square Saloon
Sneakers
Temple Billiards

**Queen Anne/Seattle Center**
Duke's Bar and Grill
Hilltop Alehouse
Kaspar's
McMenamins Pub &
  Brewery
Mecca Cafe
Paragon Bar & Grill
Space Needle
Targy's Tavern

**University District**
Big Time Brewery and
  Alehouse
The Blue Moon Tavern
College Inn Pub
The Duchess Tavern

**Wallingford**
Murphy's Pub
Pacific Inn

**Waterfront**
Ernie's Bar and Grill
(The Edgewater)

**West Seattle**
The Alki Tavern
Salty's on Alki

## ENTERTAINMENT: MUSIC/TYPE

**Alternative**
Backstage
Ballard Firehouse
Captain Cook's Pub
Colourbox
Crocodile Cafe
DV8
El Lobo Loco
Lake Union Pub
Moe's Mo'roc'n Cafe
New World Restaurant and
  Lounge
Off Ramp
RKCNDY
Re-bar
Rendezvous
Weathered Wall

**Comedy**
Comedy Underground
Giggles
Showbox

**Country**
Backstage
Riverside Inn
The Timberline
Tractor Tavern

**DJ/Dance**
Captain Cook's Pub
Colourbox
El Lobo Loco
HD Hotspurs
Iguana Cantina
Metropolis
Neighbours
RKCNCY
Re-bar
Romper Room
Sharky's
Timberline

Weathered Wall
Victor's
Vogue

**Folk/Acoustic**
Backstage
Beatnix
Crocodile Cafe
Dubliner Pub
Kerryman Pub
Madison's Cafe and Music
  House
OK Hotel
Owl 'N' Thistle
Tractor Tavern
Weathered Wall

**Jazz**
Dimitriou's Jazz Alley
Ditto Tavern
Lockstock
Newcastles
New Orleans Restaurant
OK Hotel
Old Timer's Cafe
Paragon Bar & Grill
Showbox

**Reggae/World Beat**
Backstage
Ballard Firehouse
Fenix/Fenix Underground
Kilimanjaro
Kokeb
New World Restaurant and
  Lounge
Re-bar
Under the Rail
Vogue
Weathered Wall

**R&B/Blues**
Backstage

Ballard Firehouse
Bohemian
Central
Chicago's
Detour Tavern
Doc Maynard's
Fenix/Fenix Underground
Larry's Greenfront
New Orlean's Restaurant
Newcastle's
Old Timer's Cafe
Paragon Bar & Grill
Scarlet Tree

**Rock**
Backstage
Ballard Firehouse
Beatnix
Colourbox
Crocodile Cafe
Detour Tavern
Doc Maynard's
Dubliner Pub
Gibsons
Moe's Mo'roc'n Cafe
Newcastle's
Off Ramp
OK Hotel
Owl 'N' Thistle
Romper Room
Shark Club
Tractor Tavern
Under the Rail
Waldo's

**Top 40**
DV8
HD Hotspurs
Iguana Cantina
Neighbours
Sharky's

## ENTERTAINMENT: LOCATION

**Ballard/Shilshole**
Backstage
Ballard Firehouse
Sharky's
Tractor Tavern

**Belltown/Denny Regrade**
Crocodile Cafe
Ditto Tavern
Gibson's Bar & Grill
Off Ramp
RKCNDY

Re-bar
Rendezvous
The Timberline
Under the Rail
Vogue
Weathered Wall

---

**Nightlife:** *Entertainment*                                        101

**Capitol Hill**
Beatnix
Kokeb
Moe's Mo'roc'n Cafe
Neighbours

**Downtown**
Dimitriou's Jazz Alley
Showbox

**Fremont**
Dubliner Pub

**Kent**
HD Hotspurs

**Kirkland**
Shark Club
Waldo's

**Lake Union**
Lake Union Pub

**North End**
New World Restaurant and
Lounge

**Pioneer Square**
Bohemian Cafe
Central
Colourbox
Comedy Underground
Doc Maynard's
El Lobo Loco
Fenix/Fenix Underground
Kilimanjaro
Larry's Greenfront
Metropolis
New Orleans Restaurant
OK Hotel
Old Timer's Cafe
Owl 'N' Thistle
Victor's

**Queen Anne/Seattle Center**
Chicago's
DV8
Paragon Bar & Grill
Romper Room

**Ravenna**
Scarlet Tree

**South End**
Newcastle's
Detour Tavern

**Tukwila**
Riverside Inn

**University District**
Giggles
Kerryman Pub
Lockstock

**Waterfront**
Captain Cook's Pub
Iguana Cantina

**West Seattle**
Madison's Cafe & Music
House

# Nightlife

## BARS, PUBS, AND TAVERNS

**Adriatica** New places come and go, but the Adriatica remains an oasis at the top of that endless staircase. All the ingredients are in place: a view of Lake Union and the Cascades, excellent drinks and wines, the best squid and skordalia appetizer in town, and a romantic mood you could cut with a knife. ■ *1107 Dexter Ave N; 285-5000; map:C3; full bar.*

**The Alki Tavern** A West Seattle dive that is an institution, the Alki is famous for its Taco Thursdays, when bikers from all over converge to compare hogs and tattoos. It's a rough crowd, but for local color, the Alki can't be beat. ■ *1321 Harbor Ave SW; 932-9970; map:II8; beer and wine.*

**Anthony's HomePort** A lot of glass, a lot of bar action, seafood hors d'oeuvres, and a view that won't quit. Next door to Ray's Boathouse and not nearly as crowded or pretentious. Edmonds, Kirkland, Des Moines, and Everett also have Anthony's outposts. ■ *6135 Seaview Ave NW (and branches); 783-0780; map:EE9; full bar.*

**Arnie's Northshore** A spiffy sailor's waterside hangout with great half-price appetizers during happy hour. If you get there early, you'll have a good view from the bar. ■ *1900 N Northlake Way; 547-3242; map:FF7; full bar.* ■ *300 Admiral Way, Edmonds; 771-5688; full bar.*

**Athenian Inn** A Market authentic, the modest Athenian's smoky bar is open early, commands a superb view of Elliott Bay, and attracts a wide selection of geezers. The beer list (with 16 brews on tap) will break your arm. ■ *1517 Pike Pl; 624-7166; map:J8; full bar.*

**The Attic** From Madison Park old-timers to fresh-out-of-UW Edgewater residents, everyone comes to the Attic for a good selection of microbrews, Guinness on tap, and tasty pub grub (Sunday night spaghetti is a local institution). If you're much over 22, stay away on Thursday nights, especially in the summer; you'll feel older than Methuselah. ▪ *4226 E Madison; 323-3131; map:GG6; beer and wine.*

**Belltown Billiards** Belltown Billiards is a mishmash: part high-tech bar, part high-class pool hall, part high-gloss Italian restaurant. But everyone is having too much fun to mind the confusion. Come for the chardonnay happy hour, before the crowds descend, and before the wait for a table gets too long. ▪ *90 Blanchard; 448-6779; map:G8; full bar.*

**Belltown Pub** Pile into a spacious booth, admire the wooden scull overhead, and sip micros to your heart's content, but leave the Marlboros at home: there's no smoking here at the Belltown. Some choice appetizers make lingering easy; try the steamed mussels with Italian sausage, and soak up the broth with the tasty focaccia. ▪ *2322 1st Ave; 728-4311; map:G8; beer and wine.*

**Benjamin's** Is the view better from the inside looking out, or from the outside looking in? Sparkly patrons decorate the scene at this glitzy outpost. At Lake Union's southern extremity, Benjamin's receives high marks for its good wine list. ▪ *809 Fairview Pl N; 621-8262; map:D1; full bar.*

**Big Time Brewing Company and Alehouse** Antique beer ads clutter the walls at the U District's most popular alehouse, where the brews are made on premises and five are poured on tap. The place is hopping with students, some burrowed into booths with piles of books, and others looking for love or catching a sports game on TV. The front room is nonsmoking; in the back there's a shuffleboard game, though the off-the-floor variety. ▪ *4133 University Way NE; 545-4509; map:FF6; beer and wine.*

**The Blue Moon Tavern** It's seedy, it's smoky, and it's beloved: when this lair of legends and gutter dreams appeared to be in the path of the demolition ball, a cry of protest went up and books of its shady history were quickly printed. A yearlong battle with developers produced a 40-year lease and a collective sigh of relief from the neighborhood pool players, beat ghosts, living poets, and survivors of the U District's glory days. Tom Robbins put in his time in this crusty joint, and no wonder: the graffiti-covered booths are filled with strange characters who seem to be in search of a novel. ▪ *712 NE 45th St; map:FF7; beer and wine.*

**The Bookstore . . . A Bar (Alexis Hotel)** The front bar of the Alexis Hotel is a great rainy-day hangout for sipping coffee or

Cognac. Books line the shelves, there's a wide selection of magazines and papers, or you can watch the passersby scurrying down First Avenue. The Bookstore is popular with the business crowd as well as hotel guests, and you may spot an out-of-town rock star or two on occasion. The food is fab (you can order from the Painted Table's menu as well), and anchovy lovers can partake of the city's most intense caesars. The bartenders are chatty, making it an amiable atmosphere even for the less literarily inclined. ■ *1007 1st Ave; 382-1506; map:L8; full bar.*

**The Brooklyn** If you're looking to meet a lawyer, this is the place: after work, the Brooklyn crawls with suits. There's plenty of seating at the wraparound bar, a great selection of oysters, and a good choice of beers, although this is more of a single-malt scotch crowd. ■ *1212 2nd Ave; 224-7000; map:K7; full bar.*

**Campagne** One of the best places to wind up a warm summer evening is in the courtyard terrace at Campagne. In winter the bar is a cozy, ofttimes smoky, romantic late-night refuge: a great place to sip a brandy or a glass of champagne. Popular among the restaurant crowd, Campagne is long on class and short on pretention. ■ *86 Pine; 728-2800; map:I8; full bar.*

▼

**Canlis** Men are no longer required to wear jackets in Seattle's last bastion of old-school fine dining—but most of them do anyway. You'll be transported back to another era as you sit at the elegant piano bar (where you can expect to hear every Burt Bacharach song ever written). Sip a martini or a grasshopper (it's that kind of crowd), order a pupu from the kimono-clad waitress, and dream of the days when Lyndon and Ladybird reigned. ■ *2576 Aurora Ave N; 283-3313; map:FF7; full bar.*

Bars, Pubs, and Taverns

▲

**Casa U-Betcha** The Seattle outpost of the Portland institution screams with color, from its twisting snake bar, scaled in bright metals, to its vibrant half-moon booths to its bathroom walls splashed with tropical murals. The partyers and posers often create a noise level that rules out intelligent conversation; the post-Aztec design of this space, where a balcony juts off from the oversize inverted pyramid in the back, makes it nonetheless remarkable. Whether it's the party animals (downing tequila-laced Jell-O shots) or the mythological architectural scheme, there's always something bizarre to bewilder you. Good food, too. ■ *2212 1st Ave; 441-1989; map:G8; full bar.*

**Cloud Room (Camlin Hotel)** Press the lit-up cloud in the elevator and it will take you up. This dark, clubby place features a piano bar straight out of New Jersey. The well-mixed drinks are strong and expensive, and you can count on the tinkler of the ivories to know "our song." Even on days when you're not in the clouds, most of the views are obscured by surrounding buildings. Nonetheless, the deck is a pleasant place to while away the evening. ■ *1619 9th Ave; 682-0100; map:I4; full bar.*

**College Inn Pub** The dark, cozy basement of the College Inn is the closest thing hereabouts to a campus rathskeller, since such is strictly verboten at the university a block away. Students who've reached the age of majority drink microbrewed ales by the pitcher, attack mounds of nachos, play pool and pinball to loud music, and convene for more serious symposia in the private room in back. ■ *4006 University Way NE; 634-2307; map:FF6; beer and wine.*

**Comet Tavern** The scruffy Comet is grunger's heaven and packs out on the weekends with ripped-jean rockers who keep the pool tables and dart boards in active use. Smoky and rowdy, the Comet is nothing less than an institution, and the graffiti is among the most inspired in the city. Popcorn tastes better here. ■ *922 E Pike St; 323-9853; map:HH6; beer and wine.*

**Conor Byrne's Public House** The former site of the Owl has been transformed into the most authentic-feeling Irish pub in town, where the Guinness flows freely, loosening the silver tongues of the (real and pseudo) Irishmen sitting at the bar. Celtic music on the weekends. ■ *5140 Ballard Ave NW; 784-3640; map:FF8; beer and wine.*

**Cooper's Northwest Ale House** The decor is a bit shiny and the TV intrudes, but Cooper's has four dart boards and an outstanding draft selection: 22 taps, 21 of them Northwest microbrews. The Ballard Bitter–battered fish 'n' chips are terrific. ■ *8065 Lake City Way NE; 522-2923; map:DD7; beer and wine.*

**Cucina! Cucina!** Suburbanites and frat types take over the place, and there's no shortage of tight skirts and boisterous laughter. But the wines by the glass are good, as are the pizzas, and the obvious lustfulness of the place may be bearable if you can snag a table on the waterfront deck. ■ *901 Fairview Ave N (and branches); 447-2782; map:GG7; full bar.*

**Cutters Bayhouse** It's a formula bar/restaurant appealing to the young, the rich, and the restless. The place is always hopping, so service can get inattentive (and you might have to stand during the after-work crunch). Cutters invented grazing, but it's a white-wine-and-vegetable-plate kind of place. ■ *2001 Western Ave; 448-4884; map:H8; full bar.*

**Cyclops** There's no place else quite like this eatery/tavern—from its large roving eye over the door to the gelatin molds covering its outside walls. Dotted with strange lamps made of phones, globes, and ballet shoes, the place attracts scads of artists and downtown musicians, who gather to down a brew or cheap wine by the glass, often along with a plate of pasta. ■ *2416 Western Ave; 441-1677; map:F8; beer and wine.*

**Daniel's Broiler** What could be finer than sitting at the marble-topped bar sipping a well-made Cosmopolitan, and gazing out over Lake Washington? Daniel's welcomes an older, well-heeled crowd who know that the caesar salad on the bar menu is one of the best around. ▪ *200 Lake Washington Blvd; 329-4191; map:HH6; full bar.*

**Deluxe Bar and Grill** The time-honored Deluxe is where the more mainstream Broadway boulevardiers go for stuffed baked potatoes and electric iced teas. The bar is often crammed, although the retractable wall in front allows you to sit on the sidewalk in nice weather and watch the steady stream of passersby. Nightly drink specials. ▪ *625 Broadway E; 324-9697; map:GG7; full bar.*

**Ditto Tavern** How can you not love a place that offers typewriters and paper at the table, great bands at low prices, and an intellectual Italian owner who doubles as gruff bartender and espresso maker? Whether the sounds from the makeshift floor-level stage are the voices of downtown poets or the blare of raw-edged guitars, the tiny place packs quickly. If your writings are decent, the owner may add them to his collection displayed under glass on the bar. ▪ *2303 5th Ave; 441-3303; map:G6; beer and wine.*

▼

**The Duchess Tavern** This is the kind of neighborhood tavern that former university students remember fondly decades after graduation. It's a bit more open and airy than in the past, and there are more than 20 beers on tap (about half are microbrews). The darts, the pool table, and the '60s rock make it the perfect stop for a pitcher after the game. The pizza is remarkably tasty. ▪ *2827 NE 55th St; 527-8606; map:EE6; beer and wine.*

**Duke's Bar and Grill** The singles march on through, especially on Friday and Saturday nights. Superior bartenders, a big wine list, and tasty snacks are part of the draw—although it's the only place we've ever been offered "apps." There's Duke memorabilia all over the walls, and other Duke's branches all over the place: Green Lake, Lake Union, at the Fifth Avenue Theater, and in Bellevue. ▪ *236 1st Ave W (and branches); 283-4400; map:HH7; full bar.*

**Eastlake Zoo** Young pool hustlers and older barflies have haunted the Zoo for years. The place livens up with retro rock 'n' roll and R&B bands on Sundays and cools down with classic '70s rock hits on weekdays. Plenty to do besides drink beer—play pool, shuffleboard, darts, or pinball (no video games). Free pool until 2:30pm. ▪ *2301 Eastlake Ave; 329-3277; map:GG7; beer and wine.*

**The Easy** The chic-but-casual lesbian bar Seattle has been missing. With its smooth wood surfaces, rough concrete floor, and imposing bar, this may be one of the nicest places on Capitol Hill to have a drink. A full menu of surprisingly good international food is served all day; a truncated version is served in the late hours. The Easy also houses a hopping dance club, featuring Mahogony, a drag show, on Thursday nights. The crowd is mixed in terms of gender and orientation, but this is first and foremost a lesbian bar. ▪ *916 E Pike; 323-8343; map:J3; full bar.*

### Ernie's Bar and Grill (The Edgewater)
After being remodeled a few years ago, the place has a more woodsy feel (duck wallpaper and all) to go with the Edgewater's Northwest lodge atmosphere, and all the tables now have that spectacular view. There's music in the piano bar up front on Tuesdays through Saturdays, and customers request—and sometimes sing—their favorites. ▪ *Pier 67; 728-7000; map:F9; full bar.*

### F. X. McRory's Steak, Chop, and Oyster House
There's plenty of Old World charm here, as well as more Gilded Age bravura and more bourbon than you can imagine. It's a favorite among the town's professional athletes. Fresh oysters and a solid beer collection, too. Go with a Seattle Prep grad who talks sports—loudly. ▪ *419 Occidental Ave S; 623-4800; map:P9; full bar.*

### The Fabulous Buckaroo
Upper Fremont's legendary roadhouse sports one of the city's finest displays of neon—the lassoing cowboy out front—and serves up the neighborhood's finest burgers. The helmet rack is always full, as bikers from miles around pile in for a brewski and a game of pool. One doesn't come here for MENSA meetings, though—the place can get a bit rowdy; women heading out for an evening alone might best drink elsewhere. ▪ *4201 Fremont Ave N; 634-3161; map:FF7; beer and wine.*

### Fiddler's Inn
Opened in Wedgwood in 1995, this affiliate of the Latona by Green Lake has the look and feel of a log cabin in the woods. It's a one-room, nonsmoking pub, with picnic tables set on an outdoor patio. There's acoustic music on the weekends, and a Sunday fiddle night. ▪ *9219 35th Ave NE; 525-0752; map:DD6; beer and wine.*

### The Fireside Room (Sorrento Hotel)
The clubby little bar in the lobby of the Sorrento evokes a leisurely world of hearthside chats in overstuffed chairs, an unrushed perusal of the daily newspaper, a hand of whist. Most pleasant for a late-evening drink, particularly when Dehner Franks, one of Seattle's finest young jazz pianists, is tickling the ivories. Appetizers are available until midnight. ▪ *900 Madison St; 622-6400; map:HH7; full bar.*

### Five Point Cafe
Stuffed fish on the wall, nuts in the chairs, rocks in the jukebox—you never know what you'll find here

except extra-strong drinks that have minimal impact on your wallet. With a friendly clientele that ranges from bluehairs and gays to suburban babes and Rastafarians, the place—despite its divey decor and perma-nicotined walls—gives hope that there may be world peace after all. ▪ *415 Cedar; 448-9993; map:E7; full bar.*

**Franco's Hidden Harbor** The tinselly Lake Union spots may fade in and out of fashion, but Franco's—jammed, jolly, and full of regulars—will always hold that certain appeal for Mr. Big Businessman: The double martini is a bargain. ▪ *1500 Westlake Ave N; 282-0501; map:GG7; full bar.*

**Frontier Room** Don't wear your Sunday best here: ripped jeans are de rigueur. Partyers pile into booths in the shack-like bar, or gather at tables in the dark back room, which is lit with Christmas lights. You can turn gray before a server arrives, and the line to the bar is long, but the drinks, once in hand, are thankfully strong. Despite (or perhaps because of) its skanky vibes and general seediness, it's one of Belltown's most action-packed spots. ▪ *2203 1st Ave; 441-3377; map:G8; full bar.*

**Garden Court (Four Seasons Olympic Hotel)** Spacious and grand, the formal Garden Court is the pièce de résistance of the Four Seasons Olympic. You come here to celebrate with expensive champagne, to dance on a parquet floor to the strains of a society combo (piano bar during the week), to hobnob with the pearls-and-basic-black set. Have lunch, high tea, a drink and hors d'oeuvres, or coffee and torte among the palm fronds. ▪ *411 University St; 621-1700; map:L6; full bar.*

**Grady's Montlake Pub and Eatery** Grady's is a convivial neighborhood pub: comfortable, clean, and very green—with green tables, green chairs, green carpet (though the felt on the pool tables is red, for a change of pace). Come for the good selection of micros on tap and the food, which is a cut above the usual pub fare, but stay away on Husky game days unless you're a die-hard fan. Nonsmokers beware. ▪ *2307 24th Ave E; 726-5968; map:GG6; beer and wine.*

**Harbour Public House** Simply a wonderful place to be, this friendly pub on Bainbridge's Eagle Harbor is an easy stroll from the ferry dock. In winter it is cozy and amber-lit; in summer, sunlight slants through loft windows and onto the airy waterside deck. There's a connoisseur's selection of lagers and ales along with a broad list of wines, ports, and sherries. And there's an enlightened menu of food, from traditional Cornish pasties to pasta. ▪ *231 Parfitt Way SW, Bainbridge Island; 842-0969; beer and wine.*

**Hart Brewery and Pub** Hordes of tourists crowd this cavernous brewpub south of the Kingdome. Along with ales made by Hart, Kemper, and Pyramid, you can get your souvenir mugs and T-shirts here—if you can find a server. Brewery tours available on request. ▪ *1201 1st Ave S; 682-3377; map:R9; beer and wine.*

**Hattie's Hat** Deep in the heart of Scandinavian Ballard is Hattie's Hat, home of Aunt Harriet's Room and its massive back bar brought 'round the Horn at the turn of the century. We suspect the thirsty Scandinavian fishermen aren't here for the antiques, though. ▪ *5231 Ballard Ave NW; 784-0175; map:EE8; full bar.*

**Hilltop Alehouse** The 74th Street Alehouse's newer sibling atop Queen Anne shares many of its excellent qualities: a healthy selection of beers, great pub food, and a convivial atmosphere, making the Hilltop a great contribution to the neighborhood. ▪ *2129 Queen Anne Ave N; 285-3877; map:GG7; beer and wine.*

**Hopvine Pub** Another seedy tavern transformed into a clean pub featuring lots of microbrews. There are hopvines stenciled and sculpted on the walls, wooden booths and tables stained with bright colors, and a smoking area in back. With pizza on the menu and acoustic music a couple of nights each week, this is a welcome addition to the Capitol Hill neighborhood. ▪ *507 15th Ave E; 328-3120; map:GG6; beer and wine.*

▼

Bars, Pubs,
and Taverns

▲

**Il Bistro** The amber lights cast a romantic glow that's ideal for a secret rendezvous, making this sloping bar, tucked beneath the Market, emanate warmth. A busy after-work place, it's also a quiet magnet for nocturnal sorts—from artists to jet-setters and restaurateurs—who gather around marble tables or perch at the bar, eating caesar salads, sipping well-crafted martinis, and chatting through the night, occasionally stopping to pay homage to the Market's bartender god, Murray Stenson. ▪ *93-A Pike St; 682-3049; map:J8; full bar.*

**Il Terrazzo Carmine** The romantic bar in the Merrill Place building's commendable country Italian restaurant, Il Terrazzo Carmine, is a superb spot to wind up a day in Pioneer Square. ▪ *411 1st Ave S; 467-7797; map:O9; full bar.*

**Issaquah Brewhouse** With the opening in 1995 of the Issaquah Brewhouse, the Eastside finally has a spacious, woody brewpub to rival those in Seattle. Six fresh ales on tap include Bullfrog, a wheat brew with a light citrus edge and a hint of honey; and a porter boasting of a molasses-like kick — very appealing, especially accompanying a bowl of Brewhouse chili (not too spicy, with chicken, sausage, and onions simmered in ale). Also worth ordering: the Oxford sandwich — slices of roast beef and red onion on sourdough. ▪ *35 W Sunset Way, Issaquah; 557-1911; beer and wine.*

**J&M Cafe** Pioneer Square's most popular saloon has a long bar, a crowded counter, and decent hofbrau sandwiches and burgers. There's even Jagermeister on tap. Sold and saved from eviction in 1995, it is, as always, the place to meet someone before or after a Kingdome event—if the line doesn't drive you away. ■ *201 1st Ave S; 624-1670; map:O8; full bar.*

**Kaspar's** A great place to meet friends before the opera or theater at Seattle Center, the small bar at Kaspar's offers a comfortable respite from the sporting event hordes at most area bars. Try the excellent tenderloin beef tips while sampling a glass of wine. ■ *19 W Harrison; 298-0123; map:A9; full bar.*

**Kells** Rousing sing-alongs to live Celtic music boom throughout the licensed pub side of this Irish restaurant Wednesday through Saturday. Good coddle and soda bread. ■ *1916 Post Alley; 728-1916; map:J8; full bar.*

**Kirkland Roaster & Ale House** This is the Kirkland version of the Firnstahl bars that have proven so rabidly successful elsewhere. Expect lots of boutique beers and fancy bourbons, poured by "antic bartenders" who spend a good part of their time tossing around orange juice bottles and lemons for the yupscale crowd's entertainment. From an extensive menu, the best food choices are the rich clam chowder and a burger juicy enough to destroy your shirt cuffs. ■ *1111 Central Way, Kirkland; 827-4400; map:EE3; full bar.*

**Latona by Green Lake** Years ago it was a darkened haunt for hard drinkers; now it's a light, woody, microbrew-and-cheese-bread-lovers kind of place. And, to make things extra cozy in this tiny Green Lake nook, good local jazz and folk musicians (Thursday through Sunday) make the best of a tight situation. ■ *6423 Latona Ave NE; 525-2238; map:EE7; beer and wine.*

**Leo Melina** The latest incarnation of this view space above the Market has lots of blond wood, wicker chairs, and marble tabletops—a perfect place to impress your out-of-town relatives. A seat on the outdoor deck might improve your view, but you can grow impatient waiting for service. Great appetizers, including some terrific clams and mussels. ■ *96 Union St; 623-3783; map:J8; full bar.*

**Leschi Lakecafe** Ah, the sporting life. The Lakecafe serves the jogging-sailing-cycling constituents of the Leschi neighborhood with a vast selection of beers and booze. It's best in summer, when the umbrella'd tables in the courtyard are the hottest tables around Lake Washington (and folks can munch on fish 'n' chips from the take-out window at Koby's, the Lakecafe's adjunct business). The rest of the year, the action is no less lively inside. ■ *102 Lakeside S; 328-2233; map:HH6; full bar.*

**Linda's Tavern** There might be a stuffed buffalo head over the bar, a wagonwheel chandelier, and other Wild West decor, but Linda's ain't no place to go two-steppin'. The crowd here is a multi-ethnic mix of Gen-Xers, with a smattering of just plain folks. They all come to drink beer on the little patio out back, or play pool to the strains of alternative music blaring from the stereo. Everyone is made to feel welcome—and *that's* another nice alternative. ▪ *707 E Pine St; 325-1220; map:GG6; beer and wine.*

**Louie's Cuisine of China** A favorite of bartenders around town, Louie's in Ballard is just the opposite of the usual dreary, fake-Chinese bar. Light and sleek, with polished wood tables, cushioned bamboo chairs, and ceiling fans, Louie's has a friendly atmosphere, efficient barkeeps, and free hors d'oeuvres during happy hour. ▪ *5100 15th Ave NW; 782-8855; map:FF8; full bar.*

**McCormick & Schmick's** Bankers like it because it looks like a bank. Dark-stained mahogany and cut glass provide just the right atmosphere for stockbrokers and lawyers after Irish coffees and stiff well pours. Good downtown location, great bar food. ▪ *1103 1st Ave; 623-5500; map:L8; full bar.*

**McCormick's Fish House and Bar** Polished wood and brass, stand-up counters and fresh oysters make this the closest thing to a class San Francisco bar. McCormick's crawls with attorneys and bureaucrats after 5pm. ▪ *722 4th Ave; 682-3900; map:N6; full bar.*

**McMenamins Pub & Brewery** This shiny new brewpub—Seattle's first venture for the Portland-based McMenamin brothers—is a great addition to the lower Queen Anne neighborhood that's still mourning the loss of Jake's and Harry's. Perhaps because it's so new, it feels a little stiff, but it'll be worn in soon enough from the look of things. There's a great selection of McMenamins brews, plus a seasonal representation of other local micros. Great fries, and the place is smoke-free. ▪ *200 Roy St; 285-4722; map:A6; beer and wine.*

**Mecca Cafe** The narrow bar alongside this cafe was formerly home to many a geriatric drinker. Since new owners took over a few years back, the clientele is younger, cooler, and more prone to take advantage of the hit-heavy jukebox in the corner. Dark and snug, this hideaway lined with cardboard coasters can barely hold a dozen, but it's a festive place to end a rollicking night in Queen Anne. ▪ *526 Queen Anne Ave N; 285-9728; map:GG7; full bar.*

**Morgan's Lakeplace Bistro** Bellevue's ultramod downtown hasn't been very successful at spawning bars with unique character, but Morgan's has managed to satisfy a lot of people. It's best in summer, when the doors (overlooking condo-ringed Lake Bellevue) open up and you can join the Vuarnet set out on the terrace. Good bar menu. ▪ *2 Lake Bellevue Dr, Bellevue; 455-2244; map:HH3; full bar.*

**Murphy's Pub** As Irish pubs go, it's a pretty classy place (fire-place, antiques, and stained glass). Wallingfordians (and others) pile in to play darts (real, of course, not electronic) or to catch the Wednesday open mikes and weekend Celtic music. The 'tenders are kindly. More than a dozen local brews and stouts are poured on draft, and the food's good. It's a zoo on Saint Paddy's day. ▪ *1928 N 45th St; 634-2110; map:FF7; beer and wine.*

**New Jake O'Shaughnessey's** The lights are a bit bright, and you can expect absolutely no privacy behind the huge cliff of windows, but this Mick McHugh establishment in Bellevue Square is hoppin', especially on weekends. A good selection of late-night appetizers. ▪ *401 Bellevue Square, Bellevue; 455-5559; map:HH3; full bar.*

**Nickerson Street Saloon** Alas, the legendary burgers that made the former tenant at this site, the 318, famous are no more, but you can enjoy a wide selection of beers on tap (including some lesser-known varieties) and some decent pub grub. The place has been cleaned up and the outdoor seating is nice, but we miss those 318 burgers! ▪ *318 Nickerson St; 284-8819; map:FF7; beer and wine.*

**Nikko (Westin Hotel)** Sleek, glamorous Nikko has what's got to be the best happy hour in town, at least if you're a sushi lover (they set out a free buffet in the bar, that includes sushi, from 5 to 7pm). It's a good way to start off an evening; and if you have a yen for more, well, the sushi bar itself is just a few steps away. ▪ *1900 5th Ave; 322-4641; map:H6; full bar.*

**The Old Pequliar** It's part scruffy tavern, part old English pub, and the folks on the Ballard bar circuit seem to eat it up. There's always a congenial crowd quaffing microbrews and imports. Just snag a table in the comfy pub corner and you're set. ▪ *1722 NW Market; 782-8886; map:FF8; beer and wine.*

**Old Town Alehouse** Although it's brand new, the Old Town evokes the look of Old Ballard, with an ornate antique bar and icebox, exposed brick walls, and old black-and-white photos. By sponsoring Brewer's Nights, the owners are trying to encourage patrons to learn about local microbrews; Guinness fans will like Monday night's $2 pints. The Ballard Wedge sandwiches are tasty—and the fries that come alongside are out of this world. Smoke-free. ▪ *5233 Ballard Ave NW; 782-8323; map:FF8; beer and wine.*

**Owl 'N Thistle** You can easily miss this Post Alley hideaway as you stroll from Pioneer Square to the Market, but don't. It's got all the friendliness and character of a habitual hangout: the walls are lined with black-and-white photos, antiques are stashed in corners, and there's a mini-library of outdated law

Nightlife

▼

Bars, Pubs, and Taverns

▲

books. The regulars are as varied as the decor: a mix of rockers, working stiffs, aging hippies, and the culturally inclined. ■ *808 Post Ave; 621-7777; map:M8; full bar.*

**Pacific Inn** Should you come for the brew (half a dozen on tap, a couple of dozen in bottles and cans) or for the fab cayenne-spiked fish 'n' chips? Most regulars enjoy both at this Wallingford workingman's mainstay. ■ *3501 Stone Way N; 547-2967; map:FF7; beer and wine.*

**Pacific Northwest Brewing Company** One of the first brew-pubs in Seattle, this Pioneer Square hangout, owned by a Brit, offers English-style ales instead of the familiar local varieties of microbrews. If their ads are to be believed, these ales aren't as carbonated and therefore don't make you burp into the face of the person you're trying to pick up. It's not a warm and fuzzy place, but it's a good bet if you're meeting someone before a game, or if, in warm weather, you can snag an outside table on Occidental Mall. ■ *322 Occidental Ave S; 621-7002; map:O8; full bar.*

**Palomino** It's still one of the most dramatic spaces in town: three stories high above the City Centre atrium, with gorgeous glass light fixtures and a handsome bar. If the crowd isn't quite as glossy as when Palomino first opened, it's still pretty glamorous for Seattle. It's a great spot for an after-work cocktail, and if you're hungry, the Gorgonzola cheese fries are a hit, as are the wood-fired pizzas. ■ *1420 5th Ave (City Centre); 623-1300; map:J5; full bar.*

**Paragon Bar & Grill** You'll feel as though you've gone through the looking glass and ended up in San Francisco or LA: anywhere but the top of Queen Anne. The crowd is just too sexy for their shirts; if you haven't dressed up, you'll feel out of place among the trendy young poseurs who fill the bar to capacity and then some. Paragon is *the* current place to see and be seen, and, oh yeah, the food's all right, too. Music Sundays through Wednesdays (it's too crowded on the weekends to fit in the musicians); $2 martinis during happy hour. ■ *2125 Queen Anne N; 283-4548; map:GG8; full bar.*

**Pescatore** The former site of Hiram's at the Locks is still a good bet on a sunny day, mainly for the same reason people flocked to Hiram's: drinks with a view on a patio (though there's a bar *inside*, too). There's a good selection of variations on the martini and an unusually varied spectrum of nonalcoholic cocktails as well. Pizzas are quite good here. ■ *5300 34th NW; 784-1733; map:FF9; full bar.*

**The Pink Door** We know it's kitschy, but imbibing blue martinis on the prettiest rooftop terrace in town while nibbling antipasti to the accompanying strains of Tony Yazzolino's accordion music happens to be one of our weaknesses. A variety of musical acts come by in the evenings, including multipersonalitied cabaret singer Julie Cascioppo, who does Liza Minnelli better than Liza Minnelli does. ■ *1919 Post Alley; 443-3241; map:J8; full bar.*

**Pioneer Square Saloon** One of the few bars in Pioneer Square that doesn't offer live music, and thus doesn't slap on a cover. The clientele ranges from grungers to corporate types, the taped tunes are good, and there's a dart board in the back. In the summer, the patio tables—where you can survey the tourists waddling by—are packed. Between the kindly bartenders, the good (and cheap) wines by the glass, and the unaffected air, it's the best spot in the city for making new friends. Occasional poetry readings. ■ *77 Yesler Way; 628-6444; map:N8; beer and wine.*

**Place Pigalle** Tucked in the corner of this secret gem is a slightly bohemian bar, with a well-selected list of beers, ales, wines, and eaux-de-vie. The view of the ferries rolling across the Sound is lovely, especially at sunset, and the bartenders wax intellectual. A comfortable spot to drink alone or *à deux.*
■ *Pike Place Market; 624-1756; map:J8; full bar.*

**Pleasant Beach Grill** Bainbridge Island's fancy-white-tablecloth restaurant has a simply splendid bar—cozy, woody, and full of friendly regulars. Visit in winter, when the rain is drizzling down the windowpanes, for a warming brandy on the couch in front of the fire. ■ *4738 Lynwood Center Rd NE, Bainbridge Island; 842-4347; full bar.*

**The Pumphouse** This dim, unassuming joint on the refreshingly wrong side of Bellevue's tracks fits Texas writer Jim Atkinson's memorable definition of a Bar Bar: a drinking place where people (mostly men) can bend their elbows in hard-won isolation, "the only place left on earth where you can go and be Nowhere." Aggressively non-glitzy and bleeding the neon light of beer insignias over every human face, the Pumphouse offers a long menu of eats (its burgers are best—big and juicy) to enjoy with local drafts. The crowd includes Microsoft employees, workers from nearby office termitaries, and Seattleites who eschew trendier Eastside bars. ■ *11802 NE 8th St, Bellevue; 455-4110; map:HH3; full bar.*

**Queen City Grill** Fluted lights, flowers, and a rosy glow that bathes the room make this Belltown's classiest option. On weekends it gets packed with artists, yuppies, and off-duty bartenders pretending they're in New York or San Francisco; we much prefer Queen City on weeknights, when sitting at the curved bar can be lovely. ■ *2201 1st Ave; 443-0975; map:G8; full bar.*

**Ray's Cafe** One visit to the jammed view-deck cafe atop Ray's Boathouse will assure you that Ray's doesn't lack fans. On weekends you'll probably have to wait for a seat, and harried service is de rigueur. The food (heavy on the seafood, natch) is fresh but not particularly inventive (though the happy-hour bar menu is a real steal), and the crowd is just having way too much fun. At Ray's, the postcard-perfect view's the thing, and that redeems the whole into something much better than the sum of its parts. Outstanding wine list, too. ▪ *6049 Seaview Ave NW; 789-3770; map:EE9; full bar.*

**Red Door Alehouse** During the day, suits, salesmen, and salty dogs stop in to down a cold one with a burger and fries. At night it's so crowded with the fraternity/sorority crowd, you could mistake the place for a J. Crew catalog shoot. There's a wide selection of beers (22 on tap, including Northwest microbrews) to complement some terrific (inexpensive) pub grub. Order a bowl of mussels and eat 'em in the beer garden. ▪ *3401 Fremont Ave N; 547-7521; map:FF7; beer and wine.*

**The Red Onion Tavern** Perfect in winter, when you can drink a beer beside the huge stone fireplace, this Madison Park institution is also known for its pool tables and its pizza. Mellow local crowd, except on Thursday nights in summer, when the Red Onion is invaded by the overflow of party-hearty students from the Attic down the street. ▪ *4210 E Madison St; 323-1611; map:GG6; beer and wine.*

**Red Robin** Seattle's collegiate Algonquin Club is now one outpost of the formula Red Robin burger-and-cocktail chain, but the place itself, overlooking Portage Bay, is a marvelous spot for watching the boats drift by. If you like circus burgers, exotic cocktails, and enormous desserts, you'll also be happy at any of the seven clones around town. ▪ *3272 Fuhrman Ave E (and branches); 323-0917; map:FF7; full bar.*

**Roanoke Inn** Despite its sometimes ribald reputation (rooms upstairs were once allegedly rented for immoral purposes, and gunfire was occasionally heard in the main room), this was at one time a very popular drinking spot for city swells. That was back in the early 20th century, when a ferry still connected the north end of Mercer Island with Seattle, before I-90 took all the Roanoke's drive-by business away and left it baby-sitting a dead-end route to a dark old pier. Today, the tavern is a bit more out of the way, but still venerable, with a giant black fireplace and a long front porch, where summertime patrons swap tall tales and watch Lake Washington capture moonbeams. Check out the weekly spaghetti feeds and the john, where blackboards are offered right in the stalls. ▪ *1825 72nd Ave SE, Mercer Island; 232-0800; map:II4; beer and wine.*

**Roanoke Park Place Tavern** A gathering ground where the junior gentry of north Capitol Hill can feel like just folks. Good burgers and beers, but loud music often drowns out conversation. Beware the influx of students on Thursday nights. ■ *2409 10th Ave E; 324-5882; map:GG6; beer and wine.*

**The Roost** This is such a male-oriented watering hole that you feel like you should be challenging fellow patrons to arm wrestle, rather than gulping brews and hoovering up appetizers. Decor includes framed covers from *Field and Stream*, a mounted moose head, enough neon beer signs to make the Roost visible from space, and four TV sets drowning out any shred of serious discussion on Monday nights. But as in other Mick McHugh joints, there's a broad selection of beers on tap here, and some of the grub (especially the mondo-meaty chili) is worth repeated sampling. ■ *120 NW Gilman Blvd, Issaquah; 392-5550; full bar.*

**Salty's on Alki ■ Salty's on Redondo** The spacious West Seattle bar spills over onto the bay-level patio (warmed, thankfully, by high-rise heat lamps), where you can order from a lengthy menu of seafood appetizers and gaze at the twinkling lights of Seattle. The Redondo branch has a view of south Puget Sound. ■ *1936 Harbor Ave SW; 937-1600; map:II9; full bar.* ■ *28201 Redondo Beach Dr S, Redondo; 946-0636; full bar.*

**The 74th Street Alehouse** The 74th Street Alehouse is the embodiment of truth in packaging. The main business of this establishment is beer, and the ambience is uncompromisingly tailored to suit: bar, bar stools, noisy regulars, and TV ever-tuned to the game. You can also eat—plainly, cheaply, and very well. ■ *7401 Greenwood Ave N; 784-2955; map:DD8; beer and wine.*

**Shea's Lounge** Don't let the obvious pun or the near-hidden location keep you from ferreting out this romantic little offshoot of Chez Shea. Six small tables and a minuscule bar are set in a slender, elegant, dimly lit space with enormous casement windows looking out over Market rooftops to the bay beyond. A nice selection of Italian and Spanish wines is complemented by a short but tasteful menu influenced by the flavors of Spain and Portugal. ■ *94 Pike St; 467-9990; map:J8; full bar.*

**Shuckers (Four Seasons Olympic Hotel)** Here you'll find the Establishment and celebrity hotel guests enjoying Northwest oysters and shrimp or talking to bartender's bartender David Williams, who likes fixing drinks so much he wrote a book about it. Afternoons there's a light menu of seafood and good local beers. ■ *411 University St; 621-1984; map:L6; full bar.*

**The Sloop** The big sloop painted on the east side of the building tells you that you're at one of maritime Ballard's favorite taverns. It's a low-key, comfortable place to hang out with the team after a softball game, or play pool, darts, or pinball. ■ *2830 NW Market St; 782-3330; map:EE8; beer and wine.*

**Smokie Jo's Tavern** If bars and taverns were judged on their "male dork quotient," this place would score unfortunately high. Single women patrons can expect to field every pickup line in the book. If you can get past that, though, Smokie Jo's is a wonderful anachronism: the one place in downtown Kirkland where a laid-back crowd of regulars can forget about dress codes and just hunker over a cold one. Forget the food, almost all of which has to be microwaved, and turn instead to the jukebox full of Mariah Carey and Jimmy Buffett and the restless spirit of Elvis. ■ *106 Kirkland Ave, Kirkland; 827-8300; map:EE3; beer and wine.*

**Sneakers** Sneakers is a long, narrow sports bar squeezed in between some warehouses down by the Kingdome. The food isn't very good, but it's priced so you can sit and nibble while you drink and stare at the bank of TV screens jammed between sports memorabilia and ticker tape. ■ *567 Occidental Ave S; 625-1340; map:P9; full bar.*

**Space Needle** If enjoying a truly sensational view means sipping the most expensive drink you'll ever have in your life, then spring $7 for the hop to the top (only restaurant patrons ride free)… and then drink slowly. ■ *Seattle Center; 443-2100; map:C6; full bar.*

▼

**Bars, Pubs, and Taverns**

▲

**Targy's Tavern** The kind of place where the best thing on the menu is the Rolaids, Targy's is the unofficial Upper Queen Anne Community Center, full of character and characters and a rinky-dink charm not everyone will appreciate. Sixteen kinds of beer and the best electric darts in town. ■ *600 W Crockett St; 285-9700; map:GG7; beer and wine.*

**Temple Billiards** It's not as glossy as Belltown Billiards, but that's okay with the youngish crowd that shoots pool here at the Temple. There's a decent selection of beer and wine, but it's incidental to the game, as there's not much room to do much besides play pool. ■ *126 S Jackson; 682-3242; map:O8; beer and wine.*

**Thumpers** The cozy ambience of the fireplace and oak paneling attracts a loyal gay crowd. Sample the well-chosen selection of appetizers (calamari, pâté, tempura vegetables) and enjoy a wonderful view of downtown Seattle. ■ *1500 E Madison St; 328-3800; map:HH7; full bar.*

**Triangle Tavern** Set on the angle where Fremont Place meets 35th, this popular tavern takes the eccentricities of the triangle to an extreme: everything's three-sided here (from the ashtrays to the bits of shattered tile on the bathroom counters). There's often a congested crush up front—thanks to the great, cheap food, the beer on tap, and the line of people waiting for their chance to cadge a patio table (or one in the quirky-funky dining room). ▪ *3507 Fremont Place N; 632-0880; map:FF7; beer and wine.*

**The Trolleyman** Couches and upholstered chairs abound in this renovated turn-of-the-century trolley barn, where the Red Hook is brewed next door, and a fireplace and piano add the touches that can make one forget it's pelting outside. The doors close early on weekdays. There's also a light snack menu. No smoking. ▪ *3400 Phinney Ave N; 548-8000; map:FF7; beer only.*

**Two Bells Tavern** Even the most self-conscious hipster lets it all hang out at Two Bells. Good selection of local microbrews and imported gems, plus sporadic but always creative bookings of solo guitar acts, unusual art exhibits, and poetry readings. Great burgers. ▪ *2313 4th Ave; 441-3050; map:F7; beer and wine.*

**211 Club** Up one flight at Second and Bell you'll find the city's true pool sharks strutting their stuff all day and into the night. It's a big smoky warehouse, filled with tables of every kind: two snooker, three billiard, and sixteen regular pool tables. The building looks like someplace you shouldn't be, but it's really quite safe. ▪ *2304 Second Ave; 443-1211; map:F7; beer and wine.*

▼

**Union Square Bar & Grill** One of the best after-work downtown bars, where drinks go down easy with two or three of the grill's scrumptious mini roast beef sandwiches. The barroom is long and narrow, with lots of dark wood. You may have to scramble for a table, but you'll be comfortable once you do get settled. ▪ *621 Union St; 224-4321; map:J5; full bar.*

**Bars, Pubs, and Taverns**

▲

**The Virginia Inn** What do you get when you mix arty Belltown dwellers, chic-seeking suburbanites, and babbling pensioners in a historic, brick-tile-and-avant-garde-art tavern? You get the VI, a very enlightened, very appealing, vaguely French-feeling tav with a fine list of libations (including pear cider) and character to burn. You'll have to burn your cigs elsewhere, though. ▪ *1937 1st Ave; 728-1937; map:I8; beer and wine.*

**Vito's** If you like a well-constructed cocktail (like a gigantic martini) and enjoy watching a professional bartender in action, this old-timey joint is the place to go. All dark wood and maroon leather, it attracts police detectives, lawyers, the sports crowd, and judges on the road to intemperance. ▪ *927 9th Ave; 682-2695; map:M4; full bar.*

**Wedgwood Alehouse** This congenial neighborhood pub draws a low-key local crowd who come for the decent burgers and the good sampling of microbrews. The outdoor tables in front are the draw in summer. Live music on the weekends. ▪ *8515 35th Ave NE; 527-2676; map:EE6; beer and wine.*

**Wild Ginger** The dramatic bar at one of Seattle's favorite restaurants draws a lively late-night crowd. While the space is elegant, the attitude is relaxed and casual; many of the late-night denizens are servers from nearby restaurants who come to unwind after their shifts. Live jazz on Monday nights, great Asian eats every night. ■ *1400 Western Ave; 623-4450; map:J8; full bar.*

**Wild Rose Tavern** The center of the universe for the Seattle lesbian scene, the Wild Rose has served as community center, coffeehouse, music venue, pool hall, and just plain great tavern since 1984. The look is country-lavender; the long, wooden bar scarred with the marks of good times had by all. Tables are just as likely to be filled with women reading alone, as dining with friends, or drinking in uproarious groups. The Wild Rose has an extensive, serviceable menu of mostly comfort food. The *other* sex is gladly welcomed. ■ *1201 E Pike St; 324-9210, map:J3; beer and wine.*

## ENTERTAINMENT

▼

**Bars, Pubs, and Taverns**

▲

Nirvana. Pearl Jam. Soundgarden. Alice in Chains. Candlebox. Mudhoney. The names—and the sound, "grunge" (a word long since considered passé on the local scene)—are familiar to almost anyone who has paid even the slightest attention to popular music in the '90s. Yes, they all came from here. But no, you won't find them playing regularly in the clubs like in the old days (surprise, surprise).

Nevertheless, Seattle remains one of the country's most active spots for up-and-coming rock bands. And there's more going on here than just headbanging hair bands, despite the stereotypes. The city is home to significant talents in the jazz mainstream (Kenny G) and underground (Bill Frisell, Wayne Horvitz), melodic pop (the Posies), roots-rock (Pete Droge), and western swing (Ranch Romance). Blues and R&B acts abound in the Pioneer Square clubs, many of which have banded together to form a joint cover circuit where there's one cover charge for admission to all participating venues (usually $5 to $8). Some musical styles are a bit harder to come by, but if you look around enough, you can usually find everything from reggae to folk to funk to country going on somewhere in town.

**Backstage** Despite its decidedly unhip location—in the basement of a Ballard office building—the Backstage is one of the finer showcases in the country for club-level touring talent, with bookings ranging from rock to folk to blues to alternative to reggae. (Though the club changed ownership in 1995, there was no glaring dropoff in the quality of the bookings.) The decor is rather plain, but the room has excellent sound, a spacious dance floor, and a couple hundred seats with small tables. The entrance is on the alleyway behind Lombardi's restaurant (on the 22nd Street side). Admission is usually in the $10 to $15 range, with advance tickets available for most performances. ■ *2208 NW Market St; 781-2805; map:FF8.*

**Ballard Firehouse** With the exception of the Backstage, the Firehouse is Ballard's hottest live-music spot—not to imply Ballard is Seattle's hippest district for entertainment, but the Firehouse carries its weight. The atmosphere is a little heavy on loungelike aesthetics and a little lacking in distinctive personality, save for an outdoor porch that's ideal for catching a breath of fresh air. Inside, plenty of tables and a small dance floor surround a stage that's as likely to be occupied by touring oldies acts (be forewarned that most of these bands are shades of their former selves, with few original members) as by second-rate local alternative-rock, blues, or reggae bands. ■ *5429 Russell Ave NW; 784-3516; map:EE8.*

**Beatnix** Former site of the popular gay hangout, Tugs Belmont, Beatnix has moved more in the direction of live music than its predecessor, serving as a sort of launching pad for young bands trying to break into Seattle's premier venues. Acoustic music is featured Wednesdays and Thursdays (open mike); weekend slots are usually filled by rock acts. ■ *518 E Pine; 323-1145; map:HH6.*

**Bohemian Cafe** Though it has been through frequent name changes in recent years, this modest-size restaurant/bar remains a stalwart of the Pioneer Square circuit. The venue's calling card is local favorite Isaac Scott's regular "Blue Monday" sessions. A split-level setup, with tables and the band downstairs, accompanied by an upstairs bar. ■ *111 Yesler Way; 447-1514; map:N8.*

**Captain Cook's Pub** It remains to be seen whether an alternative-rock club can succeed on the touristy waterfront, but Captain Cook's, which opened in 1995, seems eager to give it a shot. Whether it succeeds will likely depend upon whether it can start attracting more talented acts than the mediocre-at-best ones that have been featured Thursdays through Saturdays. There's dance music Sundays and Tuesdays, and free pool Sundays and Wednesdays. ■ *1414 Alaskan Way; 233-9467; map:K8.*

**Central** Once the focal point of Seattle's now legendary alternative-rock scene, the Central reverted to a more typical Pioneer Square format in 1991. The club now primarily features polished blues bands that regularly play the Square circuit, with an occasional pop act thrown in to keep things from getting too repetitive. Live music seven nights a week. ■ *207 1st Ave S; 622-0209; map:O8.*

**Chicago's** Classy, brassy, with plenty of room for dancing and mingling, Chicago's lives up to its name by featuring live R&B every Friday and Saturday, with no cover, ever. ■ *315 1st Ave N; 282-7791; map:A7.*

**Colourbox** Just about the only venue in Pioneer Square that caters to fans of alternative-rock, the Colourbox is a well-run club with decent bookings that suffers from a poor physical setting. The faux-gothic decorations do little to hide the fact that it's basically a cavernous concrete rectangle, and the sound isn't helped by that design. Nevertheless, there are too many good shows at the Colourbox to write it off, particularly if you're club-hopping in Pioneer Square and are tired of mingling with the yuppies. ■ *113 1st Ave S; 340-4101; map:O8.*

**Comedy Underground** You can't get into this palace of yuks without waiting in line. Expect national and local acts—all of high quality—and come prepared for audience involvement. Downstairs from the athlete's hangout, Swannies. ■ *222 S Main St; 628-0303; map:P8.*

**Crocodile Cafe** The Crocodile has established itself as the pride of Seattle's music scene and easily qualifies as one of the best live-music nightclubs in America. Owned by Stephanie Dorgan, whose husband is R.E.M. guitarist Peter Buck, the Croc is the spot to find the best bands Seattle's alternative-rock scene has to offer. It also features quality touring acts on a semiregular basis and has hosted quite a few high-profile surprise shows (Nirvana, Mudhoney, Mad Season, T-Bone Burnett). The space is separated into three parts: an often overcrowded concert room that holds around 300 and has the best sound of the city's rock hot spots; a cafe that operates during daytime hours (a popular lunching spot for local music-biz insiders); and a bar in the back decorated with lively kitsch. Music usually runs Tuesdays through Saturdays, and features more genre variety than the hard rock that dominates the city's other alternative-music hot spots. Cover is usually $7 or less. ■ *2200 2nd Ave; 441-5611; map:G7.*

**Detour Tavern** This rocker bar is a longtime standby in the South End, featuring local bands on weekends, a jam session on Thursdays, and the occasional roadshow (usually has-been rock and blues acts, but occasionally a worthwhile old-timer). ■ *221 Main Ave S, Renton; 226-0908; map:NN3.*

**Dimitriou's Jazz Alley** Swank, intimate, with not a bad seat in the house, this spacious jazz club is one of the coolest on the West Coast—an absolute treasure. Owner John Dimitriou, a veteran jazz producer, presents leading national acts six nights a week, with top locals frequently featured on Mondays. The best seats are up in the extended mezzanine. Cover charge varies from cheap to moderately expensive, with drink mini-

▼

**Entertainment**

▲

mums required on some nights. You can secure a seat early by making dinner reservations, but those in the know come for the music, not the food. ■ *2033 6th Ave; 441-9729; map:H5.*

**Doc Maynard's** A prototypical Pioneer Square bar, with weekend classic rock 'n' roll and R&B bands plus a regular crowd of what look like either fraternity guys or Eastside investment advisers ready to slam and shimmy. ■ *610 1st Ave; 682-4649; map:N8.*

**Dubliner Pub** Situated just north of the drawbridge in Fremont, the Dubliner features an open mike on Tuesdays, traditional Irish music on Wednesdays, and a variety of genres on Fridays. Don't dress up; this is a blue-collar, beer-drinkin' hangout—a comfortable spot, but not for those who seek highfalutin' company. ■ *3405 Fremont N; 548-1508; map:FF8.*

**DV8** Specially designed for club hounds-in-waiting, this venue formerly known as Oz caters to those 18 and not much older with Top 40 DJ dance music and occasional live "as seen on MTV" bands. It's a big maze of a room, with split levels, dark corners, and a tendency to get uncomfortably smoky (especially when the fog machine is cranked up). ■ *131 Taylor Ave; 448-0888; map:D6.*

**El Lobo Loco** Another Johnny-come-lately to the alternative-rock scene, this split-level club on the south end of Pioneer Square opened in 1995 and features a mix of live bands (of low quality, judging from early bookings) and dance music. ■ *309 1st Ave S; 343-7227; map:P8.*

**Fenix ■ Fenix Underground** By taking over the space next door formerly occupied by the Celebrity, Fenix Underground has managed to add a street-level venue to its growing little empire. The club seems to have been successful in large part because of the high profile of its owner—John Corbett, who played Chris the DJ on the late, great TV series "Northern Exposure." Musically, the clubs are more adventurous than most of the others on the Square, booking acts that tend to lean toward rock and reggae. You won't find the best music in town here, but it's often the most hoppin' scene in Pioneer Square. ■ *315 2nd Ave S; 343-7740; map:P8.*

**Gibson's Bar & Grill** On the south end of Belltown, Gibson's features rock acts Thursday through Saturday and karaoke on Wednesdays. ■ *116 Stewart St; 448-6369; map:I7.*

**Giggles** A tad more collegiate than its Pioneer Square cousin, the Comedy Underground, Giggles is a large, plain, brick room with some dozen specialty beers on tap, as well as some cheap eats. The club features up-and-coming comedy acts—usually not as funny as a good Lawrence Welk rerun, but you might just hit it on a good night. ■ *5220 Roosevelt Way NE; 526-*

5653; map:FF6.

**HD Hotspurs** This suburban dance room south of town goes the DJ route, and features Top 40 music Monday through Sunday, plus excellent barbecued ribs until 2am Friday and Saturday. ▪ *315 S Washington St, Kent; 854-5653; map:QQ4.*

**Iguana Cantina** Though the waterfront is overflowing with touristy restaurants and shops, this is one of the few places that offers any semblance of nightlife entertainment. Occupying the former location of the Pier 70 Restaurant and Chowder House, Iguana features mostly DJs spinning Top 40 tunes, with the occasional live R&B act. ▪ *2815 Alaskan Way; 728-7071; map:D9.*

**Kerryman Pub** The Kerryman occupies hallowed ground: the former site of the Rainbow, one of Seattle's best music venues in the '70s and '80s (a spot for early gigs by Soundgarden among others). Since then the site underwent a brief stint as a topless joint, but now is back in a more respectable incarnation, offering an open mike on Thursdays and live music (mostly acoustic) on weekends. Added plus: it's next door to the legendary Blue Moon Tavern. ▪ *722 NE 45th St; 545-2960; map:FF7.*

**Kilimanjaro** Relatively new on the Pioneer Square circuit is this African/Caribbean restaurant and club that caters to the world-music crowd. More often than not, this is where you'll find the best local reggae acts, as well as touring talent from Jamaica and beyond. ▪ *210 S Washington; 467-9593; map:O7.*

CLOSED

**Kokeb** At 10pm on Friday or Saturday nights, this Ethiopian restaurant closes its kitchen and shuffles the tables around to reveal a brightly lit dance floor. A whole new batch of patrons packs the floor (especially Saturdays), moving to the latest in African pop from Algeria to Zimbabwe. ▪ *926 12th Ave; 322-0485; map:HH6.*

**Lake Union Pub** It's a dive, but the punkers like it that way. So it's no surprise this place has become a hangout for the most subterranean of underground types. With a makeshift stage and a pretty sad sound system, it's not very well suited for live music, but that doesn't keep a faithful cadre of die-hard local bands (and sometimes even a few intriguing out-of-town acts) from setting up shop and rocking the house. The cover charge is never over $2. ▪ *711 Fairview N; 343-0457; map:GG7.*

**Larry's Greenfront** Probably the best of the Pioneer Square blues joints. Though they all tend to blend together because they generally book the same talent on a rotating basis, Larry's manages to stand out because of a slightly more homey atmosphere and because it occasionally books first-class West Coast touring talent. ▪ *209 1st Ave S; 624-7665; map:O8.*

**Lockstock**  Formerly known as Lox Stock & Bagel, this casually comfortable restaurant/bar on the Ave is one of the few venues for live music in the University District, which would seem to be ripe territory for such a club. Expect a jazz jam session on Wednesdays and generally mediocre local bands Thursdays through Saturdays, with an occasional touring act. ▪ *4552 University Way NE; 634-3144; map:FF6.*

**Madison's Cafe & Music House**  In 1995, Madison's became one of the most promising additions to the local club scene. It's one of the few spots worth hitting in West Seattle, and its location on the eastern edge of that neighborhood makes for relatively easy access from I-5. Madison's could well become a hot spot for the acoustic-folk scene. All ages are welcome; the cafe serves food, wine, beer, and coffee. ▪ *3803 Delridge Way SW; 935-2554; map:KK8.*

**Metropolis**  Part of the Pioneer Square lineup, Metropolis features a rather schizophrenic mix of funk, dance music, and oldies acts. ▪ *423 2nd Ave; 682-4988; map:O7.*

**Moe's Mo'roc'n Cafe**  The only real challenger to the Crocodile Cafe as kingpin of Seattle's alternative-rock scene (it was started by some former Crocodile folks), Moe's has established itself as the hottest spot on Capitol Hill since opening in 1994. It's a huge club, with a cafe in front, a long, narrow bar off to the side, and an upstairs level that features a balcony where you can view the music scene below. The concert room itself holds only about 300 comfortably, which means it fills up fast for good shows—and Moe's gets plenty of those (including a surprise Neil Young/Pearl Jam gig in the summer of '95). ▪ *925 E Pike St; 324-2406; map:L0.*

**Neighbours**  Primarily a gay dance hot spot, Neighbours has been drawing a much more diverse mix of club-hoppers recently, making it one of the most popular hangouts on Capitol Hill. A first-rate lighting-and-sound system pounds out Top 40 and disco, and the dance floor stays packed. There's a buffet Friday and Saturday nights. Entrance is in the alley; it's open after-hours on weekends, but expect to wait in line. ▪ *1509 Broadway E; 324-5358; map:HH6.*

**New Orleans Restaurant**  This Creole/Cajun restaurant with French Quarter decor in Pioneer Square is a good place to catch ragtime, Dixieland, zydeco, jazz, and R&B acts. Tuesday nights are devoted to Cajun music. Mostly local bands, though lesser-known touring acts occasionally are featured on weekends. ▪ *114 1st Ave S; 622-2563; map:N8.*

**New World Restaurant and Lounge**  The back lounge of a Chinese restaurant would seem an unlikely place to find an alternative-rock club, but in the land of alternative rock, any room is fair game. The competition seems to be running thin in the North End, however, as the New World now stands alone as prime draw for the suburban metal crowd after the closure of its longtime rival, Mad Dogs. Furthermore, the New World has tried to diversify its bookings, resulting in a mishmash reflected in the club's description of itself as "A North End original rock/R&B/reggae and karaoke room." ■ *1471 85th St NW; 789-8887; map:EE8.*

**Newcastle's** South Seattle isn't renowned for its hip nightlife spots, but this restaurant and lounge has made an attempt to bring in quality live music on weekends. Local acts ranging from rock to blues to R&B to jazz are featured. Every Thursday is "Sam's Can Jam," an open session for blues players with an admission charge of two canned food items to benefit Northwest Harvest. ■ *6932 S Carlton; 763-6446; map:KK7.*

**Off Ramp** Once a must-see stop on any tour of Seattle's hippest alternative-rock clubs (Pearl Jam played here several times), the Off Ramp has been pushed out of the spotlight lately by increased competition. Most of the best touring shows and top local acts rarely end up here anymore, which is a shame because the Off Ramp remains a good venue for live music, with its 400-person capacity, good sightlines, sunken floor, and raised area with booths in the back. The bar and restaurant at the entrance are popular for late-night snacks and just hanging out. A fine weekend feature is "Hash after the Bash," a breakfast of eggs, potatoes, and a roll served for 50 cents as the last band winds down around 1:30am. ■ *109 Eastlake Ave E; 628-0232; map:H1.*

▼

**Entertainment**

▲

**OK Hotel** If you saw the movie *Singles*, you'll recognize this place as Java Joe's, the cozy coffee shop that served as a home-away-from-home for the movie's main characters. In the back of the dining area is a warehouse-style room where live music—ranging from hard rock to free jazz–is featured, mostly on weekends. On other nights, quieter acts often play in the adjoining cabaret barroom, a recent and welcome addition to the club. ■ *212 Alaskan Way S; 621-7903; map:N8.*

**Old Timer's Cafe** Local blues and jazz seven nights a week. Full bar and typical Pioneer Square wood-and-brass decor. ■ *620 1st Ave; 623-9800; map:N8.*

**Owl 'n' Thistle** It's sort of a secret hideout in Pioneer Square, tucked away in Post Alley, but the Owl 'n' Thistle is one of the best places to meet for a drink. Since some Irish musicians bought the place, it also has become a fine live-music spot, featuring hearty Celtic folk music Thursdays through Sundays. A small poolroom is a nice escape when things get too crowded, and a dining room up front has the comfortable feel of an old professor's library. ■ *808 Post Alley; 621-7777; map:N8.*

**Paragon Bar & Grill** Since it opened in 1995, this nightspot atop the hill has been the talk of Queen Anne. It features a mix of acoustic jazz, R&B, and rock bands, in a hip and upscale (by Seattle club standards) environment. ■ *2125 Queen Anne Ave N; 283-4548; GG8.*

**RKCNDY** A classic urban warehouse-style venue, RKCNDY (pronounced "rock candy") remains one of Seattle's better locations for alternative-rock shows, though increasing competition has cut into its previous reputation as a top-tier local showcase. There's a capacity of 500 to 700, a spacious open floor, and a balcony with tables and chairs. A lounge out front (with couches) and a small game room (pool, air hockey, and a couple of pinball machines) provide areas of respite from the crowd. Be careful with your choice of shoes: the concrete floor gets a bit sticky after an evening's worth of spilled beer. ■ *1812 Yale Ave; 623-6651; map:H1.*

**Re-bar** The Re-bar may never have been known as the hottest nightspot in town, but it has been a steady standby for local clubgoers for years. Though it features live music only one night a week (the best Tuesday night gigs in town are often found here), it remains primarily a hangout for musicians as well as hipsters. Thursday is Queer Disco night, though in general the club isn't *necessarily* a gay spot. World-beat Wednesdays are popular as well, as are weekends. The finest DJs in town spin at the Re-bar. ■ *1114 Howell St; 233-9873; map:I2.*

▼

**Entertainment**

▲

**Rendezvous** You get the best of both worlds here. Just as you enter, to the right, is a smoky bar lined with some of the friendliest drunks you'll ever want to meet. Continue on through the 1940s dining room into a tiny former film-screening room, affectionately called the Jewelbox Theater. The live-music schedule here is haphazard, but it's one of the better spots in town to see a show—and certainly the most intimate. ■ *2320 2nd Ave; 441-5823; map:G7.*

**Riverside Inn** You can't get more country than this neon-splattered Tukwila institution, which features line-dancing, local bands, and the occasional mid-size touring act. For a trip to the burbs in your boots and bolo, this is, hands-down, the place to go. ■ *14060 Interurban S, Tukwila; 244-5400; map:OO5.*

**Romper Room** This lower Queen Anne club has more of a neighborhood tavern feel to it, with its wooden bar and pool-room in back. Most nights the Romper Room features recorded music, highlighted by the weekend progressive dance nights when the club stays open until 3am. Live acts occasionally are featured, usually on Monday nights. ■ *106 1st Ave N; 284-5003; map:A7.*

**Scarlet Tree** It may not be glamorous, but this shakin' little bar north of the U District is hot, funky, and ready to romp to rhythm and blues. Frequented by students, Ravenna residents, and blues fans. ▪ *6521 Roosevelt Way NE; 523-7153; map:EE6.*

**Shark Club** By importing some of Seattle's top-drawing local bands across Lake Washington, the Shark has become a prime place for Eastsiders, though it's not usually worth the trip across the bridge if you live in Seattle. ▪ *52 Lakeshore Plaza, Kirkland; 803-3003; map:EE3.*

**Sharky's** The middle-class, Top 40, rock-by-the-water theme seems to work well here at this hopping, high-volume dance club in the Beach House (formerly the Windjammer). And when it comes to moving and shaking—landside, at least— it's probably the most happening spot in Shilshole. ▪ *7001 Seaview Ave NW; 784-4070; map:EE9.*

**Showbox** Formerly the Seattle Improv, this downtown supper club features touring comedy acts plus occasional jazz shows. ▪ *1426 1st Ave; 628-5000; map:K7.*

**The Timberline** Shake a leg to country western music at this lively, popular gay and lesbian disco. Don't know how to two-step? Show up Tuesdays through Thursdays and they'll teach you—and give you line-dancing lessons as well. Closed Mondays. ▪ *2015 Boren Ave; 622-6220; map:G3.*

▼

**Entertainment**

▲

**Tractor Tavern** With its hearthlike red-brick walls and wooden bar and dance floor, the Tractor is a natural spot for down-home American music. And that's just what the club serves up—everything from roots rock to traditional folk to country to zydeco to bluegrass. There's a growing scene of quality local bands mining rootsier styles, and the Tractor pulls in a lot of the best touring acts working in those genres as well. Long underutilized during its previous incarnation as The New Melody Tavern, the club has finally taken its place as one of the city's best live-music venues. ▪ *5213 Ballard Ave NW; 782-3480; map:EE8.*

**Under the Rail** A large, open warehouse room with a capacity of over 1,000, Under the Rail theoretically should be the main spot in town for touring acts which are too big for Seattle's mid-size clubs but not big enough for the concert halls. Instead, it's a largely unused venue, apparently run by people who don't have the clout or contacts to book the touring acts that should be playing there. A frustrating tickets-for-beer sales system is another problem, creating needlessly long lines at the bar and ticket-selling counter. Still, the Rail is marginally bearable on those rare occasions when it does manage to land a band worth seeing. ▪ *2335 5th Ave; 448-1900; map:F6.*

**Victor's** This joint on the northern outer limits of Pioneer Square is primarily a sports bar, but also features a fairly spacious music room where live bands perform on Wednesdays and Fridays. ■ *75 Marion St; 622-1969; map:M8.*

**Vogue** Once a vibrant force in Seattle's alternative-rock community, the Vogue has discontinued live music, and its storied south wall of graffiti has been obscured by a new office tower. Still, this remains one of the foremost DJ/dance clubs in town, a trendy spot with up-to-the-minute music and video often playing to a capacity crowd. Patrons display black from their boots to the roots of their hair. ■ *2018 1st Ave; 443-0673; map:H8.*

**Waldo's** Hey, old-timers! Eastside room for local oldies acts waiting to be discovered by Mr. Peabody and Sherman. ■ *12657 NE 85th St, Kirkland; 827-9292; map:EE2.*

**Weathered Wall** The official name of this place is "...And the Weathered Wall, the Purity Remains...," but locals quickly tired of such pretentiousness and assigned it a more manageable title. It's one of the most visually engaging rooms in town, a gothic-decorated split-level club that features both live bands and dance music, plus the occasional offbeat poetry reading. There's also a classy third-floor room that sometimes plays host to acoustic jazz and unconventional entertainment. ■ *1921 5th Ave; 728-9398; map:H6.*

## DESSERTS, COFFEES, AND TEAS

*See also Bakeries, Candies and Chocolates, Coffee and Tea, Ethnic Markets and Specialty Foods in the Shopping chapter.*

**B&O Espresso** Legendary for espresso, extraordinary desserts, and serious conversation, this vigorous Capitol Hill coffeehouse buzzes from morning to midnight. It's a peaceful place for breakfast, for a cup of steamed latte con orange and a tart, or a plate of fried new potatoes with peppers and onions. Lunch is served, too—thoughtful, out-of-the-ordinary creations like Chinese hot noodles and Egyptian lentil soup—and you can eat contentedly off that menu until 9pm. Desserts and coffee are where the B&O really shines; these are some of the best (though they're not the cheapest) homemade desserts in town. There are also B&O outlets in the Broadway Market and Pioneer Square. ■ *204 Belmont Ave E; 322-5028; map:GG6; every day.* ■ *401 Broadway E; 328-3290; map:GG7; every day.* ■ *103 Cherry Street; 621-9372; map:N8; Mon–Sat.*

**Bauhaus** At Bauhaus, function follows form. It's a high-ceilinged place with a wall of bookshelves stocked with used art books (Bauhaus doubles as a used bookstore—though we suspect the books actually look better than they sell). Big windows afford a view of the of the Pike/Pine corridor and the

Space Needle, which appears oddly inspiring and appropriate in this context. The wrought-iron fixtures and greenish walls lend a real stylishness, as does the clientele. Sweets are typical— with the exception of single Ding-Dongs, served with reverence on a plate for a mere 50 cents. Kool-Aid is available; the vintage cold-cereal boxes displayed by the counter are, unfortunately, not. ■ *301 E Pine St; 625-1600; map:J2; every day.*

**Boat Street Cafe** Nearly hidden in the shadow of the University Bridge (look for the Bentzen Yacht Service Center sign), Boat Street draws hip profs, weekend boaters, and folks taking a break from the Burke-Gilman Trail who come here for eggs Benedict, baguette sandwiches, light dinners, or dessert and coffee served at pretty slate-topped tables. ■ *909 Boat St; 632-4602; map:FF7; every day.*

**The Boiserie** Some places are filled with such a palpable sense of history and romance that they seem to have been there forever. That's the "Bwoz," a civilized coffeehouse in the basement of the venerable Burke Museum. The walls are lined with ornate carved-pine panels from an 18th-century French chateau. At communal tables students and professors nobly study, drinking good espresso and enjoying something sweet to go along with it, while classical music lilts in the background. Tables turn as often as classes do; the place closes at 8pm most nights (5pm on weekends). Some bagels, sandwiches, and small salads are served, but the eating emphasis is on fine pastries. Outdoor tables are lovely in the spring. ■ *17th Ave NE and NE 45th St (Burke Museum); 543-9854; map:FF6; every day.*

**Boulevard Espresso** Some coffeehouses are secret community centers; you might not notice them as you whizz past in your car, but for the neighborhood they serve, they cast a very long shadow indeed. So it is with Boulevard Espresso, which holds down the corner of Genesee and 50th S—half a block from Lake Washington—and serves consistently delicious coffee, pastries, and light lunches to residents and local businesspeople alike. The corner is busy with traffic, but Boulevard, like all true hangouts, occupies a wrinkle in time. The servers know the drink orders (and the life stories) of their regulars by heart. Spontaneous chat combusts at the old wooden bar that serves as counter. Outside, trees shade picnic tables on the sidewalk and the lake can be glimpsed down the street. A person could waste a lot of time here. ■ *4922 S Genesee; 722-7217; map:JJ5; every day.*

**Bright Coffee** Bright Coffee is a bright spot perched between Fremont and Ballard—living proof that you don't have to be funky (or corporate) to be cool. Marble-topped tables, shelves of specialty food products, and tasteful artwork add to the simple elegance. There's great coffee, some Italian-leaning fare (fine focaccia), and an array of carefully selected pastries. Outdoor seating and a beer and wine license, too. Open til 9pm. ■ *4332 Leary Way NW; 706-1443; map:FF8; every day.*

**Cafe Allegro** People who got into the Allegro habit while they were at U-Dub still find themselves gravitating back. It's hard to pin down the Allegro's appeal. Perhaps it's the moody darkwood decor and often smoke-saturated air; or the cachet of the location—it's not easy to find, set on the back alley of a U District street; or the serious and interesting conversation resulting from the wonderfully international crowd of students. You may feel as if you've been left out of a private joke on your first few visits, but it doesn't take long to become a regular. ■ *4214½ University Way NE; 633-3030; map:FF6; every day.*

**Cafe Counter Intelligence** Two flights above Pike Place Market, this narrow cafe is really about personality, panache, and viewpoint, the last in the most literal sense of the word. From this urban aerie you can watch the Market bustle by, and feel its energy and its pulse in a protected, voyeuristic sort of way. Best not to be in a hurry here, or to fashionably strapped. Beyond the usual espresso permutations, you can choose blends like Bean Spasm, which marries cocoa, espresso cubes, milk, ice cream, pecans, and shaved chocolate. Even an iced latte is anything but ordinary, arriving in a huge glass with espresso ice cubes. A great place to sip for hours, as the somewhat hidden location keeps the crowd to a minimum. If you get hungry, there's a primarily vegetarian menu, focusing on healthful grains and fresh fruits and vegetables. ■ *Pike Place Market; 622-6979; map:J8; every day.*

**Café Dilettante** The name of this Seattle institution is derived from the Italian word *dilettare,* "to delight." And that's exactly what its sinfully rich truffles and buttercream-filled chocolates do—day or night. But somehow the dessert prices keep growing while the portions shrink, so you might try a rich milk shake or ice cream dish instead, then grab some chocolates to go. In any case, be prepared to splurge. The Broadway location inevitably bustles (till 1am on weekends), and the Post Alley shop has moved to a First Avenue storefront nearby (now, sadly, a retail shop only). Pssst. . .there's a small retail outlet at their candy factory (2300 E Cherry Street) with seconds at reduced prices. ■ *416 Broadway E; 329-6463; map:GG7; every day.* ■ *1603 1st Ave; 728-9144; map:I8; every day.*

**Cafe Paradiso** Enjoy good espresso drinks in huge bowls and sample sweet treats while writing, studying, or staring at the artwork or the street below from the second-story perch of this spacious coffeehouse. Enjoy the laid-back, contemplative at-

▼

Desserts, Coffees, and Teas

▲

mosphere, where there's no need to rush—Cafe Paradiso is open until 1am, 4am on weekends. ▪ *1005 E Pike St; 322-6960; map:GG7; every day.*

**Caffe Ladro** We admire Caffe Ladro for opening on the same block as an established neighborhood Starbucks, and it seems their gambit has paid off. This hangout—with plum mottled walls adorned with the work of local artists and photographers—is usually packed, especially weekend mornings, when locals vie for one of the few tables for a breakfast of homemade granola, French toast, or Italian-style scrambled eggs. The sweets and baked goods are way above average, made right there in back. *Ladro* means "thief" in Italian (a reference to the customers they "stole" from their rivals up the street?). ▪ *2205 Queen Anne Ave N; 282-5313; map:GG7; every day.*

**Caffe Vita** Another entry in the growing number of Seattle coffeehouses that roast their own beans, Caffe Vita is giving the nearby and popular Uptown a run for its money. Queen Anne–ers are rabid about this little cafe tucked in the unlikely neighborhood just north of Tower Records. Roasting is done at a second, newer location (underneath the Monorail tracks at Fifth and Denny). Baked goods are average, but the coffee is great. ▪ *813 5th Ave N; 285-9662; map:B4; every day.*

**Elliott Bay Cafe** It's a popular and somewhat contemplative place located in the basement of the fine Elliott Bay Book Company, with brick walls and padded nooks where you can huddle over coffee and a book for hours. The food (sandwiches, vegetarian chili, salads) is third in line to the atmosphere downstairs and the books upstairs, but the lattes are fine and the treats sometimes great, though pricey. If you can make it past the slow cafeteria line to a quiet corner table, you're set. ▪ *101 S Main St; 682-6664; map:O8; every day.*

**Espresso Roma** The appeal of this minimalist place is that it doesn't have any: one branch—a big, cinderblock space with a cement deck spilling out toward the Ave; the other—on Broadway, smaller but working on the same, so to speak, theme. Atmo or not, they're both always packed with students, the drinks are good, the baked goods are standard, and service is ever friendly. ▪ *4201 University Way NE; 632-6001; map:FF6; every day.* ▪ *202 Broadway E; 324-1866; map:HH6; every day.*

**Espresso to Go (ETG)** This is Fremont, summarized in a stand-up–size espresso nook with two stools and a couple of newspapers. Locals visit this place for coffee and sweet bites throughout the day. In true Fremont form, the hours are flexible: it's open from whenever the baker gets there (usually around 4am) to whenever the last person leaves (usually around 7pm). ▪ *3512 Fremont Pl N; 633-3685; map:FF7; every day.*

**The Famous Pacific Dessert Company**  These are the folks that introduced us to the ultimate indulgence, Chocolate Decadence, and for that we'll be forever indebted. But on a given night there may be fewer desserts available than you might expect—considering their massive product line and reputation. Service at the Capitol Hill spot can lag a few minutes behind your needs. But we *have* had some wonderful concoctions here: rich, incredibly silky cheesecakes, a custardy ice cream laden with chunks of chocolate, a hazelnut meringue cake with rum whipped-cream filling.  ■ *516 Broadway E (and branches); 328-1950; map:I1; every day.*

**Grand Illusion Espresso and Pastry**  Attached to the last independent theater in town is the Illusion, where UW students (and their professors) rendezvous at the small tables, the fireside couch, or, on warm afternoons, in the tiny courtyard outside. Light lunch selections such as quiche and soup change daily, and the scones, cookies, and fruit pies are favorites; however, most customers come for post-film conversation or late-afternoon quiet.  ■ *1405 NE 50th St; 525-9573; map:FF6; every day.*

**Green Cat Cafe**  The Green Cat was a neighborhood favorite from the moment it opened. The tiny triangular kitchen turns out good salads, soups, and pizza by the slice, and the staff is chatty. There's a heavy sidewalk society scene here, where people coming up from Fallout Records run into friends having lunch outside, but the crowd is not all mod; lots of joggers and casual types stop in for their morning coffee.  ■ *1514 E Olive Way; 726-8756; map:I1; every day.*

**Harvard Espresso Gallery**  Michael Lyons and Everett Patterson have created a comfortable bi-level space across the street from the Harvard Exit that has become a haven for regular film goers and arty Cornish students. They come not for the desserts but for the good espresso drinks and the we're-all-friends-here atmosphere, fostered by the proximity of the tables and the eager après-film conversation.  ■ *810 E Roy St; 323-7598; map:FF6; every day.*

**Honey Bear Bakery**  Virtually all who walk into the warm, sweet arms of the Honey Bear adopt the place as if it were their very own—from morning coffee and sugar-powdered whole-wheat sourdough cinnamon rolls to late-night steamed milk and German chocolate cake. Or stop by Saturday morning (the Bear opens at 6am) for a pumpkin or blueberry muffin to go; they'll still be warm from the oven. Earthy yuppies, ageless hippies, and just plain folk linger, converse, read, write, and listen to live acoustic music (weekends only), regardless of the lines trailing out the door. True regulars bring their own mugs to avoid the paper cups. The nonsmoking Honey Bear also serves hearty homemade soups and salads and stays open until 11pm Wednesday through Saturday. ∎ *2106 N 55th St; 545-7296; map:EE7; every day.*

**Lighthouse Roasters** People come down to Fremont from adjoining neighborhoods out of loyalty to this place. Probably not for the decor—it's an almost too spare space, too serious and with not enough kitschy furniture to be considered truly retro. We conclude it must be owner Ed Leebrick's excellent coffee (he was a former roaster for Caravelli), roasted right there on the premises. That *is* the roaster taking up all the space in the middle of the room. Another, much tinier, space (sans roaster) is located at 5416 Sand Point Way NE, 524-9348. ∎ *400 N 43rd St; 633-4444; map:FF8; every day.*

**110 Espresso and Panini Bar** Just north of the Seattle Art Museum, 110 offers swanky surroundings and coffee, too. Four stunning paintings on Lucite take up an entire wall of this busy downtown cafe, which is marked by one of the coolest signs in town: an enormous cup and saucer that says it all without saying a word. Patrons sip from multicolored, hand-constructed ceramic cups, and nosh on soups, salads, panini, and pastries. ∎ *110 Union St; 343-8733; map:J7; Mon–Fri.*

▼

▲

**Penny University** Georges Braque would have liked the decor of this Belltown cafe; the walls mix brown-hued cubist shapes and newspaper collage. A counter bar is supported with crutches, and folding theater seats (the plush red kind) provide seating in the smoking area. With the usual beverages—coffee, tea, wine, and beer—are offered an array of pastries: cakes, scones, sweet rolls, pies, and muffins. ∎ *2020 2nd Ave; no phone; map:H7; every day.*

**Procopio Gelateria** Seattle's original gelateria still serves the most civilized Italian ice cream in town, in a stylish little nook right off the Hillclimb. At least 16 flavors (seasonally rotated) of freshly made ice cream are always displayed, and if you can get past these positively first-class ices, you can choose from an assortment of luscious desserts. Beverages include a great wintertime hot spiced cider, a few Italian wines, champagne, and espresso drinks. Open summers until 10pm Monday through Thursday, midnight Friday through Saturday. ∎ *1901 Western Ave (Pike Market Hillclimb); 622-4280; map:J9; every day.*

**Queen Mary Teahouse** With a low-pressure location just beyond University Village, the Queen Mary may never be a major stop on the coffee-tea-dessert circuit, but that doesn't diminish its appeal as a refuge on wet, gray Seattle days. The small dining room is determinedly cozy, lined with pleated floral-print fabric above head-high wainscoting, and a couple of doves literally bill and coo in a glass enclosure by the door. The

first thing you lay eyes on is a display of monumental layer cakes, cheesecakes, and trifles. Indeed, baked goods are the house specialty, along with a reassuringly proper pot of tea, correctly brewed and served in fussy china. Tea, with a capital T, is available from 2pm to 5pm every day. Breakfast and lunch are served, as well as dinners (Thursday through Sunday only).
■ *2912 NE 55th St; 527-2770; map:FF6; every day.*

**Roadrunner Coffeehouse and Coyote Comics** Comics-crazed Bill Kraut and his wife, Micheal Smith, own this comics-shop within a coffee shop anchoring a cozy, tree-lined corner store-front in Wallingford. You can drink a latte served in art pottery, snack on freshly baked scones and buttery French pastries, and even enjoy a breakfast of eggs and herbs on a croissant (the eggs are fluffed into oblivion by the steaming wand on the espresso machine). Live acoustic music on Friday and Satur-day nights. ■ *2123 N 40th St; 547-3559; map:FF7; every day.*

**Simply Desserts** Simply Desserts cooks up a selection of clas-sic pastries: chocolate espresso cake, berry and fruit pies, a white-chocolate strawberry cake that wins raves from every-one, and countless variations on the chocolate cake theme— the most popular being the chocolate Cognac torte and the Bai-ley's Irish Cream cake. This small spot with an enormous rep-utation gets plenty busy evenings, when chocolate cake fans the city over sip espresso and enjoy what may be simply the best desserts around. ■ *3421 Fremont Ave N; 633-2671; map:FF7; Tues–Sun.*

**Sit and Spin** Sit and Spin is a combination laundry/cafe, and its decor reflects to some extent the spirit of Belltown—the coolification of everyday things. Lamps, tables, and conduits are all twisted together to make a large free-form sculpture that dominates the cavernous space like an out-of-control conver-sation piece. The blaring music is as likely to be Bobby Darin as something industrial (and a new 200-seat performance the-ater in back adds to the all-things-to-all-people atmo). But this is not just for the young and hip; actual families have been sighted here doing their laundry just like everyone else! We're not sure who the stacks of games are for—the kids or the artistes. The food (soups, salads, focaccia, heavy on the veg theme) is av-erage, but there are a lot of choices. Service is moody and mod.
■ *2219 4th Ave; 441-9484; map:G7; every day.*

**Speakeasy Cafe** Coffee and computers are a natural combi-nation in Seattle, and the Speakeasy, which bills itself as an "in-formation trading post," is one of the world's first Internet gathering places. While sipping lattes or nibbling pastries in this converted warehouse, log on to one of two dozen com-puters and start surfing. Communicate with the world—or the computer down the street. Check out the club scene in New

▼

Desserts, Coffees, and Teas

▲

York and LA, join a chat group, browse the Louvre's permanent collection, or research an archive of Middle English texts. User fees are nominal and members can set up their own Web home page and e-mail address care of the cafe (the staff specializes in Internet for dummies assistance). The cafe also features live music, readings, and films—real-time entertainment to complement the virtual world. Get a taste of the cafe from your home terminal: you can e-mail *cafe@speakeasy.org* (URL: *http://www. speakeasy.org*). ■ *2304 2nd Ave; 728-9770; map:F7; every day.*

**Still Life in Fremont Coffeehouse** See Restaurants chapter. ■ *709 N 35th St; 547-9850; map:FF7; every day.*

**Teahouse Kuan Yin** You can peruse the latest guide to India while sipping a Darjeeling, or study a map of Japan while letting steep a pot of matcha. It wasn't by chance that Frank Miller and Miranda Pirzada located "Seattle's first teahouse" beside Wide World Books. Former travel agents with a longtime interest in Asia, Pirzada and Miller taste-tested many teas in Asia before selecting the Kuan Yin offerings: a full spectrum of teas, including plenty of blacks and greens, a few oolongs, and some herbals. Complementing these is a multi-ethnic and very reasonably priced assortment of quiches, humbao, and pot-stickers, as well as desserts such as green tea ice cream, pies, and scones. The mood is meditative but worldly; customers are invited to sit in leisurely and lengthy contemplation. Instruction in the ways of tea drinking is dispensed generously and with a philosophical air. ■ *1911 N 45th St; 632-2055; map:FF7; every day.*

**Uptown Espresso Bar ■ Uptown Bakery** This top-notch coffee hangout, with its own adjoining bakery, turns out a range of superb muffins, scones, and other sweet-and-semihealthy treats. This spot is always busy, whether with the quiet post-movie or -theater crowd at night or friendly tête-à-têtes throughout the day. Rightfully so, as these are some of the best espresso drinks you'll find in Seattle, and the morning treats are on their way to matching that claim. No smoking. ■ *525 Queen Anne Ave N; 281-8669; map:GG7; every day.*

**The Urban Bakery** Morning, noon, and night you'll find Green Lake's urban yuppies hanging inside or out of this popular corner spot near the Green Lake shore. Enjoy excellent soups and vegetarian chili, the usual sandwiches and salads, and a world of freshly baked breads, pastries, pies, cakes, and cookies that taste as good as they look. All the requisite coffee drinks, too. ■ *7850 E Green Lake Dr N; 524-7951; map:EE7; every day.*

**Veneto's** Regulars are almost rabid about the coffee at this chrome espresso bar near QFC. In part, we think, it's because there's nowhere else like Veneto's on the Eastside. Nowhere, that is, that pulls such a *great* cuppa java. ■ *10116 NE 8th St, Bellevue; 451-8323; map:HH3; every day.*

ART IN PUBLIC PLACES *139*

GALLERIES: ART, CRAFT, NATIVE AMERICAN *141*

MUSEUMS *145*

DANCE *149*

MOVIES *151*

MUSIC SERIES *153*

OPERA *156*

THEATER *156*

# The Arts

[FREE] Seattle is known internationally for its vast and adventurous public art collections. Artworks are so liberally sprinkled throughout the city you'll find it hard to avoid going by, through, or over some of them—whether murals, sculptures, decorated manhole covers, artist-designed gateways, plazas, or bus stops. The sheer quantity of the art is mostly due to a ground-breaking 1973 city ordinance that calls for one percent of certain capital improvement funds to be spent on art; King County, Washington State, and corporate and private donors have also contributed to the collection, with works by contemporary artists from the Northwest and elsewhere. The best guide to this museum-without-walls is the Seattle Arts Commission's *A Field Guide to Seattle's Public Art*, which can be obtained at most local bookstores. Or pick up a free abridged version (essentially a list of the 256 public art sites) at any branch of the Seattle Public Library.

The art ranges widely in form, style, and personality—from traditional metal monuments to environmental pieces so subtly integrated into their settings they almost disappear. In the former category, few public sculptures have enjoyed as much unbridled affection as Richard Beyer's *Waiting for the Interurban* (1978) in Fremont—the gray, huddled band of cast-aluminum trolley riders (Fremont Avenue N and N 34th Street, map:FF7) whose distinctly homely figures have become a symbol of the neighborhood. Other additions to the landscape have gotten cooler receptions. Michael Heizer's *Adjacent, Against, Upon*, three massive hunks of granite sitting next to, leaning on, and lying atop three mammoth chunks of concrete, was the subject of a loud public outcry over spending tax dollars on rocks when it was installed at Myrtle Edwards Park (map:B9) in 1976. Now it's considered part of the waterfront. And some artworks inspire the vehement loyalty of Seattleites, as occurred in 1987 when Seafirst Bank announced the sale of Henry Moore's bronze bone forms, *Three Piece Vertebrae* (1968) (1001 Fourth Avenue Plaza, map:M6) to a Japanese investor. The art community roared in protest, and the sale was blocked.

The newest, and undoubtedly the most riveting, landmark downtown is Jonathan Borofsky's towering black *Hammering Man* (1992) (100 University, map:K7), a four-story figure whose motorized arm and hammer is set to pound four beats a minute, commemorating—so the artist intends—the city's workers. *Hammering Man* made a big impression when he arrived to guard the doorway of the new downtown Seattle Art Museum, crashing to the pavement just as he was being craned into place. The present piece is actually *Hammering Man II*, completely refabricated.

At Seattle Center in the totally renovated Coliseum, now called the KeyArena (map:B7), two major new works were installed: a 60-foot "rain wall," *Hydraulis* by Trimpin and Clark Wiegman; and *In the Event*, an equally huge video installation by Sheldon Brown, with an array of monitors mixing images under computer control.

Other notable sculptures include Alexander Calder's playful *Grand Crinkly* mobile on the plaza at Fourth and Blanchard (map:G6); Isamu Noguchi's stone doughnut *Black Sun*, through which can be spied a classic Space-Needle-in-the-sunset vista (Volunteer Park, map:GG6); Ronald Bladen's mighty minimalist *Black Lightning* at Seattle Center; Barnett Newmann's elegiac column *Broken Obelisk* in the UW's central Red Square (map:FF6); and, in a tragicomic vein, Buster Simpson's *Seattle George* (Washington State Convention Center, map:J4), a double portrait—in green ivy and steel—of our conflicted fathers, George Washington and Chief Seattle.

Harder to find but worth the effort are: Robert Irwin's *Nine Spaces Nine Trees*, a mazelike plaza of cyclone fencing that's particularly suited to its spot near the center of city bureaucracy (Public Safety Building, map:N6); Barbara Kruger's barely legible but resoundingly moral questions (..WHO IS HOUSED? WHO IS HEALED? WHO DECIDES?..) painted on the fence at Piers 62–63, map:G9) at the site of a historic warehouse bulldozed by the city in 1991. Far lighter in spirit, the inlaid bronze shoeprints of Jack Mackie's *Dancer's Series* on Capitol Hill entice pedestrians to dance from set to set—waltzing, mamboing, rhumbaing, and fox-trotting their way down Broadway (map:GG6). Farther north, the shoreline walk at the National Oceanic and Atmospheric Association (NOAA) facil-

ity at Magnuson Park (map:DD4) incorporates works by
George Trakas, Siah Armajani, Martin Puryear, Doug Hollis,
and Scott Burton—all low-profile pieces that address the frag-
ile relationship between nature and human enterprise.

The most innovative of Seattle's art projects are those in
which artists have been employed alongside architects and en-
gineers as part of the "design team" for various public facilities—electrical-power substations, police and fire precinct
stations, or the high-rise King County Jail. The first project of
this sort was the Viewland/Hoffman Substation in the North
Park district (map:DD6), an electrical power station whimsi-
cally transformed by artists Emil and Veva Gehrke, Andrew
Keating, Sherry Markovitz, and Buster Simpson, with murals,
a "garden" of wind-powered whirligigs, and a wacky viewing
chair. The biggest team project to date is the Metro transit bus
tunnel (map:I3-J6) and its terminals (opened 1990), which, with
a $1.5 million art budget, employed dozens of artists in its de-
sign and appointments, from plazas to murals, benches, and
clocks. [FREE] Buses through the 1.3-mile tunnel stop at all five
stations (International District, Pioneer Square, University
Street, Westlake, and Convention Place) frequently every day
except Sundays, when the tunnel is closed.

## GALLERIES: ART, CRAFT, NATIVE AMERICAN

Seattle's thriving gallery scene is concentrated in the historic
Pioneer Square district, with additional galleries sprinkled to
the north, especially in the vicinity of the downtown Seattle Art
Museum. [FREE] One good way to get to know many of them
is to roam with the crowd in and around Pioneer Square on the
**first Thursday** evening of each month (about 6 to 8pm), when
new shows are previewed.

**Artworks Gallery** Bright and stylish ceramics, arty furniture,
jewelry, and textiles. ▪ *155 S Main St; 625-0932; map:O8;
Mon–Sat.*

**Carolyn Staley Fine Prints** The specialty here is fine old
prints, including Japanese *ukiyo-e* woodblock prints, antique
maps, and botanical prints. Staley also hosts occasional book-
art shows. ▪ *313 1st Ave S; 621-1888; map:O9; Tues–Sat.*

**Center on Contemporary Art (COCA)** Priced out of its space
across from Seattle Art Museum, COCA relocated in 1995 to
pleasing new digs in Belltown. COCA's mission is to provide a
venue for outer-edge art, especially performance and installation works that would otherwise have little chance for survival
in the marketplace. Past shows have featured radio-operated,
self-immolating robots; assortments of tattooed, pierced,
painted, or chocolate-smeared humans; and installations in-
volving salt blocks, body bags, hair, blood, and other bodily flu-

ids. COCA's greatest source of pride is a mention on Senator Jesse Helms's blacklist, but there are a few traditional shows on the schedule as well, such as the cluttered salon-style Northwest Annual. ▪ *65 Cedar St; 728-1980; map:E8; call for event info and hours.*

**Cunningham Gallery** Named after revered and spicy photographer and University of Washington alumna Imogen Cunningham, this gallery in the UW Women's Information Center presents six one-woman shows a year, mostly by younger Northwest artists. Multiculturalism is emphasized. ▪ *Women's Information Center, University of Washington; 685-1090; map:FF6; Mon–Fri.*

**Davidson Galleries** Contemporary Northwest painters and printmakers; interspersed with shows by Russian, Czech, and Chinese artists. Upstairs, check out the antique print department with loads of work on file, as well as rotating shows of everything from Blake illustrations to Indian miniature paintings. ▪ *313 Occidental Ave S; 624-7684; map:O8; Mon–Sat.*

**Donald Young Gallery** Young moved his eminently respected gallery from Chicago to Seattle in 1991, and it instantly became the place to go for the best—and often most challenging—of contemporary American and European art. Shows are about equally divided between video works, photography, installations, sculpture, and paintings. The gallery represents a blend of American and European artists, including two Seattleites: video artist Gary Hill, a recent winner at the Venice Biennale, and glass artist Josiah McElheny. ▪ *2107 3rd Ave; 448-9484; map:H7; Tues–Sat.*

**Elliott Brown** Owner Kate Elliott has been involved with Pilchuck School and its glass art almost from its start in 1971. In her new gallery, tucked unobtrusively in a Fremont back alley, she uses her connections in the glass world to line up a stable of top names, with a commitment to making work by European artists available in the Northwest. A highlight of her 1995 roster was the first solo West Coast show of famed Czech glass artists Stanislav Libensky and Jaroslava Brychtova. ▪ *619 N 35th, #101; 547-9740; map:FF8; Wed–Sun.*

**Foster/White Gallery** Traditional paintings, sculpture, and ceramics—usually abstract and decorative—by Northwest artists living and dead. The gallery is also one of the two major local dealers in contemporary glass by Pilchuck School stars—most notably Dale Chihuly. An Eastside outpost is located in downtown Kirkland. ▪ *311½ Occidental Ave S; 622-2833; map:O8; every day.* ▪ *126 Central Way, Kirkland; 822-2305; map:EE3; every day.*

**Francine Seders Gallery** In judicious operation since 1966, Seders represents some venerable members of Seattle's art

▼

**Galleries**

▲

community, including the painters Guy Anderson, Jacob Lawrence, Elizabeth Sandvig, and Michael Spafford. New additions to the stable include generous numbers of minority artists, among them painters, sculptors, and assemblagists. ■ *6701 Greenwood Ave N; 782-0355; map:EE7; Tues–Sun.*

**G. Gibson Gallery** Gibson opened her cozy upstairs space in 1991, providing a much-needed venue for contemporary photography—by both well-known Americans and adventurous young Northwesterners. ■ *122 S Jackson, 2nd floor; 587-4033; map:O9; Tues–Sun.*

**Greg Kucera Gallery** Another of the city's top galleries. Kucera maintains a stable of young-to-middle-aged artists, some of whose reputations have spread beyond the confines of the Northwest. This is also the place to find editioned works by class-A New Yorkers such as Terry Winters or Jennifer Bartlett. Recent shows have featured prints by Frank Stella and Helen Frankenthaler. One thematic exhibit each year addresses a touchy topic: sex, religion, politics. ■ *608 2nd Ave; 624-0770; map:N7; Tues–Sun.*

**Kirkland Arts Center** In a historic brick building near the waterfront, this publicly funded center puts on nine shows each year. Each show displays challenging work by Puget Sound–area artists. A variety of art classes are open to children and adults. ■ *620 Market St; 822-7161; map:DD3; Mon–Fri.*

**The Legacy (Alexis Hotel)** Northwest Native American works, mostly by contemporary practitioners deeply devoted to reviving tribal traditions. There are elaborately hand-carved wooden masks (originally important in Northwest Coast winter festivals), bentwood boxes, silverwork, button blankets, baskets, and prints. Some pieces are antique. ■ *1003 1st Ave; 624-6350; map:L8; Mon–Sat.*

**Linda Cannon Gallery** The new kid on the block in Pioneer Square, Cannon has geared her gallery to a younger crowd of artists and collectors but hasn't taken any big risks with her stable, which includes an assortment of painters, sculptors, and some emerging glass artists from Pilchuck. ■ *520 2nd Ave; 233-0404; map:O8; Tues–Sun.*

**Linda Hodges Gallery** Contemporary paintings, and occasionally photography and sculpture, by artists from Seattle, Portland, and other Northwest burgs. The art ranges from various forms of dark fantasy to thoughtfully skewed realism. ■ *410 Occidental Ave S; 624-3034; map:O8; Tues–Sun and by appointment.*

**MIA Gallery** The penchant here is for self-taught "folk" artists, including the Reverend Howard Finster, along with others who've been to college but come on folksy. Paintings, assemblage, jewelry, and one-of-a-kind furniture. ■ *512 First S; 467-8283; map:O8; Tues–Sun.*

**911 Media Arts Center** A vital link with contemporary multimedia art that evolved out of Anne Focke's legendary experimental art center of the early '70s (called and/or), 911 emphasizes film and video works. There's the Northwest's only art video library and an editing and screening room with state-of-the-art equipment available to members. Call ahead for a schedule of evening events. ■ *117 Yale Ave N; 682-6552; map:H1; Mon–Fri.*

**Northwest Craft Center** Ceramics is the focus here, in solo or small group shows that change monthly. There are also wood items and jewelry. ■ *Seattle Center; 728-1555; map:A7; Tues–Sun (every day in summer).*

**Northwest Gallery of Fine Woodworking** One-of-a-kind tables, desks, chairs, cabinets, sideboards, screens, boxes, and turned bowls, all by local craftspeople. Cooperatively owned. There's an Eastside gallery in Kirkland, too. ■ *202 1st Ave S; 625-0542; map:O8; every day.* ■ *122 Central Way, Kirkland; 889-1513; map:EE3; every day.*

▼

**Galleries**

▲

**Sacred Circle Gallery of American Indian Art** A profit-making arm of the United Indians of All Tribes Foundation, the gallery features contemporary paintings, prints, and sculptural pieces, always flavored with tribal heritages, by a broad selection of Native American artists from the United States and Canada. ■ *Daybreak Star Cultural Arts Center, Discovery Park; 285-4425; map:FF9; Wed–Sun.*

**Seafirst Gallery** Founded in 1993, the nonprofit gallery grew out of a merger between Seafirst and Security Pacific banks which absorbed the innovative Security Pacific gallery. Seafirst is not a sales gallery and doesn't represent any particular artists; it hosts seven to eight shows a year, primarily in conjunction with other arts and civic organizations. In 1995 the gallery featured drawings, paintings, quilting, ceramics, and glassware produced by children in temporary shelters, detention centers, and in other "at risk" situations, displayed alongside pieces by professional artists who spent time helping the youngsters explore these new ways of expression. ■ *701 5th Ave, 3rd floor; 585-3200; map:N6; Mon–Fri.*

**Snow Goose Associates** In 1993 Snow Goose changed ownership and moved from a display room in a private home to a new gallery space filled with art and artifacts of Alaskan and Canadian Eskimos and Northwest Coast Indians. Annual shows include the fall exhibit of prints by Inuit artists from Cape Dorset on Baffin Island. Snow Goose has been in operation for 25 years. ■ *8806 Roosevelt Way NE; 523-6223; map:DD6; Tues–Sun.*

**Vox Populi** Rattling the cage of the art establishment, Vox Populi mounts shows that hang out on the fringes of fin de siècle art. Works range from spoofs of Northwest mysticism to flying saucer paintings to chainsaw sculpture. The gallery also keeps a selection of wild-eyed Southern folk art available on the back wall. ■ *705A E Pike St; 329-8388; map:HH6; Wed–Sun.*

**William Traver Gallery** Pilchuck School glassworks are always on view at Traver, including the annual Pilchuck glass show in December. The stunning second-story space at First and Union showcases paintings, sculptures, photographs, ceramics, and assemblages by local artists. ■ *110 Union St; 587-6501; map:G7; Tues–Sun.*

**Woodside/Braseth Galleries** Strictly Northwest fare in the city's oldest gallery (founded 1962): paintings by Mark Tobey, William Ivey, Morris Graves, Paul Horiuchi, and a varying selection of slightly younger artists, mostly abstract expressionist. ■ *1533 9th at Pine; 622-7243; map:J4; Tues–Sat.*

## MUSEUMS

**Bellevue Art Museum** BAM, sitting atop a slick shopping mall, doesn't always transcend the general ambience; but for the most part it has created its own niche with exhibits that favor Northwest artists, craftspeople, and craft traditions from around the world. Recent shows have ventured bravely into foreign territory: artists whose prime concerns are social and political instead of decorative. BAM sponsors the massively popular Bellevue Arts and Crafts Fair at Bellevue Square each July. Admission is $3 adults, $2 seniors and students, free for kids. [FREE] Tuesdays are free for everyone. ■ *Bellevue Square (Bellevue Way and NE 8th St), Bellevue; 454-3322; map:HH3; every day.*

**Burke Memorial Washington State Museum** [FREE] The most popular attractions in this pleasantly modest natural history and anthropology museum are the dinosaur skeletons and Northwest Coast Indian art and artifacts (a group of full-scale canoes among them); but the museum's holdings are strong in all the other Pacific Rim cultures. The Burke also hosts traveling shows related to its collections. Downstairs, next to the bones and butterfly wings, is the Boiserie Cafe, an especially comfy espresso spot, with imported 17th-century French wood paneling and a birdsy patio. Admission is $3, $2 seniors, and $1.50 children over six; UW students free. ■ *17th Ave NE and NE 45th St, University of Washington; 543-5590; map:FF6; every day.*

**Center for Wooden Boats** [FREE] You can sail away with the exhibits at the Center for Wooden Boats, which has its own

little harbor at the southern tip of Lake Union. This maritime museum, kept afloat financially by private donations and a contingent of volunteers, celebrates the heritage of small craft before the advent of fiberglass. Of the 75 vintage and replica wooden rowing and sailing boats in the collection, more than half are available for public use. Admission is always free. Rentals range from $8 to $25 an hour. Lessons in sailing, traditional woodworking, and boatbuilding are offered for all ages.
- *1010 Valley St; 382-2628; map:GG7; every day in summer (closed Tues, Labor Day–June).*

**The Children's Museum** [KIDS] Located on the fountain level of the busy Seattle Center House, the Children's Museum recently tripled in size. It's an imaginative learning center that stresses participation in hands-on activities and exploration of other cultural traditions, and houses a number of permanent features, including a play center, a mountain, and a global village, with child-size houses from Japan, Ghana, and the Philippines. The variety of special programs—Mexican folkdancing, Native American games, Chinese storytelling, Japanese kite making—is impressive. The Imagination Station features a different artist every month guiding activities with various materials. The newly completed Discovery Bay is geared to infants and toddlers. Admission is $3.50; annual family memberships are $40 or $55. *Center House, Seattle Center; 441-1768; map:B6; every day.*

▼

**Museums**

▲

**Frye Art Museum** [FREE] After a major renovation and expansion, the Frye reopened to wide acclaim in early 1997. It continues to showcase sentimental 19th-century German salon paintings from the collection of late Seattleites Charles and Emma Frye, but is bringing in more provocative exhibits as well. Occasionally a small but distinguished collection of late-19th- and early-20th-century European and American paintings is on display, with pieces by John Singer Sargeant, Winslow Homer, William Merritt Chase, Renoir, and others. The new exterior is very inviting, and a courtyard, cafe, an educational wing, and a gift shop, as well as higher-quality traveling exhibitions and programming have been added. Admission is always free.
- *704 Terry Ave; 622-9250; map:N3; Tues–Sun.*

**Henry Art Gallery** The Henry reopened in April 1997 after a major expansion that roughly quadrupled its size. Kicking off with an exhibit that included Kandinsky and Klee, the Henry's snappy curatorial staff continues to line up the kind of deep and fascinating exhibits, primarily of 20th-century art, for which the Henry is noted. Past shows have included a landmark exhibition of Russian modernists, and gallery-consuming installations by Ann Hamilton and Jim Turrell. The permanent collection—strong in 19th- and 20th-century paintings and photography, and textiles from everywhere—will be regularly displayed in

the expanded gallery space. A new media gallery, an outdoor
sculpture court, a 150-seat auditorium, and a children's education center have been added. Adults pay $5, seniors $3.50, and
students get in free with ID (UW faculty and gallery members
go free as well). ▪ *15th Ave NE and NE 41st St, University
of Washington; 543-2280; map:FF6; Tues–Sun.*

**Museum of Flight** [KIDS] You don't have to be an aviation buff
to enjoy the sheer physical spectacle of 20 full-size airplanes—
including a 40,000-pound B-17—suspended from the ceiling of
a stunning six-story glass-and-steel gallery. The Museum of
Flight, 10 miles south of Seattle, is notable for its size, its sophisticated design, its impressive collection, and its unique location at a working airfield. The museum has no formal
affiliation with Boeing—the aircraft-manufacturing monolith
and mainstay of the Northwest economy—apart from its location at Boeing Field and its origination in the Red Barn, Boeing's humble first home in 1909. One cannot explore the
fascinating history of Northwest aviation without paying ultimate homage to this local industry giant, however, and the airfield setting—with real aircraft taking off and landing all around
you—is one of the most thrilling aspects of the museum.

The MOF takes you from the early legends of flight
through the history of aviation, from pioneering stages to the ▼
present, with special emphasis on Pacific Northwest flight—
military, commercial, and amateur. The collection of 42 planes **Museums**
includes a replica of the Wright brothers' original glider, a 1917
Curtiss Jenny biplane, a Douglass DC-3, and the 98-foot Lock- ▲
heed A-12 Blackbird, the fastest plane ever built (it has flown
coast to coast in 67 minutes). The museum has a variety of
workshops, films, tours, and special programs. Children will especially enjoy a hangar with three explorable planes, and
hands-on learning areas with paper airplanes, boomerangs, and
other toys that fly. Adults pay $6, kids 6 to 15 $3, under 6 free.
Handicapped accessible. ▪ *9404 E Marginal Way S; 764-
5720; map:NN6; every day.*

**Museum of History and Industry (MOHAI)** [KIDS] The rambling, amiable MOHAI is a huge repository of Americana, with
artifacts pertaining to the early history of the Pacific Northwest.
There's a 1920s Boeing mail plane and an exhibit about the
great Seattle fire of 1889 (it started in a gluepot on the waterfront). There are antique cars, lace- and bustle-decked gowns,
and a half-dozen immense wooden beauties—and one mascu-
line counterpart—that once rode the prows of ships in Puget
Sound. Changing exhibits of local orientation occur throughout the year. Admission is $5.50 for adults, $3 for seniors and
children 6 to 15, $1 for children 3 to 5, free for kids 2 and un-
der. [FREE] Admission is free on Tuesdays. ▪ *2700 24th Ave
E; 324-1125; map:FF6; every day.*

**Nordic Heritage Museum** Established in a restored school-house, the Nordic Heritage Museum focuses on the history of Nordic settlers in the United States, with exhibits of maritime equipment, costumes, and photographs, including an Ellis Island installation. Periodic traveling exhibits have included a show of 18th-century Alaskan and Northwest Coast Native artifacts from the National Museum of Finland, as well as artworks by contemporary Scandinavian artists in some of the loveliest gallery space in town. The building also houses a language school and music library. Holidays bring ethnic festivals. Admission is $4 for adults, $3 for seniors and students, $2 for children 6 to 16, under 6 free. ■ *3014 NW 67th St; 789-5707; map:EE9; Tues–Sun.*

**Seattle Art Museum (SAM)** The downtown Seattle Art Museum, designed by revered American architect Robert Venturi, has drawn both praise and criticism from local folk, well-known architects, and eminent international art critics. SAM has always been known as an excellent regional museum notable for its Asian collections. Now, with 145,000 square feet of space (though only a third of it is actually *gallery* space) and many new acquisitions, the focus is worldwide, with particular strengths in Asian, African, and Northwest Coast Native American art. Each gallery is especially tailored to complement the collections—for example, dark, dramatically lit rooms for the ceremonial works of Africa and the Northwest Coast; tall ceilings with ornate moldings for European decorative arts; white loftlike spaces for New York school paintings. The Japanese Gallery features an authentic bamboo-and-cedar teahouse, where a Japanese master performs the tea ceremony for a small group of visitors twice a month (reservations are required). Elaborate climate-control systems and a big Special Exhibitions Gallery attract periodic shows from major museums (such as the Treasures of Venice from the Museum of Fine Arts in Budapest). A lecture room and a 300-seat, acoustically perfect auditorium lend themselves to lectures, films, music, and dramatic performances; there's a fully equipped art studio for children's and adult classes. And, not least, a comfortable cafe midway up the Grand Stairway is accessible without paying admission. The museum store is excellent. Suggested admission is $6 for adults, $4 seniors and students, children under 12 free; [FREE] everyone admitted free one day a month. Call for free day and special holiday hours. (Admission tickets are also good for Seattle Asian Art Museum in Volunteer Park within two days of purchase.) ■ *100 University St; 654-3100; map:K7; Tues–Sun.*

**Seattle Asian Art Museum** With the opening of the Seattle Art Museum downtown in 1991, the original building, set among the trees of Volunteer Park, was renovated as home for the mu-

▼
**Museums**
▲

seum's extensive Asian art collections. Built in 1931 by Richard Fuller and his mother, Margaret McTavish Fuller, the museum first housed their 1,700-piece collection of Asian art before growing into a more eclectic institution. Now the carefully lit galleries once again hold sacred images—the Buddha in perfect meditation, a monk at the moment of enlightenment, the Hindu deities Siva and Parvati rapt in divine love—the kind of art that draws you away from daily obsessions, that soothes the mind and expands the soul. In addition to old favorites from the collection—like the 17th-century Japanese crow screens and the Fullers' array of elaborate netsuke—see ancient Chinese funerary arts and a recently donated collection of 14th- to 16th-century ceramics from Thailand. An educational outreach gallery also has been added, with hands-on displays. The Kado tearoom, which serves selected Asian teas and fresh pastries, is open on weekends only. The Asian Art library, located near the tearoom, is available for public use. Suggested museum admission is $6 for adults, $4 seniors and students, museum members and children under 12 are free; **[FREE]** everyone admitted free one day a month. Call for free day and special holiday hours. (Admission tickets also may be used for admission at SAM downtown within two days of purchase.) ■ *1400 E Prospect, Volunteer Park; 654-3100; map:GG7; Tues–Sun.*

**Wing Luke Asian Museum** Named after Seattle's first Chinese-American city councilman, this lively little museum in the International District is devoted to the Asian-American experience in the Northwest. Particularly moving is the exhibit of photographs and artifacts relating to the internment of Japanese-Americans during World War II (it includes a replica of a prison barracks). Other exhibits are devoted to Chinese, Korean, Filipino, Vietnamese, and Laotian peoples, and their often difficult meetings with the West. Admission is $2.50 for adults, $1.50 for students and seniors, 75 cents for children. **[FREE]** Free on Thursdays. ■ *407 7th Ave S; 623-5124; map:R6; Tues–Sun.*

## DANCE

In past years, Seattle suffered a nasty trade imbalance in dance, losing Merce Cunningham, Robert Joffrey, and Mark Morris to New York and beyond. As New York loosens its stranglehold, Seattle is slowly becoming one of the more interesting regional dance centers (and Morris himself has lately taken to making annual visits to the UW World Series at Meany Hall). The wealth of distinctive choreographers who have sprung from local series to gain national attention (Pat Graney, Llory Wilson, aerialist Robert Davidson, dancer/vocalist Christian Swenson), as well as the supply of talented long-legged women in the ballet company, has led New York critics to ask for the recipe of our drinking water. Still, a lack of performance venues, concert halls, and teaching jobs here still makes for a sad attrition rate. But there are one or two cheap theaters for rent to dancers these days, and the ability to self-produce a casual, low-tech concert is helping stave off a complete exodus.

**Allegro! Dance Festival** It's hard to tell whether this 10-year-old modern dance series is flickering back to life or sputtering out completely. Since the departure of founding producer John Vadino several years ago, this small performance series—focused solely on local independent choreographers and ethnic dance troupes—has changed directors three times and changed board members with as great a frequency. Now under the leadership of Peter Staddler, formerly the publicity director for the festival, the dance series has sadly shrunk from eight annual concerts down to four, but recent concerts have featured new choreographers with satisfyingly risky and imaginative voices. ■ *Broadway Performance Hall, 1625 Broadway; 32-DANCE; map:HH6.*

**On the Boards** Plugged into David White's New Performance Network in New York City, On the Boards produces and presents cutting-edge works that merge dance, music, theater, and visual media. The sellout New Performance Series, October to May, brings in internationally known contemporary artists like Anne Teresa de Keersmaeker, Bill T. Jones, and Ron Brown, plus local greats such as Pat Graney and Robert Davidson. (For many of these sellout shows, OTB moves from their makeshift loft space in the Central District to the Moore Theatre or Meany Hall.) In late spring, the Northwest New Works Festival and the 12 Minutes Max series premiere daring experimental pieces by regional composers, choreographers, and playwrights. ■ *Washington Hall Performance Gallery, 153 14th Ave; 325-7901; map:HH6.*

**Pacific Northwest Ballet** Under the guidance of artistic directors Kent Stowell and Francia Russell—former dancers with New York City Ballet—PNB has earned recognition as one of the top five regional companies in America. Fueled by a strong, well-staged selection of classic and rare Balanchine repertory, an average six-show PNB season also features large-scale classical opuses by director Stowell and contemporary offerings by Paul Taylor, Mark Dendy, and Glen Tetley. [KIDS] Each August the company presents two fun, family-oriented, outdoor performances at Chateau Ste. Michelle, and its holiday-season *Nutcracker* is superb for all ages, thanks to sets by Maurice Sendak and an excellent reserve of young PNB school students. Unfortunately, the April PNB Offstage series, which debuts energizing new works by up-and-coming ballet choreographers from around the nation, is hanging in the lurch at

▼

**Dance**

▲

present due to budget restraints. ■ *Phelps Center, Seattle Center; 292-2787; map:A6.*

**World Dance** Five major dance groups are brought in every year as part of Meany Hall's World Dance Series, and each year the programming seems to get more complete and thrilling. The October-through-May series always includes such tried-and-true top draws as Pilobolus, the Alvin Ailey American Dance Theater, and the Paul Taylor company. There's usually one more risky choice thrown into the mix, like Lyon Opera Ballet or Garth Fagan Dance. And homeboy Mark Morris has taken to showing up here for several seasons running. ■ *Meany Hall, University of Washington; 543-4880; map:FF6.*

## MOVIES

Various versions of Seattle exist in movie dreams. Elvis Presley, of course, shared the silver screen with the Space Needle in his cheery *It Happened at the World's Fair*, while Warren Beatty witnessed a dramatic opening chase atop the Needle in the paranoia-inducing *The Parallax View*. Writer-director Alan Rudolph rechristened soggy Seattle "Rain City" in his exotic *Trouble in Mind*, while David Mamet painted the tense, psychological story *House of Games* with streetlights reflected in the city's inevitable puddles. Other feature films, including *Black Widow, Singles, American Heart*, and *Say Anything*, developed distinct visions of elemental Seattle, and works starring recent Seattle guests Jennifer Jason Leigh and Sylvester Stallone will almost certainly add to that list.

But when we speak of Seattle as a movie town, what that really means is that its residents love films. Going to them, talking about them, surreptitiously E-mailing colleagues about them. Seattle, says *Variety*, has more active filmgoers per capita than any other city in America. No wonder: the city's exhibition scene is dramatically split between plentiful national theater chains such as **Cineplex Odeon** and a vital arthouse circuit that is largely part of the homegrown **Seven Gables** mini-chain of nine theaters and 28 screens. While scores of shopping mall theaters are busy showing the same dozen titles, the Gables packs in as many American independent and international productions as it can schedule, while still accomodating above-average studio hits.

Among the most interesting of the Gables theaters are a pair of once-independent houses that helped heighten Seattle's film consciousness in the 1970s and early '80s. The **Harvard Exit** (807 E Roy Street, 323-8986) — begun by two eccentric film fans who simply wanted to see more of the movies they liked—was home to everything from the controversial *Hearts and Minds* to the first, experimental run of the lunatic *Monty*

*Python and the Holy Grail.* The **Egyptian** (801 E Pine Street, 323-4978), a grand old house converted from a Masonic temple, serves as a year-round exhibition space, but is more importantly the anchor for the annual Seattle International Film Festival.

Another Gables acquisition, the **Varsity** (4329 University Way NE, 632-3131), ingeniously dedicates one of its three screens to repertory scheduling. That allows the exhibitor to recycle second-run titles, organize blocks of movies into various cohesive series and minifestivals (tributes to Fellini, clusters of Taiwanese action flicks), and give brief bookings to deserving new movies that nevertheless lack commercial firepower.

The **Grand Illusion** (1403 NE 50th Street, 523-3935), a 90-seat house that was the birthplace of the Seven Gables chain but does not belong to it today, is an intrepid soldier in the exhibition wars, showcasing worthy, sometimes offbeat films from foreign and small distributors, as well as occasional retrospectives of such animated icons as Betty Boop.

The big kahuna in regional film action is the aforementioned **Seattle International Film Festival** (324-9996), a sprawling springtime event. Into its third decade, the Festival shows no sign of slowing down as it establishes new records for ticket sales year after year and routinely presents a slate of up to 200 features and shorts from all over the globe. Three weeks long, the Festival might seem a daunting event to first-timers who might like to check out a handful of promising movies, but the process really isn't any more difficult than buying tickets at the box office and waiting in line. (Tickets and various levels of passes can also be purchased in advance.)

While the Festival casts a big shadow, there's plenty of alternative cinema action virtually every week. The **911 Media Arts Center** (117 Yale Avenue N, 682-6552) is a fascinating hub of video and film activity, with frequent screenings and lots of helpful workshops in the nuts and bolts of production. The **Seattle Art Museum** (100 University Street, 654-3100) has been organizing extremely popular, well-researched, quarterly film series (film noir, British comedy, Judy Holliday) for 25 years, as well as presenting shorter programs on such impressive miscellany as David Lynch rarities and early works by Michael Powell. Housed in a new auditorium with 35mm capability, SAM's program remains a cornerstone of nonprofit film exhibition.

There's more: **Sanctuary Theatre**, situated in an upstairs screening room at the indispensable Scarecrow Video rental store (5030 Roosevelt Way NE, 524-8554), has a weekly program of films not available on tape and/or rarely screened in their original cut and widescreen dimensions. **Cinema Video**, held at the Velvet Elvis Arts Lounge Theatre (107 Occidental

▼

**Movies**

▲

S, 624-8477), is a monthly screening series focusing on recent experimental works by Seattle film- and videomakers.

The Rainy States Film Festival (322-3572) in February, also a focal point for Northwest filmmakers, has been a smash hit with local audiences. In general, Seattle is a haven of interesting niche-film fests taking place all the time: Asian-American, Polish, Jewish, African, gay and lesbian, children's, animation, and Native American movies all have their moment of glory during the year. The best way to find out what's happening in any particular week is by checking local arts listings.

## MUSIC SERIES

Over the past decade, Seattle has built the thriving classical music scene appropriate to a cultured cosmopolitan city. The symphony and opera are now firmly on the national map, and chamber music has become a local passion. Both early music and choral music abound. Several musicians of national or international reputation make their homes here and share their musical expertise generously. Seattle is also a regular stop for major performers on tour.

Of the **concert venues**, both sightlines and sound are respectable in almost any Seattle performance hall; however, for instrumental performances at the Opera House (3,017 seats), the acoustics are better downstairs than up. Conversely, you'll hear best in the balconies at the smaller Moore and Meany theaters. The auditorium at the Seattle Art Museum has added an elegant small concert space, seating 270, and by 1998 the city's crunch in performing space should be alleviated by the opening of the Seattle Symphony's 2,500-seat Benaroya Hall (and the attendant recital hall) opposite SAM.

**Belle Arte Concerts** The 14-year-old Belle Arte Concerts series in Bellevue has its own chamber music series of six concerts (including one for children). Some performers are locally based, all are of national, and occasionally international, caliber. Bassist Gary Karr and the Shostakovich Quartet are examples. Musical director Heidi Lehwalder has raised the overall level of performance, encouraged more adventurous programming and Northwest composers, and broadened a generally classical format to include some jazz. ■ *Venue: Lee Theatre, Forest Ridge School, 4800 139th SE, Bellevue; 454-2410; map:GG2.*

**Early Music Guild** The Early Music Guild is credited with making Seattle a center of historically informed early music performance, and has enjoyed great success as the genre becomes increasingly popular. The Guild's International Series consists of six concerts of medieval, Renaissance, baroque, and classical music, and features top international players and ensembles. Its new Recital Series, with three concerts at the Seattle

Art Museum, highlights performers whose art is best presented in an intimate venue. The organization also sponsors or assists many performances by local artists, both semiprofessional and professional. Among these are the Gallery Concerts series and Seattle Baroque Orchestra—a professional group presenting three concerts a year. ■ *Venue: various locations (mail: 1605 12th Ave, Suite 19, Seattle, WA 98122); 325-7066.*

**International Chamber Music Series** The six-concert International Chamber Music Series, presented by the University of Washington, brings to town some of the very best of the nation's chamber music ensembles (and an occasional group from abroad), with an emphasis on string quartets and trios. These popular concerts, held in the acoustically superior Meany Theater, are scheduled fall through spring. ■ *Venue: Meany Theater, University of Washington (mail: 4001 University Way NE, Seattle, WA 98195); 543-4880; map:FF6.*

**International Music Festival of Seattle** A reinvention of Seattle's beloved Santa Fe Chamber Music Festival, the International Music Festival has traveled far from its predecessor's roots. Half the musicians brought in by artistic director, conductor, and violinist Dmitry Sitkovetsky are from abroad—including superb soloists from Russia and Europe (such as pianist Vladimir Feltsman) and the New European Strings (a chamber orchestra comprised of musicians from all over Europe, with a healthy contingent of Russian-trained players). The other half are American, many local. Programming is imaginative and wide-ranging, taking place for two intensive weeks in mid-June in Seattle and Bellevue, with outreach concerts as well. ■ *Venue: various locations (mail: 93 Pike St, Suite 313, Seattle, WA 98101); 622-1392.*

**Ladies Musical Club International Artist Series** Kreisler, Rachmaninoff, Horowitz, and an astounding roster of other musical giants have performed for Ladies Musical Club since its inception in 1891. It continues its sponsorship of young artists and its educational arm. As of the 1995–96 season, LMC has joined with the UW World Series to present an expanded number of world-class musicians. ■ *Venue: Meany Theater, University of Washington (mail: 4001 University Way NE, Seattle, WA 98195); 622-6882; map:FF6.*

**Northwest Chamber Orchestra** Nearing its 25-year anniversary, NWCO, the only professional chamber orchestra in the region, continues to flourish under the management of Louise Kincaid and the musical leadership of Adam Stern. The orchestra's focus is chamber music of the 17th to 20th centuries, performed on modern instruments with attention to appropriate performance practices. Stern is pursuing "traditional adventurousness" by showcasing less familiar solo instruments (like the saxophone) and combining some concerts with singers or dancers. NWCO presents a subscription series, a chamber music series, children's performances, and special concerts. ▪ *Venue: various locations (mail: 1305 4th Ave, Suite 522, Seattle, WA 98101); 343-0445.*

**President's Piano Series** The University of Washington brings to town current pianists of international stature (plus a few new hopefuls) during this six-concert recital series. Murray Perahia is a frequent visitor; Awadagin Pratt one of the up-and-comings. ▪ *Venue: Meany Theater, University of Washington (mail: 4001 University Way NE, Seattle, WA 98195); 543-4880; map:FF6.*

**Seattle Chamber Music Festival** Founded by University of Washington cello professor Toby Saks, this popular monthlong summer series showcases local and international talent. The performances are spirited, ofttimes exceptional, and almost always sold out. Grace notes include pre-performance dining on the lawn (bring a picnic or buy a catered meal) and a minirecital before each concert. Programming sticks to the tried-and-true, but the recitals feature the performers' own choices, often rarely heard pieces. The acoustics in St. Nicholas Hall are only so-so, but for a gracious summer evening, you can't do better. ▪ *Venue: Lakeside School, 14050 1st Ave NE (mail: 2618 Eastlake Ave E, Seattle, WA 98102); 328-5606; map:CC7.*

▼

▲

**Seattle Men's Chorus** Dennis Coleman, who directs the 16-year-old, 180-member gay chorus, is one of the best choral conductors in this city of choirs. The chorus is one of the busiest in the country, with about 30 appearances a year at various events and a subscription series of three concerts. Groups or soloists who have recently come to Seattle under SMC's sponsorship are Chanticleer, the Flirtations, and Bobby McFerrin. ▪ *Venue: Meany Theater, University of Washington, or Opera House, Seattle Center (mail: PO Box 20146, Seattle, WA 98102); 323-2992; map:FF6 (Meany Theater); map: A6 (Opera House).*

**Seattle Symphony** Granddaddy of the Seattle classical music scene, the Symphony has been a barometer of the city's growing stature in the music world. Under Maestro Gerard Schwarz, the orchestra has reached a new level of consistency and artistic mastery, which should crescendo in 1998 with the scheduled opening of the Symphony's own concert hall. Schwarz has initiated several successful series since he took the helm in 1984, offering a package for every kind of music lover. Recent series include Pops, Popular Culture (with such guests as Wynton Marsalis and the Lincoln Center Jazz Orchestra), Baroque Specials, Creative Impulse (discussions between Schwarz and composers), and Musically Speaking (insightful commentary by the conductor at Sunday matinees). The symphony's Distinguished Artists series beckons such top-ranking musicians as Alicia de Larrocha, James Galway, and Horacio Gutiérrez. Also worth noting is the symphony's Discover Music Series—one-hour attention-holding concerts designed to introduce children to various themes in classical music. The symphony has a busy outreach program with special concerts in many area communities. ▪ *Venue: Opera House, Seattle Center (mail: 305 Harrison St, Seattle, WA 98109); 443-4747; map:A6.*

**Seattle Youth Symphony**  One of the premier youth orchestras in the country, the Seattle Youth Symphony is reaching new heights of performance under conductor Jonathan Shames, who became music director in 1994. These talented young musicians give three usually dazzling concerts during the winter season. Three feeder orchestras train a large number of younger musicians. ▪ *Venue: Opera House, Seattle Center (mail: 11065 5th Ave NE, Suite E, Seattle, WA 98125); 362-2300; map:A6.*

**The Tudor Choir**  In a few short years, the 24-voice Tudor Choir has established itself as an a cappella choir in the best English tradition—of the same type and virtually the same level as the Tallis Scholars. Under conductor Doug Fullington, the choir specializes in English church music of the late Renaissance, today's mystical composers, and American shape-note music. It performs a three-concert series, as well as several additional performances in conjunction with St. James Cathedral. ▪ *Venue: various locations (mail: 4203 Brooklyn Ave NE, #107, Seattle, WA 98105); 633-5018.*

## OPERA

**Seattle Opera**  Sellout audiences have come to expect fresh and innovative productions from Seattle Opera, which has become a top-flight company under the leadership of Speight Jenkins, general director since 1983. The company mounts a well-balanced program of four or five full-scale operas every season, among them a major summer production that draws an international audience. Wagner's *Ring* cycle is performed regularly. ▪ *Venue: Opera House, Seattle Center (mail: PO Box 9248, Seattle, WA 98109); 389-7676; map:A6.*

## THEATER

The slump in arts funding nationally has cast a chill in theater-crazy Seattle, too, driving long-established companies toward more conventional, easily marketable fare. Paradoxically, the result has been an explosion of experimentation among artists and companies who weren't benefiting from government and foundation largess in the first place.

Much Seattle "fringe" theater is as self-indulgent and ill-executed as fringe work elsewhere, but every season sees some of the city's best work performed in out-of-the-way venues with casts of starry-eyed and enthusiastic performers with ability out of all proportion to the hardscrabble salaries they earn. Among the fringe companies are a number that produce interesting and consistently first-rate work. These include **AHA! Theater** (2222 Second Avenue, 728-1375), presenting a half-dozen otherwise homeless companies yearly; **Alice B. Theater**, (various venues, 322-5423), offering national and home-grown productions with a gay-lesbian bias; **Annex Theater** (1916 Fourth Avenue, 728-0933), whose new scripts are staged with hell-raising attack and verve; **Greek Active** (various venues, 516-4125), a gay-lesbian troupe whose wild assaults on the classics are often performed in bars and other nontraditional stages; **Velvet Elvis Arts Lounge Theater** (107 Occidental S, 624-8477), presenting goofy original work and small touring shows, often with a campy bias; and **Northwest Asian American Theater** (409 Seventh Avenue S, 340-1445), with shows aimed at Seattle's diverse Asian communities but appealing to a broader audience as well.

Both Seattle dailies do a good job of tracking down good off-track work in their weekly entertainment supplements. *Seattle Weekly* offers a more selective, evaluative guide to the theater scene, while *The Stranger* specializes in work appealing to the younger crowd. Don't be afraid to experiment: in Seattle, biggest doesn't necessarily mean best.

## A Contemporary Theatre (ACT)

ACT—which opens in May when the Rep is just about to shut down—sticks mainly to contemporary plays, particularly new works by young American and English playwrights. More adventurous musicals are also an ACT specialty. The season always closes with *A Christmas Carol*, a Seattle tradition. The small auditorium (450 seats) and moderate-thrust stage are just right for intimate dramas. ■ *100 W Roy St; 285-5110; map:GG8.*

## Annex Theater

The Annex is the most "established" of the gaggle of companies that have opened in Seattle lately—and the most ambitious as well. With a focus on new and daring works, *nothing* is too far out: the first revival in 300 years of a tragedy of lesbian love, a musical version of *Alice in Wonderland* set in silent-era Hollywood, *The Hunchback of Notre Dame* retold by an egomaniacal avant-garde theater director. Their year-round series includes 10 mainstage shows in a 92-seat house, plus four developmental pieces in a smaller, 45-seat space. The company has a devoted young following of its own and is probably the group to keep an eye on for writing and performing stars of the future. ▪ *1916 4th Ave; 728-0933; map:H6.*

**Bathhouse Theatre Company** Perched on the shore of scenic Green Lake, this Parks Department facility houses a professional company specializing in imaginative Shakespeare stagings (*Macbeth* set in the Old West, *A Midsummer Night's Dream* at a high-school sock-hop) as well as contemporary classics suited to its intimate, 125-seat scale. The season runs year-round. ▪ *7312 W Green Lake Dr N; 524-9108; map:EE7.*

**The Cabaret de Paris** The brainchild of singer-comedian-impresario David Koch, this modest stage in a downtown French restaurant is a showcase for the brightest musical talents in town. The repertory mixes original revues (*Waiter, There's a Slug in My Latte* is a Seattle classic) with shows featuring familiar pop tunes in often zany packaging. You can order from the bar, snack à la carte, or buy a dinner-and-show package: the food is Gallic-accented, tasty, and reasonably priced. ▪ *Crêpe de Paris restaurant, Atrium Level, Rainier Square; 623-4111; map:L6.*

▼

**Theater**

▲

**The Empty Space Theatre** Revivified under the direction of nationally known playwright/actor Eddie Levi Lee, this seminal Seattle troupe has returned to its roots, presenting sleek and lively mountings of the wilder kind of new American drama along with goofy original musicals, tongue-in-cheek thrillers, and some of Lee's own loose-jointed satirical comedies about the outer fringes of American life. "Popular theater" at its best, perfectly suited to its setting: the funky, '60s-retro Fremont neighborhood. Plan to drop in to one of the lively local bars after the show; you'll probably find yourself tipping a microbrew with some of the cast. New in this theater: air conditioning! ▪ *3509 Fremont Ave N; 547-7500; map:O8.*

**Fifth Avenue Theater Company** Until the new Paramount Theater opened in 1995, this was the only house in town suitable for big touring Broadway shows. Some still play here, but the house mainstay is new productions of classic musicals (and an occasional Broadway-bound experiment) produced in collaboration with Houston's successful light opera company. Casts are strong, production values adequate (if not on the flat-out *Phantom of the Opera* level), and musical values are well-attended to by entrepreneur Frank Young. ▪ *1308 5th Ave; 625-1900; map:L6.*

**The Group Theatre Company** Founded in the 1970s to push a multicultural social agenda, this ensemble now mounts some of the most professional productions in town, without forgetting its roots in the city's lively ethnic mix. Shows range from musicals (*Falsettos*) to classic revivals (*A Raisin in the Sun*) to hard-hitting new plays. *Voices of Christmas*, an ever-changing collection of sketches and personal stories illustrating how different peoples celebrate the holidays, is an annual tradition. ■ *Center House Theater, Seattle Center; 441-1299; map:B6.*

**Intiman Theatre Company** Buoyed by a Pulitzer Prize for its staging of *The Kentucky Cycle* and a sold-out run of *Angels in America*, Intiman has taken a strong turn away from its roots in the classics toward a more engaged, contemporary repertory under artistic director Warner Shook. The company's home, the 424-seat Intiman Playhouse, isn't the friendliest space in town, but that doesn't seem to bother one of the strongest and most loyal subscriber groups around. Season runs May through December. ■ *Intiman Playhouse, Seattle Center; 626-0782; map:A6.*

**New City Theatre** Situated in the heart of Capitol Hill's lively "alternative" scene, New City is home to the resident Theater Zero company specializing in contemporary (mainly off-off-Broadway–style) writers as well as other groups presenting theater-on-the-edge. The production schedule is intermittent but year-round. ■ *1634 11th Ave; 323-6800; map:HH6.*

**On the Boards** See Dance in this chapter. ■ *Washington Hall Performance Gallery, 153 14th Ave; 325-7901; map:HH6.*

**Paramount Theater** The refurbished '20s movie palace now has a stage big enough to house touring Broadway blockbusters like *Miss Saigon* and a big enough house (3,000 seats) to make a Seattle stopover profitable for them. ■ *911 Pine St; 682-1414; map:J3.*

**Seattle Children's Theatre** [KIDS] Without question one of North America's leading theaters for youth, Linda Hartzell's SCT is prospering in its lovely Seattle Center home, the 280-seat Charlotte Martin Theater. Productions (up to nine per season) play to school groups daily, with family shows every weekend. Most of the plays are specially commissioned for the company, which employs some of the best professional actors and designers in the region. The September-through-June season is paralleled by year-round classes and workshops for aspiring school-age performers. ■ *Charlotte Martin Theater, Seattle Center; 441-3322; map:C7.*

**Seattle Gilbert and Sullivan Society** The Gilbert and Sullivan Society produces one show per year (*Patience* in 1993, *Mikado* in 1994—their 40th anniversary) in an 11-performance run in July. The cast and orchestra are volunteer performers who put on very professional productions (usually sellouts). If G & S are your cup of tea, you'll find them well served here. ■ *Bagley Wright Theater, Seattle Center; 682-0796; map:A6.*

**Seattle Repertory Theatre** The Rep is the oldest and biggest show in town, with a six-play, October-through-May season on the 856-seat Bagley Wright Theater mainstage and a three-show lineup in the modest-size PONCHO Forum space. Both venues mix recent off-Broadway and regional theater successes with the occasional updated classic and lots of Broadway-bound "commercial" fare: premieres of works by Neil Simon, Wendy (*The Sisters Rosensweig*) Wasserstein, and Herb (*Thousand Clowns*) Gardner have headlined recent seasons. The hottest ticket of all (don't plan on finding a seat unless you know someone) is for the spring workshop series, in which Broadway and screen stars often appear in hopes of getting in at the inception of a show with a future. ▪ *Bagley Wright Theater, Seattle Center; 443-2222; map:A6.*

**University of Washington School of Drama** The university's student productions are a good bet for both classics and contemporary plays—and a bargain, too ($6 to $8 a ticket). Productions featuring students of the Professional Actor Training program, rated among the nation's top three, are often directed by distinguished visiting professionals. Thesis productions by students of directing and stage production tend to be more avant-garde. The UW uses three theaters for drama—the Meany Studio Theater, the Playhouse, situated off-campus on bustling University Way, and the Penthouse, a 170-seat jewel in intimate theater-in-the-round style—one of the first such structures ever built in America. The 11-play season runs from late fall until June. ▪ *University of Washington; 543-4880; map:FF6.*

▼

**Theater**

▲

**EXPLORING CONTENTS**

**DOWNTOWN SEATTLE** *163*

**PIKE PLACE MARKET** *165*

**PIONEER SQUARE** *168*

**WATERFRONT/SEATTLE AQUARIUM** *171*

**INTERNATIONAL DISTRICT** *173*

**CAPITOL HILL** *175*

**SEATTLE CENTER** *178*

**QUEEN ANNE** *179*

**LAKE UNION** *181*

**FISHERMEN'S TERMINAL** *183*

**BALLARD** *184*

**WOODLAND PARK ZOO** *186*

**UNIVERSITY DISTRICT (UNIVERSITY OF WASHINGTON)** *188*

**BREWERY HOPPING** *191*

**WINERY TOURS** *193*

**EASTSIDE** *195*
 Woodinville *195*
 Bellevue *196*
 Kirkland *199*

**PARKS AND BEACHES** *201*

**GARDENS** *210*

**PUBLIC ACCESS** *215*

**ORGANIZED TOURS** *217*
 Air Tours *218*
 Boat Tours *218*
 Motor Tours *219*
 Walking Tours *219*

**ITINERARIES** *220*

# Exploring

## DOWNTOWN SEATTLE

*Between 1st Ave and 9th Ave, Yesler Way and Lenora St;*
*map:H9–N9*

Downtown Seattle (between the industrial sector south of the Kingdome and the Denny Regrade north of Lenora Street) is again engaged in one of its periodic building booms. Although many of the new office towers in the commercial core are corporate behemoths of the any-city style, hints of postmodernism bring the district an exciting new look, and the question of whether or not there is a Northwest architectural style is being debated by those in the know. The **Washington Mutual Tower** (Third Avenue and Seneca Street) acts as something of an environmental mirror with its hypnotic aqua facade that reflects the day's changing light. **City Centre** (Fifth Avenue and Pike Street), with ridged edges and somber gray-blue hue, elegantly dominates the Fifth Avenue skyline. Its light-filled lobby contains freestanding architectural ornaments, engaging chandeliers, and delightful glass sculptures. Three floors of exclusive shops provide excellent browsing, and the Palomino bistro tastefully drapes over both sides of the third-floor escalator. Many Seattleites are fond of **Two Union Square**, with its nautical feel and curved sides (and courtyard and waterfall inside), and the **Second and Seneca Building**, affectionately dubbed the Ban roll-on building, which sports a fat blue dome that glows at night. Towering above everything else is the 76-story **Columbia Center** (Fourth Avenue and Columbia Street). For a grand view, visit the observation platform on the 73rd floor. Check in with the security desk in the lobby ($3.50 adults, $1.75 children and seniors, weekdays only).

Five bus stations of the underground **Transit Tunnel** opened in late 1990 to ease Seattle's menacing downtown traffic problem. Each station is a showcase of underground urban glamour lined with different kinds of public art (from sculpture to poetry), the fruits of Metro's $1.5 million arts program. The controversial tunnel is outfitted with rails for future adaptation to a light-rail system.

The **Washington State Convention and Trade Center** (Eighth Avenue and Pike Street), a mammoth, glass-enclosed building, sprawls atop 12 lanes of freeway. Adjoining the complex is **Freeway Park** (Sixth Avenue and Seneca Street), one of Seattle's most original outdoor spaces. This extraordinary park forms a lid over thundering I-5—a feat of urban park innovation when it was constructed in 1976. Here, amid grassy plateaus and rushing waterfall canyons, the roar of traffic seems to disappear, and brown baggers find rejuvenating solace.

The **retail core** lies basically between Third and Sixth Avenues from Stewart Street to University Street. Few cities of Seattle's size do a better job of retaining a large, spiffy, varied retail center—anchored by the big department stores (**The Bon Marché** at Fourth Avenue and Pine Street, and the flagship **Nordstrom** at Fifth Avenue and Pine Street). High-quality boutique enclaves are **Westlake Center** at Fifth Avenue and Pine Street (which has upscale national chains—The Limited, Williams-Sonoma—as well as local enterprises) and **Century Square** at Fourth Avenue and Pine Streets. Colorful strings of smaller shops proceed up Fourth and Fifth Avenues to **Rainier Square** (Fourth Avenue and Union Street), an elegant three-story atrium at the base of the bank tower. Across University Street to the south is the **Four Seasons Olympic Hotel** (Fourth Avenue and University Street), the noble grand dame of Seattle hostelry, girded all about with boutiques of international pedigree. This is the area in which the University of Washington held court until it moved north of Lake Union in 1895. High tea in the Olympic's **Garden Court** (621-1700) makes a very civilized break for shoppers.

▼

**Downtown Seattle**

▲

Another retail district runs along First Avenue. At its north end is famous **Pike Place Market** (see listing in this chapter), which is spreading its retail tentacles southward along First and Western Avenues toward Pioneer Square. First Avenue has upscaled considerably in past years, and the shopping district now reaches beyond Virginia Street into Belltown, which is quickly becoming a veritable gourmet ghetto, with hip new restaurants, espresso bars, pubs, bistros, and bakeries nestled among a multitude of new condo complexes. **Waterfront Place** (First Avenue and Post Alley between Madison and Seneca Streets) forms a centerpiece of shops, offices, and restaurants that surround the exquisite **Alexis Hotel**. This once blighted part of town is becoming a bastion of sophisticated urban retail—a reputation that has been enhanced by the late 1991 opening of the downtown **Seattle Art Museum** in its stylish Robert Venturi–designed building (First Avenue and University Street; see listing under Museums in the Arts chapter). Outside the museum stands the imposing profile of Jonathan Borofsky's *Hammering Man*, which has taken its place in the Seattle skyline. Extending toward the waterfront from the Museum is a grand new set of stairs, Harbor Steps, designed by the famous Vancouver architect Arthur Erickson. The steps make a great place for summertime picnics and people-watching; each level has a different style of fountain, each making its distinctive sound.

## PIKE PLACE MARKET

*Pike St to Virginia St on Pike Pl; map:J7–I8; information:*
*1st Ave and Pike Pl; 682-7453*

[KIDS][FREE] If cities have souls, then Pike Place Market is certainly Seattle's. The Market that now makes available an abundant range of foods and wares—from seafood to sheep's-milk cheese to chestnuts to bok choy—opened as an experiment in August of 1907 as a response to the demands of angry housewives who were tired of high food prices padded by middlemen. Bringing farmers and consumers together proved to be immensely successful, and soon fishmongers and shopkeepers joined the farmers' wagons along Pike Place. The Market has had its ups and downs, but now, almost a century later, the tomatoes are still in the stands and the market is still the gorgeous hodgepodge it has always been.

▼
Pike Place
Market
▲

Despite relentless gentrification of the area, the oldest continuously operating farmers market in the United States still prides itself on being an incubator for small businesses— "the biggest mom 'n' pop store in town." No national or regional chain stores or franchise businesses are allowed (except Starbucks, of course, whose first store was—and still is—located here). About 125 local farmers have permits to sell their produce at day stalls, over 200 permanent businesses operate there year-round, and about 200 registered craftspeople and artists sell their wares (Market guidelines prevent infiltration of anything mass produced). The Market is open every day all year long.

The people of the Market (not the well-polished produce) are the main attraction—old seadogs who reminisce about the Market's lusty past; the boisterous produce and fish vendors who bark at the passersby; the street musicians, puppeteers, and mimes who turn the street corners into stages. The way to "do" the Market is to spend an unstructured day meandering its crannies, nibbling from its astonishing variety of ethnic and regional foods, browsing the shops, watching the people. If you visit before 9am, you can watch the place come alive as the

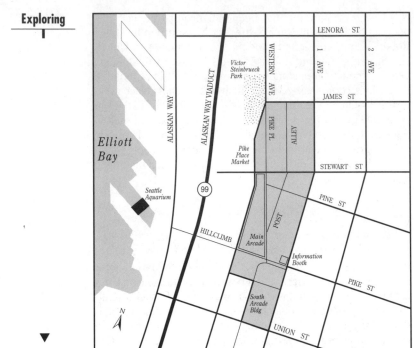

*Pike Place Market*

farmers set up; in spring and summer, shopping is best done (once most of the farmers have come) in the early morning hours. In the off-season, the vendors are less harried and you can talk them up about what's in season and how to cook it, and really get a feel for the community of people who sell at and who use the Market.

The official entrance is at the corner of First Avenue and Pike Street, at the **Information Booth** (First Avenue and Pike Place, 682-7453), where you can pick up a map, advice on sights, or a self-guided tour pamphlet. (The booth doubles as a day-of-show, half-price ticket outlet, Ticket/Ticket, open Tuesday through Sunday from noon to 6pm.) **Read All About It** (624-0140), the Market's newsstand and official gossip station, anchors this busy corner, as does **DeLaurenti** (622-0141), Seattle's landmark Italian deli with an eye-opening selection of olive oils, cheeses, imported meats, a substantial wine selection, and some of the best bread in the city. To the south is the **South Arcade**, home to the modern-looking shops and condos that have spread forth from the historical district. Walking west, down the covered corridor, past artists' stalls and vegetable stands, you'll come to the elbow of the L-shaped Market. This is the start of the **Main Arcade**—the famous Pike Place

Market sign and clock are just above you—and home of the big bronze pig (a good spot for meeting a friend). The produce vendors called "highstallers" display beautifully arranged (don't touch) international produce. Local farmers at the low stalls sell seasonal, regional produce—local berries, sweet onions, Washington apples—direct from the farm. You'll likely pass some Market veterans along here: highstaller Dan Manzo, who was "born in a lettuce crate"; Sue Verdi, who will tell you with authority how to cook the mustard greens you just bought; and Indo-Chinese farmers selling bok choy and other Asian vegetables. In the midst of this is a Market institution: **The Athenian** (624-7166), a smoky, working-class cafe that's been the favorite haunt of Market old-timers since 1909 (and a stage set during the filming of *Sleepless in Seattle*). The down-home food is okay, but the real draws are the marvelous view of Elliott Bay and the long beer list. The engraved floor tiles throughout the Market were part of a fund-raising project in 1986, when a $35 donation bought a person a little bit of immortality.

In summer, the artists' and craftspeople's tables stretch along the Main and North Arcades from Pike Place to Virginia Street and **Victor Steinbrueck Park**, the splash of green that marks the northern border of the Market (see Parks and Beaches in this chapter). Across Pike Place, you'll discover shops and ethnic eateries leading to a shady courtyard in the back where covered tables are set out for **Emmett Watson's Oyster Bar** (448-7721), a folksy seafood joint named after the infamous Seattle journalist and raconteur.

If you were to take a short detour here, up the wooden stairs to **Post Alley**, you'd find two of the gems of the ethnic restaurant scene in Seattle: the funky, likable trattoria **The Pink Door** (443-3241) (look for the pink door); and **Kells** (728-1916), a rough-hewn Irish pub. Follow Post Alley on to where it meets Pike Place at the Sanitary Market (so named because horses were not allowed inside); you'll pass Peter Lewis's wonderful **Cafe Campagne** (728-2233), just below the stylish, 65-room **Inn at the Market** (443-3600), the Market's only hotel. In the next block you'll go by the see-and-be-seen sipping bar at **SBC** (Seattle's Best Coffee) (467-7700) and the entrance to an array of shops and eating places—including a very good regional gift shop, **Made in Washington** (467-0788)—in the somewhat more sterile arcade of the **Post Alley Market Building**.

Across the street from the highstallers you'll also find **Totem Smokehouse** (443-1710, where you can pick up smoked salmon or arrange to ship it home). **Le Panier** (441-3669) is a French bakery on the corner, and wafts of garlic pour out of nearby **Cucina Fresca** (448-4758). Stop by **Piroshky Piroshky** (441-6068) for a savory pastry made (before your eyes) by Estonia-born Vladimir Kotelnikovi. **Seattle Garden Center**

(448-0431) stocks many difficult-to-find bulbs and seeds. **Sur La Table** (448-2244) is a nationally renowned cook's emporium.

Inside the **Sanitary Market** is an atmospheric, chaotic jumble of produce stands and eating places, including the **Pike Place Market Creamery** (622-5029) with its delicious dairy goods; **Jack's Fish Spot** (467-0514), which sells steaming cups of cioppino from an outdoor bar; and **Three Girls Bakery** (622-1045), the city's best sandwich counter.

Next door, to the south, is the last building in the historic stretch: the **Corner Market**, a picturesque structure of careful brickwork and arched windows that houses produce, flower stalls, and a left-of-center alternative bookstore, **Left Bank Books** (622-0195). There are a couple of restaurants hidden in its upper reaches: **Cafe Counter Intelligence** (622-6979), fine for breakfast and a lingering cup of cafe au lait, **Chez Shea** (467-9990), perhaps the most romantic nook in town, and its adjoining bistro-bar, open evenings till just after midnight. Post Alley continues on the south side of Pike Street, as it dips down below street level and passes the classy, dimly lit Italian restaurant **Il Bistro** (682-3049) and the arty **Market Theater** (781-9273).

It's almost impossible to get a parking space on congested Pike Place—local regulars don't even try—so either take a bus or splurge for a space in the spiffy 550-slot parking garage on Western, with its elevator that opens directly into the Market (some Market merchants will help defray the cost with parking stamps, free with purchase, so be sure to ask). Or try one of the lots a little farther down Western Avenue, or First Avenue to the north.

## PIONEER SQUARE

*Jackson St to Columbia St along 1st Ave; map:09–M8*

Pioneer Square, just south of downtown, has undergone several transformations since its days as an Indian village, since the whites settled it in 1852, since it was razed in the great fire of 1889, since it was rebuilt according to more architecturally coherent — and less flammable — standards. Pioneer Square went into a long decline after the 1920s when "downtown" moved uptown. It became an art gallery center in the 1960s, and was declared a historic district in the early 1970s.

Today it is one of the few extensive and stylistically consistent "old towns" in the nation, abounding in bookstores, gift shops, antique shops, nightclubs. Galleries range from fine arts to crafts to animation; museum- and history-lovers will enjoy the **Klondike Gold Rush Museum** (117 S Main Street, 553-7220). Lawyers, architects, and media folk dominate the work force, while homeless transients fill the streets, drawn by a preponderance of missions (and park benches).

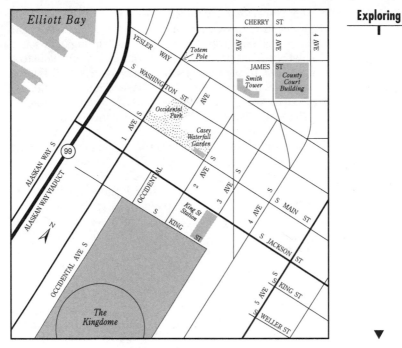

*Pioneer Square*

The real Pioneer Square, actually a triangle on the corner of First Avenue and Yesler Way, is adorned with a Victorian iron-and-glass pergola (a turn-of-the-century holdover from the days when trolley cars serviced this district) and a totem pole—a replica of the one stolen from the Tlingit tribe in 1899 in one of Seattle history's most ignominious moments. Facing the square is the **Pioneer Building,** one of the most elaborate works of the postfire reconstruction. It houses offices, a maze of antique shops on the lower level, and the headquarters of the **Underground Tour,** a touristy, subterranean prowl through the original streets of downtown (see Walking Tours in this chapter).

On the sidewalk in front of **Merchants Cafe** (109 Yesler Way, 624-1515), Seattle's oldest restaurant, is a dandy shutterbug view of **Smith Tower**, built in 1914 and distinguished for years as the tallest building west of the Mississippi. You can take the elevator up to the tower's 35th-floor observation deck to get the lay of the land. Waterward, you'll find a tasty breakfast or a late-night dinner at **Trattoria Mitchelli** (84 Yesler Way, 623-3883), an unofficial Pioneer Square landmark, open until 4am. **Al Boccalino** (1 Yesler Way, 622-7688) across the street is a wonderful nook for a romantic (and considerably pricier) Italian meal.

First Avenue is the main, tree-lined artery through the historic district, intersected by streets that terminate at the **waterfront** a block west (best chance for parking in this area is under the Alaskan Way viaduct: bring quarters). Globetrotters will love **Metsker Maps** (702 First Ave S, 623-8747), the perfect place to orient yourself to Pioneer Square, Seattle, and the world beyond. In addition to maps of every kind, there's a complete travel book section in back. Heading south you'll see **Northwest Gallery of Fine Woodworking** (corner of First Avenue S and Jackson, 625-0542), with its continually changing exhibits of exquisite handcrafted furniture and sculptures. **FireWorks Gallery** (210 First Avenue S, 682-8707) is another decor gallery, with beautifully crafted pottery, jewelry, and other handicrafts. On the same block is **Grand Central Arcade**, with two levels of tony, upscale retail—a far cry from its original function as a skid road, later "row" (this is where that term was invented) hotel. This block comes alive on weekend nights as the restaurants on its west side metamorphose into jumping nightclubs.

Across Main Street is **Elliott Bay Book Company** (First Avenue S and S Main Street, 624-6600), perhaps the finest bookstore in the Northwest and an authentic reflection of the artistic/literary sensibilities of this raw yet stylish district. There's a cafe in its basement where browsers can linger over soups, salads, and sandwiches, sip coffee, and read their purchases. Next door, **Bowie and Company** (314 First Avenue S, 624-4100) handles rare and out-of-print books and does efficient book searches. **Grand Central Mercantile** (316 First Avenue S, 623-8894), a quality kitchen emporium, and the whimsical **Wood Shop** (320 First Avenue S, 624-1763), an imaginative toy shop with great stuffed animals, are a couple of other worthy stops along this stretch.

West on Jackson Street is **Merrill Place**, Pioneer Square's high-rent district. Once Schwabacher's Hardware, the revitalized building conceals an enclave of apartments and **Il Terrazzo Carmine** (411 First Avenue S, 467-7797), an esteemed Italian restaurant with a romantic bar and a terrace overlooking a fountain. **Occidental Avenue South** is a sun-dappled, brick-lined pedestrian walkway studded with galleries. On the first Thursday of every month, this mall—indeed, all of Pioneer Square—fills up with art- (and scene-) appreciators who turn out for [FREE] **First Thursday Gallery Walks**, when galleries stay open late to preview new shows. You can pause for a nosh at the chic, high-character Italian coffee bar **Torrefazione Italia** (320 Occidental Avenue S, 624-5847), or grab a brew and some fried calamari at the **Pacific Northwest Brewing Company** (322 Occidental Avenue S, 621-7002).

South from here, you can't miss the 66,000-seat **Kingdome** (Fourth Avenue and S King Street, 296-3128), hailed by

▼

**Pioneer Square**

▲

some as fine brutalist design, lambasted by many as Seattle's oversize cement orange-juice squeezer. **F.X. McRory's Steak, Chop and Oyster House** (419 Occidental Avenue S, 623-4800) is the restaurant and watering hole of choice for game-goers, a madhouse after Seahawks and Mariners victories.

South of the Kingdome on First Avenue a neighborhood is in process, reached by the gentrifying fingers of Pioneer Square. New condos, galleries, and bars have taken their place here, including **Kagedo** (520 First Avenue S, 467-9077), an excellent Asian antiques and textiles store. Across the street is the venerable Western tack shop **Duncan and Sons** (541 First Avenue S, 622-1310). Nearby is the retail shop of the venerable outdoorswear manufacturer **C.C. Filson Company** (1246 First Avenue S, 622-3147), makers of Seattle's own highest-quality rough-and-tumble wear since the Alaska-Klondike Gold Rush.

Occidental Avenue South segues into **Occidental Park**, a Northwest attempt at a Parisian park setting with cobblestones and trees. The international feeling is enhanced by the occasional horse-drawn buggy or rickshaw-like pedicab that breezes by. A more unusual park is tucked into a corner of Second Avenue: **Waterfall Gardens**, where a man-made waterfall spills over large rocks in a cool urban grotto.

▼

## WATERFRONT/SEATTLE AQUARIUM

*Main St to Broad St along Alaskan Way; map:O9–A9*

Today Seattle's downtown waterfront is mostly a tourist boardwalk lined with kitschy souvenir shops, harbor-tour operations, and fish 'n' chips counters. All along the waterfront, however, are opportunities to watch the busy working harbor, where slow-moving container ships, hardy fishing boats, and sleek cruise ships coast against the stunning natural backdrop of the Sound. It's a worthy attraction and a fine place for an invigorating, sea-gazing stroll.

The nonindustrial waterfront is anchored at **Pier 48** (foot of Main Street) and the Washington Street Public Boat Landing. The waterfront side of the pier has an excellent interpretive display of the harbor's history, and periscopes offer grand seaward views as well. Look along this space (and directly north and south) for a thought-provoking art project/exhibit about the conflicting issues of waterfront development. Up the street is the city's main ferry terminal, **Colman Dock** (foot of Marion Street at Pier 52), where boats depart for Bremerton, Bainbridge Island, and (for foot passengers only) Vashon Island (see Ferries under Transportation in the Essentials chapter). The best way to explore the waterfront is to walk one direction and then hop aboard the **waterfront trolley** for a return ride on a quaint old streetcar that runs along Alaskan Way from Pier 70 to Main Street, a 15-minute, 85-cent ride.

At Pier 54 are a couple of Seattle's most endearing landmarks. **Ye Olde Curiosity Shop** (682-5844) displays an unabashedly zany collection of oddities, knickknacks, and miscellaneous Northwestiana of the giant-clams-and-shrunkenheads ilk. **Ivar's Acres of Clams** (624-6852), with its breezy outdoor fish bar, was the first in a diverse local chain of seafood eateries for notorious raconteur, Seattle booster, friend-to-artists, and ace fish hustler Ivar Haglund.

[KIDS] Wade through the thick of the tourist boardwalk to the compact, well-designed **Seattle Aquarium** (Pier 59, 386-4320, open daily, adults $6.95 (seniors $5.50), kids 6 to 18 $4.50, 3- to 5-year-olds $2.25). There are illuminated displays and convincing re-creations of coastal and intertidal ecosystems (and a permanent tidepool exhibit). In a domed room, you're surrounded by a tank in which sharks, snapper, octopi, salmon, and other Puget Sound inhabitants whisk by. Finally, you follow a salmon ladder to a marvelous topside vista of Elliott Bay and the superstars of the Aquarium: the cavorting seals (real hams) and the playful sea otters. The **Omnidome Theater** (622-1868), with its dramatic cinema-in-the-round, looks at nature's spectacles.

Look carefully at the fences on Piers 62/63 for a series of penetrating questions inscribed on the chain links in red—your ability to read them changes according to where you stand and the quality of the light. North, on **Pier 66**, is the site of the new Bell Street Pier, still under construction at press time. The pier will be home to the new Odyssey Maritime Museum, the Bell Harbor Conference Center, a marina (with short-term public moorage available), and a slew of new eating places (including a trio of Anthony's seafood restaurants). Plans for upland development (which will include housing, a hotel, and retail) are under way. The Port of Seattle, once headquartered at Pier 66, has since moved north to Pier 69, where it has joined the **Victoria Clipper** (see Ferries under Transportation in the Essentials chapter) in a huge white whale of a building. Next door is **Pier 70**, a picturesque barnlike structure.

Last comes **Myrtle Edwards Park** (see Parks and Beaches in this chapter), which winds back into more working piers (you'll often see container ships and auto carriers docked back here), the huge monolithic grain elevator (a waterfront landmark), and long strands of freight trains rolling by in their industrially elegant fashion. Keep walking north through **Elliott Bay Park** and you'll come to the **public fishing pier**. Farther on, this path leads to **Elliott Bay Marina** and the glitzy Palisade Restaurant (2601 W Marina Place, 285-1000), although this last is best accessed by car from Magnolia.

## INTERNATIONAL DISTRICT

*S Weller St to S Washington St between 2nd Ave S
and 12th Ave S; map:HH7*

Once known as Chinatown, this neighborhood on the southeast edge of downtown is anything but a frenetic, neon-lit miniature Hong Kong or Taipei. It's small and unpretentious, and serves neighborhood denizens with scores of tiny ethnic groceries and family-style restaurants, but offers little in the way of standard tourist attractions. Thus it makes a refreshingly *real* place to visit.

The history of white treatment of Asians in Seattle is not a pleasant one. In the 1880s, many Chinese were deported (returning only when their labor was needed to rebuild downtown after the great fire of 1889). Similarly, the Japanese were packed off to internment camps during World War II; when they returned, they found their community replaced by the interstate.

Alongside reminders of this difficult past is more inspiring evidence of the distinguished artists and writers who have emerged from this pan-Asian cultural center. Seattle's International District is both a collection of distinct ethnic communities (the Chinese have their own newspapers and opera society, the Japanese have a theater) and a cohesive melting pot (a community garden, museum, and neighborhood playground are shared by all). Look around—all over are buildings reminiscent of the type built in China's urban centers in the 1920s, businesses on the first floor and apartments with balconies above. Some larger balconies are the locations of former Buddhist temples. The influx of Southeast Asian immigrants and refugees has further enriched the mix of Chinese, Japanese, Filipinos, and Koreans. This cultural renaissance has helped infuse the district with a new vibrance. There are an increasing number of communities within this small international neighborhood, with the newest Vietnamese neighborhood

▼

**International
District**

▲

*International District*

expanding to 14th and Jackson. With an onset of new visitors to the I.D. due to the new bus tunnel terminus (Fifth Avenue S and S Jackson Street), more shopping centers and restaurants are beginning to emerge along Jackson and King Streets.

Jackson and King are the two central thoroughfares of the International District. Weekend mornings are busy with families shopping at grocery and import stores (some of which look as if they haven't changed in 50 years). This is a particularly good time for families to visit, to poke around in the mom 'n' pop markets and their yields of tantalizing Asian ingredients, and to stand in line for a jolly weekend brunch of dim sum.

A traditional Chinese breakfast can be had at **House of Dumplings** (510 S King Street, 340-0774). Or try **House of Hong** (409 Eighth Avenue S, 622-7997), a bit farther east, for dim sum. At **Kau Kau** (656 S King Street, 682-4006), glistening barbecued pork and roast ducks hang enticingly in the window. Nearby, **Shanghai Garden** (524 Sixth Avenue S, 625-1689) offers the cuisines of varying regions of China and what many consider the best Chinese food the city has to offer. Bustling **Sea Garden** (509 Seventh Avenue S, 623-2100) stays open late and specializes in seafood (try the fresh crab in black bean sauce). King Street is also home to one of the district's many traditional herbalists, the **Korea Ginseng Center** (670 S King Street, 682-5003).

A centerpiece of the neighborhood is the vast emporium called **Uwajimaya** (519 Sixth Avenue S, 624-6248), the closest thing this country has to a real Japanese supermarket/department store. Inside the tile-roofed building is a playground for the Asian gourmet, with huge tanks of live fish and rare imported produce. A cooking school here is well regarded throughout the region, and the market's second level houses **Kinokuniya** (587-2477), a branch of the largest Japanese bookstore chain in the U.S. To get an idea of the engaging contrasts of the International District, cross the street to the tiny **Hoven Foods** (508 S King Street, 623-6764) which, in much humbler fashion, sells excellent fresh tofu and soybean milk. A few doors up is **A Piece of Cake** (514 S King Street, 623-8284), a bakery that has achieved local fame for its marvelous fresh mango cake (and draws many from the suburbs into the heart of the district). Nearby is **Eileen of China** (624 S Dearborn Street, 624-0816), retailing opulent antique Chinese furnishings, from a $68,000 cloisonné elephant trunk to six-foot-tall Chinese vases and screens.

On Seventh Avenue is the **Wing Luke Asian Museum** (407 Seventh Avenue S, 623-5124), named after the first person of Asian ancestry elected to public office in Washington. With rotating exhibits and a permanent display of photographs, the museum sensitively chronicles the experience of early Asian immigrants to the West Coast. Across Jackson Street to the north is the main Japanese district, where you'll find a whimsical Japanese pre–World War II five-and-dime, **The Higo Variety Store** (604 S Jackson Street, 622-7572), presided over for the last half-century by the Murakami family. This is also where many of the I.D.'s Japanese restaurants are clustered, including **The New Mikado** (514 S Jackson Street, 622-5206) and the tiny, inexpensive **Koraku** (419 Sixth Avenue S, 624-1389). North on Sixth Avenue is **Nippon Kan Theater** (628 S Washington Street, 467-6807), known for its annual Japanese Performing Arts Series, and **Kobe Terrace Park**, with a noble stone lantern from Seattle's Japanese sister city of Kobe. Here, too, you'll get a splendid view of the district and Pioneer Square, including the **Danny Woo International District Community Gardens**, reminiscent of Asia in the compactness of their design and use of the terrain. The gardens were built in the late 1970s and parceled out to low-income elderly inhabitants of the district, who tend their tiny plots with great pride; for more information on the gardens, call 624-1802.

East of here on Jackson, the International District takes on a Vietnamese air. **Viet Wah** (1032 S Jackson Street, 329-1399) may look like a poor cousin of Uwajimaya, but it has an excellent selection of fresh and packaged foods at very low prices, and it can boast the most comprehensive selection of Chinese and Southeast Asian ingredients in town. Seattle has a well-deserved reputation for its fine Vietnamese restaurants, and this is where you'll find many of them: **Huong Binh** (1207 S Jackson, 720-4907), **Thanh Vi** (1046 S Jackson Street, 329-0208), **A Little Bit of Saigon** (1036-A S Jackson Street, 325-3663), and the tiny **Pho Bac** (1314 S Jackson, 323-4317), with its excellent beef soup.

## CAPITOL HILL

*Along Broadway, Pine St to E Roy St, and 15th Ave E; map:HH6*

Along the spine of Capitol Hill lies **Broadway**, the closest Seattle comes to the spirit of San Francisco's Castro Street. Nearly written off to urban decay, Broadway has experienced a dramatic (some would say excessive) revival in past decades, establishing it as the heady center for the city's trendy alternative boutique and street culture. Its free-stepping spirit is perhaps best expressed in Jack Mackie's inlaid bronze **Dancers' Series: Steps**, offbeat public art appearing at intervals along the sidewalk, which allow the stroller to get in step with the tango or to fox-trot down the boulevard. The haunt of punk-fashionable and mohawk-coiffed youth; a haven for black clothes, pierced body parts, and distinct attitude; Seattle's unofficial gay district; and the one place in town where the sidewalks are still filled after 10pm—that's Broadway.

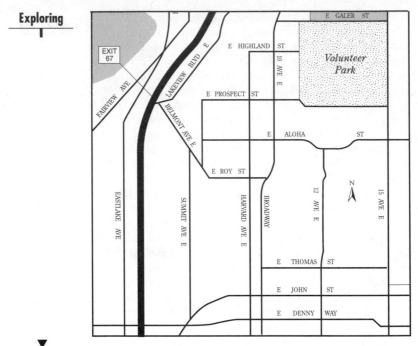

*Capitol Hill*

▼

**Capitol Hill**

▲

The commercial district extends roughly from **Seattle Central Community College** at Broadway and Pine to **Cornish College of the Arts** at Harvard and Roy, a lively 10-block walk or a slow-going drive. Best not to bring your car at all (it's a short bus ride and a great walk from downtown), since parking is tough. There are two decent parking garages, one near SCCC at the corner of Harvard Avenue and Pine Street, the other farther north, beneath Broadway Market.

The southern end of the district doesn't really begin to thicken with cars, people, and boutiques until **Dick's Drive-In** (115 Broadway E, 323-1300), one of the last remaining preserves of Broadway's less-assuming character. Food of most ethnic persuasions is available along Broadway, but one must take the minefield approach in pursuit of it. Sushi eaters should continue to stylish **Aoki** (621 Broadway E, 324-3633); Thai fanciers can find sufficiently tongue-searing dishes at **Siam on Broadway** (616 Broadway E, 324-0892); burger cravers will do well at **The Deluxe Bar and Grill** (625 Broadway E, 324-9697), full of the spirit of old-time Broadway; Italian foodies will be satisfied with trips into **TestaRossa** (210 Broadway E, 328-0878), home of the world's cheesiest stuffed pizzas; and **The Oven** (213 Broadway E, 328-2951) is a Middle Eastern fast-foodery of good quality and generous portions.

The glittering **Broadway Market** (between Republican
and Harrison, 322-1610), gargantuan Fred Meyer installation
notwithstanding, stands as an imposing symbol of the continuing million-dollar enfranchisement of once-funky Broadway.
The skylit Market features a few terrific shops and the futur-
istic **Gravity Bar** (325-7186). There's even a multiplex cinema
here, providing a pointed contrast with the old and ornate theaters that mark the north and south boundaries of the Broadway strip: **The Egyptian** (801 E Pine Street, 323-4978) and the
**Harvard Exit** (807 E Roy Street, 323-8986), both of which
screen excellent foreign films.

Vintage and imported fashion, books, and home accessories are the focus of the best of the Broadway shops. **Opus
204** (225 Broadway E, 325-1781) purveys fashions and exotica
from all over the world, while **RetroViva** (215 Broadway E, 328-
7451) and **Dreamland** (619 Broadway E, 329-8044) encourage
our kitschy, retro sides. On the other side of the street are an
excellent newsstand, **Steve's Broadway News** (204 Broadway
E, 324-7323)—well stocked for hangers-out—and a handsomely eclectic bookstore, **Bailey/Coy Books** (414 Broadway
E, 323-8842).

Finally, you'll meander to Roy Street, bounded by the quaint
stone **Loveless Building** and its sophisticated tenants, includ-  ▼
ing **Bacchus** (806 E Roy Street, 325-2888), a cozy Greek restaurant. Filmgoers and arty Cornish students gather at the **Harvard
Espresso Gallery** (810 E Roy Street, 323-7598) next door.   ▲

A fittingly schmoozy capper to a day might be a cup of coffee and a bite of dessert at any one of the coffeehouses along
the strip, which are as abundant in the pedestrian-heavy corners of Seattle as mushrooms in the rain forest. **Café Dilettante** (416 Broadway E, 329-6463) is a pricey Seattle tradition
and the cafe of choice for those who prefer to mainline their
chocolate. **Starbucks on Broadway** (434 Broadway E, 323-
7888) is another local success story, known and loved for its
mellow coffee roasts. The best coffeehouse, however, isn't on
Broadway at all, but resides on the corner of Belmont and
Olive: **B & O Espresso** (204 Belmont Avenue E, 322-5028), a
microcosm of eclectic Broadway (see also Desserts, Coffees,
and Teas in the Nightlife chapter).

The other main drag on Capitol Hill is **15th Avenue E**, a
little less flagrantly eclectic than Broadway. It starts around
Group Health Hospital at E John Street and extends north. The
strip is enlightened by a trio of good stores: **City People's
Mercantile** (500 15th Avenue E, 324-9510), a great general
store with a healthy, earthy bent; **Red and Black Books** (432
15th Avenue E, 322-7323), an issues-oriented collective bookstore; and **Coastal Kitchen** (429 15th Ave E, 322-1145), a loud,
fun, diner-cum-grillhouse with kickin' flavors from coastal regions worldwide.

Northeast of Broadway, **Volunteer Park** drapes its grassy lawns among the stately mansions of North Capitol Hill (see Parks and Beaches in this chapter).

## SEATTLE CENTER

*Between Denny Way and Mercer St, 1st Ave N and 5th Ave N; 684-8582; map:B6*

[KIDS] This 74-acre park just north of downtown, at the base of Queen Anne Hill, is the legacy of the 1962 World's Fair, one of the few to turn a profit and leave a permanent facility behind. The site was once a grounds for Indian gatherings; now it's the arts and entertainment hub of the city, and—even more significant to visitors—home of the Space Needle. The farsighted Seattle Center 2000 Master Plan has set into motion nearly $200 million worth of new construction, renovation, and improvements for over 40 Center projects, among them **Charlotte Martin Theatre**, a 480-seat children's theater which opened in 1993; the expanded and newly named **KeyArena**, a 17,000-seat arena which opened in time for the Seattle Super-Sonics 1995–96 season; and the extensive renovation of **Pacific Science Center**. In the works are improvements to the Opera House, Intiman Theater, and Bagley Wright Theatre, and the construction of the **Experience Music Project**, a museum celebrating Northwest popular music, scheduled to break ground in 1997.

[FREE] Seattle Center is open all hours with no admission charge to get onto the grounds (except during a few major festivals such as Bumbershoot), but **parking** can be a problem. The cheapest lots are located on the east side. For events at the Opera House, Arena, and the Intiman, the covered parking garage directly across Mercer Street from the Opera House affords easy access, but the egress is maddeningly long on busy nights. One way to circumvent the problem is to take the **Monorail** from downtown—a 90-second ride (see Buses: Metro Transit under Transportation in the Essentials chapter) which drops you off at the **Center House**. This cavernous building, with its vast selection of ethnic fast food, is the province of conventioneers, preadolescent hangers-out, and senior citizens dancing to the strains of a big band. On the lower level of the Center House is **Seattle Children's Museum** (see Museums in the Arts chapter), a world-class children's museum renovated in 1995, and **The Group Theatre**, Seattle's multi-ethnic, multi-cultural theater for the arts.

Next to the Center House is the **Fun Forest** (closed in winter), a small-scale amusement park with rides and an arcade. For fun of a different sort, the 520-foot elevator ride up to the **Space Needle Observation Deck** provides sufficient thrills, a history mini-lesson, and a heck of a view for your $7

($6 for seniors, $3.50 for kids 5 to 12). The ride is free if you're dining at the revolving **Emerald Suite** restaurant, but be forewarned: the restaurant is mediocre at best, and the prices reflect the stratospheric setting.

Just southwest of the Space Needle is **Pacific Science Center** (443-2880), five white buildings grouped around shallow pools and graceful white arches. The Science Center was designed by Minoru Yamasaki—the architect responsible for the inverted-pencil Rainier Square tower downtown—and features engrossing hands-on science and math exhibits for school-age children, and traveling shows aimed at all age groups. There are enough excellent displays, films, and demonstrations to keep a family occupied for most of a day. (Admission is $6 for adults, $5 for seniors and kids 6 to 13, and $3.50 for kids 2 to 5.) Other attractions include the mammoth-screen **IMAX Theater** and laser shows set to music.

Head north from the Science Center to the **Flag Plaza** (with flags commemorating all 50 states), and the **International Fountain**, shooting up enormous jets of water, sometimes synchronized with music and lights.

From here you can't miss the building that looks like a collapsed tepee. This is the **KeyArena**, formerly known as the Coliseum, the home of circuses, concerts, and the Seattle Thunderbirds hockey team, but best loved as the raucous home court of the Seattle SuperSonics basketball team. Cultural institutions reside around the fountain on the northern edge of the campus. The striking, neon-adorned **Bagley Wright Theater** (443-2210) is home of the Seattle Repertory Theatre company (you can arrange to tour the theater, [FREE]free of charge, from September to May). The Rep's old digs, the **Intiman Playhouse**, is now home to Intiman Theatre Company, while the **Opera House** accommodates the Seattle Opera, Seattle Symphony, and Pacific Northwest Ballet. Beyond the square is the **Mercer Arena** and **Memorial Stadium**, site of high school football and soccer matches.

▼

Queen Anne

▲

## QUEEN ANNE

*From Denny Way and Queen Anne Ave N up the hill to W McGraw St; map:GG7*

Seattle's Queen Anne is divided into two districts—Upper and Lower—joined by "The Counterbalance," the part of Queen Anne Avenue that climbs up the steep south slope and owes its nickname to the days when weights and pulleys helped haul streetcars up the incline. These are residential neighborhoods that demonstrate exactly what makes Seattle so livable: they're close to downtown but somehow far away, have sweeping views of two different bodies of water (depending on where you stand), and somehow retain a distinct character—a source of pride to their residents. Both Upper and Lower Queen Anne have lively commercial districts, making them fun places to explore.

**Lower Queen Anne** is anchored by Seattle Center (see listing in this chapter). This area also boasts some good restaurants: within a few blocks' radius you can eat Mediterranean, Middle Eastern, Japanese, Thai, and Mexican food. One of the city's least tasteful architectural landmarks is the huge, amorphous white building known to residents as "The Blob" (it's been home to a succession of bad restaurants, and is, at press time, a nightclub). **ACT Theater** (100 W Roy Street, 285-5110) is just up the street, and the neon-deco triplex **Uptown Cinemas** (511 Queen Anne Avenue N, 285-1022) just down. Consequently, the neighborhood abounds in late-night drop-in spots where you can sip espresso, nibble on dessert, browse for a book, or, in the case of **Larry's Market** (100 Mercer Street, 213-0778), do your grocery shopping sans the daytime crowds.

Move up the hill and the demographics become more residential. **Upper Queen Anne** is just 2 miles from Seattle's bustling core, yet its steep approach affords a measure of protection and isolation. This seems to be the territory of the big, expensive view house (and it is), but look closely: there are smaller, more modest bungalows and cottages among the condos. The big attractions up here are the glorious Elliott Bay views and the grand old-money mansions perched along a scenic loop—"The Boulevard"—on the hill's crown. Here you'll run right past **Kerry Park** (Third Avenue W and W Highland Drive), named for the timber baron, which affords a smashing view (especially at sunrise) of downtown, Elliott Bay, the Space Needle, and, on a good day, old hide-and-seek Mount Rainier. Farther west are more mansions in a crazy quilt of styles—Tudor, Dutch colonial, French gothic, shingle. The

▼

**Queen Anne**

▲

*Queen Anne*

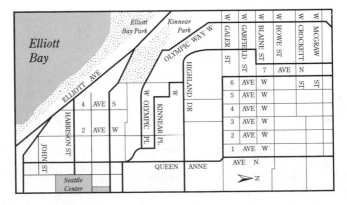

next stop, the **Betty Bowen Viewpoint** (in memory of one of the local art scene's great patrons), provides another perspective on Seattle's beauty: the Sound, West Seattle, the ferries, the islands. Kitty-corner is a little haven of peace and privacy, the rose-edged **Parsons Memorial Garden**. The rest of the loop—along Seventh Avenue W, W McGraw Street, and Bigelow Avenue—offers more fine scenery and stately homes. Below, off Olympic Way W, **Kinnear Park** rolls down the hillside toward the water with a sweeping view that includes the behemoth grain terminal, a familiar waterfront landmark marking the coming and going of some of the huge ships in the Sound.

Upper Queen Anne's thriving commercial hub, centered on two intersections at the top of the hill, is currently undergoing an expansion of the restaurant scene—as varied as the eateries, with more of a neighborhood appeal, of Lower Queen Anne. The newcomers are a welcome addition for those who call the Hill home, but other businesses—**A&J Meats and Seafood** (2401 Queen Anne Avenue N, 284-3885), **Ken's Market** (2400 Sixth Avenue E, 282-1100), and the **McGraw Street Bakery** (615 W McGraw Street, 284-6327)—have the status of local institutions. The **Queen Anne Thriftway** (1908 Queen Anne Avenue N, 284-2530), a local phenomenon, is not just an excellently stocked supermarket, but something of a singles hangout as well.

## LAKE UNION

*From Westlake at the south end of the lake up*
*Eastlake Ave E and around to Gas Works Park;*
*up Westlake Ave N to Fremont; map:FF7 to GG7*

[FREE][KIDS] Lake Union is the most central of Seattle's bodies of water, and the one most imbued with historical romance. It's also a flotsam-littered lake whose lingering boatyards are evidence of its industrial past. Its working character is passing, however, with much nostalgic gnashing of teeth, and the traditional uses of the lake are gradually giving way to spiffy view restaurants, condo complexes, and services for pleasure boats. Consequently, from different angles—a window table at a glittering eatery, the prow of a wooden rowboat, the grassy flanks of a lakeside park, or the pier of an old dry dock—schizophrenic Lake Union takes on many different guises. There's great variety in an exploration of its shores.

The southeast corner is the most accessible from downtown (via Westlake Avenue) and therefore has become the lake's commercial hub. A complex of restaurants crowds the shore, with excellent views of the lake and its docks. Further development up the south side has linked the piers with a wooden walkway and put little playgrounds here and there. These afford an accessibility to the water not previously available. The south end is also where the **seaplane charters** take off (see Air Tours under Organized Tours in this chapter), and where you can rent a classic wooden rowboat or sailboat from the **Center for Wooden Boats** (1010 Valley Street, 382-BOAT), a maritime museum that rents its exhibits for sailing on the lake (speedier vessels are available for rent from any number of other lakeside outlets).

The west shore of the lake is less accessible to pedestrians. Instead, head up the east shore, along Fairview Avenue. The efficient-looking vessels docked at Blaine Street are among nine **floating survey ships** belonging to the **National Oceanographic and Atmospheric Administration** (NOAA). You can arrange a guided tour of one on a weekday during the winter (call 553-7657).

The pretty pocket park (big enough for one blanket's worth of picnic, that's all) at the end of the next street, E Newton, marks the start of Lake Union's famous **houseboat strip**, a remnant of a floating community that once stretched along the Duwamish River and Lake Washington as well. Floating shacks were once a cheap, sequestered haven. Some houseboats are still hand-hewn in the old fashion, but over the years, enclaves of designer boxes have grown, vinelike, from the shore. (Remember: These picturesque homes and their walkways are private, so respect property rights.)

The grand park is on Lake Union's north shore: sprawling

▼

**Lake Union**

▲

*Lake Union*

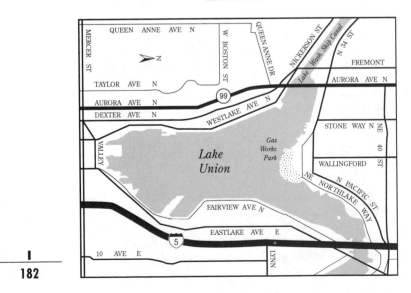

Gas Works Park, an industrial eyesore ingeniously transformed into a picnicker's and kite-flyer's heaven. Climb the grassy mound to enjoy the mosaic sundial and a view of the downtown towers just 2 miles away. The Burke-Gilman biking and jogging trail cuts east from Gas Works, a wonderful path winding clear up to Lake Washington's north edge.

Westward, past more dock trade, lies a wholly different attraction: funky Fremont, the self-proclaimed "Center of the Universe" and "Republic of Fremont." Once a seedy mini–Haight-Ashbury, this district (connected to Westlake Avenue by a bridge whose central spire houses a neon Rapunzel—flowing golden locks and all) has undergone a tremendous renaissance, making Fremont a terrific, if somewhat offbeat, outing. It boasts the city's most popular and populist sculpture, Waiting for the Interurban, and one of the most unusual, the Fremont Troll (under the north end of the Aurora Bridge), along with highly browsable antique, secondhand, and retro-kitsch stores with names like The Daily Planet (3416 Fremont Avenue N, 633-0895), Deluxe Junk (3518 Fremont Place N, 634-2733), and GlamOrama (3414 Fremont Avenue N, 632-0287). Stroll the pleasant park strip along the Ship Canal to Redhook Ale Brewery (3400 Phinney Avenue N, 548-8000), home of the Northwest's most visible microbrew. The brewery and its comfortable brewpub, the Trolleyman, are housed in the historic Fremont Trolley Car Barn, a brightly restored brick building, and are a great stop on the Fremont tour. From there, the canal path wends toward the old Scandinavian fishing enclave of Ballard, its famous locks, and the Sound beyond.

## FISHERMEN'S TERMINAL

*3919 18th Ave W, 728-3395, map:FF8*

A most authentic attraction, Seattle's bustling Fishermen's Terminal is the busiest of its kind in the North Pacific. Built in 1913, it was one of the Port of Seattle's first facilities and now houses nearly 500 commercial fishing vessels (ranging in size from 30 to 300 feet). It sits in protected Salmon Bay, the last stretch of the Lake Washington Ship Canal before it reaches the Ballard (Hiram M. Chittenden) Locks and meets the waters of Puget Sound.

Head out to the crowded piers to inspect the hundreds of trollers, gillnetters, and crab boats that make up the Northwest's most active fleet. Look for trollers (you can tell them by the two tall poles parked straight up in the air) and the big factory processors, where fish are cleaned at sea. The freshwater terminal is an optimal choice for fishermen, since the boats are protected from the corrosion and other problems of saltwater storage. Revamped in 1988, the terminal includes new docks, a large public plaza (with interpretive panels detailing the development of the local fishing industry), and **Chinook's at Salmon Bay** (283-HOOK), with its popular fish 'n' chips annex.

Fortunately, the working soul of the place remains: hardworking fishermen will be repairing their nets and scrubbing their vessels, preparing to return to the water. At **Wild Salmon Fish Market** (1900 W Nickerson Street, 283-3366), only feet from the boats, you can purchase fresh seafood for dinner. Time your visit with an incoming fishing boat and you might just be able to get an even fresher catch.

## BALLARD

*Along NW Market Street, Ballard Ave NW, and north to Shilshole and Golden Gardens; map:FF8–DD9*

Ballard began life as a company town for the Stimson Mill and has retained that independent flavor ever since it was annexed to Seattle in 1907. Hordes of Scandinavians flocked to the shores of Salmon Bay to take part in the lumber and fishing industries, creating a major enclave of Swedes, Norwegians, and Danes. Traces of the Nordic life abound, from the "Velkommen to Ballard" mural at Leary Avenue NW and NW Market Street to the Scandinavian humor of its residents, to its unofficial slogan of affirmation, "Ya Sure, Ya Betcha."

You can get a feel for the homeland along NW Market Street, Ballard's main commercial hub, from 15th Avenue NW to 24th Avenue NW. At **Norse Imports Scandinavian Gift**

*Ballard*

**Shop** (2016 NW Market Street, 784-9420), there are more trolls than you would know what to do with and lots of jokes at the expense of lutefisk and Danish drivers. The best deli is **Johnsen's Scandinavian Foods** (2248 NW Market Street, 783-8288), and at **Scandies** (2301 NW Market Street, 783-5080), Poulsbo lutefisk is available on Fridays (a tradition you may or may not want to try). The **Nordic Heritage Museum** (3014 NW 67th Street, 789-5707) displays textiles, tools, and photos from the old country and Ballard long ago.

Head southeast on Ballard Avenue NW, and you'll have a better idea of what the neighborhood looked like at the turn of the century—many of the buildings date back at least that far. This was Ballard's main drag in its early days up to the 1930s, when a ferry to the Olympic Peninsula was installed at what is now Ray's Boathouse on Seaview Avenue NW, which necessitated the east-west route that is now NW Market Street. Ballard Avenue is again best known for its saloons—now a slew of good blues taverns—which attract a crowd of an entirely different sort. **Conor Byrne's Pub** (5140 Ballard Avenue NW, 784-3640), formerly the Owl Cafe, is the oldest, and the **Ballard Firehouse** (5429 Russell Avenue NW, 784-3516) welcomes bands in this historic 1908 fire station.

The slightly industrial feel to these old streets remains, and many of the tenants of these old storefronts are woodworkers and cabinetmakers. It's still a fun stroll, though, if more for the ambience than the shopping. Some new, sleeker enterprises do exist right next to some Ballard institutions like **Vera's Restaurant** (5417 22nd Avenue NW, 782-9966) and **Hattie's Hat** (5231 Ballard Avenue NW, 784-0175), a dark little place famous for Swedish lingonberry pancakes and thirsty Scandinavians.

Across from the handsome flatiron building at 22nd and Ballard is **Marvin's Gardens**, a little pocket park dedicated to favorite local fixture and unofficial Ballard mayor Marvin Sjoberg. The columns here are from the original city hall, and were brought down by the earthquake in 1949. Nearby **Burk's Cafe** (5411 Ballard Avenue NW, 782-0091) is one of the brightest spots in the Ballard dining scene, known for its Cajun and Creole eats. One good way to get a feel for this area is to take a **Ballard Historical Society** tour. Call 782-6844 for information, or pick up a copy of their self-guided walking tour at the Ballard Chamber of Commerce (2208 NW Market Street, Suite 100, 784-9705) or area merchants.

You're never far from the water here. Down at the end of 24th Avenue NW is a lonely public pier; walk out to the end and you can see the boatyards that line the bay and the boat traffic coming in and out from the locks. [KIDS]The **Hiram M. Chittenden Locks** (3015 NW 54th Street, 783-7059) are a marvel out of an earlier industrial age. Here's where the channel connecting Lakes Washington and Union meets the Sound, the result of years of stop-and-start work that ended in 1917 when the Lake Washington Ship Canal was dedicated (and Lake Washington lowered 9 feet in the process). Now more than 100,000 boats per year (both pleasure and commercial) go by, on their way to or from the "water elevator," forming a sort of informal regatta to entertain onlookers. The descent (or ascent) takes 10 to 25 minutes, depending on which lock is being used.

Across the waterway, in **Commodore Park**, the falls generated by a **fish ladder** entice fighting salmon (sadly dwindling in number) each year, en route to their spawning grounds in Lake Washington and Cascade streams. You can watch the fishes' progress from a viewing area with windows onto the ladder: salmon in summer (peak viewing for sockeyes is in early July) and steelhead in winter. And with the salmon come the playful-but-controversial sea lions, who know a prime dining spot when they see one, feasting just off the locks much to the chagrin of salmon conservationists.

The locks are open from 7am to 9pm every day (call the **visitors center** at the number above to find out times for the daily tours). The green lawns and tree-lined waterside promenade of the park, along with the impressive rose display at the **Carl S. English Jr. Botanical Gardens**, make grand backdrops for summer picnics. (See Gardens in this chapter.)

▼

**Woodland Park Zoo**

▲

Farther north on Seaview Avenue NW, past all the view restaurants, you'll come to **Shilshole Marina**, where boat after boat after boat is moored right on the Sound's doorstep. Next on the road, **Golden Gardens Park** is the spot for a windswept beach walk in off-weather or for hanging with the suntan-lotion and boom-box crowd when it's warm.

From the Locks, travel north on 32nd Avenue NW, up to NW 77th, and then west as far as you can to a nothing-less-than-spectacular overlook of Shilshole Bay Marina and Sound, glorious Sound. Here, in any weather, you'll have a sense of the immense space of the water from your aerie high above it.

## WOODLAND PARK ZOO

*Park: 5201 Green Lake Way N; 684-4075; Zoo: 5500 Phinney Ave N; 684-4800; map:EE7*

[KIDS] Guy Phinney was an Englishman who wanted to turn his property into something resembling a proper English country estate. Woodland Park retains much of its previous owner's vision; no matter that six-lane Aurora Avenue plows right through the middle of it, dividing the property into two distinct areas. The east side of Aurora is the site of most of the sporting activities (lawn bowling, tennis, playing fields, minigolf, picnic areas, and Green Lake). The west side has the formal rose garden, the zoo's **Education Center Auditorium**, and

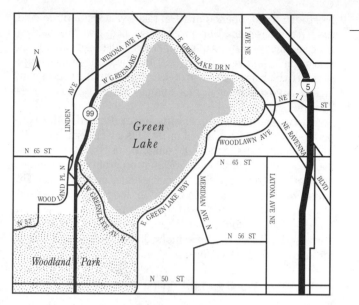

*Green Lake and Woodland Park*

the impressive **Woodland Park Zoo.**

One of the 10 best zoos in the country, the Woodland Park Zoo has evolved in the last 15 or 20 years from a traditional animals-behind-bars facility into one that provides lifelike representations of natural habitats ("bioclimatic zones" in zoo lingo). These continually evolving exhibits have garnered for the zoo more "Best Exhibit" awards than any other zoo in the nation. Among these habitats are a grassy **African Savanna** populated with giraffes, zebras, and hippos wallowing merrily in their own simulated mud-bottomed river drainage (the lions, though nearby, have their own savanna); the **Temperate Forest** with a marsh and swamp for waterfowl and waders; and **Tropical Asia**, with its **Elephant Forest**—whose 4.6 acres includes an elephant-size pool for some large-scale splashing, an Asian forest, and a replica of a Thai logging camp and Thai temple (this last serving as the elephants' nighttime home); and the new **Trail of Vines**, an adjoining 2.7-acre exhibit that takes visitors on an imaginary voyage through India, Malaysia, and Borneo with its display of orangutans, siamang apes, Malayan tapirs, and lion-tailed macaque monkeys. The **Tropical Rain Forest** explores the forest's layers from floor to domed canopy where tropical birds fly freely overhead. It's home to 20,000 plant species and more than 50 animal species—toucans and poison-dart frogs, to name a few. After the Rain Forest, visit one of the heavily planted **lowland gorilla enclosures** concealing a brooding troop of adults and their precocious offspring. The

**Northern Trail**, opened in 1994, takes visitors to three cold, rugged regions of the North with brown bears, wolves, bald eagles, and mountain goats. Interspersed with these exhibits are less inspired leftovers from the 1950s (the feline house, for instance), which await updates of their own. Coming renovations include **Australasia**, featuring animals from Australia and New Zealand.

On a tamer scale, the **Family Farm** (located in the Temperate Forest, and renovated in 1994) is a wonderful place for human youngsters to meet the offspring of other species. The zoo also offers a rich schedule of family programming, including orientation walks, classes, special events, and lectures. The **Rain Forest Cafe** is an indoor-outdoor food court (and a great place to throw a birthday party); *you* might not love the food, but the kids, no doubt, will. The entry fee for the Woodland Park Zoo is $7.50, $5.75 for seniors, $5.50 for kids 6 to 17, $2.75 for kids 3 to 5, and free for those under 2.

## UNIVERSITY DISTRICT (UNIVERSITY OF WASHINGTON)

*NE 45th St and 17th Ave NE; 543-2100; map:FF6; Visitor Information Center: 4014 University Way NE; 543-9198*

The University of Washington's parklike campus is one of the most beautiful and accessible in the nation. Just 15 minutes from downtown on the freeway, the 694-acre campus is the center of a vibrant and diverse community and is the Northwest's top general educational establishment. The university was

*University of Washington*

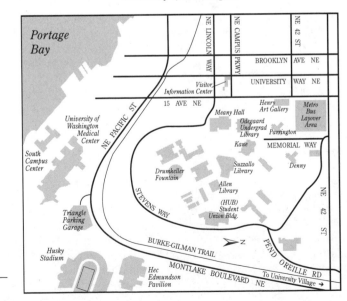

founded in 1861 on a plot of land downtown (now University Street) and moved to its present site in 1895. It is known for its medical and law schools, as well as its programs in international relations, computer science, and forestry, among others. Total enrollment is about 33,000. The university has suffered serious, state-imposed financial setbacks in recent years, but the tight budgets don't show to a casual observer—the campus has matured into a horticultural and architectural showpiece.

The **main entrance** to the university is on 45th Street and 17th Avenue NE opposite **Greek Row**, a neighborhood of stately older mansions occupied mostly by fraternities and sororities. This is also one of the entrances to the campus parking network (another is located on 15th Avenue NE and NE 41st Street), which allows you to park near your intended destination; explore a little on foot, and pay just $5 for the day. To the right of the main entrance is the **[FREE] Burke Museum** (543-5590), which houses a good collection of Native American artifacts and natural-history exhibits (see Museums in the Arts chapter), as well as a dandy basement coffeehouse and student haunt, **The Boiserie** (543-9854).

Stevens Way, flanked in April by brilliant orange azalea blossoms, wanders through campus offering strollers an impressive panorama of Lake Washington, Evergreen Point Floating Bridge, and the Cascades.

The **Husky Union Building** (the HUB) (543-1447) is where you'll find a newsstand, a cafeteria, and a branch of the University Book Store. From there King Lane leads into the heart of the campus, the **Fine Arts Quadrangle**. Home of UW liberal arts, the mellow gothic buildings and grassy lawns surrounding the Quad look like a stage set for the classic collegiate scene, and the rows of gnarled flowering cherries open spring quarter with a dazzling pink display. **Denny Hall**, the oldest building on campus, is the source of the hourly chimes which can be heard throughout the university area.

Turn left and walk down toward **Red Square**, a striking (if slippery when wet) marriage of brutalism with Siena's town square. The main parking garage is right beneath you. On your left is **Suzzallo Library** (library information, 543-9158), the main research library, with its ornate exterior and stained-glass windows. The new Allen Library addition (donated by Microsoft co-wizard Paul Allen) designed by Edward Larrabee Barnes offers a modern, marked contrast to Suzzallo's gothic style. Continuing around the square clockwise are the main administration building; **Meany Hall**, an exceptional venue for chamber music concerts and recitals; **Odegaard Undergraduate Library** (543-2060); and **Kane Hall**, site of enormous lecture classes as well as various lecture series open to the public.

If you head back between Suzzallo and the administration building, you'll reach **Drumheller Fountain** (Frosh Pond), a pleasant stopping point surrounded by the UW's acclaimed **rose gardens** and usually by a couple of stubborn geese. Look south for another winning view, the aptly named **Rainier Vista**. To the left, in what appears to be a clump of large evergreens, is the **Sylvan Theater**, a lovely hidden glade and pausing spot watched over by four towering white columns (which once graced the original University building in its downtown location). Rejoin Stevens Way at the vista, and curve around to the right, past the Forestry Department, Botany Greenhouse, and the old Architecture Department, and out the west gate of the university.

One block up is **University Way NE**, known to all as **the Ave**, a series of long north-south blocks jammed with shops and restaurants. If the UW is the brains of the U District, the Ave is its nerve center. The Ave has taken on a rather soulless quality in recent years, as family-owned businesses, funky secondhand stores, and hippie head shops have given way to franchise retailers and fast-food outlets. Pockets of cultural diversity and bohemian academia can still be found at intervals, however, as in the several art-house theaters found throughout the area (see Movies in the Arts chapter), and the vast number of unusual ethnic restaurants, excellent bookstores, and coffeehouses. In spite of rampant chainism (Tower Records, Pier 1 Imports, Starbucks), there's a decidedly underground flavor here, worth seeking out and evidenced in such stores as **Zanadu Comics** (1307 NE 45th, 632-0989) and **Cellophane Square** (4538 University Way NE, 634-2280). Duck into **Allegro** (4214½ University Way NE, 633-3030) for excellent espresso in the company of true denizens of the counterculture; or **The Blue Moon Tavern** (712 NE 45th Street), a few blocks off the Ave, where poet Theodore Roethke and novelist Tom Robbins held court for many years and Jack Kerouac (according to legend) and other beats did their inimitable thing.

Retail offerings on the Ave are hit-and-miss (with lots of vintage and import stores), but there are bright spots. **Folk Art Gallery/La Tienda** (4138 University Way NE, 632-1796) is full of select art objects and exotic crafts from several continents. On the next block is **Bulldog News** (4208 University Way NE, 632-6397), a browser's paradise where you can sip espresso while flipping leisurely through any of hundreds of periodicals on the stands. But the real bibliophile's dream is up the street at the **University Book Store** (4326 University Way NE, 634-3400), which occupies most of the block between 43rd and 45th Streets. This and the Harvard Co-op are engaged in perpetual rivalry for the title of biggest, best, and most varied university bookshop in the country.

When it comes to food, the Ave is not a paradise, but it's getting better. At the south end, **Big Time Brewery and Alehouse** (4133 University Way NE, 545-4509) offers good sand-

wiches with its brews made on the premises; **Shultzy's** (4142
University Way NE, 548-9461) purveys mostly homemade
sausages to crowds of loving fans; and **Toscana** (1312 NE 43rd
Street, 547-7679), unusually upscale for a student neighbor-
hood, serves fine Italian dishes. The area north of 50th has be-
come a haven of ethnic restaurants: **Tandoor** (5024 University
Way NE, 523-7477), an authentic Indian restaurant; **Caspian
Grill** (5517 University Way NE, 524-3434), with the fragrant
foods of Iran; and the endearing **Il Paesano** (5628 University
Way NE, 526-0949).

## BREWERY HOPPING

[FREE] Craft beers are no longer a West Coast exclusive: just
about any city with any pretensions (and some burgs with
none) has at least one brewery or brewpub. But the Northwest
is still craft-brewing heartland, with more and older breweries
and more varied and fuller-flavored brews than just about any
place west of Britain, Brussels, and Bavaria. Brewery tours and
tastings are still a favorite free or nearly-free attraction for rub-
berneckers on a budget. And most breweries stock enough
caps, mugs, sweatshirts, and other branded souvenirs for all
the beer-lovers on your shopping list.

▼

In Seattle, the old big daddy is **Rainier Brewing Com-**
**pany** (3100 Airport Way S, 622-6606, map:JJ6), a landmark industrial brewery whose big red "R" marks the south approach
on I-5 (free tours are offered weekday and Saturday afternoons). Far from the usual video torture, the introductory film
is the tour's high point—a snappy reprise of all that Rainier and
its wacky commercials have done to enliven Seattle television,
sports, and popular culture. Tastings afterward include Emerald City Ale, Rainier's covert attempt to mimic the micros' high-
ticket success.

**Brewery
Hopping**

▲

The new big daddy is **Redhook Ale Brewery** (actually
breweries), which has far outgrown the "micro" label and the
Ballard transmission shop where it started in 1982. In 1988,
Redhook moved its headquarters to the spiffy antique brick
trolley barn in Fremont (3400 Phinney Avenue N, 548-8000,
map:FF7). That location is now the company's bottling plant,
and offers the freshest pints plus good eats in the adjoining
**Trolleyman Pub**. Recently, Redhook went suburban with its
*new* main brewery, near Chateau Ste. Michelle and the
Columbia Winery in Woodinville's Fermentation Triangle. Its
**Forecasters Public House** is sprawling, airy, and a mite
stark, but a haven for bicyclists passing on the Burke-Gilman
Trail. Both Redhook breweries charge $1 for tours, but provide
a souvenir tasting glass.

The **Seattle Brewing Company** brews its Aviator Ales
and offers weekday tours at its own Woodinville plant (14316

NE 203rd Street, Woodinville, 483-3232, map:CC2); at press time, Seattle Brewing had plans afoot to open a second, smaller brewery and pub at 14655 Woodinville–Redmond Road NE, right in the Fermentation Triangle.

The strategically located **Hart Brewery & Pub**, in the shadow of the Kingdome (1201 First Avenue S, 682-3377, map:R9), brews an unbeatable range of beers: both the popular Pyramid ales and Thomas Kemper lagers (see below for Poulsbo and Kalama locations), plus seasonal specialties. Its pub is woody, noisy, and cheerful, and you should be prepared to be one of a cast of thousands hoisting a brew on game nights.

In-house pubs are adjunct operations for these larger craft breweries. At the opposite end of the spectrum are true brewpubs, which pour their potions only on their own premises. **Pacific Northwest Brewing Company** in Pioneer Square (322 Occidental Avenue S, 621-7002, map:O8), is the most upscale, with a huge, gleaming copper brew kettle for a back bar and cuisine that's many notches above usual pub grub. **Big Time Brewery and Alehouse** (4133 University Way NE, 545-4509, map:FF6) is a jolly collegiate rathskeller one block from the University of Washington, with a terrific collection of brewiana on the walls and surprisingly good ales on tap at predictably reasonable prices. (The "Bhagwan's Best" India pale ale, seasoned with cardamom and orange rind, is especially recommended.) West Seattle has its own very cozy brewpub local, **California and Alaska Street Brewing Company** (4720 California Avenue SW, 938-2476, map:JJ8), with on-tap ales named after neighborhood landmarks and with a chess set always ready for mental diversion.

The tiny **Pike Place Brewery** (1432 Western Avenue, 622-3373, map:J9) has no pub, but you can buy its popular ales on-premise or sample them at taverns all over town; because of limited capacity, some of these are contract-brewed at other plants. **Liberty Malt Supply**, just a couple of doors down (1419 First Avenue, 622-1880, map:J9), sells everything you need to brew your own. **Maritime Pacific Brewing Company** (1514 NW Leary Way, 782-6181, map:FF8), which replaced departed Redhook as Ballard's pride, likewise has no pub, but offers tours and tastings on Saturday afternoons and bottle sales every day. **Hale's Ales**, originally of Colville, then of Kirkland, has moved to Ballard as well (4301 Leary Way NW, 706-1544, map:EE8). Microbrewing pioneer Mike Hale has located his pub at the center of his brewery, with ringside seats on the operation; entering is the tour. Its taps pour all 12 of his delicately nuanced Hale's and Moss Bay ales.

The irrepressible Mike McMenamin, who has covered Portland with over 30 neighborhood brewpubs, has set his sights on Seattle. At press time, he's established three beachheads: **McMenamins Queen Anne Hill** (200 Roy Street, 285-

4722, map:GG7), **Six Arms** (300 E Pike Street, 223-1698, map:K2), and **McMenamins Mill Creek** (13300 Bothell–Everett Highway, Mill Creek, 316-0520). As you'd expect after so much practice, McMenamins has its brewing down; unlike most brewpubs, however, it also serves a fair range of competitors' products (even Rainier) and its own line of wines. Other McMenamins' pubs are in the offing, including sites in Fremont (with a movie theater as well), Green Lake, and, no doubt, a neighborhood near you.

At the opposite end of the scale from the McMenamin chain is the quirky, well-hidden **Seattle Brewers** (530 S Holden, 762-7421, map:KK7), which preceded, but couldn't preempt, the Seattle Brewing Company. Seattle Brewers is a neighborhood pub in the ramshackle industrial section of South Park. There's no sign, just a decidedly un-Botticelliesque sea nymph painted in a window, identifying the backstreet premises. Its indoor "beer garden" is brightly painted in tropical-beachfront kitsch, with parrots, palms, and howler monkeys above the bar. Open 3:30 to 7, unless someone's still drinking. Despite its name, the "Beach's Brew Nuclear Shit" goes down easier than most barley wines.

A ferry ride away is the popular **Thomas Kemper Brewery** (22381 Foss Road NE, Poulsbo, via ferry to Bainbridge Island, (360)697-1446). [FREE] Kemper produces lagers in various European styles, in contrast to the ales favored by other local micros—plus a hearty root beer and a great cream soda for teetotalers and kids. Even the latter will enjoy a free tour and tasting, and perhaps a round of croquet, volleyball, or horseshoes followed by a hearty pub lunch at its pastoral plant. True to continental tradition, more or less, Kemper really cuts loose for Oktoberfest in the last two weeks of September.

Finally, **Roslyn Brewing Company** (208 Pennsylvania Avenue, (509)649-2232) in the old coal-mining town of Roslyn (take I-90 east from Seattle), has a small taproom open on weekends from noon to 6pm. Here you can have a free taste of their flagship brew—a full-bodied lager— and buy a quart to take home. Roslyn Beer can also be quaffed at Village Pizza, the Roslyn Cafe, and The Brick. Those who want more guidance can get it from **Brewpub Tours Ltd.** (763-2739), which does what its name says.

## WINERY TOURS

[FREE] Until fairly recently, Washington vintners were used to being asked which side of the Potomac was better for growing their grapes. Now Washington State—the *other* Washington— is regularly included in any survey of the world's best wine-producing regions. With 90-some wineries, Washington is second only to California in U.S. wine production.

Although the first European grapes were planted here in the late 1800s, fledgling winemaking efforts were hurt by icy winters and limited demand, and Washington vintners resigned themselves to producing safe, sweet dessert wines from winter-hardy vines instead. It wasn't until the late 1960s that the potential of Washington's soil and climate was fully appreciated and the first real premium wines were made. Washington's initial fame came from its full-flavored whites; only in recent years have the red wines equalled and surpassed the whites in reputation. Though most of the grapes are grown in the sun-soaked Yakima River and Columbia River valleys east of the Cascades, the Seattle-area oenophile can find plenty of tastings close to home.

Most of the Western Washington wineries are concentrated on the Eastside. **Chateau Ste. Michelle** (14111 NE 145th Street, off Highway 202, 2 miles outside Woodinville, 488-3300, map:CC2) is the state's largest, occupying showplace headquarters on the 87-acre former estate of local industrialist Henry Stimson. This is a popular destination for locals and visitors alike, since the winery offers the region's most comprehensive tour and, in summer, a lively outdoor concert series. The manicured grounds are beautiful and provide lovely picnicking opportunities (you can buy picnic food to go with your wine in the gourmet shop on the grounds). The single-vineyard wines are the winery's most exciting, but winemaker Mike Januik also produces consistently well-made whites and reds with the Columbia Valley appellation. You'll get a different perspective on Ste. Michelle from across the street—at **Columbia Winery**, that is. Originally in Bellevue, this is one of the region's pioneer wineries. Its varied picnic facilities, where you can sprawl out after a wine-tasting (14030 NE 145th Street, Woodinville, 488-2776; map:BB2) are open daily and offer a pretty view of Ste. Michelle's grounds. To reach the wineries take the NE 124th exit from 405. Proceed east across the valley. Turn left at Redmond–Woodinville Road and left again on NE 145th.

▼

**Winery Tours**

▲

Now a part of Columbia Winery, **Paul Thomas Winery** (17661 128th Place NE, Woodinville, 489-9307, map:CC2) is widely recognized for both its classic vinifera wines (particularly chardonnay and merlot) and its value prices. Tastings at the new tasting room are available Friday through Sunday.

Smaller wineries provide an interesting counterpoint. To taste the wines from Silver Lake Winery, made by Chateau Ste. Michelle alum Cheryl Barber Jones, stop by **Silver Lake Sparkling Wine Cellars** (17721 132nd Avenue NE, Woodinville, 486-1900; map:CC2). There's not much to see here, but you can taste daily from noon to 5pm. **Facelli Winery** (16120 Woodinville–Redmond Road NE #1, Woodinville, 488-1020; map:BB2), inconspicuously tucked in an industrial office park, is worth a visit if just to meet one of the area's most exuberant (and entertaining) winemakers, Lou Facelli. Open Saturdays and Sundays, noon to 4pm.

Other worthwhile winery stops in the region are **Snoqualmie Winery** (1000 Winery Road, Snoqualmie, 888-4000), **Bainbridge Island Winery** (see Bainbridge Island in Day Trips chapter), **Hedges Cellars** (1105 12th Avenue NW #A4, Issaquah, 391-6056), and **Quilceda Creek Vintners** (5226 Machias Road, Snohomish, (206)568-2389). This last winery produces one of the best reds in the state, a fine cabernet sauvignon (it's the only wine they've made since 1979). Quilceda Creek is a small operation, and will show you around by appointment only. Tiny **Andrew Will** (12526 SW Bank Road, Vashon Island, 463-3290), another notable winery, is open only by appointment, and has quickly gained a reputation among wine cognoscenti for its luscious merlot and cabernet sauvignon.

## EASTSIDE

### WOODINVILLE

Not too long ago, a trip to Woodinville was considered a trek into the country. Two-lane country roads were the only way to get there and horseback was the preferred mode of transportation once you arrived. Times have changed, sort of. A trip to Woodinville takes just minutes from I-405 or 520 and while you won't see too many horses on downtown streets, Woodinville remains one of the Eastside's horsiest communities. There are, according to some, more horses per capita in Woodinville than anywhere else in the U.S.

In recent years, a host of other attractions have been added that draw visitors to the area. Woodinville is home to several of the state's larger wineries, most notably Chateau Ste. Michelle Winery; and Columbia Winery, located in the gingerbread Victorian-style house right across the street from Ste.

*Woodinville*

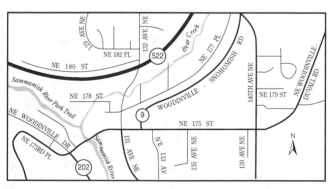

Michelle. (See Wineries Tours above.)

Running north and south from Redmond to Woodinville is a popular bike and hiking trail that winds its way alongside the slough. Be alert—you may spot some hot-air balloons coming in for a landing along the way. If you'd like to try ballooning, **Climb on a Rainbow Balloon Flights** (14481 Woodinville–Redmond Road, 364-8876) will gladly take you aloft.

For those who prefer to stay on the ground, a popular weekend bicycle trek starts at **Marymoor Park** in Redmond and rides along the slough to Woodinville, taking a short detour to Ste. Michelle winery.

Just up the road is the old one-room **Hollywood Hills Schoolhouse**, that now serves as a community center. Across the street from the schoolhouse is **Antiques at Hollywood** (14450 Woodinville–Redmond Road, 485-5555) with close to 100 dealers in one space, and **Pennsylvania Woodworks** (17705 140th Avenue NE, 486-9541), where furniture and decorative items can be purchased or custom-ordered from suppliers in the Amish country of Pennsylvania. **Between the Covers** (14450 Woodinville–Redmond Road, 481-9117) welcomes you to browse among its new and used books.

A short drive toward the center of town is **Molbak's Greenhouse & Nursery** (13625 NE 175th Street, 483-5000), a voluminous garden store (with a great gift store and cafe) which just might be the most popular downtown Woodinville stop for residents and visitors alike.

Another spot for picnicking is **Cottage Lake Park** (18831 Woodinville–Duvall Road). There's some lake access, although the county does not recommend the lake as a swimming area.

When people think of Woodinville these days, many think of **Fitz Auto Parts** (24000 Highway 9, 483-1212), just north of downtown. Acre after former horse-pasture acre of junked cars have been neatly arranged by Fitz and categorized for easy parts removal. The overall effect lifts the establishment out of the usual eyesore category associated with auto junkyards and raises it to something more like auto art.

While not technically part of Woodinville, **Theno's Dairy**, just down Woodinville–Redmond Road south of town (at 12248 156th Avenue NE, Redmond, 885-2339) is considered a traditional part of a jaunt to Woodinville. Rich and luscious ice cream packed high into all kinds of cones is as much a Theno's trademark as the life-size antique cow out front.

## BELLEVUE

It might come as something of a surprise, but there's more to Bellevue than lattes and hot tubs. This former quiet suburban hamlet has developed into a sister city of Seattle, boasting a downtown skyline of hotels and office towers. Bellevue is the heart of the Eastside, the region between Lake Washington

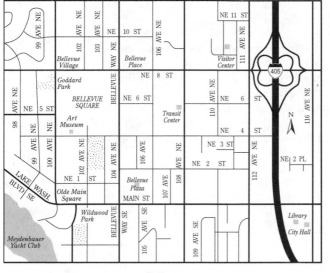

*Bellevue*

and the Cascades that is rapidly becoming the Silicon Valley of the Northwest.

While, truth be told, a lot of Bellevue does seem to be about shopping (one of the city's most recognizable landmarks is **Bellevue Place**, a hotel, restaurant, and chichi shopping complex in the center of downtown), it's managing its status as booming "edge city" by inserting little pockets of livability among the malls. Past the drive-through espresso stands, past the parking lots full of BMWs, and past the downtown skyscrapers of mirrors, granite, and glass, you'll find parks, streets lined with small shops, first-rate bookstores, and a surprising variety of ethnic food. All of which can be enjoyed without setting foot in Bellevue Square.

This is not to say there's no reason to visit the square itself. With more than 200 shops and eateries, the constantly metamorphosing **Bellevue Square** is the proverbial one-stop-shopping center. When you're there, plan to take some extra time to visit **Bellevue Art Museum** (301 Bellevue Square, 454-6021; map:HH3), housed (amazingly enough) in the top floor of the mall. The museum mounts rotating exhibits of local and national artists, from the avant-garde to the traditional. The adjoining gift shop offers a chance to find some truly unusual gifts. On nice days you can conclude a visit to Bellevue Square with a walk through **Downtown Park**, a 17-acre site in the heart of the shopping district across the street from Bellevue Square. Here's a 240-foot-long, 10-foot-high waterfall, a canal enclosing a 5-acre meadow, and a 28-foot-wide promenade, fine for strolling with or without the kids.

Art-fair lovers shouldn't miss the **Pacific Arts and Crafts Fair** (held the last weekend in July at Bellevue Square) attracting thousands of visitors and hundreds of artists from throughout the West. It is said to be the largest crafts fair in the Northwest, and local legend holds that it never rains on the weekend of the fair (Eastsiders plan their weddings and barbecues accordingly).

**Old Bellevue** (Main Street between Bellevue Way and 100th Avenue NE; map:HH3), a quiet street lined with specialty shops and restaurants, was the city's main shopping district before Bellevue Square was built in the 1940s. **Cocina del Puerco** (10246 Main Street, 455-1151), a cafeteria-style Mexican cafe, is fine for an informal lunch or dinner. For a more formal atmosphere try **Azaleas Fountain Court** (22 103rd Avenue NE, 451-0426), a restaurant of romantic Old-World elegance in an old Bellevue residence. Before leaving this part of town you might want to make a stop at **University Book Store** (990 102nd Avenue NE, 632-9500), the Eastside outlet of Seattle's famed store (minus the textbook and buy-back options).

East of town, out SE Eighth Street, is **Kelsey Creek Park**, a good place for suburban kids to get a taste (albeit a rather tame one) of the country. A demonstration farm offers up-close contact with pigs, horses, chickens, and rabbits. There are hiking trails for getting back to nature, and picnic tables for getting down to lunch. The **Japanese Gardens** once located here have been moved to Wilburton Hill Community Park (12001 Main Street); they're still dedicated to Yao, Japan, Bellevue's Sister City.

Also in the eastern part of the city is **Crossroads Shopping Center**, located at the intersection of NE Eighth Street and 156th Avenue NE. Crossroads is a midsize shopping center where the emphasis shifts from shopping to community events and ethnic foods, a comfortably low-key alternative to the city's other, glitzier mall. Visitors can play a game of chess at the giant board painted onto the floor (with giant chess pieces, no less) or choose from the menus of a growing number of ethnic eateries. Almost nobody passes up a visit to **The Daily Planet** (15600 NE Eighth Street, #33, 562-1519), one of the best newspaper and magazine stands in the area. A cinema complex (562-7230) at Crossroads offers eight first-run movies, and every Friday and Saturday night the center sponsors free live musical entertainment—featuring some of the area's most talented musicians, playing anything and everything, from jazz to polka (Thursday nights are open mike, for those who dare).

The neighborhood surrounding **Bridle Trails State Park** on the Kirkland border looks like a condensed version of Virginia equestrian country, with backyards of horses and stables. The park features miles of riding and hiking trails through vast

▼

**Bellevue**

▲

stands of Douglas fir. Day hikers can also explore **Cougar Mountain**, the forested, westernmost hill of an ancient mountain range that stretches from Lake Washington to the younger Cascades.

And for what some might describe as the quintessential Eastside experience, take a trip to Larry's Market (699 120th Avenue NE, 453-0600), where a mind-boggling array of goodies—including a sushi bar, fantastic deli, restaurant, and flowers—fuels one of the Eastside's hottest, er, social spots. Both Eastside stores (the other is in Kirkland) are open 24 hours.

## KIRKLAND

Somehow Kirkland manages a double life as friendly, low-profile town and burgeoning arts-and-boutique capital of the Eastside. The result, to date, is a city that demonstrates quite clearly the *good* reasons why people move to the Eastside. For many residents it's not the man-made attractions that account for Kirkland's high appeal, but rather its setting, hugging Lake Washington and enjoying more public access to the water than any other city on the lake's shores. Consequently, lakefront dining, lakeside walking paths, and lake cruises are staples of the Kirkland experience.

The best way to see Kirkland is to divide your time between the city's downtown area and its parks and trails. Plan a hike in the morning, followed by a browse through the antique stores or art galleries. Throw in a bookstore and some time at a corner newsstand, and you'll have a good feel for what the city of Kirkland has to offer and what the people who live there value.

There are several excellent places to hit the trails and enjoy the lake at the same time. **Saint Edward State Park** (take Market Street north and head west on Juanita Drive) is a densely forested park with a variety of trails that lead down to the beach. Also off Juanita Drive, a few miles before the state park, is **Juanita Beach Park**, a nice place for a walk any time of year. Piers surround the swimming area, pleasant places to be out over the water.

One of the best ways to experience Lake Washington is to visit **Juanita Bay Park** (access is off Market Street just south of Juanita Drive). Nature tours are offered the first Sunday of every month beginning at 1pm. These naturalist-led tours point out the great blue heron, the owls, the turtles, the beaver, and other varieties of wildlife that inhabit these natural wetlands and marshes. Even eagles have been sighted. Great care has been taken to preserve a non-intrusive atmosphere for the wildlife.

Other Kirkland shoreline parks include **O. O. Denny**, a favorite spot for wind surfers; **Waverly Park**, a secluded family-oriented beach park; and **Houghton Beach Park**, with

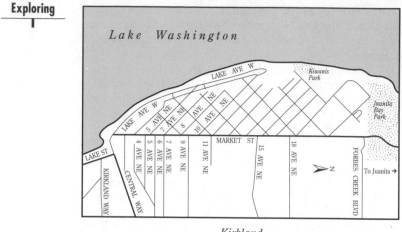

*Kirkland*

guarded swimming areas (in summer months only).

Shore up for exploring the urban wildlife with lunch at **Hoffman's Fine Pastries**, (226 Parkplace, 828-0926) a good spot for a homemade sandwich on bakery bread. **Peter Kirk Park**, which in many ways serves as the city's center, is right next door.

**Kirkland Antique Gallery** (151 Third Street, 828-4993), just off the park, is a fun stop for antique aficionados: more than 80 dealers have display space in the store, selling everything from antique tin toys to Depression-era glass. One block south of the park there are a couple of stores worth a visit: **The Dakota Art Store** (209 Kirkland Avenue, 827-7678), with wonderful art supplies and gifts for artists, and, next door, **Danish-Swedish Antiques** (207 Kirkland Avenue, 822-7899). Keep heading west along Kirkland Avenue toward the lake and you'll come to **Lake Street Bakery** (116 Lake Street, 827-0890), Kirkland's unofficial meeting and gathering spot.

Cross the street and head down to **Marina Park**, where a walk along the pier lets you look at the boats. On the way, you'll pass **DaVinci's Flying Pizza and Pasta** (89 Kirkland Avenue, 889-9000), a favorite socializing place, especially for the twentysomething crowd. In summer, the eastern wall of the restaurant is opened up, creating an open-air cafe. A quieter choice for lunch or dinner is the northern Italian **Ristorante Paradiso** (120 A Park Lane, 889-8601), where there are always extra anchovies available for the caesar salad, and incredibly good bread and pasta.

When the stomach is full, nourish the soul with a tour of the many **art galleries** in the downtown area: **Foster/White Gallery** (126 Central Way, 822-1205); **Howard Mandeville Gallery**, (120 Park Lane, Suite D, 889-8212); **Kirkland Arts**

Center (620 Market Street, 822-7161); and **Park Lane Gallery**
(130 Park Lane, 827-1462). **ALFI News** (115 Lake Street, Suite
104, 827-6486), a magazine and used-book store at the corner
of Lake Street and Central Avenue, will provide even more food
for thought.

If just looking at Lake Washington whets your appetite to
be out on the water, tour boats leave from Marina Park several
times a day from July through October. The 90-minute narrated
Lake Washington cruises are operated by **Argosy Tours** (623-
1445, $16.75 adults, $6.25 children 5 to 12), and run from May
until the end of October. While out on the water, don't miss the
chance to gawk at Microsoft founder Bill Gates's years-in-the-
making megamansion along the lakeshore in Medina, south of
Kirkland.

**Carillon Point**, south of downtown proper, was something of a controversy when construction began in 1989. The
luxury waterfront complex includes the Woodmark Hotel, specialty shops, waterfront walkways, paths, and benches. It remains a sore spot for residents who wanted to limit its scale and
density, but, at the same time, is viewed by others as a welcome
addition to the city. **Yarrow Bay Grill** (1270 Carillon Point,
889-9052) features fancy food at fancier prices, while downstairs the **Yarrow Bay Beach Cafe** offers simpler fare.

▼

Fortunately, the best thing about Carillon Point is free: the
view. Enjoy a walk around the grounds, tour the Woodmark
Hotel lobby, or rent a paddleboat and get your exercise on
the lake.

**Parks and Beaches**

▲

Round out your day in Kirkland with dinner. Residents like
**Izumi's Japanese Restaurant** in the Totem Lake area of town
(12539 116th Avenue NE, 821-1959) and **Shamiana**, serving
East Indian and Pakistani cuisine (10724 NE 68th, 827-4902).
For smashing lake views, try **Anthony's Homeport** (135 Lake
Street, 822-0225) or **Third Floor Fish Cafe** (205 Lake Street,
822-3553). For special occasions, **Bistro Provencal** (212 Cen-
tral Way, 827-3300) offers excellent French cuisine.

After dinner, drop by **Parkplace Book Store** (348 Parkplace Center, 828-6546) or, in summer, head back out onto the
lake for a sunset cruise. In either case, chances are you'll encounter just as many residents as tourists out enjoying a late
midsummer's eve in the city.

## PARKS AND BEACHES

[FREE] In 1884, Seattle pioneers David and Louise Denny donated to the city a 5-acre plot of land at what is now the corner
of Denny Way and Dexter Avenue N, and Seattle had its first
park. Since then, the park system has grown to more than
5,000 acres, many of them designed by visionary park planners
John Charles Olmsted and Frederick Olmsted, Jr. (sons of

New York's Central Park mastermind, Frederick Law Olmsted). Seattle's parks range from the classical (Capitol Hill's Volunteer Park, Washington Park Arboretum) to the recreational (Green Lake, Alki Beach) to the wild (Discovery Park, Seward Park) to the ingenious (Gas Works Park, Freeway Park). At last count there were 397 parks and playgrounds in the city of Seattle alone. The following are the best. To find out more about any of them, call the appropriate **Parks and Recreation Department** at the following numbers: Washington State Parks, (206)931-4178 (or (800)452-5687 for camping reservations and information); King County, 296-4232; Seattle, 684-4075; Bellevue, 455-6881; Issaquah, 392-7131; Kirkland, 828-1217; Mercer Island, 236-3545; and Redmond, 882-6401.

**Alki Beach** This 2½-mile strip of beach point marks the spot where the original white Seattle settlers first established homesteads. (The native American word *alki* meant "by and by," their wry comment on the pioneers' eager hopes of turning their settlement into the New York of the West.) Now the beach has many faces, depending on the season: cool and peaceful in the fall, stormy in winter, and jammed with cyclists and roller skaters in the summer. It is also regularly thronged with teenagers, who hang out along the Alki Avenue strip, lined with beachy eateries on one side, sandy beach on the other. Duwamish Head, at the north end of the strand, offers spectacular views, as does the Coast Guard-maintained **Alki Point and Light Station** (3201 Alki Avenue SW, 932-5800) at the tip of the point. [FREE] The scenic extension of Alki Beach continues southward along Beach Drive past windswept **Me-Kwa-Mooks Park** and on to Lincoln Park (see listing in this section). ▪ *Alki Ave SW; map:II9.*

**Bellevue Downtown Central Park** This 20-acre park in downtown Bellevue reflects the community's desire for an oasis in a busy urban area. Tired shoppers from Bellevue Square across the street come to sit by the fountain, enjoy the large formal garden, or stroll by the 240-foot-wide waterfall, which empties into a 1,200-foot reflecting canal. Teak benches placed throughout recall the park benches of London. ▪ *1201 NE 4th St, Bellevue; map:GG3.*

**Blake Island State Park** Once an ancestral camping ground of the Suquamish tribe, this tiny island in Puget Sound is now a densely wooded wilderness state park. There are 54 campsites, plus boat moorage (there is no ferry service to the island, except for commercial runs to the privately operated Tillicum Village, a staged-for-tourists glimpse of North Coast Indian heritage. The 15 miles of hiking trails access about 5 miles of beaches. ▪ *Information: PO Box 277, Manchester 98353; 443-1244 (Tillicum Village).*

▼

**Parks and Beaches**

▲

**Bothell Landing** This quaint little community park across the Sammamish River from the Sammamish River Trail offers rolling green lawns for family picnics and Frisbee throwing, an amphitheater (with Friday-evening concerts in the summer), a historical museum housed in a turn-of-the-century frame building, and an adult day center. Canoes and small boats can tie up at the public pier, where ducks await bread crumbs. There is limited parking at the site itself; a parking lot at 17995 102nd Avenue NE, Bothell, on the south side of the river, has additional spaces. ■ *9919 NE 180th St, Bothell; 486-8152; map:BB3.*

**Bridle Trails State Park** As its name suggests, this 480-acre park is a densely wooded equestrian paradise laced with horse trails (one links up with Marymoor Park) and even sports an exercise ring. Though you may feel like an alien if you come to do anything but ride (even the private homes in the area all seem to have stables), the park also has picnic sites. ■ *116th Ave NE and NE 53rd St, Kirkland; 827-2900; map:FF2.*

**Burke-Gilman Trail** See Bicycling under Outdoor Sports in the Recreation chapter. ■ *Gas Works Park to Kenmore Logboom Park; map:FF7–BB5.*

**Camp Long** [KIDS] West Seattle's Camp Long, run by the Seattle Parks and Recreation Department, has a variety of broader functions: as a meeting/conference facility (a lodge holds 75 people in its upper room and 35 in the basement), an in-city outdoor experience for family or group use (10 rustic bunk-bed–equipped cabins sleep up to 12 people at $24 a cabin), or simply a 68-acre nature preserve. The park also offers interpretive programs, perfect for school or Scout groups, and family-oriented nature programs on weekends. There's a climbing rock and a simulated glacier face for climbers who want to practice their technique. ■ *5200 35th Ave SW; 684-7434; map:JJ8.*

**Carkeek Park** Carkeek Park is 198 acres of wilderness in the northwest corner of the city. Forest paths wind from the parking lots and two reservable picnic areas (call 684-4081) to the footbridge spanning the railroad tracks, and then down a staircase to the broad beach. (Use caution around the tracks; trains run frequently through the park, and the acoustics can be misleading.) Grassy meadows (great for kite flying), picnic shelters, and pretty, meandering Piper's Creek are other good reasons to relax here. ■ *NW Carkeek Rd and 9th Ave NW; map:DD8.*

**Chism Beach Park** [KIDS] One of Bellevue's largest and oldest waterfront parks, Chism sits along the handsome residential stretch south of Meydenbauer Bay. There are docks and diving boards for swimmers, picnic areas, a playground, and a large parking area above the beach. ■ *1175 96th Ave SE,*

Bellevue; map:HH4.

**Coulon Park** This arboreal park on the shore of Lake Washington is the prize of Renton's park system. It has won national awards for the arresting architecture of its pavilion and restaurant concession (an Ivar's Fish Bar), but is best loved for the beach. Log booms around the swimming area serve as protective barriers for wind surfers. ▪ *1201 Lake Washington Blvd N, Renton; 235-2560; map:MM3.*

**Discovery Park** [KIDS] Formerly the site of Seattle's Fort Lawton army base, this densely foliated Magnolia wilderness has been allowed to revert to its pre-metropolitan natural order. It is full of variety and even a little mystery—in 1982 a cougar was discovered in the park, and no one knew how it got there or how long it roamed free in the 534 acres. Self-guided interpretive nature loops and short trails wind through thick forests, along dramatic sea cliffs (where powerful updrafts make for excellent kite flying), and across meadows of waving grasses. The old barracks, houses, and training field are the few remaining vestiges of the Army's presence. Discover the park's flora and fauna yourself or take advantage of the scheduled walks and nature workshops conducted by park naturalists. [FREE] There are free guided walks every Saturday at 2pm and bird tours Saturday mornings in spring and fall. Groups can also schedule their own guided walks. **Daybreak Star Arts Center** (285-4425) sponsors native American activities and gallery exhibits of contemporary Indian art in the Sacred Circle Gallery. There are two marvelously equipped kids' playgrounds, along with picnic areas, playfields, tennis and basketball courts, and a rigorous fitness trail. The network of trails is a favorite among jogging enthusiasts. ▪ *3801 W Government Way; 386-4236; map:FF9.*

**Fay Bainbridge State Park** About a 15-minute drive from the Winslow ferry dock on Bainbridge Island, Fay Bainbridge is a smallish (17-acre) park known for its camping areas and view of Mount Rainier and Seattle. The log-strewn beach has pits for fires; other features include a boat launch, horseshoe pits, and two kitchen shelters. It's a popular stop for cyclists on their way around the hilly isle. ▪ *15446 Sunrise Dr NE, Bainbridge Island; 842-3931.*

**Freeway Park** See Downtown Seattle in this chapter. ▪ *6th Ave and Seneca St; map:L5.*

**Gas Works Park** [KIDS] What do you do when the piece of property with the grandest skyline and lakeside view in the city is dominated by a greasy old gas-processing plant? You turn it into a park, of course. Gas Works Park represents urban reclamation at its finest. It's one of the city's most delightful parks, with a high grassy mound for kite flying, a large picnic shelter (call 684-4081 to reserve space), a wonderful play barn, and a front-row seat on one of Seattle's patented views. Against a sky full of dancing kites, even the looming works look oddly handsome. The threat of lurking soil pollutants, which closed the park in 1984, has been ruled out, provided you don't eat the dirt. Parents with toddlers beware. ▪ *N Northlake Way and Meridian Ave N; map:FF7.*

**Golden Gardens** Alki Beach's spiritual counterpart to the north, Golden Gardens teems with tanning humanity on summer weekends. A breezy, sandy beach, nearby boat ramp, beach fire pit, and the pretty waters of Shilshole Bay are the biggest lures, although fully half of the park's 95 acres lie to the east of the railroad tracks along the wooded, trail-laced hillside. ▪ *North end of Seaview Ave NW; map:DD9.*

**Green Lake** [KIDS] When the sun shines and the jogging, tanning, and roller-skating crowd musters en masse, the greenbelt around Green Lake looks like a slice of Southern California that's been beamed to the button-down Northwest. Even on dreary days the 2.8-mile paved circuit around the lake can be jammed with the Nike-and-Walkman set. For less competition, runners should try the outer 3.2-mile unpaved path. What is now the center of Seattle's exercise culture is the remnant of a large glacial lake that was well on its way to becoming a meadow when the pioneers arrived (hence the name). The city scrapped plans to turn it into a golf course or storm drain for I-5 and decided to bolster its declining waters with surplus from city reservoirs. This makes for balmy dunking (though on warm days the water can be rather ripe), superlative sailing and windsurfing, and great people-watching. Although the tennis courts, soccer field, indoor pool and recreation center, outdoor basketball court, baseball diamond, pitch-and-putt golf course, boat rental, thriving commercial district, and considerable car traffic around the lake make it feel like an urban beach resort, you can usually find one or two lonely grassy patches for a picnic. There's a well-equipped kids' playground on the northeast side. Limited parking can be found in three lots: the northeast lot (Latona Avenue N and E Green Lake Way N, the most crowded), northwest lot (7312 W Green Lake Way N), and the south lots (5900 W Green Lake Way N). ▪ *E Green Lake Dr N and W Green Lake Dr N; map:EE7.*

▼

**Parks and Beaches**

▲

**Hing Hay Park** Hing Hay Park (Chinese for "park for pleasurable gathering") is a meeting and gathering place for the International District's large Asian community. From the adjacent Bush Hotel, an enormous multicolored mural of a dragon presides over the park and the ornate grand pavilion from Taipei. A great place to get a feel for the rhythms of International District life. ▪ *S King St and Maynard Ave S; map:HH7.*

**Kelsey Creek Park** [KIDS] Kids are in their element at this excellent nature park, comprised of 80 acres northeast of the I-90/405 interchange. In addition to a variety of parkland habitats (marshy forests, open grassy glades, wooded hillsides), two barns and a farmyard provide an area where children can see newborn calves, goats, lambs, and piglets in the spring. Kelsey Creek and numerous footpaths (good for jogging) wind throughout. An original 1888 pioneer log cabin adds a historical dimension. There are also picnic areas and a small children's playground. ■ *13204 SE 8th Pl, Bellevue; map:II2.*

**Kirkland Waterfront** A string of parks, from Houghton Beach to Marina Park at Moss Bay, lines the shore of Kirkland's beautiful Lake Washington Boulevard. The kids feed the ducks and wade (only Houghton Beach and Waverly Beach have lifeguards); their parents sunbathe and watch the runners lope by. This is as close to Santa Cruz as the Northwest gets. ■ *Along Lake Washington Blvd, Kirkland; map:DD4.*

**Lake Sammamish State Park** The sprawling beach is the main attraction of this state park located at the south end of Lake Sammamish. Shady picnic areas, grassy playfields, barbecue stands, and volleyball courts are excellent secondary draws. Large groups must reserve day-use areas—the place can be overrun in summer. Issaquah Creek, fine for fishing, runs through the park's wooded area. ■ *20606 SE 56th St, Issaquah; 455-7010.*

▲

**Lake Washington Parks** This string of grassy beachfronts acts as collective backyard for several of the neighborhoods that slope toward Lake Washington's western shore. **Bicycle Saturdays and Sundays** take place in the summer, when the route from Colman Park to Seward Park is open to bicycles (closed to cars 10am to 6pm). **Madison Park**, the site of an amusement park and bathing beach early in the century, has shed its vaudeville image and is now a genteel neighborhood park, with a roped-in swimming area and tennis courts. If you head west on Madison and turn left onto Lake Washington Boulevard, you'll wind down to meet the beach again, this time at **Madrona Park** (Lake Washington Boulevard and Madrona Drive), a grassy strip with a swimming beach, picnic tables, a (summer only) food concession, and a dance studio. Farther on is **Leschi Park** (Lakeside Avenue S and Leschi Place), a nicely manicured city park that occupies the hillside across the boulevard. There are great views of the Leschi Marina and the dazzling spinnakers on the sailboats, as well as a play area for kids. Another greenbelt, **Colman Park** (36th Avenue S and Lakeside Avenue S), also with a play area, marks the start of the seamless strip that includes **Mount Baker Park** (Lake Park Drive S and Lake Washington Boulevard S), a gently sloping, tree-lined ravine; the hydroplane racing mecca—once a marshy slough, now a manicured park and spectator beach with boat launches—called **Stan Sayres Memorial Park**; and the lonely wilderness peninsula of Seward Park (see listing in this section). ■ *From Madison Park at E Madison St and 43rd Ave E to Stan Sayres Memorial Park at 3800 Lake Washington Blvd S; map:GG5–JJ5.*

**Lincoln Park** [KIDS] Lincoln Park, a 130-acre jewel perched on a pointed bluff in West Seattle, offers a network of walking and biking paths amid grassy forests, picnic shelters (call 684-4081 to reserve), recreational activities from horseshoes to football to tennis, and expansive views of the Olympic Mountains from seawalls or rocky beaches. There are tide pools to be inspected and beaches to roam, and the kids will delight in the playground equipment. Don't miss the (heated) outdoor saltwater Colman Pool (summer only), which began as a tide-fed swimming hole. ■ *Fauntleroy Ave SW and SW Webster St; map:LL9.*

**Luther Burbank Park** [KIDS] Luther Burbank's undulating fields and endless land-and-lake recreational areas occupy a good chunk of the northern tip of Mercer Island and make it the Eastside's favorite family park. There are picnic areas, barbecues, a swimming area, nicely maintained tennis courts, an outdoor amphitheater for summer concerts, a first-rate playground, several playing fields, docks for boat tie-ups (the haunt of the sun-worshiping teens in summer), and green meadows that tumble down to the shore. When the main beach is crowded, head north toward the point to find lonelier picnic spots. Parking is not a problem. ■ *2040 84th Ave SE, Mercer Island; map:II4.*

**Magnuson Park** This 193-acre park fronts Lake Washington just south of Sand Point Naval Air Base, with a mile of shoreline, a boat launch, a playing field, and six tennis courts. Adjacent to the north is **NOAA (National Oceanic and Atmospheric Administration**, 526-6046). You'll find a series of unique artworks along the beach (see Art in Public Places in the Arts chapter). One sculpture, **Sound Garden**, is fitted with flutelike aluminum tubes that create eerie "music" when the wind blows. The site is open every day from 6:30am and is a hauntingly wonderful spot to sit on a blue whale bench, listening to the wailing wind chimes and watching the sun come up over Lake Washington. ■ *Sand Point Way NE and 65th Ave NE; map:EE5.*

**Marymoor County Park** [KIDS] This vast expanse of flat grasslands and playfields is located in rural Redmond, a city considered by many to be the bicycle capital of the Northwest. Marymoor is home to the famed Marymoor Velodrome (see Bicycling under Outdoor Sports in the Recreation chapter) and serves as the starting point of the Sammamish River bike (or jogging or horseback-riding) trail. There are a lot of other resources here too: the Marymoor Historical Museum (885-3684), Clise Mansion, picnic facilities, a popular area for flying remote-control model airplanes, and about a zillion playing fields. ▪ *6046 W Lake Sammamish Pkwy NE, Redmond; 296-2966; map:FF1.*

**Myrtle Edwards Park** Myrtle Edwards and adjacent **Elliott Bay Park** provide a front lawn to the northern part of downtown. This breezy and refreshing strip is a great noontime getaway for jogging (the two combined form a 1.25-mile trail), picnicking on sea-facing benches, or just strolling. Parking at the Pier 70 lot just south of Myrtle Edwards is at a premium, but the Waterfront Streetcar stops nearby. ▪ *Alaskan Way between W Bay St and W Thomas St; map:B9.*

**Newcastle Beach Park** [KIDS] This Bellevue park takes full advantage of its waterfront location with a fishing dock, swimming area, and bathhouse facility (complete with outdoor showers). Walking paths—including a ¾-mile loop—weave throughout the 28 acres, and a wildlife habitat offers the chance to see animals and birds in their natural environment. ▪ *4400 Lake Washington Blvd S, Bellevue; map:JJ3.*

**Ravenna Park** This steep woodland ravine strung between residential districts north of the University District is a lush sylvan antidote to the city around it. At the west end is **Cowen Park** (University Way NE and NE Ravenna Boulevard), with tennis courts and play and picnic areas. Trails along burbling Ravenna Creek lead to the eastern end of the park and more picnic areas, a wading pool, and playing fields. The whole expanse is a favorite haunt of joggers, as is Ravenna Boulevard, the gracious, tree-lined thoroughfare that defines its southern flank. ▪ *20th Ave NE and NE 58th St; map:EE6.*

**Saltwater State Park** Folks use this 88-acre Puget Sound–front park for clamming (January to June only; call ahead for red tide report), picnicking, camping, hiking in the forested uplands, or scuba diving in the underwater reef. The views of Vashon Island and the summer sunsets are spectacular. ▪ *25205 8th Pl S, Des Moines; 764-4128; map:RR7.*

**Seward Park** [KIDS] This spectacular wilderness occupies a 277-acre knob of land in southeast Seattle and gives the modern-day Seattleite an idea of what the area must have looked like centuries ago. There are times when the park is imbued with a primal sense of permanence, especially on misty winter days when the quiet of a solitary walk through old-growth Douglas fir forest is broken only by the cries of a few birds. But other times—hot summer Sundays, for instance—Seward turns into a frenzy of music and barbecues. You can drive the short loop road to get acquainted with the park, past the bathhouse and beach facilities; **Seward Park Art Studio** (722-6342), which offers classes in the arts; some of the six picnic shelters (call 684-4081 for reservations); and some of the trailheads, which lead to the fish hatchery, the outdoor amphitheater, and into the forest preserve. Cyclists and runners can make an even better loop on the scenic 2½-mile lakeside trail encircling the park. ▪ *Lake Washington Blvd S and S Juneau St; map:JJ5.*

**Schmitz Park** Just east of West Seattle's Alki Beach is this 50-acre virgin nature preserve, full of raw trails through thickly wooded terrain. The largest western red cedars and hemlocks here are likely to be about 800 years old—seedlings when Richard the Lionhearted was leading his troops on the Third Crusade. It's a marvelous place for contemplation and nature study. No playgrounds, picnic areas, or other park amenities. ▪ *SW Stevens St and Admiral Way SW; map:II9.*

**Victor Steinbrueck Park** Pike Place Market's greatest supporter and friend is the namesake behind this splash of green at the north end of Pike Place Market. With the Alaskan Way Viaduct right below, the park can be quite noisy during peak traffic hours. It also tends to be a favorite hangout for street people. Despite those caveats, the park's grassy slopes and tables make a fine place for a Market picnic, and the view of the blue bay and ferry traffic is refreshing. ▪ *Western Ave and Virginia St; 684-4080; map:H8.*

**Volunteer Park** [KIDS] Mature trees, circling drives, grassy lawns, and lily ponds make this the most elegant of Seattle's parks—as stately as the mansions that surround it. Designed by the Olmsted brothers, and dedicated to those who fought in the Spanish–American War, Volunteer Park's 44.5 acres grace the top of Capitol Hill and offer sweeping views of the Space Needle, the Sound, and the Olympic Mountains. At the north end of the main concourse lies the elaborate **Volunteer Park Conservatory** (15th Avenue and Galer Street, 684-4743), with three large greenhouse wings filled with flowering plants, cacti, and tropical flora. [KIDS][FREE] It's open (free of charge) to the public. At the other end of the main concourse is an old 75-foot water tower, which the hardy can climb for a splendid view of the city and the Cascades. In between is the **Seattle Asian Art Museum** (1400 E Prospect, 654-3100), with one of the most extraordinary collections of Asian art in the nation. For the kids, there's a play area near the main entrance, east of the conservatory. ▪ *15th Ave E and E Prospect St; map:GG6.*

**Washington Park Arboretum** See Gardens in this chapter. ▪ *E Madison and Lake Washington Blvd E; 543-8800; map:GG7.*

**Waterfall Gardens** How many city downtowns can boast a park with a 22-foot crashing waterfall, even an artificial one?

The waterfall in this tiny Pioneer Square park was built to honor the United Parcel Service, which started in this location in 1907. It does crash (this is no place for quiet conversation), and the benches do fill up by noon on weekdays, but the park makes for a marvelous little nature fix in the middle of a busy urban day. ▪ *219 2nd Ave S; 624-6096; map:P8.*

**Waterfront Park** A park that spans three piers between the Aquarium and Pier 57 provides a break from the bustling activity of the rest of the waterfront. The park contains a tree-encircled courtyard, raised platforms with telescopes for a voyeur's view of the bay and islands, plenty of benches, and—strange for a park in this town—nary a blade of grass. ▪ *Pier 57 to Pier 61 on Alaskan Way; map:J9.*

**Weyerhaeuser/King County Aquatics Center** This aquatics center was originally built for the 1990 Goodwill Games. Its two different pools are now open for public use (except when state or national competitions are held). The diving pool stages 1-, 3-, 5-, 7.5-, and 10-meter platforms, and 1- and 3-meter springboards; the Olympic-size competition pool is one of the nation's fastest due to surge gutters that prevent much wave action; and the recreation pool is handicapped-accessible and runs a bit warmer than most for therapeutic purposes. Prices are $1.40 for the recreation pool, $2.25 for a lap swim in the competition pool. The dive pool is open to diving teams only. Call ahead for schedule. ▪ *650 SW Campus Dr, Federal Way; (206)927-5173.*

**Woodland Park** [KIDS] See Woodland Park Zoo in this chapter. ▪ *5500 Phinney Ave N; 684-4800; map:FF7.*

## GARDENS

Mild and moist of climate, the maritime Northwest ranks among the world's best places for gardening. The native flora are both abundant and varied, including towering Douglas firs and tiny calypso orchids, spectacular rhododendrons which set the mountain trails ablaze in May, and the subtle greenery of maidenhair ferns. Not surprisingly, Seattle is a green city; corporate headquarters and tiny urban yards alike are swathed in gardens that spill down sidewalk strips into vacant lots and traffic circles. Dramatic container gardens encircle tall office buildings, baskets dripping with flowers decorate window and lamppost, and community gardens, called P-Patches, beautify unused city property. Downtown roof-tops and terraces are green with gardens and Freeway Park drapes the midcity interchanges with verdant curtains of ivy, the incessant roar of the traffic obscured by whispering stands of bamboo. The University of Washington's campus is rich with trees, and its Medicinal Herb Garden is jammed with herbal simples.

Volunteer Park on Capitol Hill boasts magnificent specimen trees and a splendid Victorian conservatory overflowing with flowers.

Here are some of the area's public gardens, most of which may be visited without charge.

**The Bloedel Reserve** Since the late 1980s, this 150-acre Bainbridge Island estate has been open to the public on a limited basis. The manse, which overlooks Puget Sound, is now a visitors center where interpretive material is available to guide one's walk through the property. The parklike grounds contain a number of theme gardens, including a Japanese garden with cloud pruned pines, a Zen sand garden, and a moss garden full of intriguing native plants. A series of nature trails lead through native woods and wetlands. A small pond attracts birds in increasing numbers as its plantings mature. Not a place for a family picnic or a romp with the dog; reservations for entrance are required (and limited). Call in advance during the busy spring months. Open Wednesday through Sunday (except federal holidays) from 10am to 4pm. Admission is $6, $4 for seniors and children. [FREE] Children under five are free. ▪ *7571 NE Dolphin Dr, Bainbridge Island; 842-7631; Wed–Sun.*

**Carl S. English Jr. Botanical Gardens** [FREE] One of the region's great horticulturists, Carl English made Seattle a horticultural hotspot earlier in the century through his plant- and seed-collecting efforts. Here one can explore 7 acres of gardens containing over 5,000 species of plants, including English's personal arboretum. Rare ornamental trees and shrubs from all over the temperate world are underplanted with beds holding flowering plants in similarly rich variety. The English gardens are worth a visit even in winter, when the tapestry of bark and berry and the perfume of winter-flowering plants will brighten the grayest day. In summer the Seattle Fuchsia Society's display garden enlivens the spacious lawns, where one can picnic and watch the boats make their way through the lock systems that connect Lake Washington to Puget Sound. The garden is open from 7am to 9pm every day; guided tours of the locks, fish ladder, and garden are held daily (June 1 through September 30), and on weekends (from October 1 to May 31), but special in-depth tours can be arranged. Admission is free. ▪ *Hiram M. Chittenden Locks; 3015 NW 54th St; 783-7059; map:FF9.*

**The Gardens at Children's Hospital** [FREE] Parents, patients, and visitors alike find comfort and pleasure in the handsome perennial and mixed borders found on the hospital grounds. The main borders are found across from Lot 3 (off the main entry road), running along the sidewalk and down a staggered flight of shallow steps. Each bay of the stairway is filled with unusual border plants arranged in sensitive color runs. At every turn, plants in orchestrated combination present delightful contrasts of color, texture, and form, ably demonstrating the precepts of the English country-garden style. The grounds hold several other landscape areas, including an extensive heather collection housed near Lot 6 at the southeast corner of the hospital. The gardens are open to the public at all times. ▪ *Children's Hospital and Medical Center; 4800 Sand Point Way NE; 527-3889; map:EE5.*

**The Herbfarm** This country herb nursery has grown into a thriving family business offering herbs living and dried as well as a multitude of herbal products and herb-related gifts. Hundreds of herbs are grown on the premises, and some 17 herbal theme gardens demonstrate their looks and habits in the garden setting. A mature herb garden holds culinary and medicinal herbs as well as flowers for drying. Among the newer gardens are a fragrance garden, a cook's garden, a pioneer garden of herbs common a century or so ago, and a plot holding plants mentioned in the writings of Shakespeare. Tours of the gardens and greenhouses are offered on spring and summer weekends (or by appointment for groups). Annual events include herbal-crafts classes and workshops, and a variety of seasonal festivals; call for specific information. Picnickers are always welcome and an intimate, nationally renowned restaurant provides cooking demonstrations and meals based on the Northwest's bounty and the gardens' harvest. (Advance reservations required; see Restaurants chapter). ▪ *32804 Issaquah–Fall City Rd, Fall City; 25 miles east of Seattle; 784-2222 or (800) 866-4372.*

**Lakewold Gardens** The shores of Tacoma's Gravelly Lake are lined with wonderful old homes, among which Lakewold is outstanding for its landscaped grounds and gardens. Once the Wagner family home, Lakewold is now open to the public, its extensive plantings maintained by a nonprofit foundation. Much of the property is wooded, its native trees mingling with rare Asian species, and much of it is underplanted with a large collection of rhododendrons and azaleas. Formal gardens of roses, herbs, and topiary near the house give way to an open lawn that slopes down to the water, broken near the shore by a large alpine garden and several perennial plantings. At the garden's center stands a "wolf tree", a gnarled fir too misshapen to be cut when the old growth was logged, which now shelters a shady fern garden. Naturalistic woodland walks thread through mature stands of trees on either side, punctuated by collectors' treasures such as species peonies, blue Himalayan poppies, and towering Cardiocrinum lilies. Garden hours are 10am to 3pm Monday, Thursday, and Friday (October 1 through March), and 10am to 4pm Thursday through Monday (April 1 through September). ▪ *12317 Gravelly Lake Dr SW, Tacoma; (206) 584-3360.*

**Pacific Rim Bonsai Collection** [FREE] The corporate headquarters of America's biggest timber business also houses a
pair of significant plant collections, both open to the public (see
next listing). Frequently changing exhibits showcase the
diminutive gems of the bonsai collection, including a thousand-
year-old dwarf Sierra juniper, tiny pines, and a mature se-
quoia—usually among the tallest of trees—a mere 3 feet in
height. Many of the plants are displayed in pots, but some are
arranged in complex landscapes or miniature forests (children
find these very appealing). On alternate Sundays at 2pm from
mid-April through mid-October, professional bonsai artists
demonstrate pruning, propagation, and caretaking techniques.
Tours are Sunday at noon or by appointment. Open 11am to
4pm June through February (closed Thursday and Friday),
and 10am to 4pm March through May (closed Thursday). ■
*Weyerhaeuser Way S (Weyerhaeuser Company), Federal Way;
(206) 924-5206.*

**Rhododendron Species Foundation** The Foundation's plantings encompass the largest, most comprehensive collection of
rhododendron species and hybrids in the world. This as much
a preserve as a garden—more than 60 of the over 500 species
growing here are endangered in the wild. The Foundation's
goals—the preservation, distribution, and display of rhododendrons—are met through research and education programs. A pair of study gardens are open throughout the year,
so visitors can observe the rhododendron family's changing
beauties through the seasons; while most are spring bloomers,
others peak in winter or summer, and many deciduous species
take on magnificent fall foliage color. Ferns, an ideal companion plant, are well represented, and the Foundation hopes that
in time this collection, too, will rank among the world's most
complete. Hours and courtyard space are shared with the Pacific Rim Bonsai Collection (see listing in this section). Admission is $3.50, students and seniors $2.50. Children under 12
are admitted free. ■ *Weyerhaeuser Way S (Weyerhaeuser
Company), Federal Way; (206) 661-9377.*

**Seattle Tilth Demonstration Gardens** [FREE] Urban gardeners
find a world of practical assistance at the Tilth gardens on the
grounds of Wallingford's Good Shepherd Center. Self-guided
instructional walks lead visitors through the gardens and an impressive array of composting units. Travel at your own pace, ab-
sorbing information from the explanatory signs provided at
each step. The thriving gardens are tended organically, kept
healthy through natural pest controls and environmentally
sound horticultural practices. One Tilth program trains master
composters who take their skills to the community, teaching
apartment dwellers and home owners alike how to deal con-
structively with yard and kitchen wastes (schoolkids especially

love learning to make and maintain worm bins). Edible landscaping is a specialty here, but many of the 1,200 plants grown are ornamental (including edible flowers). A lovely dry border showcases perennials, shrubs, and bulbs that tolerate drought, pollution, and other urban challenges. This midcity oasis of living greenery serves everyone from raw beginners interested in learning how to prepare soil and sow carrots to advanced gardeners who preserve and trade heritage vegetables or rare border plants. Numerous workshops and classes are offered. [KIDS] The Children's Garden lets young green thumbs practice organic and sustainable gardening, too. ■ *4649 Sunnyside Ave N (Good Shepherd Center); 633-0451; map:FF7.*

**Washington Park Arboretum** All year round, **Washington Park Arboretum** is as full of people as it is trees. Naturalists and botanists rub elbows with serious joggers and casual walkers, for this 200-acre public park doubles as a botanical research facility for the nearby University of Washington. The Arboretum stretches from Foster Island, just off the shores of Lake Washington, through the Montlake and Madison Park neighborhoods, its rambling trails screened from the houses by thick greenbelts of trees and shrubs. More than 5,000 varieties of woody plants are arranged by family; pick up maps or an illustrated guide at the visitors center if you want to find specific trees.

From spring until autumn, the Arboretum's **Japanese Garden** is well worth a visit (call 684-4725 for event and open schedules). Found just off Lake Washington Boulevard E, which winds north-south through the park, this authentic garden was constructed in 1960 under the direction of Japanese landscape architect Juki Iida. Several hundred tons of rock hauled from the Cascades were incorporated into the design, as were stone lanterns donated by the city of Kobe and a teahouse sent by the governor of Tokyo, where tea ceremonies were performed even before the surrounding garden was completed. Nowadays visitors stroll winding paths, admiring trees and shrubs pruned as living sculptures. The graceful carp pond, spanned by traditional bridges of wood and stone and lined with water plants, is home to countless ducks, herons, and muskrats. Though the original **teahouse** was destroyed by vandals many years ago, it has since been replaced, and the tea ceremony is still performed on the third Saturday of each month. The Japanese Garden (1502 Lake Washington Boulevard E, 684-4725) is open daily at 10am, March through November; closing times vary seasonally. There is a modest entry fee ($2).

Just across the road to the north runs **Azalea Way**, a wide, grassy thoroughfare that winds through the heart of the Arboretum. (No jogging is permitted on this popular walk.) Al-

ways pleasant, Azalea Way is magnificent in April and May
when its blossoming shrubs are joined by scores of companion
dogwoods and ornamental cherries. Side trails lead through
the Arboretum's extensive camellia and rhododendron groves
(the latter collection is world-famous). Follow Azalea Way to
the copper-roofed **Visitors Center**, where you can find maps
and Arboretum guides as well as horticulturally related books,
gifts, and informational displays. **[FREE]**On Sundays at 1pm,
guided tours begin at the Center, which is open from 10am to
4pm on weekdays and noon to 4pm on weekends.

North of the visitors center, a waterfront nature trail winds
along the marshy shoreline to **Foster Island**, a sanctuary for
birds and bird-watchers and a haven for canoeists, swimmers,
fishermen, and picnickers. **[KIDS]** To explore the shoreline by
boat, rent a canoe from the **University of Washington Waterfront Activities Center**. The Arboretum is open from sunrise to sunset. ■ *2300 Arboretum Dr E; 543-8800; map:GG6.*

## Woodland Park Rose Garden
Seattle's rose garden offers gar-
deners a chance to evaluate the regional performance of several hundred kinds of roses. Two acres of permanent plantings
hold some 5,000 shrubs, both old-fashioned varieties and modern hybrids. Newest of all are the unnamed roses grown each
year in the Seattle Rose Society's trial beds. Here likely candi-
dates are tested for two years; the best of the bunch will become All-America Rose Selections. The Seattle Rose Society
offers rose care and pruning demonstrations at the appropriate
seasons (call for specific information). The zoo next door offers
some interesting landscaping as well, using both native plants
and hardy exotics to create tropical atmospheres suitable for
the animal exhibits. ■ *5500 Phinney Ave N; 684-4040;
map:EE7.*

## PUBLIC ACCESS

Seattle is home to a wealth of public access spaces. These wonderful street-end parks, shoreline beaches, and garden terraces
have been set aside for you to enjoy, thanks to land-use laws
which mandate or encourage developers to set aside common
spaces for the public.

There are more than 100 designated public access spaces
in and around Seattle. Listed below are a few of the best. With
one exception, these pockets of respite amid the urban rat race
are free. Keep an eye out, though, to discover others on your
own. They may be walkways, bikeways, viewpoints, or merely
an overgrown path between two buildings fronting the shoreline. Some have signs indicating public access, others don't.
These are the hidden and intimate spaces that give the city its
charm and reflect its unique character. For more information

about public access, call the **Department of Construction and Land Use (DCLU)** at 684-8875.

## DOWNTOWN

**Columbia Seafirst Center 73rd Floor Viewing Area** You have to shell out $3.50 to ascend to the highest viewing area in the city, but you can enjoy the panorama from the warmth of the great indoors, and it's less than you'd pay (and far less *touristy*) for a trip up the more widely visited Space Needle. Purchase tickets at the information desk on ground level. Children under 7 are free, seniors and students are $1.75. Open Monday through Friday, 8:30am to 4:30pm, except for bank holidays. ■ *701 5th Ave; map:N6.*

**Public Safety Building 12th Floor** Step off the elevator that leads to the Mayor's Office, head out the door to the rooftop terrace, and you'll find a nice spot to eat lunch—complete with terrific views of the city. You can't fight City Hall, but at least you can share the view with the top brass. ■ *600 4th Ave; map:N7.*

**One and Two Union Squares** Several levels of outdoor terraces and garden plazas offer a great place to escape the downtown bustle. The sophisticated, cosmopolitan design and landscaping include an Italian-style frieze running along a row of fruit trees three stories up from the street. The one-story rockery with cascading water is a popular place to perch and soak up the sun. ■ *600 University St (between Union and University Sts and 6th and 7th Aves); map:K5.*

▼

**Public Access**

▲

## SOUTH SEATTLE

**Diagonal Avenue South Public Shoreline Access (Terminal 108)** This 1.2-acre park on the Duwamish Waterway was developed by the Port of Seattle in the heart of the working waterfront. Tugs and tows steam up the channel only yards away, and there are interesting interpretive signs which describe the history and ecology of this estuary. You'll find a canoe-and-kayak launching site, picnic benches, and parking spaces, too. ■ *Diagonal Ave S and E Marginal Way (take a right onto Diagonal Ave S at second stoplight on Marginal Way heading south off the viaduct); map:KK8.*

## WEST SEATTLE

**West Seattle Weather Watch Park** The Alki community of West Seattle has lovingly created this small street-end park to honor its local history and pay tribute to the neighborhood's beautiful beach environment. The aptly named park offers an expansive view across Puget Sound to the Olympic Mountains. A street-side, weather-vaned cement obelisk is decorated with sea glass, photos, and personal recollections about this spot (which was formerly a ferry landing). Lavender, sea grass, and rugosa roses delight the senses. ■ *Beach Dr SW and SW Carroll St; map:JJ9.*

**Shelby Street Park** This beautiful little street-end park was dedicated in 1994 to Puget Sound's native American ancestors. Wonderful decorative salmon created by a Puyallup tribal artist grace the cement walls which terrace the lawn. There's a ramp for launching canoes and kayaks into Portage Bay, but no wheelchair access. ■ *Boyer Ave E and E Shelby St (park on Fuhrman St, south of the Canal Market store); map:FF6.FRE-MONT*

**Fremont Canal Park** Just yards off the Burke-Gilman Trail is this intimate shady spot where people feed the ducks and folks jump into the Lake Washington Ship Canal to cool off. It's a great place to watch the boat traffic ply the narrow canal. Hand-painted ceramic tiles decorate the roofed benching area. Park on Second Avenue NW. ■ *NW Canal St and 2nd Ave NW; map:FF8.*

BALLARD

**6321 Seaview Avenue NW** Here is a delightfully clean sandy beach where you can watch the sun set over the Olympics while the kids dip their toes in chilly Puget Sound. Only 40 feet wide or so, it sits between a condominium and an eagle's aerie. (Look for the blue public access sign to the right of the condo, then park on Seaview Avenue.) ■ *6321 Seaview Ave NW (several blocks north of Ray's Boathouse); map:EE9.*

## ORGANIZED TOURS

There's always more to the city than meets the eye, and tours are one way to scratch the surface of the metropolis and see what makes it run. Clearly fun for visitors, a tour is also a great chance for locals to learn something about their hometown— an angle they may never have considered at all. For instance, all environmentally inclined Seattleites should take a tour of a lumber mill, to see the other side of the story. You can tour the **Boeing plant** (544-1264) to see the source of one of the city's major employers and economies, or the **Rainier Brewery** (622-2600) to get a taste of Seattle's answer to Budweiser. Tours can be as informational as one of the **Seattle Architectural Foundation's Viewpoint Tours** (448-0106), which examine the mix of art and architecture throughout the city; as colorful as Jeri Callahan's specially tailored tours-by-water of Lake Union's quirky **houseboat neighborhood** (322-9157); or as culinarily inspired as the **Taste of the Northwest Walking Tour**, where you can cruise the stalls and shops of Pike Place Market with the chef from the Alexis Hotel's Painted Table, then sit down to a Northwest-inspired lunch (complete with Northwest wines) at the arty hotel restaurant (624-3646). Every other year in late April/early May, **Seattle Art Museum** sponsors a walk through the lofts and studios of many of the city's artists—a great way to poke into creative lives (654-3198). Use your imagination and call ahead, since some tours are by reservation only.

## AIR TOURS

**Kenmore Air** The largest seaplane operator in the area, Kenmore Air has a fleet of 19 planes that make scheduled and charter flights around Puget Sound (including sightseeing excursions over the city) from seaports on Lake Union and north Lake Washington. The popular city tour (which originates from the Lake Washington location only) lasts 20 minutes and costs $90 for three passengers, $110 for six. A one-way passage to the San Juan Islands is $70 per person on a scheduled flight, or $236 for a charter for one to three people. Go standby to the San Juans for $30 per person (a scenic round-trip flight), or sign up for a day-trip package (including lunch and ground transportation on San Juan Island) for $99 ($109 on weekends). ■ *950 Westlake Ave N; 486-8400 or (800)543-9595; map:GG7.* ■ *6321 NE 175th St; 486-1257; map:BB5.*

**Seattle Seaplanes** Formerly known as Chrysler Air, Seattle Seaplanes does its main business in charters to Canadian fishing camps, but also offers a 20-minute exhaustive airborne tour of Seattle (UW, Lake Washington, Kingdome, the waterfront, Magnolia, the Locks, Shilshole, Green Lake, and back to Lake Union) for about $40. Consider taking a flight to and from majestic Mt. Rainier ($310 for five passengers, $265 for three or fewer). Call for reservations. ■ *1325 Fairview Ave E; 329-9638; map:E1.*

▼

**Organized Tours**

▲

**Sound Flight** Up to 20 passengers can arrange their own pilot-narrated floatplane tours of Seattle, Mount Rainier, the San Juan Islands, Mount St. Helens, or the North Cascades. Prices (from $45 to $200 per person) depend on the number of people and extent of the tour. ■ *Renton Municipal Airport, Renton; 255-6500; map:MM4.*

## BOAT TOURS

**Argosy Tours** Seattle Harbor Tours changed its name to Argosy in 1994 to reflect its growing fleet and variety of reasonably priced touring options. Scheduled tours include daily, year-round, 1-hour narrated cruises along the Seattle waterfront and Elliott Bay ($13.75); a 4-hour voyage to Blake Island's Tillicum Village for a salmon bake and hyped-up look at Northwest Indian culture ($46.50); and 2½-hour tours through the Hiram M. Chittenden Locks and Lake Washington Ship Canal ($21.50). In addition, Argosy offers seasonal 1½-hour cruises around Lake Washington (departing from Kirkland), and saltwater sport-fishing trips on Puget Sound. Charters for private parties or special events are available for groups of 25 to 400. ■ *Pier 55; 623-1445; map:L9.*

**Spirit of Puget Sound** Spirit Cruises, whose luxury ships are harbored in citys throughout the Eastern seaboard, brings its newest vessel to Seattle. It's clear to us here in the West that these professionals have floating entertainment figured out. This 600-passenger luxury ship sails daily (depending on availability) for two- to three-hour lunch and dinner tours of the Sound in a style akin to that of a deep-sea cruise liner: a full-service restaurant, entertainment, and dancing. Lunch cruises run $25 to $30, dinner cruises from $47 to $55. ▪ *2819 Elliott Ave (Pier 70); 443-1439; map:D9.*

**Tall Ship Tours** Built in 1989 (though you could have fooled us), the *Lady Washington* is a classic reproduction of its earlier incarnation: an 18th-century square-rigger bearing the same name which was the first American vessel to explore the Pacific coast of this continent. The 112-foot *Lady*, with costumed crew and 6 miles of rigging, turns heads whether it's docked for tours ($8, $6 seniors and children), out for a regularly scheduled summertime sail ($20 to $35, less for seniors and children), or chartered for a party or special event. Tours run June 1 through September 30. Call for reservations. ▪ *Pier 54, Seattle Waterfront; 682-4876; map:L9.*

## MOTOR TOURS

**Gray Line of Seattle** This touring agency offers several choice trips: Mount Rainier (summer only, $39 per person); the Boeing plant ($19 per person); the popular Seattle City tours ($28 for 6 hours or $19.50 for 2½ hours); overnighters to Victoria, BC; and more. Free pickup at several downtown hotels. ▪ *720 S Forest St; 624-5813.*

## WALKING TOURS

**Chinatown Discovery** Humorous Seattle native Vi Mar conducts leisurely walking tours of the International District, providing a historical and cultural perspective (dinner, tea, or dim sum lunch at a Chinese restaurant is included in the various tour rates). Reservations required. Group rates available. Call to arrange. ▪ *236-0657.*

**See Seattle Walking Tours** Catering to those with no time to waste finding Seattle's favorite sights on their own, Terry Seidler conducts walking tours through Pike Place Market, the Waterfront, Pioneer Square, and other downtown points of interest. Custom one-, two-, and three-hour tours are available for groups, including mystery and scavenger hunts (perfect for school or Scouting groups). Call for reservations and information. ▪ *226-7641.*

**The Underground Tours** [KIDS] These tours are mostly one story down, the level of the city before it was rebuilt after the great fire of June 6, 1889. (Poor drainage at the old, lower level made the higher streets imperative.) It's all pretty cornball, but you'll get a salty taste of the pioneers' eccentricities and some historical insights in spite of the puns. The tours begin at Doc Maynard's Public House and run 1½ hours. Tour times vary seasonally. Cost is $5.95, less for students, children, and seniors. Call for reservations and information. ■ *610 1st Ave; 682-4646; map:N8.*

## ITINERARIES

Whether you're a first-time visitor or a native, here are suggestions for spending one day—or an entire week—enjoying the best Seattle has to offer. Specifics on most of the places in boldface type may be found in the appropriate chapters (Restaurants, Shopping, Lodging, Exploring, Day Trips, etc.) throughout this guide. For an individually tailored itinerary planned with your interests in mind, contact **Pacific Northwest Journeys**, a Seattle-based company that designs custom itineraries for Washington, Oregon, and British Columbia; 935-9730 or (800)935-9730.

### DAY ONE

If you have just a day in Seattle, concentrate on the city's heart: **Pike Place Market**. Ideally you're staying at the **Inn at the Market** (if you're lucky enough to secure a reservation).

**Morning:** Get an early start and watch the Market come to life. Grab a fresh croissant from **Le Panier Very French Bakery**, a latte from the original **Starbucks**, and wander among the farmers and craftspeople as they set up their wares.

**Afternoon:** If weather permits, have lunch on the terrace at **The Pink Door**; if it's shelter you're after, **Cafe Campagne**, a French-inspired bistro, makes a cozy retreat. Shoppers take note: Western and First Avenues between the Market and **Pioneer Square** are rich with treasure. Those who want to explore more of Seattle will hop a bus or take the short walk down First Avenue to Pioneer Square, the oldest part of town (you may ride free until 7pm throughout the downtown core on any Metro bus). Art lovers will want to spend a few hours at **Seattle Art Museum**.

**Evening:** Enjoy the Pacific Northwest's bounty with dinner at **Etta's Seafood**, then bring the evening to a romantic close by watching the sun set over Elliott Bay from **Shea's Lounge** (a hard-to-find aerie in the Sanitary Market Building).

### DAY TWO

**Morning:** Locals may scoff, but visitors are invariably drawn to the **Space Needle** at the **Seattle Center**. If it's a clear day, take a ride to the top, then have breakfast at the Space Needle's revolving restaurant where you can get the lay of the land along with your coffee and eggs. After breakfast, explore the rest of the Center, which is especially appealing to children.

**Afternoon:** Some of Seattle's best Thai restaurants are in the Seattle Center neighborhood. Favorites come and go, but we still love the simply named **Thai Restaurant**. Later in the afternoon, spend time exploring one of the collection of neighborhoods that make up the soul of Seattle: we suggest funky **Fremont**, a colorful, quirky, commercial and residential district bordering Lake Union and the Ship Canal, with unusual shopping, great coffeehouses, and unique public art.

**Evening:** See Seattle from the water. If you want to power your own boat, join a "Sunset Paddle" by kayak, organized by **Northwest Outdoor Center** on Lake Union, or settle in for an **Argosy** boat tour of Seattle Harbor (take their "Rich and Famous" tour of Lake Washington if you yearn to see how the other half lives). Enjoy a late dinner in burgeoning, boisterous **Belltown** at **Marco's Supperclub**, and, if you're still raring to go, a nice loud band and a beer in the jam-packed **Crocodile Cafe**.

## DAY THREE

You won't need your passport to travel out of the country on one of Seattle's most popular day trips: **Victoria, BC**.

**Morning:** Rise and shine for an early **Victoria Clipper** departure. You'll arrive by midmorning; spend the next couple of hours learning about the history of the Pacific Northwest at the fascinating **Royal British Columbia Museum**. Then take a narrated horse-drawn carriage tour of **Beacon Hill Park**.

**Afternoon:** Cruise in a tiny water taxi on the Inner Harbour to **Barb's Place** for great fish 'n' chips, then walk it off on your way back to town. Next, hop on a bus to **Butchart Gardens** to marvel at the horticultural displays. Once back in Victoria, fortify yourself with afternoon tea at the **Bedford Regency** before taking an evening boat back to Seattle.

**Evening:** If high tea leaves you hungry, grab a burger at **The Two Bells Tavern**, and throw off any lingering proper British atmosphere with a nightcap at the **Frontier Room**.

## DAY FOUR

More Seattle neighborhoods, and a chance to taste some of Washington's best exports.

**Morning:** Breakfast at **Mae's Phinney Ridge Cafe**, a Seattle morning institution, then head for the nearby **Woodland Park Zoo**. The animals are most active in the morning (the zoo opens at 9:30am) and weekday morning crowds are sparse.

**Afternoon:** Have a picnic at **Green Lake** or sit out on the patio at **Duke's Greenlake Chowderhouse**, and watch all the walkers, runners, bladers, and bike riders jostle for space on the path around the lake. Inspired? Rent a bike at **Gregg's Greenlake Cycle** and head out on the **Burke-Gilman Trail** to **Woodinville**, where you'll be able to visit two wineries and a brewery before heading (carefully!) back to Seattle.

**Evening:** Yes, we know it's a touristy cliché, but **Ray's Boathouse**, with its waterside view of the Olympics, really does have some of the best seafood in town. After dinner, stop in at **Old Town Alehouse** on historic Ballard Avenue for some acoustic jazz or blues.

## DAY FIVE

It's time to hop on a ferry and explore the **Kitsap and Olympic Peninsulas** to the west of Seattle. **Port Townsend** makes a good day trip.

**Morning:** Take the ferry from downtown to **Bainbridge Island** and breakfast at **Streamliner Diner**. If you've planned in advance and made reservations, visit **The Bloedel Reserve**. Otherwise, explore the forest trails and coastline at **Fort Ward State Park**. From Bainbridge, it's about an hour's drive to Port Townsend.

**Afternoon:** How about a picnic at scenic **Chetzemoka Park**? Or have a bite to eat at **Blackberries** at **Fort Worden**, then explore the turn-of-the-century former Army base-turned-cultural center. Browsing in the shops and galleries along **Water Street** makes for a pleasant afternoon. On summer weekends, allow room in your schedule to attend a classical concert in a barn at the **Olympic Music Festival** in **Quilcene**.

**Evening:** Make your way back to Bainbridge, perhaps with stops in **Port Gamble** and **Poulsbo**. Enjoy a burger with a waterfront view at the casual, convivial **Harbour Public House** on Bainbridge before taking the ferry back to the hustle and bustle of Seattle.

## DAY SIX

Today you'll head to the hills: the **Cascade Range** to the east of Seattle.

**Morning:** Get an early start and have breakfast on the road at the **Mar-T Cafe** in **North Bend**. If you'd just like to spend the morning hiking, try the hikes to Talapus and Olallie Lakes (Exit 45 off I-90). For a longer hike, take the Denny Creek Trail to Melakwa Lake, with lots of scenic views and waterfalls (Exit 47 off I-90).

**Afternoon:** Lunch on the trail, or, if you're feeling flush and lucky, try for reservations at **The Herbfarm** (you should stop here anyway to check out the 17 herbal theme gardens, farm animals, and intriguing gift shop). Another scenic stop on the way back to Seattle is stunning **Snoqualmie Falls**.

**Evening:** Once back in town, visit another Seattle neighborhood, perhaps **Madison Park**, an oh-so-chichi neighborhood on the shores of Lake Washington. Sample satisfying Italian- and French-inspired cuisine at charming **Sostanza**, and continue south on Lake Washington Boulevard to **Leschi Marina** for an after-dinner drink at the elegant bar at **Daniel's Broiler**. The evening light reflecting off the lake is gorgeous, and if it's clear, you can gaze at the Cascades where you began the day.

### DAY SEVEN

Time to hit the road again: **Mount Rainier**'s been looming all week. Today you go to the Mountain.

**Morning:** Again, an early start is in order. It takes about 2½-hours to reach **Mount Rainier National Park** from Seattle. If you're up for an Ironman type of day, start off at the visitors area, **Sunrise**, and take the 4-mile **Sourdough Ridge Trail** to stretch your legs.

**Afternoon:** Picnic on the trail. Back in the car, cross **Cayuse Pass** and continue south to **Grove of the Patriarchs**, a great 1-mile walk through a stand of thousand-year-old trees. Continue around the mountain to **Paradise**, where there is a plethora of hiking options, from guided nature walks to more strenuous half-day hikes (less hardy souls should head straight to Paradise from Seattle).

▼

**Evening:** After a shower (and maybe a nap), end your stay in Seattle at the marvelous pan-Asian restaurant **Wild Ginger**, perhaps seated at the fragrant satay bar, where Seattle's locals and vistors convene for an exotic repast.

▲

# SHOPPING

**Shopping Areas** *227*
  Downtown Seattle *227*
  Historic Districts *227*
  Neighborhoods *228*
  Suburban Malls *229*

**Accessories and Luggage** *230*

**Antiques** *231*

**Apparel** *234*

**Auctions** *240*

**Bakeries** *241*

**Body Care** *245*

**Books/Magazines/**
  **Newspapers** *246*

**Cameras/Photo Supplies** *254*

**Candies and Chocolates** *256*

**Children's Clothing** *257*

**Coffee and Tea** *258*

**Computers/Software** *260*

**Consignment and**
  **Discount** *261*

**Department Stores** *264*

**Ethnic Markets and Specialty**
  **Foods** *265*

**Fabric and Knitting**
  **Supplies** *270*

**Florists and Nurseries** *271*

**Furniture** *276*

**Gifts** *278*

**Hardware** *282*

**Health Food** *283*

**Home Accessories** *285*

**Imports** *287*

**Jewelry** *289*

**Kitchenware** *291*

**Lingerie** *292*

**Meat** *293*

**Outdoor Gear** *294*

**Records, Tapes, and CDs** *301*

**Seafood** *304*

**Shoes** *305*

**Specialty Size Clothing:**
  **Large/Tall/Maternity/**
  **Petite** *307*

**Stationery and Art Supplies**
  *308*

**Stereos/Audio Equipment** *310*

**Toys** *310*

**Video** *314*

**Vintage/Retro** *315*

**Wine and Beer** *317*

# Shopping

*DOWNTOWN SEATTLE*

See Downtown Seattle in the Exploring chapter.

*HISTORIC DISTRICTS*

Let yourself be taken in by the unaffected charm of **Pike Place Market** (Western Avenue between Virginia and Pike Streets, open every day, all year long; map:J8), the most unusual and important shopping area in town (see Pike Place Market in the Exploring chapter). This is the spot for food—mainly fresh produce and seafood—and in the several arcades and labyrinthian passageways that make up its layout, you'll find vintage apparel, antiques, and arts and crafts; it's like a street fair every day. Recent years have also brought on an upscale overspill of shops as the Market's **South Arcade** (south on First Avenue from the main entrance of the Market to Union Street; map:I8) marches southward along First Avenue.

Another egress from the Market is toward the **Waterfront** (Alaskan Way from Pier 52 to Pier 70; map:M8–D9) via an appealing lineup of retail along **Pike Market Hillclimb** (Pike Street to Pier 59; map:J8). Just south along this shore, you'll meet up with legions of furniture and home design shops, and if you double back and meander northward, the boardwalk ends at **Pier 70** (Alaskan Way and Broad Street; map:O9), a lovely old barn of a pier with Northwest crafts emporiums and more scrimshaw than you've seen in your life. (See Waterfront/Seattle Aquarium under Major Attractions in the Exploring chapter.)

**Pioneer Square** (between Second Avenue and the waterfront, from Cherry Street to King Street; map:N8) is where

Seattle got started in 1852; now the area boasts the Northwest's most prestigious concentration of art galleries and a dizzying proliferation of shops—some tourist-schlocky, but most quite respected (and frequented) by Seattleites.

Historic areas farther afield in the greater Seattle area have also been recast as shopping districts. **Gilman Village** (Issaquah, Exit 17 off I-90) is a minitown of shops and restaurants, most of which are in turn-of-the-century-type structures, connected by a charming boardwalk to create a small-specialty-shop-and-ladies'-luncheon kind of place. Stores here feature high-end merchandise and the glorious backdrop of the Cascade foothills. Edmonds's historic offering, **Old Milltown** (201 Fifth Avenue S, Edmonds), is another collection of quaint shops; **Country Village** (Exit 26 off I-405; map:BB3) in Bothell purveys a hearty dose of country gift shops and home decorations.

*NEIGHBORHOODS*

▼

**Shopping
Areas**

*Historic
Districts*

▲

The University District's "**The Ave**" (along University Way NE from NE 41st Street to NE 50th Street; map:FF6) features a concentration of book, record, and ice cream stores, plus some interesting boutiques and ethnic restaurants. Though its student/bohemian flavor is being eaten up by a combination of deadbeat culture and advancing chain stores, the retail blocks still yield some good browsing, and the shopping district is slowly spreading in a northerly direction (see University District (University of Washington) in the Exploring chapter). Genteel **University Village** (NE 45th Street and 25th Avenue NE; map:FF6), down the 45th Street viaduct from the UW campus and the shopping mall closest to downtown, is home to especially good gourmet and specialty food stores, and, since the 1995 expansion, to an Eddie Bauer outlet and a gargantuan Barnes and Noble. Two neighboring districts also serve University folk with good shopping: **Roosevelt** (Roosevelt Way NE from NE 55th Street to NE 70th Street; map:EE6), a strip with stereo stores, vintage-clothing stores, and diverse restaurants; and **Wallingford** (along N 45th Street from Stone Way N to Latona Avenue NE; map:FF7), which, with a refurbished and converted school building, **Wallingford Center** (N 45th Street and Wallingford Avenue; map:FF7), as its showpiece, caters to its constituents with funky gift shops and quirky, slightly "alternative" retail (an erotic bakery, for instance, as well as the city's first condom store).

South of Portage Bay and the Ship Canal, head for **Broadway** (from E Pine Street north to E Roy Street; map:HH6), center of the punk-stylish universe in Seattle and the best sidewalk-filling, see-and-be-seen shopping scene in town. Vintage clothing, chic apparel, espresso, and housewares predominate, as do a multitude of restaurants (see Capitol Hill in the Exploring chapter). Five blocks east is the neighborhood commercial district of **15th Avenue East** (E Denny Way to E Mercer Street; map:HH6), which embodies the homegrown, untrendy element of Capitol Hill's collective personality: mom-and-pop businesses, a health-food grocery, consignment shops, and a collective-run issues-oriented bookstore. South of here, Madison Street intersects 15th Avenue on its way from downtown to **Madison Park** (along E Madison Street from McGilvra Boulevard E to 43rd Avenue E; map:GG6). Here, the lakeside shopping/restaurant enclave reflects the family orientation and upward mobility of the neighborhood. Closer to downtown is **Madison Valley** (along E Madison Street from Martin Luther King Jr. Way to 32nd Avenue E; map:GG6), a pleasant, upscale, and highly browsable retail pocket that attracts the landed gentry from the nearby Washington Park and Broadmoor residential districts.

Across town is **Queen Anne Hill**, whose lower slopes around Queen Anne Avenue North and Mercer Street are studded with shops and restaurants. Seattleites are rediscovering the many good restaurants at the top of the hill, and new retail establishments are cropping up everywhere. Down the northern slope of Queen Anne Hill and across the Lake Washington Ship Canal lies **Fremont** (Fremont Avenue N and N 34th Street; map:FF7), a funky neighborhood known to its residents as "The Artists' Republic of Fremont" and noted for antique-and-kitsch stores, retro boutiques, and some of the city's better pubs. Finally, Eastsiders in search of the neighborhood shopping experience head for **Old Bellevue** (Main Street at Bellevue Way; map:HH3), where traditional shops on flower-lined streets cater to the carriage trade; or the **Kirkland Waterfront** (along Lake Washington Boulevard NE from Second Avenue S to Central Way; map:EE4), a stretch of retail hugging the shore of Moss Bay.

## SUBURBAN MALLS

The standard-setter for the region, and one of the best of its kind in the nation, is glittering **Bellevue Square** (NE Eighth Street and Bellevue Way, Bellevue; open Monday through Saturday until 9:30pm, Sundays until 6pm; map:HH3). Surrounded by plenty of parking, Bellevue Square offers a sunny, spacious interior, the Big Three department stores (Nordstrom, The Bon, and J.C. Penney), and a growing number of exceptionally high-quality shops. Bellevue Square developer Kemper Freeman is also the name behind the sprawling complex called **Bellevue Place** (NE Eighth Street and Bellevue Way, Bellevue; open every day until 6pm, Fridays until 9pm; map:HH3), with 20 shops and a number of excellent restaurants, some of which occupy the dramatic glass-walled Wintergarden atrium.

**Northgate Mall** (off I-5 at the Northgate exit; open Monday through Saturday until 9:30pm, Sunday until 6pm; map:DD7), the first mall in the nation when it opened in 1950, is now modern and quite complete. Its South End, climate-controlled counterpart is **Southcenter** (off I-5 at Southcenter exit; open Monday through Saturday until 9:30pm, Sunday until 6pm; map:OO5). Near Southcenter is the **Pavilion Mall** (179000 Southcenter Parkway; open weekdays until 9:30pm, Saturdays until 9pm, and Sundays until 6pm; map:OO5), where every store deals in discounted merchandise.

Other suburban shopping ghettos are the new discount mega-mall, the **Supermall of the Great Northwest** (1601 15th Street SW, Auburn; open Monday through Saturday until 9:30pm and Sunday until 6pm), **Sea-Tac Mall** (Federal Way, 320th Street exit off I-5; open Monday through Saturday until 9pm and Sunday until 6pm); **Alderwood Mall** (Lynnwood, Alderwood Mall exit off I-5; open Monday through Saturday until 9:30pm, Sunday until 6pm; and on the Eastside, **Kirkland Park Place** (Kirkland, exit 18 off I-405; open weekdays until 8pm, weekends until 6pm; map:EE3); **Factoria Square** (Bellevue at I-90 and I-405 interchange; open weekdays until 9pm, weekends until 6pm; map:II3); **Totem Lake** (Kirkland, 124th Street exit off I-405; open weekdays until 9pm, Saturdays until 6pm, Sundays noon to 5pm; map:CC3); and one that stands out from the crowd with a unique blend of suburban retail mall and indoor fresh-food marketplace, **Crossroads Mall** (Bellevue, NE Eighth Street and 156th Avenue NE; open Monday through Saturday until 9pm, Sunday until 6pm; map:HH2).

## ACCESSORIES AND LUGGAGE

**Bergman Luggage** If it's made of leather or intended for travel, Bergman has it at discount prices: portfolios, bags, attaché cases, carry-ons, wallets, travel accessories, and suitcases galore. There's something for every pocketbook, and a complete luggage repair service at the Third Avenue store. ▪ *1930 3rd Ave (and branches); 448-3000; map:H7; every day.*

**Byrnie Utz Men's Hat Store** Byrnie Utz provides that civilized flourish that has all but disappeared from modern dressing. With close to a quarter million hats in inventory and thousands of styles to choose from, you can find everything from Harrison Ford's hat in *Raiders of the Lost Ark* to John Wayne's Stetson. This is one of the last full-line hat shops on the West Coast and one of the largest in the United States, and now carries a selection of women's hats, too. ▪ *310 Union Ave; 623-0233; map:K6; Mon–Sat.*

**The Coach Store (Four Seasons Olympic Hotel)** Classic, beautifully crafted, built-to-last bags, belts, briefcases, luggage, and accessories are displayed on floor-to-ceiling bookshelves. In fall and winter, Coach leather coats are available, too. Salespeople are helpful and down to earth; prices are not. ■ *417 University St; 382-1772; map:L6; Mon–Sat.* ■ *Bellevue Square, Bellevue; 453-0141; map:HH3; every day.*

**Fast Forward** Funky, upbeat jewelry, clothing, and accessories (for your wardrobe and your home) make Fast Forward a store geared toward progressive urbanites who want to stand apart from the crowd. A good selection of scarves and hats for women as well as way-out men's and unisex fashions from Todd Oldham, John Paul Gaultier, and some local fashion folk. ■ *1918 1st Ave; 728-8050; map:H8; every day.*

**Metro Man** This is the place to shop for the little "nonessentials" that make life worth living. They stock an armload of leather belts and a thoughtful collection of contemporary watches, men's silk loungewear, and a multitude of styles of men's underwear. Do you dare to give postcard-printed boxers? You'll find them—and more—here. ■ *401 Broadway Ave E (Broadway Market); 328-1417; map:GG7; every day.*

**WE Hats** A delightful mix of kitsch and quality. The walls are covered with wacky hats, including WE's own popular "court jester." Well-made fedoras, top hats, and berets make for a great browse. Get your Tilley canvas hat here (complete with lifetime guarantee), your Hillary Rodham Clinton look-alike by Kaminsky, and even politically correct chapeaux made from recycled soda bottles (the hat of choice for the Pepsi Generation, no doubt). Earrings, umbrellas, nylons—even with a spiderweb design—and great glasses round it all out. Consider stopping by WE's factory showroom at 2601 Elliott Avenue. ■ *105 1st Ave S; 623-3409; map:N8; every day.*

## ANTIQUES

**Almost Antiques** A modest Ballard storefront with scrolled signage on the side of the building, Almost Antiques has room after room of gilt mirrors, tapestried love seats, lamps, and dining sets. Lots of quality furnishings in mahogany, maple, walnut, and cherry. There's crystal, china, sterling, and quality flatware, too. ■ *6019 15th Ave NW; 783-5400; map:EE8; every day.*

**Antique Importers** Direct importing from Denmark and occasionally from England (each item hand-selected by the store's own buyers) ensures that the stock of pine and oak furniture and stained glass is of excellent value and respectable quality. High-ish prices; mostly standard items, with a few rare finds, including some interesting cast-iron pieces. New shipments arrive often. ■ *640 Alaskan Way; 628-8905; map:M8; every day.*

**Antique Liquidators** Without a doubt this is the largest antique store in town, with 22,000 square feet of sales and storage space. New merchandise arrives constantly to meet the high demand for practical furnishings (mostly Danish and English; lots of chairs and drop-leaf tables). Browsing among the antique kitchen accessories is great rainy-day fun. Endless variety and good prices, but don't expect perfect quality. ▪ *503 Westlake Ave N; 623-2740; map:D2; every day.*

**The Crane Gallery** Crane is highly respected in the business for its fine Asian antiques and artifacts. Paintings, ceramics, bronzes, ivory, jade, and furniture from around the Orient are museum quality and priced accordingly. ▪ *1203-B 2nd Ave; 622-7185; map:L7; Mon–Sat.*

**Daily Planet** A medley of vintage collectibles and art deco memorabilia covers every square inch of this eccentric Fremont enclave. For over 25 years, owners Richard Friend and Jan Cole have filled this unique shop with a cornucopia of: jukeboxes, victrolas, lamps, chandeliers, carpets, light fixtures, furnishings, and other memorable objects. ▪ *3416 Fremont Ave N; 633-0895; map:FF8; every day.*

**David Weatherford Antiques and Interiors** A Capitol Hill mansion provides a resplendent showplace for exquisite 18th-century English and French furniture, as well as Oriental rugs, porcelain, screens, and art glass. A resident design team advises clients on integrating antiques gracefully with their present furnishings. The downtown location in the Washington Mutual Tower specializes in commercial collections. ▪ *133 14th Ave E; 329-6533; map:HH6; Mon–Sat.* ▪ *1200 2nd Ave; 233-0796; map:L7; Mon–Fri.*

**Eileen of China** Those looking for Asian opulence will find it at this large International District store stocked with Chinese antiques that make a statement: a $68,000 cloisonné elephant trunk, 6-foot-tall Chinese vases, grand armoires, and hand-painted screens. ▪ *624 S Dearborn; 624-0816; map:R7; Mon–Sat.*

**Greg Davidson Antique Lighting** It's dark inside Greg Davidson's cavernous antique lighting store. All the better to get the feel of the warming glow from a Tiffany-Handel lamp as it shines through its graceful shade. A handful of fine furnishings set off a collection of mostly American fixtures, standing and desk lamps, and chandeliers. Whether your fuel of choice is gas, kerosene, or electricity, Davidson (who can be found wiring and repairing in the open recesses of the shop) has an expert eye for Arts & Crafts and Victorian pieces and leaves you in peace as you inspect his valuables. ▪ *1307 1st Ave; 625-0406; map:K8; Tues–Sat.*

▼

**Antiques**

▲

**Honeychurch Antiques** John Fairman runs this excellent shop, whose second location is in Hong Kong—hence, the largest selection of 19th-century Japanese and Chinese furniture in the Northwest. The store's attraction lies in its tasteful blend of Asian fine art, folk art, and furniture with a reputation for integrity and quality that is well deserved. The shop puts on bimonthly shows of early Chinese ceramics and Japanese woodblock prints. ▪ *1008 James St; 622-1225; map:N4; Mon–Sat.*

**Jean Williams Antiques** A distinctive collection of French, English, and American 18th- and 19th-century furnishings is showcased in this commodious Pioneer Square storefront. Handsome fireplace mantels, mirrors, and other classic accent pieces fill the crannies, distinguishing this shop as extremely well stocked. You can get French and English handmade reproductions here at half the cost of genuine antiques. ▪ *115 S Jackson St; 622-1110; map:O9; Mon–Sat.*

**Marvel on Madison** Marvel on Madison truly *is* a marvel: small and filled with lovely Japanese antiquities. Screens, tea sets, tansu chests, and a unique collection of jewelry set with Chinese semiprecious stones are all personally selected by owner Marvel Stewart. Affordably priced. ▪ *69 Madison St; 624-4225; map:M8; Tues–Sat.*

▼

▲

**N. B. Nichols and Son** The sign in Post Alley sums it up: "Antiques, Fine Imported Objects, Extraordinary Junk." From 11th-century BC Egyptian antiquities to English garden figurines, this store stocks the junk of the world. Don't expect to find flawless treasures; do expect an interesting conglomeration of European, Asian, and African Old World belongings—some truly lovely. ▪ *1924 Post Alley; 448-8906; map:I8; Mon–Sat.*

**Partners in Time** Two locations offer antique pine furniture imported from England, Austria, Germany, and Holland. Also Asian carpets, Japanese porcelain, and other collectibles. ▪ *1201 2nd Ave; 343-3300; map:M8; every day.* ▪ *1332 6th Ave; 623-4218; map:K5; every day.*

**Pelayo's** Pedro Pelayo specializes in Danish country pine furniture from the 19th and 20th centuries, as well as pieces from England and Central Europe. Scandinavian crockery, bric-a-brac, wine jugs, and benches can be found, along with brass and copper accessories and more than 100 Russian items. Two locations. ▪ *7601 Greenwood Ave N; 789-1999; map:EE8; every day.* ▪ *8421 Greenwood Ave N; 789-1333; map:EE8; every day.*

**Stuteville Antiques** You may remember Marshall Stuteville from Globe Antiques. He brings to his own shop an impressive collection of Georgian period furniture as well as Continental and American pieces. The authenticity of every item, including the smaller silver and porcelain items, is evident. He also offers a restoration service. ■ *1518 E Olive Way; 329-5666; map:HH6; Tues–Sat, or by appointment.*

**Two Angels Antiques** Steve Glueck and Sally Maryatt's exceptional shop, directly across the street from the Seattle Art Museum, is a veritable art museum itself. Whimsical, creative window displays will draw you inside. Once in, the fabulous furnishings and objects d'art are further proof that serious antiques—even extraordinarily expensive, museum-quality treasures such as a pair of 15th-century angels, or a string of period chairs hanging carefully from the high ceiling—can be fun, too. ■ *1301 1st Ave, Seattle, WA 98101; 340-6005; map:K8; Mon–Sat.*

**Wicker Design Antiques** The store offers limited hours, but not limited service; its dealers are among the handful of experts on the West Coast who buy, sell, and restore old wicker furniture—chairs, sofas, rockers, and the occasional Victorian baby buggy. Finder service, too. ■ *515 15th Ave E; 322-2552; map:HH6; Wed–Sat, or by appointment.*

## APPAREL

**A Grand Affair** It's fun to dress up in sequined outfits, especially if you don't have to *buy* them. This shop is one of the few that rents glitzy bridal and formal wear, including Bob Mackie creations. The standard five-day rental conveniently takes party-goers from the night before the event to the Monday after, and includes coordinated jewelry and a handbag. A special-event registry system ensures that your outfit won't be worn by anyone else. Tux rentals, too. ■ *10218 NE 8th St, Bellevue (and branches); 453-7300; map:HH2; Tues–Sat.*

**AKA Eddie Bauer** AKA, offspring of Seattle's own hometown son, offers an alternative look to the renowned outdoor-wear clothier's reliable classics. Here you'll find private label, dress sportswear for men and women with a casual attitude toward comfort and the workplace. Slacks, sport coats, sweaters, and accessories, all in natural fabrics. ■ *Bellevue Square, Bellevue; 637-0870; map:HH3; every day.* ■ *University Village; 526-8594; map:FF6; every day.*

**Abercrombie & Fitch (Four Seasons Olympic Hotel)** When aristocrats dress sporty, it's usually in something bearing the Abercrombie & Fitch label. These days, Abercrombie & Fitch lean toward the mainstream; now even the plebes among us can afford to pay a bit more for clothes this well-crafted. ■ *421 University St; 623-2175; map:K6; every day.*

**Ann Taylor** Classic, reliable, timeless. Here's the place to go for luxurious fabrics, accessories, and fine footwear from the custom-shoe salon. The Bellevue Square location is considerably bigger, affording greater choices. ▪ *1420 5th Ave (City Centre); 623-4818; map:J5; every day.* ▪ *Bellevue Square, Bellevue; 455-3470; map:HH3; every day.*

**Baby & Co.** With pricey playclothes evocative of New York and Paris street life, Baby & Co. offers fun and whimsy. Besides trappings for the fashionably daring, the store carries handsome pieces in silk, rayon, and cotton. Mainly selections for women; menswear is down to a trickle. ▪ *1936 1st Ave; 448-4077; map:I7; every day.*

**Banana Republic** The new downtown location—a multimillion-dollar redo of the former Coliseum Theater—makes this the Big Banana, outranking all others. Just past the velvet curtains of the entryway lies a gold mine of wearable casual clothes, all extremely well constructed of all-natural, washable fabrics. Peruse the sale racks for surprisingly affordable fashions. ▪ *500 Pike St (and branches); 622-2303; map:J6; every day.*

**Barneys New York** Grab hold of your credit card, take a deep breath, and plunge into Barneys world. The leader of New York City retailers and the pride of distinctive shoppers, Barneys mixes, as *Money* magazine says, haute and hip, bold architectural design, and phenomenal customer service. You'll be fighting your conscience trying to hold yourself back from purchasing something sumptuous—say, a choice Armani leather vest. Fine body care products, too. ▪ *1420 5th Ave (City Centre); 622-6300; map:J5; Mon–Sat.*

▼

▲

**Betsey Johnson** A little twist-and-shout and a clothing "Twilight Zone" mixed into one. Seattle's fashion scene gets an extra-high-voltage jolt of fun with stretch, funk, spandex, short flippy skirts, snakeskin corsets, and leggings, all displayed in an ultrabright retail space just ready for adventuresome boundary-testers. ▪ *1429 5th Ave; 624-2887; map:J5; every day.*

**Bonneville's** Beauty and a sure sense of style pervade Bonneville's, both in ambience and in merchandise. Colorful and unusual scarves; sequined, beaded, or appliquéd tops; and tons of accessories are displayed side by side with Oriental carpets, antique wood furniture, silk flowers, and Japanese parasols. Truly lovely stuff. ▪ *114 Lake St, Kirkland; 822-7002; map:EE3; Mon–Sat.*

**Brooks Brothers** Ensconced in the heart of downtown Seattle, Brooks Brothers's famous conservative lines of men's casual and dress fashions are well geared to the city's climate. Tremendous depth of inventory, a fine special-order system, two terrific sales a year (two weeks in June and the week after

Christmas), and gracious service amid sedate surroundings are the store's trademarks. Some good women's lines in among the button-downs. A growing line of casual wear and big and tall sizes, too. ■ *1401 4th Ave; 624-4400; map:K6; Mon–Sat.* ■ *Bellevue Square, Bellevue; 646-9688; map:HH3; every day.*

**Burberrys** The famous trench-coat maker's Seattle outlet carries a full line of men's furnishings and assorted women's separates (primarily skirts and sweaters), as well as coats, umbrellas, handbags, and scarves—all endowed with the trademark Burberry plaids. ■ *409 Pike St; 621-2000; map:J6; every day.*

**Butch Blum** Along Seattle's version of "Fifth Avenue" is this oasis for men wanting the fashion-forward, predominantly European clothes of established designers in addition to the wearables of avant-garde newcomers to the business. The minimalist interior won't deter you from the inviting lines exclusive to Seattle; you can depart without fear of seeing yourself cloned everywhere. Owners William and Kay Smith-Blum employ a friendly, helpful staff. ■ *1408 5th Ave; 622-5760; map:K6; Mon–Sat.*

**C. P. Shades** You'll want to parade yourself in front of the amazing wall-size mirror to admire the easy elegance of these natural-fiber casual clothes. This San Francisco–based company manufactures its own sumptuous, easy-to-care-for fabrics for women. Flowing silky rayons, textured cottons, and velvets distinguish these dresses, pull-on pants and skirts, tunics, and vests—all carefully dyed in sophisticated, dusky shades. ■ *2025 1st Ave, #A; 448-9218; map:G8; every day.*

**Dakota** Less is more at Dakota, two handsome shops that favor classic women's clothes and accessories with a contemporary touch—all from American designers. ■ *2025 1st Ave; 441-3177; map:K4; every day.* ■ *Bellevue Square, Bellevue; 462-1677; map:HH3; every day.*

**Darbury Stenderu** Stenderu stresses the *wearable* in wearable art, fashioning her hand-painted, block-printed, and screened silks and velvets in simple designs on everything from T-shirts to evening gowns. Unusual fabrics in deep colors prevail in formfitting velvet shifts and billowy silk tunics; fabric is also available by the yard. One-of-a-kind jewelry items set the clothes off nicely. A visit to this singular shop, surrounded by color and texture, is a treat for the senses. ■ *2121 1st Ave; 448-2625; map:J8; Mon–Sat.*

**Design Products Clothing** Sumptuous sweaters, casual pants and skirts, and an outstanding array of blouses offset softly tailored apparel at Design Products Clothing. This snazzy boutique in Pioneer Square also carries a limited selection of distinctive menswear (mostly ties and socks) and some local designer clothing, including Deliane Klein's. ▪ *208 1st Ave S; 624-7795; map:O8; Mon–Sat.*

**Dita Boutique**  Dita's has a wide array of innovative silhouettes, many imported from Italy, Germany, France, Belgium, and Japan. Here, 20- and 60-year-olds shop side by side; the selections are rooted in style, not age. ▪ *1525 1st Ave, #2; 622-1770; map:HH6; every day.*

**The Forum Menswear**  A fashionable guy's paradise, from the chic eye-opening "gotta have it" ensemble displays, to the astounding selection of moderate-to-expensive suits and accessories for men. Lines include Jhane Barnes, Calvin Klein, Reunion, and Axis. European socks, belts, and ties finish the look. Salespeople are anxious to befriend. ▪ *95 Pine St; 624-4566; map:I8; every day.*

**The Gap**  The store that taught a younger generation how to shop for coordinates. Seasonal color palates mark the arrival of new merchandise, from periwinkle casual linen shirts and polos, to off-white, stone-washed chinos, to taupe and natural Gap underwear. Accessories cover the realm of sweaters, ties, and shoes. Expect great buys just before the next color shipment arrives. Gap Kids, upstairs at the downtown location, has set the trend with other major retailers by offering kid-size fashions. ▪ *1531 4th Ave (and branches); 625-1470; map:I6; every day.*

**Helen's (Of Course)**  Fashions from the pages of *W* fill this marble showcase, with labels from the world's most famous couture houses (Oscar de la Renta, Escada Boutique) while saleswomen from the pages of *Modern Maturity* tend to long-time clients. Helen's is the choice for Seattle's worldliest—and wealthiest—fashion mavens. Others shop the "sale" room in back for a chance to max out their credit cards. ▪ *1302 5th Ave; 624-4000; map:K6; Mon–Sat.* ▪ *Bellevue Place, Bellevue; 462-1400; map:HH3; Mon–Sat.*

**J. Crew**  J. Crew is known as the mail-order company that made the plaid-shirt-and-blue-jeans combination a look to emulate in men's and women's fashions. Bellevue hosts the only J. Crew in the Seattle metropolitan area—and this store is a standout. Crisp, clean design, uncluttered spaces, and inviting, plush, black side chairs reflect a casual elegance. From rugged flannel outerwear and corduroy jackets to silk charmeuse and sheer knit cardigans, J. Crew offers comfort and style. ▪ *Bellevue Square, Bellevue; 451-2739; map:HH3; every day.*

**Jessica McClintock Boutique**  Specializing in the most up-to-date in bridal wear, ultrafeminine dresses with lots of lace, sweeping skirts, velvet, and satin. If you don't see it in the store, full-color catalogs will help you make the best choices. ▪ *Westlake Center; 467-1048; map:I5; every day.*

▼

Apparel

▲

**Laura Ashley (Four Seasons Olympic Hotel)** Laura Ashley invented the look that defines a type: demure and country elegant. At the Seattle outpost in the Four Seasons Olympic Hotel, you shop for the ever popular floral-print smocks, dresses, pajama pants, and handsome velvets, as well as home decorations made from the same signature prints. Kids' and infants' clothes, crisp nighties, and imported bridal gowns too. ▪ *405 University St; 343-9637; map:L6; Mon–Sat.*

**Local Brilliance** Beneath painted clouds and satin green drapes, Local Brilliance showcases the best Northwest designers, and then some, so you can get originals at fairly affordable prices. Jewelry, belts, scarves, and even handbags shaped like pigs from local designers Jupiter and Mars. ▪ *1535 1st Ave; 343-5864; map:I8; every day.*

**Lord's** Look for Zanella slacks from Italy and the Northwest exclusive of the St. Croix line at this fine men's shop. Servicing Bellevue for nearly 30 years, Lord's carries beautifully cut suits and sport coats, as well as a larger-than-ever sportswear selection. ▪ *10520 NE 8th St (Bellevue Place); 454-1234; map:HH3; Mon–Sat.*

**Mario's of Seattle** Mario's cavernous setting proffers cutting-edge fashion and full service, from stunning shirts and sweaters to a dazzling array of Italian suits and shoes. Look here for Kenneth Cole, Basco, and Giorgio Armani for men; Donna Karan and Zanella for women. After shopping, sate your *other* appetite upstairs at the mezzanine cafe, Baci. ▪ *1513 6th Ave; 223-1461; map:J5; every day.*

▼

**Apparel**

▲

**Marlee** Marlee carries many local, very affordable designers, including Marylou Ozbolt, Storer, Seattle Gear, and dozens of others, as well as lines of playwear and dressier clothes and a few career-dressing styles. There is a large display of belts, and lots of affordable fun-to-wear jewelry to finish off any outfit. ▪ *University Village; 522-6526; map:FF6; every day.*

**Nelly Stallion** Original, elegant, savvy. Nelly's buyer prowls the garment district of New York and flies the finds to this stunning shop before anyone else in Seattle has them. Consequently, Nelly Stallion has won the hearts of the area's most stylish, who look upon the annual sales as seasonal must-attend events. High points are the beautiful separates, pretty lingerie, and vintage fashions. ▪ *1622 Queen Anne Ave N; 285-2150; map:FF6; every day.*

**Newport House** It's one of the stores on the Bellevue Ladies Circuit, but Newport House, with its sporty bent, appeals to a slightly younger clientele. Elegant, upper-end lines like David Dart, Kenar, Ballinger Gold, and Mac Akimo fill the racks. It's the reason to go to Factoria. ■ *Factoria Square, Bellevue; 747-6333; map:II3; every day.*

**Nubia's** These stores are named after the affable and knowledgeable owner who considers them a labor of love. Nubia's Colombian roots show up in her eclectic inventory; here she weaves a theme of Latin and Asian styles with relaxed sophistication. The best natural textiles distinguish the garments, whether knit sweaters and skirts or elegant silk pieces fashioned by Nubia herself. Accessories, scarves, and designer jewelry complement the clothing. ■ *1507 6th Ave; 622-0297; map:J5; Mon–Sat.* ■ *4116 E Madison; 325-4354; map:GG6; Mon–Sat.*

**Opus 204** A striking array of art, wearable and otherwise, distinguishes this outstanding Capitol Hill boutique. Owner Vija Rekevics assembles unique fashion and artifacts from all over the world. The clothes are of beautiful wools, cottons, linens, rayons, and silks, including Vija's own custom designs. Often spare and simple in design, always interesting. Some children's apparel as well. ■ *225 Broadway E; 325-1782; map:GG7; every day.*

**Pendleton** For Pendleton Wool lovers, this shop has it all: a wide selection of classic clothing for men and women, along with scarves and accessories. ■ *Bellevue Square, Bellevue (and branches); 453-9040; map:HH3; every day.*

▼

**Apparel**

▲

**Talbots** Fine women's fashions from the famous mail-order house. These clothes are classic for casual and special occasions. (This is the place for not-too-foofy bridesmaid dresses.) You'll think "pretty and preppy" as you browse the silks, wools, argyles, and gabardines. Petite and large-size sections, and Talbots Kids, too. ■ *Rainier Square; 464-1456; map:K6; every day.* ■ *Bellevue Square, Bellevue; 455-5058; map:HH3; every day.*

**Totally Michael's** Part of the Seattle clothing scene since 1971, the experienced and friendly owners, Michael and Carol, carry exciting clothing for sophisticates at work (beautifully tailored suits and separates), at play (relaxed, oh-so-chic casuals), and after dark (evening and party dresses). You'll find local designers represented along with Hind & Malee and Tamotsu. ■ *1525 6th Ave; 622-4920; map:K6; Mon–Sat.*

**Uno/Duo** Walking into Uno/Duo is like stepping into a Soho loft; cavernous rooms with brick walls and creaky wood floors, draperies over doorways, and hip music playing—tasteful yet understated. Uno/Duo offers an eclectic range of merchandise, with options for men and women including casual wear, Italian-tailored garments, costume jewelry, watches, and elegantly funky shoes. Especially fun are the far-out men's ties and undergear. ■ *2209 1st Ave; 448-7011; map:I7; every day.*

**Urban Outfitters** Appealing to the younger generation, Urban Outfitters' primary goal is to clothe the youthfully grungy in jeans, tops, and accessories: a visual deconstructionist's dream come true. If you're seeking casually hip clothing, an unusual card, a trendy book, or cool apartment accoutrements, you'll find them here. Don't let the shattered-glass entrance or the tattooed help deter you; nongrunge types have also been seen shopping here. ▪ *401 Broadway Ave E; 322-1800; map:GG6; every day.*

**What's That?** Owner Lenoir Perara specializes in dressing women in moderately priced alternative clothing with accessories to complement the looks. Suits have softer lines here, and casual clothes are chosen with a creative flair. Perara has a keen eye for fashion and obtains her stock from all over the world. ▪ *8117 161st Ave NE, Redmond; 881-3034; map:EE1; Mon–Sat.*

## AUCTIONS

▼

**Apparel**

▲

**Bushell's Auctions** Mary Bushell's auction house is open to all, with auctions every Tuesday at 10am and occasionally again at 7:30pm, depending on what's being sold (there are more antiques in the evenings). The merchandise (which comes from estate liquidations and private sales) changes weekly and consists of a great variety of household items, some antique, some contemporary: dishes, glassware, rugs, bedroom sets, and more. Treasures can be found here, and an occasional box of great junk that sells for a couple of bucks. Previews are noon to 5pm Fridays, 8am to 7pm Mondays. ▪ *2006 2nd Ave; 448-5833; map:H7; Mon–Fri.*

**Pacific Galleries** Twice a year the owner flies to Europe to bring back housewares, art, and furniture, which are featured in the monthly auctions. Many of these are antiques—Pacific Galleries is the largest such auction gallery in the Northwest. They auction items in every price range, from 50 cents to thousands of dollars. Preview from the catalog, but it's far better to get a look when the house opens for viewing, the weekend before each auction. This is one show you might not want to miss. The stage is set, and you're in the live audience, expecting Bob Barker to round the corner as you twitter on your folding chair, sitting on your hands to keep from entering the fray. ▪ *2121 3rd Ave; 441-9990; map:H7; call for schedule/by appointment.*

**Satori Fine Art Auction** An auction here in this cozy showroom used to be a low-key, refined affair; now it's a good-humored show, as much fun to watch as to take part in. The items are on consignment from private estates and may include European antique furniture, coins, jewelry, or fine art by old masters, as well as new porcelain, Oriental rugs, even some real estate. Satori is specializing in Northwest fine art. Pilchuck and other art glass is often for sale. Preview items from 10am to 6pm on Wednesdays, Thursdays, and Fridays, and 10am to 1pm on Saturdays; auctions are Saturdays and Sundays at 1pm. ■ *2305 5th Ave; 443-3666; map:F6; call to confirm auction dates.*

## BAKERIES

**A La Francaise** Buttery croissants and fine French bread are still the hallmarks of this long-established French bakery. The University Village retail shop carries a selection of all-butter pastries, fresh-fruit tarts, and a wonderful sour-cream chocolate cake with ganache icing. The Pioneer Square store has many of the same items, but in single slices for the downtown crowd. ■ *University Village; 524-9300; map:FF6; every day.* ■ *415 1st Ave S; 624-0322; map:O8; every day.*

**A Piece of Cake** It's adored for its light, fresh, fruit-filled sponge cakes (mango is the best). This International District favorite also bakes napoleons and Black Forest cakes, as well as authentic Chinese pastries. ■ *514 S King St; 623-8254; map:R6; Wed–Mon.*

**Bagel Oasis** This is the bagel shop transplanted Easterners rave about. Boiled before they are baked, the bagels are crisp-skinned outside and chewy inside, as authentic as you'll find this side of the Mississippi. No gimmicks here; the bagels come in eight traditional flavors, from salt to sesame seed to pumpernickel, along with a big, oniony bialy. A third store recently opened downtown at Fourth and Seneca. ■ *2112 NE 65th St; 526-0525; map:EE7; every day.* ■ *462 N 36th St; 633-2676; map:FF8; every day.*

**Bainbridge Bakers** Many islanders start their morning commute here with a pull-apart—an eight-grain whole wheat roll sweetened with raisins. If that sounds too healthy, just as tempting are the muffins, scones, Danish, and cinnamon rolls. The line often winds out the door, but the chatter is neighborly. The bakery's success has spawned a cafe located in Eagle Harbor Books one block north. ■ *140 Winslow Way, Bainbridge Island; 842-1822; every day.*

**Ballard Baking Company** Good breads, traditional cookies, and tempting pies fill the display cases in this little storefront, younger sister to the Greenwood Bakery. You'll find croissants, fruit tarts, and a large assortment of cookies. Coffee and newspapers invite you to linger. ■ *5909 24th Ave NW; 781-0091; map:EE9; every day.*

**Borracchini's Bakery & Mediterranean Market** See Ethnic Markets and Specialty Foods in this chapter. ■ *2307 Rainier Ave S; 325-1550; map:II6; every day.*

**Boulangerie** At this authentic French bakery you can count on excellent crusty loaves, buttery croissants, and heavenly brioche. The seigle noix—a dense, light rye bread with walnuts—is superb with cheese, which they sell as well. The place bustles, but service is quick. ▪ *2200 N 45th St; 634-2211; map:FF7; every day.*

**Brenner Brothers Bakery** Excellent challah, rich cream puffs, cheese pastries, and filled strudels are just some of the offerings in this kosher bakery. There's a deli with a small selection of specialty foods, too: rye bread, lox, pastrami, matzo, and other kosher supplies. ▪ *12000 NE Bellevue–Redmond Rd, Bellevue; 454-0600; map:GG3; every day.*

**Carolyn's Cakes** Owned by the same family for 50 years, this old-fashioned bakery still bakes some of the best pies you'll find on any holiday table. Generations of families have swooned over the creamy pumpkin pie, the rich brandied mincemeat, the wild blackberry, and the fresh rhubarb. Equally good are the cakes and cookies and the fluffy dinner rolls. ▪ *518 15th Ave E; 322-1152; map:GG6; Tues–Sat.*

**The Crumpet Shop** Better than an English muffin, these English griddle cakes are made from a yeasted batter using no fat, sugar, butter, or cholesterol. Get yours toasted, with butter and jam, and the crumpet's hole-y surface will catch every last drip of topping. Or try them as a sort of open-faced sandwich with tomatoes and ricotta or "green eggs and ham" (with pesto). ▪ *Pike Place Market; 682-1598; map:J8; every day.*

▼

**Bakeries**

▲

**Dessert Works** Everything here is made to order, but you can't miss with such tempting treats as white coconut cake, pecan caramel tart, or the strawberry bagatelle made with layers of white velvet cake and strawberries in white chocolate mousse. ▪ *6116 Phinney Ave N; 789-5765; map:EE7; Tues–Sat.*

**The Erotic Bakery** A little bit naughty and a little bit fun, the bakery does a bang-up business making cakes for men's and women's stag parties, anniversaries, or other (truly!) memorable occasions. White or chocolate cakes are topped off with buttercream frosting and a marzipan sculpture of your most, er, edible body parts. ▪ *2323 N 45th St; 545-6969; map:FF7; every day.*

**Grand Central Baking Company** The craze for Italian rustic bread started here, and this is still one of the best. Thanks to raves from *Sunset, Bon Appetit,* and *The New York Times,* legions of fans stop by to pick up their daily bread. The Como Loaf, a moist, crusty loaf of Italian-style bread, "may be to Seattle what sourdough is to San Francisco," according to one review. Rosemary rolls, whole grain and walnut loaves all have big followings. The bakery also offers scones and other pastries, and Grand Central does a brisk lunch business with sandwiches on the same fine breads. ▪ *214 1st Ave S; 622-3644; map:O9; Mon–Sat.* ▪ *138 107th Ave NE, Bellevue; 454-9661; map: HH3; every day.*

**Greenwood Bakery** Sister to Ballard Baking Company, this modest bakery has evolved into a neighborhood institution with a fiercely loyal clientele. The fruit tart with Grand Marnier custard is a favorite, and the award-winning sourdough Pain au Levain is an excellent excuse for a sandwich. Cookies are small and traditional; pastries border on decadent. ▪ *7227 Greenwood Ave N; 783-7181; map:EE7; every day.*

**Hoffman's Fine Pastries** June and Ed Hoffman's tiny, six-table bakery makes up in quality what it lacks in size. Buttery croissants, oh-so-tender scones, cookies, and Danish fill the cases. Their specialty cakes have earned them local renown, especially the Princess Torte—a surprisingly light concoction of sponge cake, Bavarian cream, raspberry filling, and bright green marzipan icing. ▪ *226 Parkplace Center, Kirkland; 828-0926; map:EE3; every day.*

**Honey Bear Bakery** See Desserts, Coffees, and Teas in the Nightlife chapter. ▪ *2106 N 55th St; 545-7296; map:FF6; every day.*

**Il Bacio Italian Pastry** It's hard to go wrong in this Redmond bakery. From almond or anise biscotti to light and fluffy tiramisu to apple-filled puff pastry sfogliatelle, the choices are numerous. Fancy cakes include Delizia—almond paste on two sponge layers with raspberry and apricot fillings—and Gianduia—sponge cake with chocolate hazelnut cream filling. ▪ *16564 Cleveland St, Redmond; 869-8815; EE1; Mon–Sat.*

**La Panzanella** Ciro Pasciuto started making his naturally fermented rustic Italian bread a few years back, and could hardly keep up with the demand. Now he's opened a retail shop on Capitol Hill where he offers his famous "Ciro bread," Italian pastries, seasonal fruit tarts, and small pizzas, panini, and crostini appetizers to take out. ▪ *1314 E Union St; 325-5217; map:HH7; Mon–Sat.*

**Larsen's Danish Bakery** The best Scandinavian bakery in town is even more visible with products available in most QFCs. Quality is high, with moderately priced Danish pastries, coffee cakes, kringles (a large pretzel-shaped puff pastry with almond paste in the center), light cookies, and great breads, particularly the eight-grain and Swedish rye. ▪ *8000 24th Ave NW; 782-8285; map:EE9; every day.* ▪ *5530 208th SW, Lynnwood; 771-4806; ; every day.*

**Le Panier Very French Bakery** In addition to some of the most enticing aromas in town, Le Panier's hearth ovens turn out fine baguettes (arguably Seattle's best); decorative epis; unusual breads (notably the onion and the hazelnut); heavenly amandine croissants; fruit tarts; and flavorful feuilletes (puff pastry pockets with savory or sweet fillings). ■ *Pike Place Market; 441-3669; map:J8; Mon–Sat.*

**London's Bakehouse** What can two guys from New York teach bread-savvy Seattle? Quite a lot, as it turns out, with 15 varieties of bread, as well as pastries and coffee cakes. The farm bread is a rustic French white-wheat-sourdough blend wonderful for sandwiches. Also tops are the onion black caraway rye, the Kalamata olive with fresh rosemary, and the raisin pecan breads. ■ *10640 Main St, Bellevue; 688-8332; map:HH3; Mon–Sat.*

**Macrina Bakery and Cafe** After introducing Seattle to rustic Italian breads at Grand Central Baking Company, Leslie Mackie opened her own bakery in Belltown. In addition to the rustic loaves you'd expect, Mackie has added a range of specialty breads—a pillow-soft potato bread, a wonderfully seedy Vollkorn (try it with a ripe camembert), a cinnamon-apple swirl Monkey Bread, an olive loaf, and several others. Macrina's Budapest Coffee Cake with a cocoa walnut swirl uses low-fat yogurt and buttermilk in place of sour cream. Besides the European-style pastries, Macrina offers breakfast and lunch in the Euro-stylish cafe. ■ *2408 1st Ave; 448-4032; map:F8; Mon–Sat.*

**Madison Park Bakery** Truly a neighborhood bakery, the shop has room to sit down with a cup of coffee and a good cinnamon roll, a mini–pecan cup (like the center of a sticky bun), or a selection of cookies or pastries. ■ *4214 E Madison St; 322-3238; map:GG6; Tues–Sat.*

**McGraw Street Bakery** Loyal Queen Anne residents flock here for what many believe are the best pastries around. Friendly owners Debra and Mark Dubief (who seem to know everyone by name) and their helpful employees (who cheerfully dole out marionberry coffee cake and chocolate cinnamon Danish while pulling lattes with aplomb) make this an early morning must-stop for commuters and a great neighborhood place to while away the afternoon over a sandwich (with bread made from scratch, natch). ■ *615 W McGraw St; 284-6327; map:GG8; every day.*

**John Nielsen Pastry** A marvelous downtown bakery and old-fashioned coffee shop with authentic Danish pastries, petits fours, and specialty cakes at great prices. Come early for a breakfast pastry, hot from the oven. ■ *1329 3rd Ave; 622-1570; map:K7; Mon–Sat.* CLOSED

**Patisserie Alinea** Started by a brother and sister from Norway, this Factoria shop produces truly beautiful desserts. These are special occasion cakes—dark chocolate torte, Delice raspberry mousse cake, or Mont Blanc, a white chocolate mousse cake with almond meringue, among others. ▪ *3610-C 128th Ave SE, Bellevue; 746-2724; map:II3; every day.*

**Seattle Bagel Bakery** For some people, the best bagel in town—and certainly the largest bagel around—is at this take-out and lunch-in spot next to the Harbor Steps. From plain to pesto to poppy seed, plus the baker's improvisational whims such as allium or honey walnut. ▪ *1302 Western Ave; 624-2187; map:K8; every day.*

**Simply Desserts** See Desserts, Coffees, and Teas in the Night-life chapter. ▪ *3421 Fremont Ave N; 633-2671; map:FF7; Tues–Sun.*

**60th Street Desserts** Primarily a wholesaler to many of Seat-tle's better restaurants, the bakery offers its superb tarts, cheesecakes, and tortes retail by advance order. The desserts change seasonally and include apricot-almond tart, Key lime cheesecake, and a dense, fudgelike Mocha Decadence. Any desserts deemed less than perfect are sold as seconds for a fraction of the price, subject to availability. ▪ *5758 35th Ave NE; 527-8560; map:EE6; Mon–Fri only for phone orders.*

**Spot Bagel Bakery** Lots of folks like this little spot in Walling-ford Center despite the sometimes slow service. These big, doughy spheres are infused with orange, poppy seeds, jalapeño, or seeded with chopped garlic cloves. Open-faced bagel-melts with tuna, turkey, ham, or vegetables and melted cheese make a gooey, filling lunch. A new shop has opened on the top of Queen Anne hill. ▪ *1815 N 45th St (and branches); 633-7768; map:FF7; every day.*

▼

**Bakeries**

▲

## BODY CARE

**Garden Botanika** Three environmentally concerned North-west natives began this skin- and body-care company in late 1990 and there are now over 100 stores nationwide (with four in the greater Seattle area). No animal products, no contro-versial animal testing, no petroleum products, and minimal packaging. ▪ *Westlake Center (and branches); 624-8292; map:I5; every day.*

**The Herbalist** The Herbalist—which has moved into a (larger) storefront location a block away from PCC in Ravenna—stocks all kinds of natural body-care supplies, including essential and massage oils, natural cosmetics, vitamin supplements, and a va-riety of herbs to cure, clean, and calm. A good selection of books and potpourri supplies, too; service is friendly and help-ful. ▪ *2106 NE 65th St; 523-2600; map:FF6; every day.*

**Nordstrom at Bellevue Square** No longer guarded in glass counters by a highly coiffed sales staff, those illusive, enigmatic cosmetic brands—from Chanel to Clinique—are now fully exposed, ready to be tinkered with. In addition, you may sample the lotions, powders, and pencils of Lancome, Estee Lauder, and MAC, among others, while roaming freely from station to station, trying a little of this, a little of that, without the cloying ministrations of the Made-up Ones—a welcome alternative to the traditional department store cosmetics counter. ■ *Bellevue Square, Bellevue; 455-5800; map:HH3; every day.*

**Parfumerie Elizabeth George** First, Elizabeth George tests your skin's pH content, then she matches the right fragrance to your skin and helps you learn to wear it. She's spent over 10 years at her craft, purveying one of the top lines of designer-matched scents (less expensive versions of the originals), and specializing in custom and hard-to-find perfumes. Beautiful atomizers and a line of lotions and bath products. ■ *1424 4th Ave; 622-7212; map:J6; Mon–Sat.*

**Parfumerie Nasreen** Fittingly situated off the lobby in the Alexis Hotel, Parfumerie Nasreen is the only all-perfume store in the city, stocking close to 400 different fragrances, many from exotic lands, in all price ranges. ■ *1005 1st Ave; 682-3459; map:M8; Mon–Sat.*

▼

**Body Care**

▲

**The Soap Box** A fragrant emporium of perfumed soaps, bath oils, lotions, unique and beautiful imported items from all over, and other novelties for the bath. You can always find a gift here; they'll mix any scent you like into a lotion, oil, or bubble bath brew. There's a branch in Pike Place Market, and an even tinier version downtown at Third and Marion. ■ *4340 University Way NE (and branches); 634-2379; map:FF6; every day.*

**Tenzing Momo & Co.** If you get past the thick cloud of incense that lingers in the doorway of this small Pike Place Market shop, you'll discover a serious natural apothecary. Herbal body-care products line the shelves, and the staff is extremely knowledgeable about the properties (and mysteries) of the dozens of varieties of herbs, tinctures, and elixirs they carry, including natural remedies for PMS, dandruff, athlete's foot, or whatever ails you. ■ *93 Pike Place Market; 623-9837; map:J8; Mon–Sat.*

## BOOKS/MAGAZINES/NEWSPAPERS

**All for Kids Books and Music** In this jam-packed store near the University Village (with another branch in Issaquah), classics and classics-to-be are given equal attention. All for Kids seems to embrace the evolving concept of interactive children's books, stocking plenty of kits, tapes, and activities as well. There's a music or reading event every day, except in August. ■ *2900 NE Blakely St; 526-2768; map:FF6; every day.* ■ *170 Front St, Issaquah; 391-4089; every day.*

**Bailey/Coy Books** Bailey/Coy offers a wide spectrum and an eclectic mix, well suited to the Broadway crowds: fiction and literature (including mystery and sci-fi), poetry, lesbian and gay studies, women's studies, and philosophy. Look here also for coffee table books, child care, gardening, cooking, and a good selection of literary magazines. ▪ *414 Broadway E; 323-8842; map:GG7; every day.*

**Barnes & Noble Books** B&N is one super superstore (though you might forget you're actually *in* a store when you see its library-like dark wood detailing, deep green carpeting, and upholstered chairs tucked among the bookcases). The selection is generally excellent (though the staff is not generally knowledgeable), and they do a good job of showcasing local authors. The new University Village location rivals St. Peter's for size and sheer overwhelmingness, and B&N even has the courage to put chairs and tables right next to the magazine racks. Starbucks cafes come attached. ▪ *626 106th Ave NE, Bellevue (and branches); 451-8463; HH3; every day.*

**Beatty Bookstore** Among the largest general used-book stores in Seattle, Beatty has a huge inventory that includes one of the best bibliography sections on the West Coast. Excellent regional, art, philosophy, and cookbooks, too. They pay well for the used books they buy, ask fair prices for the books they sell, and are very knowledgeable about their inventory. ▪ *1925 3rd Ave; 728-2665; map:I6; Mon–Sat.*

**Beks Bookstore** An uptown bookstore to match its location: good selections of contemporary fiction, current nonfiction best sellers, business, travel, and coffee table volumes. Service is friendly and knowledgeable and they'll special-order anything you can't find. The smaller shop in the Washington Mutual Tower makes a great spot to grab a potboiler or magazine for the commute home. ▪ *1301 5th Ave (Rainier Square); 624-1328; map:K6; Mon–Sat.* ▪ *1201 3rd Ave (Washington Mutual Tower); 224-7028; map:K7; Mon–Fri.*

**Beyond the Closet Bookstore** Filling an important niche in the community, Beyond the Closet carries all manner of gay and lesbian books both by gay and lesbian authors and regarding gay or lesbian subjects—from the political to the everyday to the explicit. The fiction section is notable for the lesser-known authors and books from small presses, though it also carries best sellers if they're appropriate. ▪ *1501 Belmont St; 322-4609; map:K1; every day.*

**Blackbird** Joseph Antoine-Zimbabwe sells strictly African and African-American literature from his small, well-stocked store on Lake Washington. ▪ *1316 E Pike St; 325-3793; map:HH6; every day.*

**Borders Books & Music** The best of the chain superstores, Borders models itself after the best of the independents, including a staff who actually know something about books. The large general inventory is enhanced by a wide and varied Northwest section and a sensible, comfortable store layout. After choosing this week's good read, head upstairs to the music section and browse through the impressive array of CDs. The store also features regular events and signings and a small cafe. ■ *1501 4th Ave (and branches); 622-4599; map:J6; every day.*

**Bowie & Company Booksellers** Here you'll find the oldest and rarest books in town (dating to 1475). M. Taylor Bowie, known for his outstanding collection of antiquarian books, stocks a wide range of out-of-print books, maps, and west-of-the-Mississippi ephemera. It's not exclusive: there are items ranging from $5 to $70,000. A catalog is issued frequently for mail orders. Appraisals are available (informal ones are free of charge), as is a good book-search service. ■ *314 1st Ave S; 624-4100; map:O8; every day.*

**Bulldog News and Fast Espresso** Between 1,800 and 2,700 publications are stocked at this indispensable Ave newsstand: periodicals, foreign magazines, and newspapers. They also sell espresso to sip while you browse. The other branch is a kiosk at the heart of Broadway Market. ■ *4208 University Way NE; 632-6397; map:FF6; every day.* ■ *Broadway Market; 322-6397; map:HH6; every day.*

**Chameleon** If you're lucky, you'll get to hear owner Al Frank practicing jazz riffs on his upright piano as you browse through his carefully chosen collection of used books. The once-general stock has begun to lean toward the rare and antiquarian, and includes a fine selection of volumes on art and architecture, science and medicine, and illustrated books, among others. Sets, fine bindings, books on books, and first editions, too. Fair prices for trades. ■ *514 15th Ave E; 323-0154; map:GG6; every day.*

**Cinema Books** A specialty bookstore located under a movie theater could sell only one thing: film-related books. You'll also find magazines, screenplays, posters, stills, and technical books for filmmakers. Truly a movie-lover's paradise. ■ *4753 Roosevelt Way NE; 547-7667; map:FF6; Mon–Sat.*

**David Ishii, Bookseller** This small, crowded Pioneer Square shop features finely selected books reflecting the tastes and interests of the proprietor—David Ishii is Seattle's fly-fishing and baseball guru. His eclectic collection of used, out-of-print, and scarce books is the region's largest on these subjects. Baseball fans can buy Everett AquaSox tickets here, too. ■ *212 1st Ave S; 622-4719; map:O8; every day.*

▼

**Books/ Magazines/ Newspapers**

▲

**East West Book Shop** Based on the East West store in Palo Alto, Seattle's version is a good place to thumb through alternative and off-the-wall books by authors who are either crazy or geniuses, and sometimes a bit of each. One of the most comprehensive Jungian psychology selections in town. Friday night speakers forums focus on topics ranging from spiritual healing to near-death experiences. ■ *1032 NE 65th St; 523-3726; map:EE7; every day.*

Shopping
I

**Elliott Bay Book Company** [KIDS] Since opening in 1973, Seattle's premier bookstore has never stopped growing beyond the boundaries of its original rough-hewn one-room shop in Pioneer Square. Today, it still offers a relaxed, literary atmosphere, but you need a map to navigate your way around the ever changing nooks of books. The children's section has expanded to fit a large area of the store; up front, travel has its own room for a wide-reaching choice of maps, atlases, and foreign language references. Regardless of where your favorite niche ends up, you'll find an excellent selection.

Elliott Bay stocks over 150,000 titles. Service is smart and efficient; they'll field any question, and wrap and send your entire gift list. [FREE] The free quarterly newsletter, *Book Notes*, runs book reviews and staff recommendations, profiles authors, and announces recent paperback releases. Readings and signings, drawing the nation's premier authors, occur six days a week. These are free, but tickets are often required to ensure a place—these readings are popular; the schedule is printed out on your receipt. Kids' readings take place the first Saturday morning of each month. And the homey basement cafe is the perfect place to dive into your new purchases. ■ *101 S Main St; 624-6600; map:O8; every day.*

▼

Books/
Magazines/
Newspapers

▲

**Fillipi Book and Record Shop** A store to lose yourself in. The superb selection of used and rare books, records, and sheet music is constantly being updated, and they can get virtually anything. Prices, however, tend to be higher than elsewhere in the city. ■ *1351 E Olive Way; 682-4266; map:HH7; Tues–Sat.*

**Flora and Fauna** This Pioneer Square basement offers the largest selection of books on natural history, gardening, and the life sciences that you'll find anywhere on the West Coast, possibly in the country. New, used, and rare books—it's all here, aardvarks to zinnias, in more than 25,000 titles. Buy or sell. ■ *121 1st Ave S; 623-4727; map:N8; Mon–Sat.*

**Fremont Place Book Company** Located in the heart of this now-trendy grassroots neighborhood, Fremont Place is a small, bright bookstore anchored in its tight community. New and contemporary fiction, women's studies, gay and lesbian literature, and regional books are the areas of emphasis, along with a small but well-chosen children's section. Throughout the store you can find tags with good staff recommendations subtly pasted to the shelves. The store also showcases a selection of colorfully painted T-shirts. ■ *621 N 35th St; 547-5970; map:FF8; every day.*

**The Globe Books** You'll find a broad selection (new and used) in the humanities (especially literature and reference books) and a growing section of natural science books in this U District bookstore. Don't be intimidated by the specialized inventory; this is a wonderfully unstuffy place and a real labor of love. Browse through the antique maps and replicas, too. Trades are welcome. ■ *5220 University Way NE; 527-2480; map:FF6; every day.*

**Half-Price Books and Tapes** No evasiveness here. Half-Price sells books at, well, half-price. They will also buy your used books, with someone on call at all hours for pricing. There's a large selection of classical literature, as well as a huge line of discounted new and used software, with branches in Bellevue (in Crossroads Mall), Tukwila (16829 Southcenter Parkway), and Edmonds (23632 Highway 99). ■ *4709 Roosevelt Way NE (and branches); 547-7859; map:FF7; every day.*

**Horizon Books** Don Glover has been buying and selling used books from his nook-and-cranny 15th Street shop since 1971, offering an emphasis on literature, criticism, history, mystery, and philosophy. His second store (6512 Roosevelt Way NE) is well-stocked, neatly laid-out, and imminently browseable, and a third location is now open in Greenwood (8570 Greenwood Avenue N). ■ *425 15th Ave E (and branches); 329-3586; map:GG6; every day.*

**Island Books** [KIDS]A good general bookstore with a lot of personal service. Besides a fine assortment of children's books, nice touches for kids include a playhouse and story hours on Saturdays throughout the year. ■ *3014 78th St SE, Mercer Island; 232-6920; map:II4; every day.*

**Kinokuniya Bookstore** Upstairs at Seattle's largest Asian grocery store, Uwajimaya, is an extraordinary landscape of Japanese books and magazines comparable in size to many English-language bookstores in town. There's a great selection of books in English—mostly by Japanese authors or on Japanese subjects—spanning a variety of topics, including alternative medicine, travel, language (tapes, too), fiction, children's books, and cookbooks. ■ *519 6th Ave S (above Uwajimaya); 587-2477; map:Q7; every day.*

**Left Bank Books** From buttons to bumper stickers to books, variety is the rule in this alternative bookstore in the Corner Market building. The emphasis is on politics of a reddish hue; there are also good new and used social science, contemporary poetry, fiction, gay and lesbian, and philosophy sections. ■ *Pike Place Market; 622-0195; map:J8; every day.*

**M Coy Books** Michael Coy takes bookselling seriously, and he's crafted his retail business into a fine art. He knows how to make you feel good about books and has a talent for suggesting other titles that will interest you (discuss them over a latte at the espresso bar in back). The Pine Street store (one block east of Pike Place Market) carries a spectrum of books with an emphasis on contemporary literature, photography, art, gardening, and interior and graphic design. ▪ *117 Pine St; 623-5354; map:J8; every day.*

**Madison Park Books** On a corner in the cozy Madison Park neighborhood, this pleasant, roomy shop with a patient and helpful staff is a good choice for browsing new titles. There's a nice array of large-format coffee table volumes, with a concentration on art and photography, and cookbooks and garden books are well represented. Kids' selections are thoughtfully chosen. ▪ *4105 E Madison St; 328-7323; map:GG6; every day.*

**Magus Bookstore** If you can't find a used book here, it probably doesn't exist. A staple in this student-dominated neighborhood, Magus carries everything from classical literature to engineering and has a large science-fiction selection and tons of Cliff Notes, as well as a poetry section that would do any new-book store proud. ▪ *1408 NE 42nd St; 633-1800; map:FF6; every day.*

**MisterE Books** This Pike Place Market shop specializes in mystery (hence the name), fantasy, horror, and signed editions by the likes of Ray Bradbury, Harlan Ellison, and Maurice Sendak. Authors' signings and lots of kids' books, as well as hard-to-find collectors' volumes and an ecclectic array of LPs, too. ▪ *Pike Place Market; 622-5182; map:I8; every day.*

**Open Books** The store's subtitle—A Poem Emporium—says it all. Christine Deavel and John Marshall (they are both poets, the editors of *Fine Madness* magazine, and devoted to their craft) closed the original Open Books, a general bookstore, and opened this clean little place a couple of blocks east. If you're not a dedicated poetry reader when you go in, volume after volume of new, used, and out-of-print poetry (as well as poetry on tape) just might convert you. Open books puts poetry in the forefront by proximity of a neighboring arena for readings. It's quiet and inviting, and the proximity of an adjoining wine bar increases the allure of reading and contemplation. There are obscure poets here, classics, and contemporary greats, but Deavel and Marshall are not too proud to carry *Poetry for Cats.* ▪ *2414 N 45th St; 633-0811; map:FF7; Tues–Sat.*

**Parkplace Books** [KIDS] Co-owner Ted Lucia is a book rep who decided to open his own account. He and his wife, Kathi, own this general bookstore that pays close attention to children's books, mystery, and fiction. Open and airy and impeccably organized, the store also has a friendly staff worthy of a book rep's knowledge. ■ *348 Parkplace Center, Kirkland; 828-6546; map:EE3; every day.*

**Peter Miller Architectural and Design Books and Supplies** In an elegantly spare space, Peter Miller's shop carries not only the best local selection of new, used, and out-of-print architectural books (one of few such specialized outlets in the country), but also a collection of European and Japanese gadgets and drafting supplies. Ask about the catalog. ■ *1930 1st Ave; 441-4114; map:H8; every day.*

**Queen Anne Avenue Books** Its selection fits into a cozy space, but the staff at this pleasant neighborhood shop more than make up for the squeeze with their intelligence, good recommendations, and overall geniality. Special orders are handled quickly and efficiently. ■ *1629 Queen Anne Ave N; 283-5624; map:GG8; every day.*

**Read All About It** An enormous selection of local, national, and international papers and magazines is displayed at this colorful newsstand in Pike Place Market (across from DeLaurenti). A Market institution with a jolly staff. ■ *Pike Place Market; 624-0140; map:J8; every day.*

**Red and Black Books** [KIDS] As much of an awareness outlet as a bookstore, this volunteer collective shelves books you may not find in other stores. Books, newspapers, pamphlets, and buttons cover politics, race, gay/lesbian issues, and, for that matter, almost any issue with a radical bent. Multicultural fiction and nonfiction for all ages, and a kids' play area. ■ *432 15th Ave E; 322-7323; map:GG6; every day.*

**Seattle Mystery Bookshop** Bill Farley set up his subterranean store in Pioneer Square in 1990 with a shivering collection of thrillers. The whodunit crowd will love this well thought-out, well laid-out shop. From the latest releases to Sherlock Holmes, a clever display of first-in-a-series to out-of-print editions, you'll find them here. Today's most popular mystery writers often drop in for signings. ■ *117 Cherry St; 587-5737; map:N8; every day.*

**Second Story Books** A terrific little general bookstore with excellent children's, regional, and fiction sections. Ask about joining the rental library, or come for an autograph party. Good displays draw you in, and big, comfy armchairs invite you to stay. ■ *1815 N 45th St (Wallingford Center); 547-4605; map:FF7; every day.*

**The Secret Garden Children's Bookshop** [KIDS] The Secret Garden is the oldest exclusively children's bookstore in the city, and in its big new Ballard location it continues to grow, with expanded parenting and children's nonfiction sections.

The selection is fine here; special events (musical performances, classes, signings, and the occasional reading) are entertaining. The Secret Garden is involved in literacy efforts, with programs for teachers and parents and book fairs for local schools. ■ *6115 15th Ave NW; 789-5006; map:EE8; every day.*

**Shorey Bookstore** Shorey's, one of the world's largest general antiquarian bookstores, has been in existence since 1890 and has an inventory now numbering over a million. You can find everything here, from 95-cent paperbacks to $10,000 rare printings. The staff conduct effective searches for out-of-print titles. ■ *1411 1st Ave; 624-0221; map:J8; every day.*

**Steve's Broadway News** Steve Dunnington's news nook has become a newshound's source for current issues of periodicals, from regional magazines to Australian dailies. No back issues. Open every day from 8am until 11pm, 364 days of the year (closed Christmas). ■ *204 Broadway E; 324-7323; map:GG7; every day.*

**Tower Books** Russ Solomon's chain that's not exactly a chain—as the selection is bought locally—Tower has an outstanding computer-book selection, as well as an excellent general-book selection with a bias toward genres: mysteries, sci-fi, and sports. Open until midnight every day of the year, even holidays, with a branch in Bellevue (downtown at 10635 NE Eighth). ■ *20 Mercer St; 283-6333; map:GG8; every day.*

**Twice Sold Tales** What began as a one-room shop on Capitol Hill's John Street (luring in bus-stop customers with racks of 50-cent books and a sign reading "you can always catch the next bus") has overflowed into the store next door and two other (separately owned) locations (in Pioneer Square and Wallingford). No musty stacks of old science texts here; the shelves offer a generous collection of fiction, poetry, cooking, and more—interspersed with cartoons, cat humor, and pop philosophy. The stores are known for fair prices when buying books, though this is reflected in the retail prices, which some people feel are high. Things are never dull at the John Street location; a bubble machine runs constantly out a front window, cats are suspended overhead on specially designed highways that bridge the tall bookcases, and the owner (and her employees) are opinionated and loud. ■ *905 John St (and branches); 324-2421; map:GG7; every day.*

**University Book Store** [KIDS] The largest bookstore in Washington also happens to be the largest college bookstore in the U.S. The U Dub's primary bookstore has a vast selection (especially the gardening, arts, and design departments) that *is* a bit overwhelming at first. Don't hesitate to ask for help: customer service goes beyond expected boundaries—with free

▼

Books/
Magazines/
Newspapers

▲

book shipping *and* parking validation; and in the rare event that your title is not in stock, staff will promptly special order it. But browse on your own, too, especially the large remaindered section. The store often sponsors large events or readings in conjunction with the University and, if you want a computer, a camera, or a Husky dressed in purple and gold, you'll find them here, too. The branch across the lake is smaller and does not carry textbooks or have the buy-back service; it does carry an extensive general literature and children's selection. In 1995, a new branch opened in downtown. Catering to corporate Seattle, it features an awesome selection of business and computer titles. ■ *4326 University Way NE; 634-3400; map:FF6; every day.* ■ *990 102nd Ave NE, Bellevue; 632-9500; map:HH3; every day.* ■ *1225 4th Ave; 545-9230; map:K6; Mon–Sat.*

**Wessel and Lieberman Booksellers** Beyond books for reading, there are books for collecting. This high-quality shop specializing in first-edition fiction, Western Americana (especially Northwest and Native American history), and books on books has quickly become a favorite among Seattle book collectors, thanks to the personal attention of Mark Wessel and Michael Lieberman. In an increasingly electronic age, it's exciting to see due respect given to the craft of making books. And Wessel and Lieberman's presentations of books as art objects—miniature books, take-apart books, books in cigar-box covers, and a rotating exhibit of artists' books—give bibliophiles yet another reason to visit often. ■ *121 1st Ave S; 682-3545; map:N8; Mon–Sat, every day in summer.*

▼

**Books/
Magazines/
Newspapers**

▲

**Wide World Books and Maps** All of the employees are seasoned wanderers, so advice on specific trips and travel in general is part of the service. Aside from a vast array of travel books, you'll find a complete range of accessories, including globes, maps, language tapes, a passport photo service, and luggage. The serene Teahouse Kuan Yin next door is the perfect place in which to contemplate future journeys. ■ *1911 N 45th St; 634-3453; map:FF7; every day.*

## CAMERAS/PHOTO SUPPLIES

**The Camera Show** The continually changing stock at this used-camera shop presents cameras and gear from collector's items to late-model equipment. Proprietor Ed Olson buys and sells photographic equipment, and he knows virtually everything about the trade. Hours are limited: 12pm to 6pm, five days a week. ■ *7509 Aurora Ave N; 782-9448; map:EE7; Tues–Sat.*

**CameraTech** Once a camera-repair shop and photography gallery, CameraTech now concentrates mostly on repairs (the hired techs occupy part of the former gallery space). Free testing and estimates of your used equipment are part of the deal here, and a good selection of refurbished cameras are offered for sale alongside racks of accessories. ▪ *5254-A University Way NE; 526-5533; map:FF6; Mon–Sat.*

**Cameras West** The best discount prices in town and a good selection of major brands make this *the* place for amateurs to shop for a new camera. Cameras West also carries a large inventory of video equipment, with branches in Bellevue, Southcenter, and Northgate Mall. ▪ *1908 4th Ave (and branches); 622-0066; map:I6; every day.*

**Glazer's Camera Supply** The city's oldest professional-grade camera store, Glazer's is on par with any of the best in the photo districts across the nation. There's a complete rental department—from studio lights to large format cameras, a full line of film and paper, and a most knowledgeable staff. ▪ *430 8th Ave N; 624-1100; map:D3; Mon–Sat.*

**Ivey Seright** The primo photo lab in the Northwest caters to the commerical photographer, but will gladly accept (for a price, though you'll definitely get your money's worth) business from the casual photographer. They'll process all formats of film, print up to mural size, and are conveniently located right next to Glazer's. ▪ *424 8th Ave N; 623-8113; map:D3; Mon–Sat.*

**Moonphoto** Moon does black and white processing and printing only. Additional services include retouching and restoration of old photos, and printing old negatives. ▪ *431 Westlake Ave N; 682-7260; map:E3; Mon–Fri.* ▪ *7704 Greenwood Ave N; 783-3377; map:EE8; Mon–Sat.*

**Optechs Camera Supply** Another professional-grade camera store, Optechs is Number Two (after Glazer's) and tries much harder. What started out as a tiny shop has grown into a full-service photo center catering to the evolving pro. There's a rental department, film and paper, and a highly educated staff. ▪ *433 Fairview Ave N; 343-9900 or (800)527-6611; map:E1; Mon–Sat.*

**Photographic Center Northwest** The only rental darkrooms in Seattle are available here. Do-it-yourselfers can try black-and-white, color, and Cibachrome printing from both slides and negatives. PCN offers classes and workshops and will do the printing for you at slightly lower prices than other labs. ▪ *2617 5th Ave; 441-7030; map:D7; every day.*

**Photo-tronics** The place to go for complete repair of most still and video cameras, Photo-tronics is also the warranty center for most major brands. A knowledgeable staff offers in-house repair with a very reasonable turnaround time. ▪ *223 Westlake Ave N; 682-2646; map:F4; Mon–Sat.* ▪ *13281 NE 20th St, Bellevue; 643-1131; map:HH3; Mon–Sat.*

▼

Cameras/
Photo
Supplies

▲

**ProLab** Serving both the commercial and portrait photographer, ProLab processes and prints all formats. There's extensive in-house automation options for economy services. ▪ *123 NW 36th St; 547-5447; map:FF8; Mon–Sat.*

**Rainier Photographic Supply** You'll find a stockhouse of film, paper, and darkroom chemistry supplies at this photographic specialty shop. Buy in quantity and the good prices get even better. ▪ *8730 Rainier Ave S; 722-8700; map:JJ6 ; Mon–Sat.*

**Warshal's** While Warshal's may be known primarily as a sporting goods store, photographers in-the-know shop and trade here. Expect less stock on hand than other photo houses, and bear in mind that this is a great source for 35mm and medium-format equipment, film and paper. ▪ *1000 1st Ave; 624-7300; map:M7; Mon–Sat.*

## CANDIES AND CHOCOLATES

**Cafe Dilettante** See Desserts, Coffees and Teas in the Nightlife chapter. ▪ *416 Broadway E (and branches); 329-6463; GG7; every day.* ▪ *1603 1st Ave; 728-9144; map:GG7; every day.*

**Chocolaterie Bernard C** The only Bernard Callebaut store in the U.S., this sleek gem houses the renowned Belgian Callebaut chocolates, made by Bernard's Calgary confectionery. Sauces, baking supplies, and ice cream bars too. Bernard occasionally travels to Kirkland to conduct candy-making classes at the store. ▪ *128 Central Way, Kirkland; 822-8889; map:EE3; every day.*

**The Confectionery** A Candyland of treats gleaned from around the world. Chocolates from Fran's, Dilettante, Joseph Schmidt, and Baker's, plus Valrhona and Perugina bars, licorice, gummies, Jelly Bellies, hard candies, taffy, kosher, low-cal, and sugarless candies. Fun selection of gift tins, bags, and piñatas. ▪ *University Village; 523-1443; map:FF6; every day.*

**Fran's Chocolates** In a jewel box of a store on East Madison are the crème de la crème of locally made truffles and creams. Fran Bigelow, whose renown has spread from Seattle throughout the nation, hand dips her delectable creations in fine Belgian chocolate and offers them at great prices. Tortes, ice cream, and Gold Bars, of course. Hand-painted gift boxes. In season, look for fresh figs stuffed with ganache. ▪ *2805 E Madison St; 322-6511; map:GG6; Tues–Sat.*

**Godiva Chocolatier** These are the only shops in the Northwest devoted exclusively to Godiva—the chocolate as rich in cachet as in calories. Chocolate sauces and espresso, as well. In Westlake Mall and Bellevue Square. ▪ *Westlake Mall; 622-0280;*

map:J6; every day. ▪ *Bellevue Square, Bellevue; 646-8837; map:HH3; every day.*

**Schober Chocolates** Extraordinary Teuscher chocolates are flown in weekly from Switzerland for true connoisseurs. Look for Dom Perignon champagne truffles, white truffles, and cherries with Cognac. Sugarless chocolates, too. Pricey, but worth it. ▪ *1420 5th Ave (City Centre); 682-7295; map:K6; Mon–Sat.* ▪ *Bellevue Square, Bellevue; 462-6135; map:HH3; every day.*

**The Sweet Addition** It's licorice heaven, but dozens of chewy, gummy, hard, and sugarless candies tempt shoppers just as much. Look for Portland's Moonstruck truffles here, plus other fine chocolates. The Addition also serves homespun pies, towering cakes, and soup/salad/sandwich–style lunches. ▪ *Gilman Village, Issaquah; 392-5661; every day.*

**Temptations** [KIDS] A great place to find party treats or to fill up a stocking or Easter basket. It's all here: jelly beans, hard candies, gumballs, cordials, covered espresso beans, dried fruits, nut confections, gumballs, and chocolates from Fran's, Boehm, and Joseph Schmidt. ▪ *10116 NE 8th St, Bellevue (QFC Village); 455-4844; map:HH3; every day.*

▼

## CHILDREN'S CLOTHING

**Boston Street** Snazzy duds for stylish kids sizes 0 to 14. Much of the clothing here is locally made and one of a kind—pretty smocks and tiny jean jackets. They also carry the colorful Cotton Caboodle label and pint-size accessories and umbrellas. Great gifts for your favorite niece or nephew. Some of the best baby duds around. ▪ *101 Stewart St; 728-1490; map:I8; every day.* ▪ *1815 N 45th St; 634-0580; map:FF7; every day.*

▲

**Fine Threads** Here's the best selection of classic, high quality boys' and young men's clothing in the Northwest (Fine Threads carries sizes for males ages 4 to 104). This is where to shop for his first suit—if you are willing to pay a man's price. ▪ *University Village; 525-5888; map:FF6; every day.*

**The Kids Club** These two stores feature colorful (if slightly expensive) childrens' and infants' clothes and shoes. They also have an abundance of baby paraphernalia—from car-seat covers to bottle warmers to snugglies. The Crossroads location, which is larger and has a better selection, even has a kiddie hair salon (The Hair Chair) to keep the kids occupied while Mom shops (the U Village store has a big TV with videos running to accomplish the same purpose). ▪ *University Village; 524-2553; map:FF6; every day.* ▪ *Crossroads Mall, Bellevue; 643-5437; map:HH1; every day.*

**Kids in the Park** At this imaginative little shop in Madison Park, the emphasis is on high-end European children's clothing and accessories. Plenty of cute little-girl wear: slips, nighties, bathing suits, and tiny leotards. ▪ *4105 E Madison St; 324-0449; map:GG6; Mon–Sat.*

**Kym's Kiddy Corner** Though it looks like a shabby consignment store from the outside, Kym's sells both new and (usually in good condition) consignment clothes, toys, and equipment, and offers some of the best prices in town. Whether it's mittens or swimsuits you're after, they are usually well supplied—even at the height of the season when everyone else is out of stock. ▪ *11721 15th Ave NE; 361-5974; map:CC7; every day.*

**Li'l People** Whimsy and cotton knits prevail here. Baggy bloomers and leggings in charming prints and bright solid hues, patchwork cardigans, fleece jumpsuits, and inventive headgear (the best selection of sun hats in the city) for Jughead or Veronica. ▪ *Westlake Center; 623-4463; map:I5; every day.* ▪ *Bellevue Square, Bellevue; 455-4967; map:HH3; every day.*

**Me 'N Mom's** Carrying sizes newborn through 14, this store concentrates on sizes 6X and under. It specializes in 100 percent cotton playwear, such as the exclusive line Flapdoodles. Both new and consignment; and there's always a healthy section of sales merchandise. Get your kid's hair cut while you shop—the store adjoins the unparalleled kids' hair salon, L'il Klippers. ▪ *1021 NE 65th St (Roosevelt Square); 524-9344; map:EE6; every day.*

▼

**Children's Clothing**

▲

**The Shoe Zoo** The kids' shoe store to use if you want comprehensive selection with salespeople who really pay attention to your child. They specialize in old-fashioned service (they keep a file of kids' previous purchases so you don't have to remember your child's shoe size in a particular brand every time) with a good selection of everything from Buster Browns for dress-up to the lastest version of kid-Teva's. ▪ *University Village; 525-2770; map:FF6; every day.* ▪ *Gilman Station (across from Gilman Village), Issaquah; 392-8211; every day.*

## COFFEE AND TEA

**MarketSpice** MarketSpice, famous for its aromatic teas in more than 50 flavors, also carries an extensive line of coffee beans, and more than 200 different spices from all over the world (including hard-to-find items like juniper berries). In the Main Arcade. ▪ *Pike Place Market; 622-6340; map:J8; every day.*

**Pegasus Coffee** Both the original Pegasus on Bainbridge Island and the downtown shop receive around 20 freshly roasted varieties of coffee daily. They have an expanded tea selection and offer home-baked goods, too. Pegasus coffees can be found

in local retail stores, such as Larry's Markets. ▪ *131 Parfitt*
*Way SW, Bainbridge Island; 842-6725; every day.* ▪ *711 3rd*
*Ave; 682-3113; map:N7; Mon–Fri.*

**The Perennial Tea Room** For the largest selection of teapots
(from China, Japan, the Philippines, and an impressive collection of handcrafted pots by Northwest artisans), look no further
than the Perennial Tea Room. Shop owners Julee Rosanoff and
Sue Zuege operate on the "tea is fun" principle and consider it
their mission to help us love loose teas. With 55 tea varieties
plus infusers, kettles, cozies, and tea-centric books, their mission is more than accomplished. ▪ *1910 Post Alley; 448-4054;*
*map:I8; every day.*

**Seattle's Best Coffee (SBC)** The largest local rival to Starbucks roasts its coffees on Vashon Island. SBC (which
changed its name from Stewart Brothers Coffee at the behest
of the trademarked Stewart's Private Blend in Chicago) de-
votes most of its business to selling wholesale to restaurants;
however, their coffee bars are among the most stylish places
in the city in which to sip Seattle's black gold. ▪ *1530 Post Al-*
*ley (and branches); 467-7700; map:J8; every day.*

**Starbucks** With more than 600 stores (100 of them in Washington alone) in the U.S. and Canada, Starbucks can be credited with establishing Seattle as the notorious coffee-swilling
town that it is. Good blends and varietals (nearly 50 of them)
are the reason. You'll also find the best in brewing accessories,
several imported teas, and coffee by the cup. A few branches
serve sandwiches (made out-of-house); others offer various
sweets and breakfast breads. ▪ *Pike Place Market (and*
*branches); 448-8762; map:J8; every day.*

▼

**Coffee
and Tea**

▲

**The Tea Cup** Though Seattle is a long way from kicking the coffee habit, teahouses are on the rise. The Tea Cup serves more
than 100 different teas (including a tea latte), all of which can
be purchased for home consumption. Inside, sippers can either
park at the stand-up bar or at one of the two tables. The more
adventurous can sit outside on the storefront benches and observe the bustle of Queen Anne. ▪ *2207 Queen Anne Ave N;*
*283-5931; map:GG7; every day.*

**Teahouse Kuan Yin** See Desserts, Coffees, and Teas in the Nightlife chapter. ▪ *1911 N 45th St; 632-2055; map:FF7; Wed–Mon.*

**Torrefazione Italia** Torrefazione has become the *dernier cri*
in Seattle in much the same way Starbucks did nearly 20 years
ago. The retail trade at Umberto Bizzarri's three-outlet operation (also at 622 Olive Way and Rainier Square) is small and exclusive, and its coffee is light and smooth. Bizzarri, who learned
the craft from his father in Perugia, is passing on the trade to
his son Emmanuele. ▪ *320 Occidental Ave S (and branches);*
*624-5773; map:P8; Mon–Sat.*

**Tully's Coffee** A young coffee company that is Northwest based, Tully's is expanding rapidly. (At press time, there were 10 stores in operation, including one at 1000 Second Avenue and on Mercer Island.) What differentiates Tully's from other coffees is the roasting—which is mild but not too light, yielding a strong cup that won't knock you over. Most stores offer a variety of sweets and panini sandwiches and the walls are filled with shelves of cups and coffee-makers, reminiscent of other Seattle coffee chains. Their ginger peach tea (served hot or cold) makes a blissfully cooling summertime treat. ▪ *4036 E Madison St (and branches); 329-6659; map:GG6; every day.*

## COMPUTERS/SOFTWARE

**The Computer Store** If you're a Mac aficionado (or planning to become one), you'll appreciate the fact that Macs are all this store carries. There's a friendly atmosphere here, in addition to a good selection of desktops and Powerbooks. Prices and service are commendable, and the staff really know their Apples. The Computer Store even carries Radius, one of the first Mac clones. ▪ *6406 Roosevelt Way NE; 522-0220; map:EE6; Mon–Sat.*

**Doppler Computer** Ballard Computer, the Seattle institution, is no more. After several years of rapid expansion, Ballard declared Chapter 11 and almost closed its doors for good. Enter Doppler Computer, the company that has taken over three of Ballard's old locations. (The flagship store remains, as do locations in Issaquah and Mount Vernon; the Kirkland and Tukwila stores are gone.) Although the selection is reduced, it's still a great alternative to the superstores. The Ballard store now stocks mainly Compaq and AST desktops (no more Macs) and a few different laptops, plus a good selection of peripherals and software. The staff is friendly and knowledgeable and the service is good. One welcome improvement: you can now actually get the attention of a salesperson. ▪ *5424 Ballard Ave NW (and branches); 781-7000; map:EE8; every day.*

**Egghead Software** Egghead, the Northwest-based computer chain that pioneered the idea of the all-software discount store, still does it best. Even though they are now a big national chain, the staff are knowledgeable, the selection is amazing, and the prices are great. If you're looking for software, this is the place to go; there are plenty of locations to choose from. ▪ *1201 4th Ave (and branches); 623-4851; map:L6; every day.*

**The Future Shop** A national chain, the Future Shop has probably the best selection of desktops—including models from Compaq, AST, Apple, Packard Bell, and IBM—laptops, peripherals, and software in the area, all at the lowest prices. (Blame these guys for Ballard Computer's financial woes.)

Wondering what gives this superstore the edge over the other big boys? Pssst..the staff actually know the difference between RAM and ROM. ■ *13201 Aurora Ave N; 363-7312; map:DD7; every day.* ■ *14505 NE 20th St, Bellevue; 644-1984; map:GG2; every day.*

**Office Max** Office Max is another national chain that has a good selection of hardware (including a few Apple models) and software, but what really sets these guys apart from the rest is their great selection of computer supplies and furniture. They have tons of different laser, inkjet, and dot matrix papers and more sizes of laser printer labels than you could possibly want. Are you looking for a nice chair or desk? Office Max also has a fine selection of ergonomic furniture in a range of prices. ■ *2401 Utah Ave S; 467-0071; map:II7; every day.* ■ *14515 NE 20th Street, Bellevue; 641-1418; map:GG2; every day.*

## CONSIGNMENT AND DISCOUNT

**Alexandra's** Upscale, downtown, with a good selection of stylish women's clothes and men's sportswear, too. You'll find Armani, Ellen Tracy, DKNY, et al; expensive, good-quality re-sale clothing at fair prices. Suits are $50 on clearance to $400 for top of the line. The professional women's wear is comple-mented by a great rack of party wear, from gold lamé to mother-of-the-bride–type dresses, all in excellent condition. ■ *415 Stewart St; 623-1214; map:I6; every day.*

**The Clothes Connection** A women's consignment shop with a pleasant atmosphere worth going out of your way to visit. A wide selection of dresses, suits, and casual clothes are always available at a range of prices. ■ *11026 NE 11th St, Bellevue; 453-2055; map:HH3; Tues–Sat.*

**Dark Horse Boutique** Dark Horse is a large shop with racks and racks of resale clothes (women's mostly, with a small se-lection of men's clothing). Expect a variety of labels and a range of quality. You can get a bejeweled halter top or a wool blazer—depending on which rack you check and what day you check it. ■ *11810 NE 8th St, Bellevue; 454-0990; map:HH3; Mon–Sat.*

**The Down Factory (Don Shingler Inc.)** The Down Factory manufactures and markets down everything: sleeping bags, booties, hand warmers, and outerwear for both children and adults. Don Shingler has been selling quality garments at rea-sonable prices for over 60 years. ■ *3427 4th Ave S; 467-7072; map:HH6; Mon–Sat.*

**Fury** When the moneyed Madison Park matrons clean out their closets, it's your lucky day. This Madison Valley women's shop offers a nice collection of casual and elegant: slacks,

▼

▲

jackets, dresses, and party wear—all in good shape and priced to sell with all the accessories to go along with them. The staff are happy to help you find the right look for the right occasion. ■ *2810 E Madison St; 329-6829; map:GG6; Tues–Sat.*

**Gentlemen's Consignment** Open since 1987, this men's-only consignment shop sells moderate to upper-end clothing, emphasizing business clothes and accessories. The atmosphere is classy, the clothes high quality. You can find Polo, Armani, and a lot of Nordstrom labels, as well as tailor-made suits in sizes 36 to 56. Suspenders, belts, cufflinks, and ties finish the look. ■ *2809 E Madison St; 328-8137; map:GG6; Tues–Sat.*

**Kathy's Kloset** Kathy Robertson's has long had a great reputation among consignment shoppers, who come here for classic, professional, and fun clothing. There is a high-quality selection of women's clothes, with jewelry, purses, and shoes to complete the outfit. Kathy accepts only quality seasonal clothing, and it shows. An excellent stop for school or work wear. ■ *4751 12th Ave NE; 523-3019; map:FF7; every day.*

▼

**Consignment and Discount**

▲

**Kids on 45th** A large resale and new cotton-clothing store just for kids. Plenty of playwear and accessories, plus a great selection of infant furniture, car seats, and equipment. The mix changes from week to week, but there's always a good stock of clothes from infant to 4T. ■ *1720 N 45th St; 633-5437; map:FF7; every day.*

**Loehmann's Women's Clothing and Accessories** This women's off-priced clothing store has it all—casual, business, and party wear, lingerie, coats, accessories, and plenty of shoes—all new. There are name brands and good deals, but you have to hunt a little. Selection changes often, so if at first you don't succeed. ■ *3620 128th Ave SE, Bellevue; 641-7596; map:II2; every day.*

**Marshalls** The quality and selection at this off-priced department store chain are consistent. There's something for everyone—women's, men's, children's, shoes for all, and a smattering of household and gift items. The stores are well organized and the prices always a bargain. ■ *15801 Westminster Way N (and branches); 367-8520; map:BB7; every day.*

**Nordstrom Rack** The Rack carries clearance merchandise from the Nordstrom stores at a big discount, and that's not all. Additional lines are bought in bulk just for the Rack. That means good prices and good selection on quality clothes. Work clothes, play clothes, outerwear, underwear, and miles of shoes. The downtown Rack is huge, with a whole floor just for footwear. There are tailor and shoe repair services, too. ▪ *1601 2nd Ave (and branches); 448-8522; map:I7; every day.*

**The Other Place** The well-dressed woman can find a wardrobe of suits, dresses, and accessories at this resale shop south of Northgate. Stylish and classy, the clothing is midrange to high end, all in good condition. ▪ *8320 5th Ave NE; 527-0766; map:DD7; Mon–Sat.*

**Pavilion Mall** There's nothing but bargains in this discount shopping mall near Southcenter. Under one roof you find shops that specialize in kids' clothing, linens, luggage, coats, cosmetics, imports, crafts, jewelry, home furnishings, and almost anything else you can think of. Particularly notable are the Bergman's and Marshalls outlets and a large Burlington Coat Factory. ▪ *17900 Southcenter Pkwy, Tukwila; 575-8090; map:OO5; every day.*

**Price Costco Wholesale** You have to be a member to shop, but cards are now issued through numerous businesses and credit unions. There's a good selection of everything—tires, sporting goods, sundries, jewelry, books, computers and other electronic goods, appliances, furniture, office supplies, and clothes for the whole family. The main sections of these warehouse stores are stocked with food—fresh, frozen, canned, and packaged (there's a substantial meat department and bakery)—sold in enough-to-feed-an-army–size portions. ▪ *4401 4th Ave S (and branches); 622-1144; map:II7; every day.*

▼

**Consignment and Discount**

▲

**Ragamoffyn** A fine women's boutique in downtown Kirkland that hardly seems like a resale shop. Behind the beautiful merchandising is a large selection of high-end clothes (like a rack of more than 30 pair of perfectly pressed off-white slacks). A great stop for a classy business suit or a pretty party dress, all at surprisingly low prices. ▪ *132 Park Lane, Kirkland; 828-0396; map:EE3; Mon–Sat.*

**Re-Dress Consignment Shop** In addition to the work and play clothes, and a small selection of formal wear, Re-Dress carries a selection of kids' clothes—newborn through size 14. Friendly, helpful staff and midrange clothes (from Jones New York to the Gap and everything in between) at excellent prices. ▪ *513 156th Ave SE, Bellevue; 746-7984; map:HH1; every day.*

**Take 2 Consignment** The shops on Capitol Hill and in Fremont feature selectively chosen merchandise and factory seconds. The clothes are good-quality, stylish, and fun, and the prices are terrific. Best of all, Take 2 doesn't even feel like a consignment store, thanks to roomy display areas, nice dressing rooms, and helpful salespeople. ▪ *430 15th Ave E; 324-2569; map:HH6; every day.* ▪ *460 N 36th St; 632-1194; map:FF8; every day.*

## DEPARTMENT STORES

**The Bon Marché** The Bon is big (nine floors on a city block) and offers a full complement of services: tire center, free delivery in the downtown area, shoe repair, optometrist, post office, picture framing, cafe and deli, beauty salon, liquor store, and bakery. It's the everyman's department store in town, specializing in good-looking, moderately priced merchandise, and a lot of it. The Cube and the Tiger Shop stock excellent selections for juniors, including a good representation of local sportswear manufacturers. Toytropolis is a miniature FAO Schwartz with a play area for kids. Particularly noteworthy are all women's departments (they have one of the largest Liz Claiborne selections on the West Coast); the linen, lingerie, and fine furniture departments are large, varied, and attractive. You can find Baccarat crystal in glassware. Prices are generally lower here than at the other department stores in town. And the bathrooms are more like suites in a grand hotel. ▪ *3rd Ave and Pine St (and branches); 506-6000; map:I6; every day.*

**Nordstrom** Perhaps *the* locally owned success story, Nordstrom owes much of its popularity to its famous emphasis on service. The concierge booth located on the main floor, provides visitors with maps and brochures, and the downtown store even provides valet parking. An extremely helpful sales staff are well informed about current (mainstream) fashions and the store's merchandise—and dress to emphasize the point.

Nordstrom started business as a shoe store, and shoes are still its specialty. These shoe departments are the best in the city, with a tremendous range of style and price and no shortage of hard-to-find sizes. Women's fashions are displayed in a series of departments, each with a well-defined feeling all its own—Savvy, Collectors, Gallery, Brass Plum, Petites, Point of View, and Individualist Sportswear, among others. The Bellevue and Tacoma stores have an Encore department, with clothing specifically for larger women. Men can outfit themselves to Northwest Ivy League specifications (and in the popular Nordstrom-label suit, a Seattle wardrobe mainstay) in a variety of departments (including Ralph Lauren's Polo, in the downtown and Bellevue stores). Even Chanel has a berth, a Northwest exclusive on the second floor of the downtown store. If you hate to shop, or need help creating a "new you," a Nordstrom "Personal Shopper" will help find just what you require (accompanied by the necessary underclothing, shoes, and other accessories, of course), absolutely free of charge.

A smattering of beautifully chosen gifts and gourmet foods is found in the Boardwalk department. And the Nordstrom Cafe is often packed at lunch under the rigidly enforced

▼

**Department Stores**

▲

"seven-minute food rule." Watch for the excellent sales throughout the store, which have come to be known as not-to-be-missed Northwest events: Nordstrom's anniversary (July), half-yearly for women (June and November), and half-yearly for men (June and January). Though they don't flaunt it, Nordies will not be undersold—just ask a sales clerk about that little-known policy. ■ *5th Ave and Pine St (and branches); 628-2111; map:J6; every day.*

## ETHNIC MARKETS AND SPECIALTY FOODS

**Beacon Market** A large, full-line Asian grocery store with row after row of canned and dried foods from Taiwan, Thailand, the Philippines, Japan, Korea, and Singapore. The produce section is good, with offerings like long beans and green papaya. Look for interesting species at the smallish seafood counter (lion fish, golden thread fish). Tilapia and catfish swim in the live tank (and you can't beat *that* for freshness). Reasonable prices draw customers from all over the area. ■ *2500 Beacon Ave S; 323-2050; map:II6; every day.*

**British Pantry Ltd.** A cheerful outpost of civility, British Pantry stocks must-haves like mushy peas, pork pies, curries, Fortnum and Mason teas, biscuits, and the like. A tearoom/ restaurant and English gift shop complete the picture. ■ *8125 161st Ave NE, Redmond; 883-7511; map:EE1; every day.*

**Borracchini's Bakery and Mediterranean Market** People have been thronging to this Ranier Valley institution for years for the good selection and better prices on imported Italian foods and wines. There are fresh and frozen pastas, deli meats and cheeses, and of course, the famous bakery, which turns out reasonably priced country breads. Tens of thousands of birthdays, retirements, and anniversaries have been celebrated with a Borracchini's sheet cake. The process is straightforward: you choose the cake (white, chocolate, banana, or carrot), the filling (lemon, raspberry, custard, mocha, or one of four others), and the message, and the expert decorators do the rest. ■ *2307 Rainier Ave S; 325-1550; map:II6; every day.*

**Continental Store** A German deli with excellent cheeses, sausages, mustards, sauerkrauts, breads, pastries, chocolates, and pickled everything. Small gift area, too. ■ *5014 Roosevelt Way NE; 523-0606; map:FF7; Mon–Sat.*

**Cucina Fresca** A hip, attractive source for lunch or dinner to go. Try some of the potato and roasted onion ravioli, a towering slice of lasagne, or the thickly sliced roasted eggplant with mint and olive oil. Good fresh noodles are always available, some with alluring flavors like red pepper or lemon. Prices are somewhat spendy. ■ *Pike Place Market; 448-4758; map:I8; every day.*

**DeLaurenti** A Market anchor for over 50 years, DeLaurenti is a popular source for international foodstuffs, mostly Mediterranean. The narrow aisles are dense with canned goods, olives, olive oils, imported pasta, and truffles. The deli is noted for its excellent meats and the Market location has over 160 kinds of cheese (this is the exclusive West Coast source for Neal's Yard handmade English farm cheeses). Bakers love the imported chocolates, dried fruits, and such. The wine department is known for its Italian labels and good selection; the Bellevue location has fewer bottles. The baked goods department features breads from some of the area's best bakers, although they're all marked DeLaurenti. Great service. ▪ *Pike Place Market; 622-0141; map:J8; Mon–Sat.* ▪ *317 Bellevue Way NE, Bellevue; 454-7155; map:HH3; Mon–Sat.*

**El Mercado Latino** The front of this diminutive store in the Sanitary Market boasts a green grocery stocked with vegetables and fruits used in Caribbean, South American, Spanish, Creole, and Thai cuisines. Chiles are a specialty, with six to eight fresh varieties and more dried and canned. Many hard-to-find spices, dried edible flowers, as well as beans and fruit drinks. Bring your cookbook with you, as the help is friendly. ▪ *Pike Place Market; 623-3240; map:J8; every day.*

**George's Sausage and Delicatessen** A true Polish grocery with a faithful clientele. Come here for Hungarian peppers, Polish sauerkrauts, pickled vegetables, mustards, preserves, juices, and candies. George's own authentic kielbasa sausage, blood sausage, and potato salad are made in the back. Reasonable prices, friendly service. ▪ *907 Madison St; 622-1491; map:M3; every day.*

**Husky Deli** A wonderful deli and market that's been in the West Seattle Junction since the 1930s. The Miller family offers only the best-tasting foods, and there's a wide array of fancy mustards, dressings, crackers, and candies. They also make some of the greatest homemade ice cream in the city, a whopping 40 flavors, offered by the cone or the half gallon (the large, hand-dipped Husky milk shakes are not to be missed). Premium cold cuts and cheeses, plus some scrumptious sandwiches and salads to go. There's a small lunch bar and sidewalk seating. Catering, too, at very reasonable prices. ▪ *4721 California Ave SW; 937-2810; map:KK8; every day.*

**Kilimanjaro Market** This quirky little market stocks foods direct from Africa and the Caribbean. You'll find red palm oil, Nigerian uda, and tapioca strips, plus imported toiletries and jewelry. Know what you need and how to recognize it, as the help is spotty. ▪ *12519 Lake City Way NE; 440-1440; map:CC6; every day.*

▼

**Ethnic Markets and Specialty Foods**

▲

**Kosher Delight** Owner Michel Chriqui runs a sparkling Glatt (highest rated) kosher deli. Customers can nosh on several kinds of knishes, lox, bagels, kosher tofu "cream cheese," and other eat-in fare. Closed on the Sabbath. ■ *1509 1st Ave; 682-8140; map:J8; Sun–Fri.*

**Larry's Market** A supermarket that's really a high-style specialty market, Larry's is a treasure. If you're looking for something unusual, especially if it's au courant, you'll likely find it here. In addition to regular supermarket offerings, there's organic produce, lots of ethnic foods and spices, a line of Oriental macrobiotic products, and a Biofoods section with natural and organic foods, created by owner Larry McKinney and his family. The Queen Anne store has an exemplary meat-and-seafood counter. The cheese selection runs from 200 to 400 varieties, depending on the store. Queen Anne, Totem Lake, and Bellevue have temperature-controlled wine rooms; Bellevue offers cooking classes. Branches are in North Seattle, Queen Anne, Totem Lake, Bellevue, Sea-Tac, and Lakewood in Tacoma. ■ *10008 Aurora Ave N (and branches); 527-5333; map:DD7; every day.*

**Medina Grocery and Deli** A spotless store with imported Turkish, Greek, Pakistani, and Indian foods, plus halal meats (butchered according to Islamic dietary laws). There's a fine selection of beans and spices, plus cheese from Cyprus, French feta, olives, dried apricot paste, rose jam, and more. ■ *1421 NE 80th St; 527-2139; map:EE6; every day.*

**The Mexican Grocery** When it's time to move beyond burritos, you'll find the necessary Mexican ingredients in this tidy little store in the Market's Soames-Dunn Building. Chichirrones, mole, Mexican chocolate, corn husks, and over a dozen kinds of dried chiles are available here, along with Mexican canned goods and fresh salsas. The Grocery's own La Mexicana fresh tortillas come in corn, flour, organic blue corn, or red chile flavors. Call ahead for uncooked hominy for posole and masa dough for tamales. ■ *Pike Place Market; 441-1147; map:J8; every day.*

**Olsen's Scandinavian Foods** Owned by the Olsen family for nearly 30 years, this sparkling Ballard shop has more than lefse, lingonberries, and lutefisk. They make their own Scandanavian cold cuts and pickled herring, and import cheeses, cod balls, Swedish caviar pastes, soup and pudding mixes, and more. Just-baked Scandinavian cookies and fragrant cardamom rolls are a specialty. ■ *2248 NW Market St; 783-8288; map:FF8; every day.*

**Oriental Mart** This is a fine place to find basic ingredients for Filipino, Korean, Indonesian, Vietnamese, Chinese, and Japanese cooking. Owner Mila Apostol, from the Philippines,

▼

Ethnic
Markets
and Specialty
Foods

▲

is always glad to help with recipes (yours or hers). The lunch counter has Filipino lunches, like adobo chicken, and suman—a rice dessert wrapped in banana leaves. Located in the Corner Market (enter where you see the jumping paper snakes). ▪ *Pike Place Market; 622-8488; map:J8; every day.*

**Pacific Food Importers (PFI)** The price is right at this wholesale importer's outlet. Look here for real deals on European cheeses, meats, dried pastas, bulk beans, lentils, and spices. The selection of Greek and Italian olive oils is extensive, and no one can beat their bulk feta cheese prices or the price for Kalamata olives. Bring your own lidded container and they'll add brine to preserve your purchase. The decor is early warehouse; service is friendly. Be mindful: meats, cheeses, and olives have a 1-pound minimum; meats and cheeses are sold unsliced (PFI doesn't have a slicer). Come early on Saturdays, as the checkout lines are long and closing time is 2pm. ▪ *1001 6th Ave S; 682-2022; map:II7; Tues–Sat.*

**Pasta & Co.** See the Restaurants chapter. ▪ *University Village (and branches); 523-8594; map:FF6; every day.*

**Pike Place Market Creamery** Locals come here for exceptional dairy foods and eggs. You'll find Russian yogurt, kefirs, goat and soy milk products, plus rich heavy cream, unsalted butter, and ice creams. You'll find naturally colored araucana chicken eggs, fresh duck, goose, and quail eggs, and more. Located in the Sanitary Market. ▪ *Pike Place Market; 622-5029; map:J8; every day.*

**Quality Cheese** Peerless quality and a superb selection distinguish this old-fashioned cheese shop, which has been in the Corner Market since WWII. Owner Nancy Rentschler hand-selects her cheeses from the U.S. and Europe, and champions local handmade varieties like Sally Jackson's goat milk cheeses. ▪ *Pike Place Market; 624-4029; map:J8; every day.*

**Rooz Market** A real find for those who love the fragrant complexities of Persian cuisine. Zohreh Kashmeri stocks her store with pussywillow water, sourgrape juice, dried limes, pomegranate molasses, Persian teas—and a lot more you won't find anywhere else. A deli case offers Bulgarian feta cheese, mortadella, dolmeh (stuffed grape leaves), and Salad Olovier (an extraordinary potato and chicken salad made by the owner). Persian breads, cookbooks, music, and videos from before and after the Iranian revolution, too. ▪ *12332 Lake City Way NE; 363-8639; map:DD6; every day.*

**Scandinavian Specialty Products** A smallish store in north Ballard, Scandinavian Specialty Products stocks an incredible array of imported Scandinavian vegetables, jams, fish, cheeses, coffees, and flatbreads, and attracts customers from all over the

U.S. One wall is dense with Norwegian and Swedish candies and chocolates. Owners Ruby and Herb Anderson make authentic Norwegian meat rolls and sausages, fresh fish pudding, and rřmmegrřt, a sour cream pudding. Quality is tip-top, as Herb is a former food inspector for the Department of Health. At Christmas, look for traditional treats. They even have marzipan pigs. ■ *8539 15th Ave NW; 784-7020; map:DD8; Mon–Sat.*

**The Souk** Four Pakistanis operate this esoteric store with a tremendous inventory of Middle Eastern and Indian delicacies: dal and lentils in every color, bulghur sold by coarseness, unusual flours, spice pastes, and lots of chutneys. There's a Pinehurst location, too. ■ *Pike Place Market; 441-1666; map:J8; every day.* ■ *11730 Pinehurst Wy; 367-8387; map:DD6; every day.*

**Trader Joe's** A panoply of vogue foods, at very reasonable prices. This outpost of a California specialty chain buys direct from producers so middleman costs are eliminated. Coffees, juices, wines, a rainbow of pastas, lentils and beans, and wonderful bottled and canned goods make this a store worth investigating. Seafood is chemical-free and flash-frozen. A frozen entree section—with ready-to-heat phad Thai, nasi goreng, lasagne and gnocci, and more—offers inexpensive convenience. Here, the quality is good but some of the flavors are hit-and-miss. ■ *15400 NE 20th, Bellevue; 643-6885; map:GG3; every day.*

**Tsue Chong (Rose Brand) Company Inc.** In Rose Brand's unassuming Chinese noodle shop, they sell high-quality fresh and dried noodles, steamed noodles for frying, slender soup noodles, fresh wonton wrappers, and fortune cookies in 11 flavors. You can order custom fortunes if you like. ■ *801 S King St; 623-0801; map:R5; Mon–Sat.*

**Uwajimaya** The cornerstone of the International District, this large, sparkling supermarket sells all kinds of Asian foods, plus makeup, small electrical appliances (rice cookers, woks) and housewares. The real distinction comes with the extensive canned goods, fresh-shellfish tanks, and produce department—you'll find geoduck, live prawns and crabs, bitter melon, water chestnuts, durian, and all the makings for sushi. Service is quite knowledgeable. The Bellevue store has a fine Asian bakery case and deli, plus live-fish tanks in the seafood section. ■ *519 6th Ave S; 624-6248; map:R7; every day.* ■ *15555 NE 24th St, Bellevue; 747-9012; map:GG1; every day.*

**Viet Wah Supermarket** If you can stand a little funkiness, this is truly one of the best Chinese and Southeast Asian grocery stores in town. You'll find all the ingredients you need (and will be seduced by the vast quantities you *don't* need) to stock an

▼

Ethnic
Markets
and Specialty
Foods

▲

estimable Asian pantry. Mega-produce, fresh seafood, and a butcher shop, too (the chicken is so cheap it's nearly free). There's a Chinese herbal pharmacy near the entrance. ■ *1032 S Jackson St; 329-1399; map:HH6; every day.*

**Welcome Supermarket** A completely authentic International District grocery with a fine array of Asian greens and a low-priced rice selection, including bags of Thai black sticky rice. Seafood, meats, and canned goods, too. ■ *1200 S Jackson St; 329-7044; map:HH6; every day.*

## FABRIC AND KNITTING SUPPLIES

**Calico Corners** First- and second-quality—second quality has only very minor flaws—decorator fabric for the home. If you don't see material you like, order from their samples selection. Their workrooms will do the sewing for you if you don't want to do it yourself. ■ *104 Bellevue Way SE, Bellevue; 455-2510; map:HH3; every day.* ■ *3225 Alderwood Mall Blvd, Lynnwood; 778-8019; every day.*

**Designers' Fabrics** Catering to the kind of folks who sew their own dress-for-success suits or one-of-a-kind wedding dresses, this Eastside fabric store is excellent (especially if you're looking for silks). It offers a large selection of bridal fabrics and imported laces and the staff can give the customer the know-how to create a masterpiece. ■ *2251 140th Ave NE, Bellevue; 747-5200; map:HH1; every day.*

**In the Beginning Fabrics** There's no end to the superb selection of calicoes, cottons, natural dress fabrics, and decorator chintz. Their specialty, if we must, is quilts; they sell the fabrics, teach the classes, and supply yards and yards of resource materials for seamstresses of all designs. The knowledgeable sales staff go out of their way to answer questions of any dimensions. ■ *8201 Lake City Way NE; 523-8862; map:EE7; every day.* ■ *14125 NE 20th Street, Bellevue; 865-0155; map:GG2; every day.*

**Jehlor Fantasy Fabrics** The stuff dreamwear's made of: liquid sequin, imported hand-beaded laces, lamé, metallic glitz. This fantastical fabric store for bridal wear, evening clothes, and costumes is the place to go for metallic brocade and stretch velvet. ■ *730 Andover Park W; 575-8250; map:NN5; every day.*

**The Loft** A complete quilting department is featured here, along with good general troubleshooting and advice. The Loft now offers decorator fabrics from Kona Bay, Hoffman, Kaufman, and others, many suitable for draperies and light upholstery. For those too lazy to take a class, ready-made Amish quilts are sold here. ■ *709 NW Gilman Blvd, Issaquah; 392-5877; every day.*

▼

**Ethnic Markets and Specialty Foods**

▲

**M. L. Mallard** The strengths in Kerry Ferguson's stylish shop are the beautiful knitting yarns, original patterns for knitting and needlepoint projects, and a wide range of esteemed classes for beginners (including sweater, needlepoint, and crochet). The staff know their stuff, are handy with the needle, and are ever patient and helpful to neophyte knitters. ▪ *1012 Western Ave; 621-0632; map:L8; Mon–Sat.*

**Seattle Fabric** Here you'll find a full stock of fabric, patterns, and accessories for creating your own outdoor clothing and equipment: Gore-Tex and cozy Synchilla (as well as less expensive lookalikes), sturdy canvas, and waterproofed nylon— in a wide array of colors. A full range of grommets, buckles, clips, cords, and Velcro is available for creating the hardiest of gear. ▪ *3876 Bridge Way N; 632-6022; map:FF7; Mon–Sat.*

**Shamek's Button Shop** The only button shop on the West Coast carries bone, wood, plastic, glass, pewter, and coin buttons, along with shell, tusk, and horn. Custom-made belts are the most expertly crafted in town, and the buckle selection is like nobody else's. Good buttonhole service. ▪ *1201 Pine St; 622-5350; map:J2; Tues–Sat.*

**Tricoter** Tricoter specializes in high-fashion knitting, with a dazzling selection of fine yarns from Germany, Japan, France, and Italy. Soft angoras and other specialty fiber yarns—including a nice array of metallics—are the stars here. Good design and finishing classes, for novices as well as more advanced knitters, as well as needlepoint canvases and threads and needlepoint classes, too. There's a small but exquisite selection of unusual buttons, and a custom-design knitwear service. ▪ *3121 E Madison St; 328-6505; map:GG6; Mon–Sat.*

**The Weaving Works** Seattle is a big city for needle arts, and Weaving Works is a wonderful find. It's crowded with yarn and everything you need for dyeing, spinning, weaving, and knitting—including advice and classes. The Weaving Works also carries basketry and papermaking supplies. ▪ *4717 Brooklyn Ave NE; 524-1221; map:FF6; every day.*

**Yarn Shop in Old Bellevue** Anything you might want for knitting can be found here: yarns, needles, books, small classes, and customer service from knowledgeable and patient employees who can answer any question. ▪ *106 102nd Ave SE, Bellevue; 454-3636; map:HH4; Mon–Sat.*

▼

**Florists and Nurseries**

▲

## FLORISTS AND NURSERIES

*A number of specialized nurseries are open only on selected days and by appointment. Call before you go to:*

**Bassetti's Crooked Arbor Gardens** (18512 NE 165th Street, Woodinville), 788-6767, for dwarf conifers, alpine plants, and displays; **The Greenery** (14450 NE 16th Place, Bellevue), 641-1458, specializing in species rhododendron, dwarf hybrids, and Northwest native shrubs and ferns; **Herban Renewal** (10437 19th Avenue SW, Seattle), 243-8821, for organically grown herb plants for culinary, healing, or ornamental uses (classes, too); and **Stone Hollow Farm** (21302 SE First Street, Redmond), 391-2218, for hard-to-find drought-tolerant perennials and herbs.

**Bainbridge Gardens** Here's a country nursery with a fine selection of woody plants, theme gardens for herbs, perennials, grasses, and a well-stocked garden gift shop. The restored Harui Memorial Garden (begun in 1908, abandoned during WWII) showcases bonsai trees, while a nature trail loops through native woods. Wreath machines may be reserved (no fee) in November and December so customers can assemble their own Northwestern holiday gifts (UPS service on site as well). A small outdoor cafe offers beverages, snacks, and light lunches in spring and summer. ■ *9415 Miller Rd NE, Bainbridge Island; 842-5888; every day.*

**Ballard Blossom** Seattle's largest florist shop, family run since 1927, offers a cheerful abundance of fresh flowers, potted plants, and seasonal gift items. The friendly staff can send certain selections anywhere in the world, while personally chosen arrangements can be delivered areawide. ■ *1766 NW Market St; 782-4213; map:EE8; Mon–Sat (open Sun in Dec.).*

**Bamboo Gardens of Washington** Forty species of bamboo plants, and bamboo products from poles to fences to deer scarers to water pipes: you can find them all here, along with lots of how-to advice for planting your own bamboo landscape. ■ *196th & Redmond–Fall City Rd, Redmond; 868-5166; map:EE1; every day.*

**Bay Hay and Feed** A funky storefront that has served the Rolling Bay neighborhood of Bainbridge Island for more than a century, Bay Hay and Feed currently stocks hay and other animal feeds, but also carries a great selection of farm- and garden-related toys, gifts, books, and clothing. The small nursery is ably staffed and offers a full range of edible and ornamental plants, including some collector's treasures. Rustic lawn furniture, hand tools, and unusual clay pots are specialties. Lots of natural and earth-safe pesticides. ■ *10355 Valley Rd, Bainbridge Island; 842-2813; every day.*

**Chases Downtown Florist** In business for 15 years, this small shop in the Washington Mutual Tower does distinctive, classy arrangements in the French country style. Exotic flowers are a specialty, and there is a large selection of flowers on hand at all times. You can order 300 roses on the spur of the moment, and they'll say, "No problem." Chases carries a few gift items, seeds, and pot plants as well. Arrangements from $25, area- and worldwide delivery. ▪ *1201 3rd Ave; 625-9500; map:K7; Mon–Fri.*

**City Flowers Inc.** City Flowers' gorgeous arrangements follow French country and English garden styles, often including wildflowers, but with no 'mums, no carnations, and nothing cutesy. A few cards or potpourri at the tiny downtown shop, more gifts at the Bellevue store. Arrangements from $22, area- and worldwide delivery. ▪ *1191 2nd Ave; 622-6760; map:L7; Mon–Fri.* ▪ *10500 NE 8th Ave, Bellevue; 454-0882; map:HH2; Mon–Sat.*

**City People's Garden Store** An urban nursery for the serious gardener, City People's offers not only plants (though the choices are very good here in garden plants, and foliage and flowering houseplants), but seeds, garden carts, compost bins, trellises, and drip irrigation systems. Other strengths include gifts, gardening tools, books, furniture, ornaments, organic and nontoxic fertilizers, a fine landscaping service, and a full-service florist's shop. ▪ *2939 E Madison St; 324-0737; map:GG7; every day.*

**Cottage Creek Nursery** With more than 20 years in business to its credit, this nursery specializes in old garden roses and English roses, as well as many other difficult-to-find blooms among the 600 rose varieties offered. At the height of the seasonal frenzy, you may choose from as many as 300 different perennials just right for a cottage garden. ▪ *13232 Avondale, Woodinville; 883-8252; map:BB1; every day.*

▼

**Florists and Nurseries**

▲

**Crissey Flowers and Gifts** First opened in the 1890s (and taking the Crissey name some 50 years ago), this is surely the oldest established florist in the city, specializing in English garden–style arrangements and the tropical hi-style—a synthesis of Dutch and Japanese traditions. From private dinner parties to corporate galas, weddings to wakes, this is a full-service florist that does everything with excellence. ▪ *416 University (Rainier Square); 728-6661; map:L5; Mon–Sat.* ▪ *2100 5th Ave; 448-1100; map:G6; Mon–Sat.*

**Furney's Nursery** Basic garden furnishings are the mainstay here, especially trees and shrubs, available in pots or as large, field-grown specimens. Look here first for fruit trees, shade and flowering trees, hedge plants, and evergreens. Bulk ground covers are another specialty, as are roses of all kinds, including standards, climbers, and David Austins. ▪ *21215 Pacific Hwy S (and branches); 878-8761; map:PP6; every day.*

**Kimura Nursery** Indoor gardeners appreciate this full-service nursery for its bargain prices on recycled office- or houseplants. These are the horticultural equivalent of secondhand books; you won't find a 20-foot fig tree for a hundred bucks anywhere else. A modest budget will stretch a mile here, where prices average 50 to 70 percent off retail. Kimura's also features imported Japanese bonsai and an Oriental garden–design service. ▪ *3860 NE Bellevue–Redmond Rd, Bellevue; 881-6508, Bellevue, WA 98008; map:FF1; every day.*

**Martha E. Harris Flowers and Gifts** Expect extravagant, dramatic, bountiful arrangements from Martha Harris, whose Euro-Northwest style is not of the arrange-by-numbers sort: each is an original. Parties and weddings are her specialties. The gift shop offers fine accessories, jewelry, and accent pieces for the home. ▪ *4733 University Village Plaza NE; 527-1820; map:FF6; every day.*

**Maxine's Pickity Patch** Maxine's folksy-sweet arrangements evoke an English garden style as envisioned by Martha Stewart, and her shop is an outlet for fine local and European crafts in addition to many gardening books and miscellany. Deliveries are areawide, but there is no wire service. Funeral floral arrangements are anything but funereal. ▪ *6405 Roosevelt Way NE; 523-4200; map:EE6; Mon–Sat.*

**Megan Mary Olander Florist** Loose, elegant arrangements in the European country garden style characterize this little shop in Pioneer Square. Border perennials and wildflowers are often included among the hothouse beauties, all of which can be bought by the stem (the pleasant staff offer expert advice and assistance if required). Olander also carries a pretty assortment of containers which display exuberant bouquets to advantage, as well as French ribbon, dried wreaths, and tussy-mussies. Weddings and corporate accounts are specialties, but walk-ins are welcome. ▪ *222 1st Ave S; 623-6660; map:O8; Mon–Sat.*

▼

**Florists and Nurseries**

▲

**Molbak's Greenhouse and Nursery ▪ Seattle Garden Center** Lavish holiday displays bring visitors here in droves, but Molbak's is always an attraction for those who love to drink in the scent of growing things amid the sounds of water and singing birds. This is rich ground for the novice and expert gardener, who will find plenty to explore among the hundreds of houseplants and the full range of outdoor plants (everything from trees to ground cover). Molbak's also offers gifts, patio and garden furniture, a Christmas shop, garden store, and distinctive floral designs. Seattle Garden Center (Molbak's Pike Place Market store) serves the urban gardener well and boasts an outstanding selection of garden seeds. ▪ *13625 NE 175th St, Woodinville; 483-5000; map:BB2; every day.* ▪ *Pike Place Market; 448-0431; map:J8; every day.*

**Oasis Water Gardens** Everything you might need for your water or bog garden: hardy lilies, tropical lilies, lotus, goldfish, koi—and all the neccessary pumps, fountains, and statuary to bring your garden to life and show it off to best advantage.

■ *404 S Brandon; 767-9776; map:LL5-LL6; Tues–Sun (Tues-Sat in winter)*.

**Pike Place Flowers** Here you'll find contemporary, original, and tropical hi-style arrangements (and no carnations or pom-pons). You can buy bunches of flowers for as little as $2 and arrangements for $10 and up ($25 minimum on deliveries, area- or worldwide). Staff are enthusiastically helpful. ■ *1st Ave and Pike St; 682-9797; map:J8; every day*.

**Sea-Tac Dahlia Gardens** Dahlia aficionados flock here to gawk and take pictures, but they *really* come to order bulbs for next season's planting. An incredible variety of dahlias covers an acre, and information on all aspects of raising and nurturing dahlias is yours for the asking. There's a self-serve road stand, and cut flowers are a specialty. ■ *20020 Des Moines Memorial Dr; 824-3846; map:PP7; every day (in summer months only)*.

**Swanson's Nursery and Greenhouse** A riot of exuberant color greets you at Swanson's. With 5 acres of display gardens, this excellent full-service nursery includes uncommon plants of all kinds. Perennials are a specialty, but in every category, from trees and shrubs through ground covers to houseplants, Swanson's emphasizes choice offerings over sheer quantity. A cafe in the gift shop offers light meals and espresso amid European garden tools and handsome planting containers. Rustic log furniture is available in spring. ■ *9701 15th Ave NW; 782-2543; map:DD8; every day*.

**Village Green Perennial Nursery** Walk through the fragrant English cottage gardens, choose among the extensive perennial selections, and browse in the small garden store. Owner Teresa Romedo offers a design-and-landscaping service in addition to classes on culinary herbs and flower-drying techniques (among other garden-related topics). The pretty site may be rented for private gatherings. Ask about the twice-yearly high teas. ■ *10223 26th Ave SW; 767-7735; map:LL8; Tues–Sun (Apr 1–Oct 1)*.

**Wells-Medina Nursery** The perennial-lover's favorite nursery, regionally famed for depth and variety, this is also the place to buy choice shrubs—the selection of rhododendrons and Japanese maples is unmatched in the area. Look here for unusual vines, bulbs, and ground covers as well, and check out the long demonstration border; the best things sell quickly, so browse often to keep up with what's new. The excellent plant range and prices are complemented by a knowledgeable and helpful staff. ■ *8300 NE 24th St, Bellevue; 454-1853; map:GG3; every day*.

**West Seattle Nursery** All the basics are here, but these folks take a few risks, too, stocking collector's plants, uncommon annuals and perennials (in growing quantities), as well as some offbeat decorative items. Interesting foliage plants are in good supply, both houseplants and border perennials, and West Seattle Nursery carries a full line of natural pesticides and garden-care products. ■ *5275 California Ave SW; 935-9276; map:KK8; every day.*

**Young Flowers** Mark Young has kept this busy downtown corner exciting for several years now with knockout displays of fresh and unusual flowers. Most of the arrangements here are natural in style, European in flavor; if you want drama, charm, spunk, or sheer romance, just ask—he can do that, too. Buy by the stem, and the staff will gladly share tips on assembling your own floral creations. No weddings, but they handle lots of parties and corporate accounts. Fair prices and lovely products, fully guaranteed. ■ *1111 3rd Ave; 628-3077; map:L7; Mon–Fri.*

## FURNITURE

**Abodio** Furnishings that are loosely modeled on the pattern of contemporary simplicity pioneered by Conran's fill this waterfront warehouse. The main floor is a maze of wall systems, country and modern beds, computer cubicles, rugs, and couches. Abodio specializes in contemporary and upbeat traditional pieces, with a good supply of kids' furniture. Prices are in the middle range. Another, expanded store, opening downtown at press time (217 Pine Street, 343-3030), features a new line of high-end furnishings called "Studio Abodio." Meant to be Abodio's flagship store, it will also house a Euro-style bistro. ■ *5961 Corson Ave S (and branches); 763-5000; map:K8; every day.*

**Cape Cod Comfys** In this small Fremont shop you'll find comfortable cedar resort furniture that actually works well indoors, too. Owner Dwight Jacobson makes the low-slung Adirondack chairs—the ultimate in casual reclining, with their wide, flat arms perfect for holding a tall, cold drink and a book on a balmy summer day (child-size chairs are available). He also sells sturdy hammocks for slinging between two trees in the shade. ■ *3413 Fremont Ave N; 545-4309; map:FF7; every day.*

**Current** If your taste runs to high-tech black matte, Memphis design geometry, or neoclassical granite, you'll be in contemporary heaven at Current. The store specializes in state-of-the-art lighting, avant-garde wall units, chairs, desks, tables, rugs, and beds. The unfinished concrete-and-brick interior is an appropriately spare showroom for Current's Italian imports. ■ *1201 Western Ave; 622-2433; map:K8; every day.*

**Del-Teet Furniture** Del-Teet's Bellevue showroom sports an emphasis on classic-contemporary Northwest items in addition to its stock of gifts and accessories. Furniture can be custom-made here, and an interior design service is provided for clients. ■ *10308 NE 10th St, Bellevue; 462-5400; map:HH3; every day.*

**Expressions Furniture**  In stores across the country, including Seattle and Kirkland locations, Expressions offers a sort of mix-and-match method of furniture shopping: customers select from more than 50 styles of solid oak sofa and chair frames, then choose from a staggering array of fabrics, including velvet, leather, and wovens, with which to cover them. The store is staffed by interior designers eager to share their expertise; home accessories are scattered throughout to complement the upholstery groups on display. ■ *1001 Western Ave; 625-1660; map:M8; every day.* ■ *132 Central Way, Kirkland; 889-8989; map:EE3; every day.*

**The Great Northwest**  Here you'll find the popular peeled Douglas fir furniture from Chicken and Egg Productions. Besides the rocking chairs, benches, and beds made by Chicken and Egg (whose profits from the log furniture line go to nonprofit organizations, including the Children's Trust Program), the store has plenty of Northwest-originated home furnishings and accessories, as well as Pendleton blankets, specialty foods, and jewelry. There's a lot of square footage in which to browse. ■ *1426 Alaskan Way; 623-6144; map:M8; every day.*

**Kasala**  Kasala emphasizes moderate prices and modern, space-conscious lifestyles. Its collection includes contemporary, trendy European home accessories—concentrating on lighting systems—glassware, gift items, and furniture. ■ *1505 Western Ave; 623-7795; map:J8; every day.* ■ *1014 116th Ave NE, Bellevue; 453-2823; map:GG3; every day.*

**Masins**  Talk about staying power: the Masin family has been in the business nearly 70 years and have been selling furniture from the Pioneer Square location since the late '30s. This traditional store's extensive showrooms display the full range of classic furnishing styles from such names as Baker, Henredon, Drexel Heritage, and Karastan. The proficient staff offer free in-home consultations. ■ *220 2nd Ave S; 622-5606; map:O8; every day.* ■ *10245 Main St, Bellevue; 450-9999; map:GG2; every day.*

**Modele's**  Roche Bobois customers, who have yet to realize the très expensive furniture store has moved down the street, would be smart to take a look inside its replacement on the ground floor of the elegant National Building. Owner Deb Bluestein runs the only high-end furniture consignment store in town. Why buy new when you can buy honestly priced pre-owned furniture that looks this good? Stock changes weekly (if not more often) and moves quickly as buyers get hip and the client-base continues to grow. Occasional new pieces are also displayed, along with pre-owned carpets and artwork. A small, artful stock of new home accessories (table linens, vases, and candles among them) make for good browsing. ▪ *1006 Western Ave; 287-9942; map:L8; every day.*

**Pennsylvania Woodworks** Many of the pieces here are individually made by the Amish; hence these are simple, traditional designs in solid woods (no veneers). Prices reflect the handcrafting, and if the store doesn't have what you want, the pleasant sales staff will be happy to place a special order. Admire the Amish-made quilts and rugs, and don't leave without buying a little Amish-style trinket (say, a candle holder, a kitchen hook) fit for the slimmer purse. ▪ *355 NW Gilman Blvd, Issaquah; 557-4776; every day.* ▪ *17705 140th Ave NE, Woodinville; 486-9541; map:BB1; every day.*

**Roche Bobois** Roche's European dining rooms, bedrooms, and living rooms are first-cabin luxury, bringing elegance and selection to those who can afford to invest in the stunning selection of Italian leathers and high-gloss lacquers. Service is professional, as befits the inventory. The new, larger location is a block south of the original Western Avenue digs. ▪ *903 Western Ave; 622-7166; map:M8; every day.*

▼

**Furniture**

▲

## GIFTS

**Belle Provence** Tucked inside quaint Country Village is this spirited and artful shop. Antique-reproduction jewelry, Hungarian porcelain, Limoges boxes, Beatrix Potter and other children's books, and fragrant potpourris line the shelves and provide both collectors and browsers a shopping experience abundant with possibilities. ▪ *Country Village, Bothell; 483-4696; map:AA4; every day.*

**Bitters Co.** It looks much like a fashionably restored garage, but sisters Amy and Katie Carson turned this stylishly simple space (named for their mother, whose maiden name was Bitters) into a classic Fremont showplace. Scouring the world, the U.S., and their adopted city with a well-honed, no-chotchkes-need-apply fashion, they stock their store with antique tools and buttons, gourds, fabrics, ceramic wares, weathered wood furnishings, artistic textiles, jewelry, and other pretties. Gifts both functional and eye-catching. ▪ *513 N 36th St; 632-0886; map:FF8; Tues-Sun.*

**Burke Museum Store** Housed inside the Burke Museum at the northwest corner of the UW campus, the gift store follows the museum's lead. Look for its permanent collection of Northwest Coast Native American art, silk-screen prints, basketry, and wooden boxes, and don't miss the geological specimens and dinosaur replicas. ▪ *University of Washington; 685-0909; map:FF6; every day.*

### Crackerjack Contemporary Crafts
Showcasing many local artists, Crackerjack, which holds a central position in classy Wallingford Center, is a gift-buyer's paradise. You-didn't-buy-*this*-at-a-department-store stuff for the cook, the gardener, the musically inclined, and the collector. Artsy handcrafted renderings of everthing from espresso cups to fine glassware to funky hats to hanging earrings. ▪ *1815 N 45th St (Wallingford Center); 547-4983; map:EE6; every day.*

### Explore More Store (Pacific Science Center)
Don't let the educational benefits of browsing here deter you from a visit—it's fun, too. The shop ties in with the Pacific Science Center exhibits, so you'll find minerals, astronomy paraphernalia, dinosaur items, and other science-related toys and books for children. The collection of crystals is extensive and affordable, compared with those of the New Age specialty stores. ▪ *Seattle Center; 443-2870; map:C7; every day.*

### FireWorks Gallery
No old grandmom gifts here; if it's clever, quirky, and fun, they've probably got it. FireWorks displays a compelling array of ceramics, glass, and other hand-crafted wares—from the wild and whimsical to the elegantly functional. A browse through the shop is your best introduction to the work of choice local artisans, as well as that of outside talent. Great off-beat jewelry, fiber art, and woodwork. A lot of fun at Christmas (there's tree trimming stuff like you've never seen). A fabulous selection of menorahs sure to become modern-day family heirlooms. ▪ *210 1st Ave S; 682-8707; map:O8; every day.* ▪ *Westlake Center; 682-6462; map:I5; every day.* ▪ *Bellevue Square; 688-0933; map:HH3; every day.*

### Flying Shuttle
Wondrous finds at this contemporary wearable-crafts gallery in Pioneer Square specializing in handsome, handwoven clothing and jewelry crafted from a wide range of media, including paper, glass, ceramics, and beads. A wonderful place to find a gift. ▪ *607 1st Ave; 343-9762; map:N8; every day.*

### Fox Paw
With her assortment of artwork, jewelry, books, photo frames, note cards, linens, and lace, owner Linda Allen has created an eclectic place to shop. Esoteric music and exceptional gifts, clothing, and home furnishings. ▪ *160 Winslow Way W, Bainbridge Island; 842-7788; every day.*

### Gargoyles
A gothic mood prevails in this small, candle-lit shop specializing in—guess what?—gargoyles. The statuary comes from artists all over the country (some local) and a few sweet-faced angels are thrown in for good measure. Candleholders, shelf brackets, fountains, and statues of all sizes are available in a wide variety of weights and finishes. Truly remarkable (if

spooky) stuff. ▪ *4550 University Way NE; 632-4940; map:FF6; every day.*

**Made in Washington** And everything *is*—from crafts and local books to foodstuffs and wine: the selection is vast. Gift packages can be assembled for those who have the misfortune to live anywhere else. ▪ *Pike Place Market (and branches); 467-0788; map:J8; every day.*

**Museum of Flight Store** A barnstorm of aviation books: general, space, military, and literary. Models and posters are geared to all ages, from small plastic planes for kids to fairly complex airplane models for adult hobbyists. There's also a small outlet at —where else?—Sea-Tac airport. ▪ *9404 E Marginal Way S; 764-5720; map:LL6; every day.*

**The Nature Company** Right in the heart of the city is a paradise for the nature lover. Shoppers lose themselves as they handle telescopes and globes, study minerals and fossils, play with nature-related toys, sort through posters and books, and check out distinctive timepieces. Like walking through the catalog, only better. ▪ *2003 Western Ave; 443-1608; map:H9; every day.* ▪ *Bellevue Square, Bellevue; 450-0448; map:HH3; every day.*

**Nido** Andrea Stuber-Margelou has a knack for selecting an eclectic collection of one-of-a-kind home accessories. You'll find body-care products, architectural artifacts, jewelry, candles, and Victorian and chic European furniture side by side here. Definitely not for the budget-conscious. ▪ *1920½ 1st Ave; 443-1272; map:I8; Mon-Sat.*

**Northwest Discovery ▪ Elements Gallery** An Eastside showcase for local artists' work, which features a fine woodwork collection of boxes, cribbage boards, and mirrors. Porcelain, silver, gold, and beaded jewelry are of distinctive design and reasonably priced. Elements, in a more refined gallery atmosphere, displays handblown glass, pottery, and wall art. ▪ *142 Bellevue Square, Bellevue; 454-1676; map:HH3; every day.* ▪ *10500 NE 8th St, Bellevue; 454-8242; map:HH3; Mon–Sat.*

**PANACA Gallery** The focus of PANACA (Pacific Northwest Arts and Crafts Association) is crafts and artifacts: handcrafted pottery, blown glass, baskets, and handmade jewelry, beautifully produced by Northwest and Southwest craftspeople. ▪ *Bellevue Square, Bellevue; 454-0234; map:HH3; every day.*

**Phoenix Rising** Maureen Pierre's Phoenix has risen steadily at the north end of Pike Place Market since she opened her fine crafts gallery in 1989. Her forte is carefully chosen and beautifully displayed functional art (glass, ceramics, jewelry, and even a smattering of handcrafted furnishings), works that have garnered the shop national acclaim and make for very original gifts. A full complement of Northwest artists are represented. While you can spend a bundle for a bauble, 25 percent of the stock is in the $50-and-under range. ▪ *2030 Western Ave; 728-2332; map:H8; every day.*

**Portage Bay Goods** Combine good taste with do-good '90s environmental and social awareness and you've got this warmly inviting shop where you might browse comfortably for an hour among the crafts and handmade items. Much of the stock here is made from recycled materials or bought from international cooperatives—and it's all beautifully displayed on recycled wooden pallets; Spanish pottery, English pewter, Scottish yarns. The main display case, a hand-crafted boat-like structure with a central column that's been transformed into a "tree" is *alone* worth a look. ▪ *1121 Pike St; 622-3212; map:K3; Mon–Sat.*

**Three Furies** A little slice of a shop on bustling Broadway, Three Furies is not, as its name might suggest, owned by the three terrible, winged goddesses of Greek and Roman mythology. Instead, this artful, affordable shop—stocked and run by a trio of friendly folk—offers winged angel wall statuary, a multitude of lovely frames, small lamps, miniature wooden boxes, pretty cards, handmade soaps, and a number of interesting crafts and seasonal surprises. ▪ *603 Broadway Ave E; 860-1518; map:HH6; every day.*

**Tilden** Tilden has earned its reputation as a classic gift store by continuing to focus on items that make the best gifts: textiles, crystal, candles, glass, note cards, art jewelry, and housewares. All displayed well and priced with integrity. ▪ *401 15th Ave E; 323-7526; map:HH6; every day.*

**The Weed Lady** Set in an old-fashioned, arbor-guarded house off the main street, this shop is fragrant with potpourris, dried everlastings, and soaps. Small pottery pieces are displayed on wooden shelves and around the floor. The owner is especially creative with dried floral arrangements and does outstanding work for weddings (ask to see her photo album). The Weed Lady offers fall and spring classes in floral design, and her garden in the back of the store is a quiet oasis among the small-town–suburban flow that is Edmonds. ▪ *122 4th Ave S, Edmonds; 775-3800; every day.*

**Ye Olde Curiosity Shop** This "world-famous" Seattle attraction (since 1899) is a novelty stop for more than tourists. It's a veritable kitsch museum, housing a remarkable collection of Northwest Indian and Eskimo art, ivory, and soapstone, plus imports, totem poles, and other curios. Weird and wonderful things are found among the souvenir junk, such as shrunken heads from the Jivaro tribe of South America. ▪ *Pier 54, Alaskan Way; 682-5844; map:N9; every day.*

▼

Gifts

▲

## HARDWARE

**Chubby & Tubby** To call Chubby & Tubby a hardware store doesn't do it justice, since this local chain, with branches in North Seattle and White Center, virtually carries one of everything—from clothes to croquet sets—at workingfamily's prices. There's a large lawn and garden section (C & T is *the* place for good, cheap Christmas trees), and a great selection of sport shoes, including hard-to-find Converse colors. ▪ *3333 Rainier Ave S (and branches); 723-8800; map:II6; every day.*

**City People's Mercantile** ▪ **City People's Garden Store** See Florists and Nurseries in this chapter. ▪ *500 15th Ave E; 324-9510; map:GG6; every day.* ▪ *3517 Fremont Ave N; 632-1200; map:FF8; every day.* ▪ *2939 E Madison St; 324-0737; map:GG6; every day.*

**Greenwood Hardware and Glass/True Value** An excellent, full-line hardware store with an extensive line of lawn and garden tools, paint, fittings, and fixtures. The friendly salesperson who says, "If you don't see it, it's somewhere" is right on the mark. ▪ *7201 Greenwood Ave N; 783-2900; map:EE7; every day.*

**Hardwick's Swap Shop** A spacious hardware store with an old-time feel and an up-to-date selection. All the new supplies to keep your home running, plus plenty of used and bargain merchandise to make for low-cost shopping—Hardwick's even carries used furniture (hence the name) as a sideline. ▪ *4214 Roosevelt Way NE; 632-1203; map:DD7; Tues–Sat.*

**Kirkland True Value Hardware** Kirkland Hardware draws clientele from all over the Eastside with a variety of quality paints, electrical and plumbing items, lumber, and housewares. There's also an extensive lawn and garden section. Good prices, some great bargains, and a clean, friendly atmosphere. ▪ *424 Kirkland Ave, Kirkland; 822-6011; map:EE3; every day.*

**Madison Park Hardware** Madison Park Hardware is a center of commercial (and sometimes, it seems, *social*) life in this close-knit, single-family neighborhood. Every square inch of this store is packed with goodies. There is a selection of kitchen and gift items, decorator baskets, toys, and pet supplies to supplement the standard hardware fare. Usually closed most of January. ▪ *1837 42nd Ave E; 322-5331; map:GG6; Mon–Sat.*

**McLendon's** Well worth a special trek to Renton, this hardware mega-emporium has been in business for 70 years, making it an area institution. The great thing about McLendon's is that it's almost exclusively a hardware store, not an everything store. There are aisles and aisles of pipes, caulking, tools, and

▼

**Hardware**

▲

electrical and plumbing supplies. Lots of paint and lumber, too.
■ *710 S 2nd St, Renton (and branches); 235-3555; map:MM3; every day.*

**Pacific Iron and Building Materials** If you can't find it anywhere else, you'll find it here: doors, hardwoods, piles of cabinet fronts, sheets of stainless steel and steel plate cut and sold by the pound. If you're serious about doing it yourself, you can get help here. ■ *2230 4th Ave S; 628-6256; map:II7; every day.*

**RR Hardware** An old-time hardware store is a real find these days. The narrow, high-stacked rows hold a little bit of everything. New, used, and to-be-repaired are all mixed together. There are plenty of manual lawnmowers for sale, and even a stack of recycled hard hats—just $3.19 each. ■ *6512 15th Ave NE; 522-7810; map:EE6; every day.*

**Stephenson Ace Hardware** A friendly, neighborhood hardware store, complete with helpful staffers. The shelves are stocked with basic lawn and garden, variety, and paint supplies. The electrical and plumbing sections are extensive and include hard-to-find items. ■ *9000 Roosevelt Way NE; 522-3324; map:DD7; every day.*

**Stoneway Hardware & Supply** Big, well-stocked, no-frills Stoneway carries lawn and garden, lumber, electrical and plumbing supplies, paint, and even ducting. The staff at both locations clearly know their stuff. If you have a job to do, this is the place to go. ■ *4318 Stone Way N; 545-6910; map:FF7; every day.* ■ *7330 35th St NE; 524-9099; map:EE6; every day.*

**Tashiro's Sharp Japanese Tools** Tashiro's is small, and it hardly carries everything, but it's a must-see if you're a tool fanatic. This place specializes in high-quality Japanese woodworking tools, and if you're lucky, you'll get a demonstration. ■ *2939 4th Ave S; 621-0199; map:Q6; Mon–Sat.*

**Tweedy and Popp Ace Hardware** A clean, well-stocked neighborhood hardware store with a little of everything. Though it is an Ace Hardware, Tweedy and Popp refuses to don the sterile, modern look of a chain. There are plenty of housewares, plumbing, electrical, and lawn and garden supplies to keep your house humming. ■ *1916 N 45th St; 632-2290; map:FF7; every day.*

## HEALTH FOOD

**Alfalfa's** A newcomer out of Colorado, Alfalfa's is the wave of the future in the grocery business: a complete grocery store devoted to natural food and the environment. There's organic produce, a meat and seafood department complete with sushi, and a large cruelty-free cosmetics and vitamins section. Aisles of canned and packaged foods include often hard-to-find items.

The deli/bakery offers a changing selection of both hot and cold entrees, salads, sandwiches, and desserts to take out or eat in, and the juice bar also pulls a good espresso. ▪ *5440 Sand Point Way NE; 525-3941; map:FF5; every day.*

**Central Co-op Grocery** Since 1978, this Capitol Hill independent co-op has offered bulk foods, organic produce, and a wide range of macrobiotic products. It is an excellent source for special dietary needs (salt-free, sugar-free, wheat-free, and other alternatives). Nonmembers are welcome, but pay a slightly higher price. At press time, plans are in the offing for a second store. ▪ *1835 12th Ave; 329-1545; map:GG2; every day.*

**The Grainery** Not exactly a working mill, this Burien store *will* grind your grain into flour. There's a large selection of whole grains, or you can purchase flours in bulk. You'll find beans, raw honeys, and vitamin and mineral supplements, as well as flour grinders, juicers, and bread machines. ▪ *13629 1st Ave S, Burien; 244-5015; map:OO8; Mon–Sat.*

**Larry's Markets** All things to all people, Larry's has a department devoted to natural foods. In the Bio section you'll find packaged foods, frozen products, juices, vitamins, supplements, homeopathic treatments, and aromatherapy oils. Elsewhere in the store are a large bulk food section, an extensive selection of organic produce, organic milk, and fertilized eggs. ▪ *10008 Aurora Ave N in Oak Tree Village (and branches); 527-5333; map:DD7; every day.* ▪ *699 120th Ave NE, Bellevue; 453-0600; map:HH3; every day.*

▼

**Health Food**

▲

**Magnano Foods** A great place in the mezzanine of Pike Place Market's Main Arcade for bulk pasta, rice, beans, flours, grains, dried fruits, nuts, coffees, teas, and spices—some of it organic. Bulk olive oil is a bargain. ▪ *Pike Place Market; 223-9582; map:J8; Mon–Sat.*

**Marlene's Market and Deli** Marlene's has been a full-service market/deli/health-food store operating in south King County for more than 20 years. It offers organically grown produce, bulk grains, spices, natural cosmetics and body-care products, vitamins, herbs, and books. A natural foods deli and bakery adjoins the store. ▪ *31839 Gateway Center Blvd S, Federal Way; 839-0933; map:SS6; every day.*

**Nature's Pantry** The Eastside's finest and most comprehensive natural foods store (there's even a small Mercer Island branch, 232-7900) features all-organic produce, natural foods groceries, vitamins, natural cosmetics, and a sit-down deli/bakery with whole-grain baked goods. The Crossroads Shopping Center store has a state-of-the-art juice bar. ▪ *10200 NE 10th St, Bellevue (and branches); 454-0170; map:GG3; every day.* ▪ *Crossroads Shopping Center, Bellevue; 957-0090; map:HH1; every day.*

**PCC Natural Markets** The name change from Puget Consumers' Co-op reflects the growth and upgrading of this over-30-year-old cooperative into a full-line natural foods grocery store with seven branches (Fremont, Green Lake, Kirkland, Ravenna, Seward Park, View Ridge, and West Seattle). Up to 10,000 people join the co-op each year, but nonmembers can shop here, too (though they pay a surcharge). Produce, much of it organic, is centrally displayed, and each store carries over 200 whole foods available in bulk. PCC has a wide range of vitamins and supplements, packaged goods, frozen foods, beer and wine, and additive- and chemical-free meats, all at competitive prices. All but the Green Lake store have delis that offer heat-and-eat entrees, salads, desserts, sauces, and fresh pastas in addition to meats and cheeses. At press time, a new, full-service, Green Lake store is slated to open at N 74th Street and Aurora Avenue N. ■ *6504 20th Ave NE (and branches); 525-1450; map:EE7; every day.*

**Rainbow Grocery** This folksy little market features natural food products and healthy cosmetics at competitive prices. Much of the produce is organic, and the fine dairy department offers hormone-free milk and several varieties of cheese— some rennet-free. Great, friendly service. ■ *409 15th Ave E; 329-8440; map:HH6; every day.*

## HOME ACCESSORIES

**The Best of All Worlds** This downtown shop is crowded with fine and esoteric stuff for the home: wrought-metal birdcages, tapestry pillows, sumptuous and unusual tabletop accessories, French flatware, and linens from all over the world. A nice eye for detail distinguishes the merchandise here as something special. ■ *523 Union St; 623-2525; map:K6; every day.*

**Crystallia** It's one of the most complete selections of world-renowned crystal, glass, and Lucite accessories you'll find in the Northwest—Waterford, Orrefors, Lenox, Baccarat. Service is great, and if they don't have what you're looking for, they'll find someone who does. ■ *Bellevue Square, Bellevue; 454-5687; map:HH3; every day.*

**Design Concern** An eclectic array of items fills this sleek, contemporary, two-level store, but all share at least one feature: unique, functional, top-notch design. Pens and desktop accessories, hand-crafted jewelry, watches, leather goods, and housewares and glassware from around the world make browsing a pleasure here. ■ *1420 5th Ave, #201 (City Centre); 623-4444; map:J8; every day.*

**Domus** Bellevue Square's best housewares store carries an extremely well-chosen lot—wine glasses, linen towels, jewelry, note cards, furniture, china, aprons, cutlery. Affordable, with a sleek, modern inclination. You could lose yourself in here for hours. Domus's sister store (also in Bellevue Square), Kitchen Kitchen, is chock-full of kitchen wares. Both offer bridal registry. ■ *Bellevue Square, Bellevue; 454-2728; map:HH3; every day.* ■ *912 Northgate Mall; 367-1731; map:DD7; every day.*

**Egbert's** You'll rarely see the same thing twice at this unlikely Belltown address, but you can be assured of finding creative, fine-quality items all the time. An Italian leather chair sets off a Scandinavian light wood dining room table; jewelry from around the world approaches museum quality; African art mixes with folklore-inspired bronzes. There is even some clothing thrown in for good measure. The potpourri style is executed quite successfully by owner Jim Egbert, whose eclectic tastes run the gamut from whimsical to functional. ■ *2231 1st Ave; 728-5682; map:G8; Mon–Sat.*

**Frank and Dunya** Quirky Frank and Dunya are the owners' departed dogs, and their likenesses perpetually, cheerfully greet all comers. The store is filled with handmade furniture and mostly locally crafted jewelry and accessories. Everything in here is a character piece—overwhelmingly so. Expensive and well worth it. ■ *3418 Fremont Ave N; 547-6760; map:FF7; every day.*

▼

**Home Accessories**

▲

**Hold Everything** The Williams-Sonoma people have come out of the kitchen. Just walk into the store and you'll feel more organized. They carry places to put stuff—cedar shoe racks, hanging sweater bags, folding bookshelves, expando spice risers, and modular furnishings to house your computer, VCR, or CD collection. Catalog, too. ■ *1420 5th Ave, #202 (City Centre); 682-8915; map:J6; every day.*

**J.F. Henry Shop** J.F. Henry's bright interior attracts West Seattle shoppers looking for popular and traditional place settings: Noritake, Mikasa, Lenox, and other mainstream collections, plus a bountiful assortment of glassware, crystal, and accessories. Brides can register here. ■ *4540 California Ave SW; 935-5150; map:II9; Mon–Sat.*

**Keeg's** When Keeg's left its flagship Capitol Hill digs and headed to the Eastside in 1995, the Seattle contingent was up in arms. In Bellevue, Keeg's continues to supply all the pricey necessities for modern small-scale living: glassware, leather accessories, contemporary lighting, rugs, flatware, tables and chairs, and more, including wrapping paper and note cards. ■ *10575 NE 12th, Bellevue; 635-0655; map:GG3; every day.*

**Market Graphics** From Leonardo to pop art, Market Graphics carries contemporary and classic art reproductions. There are museum art posters and black-and-white photographic reproductions, framing, and small gift items, as well. The helpful owners provide special service to businesses decorating with posters. ■ *1935 1st Ave; 441-7732; map:I8; every day.*

**Miller-Pollard Interiors** Miller-Pollard is a Seattle treasure, and continues to delight browsers with its restrained good taste. Clean-lined antiques (with a special affection for Danish pine) intermix with comfortable chintz pillows; country-kitchen tables are bedecked with wooden bowls; table linens complement the flatware, dinnerware, and stemware. Design consultation available. ■ *University Village; 527-8478; map:FF6; every day.* ■ *4218 E Madison St; 325-3600; map:GG6; Mon–Sat.*

**Pottery Barn** Another Williams-Sonoma offspring specializing in tabletop and living space accoutrements for the Modern Home: stenciled cotton rugs, bold vases, and a panoply of glass- and stemware, both practical and fun. ■ *1420 5th Ave, #200 (City Centre); 682-9312; map:J6; every day.*

**The Well Made Bed** Talk about the stuff that dreams are made of. Elegant dreams. Comfortable dreams. *Expensive* dreams. But when you spend a third of your life between the sheets, shelling out bucks for good bedding makes all the sense in the world. Sheets, pillow slips, comforters, dust ruffles, and custom-fitted or ready-made duvets are sold by staff who are eager to provide you with individual attention. They can special-order bed linens from any American manufacturer. ■ *2671 University Village; 523-8407; map:FF6; every day.* ■ *990 102nd NE, Bellevue, WA 98004; 455-3508; map:HH3; every day.*

▼

▲

**Zanadia** Zanadia carries a wide range of contemporary, reasonably priced kitchen and life-style accessories, as well as rugs, clocks, mirrors, magazine racks, picture frames, and other can't-do-withouts. Lots of seasonal stuff and a smattering of furniture, too. ■ *1815 N 45th St (Wallingford Center); 547-0884; map:EE6; every day.*

## IMPORTS

**Alhambra** It's like walking into a becalmed Middle Eastern bazaar; heavy rugs draped over big wooden chests, cases full of gleaming silver, and ephemera from exotic locales spread throughout the store. The owners are from Turkey, where they travel twice a year to find hand-knit sweaters, gloves, hats, and unique home accessories. The jewelry ranges from contemporary imports to vintage pieces: onyx, Russian amber, Indonesian, African, and Nepali designs. There's a small but well-chosen selection of women's natural-fiber clothing. The atmosphere is dreamy, as befits the prices, which for the most part hover in the stratosphere. ■ *101 Pine St; 621-9571; map:J8; every day.*

**Anglomania ▪ Cottontail Corner** Owner Susan Jarrett loads up with authentic British goods on her twice-yearly jaunts to the mother country. A proper collection of English bone china (Royal Doulton, Royal Albert, and other lines), Irish porcelain, books, tea biscuits, and much more fill the shelves. A second store, Cottontail Corner, carries nothing but Beatrix Potter merchandise. ▪ *Gilman Village, Issaquah; 392-2842; every day.* ▪ *Gilman Village, Issaquah; 392-3818; every day.*

**Asia Gallery** Owner Tony Ventura sells Asian antiques, folk arts, ethnic textiles, and some contemporary (mostly Asian) jewelry from his artfully cluttered shop in the shadow of the Seattle Art Museum. Estate pieces new and old are available for from $1 to $10,000. ▪ *1220 1st Ave; 622-0516; map:K7; Mon–Sat.*

**Cibol** The good-looking, low-priced, imported clothing in this small Market shop (on the mezzanine level of the Main Arcade) comes from Latin America, India, and Bali. Alpaca sweaters are great deals: a lot of color and warmth at very reasonable prices. The accessories are imports, too. ▪ *Pike Place Market; 682-5640; map:J7; every day.*

**Folk Art Gallery/La Tienda** One of the nation's premier import shops, La Tienda is loaded with clothing, crafts, jewelry, and musical instruments from everywhere, including a fair amount of work from United States folk artists. The displays are fascinating—shelves of hand-thrown pottery, a few imported children's toys, African drums, silk scarves—and the owner is delighted to speak Spanish with customers. ▪ *4138 University Way NE; 632-1796; map:FF6; every day.*

▼

**Imports**

▲

**Galway Traders** Goods from Ireland and art from the American Southwest share space in this house-turned-shop. Successfully, too: the six rooms are filled to the brim with crafts, imports, and foodstuffs. From Ireland come woolens, capes, Aran sweaters (the best collection in the area), Belleek china, dolls, books, and a large collection of Celtic recordings. From the Southwest come Navajo pottery and haunting Indian tapes, gorgeous tiles, and other art. You can even pick up the makings of a meal: oatmeal and Irish tea, blue corn tortillas and salsa. ▪ *7518 15th Ave NW; 784-9343; map:EE8; every day.*

**Hands of the World** A bright shop in the lower level of Pike Place Market's Main Arcade, Hands of the World carries beautiful crafts and home accessories imported primarily from third world countries. The emphasis is on jewelry and art, including masks and carvings, along with a great selection of scarves and other imported accessories. Closed Sundays January through April. ▪ *Pike Place Market; 622-1696; map:J8; every day.*

**Higo** Think of a Japanese Woolworth's in the International District, and that's Higo, a 50-plus-year-old Seattle institution. There are soup bowls, chopsticks, rice steamers, and other utensils along with kimonos, shoes, and postcards of Mount Fuji. ▪ *604 S Jackson St; 622-7572; map:Q6; Mon–Sat.*

**Monsoon** Nancy and Eric Gorbman travel abroad to bring back treasures from Indonesia, Thailand, and India, but they don't exclude local designers. Lovely accessories include a marvelous selection of sterling silver jewelry set with stones. Tons of beads from everywhere. ▪ *4536 University Way NE; 633-2446; map:FF6; every day.*

**Prima Mexico** Mexican furniture, pottery, jewelry, and folk art are the order of the day at Prima Mexico. It's all handcrafted in Mexico and imported directly to the United States. Especially popular are the pottery selections—in all sizes, shapes, and colors—and the masks from all over Mexico, made of stone, wood, or metal. ▪ *68 Madison St; 682-6294; map:M8; Mon–Sat.*

**The Ring of Fire Gallery** Inhale the scent of Asia wafting from the Wild Ginger restaurant next door as you browse through Chris McGinnis and Jacquelyn Loree's carefully selected contemporary artifacts. Much of the merchandise in this handsome gallery setting comes from Africa, Asia, and Indonesia. ▪ *1408 Western Ave; 682-9641; map:J8; every day.*

▼

Jewelry

▲

## JEWELRY

**Alvin Goldfarb Jeweler** The owner learned his trade as a gemologist at Friedlander, his wife's family's business. Today Alvin Goldfarb provides unerring personal attention and quality. Many of Bellevue's affluent won't go anywhere else. ▪ *305 Bellevue Way, Bellevue; 454-9393; map:HH3; Mon–Sat.*

**Ben Bridge** The best place for diamonds is Ben Bridge, in the same downtown location since 1912. Their diamonds range from inexpensive to expensive, and service is very informative. Mountings are fairly traditional, but custom design work is offered. ▪ *409 Pike St (and branches); 628-6800; map:J6; every day.*

**Carroll's** Carroll's, in business for over a century, sparkles with unusual finds from all over the world; it's one of the most fascinating and lovely gem stores in Seattle. You might discover an antique silver picture frame or a set of antique Oriental gaming pieces. There's also a classy selection of watches, rings, bracelets, necklaces, and gemstones. ▪ *1427 4th Ave; 622-9191; map:K6; Mon–Sat.*

**Facere Jewelry Art** Proprietor Karen Lorene, the city's leading authority on antique jewelry, specializes in Victorian jewelry art here in this small space on the main level of City Centre. Along with exquisite old pieces, some dating from the late 18th century, she offers a beautifully displayed collection of art deco rings, as well as contemporary works by local designers and jewelry artists from around the country. ▪ *1420 5th Ave (City Centre); 624-6768; map:K6; Mon–Sat.*

**Fox's Gem Shop** If there really were a diamond as big as the Ritz, here's where you'd find it. Fox's is an elegant shop with stiff prices. Their specialties: glittering gemstones and dazzling diamonds. You dress up to shop here. The gift section has silver for all occasions and a large selection of clocks. If you like to give gifts that bear the name Tiffany, Fox's has your little blue boxes—and the gems that go in them. ▪ *1341 5th Ave; 623-2528; map:K6; Mon–Sat.*

**Friedlander Jewelers** Though the downtown store (a Seattle landmark since 1886) closed its doors after 100 years in business, Friedlander's is still going strong in a mall near you. Besides an overwhelming selection of watches, rings, and fine crystal, the shop offers custom design and repair. ▪ *Northgate Mall (and branches); 365-8740; map:DD7; Mon–Sun.*

**Gem Design Jewelers** Owners Shauna and Richard Miller deal in original and custom designs and stone remounting. Also a nice line of earrings, gold necklaces, and individual colored stones, diamonds, and pearls. ▪ *14310 NE 20th St, Suite B, Bellevue; 643-6245; map:GG3; Tues–Sat.*

**Gold & Silver Shop** Traditional to ultramodern jewelry is fabricated in-house here. Diamonds are an especially good value because the shop buys directly from contacts in Israel. Gemstones, too. ▪ *526 1st Ave N; 284-2082; map:A7; Tues–Sat.* ▪ *Bellevue Square; 462-8202; map:HH3; every day.*

**Goldman's Jewelers** Goldman's carries exciting, state-of-the-art jewelry, much of it made by local artists. Expect to find unusual gems and colored stones, custom and artist inlay work, and an extensive clock selection. Goldman's ships all around the world. ▪ *1521 1st Ave; 682-0237; map:J7; Mon–Sat.*

**Lillian's Pearl Shop** Lillian's has a broad assortment of cultured pearls in many colors and sizes. The shop strings pearl necklaces to any length (and can repair broken strings); also jade and lapis pieces. Hours are short: from 11am to 4pm. ▪ *1411 4th St; 682-1043; map:L6; Mon–Fri.*

**Michael Farrell, Jeweler** A friendly shop, always full of clients buying and admiring the excellent selection of vintage watches. There's an impressive collection of sterling silver hollowware, as well as vintage American signature jewelry. They also do custom repairs. ▪ *324 15th Ave E; 324-1582; map:HH6; Mon–Sat.* ▪ *5420 Sand Point Way NE; 524-8848; map:EE5; Mon–Sat.*

**Philip Monroe Jeweler** The top of the line when it comes to custom jewelry (which makes up 95 percent of its business), this small shop has an air of restrained elegance. Occasionally the lovely selection of unusual and antique jewelry hangs from the arms of exquisite Oriental figurines. Antiques and art objects. ▪ *519 Pine St; 624-1531; map:J5; Mon–Sat.*

**Turgeon Raine Jewelers** Norman Turgeon and Jerry Raine have some of the finest custom and designer jewelry in town. From the new classics (like tension-set diamonds) to the old (modern twists on antique pieces), you'll find something to please. Don't let the elegant digs and the guard at the door scare you off: they take all comers, and the personable sales staff will make you feel at home among the precious baubles, bangles, and beads. Expensive? Sure. Worth it? Indeed. ▪ *1407 5th Ave; 447-9488; map:K5; Mon–Sat.*

## KITCHENWARE

**City Kitchens** A general-purpose kitchen store, City Kitchens sells selected commercial and specialty cookware lines at some of the lowest prices in the city. ▪ *1527 4th Ave; 382-1138; map:J6; every day.*

**A Cook's Tour** This spacious, gadget-filled waterfront store has everything you need for a well-equipped kitchen, from linens to storage containers to stockpots. The helpful staff, the long hours (until 10pm every night during the summer), and the salty air make this a particularly relaxing place to shop. ▪ *Pier 56; 622-2838; map:K9; every day.*

**Grand Central Mercantile** A gold mine of imported kitchenware, cooking accessories, and dinnerware, plus a broad selection of cookie cutters and gadgets. ▪ *316 1st Ave S; 623-8894; map:O8; every day.*

**Kitchen Kitchen** A spinoff of the home accessories store Domus, Kitchen Kitchen carries everything for the kitchen, from the practical to the frivolous. Mixing bowls, pots, and cookbooks vie for space with cookie cutters and refrigerator magnets. ▪ *Bellevue Square, Bellevue; 451-9507; map:HH3; every day.*

**Kitchen 'n Things** Located in the heart of Seattle's Scandinavian community, this shop offers high-quality cookware and tableware, as well as hard-to-find Scandinavian cooking implements—ebilskivers, lefse rolling pins, and krunkake irons. ▪ *2322 NW Market St; 784-8717; map:FF8; every day.*

**Mr. "J" Kitchen Gourmet** A veritable warehouse of domestic and imported pots, pans, glassware, plates, flatware, cooking aids, food processors, and cookbooks. Classes are offered in

▼
Kitchenware
▲

their well-equipped demonstration kitchen. ■ *10116 NE 8th St, Bellevue; 455-2270; map:HH3; every day.*

**The Mrs. Cooks** Concentrating on top-quality cookware and utensils, this neighborhood kitchen store also offers a respectable collection of cookbooks, giftware, and linens. ■ *University Village; 525-5008; map:FF6; every day.*

**Sunshine Kitchen Company** Owner Hal Sadis opened his kitchen supply shop in the same building as the Sunshine Bakery; the aroma of baking brioches and baguettes will inspire you to purchase his crockery, copper molds, heavy kitchen equipment, and other necessities. ■ *14625 NE 20th St, Bellevue; 641-4520; map:GG2; every day.*

**Sur La Table** Things at Sur La Table haven't been quite the same since owner Shirley Collins sold Seattle's beloved cookshop to Carl and Renee Behnke in 1995. In its newest incarnation, the store is far less cramped, with wider aisles for browsing (losing much of its beloved Continental appeal). Nonetheless, Sur La Table has most of the essential (and nonessential) equipment for cooks: candy molds, Cuisinarts, cake pans, muffin tins, copper pots, dishtowels, potholders, imported aprons, and lots of cookbooks. For those whose hearts break at the Bon Marchéification of the shop, we suggest ordering from the catalog: (800)243-0852. ■ *Pike Place Market; 448-2244; map:I8; every day.*

▼

**Kitchenware**

▲

**Williams-Sonoma** A long-standing favorite of cooks nationwide, this catalog retailer stocks high-quality cookware, as well as linens, glassware, cookbooks, and specialty food items in its handsome L. L. Bean-meets-Martha Stewart–style stores. ■ *Westlake Center; 624-1422; map:I5; every day.*

## LINGERIE

**Ann Marie Lingerie** Fine lace bras and other elegant lingerie on display in this equally elegant Madison Park shop subtly encourage you to splurge on fancy underthings. What price glamour? Little nothings from Valentino, Chantel, and Aubade will make you (and yours) feel like a million. Ann Marie Spiers' Gentleman's Night (an annual, in-store, invites-only, pre-Christmas bash) is a must for the man whose woman should have everything. ■ *4000 E Madison St; 323-6027; map:GG6; Mon–Sat.*

**Nancy Meyer** With about as much square footage as the walk-in closets of some of its patrons, this eclectic boutique manages to stock a surprising selection of the finest designer and imported lingerie. The tasteful luxury displayed here has made it a favorite among the physically and fiscally fortunate. ■ *1318 5th Ave; 625-9200; map:K6; Mon–Sat.*

**Victoria's Secret** Men live for the catalog, with its quasi-whole-
some take on pulchritude; but women have grown to expect
two things from VS: cotton that isn't frumpy and tasteful lingerie that doesn't cost a fortune. Intimate apparel here runs the
gamut from sport bras to skimpy silk nighties to hug-size
bathrobes. ▪ *Westlake Center (and branches); 623-6035;
map:I5; every day.*

## MEAT

**A& J Meats and Seafoods** Regarded as the best in town, A&
J Meats has a wonderful selection of specialty items as well as
top-quality basic cuts (the beef and lamb are superb). They
make all their own wieners and lunch meats (both pure beef),
chicken cordon bleu, stuffed pork chops, meat loaves, and
sausages of all types (including fruit-spiked varieties). They
also do their own applewood smoking. ▪ *2401 Queen Anne
Ave N; 284-3885; map:GG8; Tues–Sat.*

**Bavarian Meats** German is definitely spoken here in the north
end of Pike Place Market, where you'll find a large selection of
sausages—from bratwurst to knackwurst—along with deli
meats and German specialty foods. ▪ *Pike Place Market; 441-
0942; map:J8; Mon–Sat.*

**CasCioppo Brothers Italian Meat Market** Seattle's only Ital- ▼
ian meat vendor and a longtime Ballard tradition carries sev- **Meat**
eral lines of imported Italian specialty foods. The Italian
sausage is spicy and excellent (it's the choice of many Italian ▲
restaurants in town), and some customers consider the homemade pepperoni the hottest in the world. ▪ *2364 NW 80th St;
784-6121; map:EE8; every day.*

**Don & Joe's** Located under the clock in the Main Arcade, Don
& Joe's is the best butcher in the Market (some might say in
town). Their smoked ham, fresh turkeys, and lamb chops are superb. Lamb's tongue, sheep's head, sweetbreads, and tripe can
be yours for the asking and they'll even give your veal
tenderloin the "mother-in-law treatment"—tenderizing it with the
flat-side of a cleaver. Friendly service ensures hordes of satisfied
regulars. ▪ *Pike Place Market; 682-7670; map:J8; Mon–Sat.*

**Fischer Meats and Seafoods** This 1910 Issaquah institution is
the place to go for chicken—it's delivered fresh daily, as is the
seafood. Fischer also makes its own German, Italian, potato,
and smoked sausages, as well as beef and turkey jerky. ▪ *85
Front St N, Issaquah; 392-3131; Mon–Sat.*

**The Incredible Link** Jimi Dorsey and his extended family make
sausages that actually live up to their name. Their Pike Place
Market sausage kitchen (you can watch the preparations
through the glass-front window in the heart of the market)

adjoins the small retail shop. These incredible links have no nitrates, preservatives, fillers, MSG, or meat by-products and include incendiary Louisiana hot links, chichi chorizo, and English bangers, among others. For those who just say no to red meat, there are links made with seafood, chicken, or turkey (and there's even a veggie version complete with fruit, rice, sunflower seeds, and tofu). Jimi and crew will even custom-make sausage to your specifications. Try a grilled sausage sandwich and you won't have to be convinced to take home a pound or two. ■ *Pike Place Market; 622-8002; map:J8; every day.*

**Market House Corned Beef** A very unpretentious place that has been selling simply terrific corned beef since 1948. The emphasis here is on wholesale, but they do retail corned beef in any amount. ■ *1124 Howell St; 624-9248; map:I2; Mon–Sat.*

**Seattle Super Smoke** Seattle Super Smoke caught on so feverishly with Seattle palates that it had to move to much larger quarters. Its main business is wholesale, but you can also buy this deeply smoky, alderwood-redolent poultry and meat from a retail deli. The barbecue sauce is a fine accompaniment. ■ *2454 Occidental Ave S; 625-1339; map:II7; Mon–Fri.*

**Torino Sausage Company** A family-run company since the mid 1930s, Torino specializes in freshly made sausages and salami (with no added preservatives). ■ *1024 Andover Park E; 575-9353; map:NN5; Mon–Fri.* ■ *1101 Madison St; 623-1530; map:M3; Mon–Sat.*

## OUTDOOR GEAR

**Alpine Hut** Alpine Hut is a great place to find good deals on all kinds of ski gear in winter, wet suits and bike wear in summer. The owner is friendly and the store aims to please. ■ *2215 15th Ave W; 284-3575; map:GG8; Mon–Sat.*

**Crossings** While the emphasis is on sailing, these crew outfits work nicely for *almost* any kind of boating endeavor. The outerwear keeps you dry on deck and the natural fiber fabrics keep you dapper. Landlubbers and water-fiends alike will appreciate the handsome collection of general outerwear for both men and women. ■ *2140 Westlake Ave N; 283-1645; map:GG7; every day.*

**The Crow's Nest** This large marine hardware store, with branches at Shilshole and in Everett, specializes in yachting accessories, clothing, foul-weather gear, and hardware. ■ *1900 N Northlake Way (and branches); 632-3555; map:FF7; every day.*

**David Morgan** Here is where you buy plush, functional Scottish waxed cotton jackets and Buxton riding coats. Also look for British ordinance survey maps, C. C. Filson clothing (the prime outdoorwear made in Seattle), Akubra hats, and Welsh wools. Everything for the well-heeled huntsman or all-purpose outdoorsman, plus Celtic and Northwest Coast Native American jewelry. ▪ *11812 Northcreek Pkwy N, Suite 103, Bothell; 485-2132; map:BB4; Mon–Sat.*

**Easy Rider** The largest West Coast manufacturer of canoes and kayaks (in business for over 25 years), Easy Rider offers its complete line of 50 different styles, factory direct to the public. Factory pickup offers good savings on first-quality vessels, with even better savings off seconds. There are whitewater, lake, saltwater, all-purpose, family, and hunting styles in 12½- to 22½-foot lengths. ▪ *15666 W Valley Hwy, Tukwila; 228-3633; map:NN5; Mon–Sat.*

**Eddie Bauer** Once Seattle's very own, Eddie Bauer is now a national chain (owned by Spiegel Inc.) with a like-size reputation. You used to shop here for fine goose-down sleeping bags, comforters, and pillows, but now you come for outdoor fashion: goose-down jackets, vests, and parkas, along with shorts, rugby shirts, and other sportive ensembles. All are very high quality, dependable, and pricey. In addition, Eddie Bauer's 200 stores sell some fishing rods, backpacking equipment, sports accessories, knives, sunglasses, and shoes. The downtown Eddie Bauer's lower level is devoted to their latest venture: furniture and home accessories—sturdy, hunting-lodge–style designs for the rugged indoorsman. The bargain basement has moved to Silverdale. ▪ *Rainier Square (and branches); 622-2766; map:K6; every day.*

**Elliott Bay Bicycles** Intimidating to novices, Elliott Bay is the Cadillac of bike stores. It's regarded as something of a pro shop; it sells bikes to cyclists who know what they're doing and do enough of it to justify the high prices. Among its other attributes, the shop is home base for Bill Davidson, a nationally known frame-builder. ▪ *2116 Western Ave; 441-8144; map:G8; every day.*

**Fast Lady Sports** Fast Lady has the most complete selection of women's clothing and footwear for running, cycling, swimming, tennis, and aerobic workouts. The friendly staff dispense accurate information and advice. ▪ *2701 University Village; 522-2113; map:FF6; every day.* ▪ *5 Lake St, Kirkland; 889-9433; map:GG2; every day.*

**Feathered Friends** These are the top-of-the-line down products in the city; their Gore-Tex and down clothes have been leading climbing expeditions for years. The 10th Avenue branch sells bedding and comforters; the one on Capitol Hill specializes in sporting goods, sleeping bags (made to order), and climbing equipment. ▪ *1516 11th Ave; 324-4166; map:HH6; every day.* ▪ *1415 10th Ave; 328-0887; map:J7; Mon–Fri.*

▼

Outdoor Gear

▲

**C. C. Filson Co.** One of the few Seattle businesses around since the turn of the century, Filson sells rugged wearables which are enjoying something of a rebirth since the opening of a retail store just south of downtown Seattle. Heavy wool jackets and vests, canvas hunting coats, oil-finish hats, and wool pants are the style here. The original C. C. Filson sold clothes to the men headed north to Alaska during the Gold Rush, and today's clothes are still attractive and tough—not necessarily in that order (one jacket style, the Cruiser, hasn't been much changed since Filson designed and patented it in 1914). Complete line of handsome luggage (including gun bags), too. At Filson they take themselves rather too seriously, but after nearly 100 years in business, why shouldn't they?. ■ *1246 1st Ave S; 622-3147; map:II8; Mon–Sat.*

**Gregg's Greenlake Cycle** Gregg's is a high-volume, high-pressure Seattle institution, perhaps (at least initially) by virtue of its Green Lake location. With such a large inventory, it can handle the entire family: bikes for kids, all-terrain, and Japanese-, Italian-, and American-made racing cycles, along with Seattle's largest collection of touring bikes. Because of its sheer volume, it's the best first stop when you're hunting for a bicycle. If you do buy from Gregg's, you'll get good follow-up service. The Green Lake location has a large clothing and accessories department and rents bikes, roller skates, in-line skates, and snow boards. There are branches in Bellevue and on Aurora. ■ *7007 Woodlawn Ave NE (and branches); 523-1822; map:EE7; every day.*

▼

**Outdoor Gear**

▲

**Il Vecchio** Visually, George Gibbs's bicycle shop in Leschi looks more like an art gallery than a bike shop. The award-winning Weinstein-designed store is minimalist in appeal—there are very few bikes here—and maximalist in quality (and price): Italian racers, De Rosa and Pinarello, and American-made Merlin and Landshark. ■ *140 Lakeside Ave; 324-8148; map:HH6; Tues–Sat, or by appointment.*

**The Magic Spoke** Sally Hildt has gained a reputation for her quick, honest bicycle repairs and wheel building. All types of bikes and bicyclists benefit from this thorough-service ethic. ■ *7009 Roosevelt Way NE; 527-2100; map:EE6; Tues–Sat.*

**Marley's Snowboards and Skateboards** If you aren't enthusiastic about snow-boarding when you walk into this darkish subterranean store, you will be by the time you walk out. Co-owner Ian Fels, a skier who took up snow-boarding eight years ago and never looked back, is a friendly, talkative guy who can tell you anything you need to know about getting radical or getting started. Marley's carries top brands that cover the price range from reasonable to jaw-dropping. There's a wide selection of those baggy, comfortable clothes that are de rigueur for snow boarders. In summer the emphasis switches to skateboards. ■ *3519 Fremont Pl N, #B; 634-2933; map:FF7; every day.*

**Marmot Mountain Works** Marmot outfits the skier, backpacker, and mountaineer with cross-country skis, packs, tents, boots, crampons, ice axes, and more—all for sale or rent. Prices for outerwear are some of the highest around; however, deals can be found on some ski accessories, such as climbing skins for the backcountry. An excellent selection of climbing hardware. ■ *827 Bellevue Way NE, Bellevue; 453-1515; map:HH3; every day.*

**McHale & Co.** Mountaineer Dan McHale has been designing backpacks for professional climbers since 1971, and his expertise is renowned here among experts and weekend trailhounds alike. The store and workshop near the Ship Canal cater to serious backcountry skiers and hikers, with a full line of rucksacks, fanny packs, and internal-frame packs, including a popular model that converts to accommodate bigger loads. McHale's packs are built with comfort in mind, and they customized to ensure proper fit. ■ *29 Dravus St; 281-7861; map:FF8; Tues–Sat.*

**Mercer Island Ski and Cycle** The island's full-service neighborhood bike shop (which offers ski rental and ski clothing as well) upholds its reputation as the place to go for mountain bikes (a smaller selection of road bikes are available, too). Back when it was known as Mercer Island Cyclery, it was credited with starting the craze in this area. The shop is small; you're always bound to be talking to one of the owners—enthusiastic cyclists who are eager to help. There's now a second Ski and Cycle location in Issaquah (391-7547). ■ *7656 SE 27th St, Mercer Island; 232-3443; map:JJ4; every day.*

**NBN OUTLET** NBN, as most snow boarders know, is short for "No Billy No," which used to be the typical response to co-owner Christine "Tuna" Wood's big dog, Bill, but is now a hot line of reasonably priced snow-board wear. Wood and co-owner Ross Jurgensen run the business out of this Ravenna outlet, which carries seconds and overruns (though with such big baggy clothes, who can tell the difference?); a number of local stores also carry the line. These are the comfortable clothes that shredheads favor (most in comfortable earth tones): big fleece jackets, waterproof shorts, baggy shirts—as well as clothing for wake-boarding, an up-and-coming mixture of waterskiing and surfing. ■ *6326 22nd Ave NE, 98115; 522-0363; map:EE6; Thurs–Sat.*

**The North Face** A well-known name in backpacking equipment design, The North Face also has down clothing and bags, outdoor apparel, and skiwear. The store has every map and

▼

Outdoor Gear

▲

book imaginable to plan your mountaineering trip. The feeling here is of a yuppified REI (and prices are high, high, high), but that doesn't mean they aren't serious about products and service. ■ *1023 1st Ave; 622-4111; map:L8; every day.*

**Pacific Water Sports** A landbound spot on the Pacific Highway South strip is an unlikely location for this burgeoning water-play shop. Here, advanced and novice paddlers outfit themselves with the boat (kayak or canoe), the suit (wet or dry), and even the class (sea or whitewater). Excellent instruction ranges from canoe basics to intensive whitewater excursions. Exceptionally friendly service and advice. Rentals, too. ■ *16055 Pacific Hwy S; 246-9385; map:006; Mon–Sat.*

**Patagonia** It's all sleek-wood glamour and high-quality outdoor fashion at this handsome retail outlet. Here at Seattle's own Patagucci Central, you'll feel like a million bucks in stretch Synchilla and Capilene fleece, and you'll be oh so politically correct in your made-with-only-organically-grown-cotton garments. Tyke sizes, too. In fashion colors, built for comfort and style and made to last—with price tags to prove it. ■ *2100 First Ave; 622-9700; map:H8; every day.*

▼

**Outdoor Gear**

▲

**Patrick's Fly Shop** Fishing enthusiasts think of this shop as the premier source of information on area fly-fishing and how to tie those flies. As well they should: it has been around for over 50 years, making this the oldest fly-shop in the state. Patrick's offers workshops as well as old-fashioned friendly fishing stories and advice. ■ *2237 Eastlake Ave E; 323-3302; map:GG7; Mon–Sat.*

**R& E Cycles ■ Mountain Bike Specialists** Dan Towle and Estelle Gray bought this thorough operation a couple of years ago and are restoring it to its former glory. They specialize in hand-built Rodriguez frames (the original "R" in "R–&–E"), tandems, racing bikes, and wheel building. Mountain Bike Specialists has moved down a few doors and has been thoroughly renovated and enlarged. Repairs are done down the street at Seattle Bike Repair (527-0360), and seconds and used bikes are sold at 2nd Gear around the corner. Hours are unusual: the shop opens at noon, but is open mornings by appointment. ■ *5627 University Way NE; 527-4822; map:FF7; every day in summer; Tues–Sun in winter.* ■ *5601 University Way NE; 527-4310; map:FF7; every day in summer; Tues-Sun in winter.*

**REI (Recreational Equipment Inc.)** At the nation's largest co-op (15 West Coast stores, just over two million members) you'll find basically everything you need for mountaineering, backpacking, camping, cross-country skiing, and other outdoor pursuits. In the fall of 1996, the Capitol Hill store is moving to a high-visibility two-level location just off I-5 (222 Yale Avenue N), and REI is promising Seattle the moon—a 60-foot indoor climbing wall, mountain bike and hiking test paths, a deli/cafe, and an even wider assortment of items and brands (we hope they'll improve their service along with their space.) As it is, the store is an excellent source for maps, trail food, and outdoor books. Anyone can shop here, but members pay only $15 to join and receive at least a 10 percent yearly dividend on their purchases. Founded in 1938 by a group of Seattle mountaineers who wanted to import European equipment, the co-op was presided over for years by Everest-conqueror Jim Whittaker, and it is still staffed by knowledgeable (if somewhat flaky) outdoorspeople. Rentals at good prices, too. There are smaller branches in Bellevue, Federal Way, and Lynnwood. ■ *1525 11th Ave (and branches); 323-8333; map:HH7; every day.*

**Recycled Cycles** An idea whose time has come. At Recycled's pleasant Boat Street location, old bikes are taken in, cleaned up, given new parts where necessary, and put back on the market. Though the focus is on mountain, road, and 10-speed bikes, no bike is too old, specialized, or goofy-looking—even old Schwinn beaters, track bikes, or bikes that Mary Poppins would have liked. ■ *1011 NE Boat St; 547-4491; map:FF7; every day.*

**Ricky Young Surfboards** Yes, there's surfing in Washington (and Oregon). Ricky Young, a nationally ranked surfer in the '60s, is the sport's top local promoter and adviser. Young manufactures his own boards, sells a California line for both short- and long-board surfers, and carries Cascade Boards from Hood Canal (accessories and rentals, too). This is a *real* surf shop. ■ *14 102nd Ave NE, #2, Bellevue; 453-2346; map:GG3; Mon–Sat.*

**Seattle Athletic and Exercise** Everything from 1-pound weights to $7,000 exercise machines, including exercise mats, rowing machines, treadmills, and other high-quality exercise equipment. Customers are trained in use of their new purchases. Branches are in Bellevue and just south of Southcenter Mall. ■ *842 Northgate Way (and branches); 364-5890; map:DD2; every day.*

**Snowboard Connection** No fancy neon ski outfits here, just the latest in equipment and accessories for this growing downhill craze. Boards by K2 and Gnu (and perhaps a dozen other companies), tuning, and great advice from shredheads who really know the sport; T-shirts, boots, and basic, functional warm clothing, too. New products arrive daily. ■ *604 Alaskan Way; 467-8545; map:O9; every day.*

**Super Jock 'N Jill** Sports-medicine clinics and doctors send their patients here for proper shoe fitting: these salespeople know their merchandise and understand the mechanics of running and power walking. A podiatrist is in the store once a week

▼

Outdoor Gear

▲

to answer questions and help with problems. The selection of other merchandise (running gear, bathing suits) is smaller, but often this is the one place in town to carry a specific item. They are also a good source on races, routes, and training. ■ *7210 E Green Lake Dr N; 522-7711; map:EE7; every day.*

**Swallows' Nest** Some local climbers claim they spend more time at the Swallows' Nest than they do in their own homes. This excellent store outfits backpackers, cross-country and backcountry skiers, mountaineers, and even fly-fishers with rental or sales equipment, and carries everything else needed to make the trip safe and fun. The truly helpful and experienced salesfolk have been carefully schooled in boot fitting; and they have tried out most of the skis and can honestly tell you the differences (the store also sponsors a couple of ski-demo evenings at Snoqualmie Pass every winter). They have also probably been where you want to go. ■ *2308 6th Ave; 441-4100; map:G6; every day.*

**Swiftwater** This little Fremont storefront specializes in rafts and inflatable kayaks. They'll rent you one, sell you one, or help you organize a trip on one. These guys know their rivers, and there are lots of lifejackets for sale for those that don't. ■ *4235 Fremont Ave N; 547-3377; map:FF7; Closed Wed and Sun.*

**Warshal's Sporting Goods** A downtown dinosaur, Warshal's has been holding down the corner of First and Madison forever. You come here for virtually any sporting-goods need, along with unadvertised discounts, hunting and fishing licenses, and a fine selection of darkroom supplies and photography equipment. The regular-joe atmo appeals in this high-gloss part of town. ■ *1000 1st Ave; 624-7300; map:M7; Mon–Sat.*

**Wedgwood Cycle** Challenging Gregg's hegemony on the new-bike market, Wedgwood now has two locations—the old Wedgwood location, and a bright new store in Ballard. Prices here are quite reasonable (more so than in other parts of town), and the staff are friendly and knowledgeable. Wedgwood carries good brands such as Kona and Gary Fisher, as well as parts and accessories (including the spiffy Timbuktu bags that bike messengers favor). ■ *8507 35th Ave NE; 523-5572; map:EE6; every day.*

**West Marine Products** West Marine has a well-established reputation as a sailing-equipment supplier, with a full line of marine supplies for powerboats and sailboats, and accessories for both: binoculars, winches, line (for sails or for tying up), outboards, dinghies, sports boats up to 12 feet, and more. ■ *6317 Seaview Ave NW; 789-4640; map:EE9; every day.* ■ *1000 Mercer St; 292-8663; map:D2; every day.*

**Wiley's Waterski Shop** Wiley's sells waterskis out of a garage-like South End store. Wet suits, dry suits, slalom skies, ropes, and life preservers complete the selection. They will custom-make bindings for customers. ▪ *1417 S Trenton St; 762-1300; map:LL6; Mon–Sat.*

**Wright Brothers Cycle Works** You can have reliable bike repairs done here or, for a small fee, join this cooperative and do your own bike maintenance with Wright Brother's tools and space. Owner Charles Hadrann and his staff are known for wheel building, informative repair classes, and good advice. There's an ever growing selection of tires, and prices on parts are fair. Closed Sundays and Mondays in winter. ▪ *219 N 36th St; 633-5132; map:FF7; Tues–Sun.*

## RECORDS, TAPES, AND CDS

**Bop Street Records & Tapes** In the site of the old Ballard Record Store, you'll find a stock of albums, 78s, CDs, cassettes, and tens of thousands of 45s. State-of-the-art filing system. ▪ *5512 20th Ave NW; 783-3009; map:EE7; Mon–Sat.*

**Bud's Jazz Records** Established in 1982 by Chicago refugee and jazz buff Bud Young, Seattle's first and only jazz, all-jazz, and nothing-but-jazz store is the biggest of its kind west of Chicago. It has one of the best inventories in the country; with around 15,000 titles, Bud's is *the* place. Here musicians argue over the unlisted sidemen on old Charlie Parker records, and Bud's keeps an exhaustive jazz library to settle the argument. The free search service has a great track record. ▪ *102 S Jackson St; 628-0445; map:O8; every day.*

**Cellophane Square** Here's the closest thing to Berkeley's Telegraph Avenue selection in used folk, rock, and international music. A lot of stock, both vintage and new, and fast turnover, quality merchandise, and friendly, knowledgeable staff. The larger U District location is unbelievably spacious and bright. ▪ *4538 University Way NE; 634-2280; map:FF7; every day.* ▪ *Bellevue Square, Bellevue; 454-5059; map:HH3; every day.*

**Ear Wax** Owners Sarah Green and Melissa Follett bring years of combined experience at local record stores to one of the few women-owned record stores in Seattle. Ear Wax has moved from its digs in Wallingford Center down the street, but it's still refreshingly free of the teenage posturing that usually goes on in music stores. The CD selections are intelligently chosen, and the staff are willing to do special orders or seek out a lesser-known band's recordings. Used CDs are guaranteed, and trade-ins get a fair payment in cash or credit. ▪ *1622 N 45th St; 632-0622; map:FF7; every day.*

**Exotique Imports** Exotic is definitely the operative word here. You'll find the latest alternative dance tracks, on new or used vinyl and (some) CDs, along with obscure bands from the early to mid-'80s, and '70s one-hit wonders. An intricate filing system guarantees that if you're looking for something specific, you'll probably find it. ■ *2400 3rd Ave; 448-3452; map:F7; every day.*

**Fallout Records** If you're into punk rock, this is really the only place in town you need to know. Mostly vinyl (which many fans feel suits punk's sound best), some CDs, and a staff that, while not particularly friendly, know every obscure label, band, and recording ever made. One side of the store is devoted to music, the other to comics. Intimidating, somewhat young, but classic. ■ *1506 E Olive Way; 323-2662; map:I1; Tues–Sun.*

**Golden Oldies** An enormous selection of rock, country western, big band, and jazz albums and singles. They've got music from 1910 to the present, but the main attractions are hits from the '40s, '50s, '60s, and '70s. These historians will search nationwide for your favorite record from seventh grade. ■ *201 NE 45th St (and branches); 547-2260; map:FF7; every day.*

**Orpheum** A good choice for the latest alternative releases, boxed-set CDs, a large inventory of tapes, and used albums. The upstairs loft carries a respectable selection of hard-to-find rap, hip-hop, techno, and rave music. ■ *618 Broadway; 322-6370; map:HH6; every day.*

**Park Avenue Records** A mainstay in the busy Queen Anne shopping district, Park Avenue carries a huge selection of used albums and CDs. They buy entire collections, so the inventory is eclectic and varied—jazz, blues, rock, and grunge; imports and local labels, too. Service is knowledgeable and helpful. ■ *532 Queen Anne Ave N; 284-2390; map:GG8; every day.*

**Platters** It's a business built on steady customers—and no wonder. Here's where to find the city's largest stock of 12-inch singles (their specialty) and unused oldie 45s. In these days when vinyl may or may not make a comeback, if anyone's got it, Platters does—including current releases and imports. Open 10am to 4pm. ■ *8018 15th NE; 523-9900; map:EE6; every day.*

**Retrospect Records** Since opening in Seattle in 1992, Retrospect has garnered a reputation as the best place for vinyl recordings in the city. New, used, rare, 45s—they've really got it all, including a great punk rock section and new and used CDs and cassettes. (If you're not lucky enough to own a turntable, they've got a few used ones for sale.) Looking for something out of the mainstream? You'll likely find it here, as well as unusual posters, T-shirts, and collector's items such as books, magazines, and picture discs. They won't, as a rule, do special orders, but you'll probably find something you like here anyway. With enthusiastic and knowledgeable employees and a real feel for the musicalia, this place *rocks*. ■ *1524 E Olive Way; 329-1077; map:I1; every day.*

**Rubato Records** Lots of tapes, used CDs, and vinyl in this shop tucked away in a downtown Bellevue back alley. A really good place to find mid-'80s alternative and pop albums that never made it onto CD. ■ *136 105th Ave NE, Bellevue; 455-9417; map:HH3; every day.*

**Silver Platters** Silver Platters reputedly has the country's largest selection—virtually everything on the market—of compact discs. There's also a large selection of laser videodiscs. Silver Platters is in the Northgate and Southcenter neighborhoods, too. ■ *14603 NE 20th St, Bellevue (and branches); 643-3472; map:GG1; every day.*

**Sub Pop Mega Mart** Most people know that Sub Pop—a local record label—was at the center of the Seattle music scene as it exploded across the U.S. in the early '90s. But Sub Pop was signing good local bands long before national recognition, and continues to take on promising new groups that often graduate to major labels. Their retail store at the southern fringe of Belltown houses all of the label's releases (including some rare ones) and some major-label albums of early Sub Pop bands— but sees a lot of tourist action as well for the t-shirts, hats, and sweatshirts. Sub Pop–label albums are sold at mail-order prices, meaning that Sub Pop's own cost a few bucks less here than elsewhere. They will play almost anything you want to hear before you buy. They will not tell you where Kurt Cobain's house is. Don't ask. ■ *1928 2nd Ave; 443-0178; map:G8; every day.*

▼

**Records, Tapes, and CDs**

▲

**Tower Records** One side of this Records R Us emporium is classical—a well-priced, good selection. The popular side has pop and a wall of jazz. It's a good first-look place for folk, country, children's, and women's music. There's also a strong rock (local, classic, and alternative) orientation. Cutouts, too. Tower may be the supermarket of record stores, but there's always at least one good, informed clerk on duty, and it's open until midnight every night. Also in the U District, Bellevue, and Tacoma. ■ *500 Mercer St (and branches); 283-4456; map:B4; every day.*

**Wall of Sound** Rhythm's the thing at this Belltown shop: they carry the best overall selection of world music in town, by artists from South America, Europe, Africa, and Asia. Knowledgeable staff will help you find your way around an eclectic candy store of new and used recordings, including great selections of avant-jazz, acid jazz, ambient, trance, and soundtracks. A good place to keep in touch with local and regional happenings in these styles of music—and don't let out the cat. ■ *2237 2nd Ave; 441-9880; map:F7; every day.*

**City Fish** Great quality and service earned City Fish its reputation and faithful clientele. This Main Arcade purveyor does a brisk business in local fish and shellfish, plus some exotics like Louisiana crawfish. Line-caught king salmon and Dungeness crab are specialties. Overnight shipping to anywhere in the country. ■ *Pike Place Market; 682-9329; map:J8; every day.*

**Jack's Fish Spot** Point to an oyster in the tank, and Jack's crew will pluck it and shuck it on the spot. This fine seafood shop has the only live-shellfish tanks in the Market, with loads of live Dungeness crabs, clams, lobsters and oysters. They smoke their own salmon, run a walk-up oyster bar, and have great fish 'n' chips. ■ *Pike Place Market; 467-0514; map:J8; every day.*

**Mutual Fish Company** Mutual Fish is where many of the city's best restuarants buy their seafood, and it's easy to see why. Top quality and a dazzling selection are the result of the undivided attention of the Yoshimura family. Fresh-tanks are full of several types of local oysters and crabs, and the seafood cases present the best from the West and East Coasts. Seattleites are pleased to find mahi-mahi, tilefish, Maryland softshell crabs (in season), and other exotics. Prices are good, and they'll pack for air freight or carry-home. ■ *2335 Rainier Ave S; 322-4368; map:II6; Mon–Sat.*

**Pike Place Fish** This is the spot with fish flying overhead. (While it's great fun to watch, serious fish cooks don't insist their salmon be hurtled over a cheering crowd.) There's a good selection of fresh fish and shellfish, plus smoked and kippered seafood, and some local rarities like the homely geoduck (a must-see for tourists). Pike Place Fish will pack and ship for the traveler. Located in the Main Arcade, by the bronze pig. ■ *Pike Place Market; 682-7181; map:J8; every day.*

**Port Chatham Packing Company** People flock here for wild Alaskan seafood that's been smoked to satiny perfection. For years Port Chatham has been turning out some of the best alderwood-smoked salmon anywhere, as well as supplying an eye-popping array of smoked shellfish, trout, gourmet seafood pâtés, and caviar. The Ballard location is off the beaten track, but there are enough branches in downtown Seattle (and nearby cities) to take care of your gift needs for the next decade. Phone orders and shipping are no problem. Kosher. ■ *632 NW 46th St (and branches); 783-8200; map:FF8; Mon–Sat.*

**Queen Anne Thriftway** When food dignitaries come to town, they head here. Fish guru Rick Cavanaugh runs one of the best seafood departments in the U.S. (Julia Child orders from him):

pristine stock and 20 to 30 kinds of fish and shellfish, from here and all over. Savvy cooks call ahead to tailor their menus to what's in that day. Special orders welcome; free packing for travel. ▪ *1908 Queen Anne Ave N; 284-2530; map:GG7; every day.*

**Seattle Caviar Company** Diamonds may be a girl's best friend, but when it comes to caviar, Betsy Sherrow, owner of this Lake Union caviar importer, will be yours. Sherrow sells the finest beluga, osetra, and sevruga caviar from the Caspian Sea, in addition to Northwest fresh American malossol caviar and all the froufrou accoutrements of fussy roe-eating (such as pretty mother-of-pearl spoons and caviar *presentoirs*). Want to impress your friends and business associates? She gladly arranges beautiful gift packages, and even handles shipping. ▪ *3147 Fairview Ave E; 323-3005; map:GG7; Mon–Fri, Sat by appointment.*

**University Seafood & Poultry** Good prices and impeccable quality are the hallmarks of Dale Erickson's U District fish market. The selection includes salmon, halibut, and ling cod, plus varieties like local sturgeon. An amazing array of caviars, from flying fish to Columbia River sturgeon to beluga. Hard-to-find game birds, free-run chickens, and the freshest eggs. Prices are not posted, but are in line with supermarket prices. The fishmongers at the counter are friendly, and are all good cooks with recipes to share. Kids love to feed Eli, the store's mascot eel. ▪ *1317 NE 47th St; 632-3900; map:FF7; Mon–Sat.*

**Uwajimaya** See Ethnic Markets and Specialty Foods in this chapter. ▪ *519 6th Ave S; 624-6248; map:R7; every day.* ▪ *15555 NE 24th St, Bellevue; 747-9012; map:GG1; every day.*

## SHOES

**Bally of Switzerland (Four Seasons Olympic Hotel)** Bally's white marble entryway and beige interior are forbidding: a cathedral for shoes. But the staff are friendly and the merchandise is superb. For women: black leather boots edged with gold chain in addition to office and ballet wear. For men: Euro-style low boots, casual tassled loafers, and dressier leathers. Velvet scarves, golf sweaters, and briefcases are a few of the other expensive items. ▪ *1218 4th Ave; 624-9255; map:L6; Mon–Sat.*

**Church's English Shoes** Church's offers an enticing selection of proper English men's shoes. A variety of textures (woven, alligator) and styles (loafers, two-toned) punctuate the perfect-for-the-fancy-office footwear (in brown, black, and cream leathers). Also, much casual weekend wear from Clark's of England. Prices are not scaled for the budget-conscious. ▪ *520 Pike St; 682-3555; map:J5; Mon–Sat.*

**Duncan and Sons Boots and Saddles** In business since 1898, this family-run boot shop carries more than 30 styles of boots for men, women, and children. Prices run from $90 to $350. Most of the boots are handmade in Texas. ▪ *541 1st Ave S; 622-1310; map:P9; Mon–Sat.*

**Enzo Angiolini (Bellevue Square)** These Italian leather women's shoes are in step with the latest trends, at remarkably reasonable prices. Careful attention to details—like the leather buttons and colors (the chocolate brown is beautiful)—make Enzo Angiolini elegant as well as fashionable. Leather picture frames, belts, and bags, too. ▪ *2042 Bellevue Square, Bellevue; 450-5582; map:HH3; every day.*

**Joan & David Shoes** Expensive and irrefutably stylish, a pair of Joan & David shoes makes a perfect investment. From white-and-silver summer sandals to silk black opera shoes to smart leather boots, the shoes are oh so appropriate, yet wear like minor jewels. A tasteful selection of bags and accessories and a few pieces of elegant clothing complement the shoes. Watch for the twice-yearly sales. ▪ *1420 5th Ave (City Centre); 624-2427; map:K6; every day.*

**John Fluevog Shoes** Pink patent leather, platform Mary Janes, square toes, and flared heels—Fluevog's footwear is the hippest in town. The Canadian owner does the designs; the shoes are made in England, Poland, Mexico, and Spain. For dance-club divas and daring souls. ▪ *1611 1st Ave; 441-1065; map:I8; every day.*

**Maggie's Shoes** Maggie journeys to Italy and picks out the latest from the country that knows fine legs deserve fine footwear. She also carries Argus, a nice French-made shoe. Subtle browns, blacks, deep blues, and creams; brushed suede; and elegant buttons and straps make Maggie's women's and men's shoes most desirable. Quite reasonable prices. ▪ *1927 1st Ave; 728-5837; map:I8; every day.*

**Mephisto** They're not beautiful, but *boy* are they comfortable. Mephisto's upscale French walking shoes have loyal fans who defend them against fashion snobs. With moss-soft cushioning and carefully crafted soles, Mephisto shoes are worth the pricey tag. ▪ *2025 1st Ave; 441-1182; map:H8; Mon–Sat.* ▪ *318 Occidental Ave; 223-0135; map:O8; every day.* ▪ *10129 Main St, Bellevue; 462-0782; map:HH3; every day.*

**M. J. Feet's Birkenstock Store** This is where you get those sturdy Birkenstock sandals in all colors and styles. The cheerful shops carry a lot of jazzy socks and tights by Hue, plus a small selection of clothing. They're also good places to get hard-to-find, beautiful Ellington schoolbags. Great repair service, too. ▪ *1514 Pike Pl; 624-2929; map:J5; every day.*

- *4334 University Way NE; 632-5353; map:FF6; every day.*
- *15600 NE 8th St, Bellevue; 747-8221; map:HH1; every day.*

**San Marco** Shoes are displayed as art at San Marco, carefully set atop wavy pieces of plastic and fake rock. Such artful attention is warranted: the women's shoes and small selection of men's footwear are daring and glamorous. Strappy, shiny pieces from Petra, deeply colored, soft suede Arche shoes, and DKNY footwear can be counted on. The employees are stylish and kind. End-of-summer and end-of-winter sales. ■ *1509 6th Ave; 343-9138; map:J6; every day.*

**Ultima** Ultima's men's and women's stores merged into one at this new location offering sexy shoes from London to Italy. Of special note are the Kikit, Kenneth Cole, Via Spiga, and Sacha lines. Women may choose between red suede and ivory Edwardian bows. The men's section offers several fine lines at reasonable prices for the well-shod male. Soft leather Kenneth Cole bags are available, too. ■ *1427 5th Ave; 467-9459; map:J6; every day.*

**The Woolly Mammoth** This University District shop has outfitted generations of students of both sexes with sturdy, rainproof walking shoes and durable backpacks. The Woolly Mammoth mostly carries comfortable brands like Rockport, Bass, and Timberland, the stylish-yet-sensible White Mountain label, and clogs for women. A second store up the street, called The Annex, carries trendier stuff—Doc Marten's, Converse, and the like. ■ *4303 University Way NE; 632-3254; map:FF6; every day.* ■ *4309 University Way NE; 547-3192; map:FF6; every day.*

## SPECIALTY SIZE CLOTHING: LARGE/TALL/MATERNITY/PETITE

**High & Mighty Store** Over 23 years of expert, personalized service and good brands such as London Fog and Crown distinguish this shop for tall and large men. ■ *Southcenter Mall; 246-8434; map:OO5; every day.*

**Motherhood Maternity** In addition to reasonably priced pajamas, swimsuits, leggings, and jeans, Motherhood Maternity offers formalwear in velours and velvets, with sequins and rhinestones. ■ *Bellevue Square, Bellevue; 454-1355; map:HH3; every day.*

**Village Maternity** Village Maternity stresses versatility, affordability, and long-term wear; most clothes can be worn even after the baby comes. A good mix of sporty, dressy, and business clothes includes the popular Japanese Weekend line. Supplies for the nursing mother are in abundance and there are some all-cotton children's clothes, too. ■ *University Village; 523-5167; map:FF6; every day.*

**Wallaby Station** This is the only shop we know of in town that carries quality clothing for men 5 foot 8 and under, including formalwear and a fine selection of suits and sport coats by Perry Ellis, Palm Beach, and Henry Grethel. This 20-year-old establishment sells casual clothing, too: jeans, sweaters, and Hawaiian-print shirts, as well as robes and other accessories—even a line of ties appropriately proportioned a few inches shorter. ▪ *1022 1st Ave; 624-3882; map:L8; every day.*

**Your Hidden Closet** It's a great idea: a women's large-size consignment shop, so weight droppers can drop their larger clothes, too. Still going strong as it nears its 10th anniversary (though it's now in a new location), the shop boasts designer labels like Liz Claiborne and Carol Little, plus a wide range of merchandise (including lingerie, shoes, scarves, and purses) in a correspondingly wide range of quality. ▪ *10129 Main St, Bellevue; 453-5999; map:HH3; Mon–Sat.*

## STATIONERY AND ART SUPPLIES

**All Wrapped Up** A comprehensive greeting-card selection and every gift-wrapping accessory imaginable keep customers rolling into this downtown card shop. But it's the little extras—Gumby, Slinky, Teaberry gum, and old musicals on the sound system—that give this place personality and bring back your childhood memories. Custom calligraphy and party invitations, too. ▪ *201 Pine St; 447-CARD; map:I7; every day.*

**Dakota Art Store** This welcome addition to the art supply market quickly became a favorite stop-off for professional artists and students when the Roosevelt Square store opened in 1990. Dakota now has branches on Capitol Hill and in Kirkland. They also stock supplies for children's art projects. ▪ *1030 NE 64th St; 523-4830; map:EE6; every day.* ▪ *819 E Thomas; 325-8490; map:HH6; every day.* ▪ *209 Kirkland Ave, Kirkland; 827-7678; map:DD3; every day.*

**Daniel Smith** Serious artists like Dan Smith's cavernous warehouse for paints, brushes, paper, and printmaking supplies (and many years of catalog sales bear this out). Weekend craftspeople are known to shop here, too, for projects and reasonably priced framing. ▪ *4130 1st Ave; 223-9599; map:JJ7; every day.*

**de Medici/Ming Fine Paper Company** Walking into this shop is like going into your Victorian great-aunt's attic (albeit a well-kept one) and finding some of the stationery she used for bread-and-butter notes. Handmade Japanese rice paper pressed with butterfly wings vies for your attention with rare Italian and vintage Chinese ceremonial papers. For the really passionate, there are papermaking classes and calligraphic

▼

**Specialty Size Clothing**

▲

services. No ordinary stationer, this. ■ *1222 1st Ave; 624-1983; map:L7; every day.*

**Elliott Bay Stationery Store** Leather anything and everything for the office: photo frames, desk sets, appointment books, and planners. Boxed writing paper for conservative occasions, and all sorts of custom printing. ■ *Westlake Center; 587-4001; map:I5; every day.* ■ *2724 1st Ave S; 624-4423; map:II7; Mon–Fri, Sat by appointment.*

**Metropolis** Contemporary greeting cards (many by Northwest artists and photographers), gift wrap, and party supplies for every possible occasion are the specialties at Metropolis. The store is popular, as is the branch in Wallingford Center. ■ *7220 Greenwood Ave N; 782-7002; map:EE8; every day.*

**Paper Cat** This is a one-stop stationery shop where you'll find loads of greeting cards, notepaper, stickers, wrapping paper, and thousands of rubber stamps. A selection of fine imported stationery and handmade note cards, too. ■ *214 1st Ave S; 623-3636; map:N8; every day.*

**The Paper Tree** A tasteful selection of note cards, stationery, invitations, and frames is coolly displayed in this mall nook. Handsome desk accessories and fine writing instruments augment the inventory—although the shop would probably survive just fine solely on its custom-order business. ■ *Bellevue Square, Bellevue; 451-8035; map:HH3; every day.*

**Seattle Art** There's always a number of hip-looking art students in black having a cigarette by the door. Extensive paper department, a room full of graphic and traditional art supplies, and lots of books. ■ *1816 8th Ave; 223-2787; map:I4; every day.*

**Seattle Pen** One of only a few "pens only" stores on the West Coast. You'll find a terrific collection of vintage fountain pens, ink, and leather pen cases. Owner Todd Craver provides repairs when needed and engraves at the store. ■ *1424 4th Ave, Suite 527; 682-2640; map:J6; Mon–Sat.*

**Silberman/Brown** This stationer's stationer offers an elegant array of stationery and desk accessories, with several choices for special-order monograms and engravings. Invitations for all occasions and a handsome selection of picture frames are hallmarks. Very accommodating, and they even carry the hard-to-find and hard-to-live-without Filofax line. ■ *Rainier Square; 292-9404; map:K6; Mon–Sat.* ■ *10220 NE 8th St, Bellevue; 455-3665; map:HH3; Mon–Sat.*

**Stampola** The idea is pretty straightforward: just shelf after shelf of rubber stamps, arranged by subject matter from '40s-style sports figures to architecture and everything you could possibly dream up in between. You won't find any teddy bears

▼

▲

or balloons here, nothing pedestrian or cute, but you will find great designs by bizarro illustrator Ken Brown and plenty of other intriguing stuff to go stamp crazy with. A move from their tiny shop in Fremont to larger digs in Greenwood means that stamps are now manufactured on the premises. ■ *8544 Greenwood Ave N; 706-7448; map:DD8-EE8; every day.*

## STEREOS/AUDIO EQUIPMENT

**Car Toys** The ultimate in car stereos sounds good enough to go in your living room. Car Toys does a great deal of business in custom work; however, for the less obsessed, they carry more common brands like Alpine, Sony, and Rockford Fosgate. Branches are in Bellevue, Lynnwood, and Southcenter. ■ *307 Broad St (and branches); 443-2726; map:D7; every day.*

**Definitive Audio** The smart-not-slick sales at Definitive reflect a certain Zen approach, and indeed, one of the owners is a philosophy major. This is Seattle's oldest dealer in high-end systems; prices are on the same end. ■ *6017 Roosevelt Way NE; 524-6633; map:EE6; Tues–Sat.*

**Magnolia Hi-Fi** An almost undisputed favorite that has created a virtual electronics ghetto on Roosevelt (and with branches in Bellevue and Southcenter), Magnolia stocks several durable brands and can put together systems for the uninitiated. Excellent follow-up service. ■ *6322 Roosevelt Way NE (and branches); 525-0080; map:EE6; every day.*

**Speakerlab** Whether it's for your home, office, or car, Speakerlab's specialty is, naturally, speakers. They'll custom-design a set for you, or sell you a kit to make your own. The small store also sells a selection of audio and video equipment in all price ranges. ■ *6307 Roosevelt Way NE; 523-2269; map:EE6; every day.*

## TOYS

**American Eagles** The largest hobby shop in the country specializes in historical hobbies and model railroads. Owner Michael Edwards stocks over 87,000 different items, including a regiment of 22,000 miniature soldiers, and lots and lots of models. ■ *2220 NW Market St; 782-8448; map:EE9; Mon–Sat.*

**Archie McPhee** Contemporary kitsch at its wacky best. Home to glow-in-the-dark dinosaurs, rubber slugs, and the famous boxing nun puppets, Archie McPhee's is a great place to stock up on cheap toys and party favors or just to browse the memorable catalog. Plenty of grown-ups confess shameful inclinations to losing themselves among the whoopie cushions. In addition to its waterfall, the recently renovated Tiki Hut is stocked with a variety of vintage vending machines featuring the chicken that lays magic eggs. ▪ *3510 Stone Way N; 545-8344; map:FF7; every day.*

Shopping
I

**City Kites/City Toys** Participation is the name of the game at this Hillclimb shop loaded with books, kites, puzzles, games, and a real supply of gizmos. When the energetic staff aren't throwing toys to each other, they're throwing them to customers as they come through the door. Lots of hands-on toys and ongoing demos. Summer weekends are wonderfully crazy. ▪ *1501 Western Avenue; 622-5349; map:J8; every day.*

**The Disney Store** A place that drives parents Disney. Nonstop patter from multiple video screens playing the latest Walt Disney clips. The G-rated clerks also sell Disney-inspired gadgets and garb. Kids love the sing-along tapes featuring songs from Disney hits. ▪ *Westlake Center; 622-3323; map:I5; every day.* ▪ *Southcenter; 241-8922; map:OO5; every day.* ▪ *Bellevue Square; 451-0540; map:HH3; every day.*

**Don's Hobbies** A gold mine for the hobbyist, Don's has radio-controlled boats, model airplanes, motorized race cars, and American and European electric trains in all the usual gauges. Models of all kinds and system toys by Fischer, Brio, and more draw a faithful clientele from all over. ▪ *2943 NE Blakeley; 525-7700; map:FF6; Tues–Sat.*

▼

**Toys**

▲

**Eastside Trains** Trains, trains, and more trains. The business chugged along for years out of the owner's home. Now it's full speed ahead in its Kirkland retail location. For train lovers young and old, this is a shop like no other, where you'll find train-related shirts, hats, and videos, too. ▪ *217 Central Way, Kirkland; 828-4098; map:EE3; Mon–Sat.*

**FAO Schwartz** From the mechanical clocktower—a two-story high, singing, prancing, toy-sculpture that greets you at the door—to the animal-stuffed jungle room with its talking tree, the pre-school area with toddler toys to interest one-and-all, and the Barbie room (a very pink, fantagorasmasmic display of every Barbie doll and contraption ever made), it's clear why FAO is the biggest toy show in town. The staff is so earnest and cheerful, you'll wonder whether they're watching a video of Tom Hanks in *Big* during coffee breaks. The Bellevue Square store, as befits its mall location, is slightly less ostentatious. ▪ *6th and Pike (City Centre); 442-9500; map:J5; every day.* ▪ *Bellevue Square, Bellevue; 646-9500; map:HH3; every day.*

**Fantastic Games and Toys** Fantastic takes prides in carrying only items that chains don't: You won't find Monopoly here. You will find pewter figures, origami, puzzle boxes, and lava lamps, as well as a selection of novelty toys (windup walking teeth), seasonal items (squirt guns), and small toys (dice). ■ *3333 184th St SW, Lynnwood; 775-4871; every day.*

**Great Winds Kite Shop** Kites of all kinds live in this friendly Pioneer Square shop. It's a whimsical and wonderfully colorful place where you can also get kite-making kits, wind socks, boomerangs, and plenty of good advice from a well-seasoned, experienced staff. ■ *402 Occidental Ave S; 624-6886; map:P9; every day.*

**The Great Wind-up** For the kid in every adult. The Great Wind-up is full of every kind of windup (collectible tin items, too) and battery-operated animated toy imaginable (you can hear the whirring and chirping from a few doors away). Home to everyone's favorite nostalgia toys: Slinky, Sea Monkeys, Pez, and Gumby. In the Economy Market Atrium. ■ *Pike Place Market; 621-9370; map:J8; every day.*

**Imagination Toys** A real find for wonderful, well-made toys by Brio, Gund, and the ever popular Lego. This family-run store also carries activity toys by Playmobil, train sets, games, and puzzles. They feature a wide assortment of musical instruments ranging from ukuleles to keyboards. ■ *1815 N 45th St; 547-2356; map:FF7; every day.*

▼

**Toys**

▲

**Learning World** A fine purveyor of basic, educational toys (craft supplies, chemistry sets, abaci, and flash cards), Learning World also sells Fisher-Price and Playskool brands. Other branches are as close as Sea-Tac Mall, Lynnwood, and Bellevue Square, and as far away as Anchorage, Alaska. The store is a real find for teachers and those interested in primary education. ■ *310 Westlake Ave N (and branches); 464-1515; map:D2; every day.*

**Magic Mouse** Top-of-the-line toys, chosen by "a professional child," fill the shelves of this marvelous Pioneer Square store: Steiff animals, Corolle dolls, Brio wooden train sets, and Marklin electric trains. The stuffed-animal collection includes over 100 styles of teddy bears alone. There is a selection of developmental baby and preschool toys, art supplies, games and puzzles, kids' books, windup toys, stocking stuffers, and literally hundreds of different decks of cards. ■ *603 1st Ave; 682-8097; map:N8; every day.*

**Mr. Peepers** They begin with an extensive selection of dollhouses (ranging from $1 to $30,000) and carry out the theme with an assortment of miniature furniture and dolls. Hobbyists will find building components to construct their own. Christmas decorations are the other big deal. ■ *6200 Sand Point Way NE; 522-8202; map:EE5; Mon–Sat.*

**Pinocchio** Pinocchio features puzzles, interactive play media (such as Playmobil), nature-exploring aids (binoculars and science workbooks), a wide variety of paints (nontoxic water-colors and tie-dying kits), and Madame Alexander collectible dolls (which range from $50 to $250). The books in stock are geared more toward adults reading bedtime stories to the little 'uns than older children who read on their own. ▪ *4540 Union Bay Pl NE; 528-1100; map:FF6; Mon–Sat.*

**Play It Again Toys** Clean, shrink-wrapped, used toys for half the price of retail. Toddler toys include Fisher-Price and Playskool; baby strollers and tubs; and outdoor equipment and bikes. Items with signs of wear are priced accordingly. ▪ *16003 Redmond Way, Redmond; 881-6920; map:EE1; every day.*

**Teri's Toybox** Teri Soelter's small shop in downtown Edmonds is chock-full of wonderful stuff, and is a great place to gift-shop (ask for wrap and they'll gladly tuck your purchase into a gaily beribboned gift bag). Collectible dolls are handsomely displayed, and you're sure to find something for every kid on your list: art and jewelry-making supplies, educational toys, stuffed animals, building blocks, kiddy carpenter's tools, cassette tapes and CDs, and more. ▪ *526 Main St; 774-3190; every day.*

**Thinker Toys** The intelligently chosen, upper-end inventory has a little bit of everything: kites, games, trains, dolls, books, 3-D puzzles. Kids of all ages will go bonkers in the mind-boggler section. ▪ *10680 NE 8th, Bellevue; 453-0051; map:HH2; every day.*

▼

**Toys**

▲

**Top Ten Toys** Both parents and kids love the sections of toys devoted to the youngest and most demanding—the toddler area, the infant area, and the 2's area. With mobiles hanging off every light fixture that isn't hanging a kite, this one-of-a-kind store is literally filled to the rafters with goodies. Look for the trike and wagon room, the jungle gym equipment, and the unexciting but most necessary Safety First line for parents (featuring electrical-outlet covers and cabinet safety locks). ▪ *104 N 85th; 782-0098; map:EE7; every day.*

**Tree Top Toys** Tree Top aims directly for a child's imagination with a supply of dress-up clothes such as sequined ballerina outfits and Robin Hood garb. Cooking texts offer cultural education with recipes featuring ethnic foods, but the main draw is a giant Brio train that promises to fascinate children long past the necessary shopping visit's allotted time. ▪ *Lake Forest Park Center; 363-5460; map:BB5; every day.*

**Wood Shop Toys** Since 1972 Wood Shop Toys has provided well-crafted, sturdy wooden toys by Pacific Northwest artisans, stocked side by side with imported European toys including pull toys, dolls, and trucks, as well as old-fashioned board games. Its line of Folkmanis puppets come in wonderful animal shapes, and look like mere stuffed animals until a child's hand slipped inside brings them to life. ▪ *320 1st S; 624-1763; map:N8; every day.*

## VIDEO

There's nothing like meandering through a well-stocked video rental shop owned and operated by people who simply love movies and staffed by individuals enthusiastic about their jobs. Several such independent stores have staked out neighborhood turf in Seattle, and serve as little meccas for discriminating film buffs.

Downtown Seattle has **Harbor Video** (2113 Third Avenue, 443-5435), which boasts a tidy inventory of nearly 3,000 titles. And while **Borders Books & Music** (1501 Fourth Avenue, 622-4599) doesn't fit the mom-and-pop profile of most of the stores in this listing, the mammoth bookseller in the heart of the city does feature a huge selection of videos in a civilized setting. **Tower Video** (500 Mercer Street, 283-4456), across from the northeast corner of Seattle Center, also has a wide array of foreign and older movies, as well as television classics that are awfully fun to peruse.

▼

**Video**

▲

In the North End, the **Maltese Falcon** (9911 Aurora Avenue N, 524-1940) claims to have "the 3,000 best movies ever made," and it may be so. With its classicist bent, the Falcon is especially rich in film noir and international offerings.

On the Eastside, **Tower Video** has a decent companion store in Bellevue (10635 NE Eighth Street, 451-2557), while nearby Kirkland and Woodinville each have a shop (with separate owners) called **Critics' Choice**. The long-time Kirkland operation (308 Park Place Center, 827-9263) has the largest laser disc collection on the Eastside. The newer Woodinville store (14134 NE Woodinville–Duvall Road, 486-5597) has a pleasingly diversified stock.

**Backtrack Video and Records** Backtrack is the cult video shop to end them all. They have been touting the glories of Edward D. Wood Jr.'s *Plan 9 from Outer Space* long before Tim Burton. They deal in vintage: the best and the weirdest of sci-fi, film noir, and horror from the 1940s through the 1970s. ▪ *5339 25th NE; 524-0529; map:EE6; Tues.–Sat.*

**Scarecrow Video** Scarecrow, now in the University District (having moved from its original Green Lake neighborhood digs), is widely regarded as the video center of the universe. This lively, hip shop was born when the owners decided to make available to the public their own personal collection of American classics and hard-to-find foreign fare (such as R.W. Fassbinder's seven-volume *Berlin Alexanderplatz*). Buy a cup of coffee from the store's espresso stand, the Ruby Slipper, chat with the knowledgeable employees and browse shelves of rentals conveniently organized by national cinemas (French, German, Mexican, etc.), silent works from around the world, wonderful comedy collections, all kinds of niche interests, and such '90s cult goodies as Taiwanese martial arts pictures. ■ *5030 Roosevelt Way NE; 524-8554; map:FF7; every day.*

**Video Isle** The staff at Queen Anne's Video Isle would be quick to tell you (rightfully so) that there are some good alternatives to Scarecrow. Besides having plenty of popular recent releases on hand, the Isle carries lots of obscure international titles, gay and lesbian movies, and documentaries. A second store in the Fremont–Wallingford area is a touch more bohemian, but the friendly, helpful folks at either location will go out of their way to get their hands on what you're looking for. ■ *2213 Queen Anne Ave N; 285-9511; map:GG8; every day.* ■ *4459 Fremont Ave N; 548-0502; map:FF8; every day.*

**Videophile Inc.** Videophile is the one old stalwart that was among the first rental outfits for true cinephiles, and old ties have kept customers coming back. At press time, however, the Broadway store is moving to Roosevelt, and will now deal almost exclusively in laser discs. ■ *1028 NE 65th St; 522-3035; map:EE6; every day.*

## VINTAGE/RETRO

**Deluxe Junk** Not to be taken too seriously, Deluxe Junk is trashy, exuberant, and kitschy, specializing in furnishings and housewares from the '50s. The clothes, from the 1930s through the 1960s, have, if not grace, a lot of style, and the stock rotates seasonally (heavy tweed coats and handmade sweaters in winter, cool cotton shirts and straw hats in summer). This former funeral parlor also has lots of space for other funky goodies and collectibles. ■ *3518 Fremont Ave N; 634-2733; map:FF8; every day.*

**Fremont Antique Mall** Mark Salo let the community of Fremont shape the contents of his antique store in the basement of the Fremont Building. The results? It's more a place for collectibles than antiques. There are nearly 50 dealers, with vintage clothing and toys, dinnerware and appliances from the 1950s, Oriental rugs, and even a little bit of the *real* stuff here and there. ■ *3419 Fremont Pl N; 548-9140; map:FF7; every day.*

**Funk You** Seattle's only vintage store devoted to the 1960s and '70s, Funk You carries items you still might not be ready to wear again. Excellent selection of hot pants, tube tops, platform shoes, and leisure separates. The Charlie's Angels posters say it all, as does the groovy music. ■ *612 E Pine; 329-7963; map:K1; Mon–Sat.*

**Guess Where** Who knows what you'll find among this broad selection of men's clothing and accessories, all high quality. Perhaps a vintage alligator trunk, perfectly broken-in cowboy boots, a Ward Cleaver cardigan, or a groovy Hawaiian shirt. A few contemporary items and some furnishings (lamps, mirrors, wrought-iron, a camelback sofa) are mixed in, too. ■ *615 N 35th St; 547-3793; map:FF7; every day.*

**Isadora's** Laura D'Alesandro's shop is distinguished by her understanding of, and passionate attention to, a period (the 1900s to the 1950s), and there's no "filler." The museum-quality clothing at Isadora's is elegant and truly stunning, including gowns and tuxedos. ■ *1915 1st Ave; 441-7711; map:I8; every day.*

**Le Frock** Le Frock is like an older sister's stuffed closet—lots of stuff you like and a couple of things you might not. There's a healthy complement of men's clothes, but the women's selection is better. Dresses, skirts, vests, shoes—all in good condition. Prices are moderate but fair. You need a certain amount of imagination to shop the bargain balcony, but the price is definitely right. ■ *317 E Pine; 623-5339; map:K2; every day.*

**Madame & Company** Vintage clothing is treated with respect, knowledge, and love by the people at Madame & Company, a fact recognized by collectors, shoppers, and Hollywood costumers, all of whom frequent the store. Mother-daughter owners Carol and Deborah Winship carry inventory up to the 1940s (you'll be carefully screened if you want to see the 19th-century museum-quality pieces in the back). Lingerie, evening wear, and antique wedding dresses are carefully restored before being marked for sale. Check out the lace yardage, collars, buttons, hats, or just indulge yourself in a highly satisfying browse. ■ *117 Yesler Way; 621-1728; map:N8; Tues–Sat.*

▼

**Vintage/ Retro**

▲

**Pin-Down Girl** Among the vintage stores that have sprung up in Belltown, this is one of the best. First you'll probably notice the vintage motorcycles (for sale) in the center of the room, but then you'll get lost in rack after tidy rack of casual, hip clothes—mechanic's jackets, jeans, Nordic sweaters, and flannel and leather jackets. Next door at Speedboat (the conjoined shops have one owner) are all manner of brightly colored shirts—both eyesores and vintage gems—as well as glitzy dresses and a good collection of bowling-ball bags. ■ *2224 2nd Ave; 441-1248; map:G7; Mon–Sat.*

**Retro Viva** A funky shop with men's and women's clothing (new and used) and accessories from every era, Retro Viva is your first stop when you need a leopard-skin bra from the 1960s. Jewelry—some costume, some collector's—fills the display cases. Clothing is well priced, and customers are told if a piece is damaged. Other stores are on Broadway and the Ave. ■ *1511 1st Ave (and branches); 624-2529; map:J8; every day.*

**Rhinestone Rosie** Rhinestone Rosie rents, buys, and sells an exceptionally large and complete inventory of rhinestone treasures in all colors, shapes, and sizes. Her specialty is buying broken pieces of jewelry and repairing them herself before selling them for low prices; hers is the only store on the West Coast with this rhinestone repair service. If you have lost a stone out of a favorite piece, she can probably find a replacement for you. ▪ *606 W Crockett St; 283-4605; map:GG8; Tues–Sat.*

**Ruby Montana's Pinto Pony** The five-and-dime of vintage objects, Ruby Montana sells wonderfully awful things that you just can't live without. Ruby specializes in collectibles and popular culture must-haves from the '40s and '50s: kidney-shaped sofas, lava lamps, marlin and mooseheads to hang on walls, and she's got the largest salt-and-pepper-shaker selection on the West Coast. There's also a treasure trove of vintage 1970s and 1980s smaller merchandise: note cards, lamps, clocks, and other novelties. Postcards galore and dinnerware, too. ▪ *603 2nd Ave; 621-7669; map:O7; every day.*

**Vintage Voola** This is not one of those stuffed-to-the-rafters vintage shops; it feels instead like an eccentric friend's personal collection of retro furniture, clothing, and accessories. The dresses are in perfect condition, as are the hats. There's a rack of eye-catching drapes in bright colors, carefully cleaned and hung—someone smart *knew* they'd be back in style someday. ▪ *705B E Pike St; 324-2808; map:K1; every day.*

**Wrinkled Bohemia** If you are sick of rifling through tables of junk at flea markets and rack after rack of clothing at Goodwill, go to Wrinkled Bohemia—it's like they've already done it for you. A basket of Bakelite-handled utensils, a couple of perfect vintage leather jackets, exquisite furniture from recent eras are just a few of the gems you might find on any given day. This place reeks of someone's good taste (in this case, that of owners Brian Balmert and Laura Michalek), but the prices are surprisingly reasonable. ▪ *1125 Pike St; 464-0850; map:K2; Mon–Sat.*

## WINE AND BEER

**Brie and Bordeaux** Brie and Bordeaux are among the luscious luxuries at this charming shop near Green Lake—which offers a thoughtful selection of wines to complement food. In one part of the store are 350 labels from smaller Italian, French, Northwest, and California wineries not typically found in grocery stores. The other half of the shop is devoted to cheese. ▪ *2108 N 55th St; 633-3538; map:FF6; every day.*

**City Cellars Fine Wines & Foods** Owners Jeff Triestman and Polly Young have traveled extensively in Europe and brought

▼

Vintage/
Retro

▲

back a love of good food and wine. Their shop carries specialty food items and includes a wide selection of Italian wines. Their Bungalow Wine Bar and Café, located seven blocks east (2412 N 45th St), is open until late evenings Tuesday through Saturday for appetizers, desserts, and tastings by the glass (with more than 60 selections from which to choose). ■ *1710 N 45th St; 632-7238; map:FF7; every day.*

**DeLaurenti Specialty Foods** See Ethnic Markets and Specialty Foods in this chapter. ■ *Pike Place Market; 340-1498; map:J8; Mon–Sat.* ■ *317 Bellevue Way NE, Bellevue; 454-7155; map:HH3; Mon–Sat.*

**Esquin Wine Merchants** Owner Rand Sealey's goal is finding the best values for the money; his monthly specials reflect the best wines from all regions at some of the best prices in town. He seeks out the special or unique, occasionally acquiring wines no one else has. His French, Italian, Australian, and American selections are all good. You'll find close to 500 labels, case discounts, free twice-weekly tastings, and outstanding sales. Many choices in the $5 to $15 range. ■ *1516 1st Ave S; 682-7374; map:II7; Tues–Sat.*

**European Vine Selections of Washington** Providing low-cost, low-overhead wines is the focus of this Capitol Hill shop. The supply is limited but very carefully selected, and the owners/managers sample virtually every wine they sell so that they know what they're recommending. ■ *522 15th Ave E; 323-3557; map:GG6; Tues–Sun.*

**La Cantina** Although under separate ownership, both stores are exactly what a small specialty shop is all about. Owners are knowledgeable, and in getting to know regular customers are able to make suggestions based upon the customers' tastes. With an emphasis on French bottlings, this is the shop for fine Burgundies and Bordeaux. The Bellevue store offers discounts through its buying club. ■ *University Village; 525-4340; map:FF6; every day.* ■ *10218 NE 8th St, Bellevue; 455-4363; map:HH3; Mon–Sat.*

**Larry's Markets** True to Larry's gourmet mission, the wine sections are among the largest in any Seattle-area grocery store. The Northwest selection is particularly extensive. In recent years, Larry's has developed an aggressive direct-import program which, while providing some good values, has necessitated a reduction in the depth of its California and European selections. ■ *10008 Aurora Ave N in Oak Tree Village (and branches); 527-5333; DD7; every day.*

**McCarthy and Schiering** Dan McCarthy (at Queen Anne) and Jay Schiering (at Ravenna) actively seek out the newest and most promising producers from Europe and the U.S. Come here to discover the rising stars in the wine world. Regular in-store tastings, a knowledgeable staff, and a special rate for "Vintage Select" club members add appeal. A good place to find a rare bottle; California and the Northwest are as well represented as France. ■ *6500 Ravenna Ave NE; 524-9500; map:EE6; Mon–Sat.* ■ *2209 Queen Anne Ave N; 282-8500; map:GG8; Tues–Sat.*

**Pete's Supermarket** Don't let the "Supermarket" in the name put you off. This surprising little store, tucked away off Eastlake near Lake Union, packs an amazing amount of wine into its narrow aisles. Owner George Kingen jokes that every new wine brought in replaces a grocery item. The store has the best deals in town on champagne, and also offers good values on Northwest, California, French, and Italian wines. The roomy Bellevue shop (Pete's Wines Eastside) is devoted solely to wine, with the same good prices and special-order service. ■ *58 E Lynn St; 322-2660; map:GG7; every day.* ■ *134 105th NE, Bellevue; 454-1100; map:HH3; every day.*

**Pike & Western Wine Merchants** If you think of Pike Place Market as a grocery store, think of Pike & Western as its wine section. While still one of the best places to learn about *Northwest* wines, Pike & Western boasts a staff knowledgeable about wines from the rest of the world. They make a concerted effort to offer the best values, and are especially adept at helping shoppers match wines to the dinner ingredients they've purchased elsewhere in the Market. Owner Michael Teer uses his knowledge of wine and food to help some of the city's best restaurants craft their wine lists. ■ *Pike Place Market; 441-1307; map:J8; every day.*

**Queen Anne Thriftway** Seattle-area grocery stores have developed amazingly large cellars, and this superlative independent is one of the best. Its purchase and upgrading of two other Thriftways (Admiral in West Seattle and Procter in Tacoma) show the store's commitment to fine food and wine. Wine manager Jeff Cox oversees an ever changing selection including many of the current hits. In addition, Thriftway carries over 100 varieties of beer, including an extensive selection of microbrews. Open 24 hours (though no alcohol is sold between 2am and 6am). ■ *1908 Queen Anne Ave N; 284-2530; map:GG7; every day.* ■ *2320 42nd SW, West Seattle; 937-0551; map:II9; every day.*

# LODGINGS

**LODGINGS CONTENTS**

**DOWNTOWN/SEATTLE CENTER** *323*

**UNIVERSITY DISTRICT/NORTH END** *332*

**CAPITOL HILL** *332*

**QUEEN ANNE HILL** *335*

**WEST SEATTLE** *335*

**EASTSIDE** *336*

**AIRPORT AREA** *338*

**BAINBRIDGE ISLAND** *340*

# Lodgings

## DOWNTOWN/SEATTLE CENTER

**Alexis Hotel** ★★★ When the Sultan of Brunei showed up in Seattle for the APEC conference, this is where he stayed. And if it's good enough for the richest man in the world, you'll probably like it here, too. The Alexis is a gem carved out of a lovely turn-of-the-century building in a stylish section of downtown near the waterfront. It's small, full of tasteful touches, and decorated with the suave modernity of Michael Graves's postmodern colors. You'll be pampered here, with Jacuzzis and real-wood fireplaces in some of the suites, a steam room that can be reserved just for you, and nicely insulated walls between rooms to ensure privacy. Request a room that faces the inner courtyard—those facing First Avenue can be noisy, especially if you want to open your window. Amenities include complimentary continental breakfasts, a morning newspaper, shoe shines, and a guest membership at the nearby Seattle Club ($12). The Painted Table serves innovative Northwest cuisine (see Restaurants chapter). Pets are accepted.

At press time, the Alexis was planning to begin a major renovation, converting the neighboring Arlington Suites into additional hotel rooms. Plans are to increase the amount of rooms to 109; a few suites will retain kitchens for long-term stays. Small meeting rooms will also be added, although this will by no means turn the Alexis into a convention-oriented hotel. ■ *1007 1st Ave; 624-4844 or (800) 426-7033; map:L8; $$$; AE, DC, MC, V; checks OK.* &

**Best Western Executive Inn** ★ The lobby of this cheerful motor inn is welcoming, with a gas fireplace and rustic twig furnishings. Spacious rooms are done up in mauves and teals (try for a room with a view of the Space Needle). There's no charge for children under 18, and the parking is free. Proximity to the monorail at the Seattle Center and a free downtown shuttle from the inn make the location feasible even without a car. The inn has a spa and workout room, as well as an informal restaurant and lounge. ▪ *200 Taylor Ave N; 448-9444 or (800)351-9444; map:F5; $$; AE, DC, MC, V; checks OK.* &

**The Claremont Hotel** ★ Budget travelers from all over keep the Claremont heavily booked year-round. The location can't be beat: three blocks from the Market, a block and a half from Westlake Center and the monorail. A recent makeover has added an elegant touch to many of the rooms. Prices edge over $100 for kitchen suites, but whole families can comfortably fit in the apartment suites, which feature a full kitchen, a separate bedroom, and a pull-out couch. For a moderately priced splurge, spring for one of the corner king bedroom suites on an upper floor with a view of downtown and the Market. ▪ *2000 4th Ave; 448-8600 or (800)448-8601; map:H6; $$; AE, DC, MC, V; no checks.*

**Crowne Plaza Hotel** ★½ This hotel bends over backward for the repeat and corporate visitor. The top "Executive Floors" are corporate, comfortable, and very clean in striking maroons, mauves, and dark wood. Business travelers taking advantage of executive services receive a lot of individual attention in addition to free papers, a lounge, complimentary breakfast, and their own concierge desk (all at only slightly higher prices). Lower-floor guest rooms are spacious, if not especially visually appealing. The lobby and lounge don't have a lot of charm, reminding you that this is a Holiday Inn after all—albeit an upscale version. There is a full range of meeting facilities, and the location is convenient: right off the freeway and about four blocks from the Convention Center. ▪ *1113 6th Ave; 464-1980 or (800)227-6963; map:L5; $$$; AE, DC, MC, V; checks OK.* &

**The Edgewater** ★★ Alas, you can't fish from the famous west-facing windows of this waterfront institution anymore. You can, however, still breathe salty air and hear the ferry horns toot. The lobby and rooms have a rustic tone, with bleached oak and overstuffed chairs, plaid bedspreads, and lots of duck motifs and antler art. It's like a lodge on a busy (and sometimes noisy) Northwest waterfront, but with a reputable restaurant (Ernie's), a decent bar with a piano, and an uninterrupted view of Elliott Bay, Puget Sound, and the Olympic Mountains. Waterside rooms have the best views, but can get hot on summer afternoons. At press time, it remains the only hotel on the waterfront, allowing the Edgewater to command prices approaching outrageous. The cruise ship–style Sunday brunch served here is a veritable extravaganza. ▪ *Pier 67, 2411 Alaskan Way;*

*728-7000 or (800)624-0670; map:F9; $$$; AE, DC, MC, V; checks OK.* ⟨

**Four Seasons Olympic Hotel** ★★★★ Elegance is yours at Seattle's landmark hotel, where grand borders on opulent, and personal around-the-clock service means smiling maids, quick-as-a-wink bellhops, and a team of caring concierges who ensure your every comfort. Luxury extends from the 450 handsome guest rooms and suites tastefully furnished with period repro-ductions (executive suites feature down-dressed king-size beds separated from an elegant sitting room by French doors) to the venerable Georgian Room (see Restaurants chapter), where the talents of chef Kerry Sear, the decorum of liveried waiters, and the strains of a grand piano create a fine-dining experience you won't soon forget. Enjoy afternoon tea in the Garden Court or relax in the solarium spa and pool (where a licensed masseuse is on call). The hotel even goes out of its way for kids, right down to a teddy bear in the crib and a step stool in the bathroom. There are several elegant meeting rooms and fine shops in the retail spaces off the lobby. The hotel's prices are steep, especially considering there are few views, but this is Seattle's one world-class contender. ■ *411 University St; 621-1700 or (800)821-8106; map:F9; $$$; AE, DC, MC, V; checks OK.* ⟨

**Hotel Vintage Park** ★★½ Part of the San Francisco–based Kimpton Group, the Vintage Park is a personable, well-run, classy downtown hotel, with genuinely attentive service. There are two kinds of rooms: those facing inward and those facing outward (the exterior rooms tend to have a little more space, but forget about a view). Unfortunately, Vintage Park is located on a busy I-5 entrance ramp and soundproofing only seems to help on the upper floors. The hotel's only suite, on the entire top floor, gives a new fun twist to elegance. Everywhere else, they've carried their vintage theme to the limit with rooms named after wineries, burgundy upholstery, and green-and-ma-roon bedspreads. All rooms have robes, hair dryers, irons and ironing boards, and phones in the bathrooms. There is 24-hour room service (lightning fast) from their Italian restaurant, Tulio (see Restaurants chapter). The hotel provides coffee in the morning and complimentary fireside wine-tasting in the evening—classic Kimpton. ■ *1100 5th Ave; 624-8000 or (800)624-4433; map:L6; $$$; AE, DC, MC, V; checks OK.* ⟨

**Houseboat Hideaway** ★★ A stay on one of these two Euro-pean-style canal barges could be the quintessential Seattle ex-perience. You're moored on the south end of Lake Union, with unencumbered lake vistas and all the comforts of home: a sparkling kitchen, a big nestlike bed, TV and VCR. Yes, the toi-let's a marine head, but it's a small price to pay. The smaller boat sleeps two cozily, while the larger one will fit up to six.

■ *2144 Westlake Ave N; 323-5323; map:A1; $$$; AE, MC, V; checks OK.*

**Inn at the Market** ★★★ The setting—perched just above the fish, flower, and fruit stalls of Pike Place Market with a view of Elliott Bay, and adjacent to Seattle's oh-so-special French-inspired restaurant, Campagne (see Restaurants chapter)—is unsurpassed. This small hotel (65 rooms) features personalized service that approximates that of a country inn. Despite the ideal location, you won't feel oppressed by conventioneers—conference facilities consist of one meeting room and one outdoor deck. The architecture features oversize rooms, bay windows that let occupants of even some side rooms enjoy big views, and a comfortable, pretty lobby. There is no complimentary breakfast (just coffee), but room service for that meal can be ordered from Bacco in the courtyard; room service dinner comes from Campagne. ■ *86 Pine St; 443-3600 or (800)446-4484; map:I7; $$$; AE, DC, MC, V; checks OK.* &

**Inn at Virginia Mason** ★ The Inn at Virginia Mason has been working hard to let the public know it's not just a place for friends and family of Virginia Mason's patients. The location is convenient to the Convention Center, yet offers respite from the downtown bustle (if not from ambulance sirens). The standard rooms are on the small side, although comfortably and tastefully furnished, but the suites ($135-$200) are fairly priced for what you get. Try for the one on the rooftop floor with a fireplace in the living room, bar, TVs, and a behind-the-city view of Puget Sound. The pleasant Rhododendron Restaurant is available for meals, but you're also an easy walk from downtown shops and restaurants. ■ *1006 Spring St; 583-6453 or (800)283-6453; map:HH7; $$$; AE, DC, MC, V; checks OK.* &

**Marriott Residence Inn—Lake Union** ★½ It's not exactly on the lake, but rather across busy Fairview Avenue. Still, the 234 rooms, half of which are one-bedroom suites boasting lake views (request one on the highest floor possible), are spacious and tastefully decorated. All rooms have fully outfitted kitchenettes, and a continental breakfast and evening dessert are presented in the lobby—a light, plant-filled courtyard with an atrium and waterfall. There isn't a hotel restaurant, but there are plenty of lakeside eateries across the street at which guests may charge meals to their rooms. Amenities include meeting rooms, lap pool, exercise room, sauna and steam room, and spa. ■ *800 Fairview Ave N; 624-6000 or (800)331-3131; map:D1; $$$; AE, DC, MC, V; checks OK.* &

**Mayflower Park Hotel** ★★ Step out of the heart of the downtown shopping district and into the coolly elegant lobby of this handsomely renovated 1927 hotel. On one side of the lobby sits

▼

**Downtown/
Seattle
Center**

▲

Oliver's (a perfectly civilized spot for a perfect martini) and on the other is Clipper's, one of the prettiest breakfast places in town. Rooms are small, still bearing charming reminders of the hotel's past: lovely Oriental brass and antique appointments; large, deep tubs; thick walls that trap noise. Modern intrusions are for both better and worse: double-glazed windows in all rooms keep out traffic noise, but there are undistinguished furnishings in many of the rooms. The slightly bigger deluxe rooms have corner views; ask for one on a higher floor or you may find yourself facing a brick wall. ■ *405 Olive Way; 623-8700 or (800)426-5100; map:I6; $$$; AE, DC, MC, V; checks OK.* ♿

**MV *Challenger* ★★** A luxury liner it's not, but if you've got a thing for tugboats, the boat-and-breakfast MV *Challenger*, Captain Jerry Brown's handsomely restored, 96-foot workhorse, is for you. Everything—from the spotless galley to the eight cabins—is shipshape. Lounge topside on a deck chair, inside around the fireplace, or step out and explore the docks, restaurants, and shops just a stroll away. For utmost quiet and comfort, reserve one of the cabins on the tug's upper deck or consider renting space aboard one of two yachts moored alongside the tug (rates include an exceptional breakfast aboard the *Challenger*). We've all heard tales of notoriously temperamental sea captains, and though his boat rarely leaves its Lake Union dock, Captain Brown has been known to exercise that prerogative inappropriately. That said, we've ascertained that the majority of guests will find him a most gracious host. ■ *Yale St Landing, 1001 Fairview Ave N; 340-1201; map:C1; $$; AE, MC, V; checks OK.*

**Pacific Guest Suites** [*unrated*] Pacific Guest Suites rents condos in Seattle, Bellevue, Redmond, Everett, and Renton. Most of the locations have amenities such as swimming pools, fitness centers, fireplaces, Jacuzzis, and weekly maid service. Ideally suited to long-term business stays, the condos are also perfect for families on vacation, as the minimum stay is only three days (although the nightly rate drops the longer you stay). ■ *Administrative Office, 411 108th Ave NE, Bellevue; 454-7888 or (800)962-6620; $$; AE, DC, MC, V; checks OK.*

**Pacific Plaza Hotel ★** The Pacific Plaza offers a welcome respite from astronomical downtown hotel prices. For those who care more about location and budget than amenities, this is the perfect place. Rooms start at well under $100, even in summer, and include a generous continental breakfast. The ambience brings to mind a good budget hotel in a European city: long hallways; simple, comfortable rooms; and small, clean bathrooms. Light sleepers may wish to stay elsewhere, as the Pacific Plaza is not air-conditioned and opening the windows invites traffic noise. ■ *400 Spring St; 623-3900 or (800)426-1165; map:L6; $$; AE, DC, MC, V; checks OK.*

▼

Downtown/
Seattle
Center

▲

**Pensione Nichols** ★ Its location is both the best and the worst feature of Pensione Nichols. Its perch, just above the Pike Place Market, outweighs the fact that its entrance is right next to an X-rated movie theater. Some of the rooms face First Avenue and can be quite noisy; and while the other rooms don't have windows, they do have skylights and are much quieter. Ten guest rooms ($60 single, $85 double) share three bathrooms (with a fourth in the works). The large common room at the west end of the third floor has a gorgeous view of the Market's rooftops and Elliott Bay beyond; it is here that the bountiful breakfast—including fresh treats from the Market— is served. Unusual antiques abound (the Nichols also own the N. B. Nichols antique store in Post Alley). Also available: two wonderful suites with private bath, full kitchens, bedroom alcove, and a living room with that great view. ■ *1923 1st Ave; 441-7125; map:H8; $$; AE, MC, V; checks OK.*

**Pioneer Square Hotel** ★★ Renovations have transformed this formerly seedy hotel into a handsome, comfortably appointed, moderately priced lodging—a boon for budget-minded travelers intent on staying in downtown Seattle. The furniture is a rich, elegant cherry wood, and each room has two armoires (one to use as a closet—since the former closets have been transformed into spacious bathrooms—and one for the TV). There's a small sitting alcove in these surprisingly quiet rooms (the hotel is in close proximity to the Alaskan Way Viaduct). Quibbles? The front desk staff could use some polish and the complimentary continental breakfast may be picked over if you sleep past 7:30am. The neighborhood may not suit timid travelers, but for those willing to embrace the urban melting pot of Pioneer Square, this is a great new choice. ■ *77 Yesler Way; 340-1234 or (800)800-5514; map:N9; $$; AE, DC, MC, V; no checks.* &

▼

**Downtown/ Seattle Center**

▲

**The Renaissance Madison Hotel** ★★½ The former Stouffer Madison, now part of the Renaissance chain, successfully conveys a sense of warmth and intimacy. The lobby is tasteful and uncluttered, upstairs hallways are softly lit, and the rooms are elegantly furnished, with lots of marble and wood; most offer great city views. Avoid rooms on the freeway side; although the windows are soundproofed, the hum of traffic seeps in. Guests enjoy complimentary coffee and morning newspaper, a rooftop pool, and free in-town tranportation. The pricey "Club Floors" offer exclusive check-in privileges, concierge services, hors d'oeuvres and a continental breakfast at the Club Lounge, a library, and the best views. Prego, on the 28th floor, offers a fine selection of seafood to complement the view. ■ *515 Madison St; 583-0300 or (800)278-4159; map:M5; $$$; AE, DC, MC, V; checks OK.* &

**Seattle Sheraton Hotel and Towers** ★★½ Seattle's Sheraton is an 840-room tower rising as a sleek triangle, the Convention Center in its shadow. It, too, aims at the convention business, so the rooms are smallish and standard, and much emphasis is placed on the meeting rooms and the restaurants. 1995 saw nearly $4 million in renovation with the completion of the new Gallery Lobby & Oyster Bar, the redesign of the casual Pike Street Cafe (formerly Banners) known for its 27-foot-long dessert spread, and the transformation of Gooey's nightclub into Schooners Sports Pub (complete with large screen TVs, Northwest microbrews, and accompanying pub fare). The outstanding four-star restaurant, Fullers, is an oasis of serenity adorned with fine Northwest art (see Restaurants chapter). Service is quite efficient. Convention facilities are complete, and the kitchen staff can handle the most complex assignments. Discriminating business travelers can head for the upper four "VIP" floors (31–34), where a hotel-within-a-hotel offers its own lobby, concierge, and considerably more amenities in the rooms (same size as economy). The top floors feature a health club and a private lounge with a knockout city panorama. You pay for parking. ■ *1400 6th Ave; 621-9000 or (800)204-6100; map:K5; $$$; AE, DC, MC, V; checks OK.* ᕂ

**Sixth Avenue Inn** Catering to tourists and conventioneers, this sprightly motor inn is done up in blues and tans. Some rooms have brass beds, and service is professional and friendly. There's less street noise on the east side, and you'll find room service, a restaurant, free parking, and a good location with nearby retail on one side of the hotel, movie theaters on the other. ■ *2000 6th Ave; 441-8300 or (800)648-6440; map:H5; $$; AE, DC, MC, V; checks OK.*

**Sorrento Hotel** ★★★½ Occupying a corner just east of downtown in Seattle's First Hill neighborhood, the Sorrento is an Italianate masterpiece that first opened in 1909, was remodeled to the tune of $4.5 million in 1981, and has just completed a makeover for the millennium, adding top-notch service touches like fax machines, in-room voice mail, and a small on-site exercise facility. The 76 rooms come decorated in muted good taste with a slight Asian accent. We recommend the extravagantly large 08 series of suites, in the corners. Suites on the top floor make elegant quarters for special meetings or parties—the showstopper being the 3,000-square-foot, $1,000-a-night penthouse, with a grand piano, patio, Jacuzzi, view of the bay, and luxurious rooms. A comfortable, intimate fireside lobby lounge is a civilized place for afternoon tea or sipping Cognac while listening to jazz piano or classical guitar. Chef Eric Lenard showcases Northwest lamb, among other local culinary treasures, at the manly Hunt Club (see review in restaurants section). Some may find the location—uphill five blocks from the heart of downtown—inconvenient, but we find it quiet and removed. ▪ *900 Madison St; 622-6400 or (800)426-1265; map:M4; $$$; AE, DC, MC, V; checks OK.*

**Warwick Hotel** ★ The Warwick is part of an international chain that aims its pitch at the corporate traveler; unfortunately, the result is somewhat characterless. Rooms are large and comfortable, with floor-to-ceiling windows (reserve a room above the sixth floor for a great view) and marble bathrooms. The pool in the health club is too shallow for play and too short for laps, but a spa and sauna will help you unwind. If you've got the bucks, splurge for the Queen Victoria Suite, with its elegant appointments and panoramic view (good for private parties, too). The restaurant, Liaison, has decent service and rather good, if unimaginative, food. As at most downtown hotels, you pay for parking, but there's 24-hour courtesy van service for downtown appointments. The Warwick is one of the few city hotels that allow small pets (ask first). ▪ *401 Lenora St; 443-4300 or (800)426-9280; map:H6; $$$; AE, DC, MC, V; checks OK.* &

**WestCoast Camlin Hotel** ★ Like many older hotels in Seattle, this 1926 grande dame has been remodeled and sound-proofed with double-glazed windows. (The elevator and the ventilation system, however, both hark back to an earlier era.) Though its conference facilities are limited, the Camlin appeals to the business traveler, with large rooms that have small sitting/work areas, spacious closets, and spotless bathrooms; those whose numbers end in 10 have windows on three sides. Avoid the Cabanas (they're small and dreary and for smokers) and room service, which is quite slow. There's rooftop dining, and a piano bar in the Cloud Room, a retro-chic cocktail lounge favored by both locals and out-of-towners. ▪ *1619 9th Ave; 682-0100 or (800)426-0670; map:J4; $$; AE, DC, MC, V; checks OK.*

**WestCoast Plaza Park Suites** ★★ For better or for worse, this suites-only hotel is a step away from the Washington State Convention Center. Each room is, in one way or another, a suite (even the studios) with a living room, kitchenette, and a downy bedroom (sporting a *second* TV). Some have fireplaces, others boardrooms, some even have Jacuzzis, and while all are large, the somewhat bland decor could use a splash of something. Expect all the amenities of a full-service hotel: conference rooms, exercise rooms (sauna and Jacuzzi, too), and laundry and valet service. Personal needs are gladly met—from groceries to an extra phone line for your modem. There's no restaurant, but an extensive continental breakfast is included. There's even a shop in the lobby that stocks frozen dinners to nuke in your microwave. The Plaza Park is great for corporate clients on long-term stays or families on vacation who want a little room to spread out (and an outdoor pool for the kids). ■ *1011 Pike St; 682-8282 or (800)426-0670; map:K3; $$$; AE, DC, MC, V; checks OK.* &

**WestCoast Roosevelt Hotel** ★ Gone is the grand skylit lobby that so distinguished the Roosevelt when it first opened its doors in 1930; the space is now inhabited by Von's Restaurant. The new lobby is low-ceilinged and cramped, but elsewhere the WestCoast installation has somewhat preserved the Roosevelt's art deco sensibilities. The hotel's 20 stories have been redivided for the contemporary traveler, but studios are still almost comically small. The deluxe rooms are a better choice, with adjoining sitting areas; the 13 suites each contain a Jacuzzi and a separate sitting area. Nine floors are nonsmoking. Considering its proximity to the Convention Center and the shopping district, the Roosevelt's prices—$95 to $170—are decent, but the service could be more polished. ■ *1531 7th Ave; 621-1200 or (800)426-0670; map:J5; $$$; AE, DC, MC, V; checks OK.* &

**WestCoast Vance Hotel** ★ Another WestCoast mission to save a forgotten downtown hotel. Most of the $7 million restoration done in 1990, it seems, was spent in the lobby—making for a very pretty entrance. The rooms are small and spartan, and are showing serious signs of wear: carpet stains, scuff marks, and the occasional chipped paint. Standard rooms, at $95 for a double, are no bargain, as there's barely enough room to swing a cat (the bathrooms are shoehorned into two former closets; claustrophobics should shower elsewhere). Better to spend $20 more for a superior room, which at least has a small sitting area. The north-facing rooms above the fifth floor are best, with a view toward Queen Anne and the Space Needle. Room service comes from the Italian restaurant next door, Salute in Città. ■ *620 Stewart St; 441-4200 or (800)426-0670; map:I6; $$; AE, DC, MC, V; checks OK.*

**Westin Hotel** ★★½ Westin's international headquarters is in Seattle, so this flagship hotel has quite a few extras. The twin cylindrical towers may be called corncobs by the natives, but they afford spacious rooms with superb views, particularly above the 20th floor. The size of the hotel (with 877 rooms and 48 suites) contributes to some lapses in service, however: we can attest to long lines for check-in and occasional difficulties getting attention from the harried concierge staff. Convention facilities, spread over several floors of meeting rooms, are quite complete. There is a large pool and an exercise room supervised by conditioning experts. On the top floors are some ritzy, glitzy suites. The location, near Westlake Center and the monorail station, is excellent, as is a meal at Nikko, a superb Japanese restaurant on the premises (see Restaurants chapter). ■ *1900*

▼

Downtown/
Seattle
Center

▲

*5th Ave; 728-1000 or (800)228-3000; map:H5; $$$; AE, DC, MC, V; checks OK.* &

## UNIVERSITY DISTRICT/NORTH END

**Chambered Nautilus** ★★ This blue 1915 Georgian colonial in a woodsy hillside setting in the University District offers six airy guest rooms beautifully furnished with antiques. Four have private baths, and four open onto porches with tree-webbed views of the Cascades. All rooms have robes, desks, flowers, and reading material. This location, just across the street from shared student housing units and a few blocks from Fraternity Row, can get noisy during rush. Other times, though, it's surprisingly quiet. Innkeepers Bunny and Bill Hagemeyer serve a full breakfast, complimentary afternoon tea, and even homemade lollipops. A spacious public room, meeting facilities, a library of 2,000-plus volumes, and an enclosed porch/ reading room with soothing chamber music round out this tasteful inn. Smoking is allowed on the porches and outside. Make prior arrangements for kids under 12. ▪ *5005 22nd Ave NE; 522-2536; map:FF6; $$; AE, DC, MC, V; checks OK.*

▼

University District/ North End

▲

**The College Inn Guest House** With the glorious grounds of the University of Washington practically at your doorstep, you can excuse a little noise (there's a cafe and pub on the premises) and the dormlike quality of the toilet and bathing facilities (separate-sex, rows of showers, down the hall). Housed in the upper three floors of a renovated 1909 Tudor building that's on the National Register of Historic Places, the College Inn is designed along the lines of a European pension: it's devoid of TV and radio (though most rooms have phones). Each of the 25 guest rooms offers a sink, a desk, and a single or double bed. The best of the lot even have window seats. A generous continental breakfast (included in the bargain rates) is served upstairs in the communal sitting area. ▪ *4000 University Way NE; 633-4441; map:FF6; $; MC, V; checks OK.*

**Edmonds Harbor Inn** ★ Strategically located near the Edmonds ferry and train terminals, the inn is an attractive choice for a night in this charming, waterside Seattle suburb. The inn features 61 large rooms (with views, unfortunately, of the surrounding business park rather than the picturesque Sound), oak furnishings, continental breakfast, and access to an athletic club just next door. If you're traveling with youngsters in tow, the rooms with modern kitchenettes, coupled with the inn's extremely reasonable rates, will be particularly appealing. Get directions—the place is near the harborfront, but a little difficult to find in the gray sea of new office and shopping developments. ▪ *130 W Dayton St, Edmonds; 771-5021 or (800)441-8033; $$; AE, DC, MC, V; checks OK.* &

**Lake Union B&B** ★★ Shoes off. If you don't have any socks, they're provided. Then sink into the white cloud of carpet and couches in this modern three-story house near Gas Works Park, and enjoy a glass of wine by the fireplace. There are three rooms, each with TV, queen-size feather bed, and carefully ironed sheets. Upstairs, two stunning rooms offer Lake Union views. The larger suite also boasts a solarium, fireplace, Jacuzzi, and private bath—and is probably Seattle's finest *affordable* guest room. The sauna in the bathroom downstairs has piped-in music. Owner Janice Matthews, a former restaurateur, gladly prepares private dinners on request. The two-night minimum is often waived. ▪ *2217 N 36th St; 547-9965; map:FF7; $$; MC, V; checks OK.*

**Meany Tower Hotel** ★ The best thing about the Meany is the 1930s octagonal tower design—every window is a corner window. Inside, the whole place—lobby and rooms—is turned out in shades of peach. Guest rooms are nothing special, though each has a bay window with a view—some better than others—and those on the south side are sunny. You're one block from shopping on the Ave and two blocks from the University of Washington campus. There's a serviceable restaurant, The Meany Grill, with a bar and a big-screen TV in the lounge for sports fans. ▪ *4507 Brooklyn Ave NE; 634-2000 or (800)899-0251; map:FF7; $$; AE, DC, MC, V; checks OK.* ♿

**University Inn** ★★½ A remodel in 1993 added a south wing, more than doubling the number of guest rooms at this bright, clean, well-managed University District establishment. Rooms in the new wing are more spacious and have king-size beds. North-wing rooms, even after a remodel of their own, are standard, with shower stalls in the bathrooms (no tub). Some have small balconies overlooking the heated outdoor pool and hot tub. Other amenities include a complimentary continental breakfast, free morning paper, a small fitness room, and free off-street parking. ▪ *4140 Roosevelt Way NE; 632-5055 or (800)733-3855; map:FF7; $$; AE, DC, MC, V; checks OK.* ♿

## CAPITOL HILL

**Bacon Mansion/Broadway Guest House** ★★ Built by Cecil Bacon in 1909, this Edwardian-style Tudor mansion (formerly known as the Broadway Guest House) is now a fine bed and breakfast. Most of the original wood was destroyed in a fire, but the mansion has been skillfully restored. Seven rooms in the main guest house (five with private bath) are appointed with antiques and brass fixtures. The top of the line is the Capitol Room, a huge suite on the second floor with a sun room, fireplace, four-poster bed, and a view of the Space Needle. The basement Garden Room (which stays pleasantly cool in summer) has 8-foot ceilings and a kitchenette. The Carriage House, a separate, two-story building with hunter green decor, is appropriate for a small family or two couples (at press time, plans were afoot to convert the Carriage House into two units). Proprietor Daryl King is an enthusiastic, friendly host. ■ *959 Broadway E; 329-1864 or (800)240-1864; map:GG6; $$; AE, MC, V; checks OK.*

**Capitol Hill Inn** ★ One of the most conveniently located B&Bs in the city—within walking distance of the Convention Center and Broadway shops and restaurants (as long as you don't mind hills). Unfortunately, you give up any charm of a neighborhood for this convenience. The 1903 Queen Anne–style home itself is a lovely place run by pleasant mother/daughter team Katie and Joanne Godmintz, who restored the inn down to its custom-designed wall coverings, period chandeliers, carved wooden moldings, sleigh and brass beds, and down-filled comforters. There are four rooms upstairs (two with full baths, two with toilets and sinks and a shower down the hall), and two rooms downstairs in the daylight basement (with private bath, fireplace, and Jacuzzi). The Godmintzes live on the third floor. ■ *1713 Belmont Ave; 323-1955; map:HH6; $$ ; AE, MC, V; checks OK.*

**Gaslight Inn and Howell Street Suites** ★★½ Praised by repeat guests and bed-and-breakfast owners alike, the Gaslight is one of the loveliest, most reasonably priced, and friendliest bed and breakfasts in town. Trevor Logan and Steve Bennett have polished this turn-of-the-century mansion into a 10-guest-room jewel, 5 with private baths, 2 with fireplaces, each decorated in a distinct style—some contemporary, some antique, some art deco, some mission. Outside are two sun decks and a large heated swimming pool. The Howell Street Suites next door (five full and one studio) are outfitted with kitchens, contemporary furnishings and antiques, a coffee-maker, wineglasses, fruit, and flowers. Targeted at businesspeople, the suites also offer phones, fax availability, off-street parking, maid service, and laundry facilities. There's a hot tub and a garden area between the two houses. No pets, kids, or smoking (you may light up outdoors, though). ■ *1727 15th Ave; 325-3654; map:HH6; $$; AE, MC, V; checks OK.*

**Roberta's** ★★ Roberta is the gracious, somewhat loquacious lady of this Capitol Hill house near Volunteer Park and a few blocks from the funky Broadway district. Inside it's lovely: refinished floors throughout, a comfortable blue couch and an old upright piano, books everywhere, and a large oval dining table and country-style chairs. Of the five rooms, the blue-toned Hideaway Suite (the entire third floor)—with views of the Cascades from the window seats, skylights, a sitting area with a futon couch and a small desk, and a full bath with a tub—is our favorite. Others prefer the Peach Room with its antique desk, bay window, love seat, and queen-size oak bed. Early risers will enjoy the Madrona Room, with its morning sun and bath. In the morning, Roberta brings you a wake-up cup of coffee, then later puts out a smashing, full, meatless breakfast. No children. You may smoke on the porch. ■ *1147 16th Ave E; 329-3326; map:HH6; $$; AE, DC, MC, V; checks OK.*

**Salisbury House** ★★ A welcoming porch wraps around this big, bright Capitol Hill home, an exquisite hostelry neighboring Volunteer Park. Glossy maple floors and lofty beamed ceilings lend a sophisticated air to the guest library (with a chess table and a fireplace) and living room. Up the wide staircase and past the second-level sun porch are four guest rooms (one with a canopy bed, all with queen-size beds and down comforters) with full private baths. Breakfast is taken in the dining room or on the sunny terrace. Classy, dignified, non-smoking, and devoid of children (under 12) and pets, the Salisbury is a sure bet in one of Seattle's finest neighborhoods. ■ *750 16th Ave E; 328-8682; map:HH6; $$; AE, DC, MC, V; checks OK.*

## QUEEN ANNE

**The Williams House** ★ Over the course of its 90-odd-year history, this south-slope Queen Anne residence has been a gentlemen's boardinghouse and an emergency medical clinic for the 1962 Seattle World's Fair. Today, owners Doug and Sue Williams offer five guest rooms, four with views (three have private baths, the other two have a bath each, down the hall). The enclosed south sun porch is a nice gathering spot. Brass beds, original fixtures, fireplaces, ornate Italian tiles, and oak floors mirror the home's Edwardian past. A full breakfast is served in the first-floor dining room. Children are welcome by prior arrangement and there is a limited smoking area. ■ *1505 4th Ave N; 285-0810 or (800)880-0810; map:GG8; $$; AE, DC, MC, V; checks OK.*

## WEST SEATTLE

**Villa Heidelberg** ★ Leaded-glass windows, beamed ceilings, Puget Sound views, and a wraparound covered porch distinguish this 1909 mini-mansion in West Seattle, built and named by a German immigrant. The four guest rooms share two bathrooms. Of the two with king-size beds, one has an Olympics-facing sun deck, the other has a fireplace and a phone. The other rooms have a four-poster double bed and two twin beds, respectively. Owners John and Barb Thompson serve a breakfast of popovers and fruit, waffles, or French toast. Look for extras like a bouquet of roses on the table, grown in the beautifully

▼

**West Seattle**

▲

landscaped garden. ▪ *4845 45th Ave SW; 938-3658 or (800)671-2942; map:II9; $$; AE, MC, V; checks OK.*

## EASTSIDE

**Bellevue Club Hotel** ★★½ The new hotel addition at the former Bellevue Athletic Club promises to give the Hyatt Regency a run for its money, especially among well-heeled business travelers. Each of the 67 rooms is beautifully decorated, featuring striking modern furnishings and pieces by Northwest artists. The oversize limestone and marble bathrooms are absolutely fabulous, complete with spalike tubs and separate shower stalls. The lovely garden rooms open onto private patios. Other rooms overlook the five tennis courts. All of the extensive athletic facilities are available to hotel guests, including an Olympic-size swimming pool, indoor tennis, racquetball, and squash courts; and aerobics classes. ▪ *11200 SE 6th, Bellevue; 454-4424 or (800)579-1110; map:HH3; $$$; AE, MC, V; checks OK.* &

**The Bellevue Hilton** ★★ With every amenity in the book, the Bellevue Hilton is the best bet on the Eastside's Hotel Row. Rooms are tastefully done in warm colors. Amenities include use of a nearby health-and-racquet club, free transportation around Bellevue (within a 5-mile radius), room service (until late evening), a Jacuzzi, a sauna, a pool, cable TV, and two restaurants. Working stiffs will appreciate the modem hookups and desks in every room; computer, fax machine, and copy machine are also available. ▪ *100 112th Ave NE, Bellevue; 455-3330 or (800)BEL-HILT; map:HH3; $$$; AE, DC, MC, V; checks OK.* &

**Hyatt Regency at Bellevue Place** ★★ Hyatt Regency is just one part of Kemper Freeman's splashy, sprawling retail-office-restaurant-hotel-health–club complex called Bellevue Place. The 382-room hotel with 24 stories (the highest in Bellevue) offers many of the extras: pricier "Regency Club" rooms on the top two floors, two big ballrooms, several satellite conference rooms, use of the neighboring Seattle Club (for a $10 fee), and a fine restaurant, Eques. The best rooms are on the south side above the seventh floor. ▪ *900 Bellevue Way NE, Bellevue; 462-1234 or (800)233-1234; map:HH3; $$$; AE, DC, MC, V; checks OK.* &

**La Residence Suite Hotel** ★ Conveniently located across from the region's best shopping (Bellevue Square), this 24-room facility is a homey alternative to commercial super-hotels on the Eastside. There's leather furniture in the living rooms, two phones in each room, with free local calls, and a fax and copy machine (at no charge) for business use. Rooms have kitchens, separate bedrooms, and large closets, making the hotel popular

▼

**Eastside**

▲

for longer stays (there is no minimum stay and rates drop after eight days). Laundry facilities and free parking. ■ *475 100th Ave NE, Bellevue; 455-1475 or (800)800-1993; map:HH3; $$$; AE, DC, MC, V; checks OK.* ᕾ

**Marriott Residence Inn—Bellevue** ★★ A quiet cluster of suites just off 520 in east Bellevue, the Eastside version of the Residence Inn feels more like an apartment complex than a hotel. Well suited to business travelers, the place is also great for families. All suites have fireplaces and full kitchens with separate living rooms and bedrooms; a complimentary continental breakfast is provided in the main building. The complex has an outdoor pool, three spas, and a sports court, and passes to a nearby health club are provided. They'll even do your grocery shopping for you. Travelers with smaller budgets might try the moderately priced basic hotel rooms next door at the Courtyard by Marriott (869-5300). ■ *14455 NE 29th Pl, Bellevue; 882-1222 or (800)331-3131; map:GG2; $$$; AE, DC, MC, V; checks OK.* ᕾ

**Shumway Mansion** ★★ When Richard and Salli Harris heard that developers wanted to demolish this historic 1909 building to make room for condos, they hauled the four-story house to a safe location near Kirkland's Juanita Bay. Now it's a gracious bed and breakfast with an equal emphasis on seminars and receptions. The eight guest rooms are furnished with antiques, and public rooms overlook the bay (just a short walk away) and the lower parking lots. The ballroom downstairs is often used for weddings or special meetings, opening onto a flowering patio in summer. A full breakfast is served in the dining room on table linens. Guests can use the Columbia Athletic Club a block away for no charge. Children over 12 are welcome. No pets or smoking. ■ *11410 99th Pl NE, Kirkland; 823-2303; map:DD3; $$; AE, MC, V; checks OK.* ᕾ

**WestCoast Bellevue Hotel** ★ The former Best Western Greenwood Hotel underwent a change in ownership in 1993, and is now part of the WestCoast chain (which seems to be buying up hotels throughout the Northwest faster than you can say "bargain rates"). Since then it has been spruced up with new carpeting, draperies, bed-dressings, and has remodeled bathrooms throughout. Just a jump off I-405, this mid-scale hotel offers, in addition to 176 very reasonably priced guest rooms, 16 two-level townhouse suites ($85), featuring loft bedrooms with king-size beds. Rooms facing the courtyard are much more pleasant, of course, than those with parking lot vistas. Eats and drinks are available here at the Eastside Bar & Grill. ■ *625 116th Ave NE, Bellevue; 455-9444 or (800)426-0670; map:HH3; $$; AE, DC, MC, V; checks OK.* ᕾ

**Woodmark Hotel** ★★★ The Woodmark, on the eastern shore of Lake Washington, holds claim to being the only lodging actually on the lake. From the outside it resembles a modern office building, but on the inside one encounters the soft touches of a fine hotel: 100 plush rooms (the best with lake views and the sounds of honking geese and quacking ducks) with fully stocked minibars and refrigerators, VCRs (complimentary movies are available at the front desk), terrycloth robes, oversize towels, and service (from laundry to valet) to match. You'll get a complimentary newspaper with the full breakfast. Downstairs on the lake level there's a comfortable living room with a grand piano and well-tended fire. The hotel has its own restaurant, Waters (see Restaurants chapter), featuring Northwest cuisine and a variety of bubbly and nonbubbly mineral waters (hence the name). Check out the nearby specialty shops or rent a boat from the marina. Business travelers can take advantage of extra amenities such as a pager for offsite calls, a cellular phone, and complimentary use of a laptop computer and printer. Parking access is a bit of a maze. ■ *1200 Carillon Point, Kirkland; 822-3700 or (800)822-3700; map:EE3; $$$; AE, DC, MC, V; checks OK.* &

▼

## AIRPORT AREA

**Eastside**

▲

**Doubletree Suites/Doubletree Inn** ★ The Doubletree, fixed between I-5 and Southcenter shopping mall, is two hotels. The handsome luxury suites ($116 to $174) have refrigerators, TVs with pay-per-view movie options, and small wet bars. Southeast-facing rooms have views of Mount Rainier. There's an indoor heated pool, Jacuzzi, and a sauna here; the outdoor pool is across the street in a secluded courtyard at the Doubletree Inn, the older, more plebeian sibling. The woody Northwest lobby is nice, and rooms here ($82 to $92), which recently underwent a facelift, are somewhat average; avoid the north-facing ones, which hum with the sounds of I-5. Service is quite friendly. ■ *16500 Southcenter Pkwy, Tukwila; 246-8220 or (800)DBL-TREE; map:PP4; $$; AE, DC, MC, V; checks OK.* &

**Holiday Inn of Renton** ★ A spirited, friendly staff gives this average mid-rise, corporate-oriented hotel some personality. Guest rooms and public areas are regularly spiffed up with new paint, carpet, draperies, and such, helping keep the place aesthetically up to date. There's a restaurant and lobby lounge. Spend the night before you leave from the airport, and you can park here free while you're away. ■ *800 Rainier Ave S, Renton; 226-7700 or (800)521-1412; map:NN4; $$; AE, DC, MC, V; no checks.* &

**Sea-Tac Red Lion Inn** ★ In true Red Lion tradition, it's gargantuan (850 rooms) and caters to conventioneers. You may pass Willy Loman in the dark, cavernous halls, but the tower rooms have been rather nicely done up in brighter shades. The east-facing rooms have views of the Cascades. Suites are available for parties. Three full restaurants, two lounges, and around-the-clock airport limo and room service. ■ *18740 Pacific Hwy S; 246-8600 or (800)RED-LION; map:PP6; $$$; AE, DC, MC, V; checks OK.* ⟨

**Seattle Airport Hilton Hotel** ★★ In this streamlined four-winged building camouflaged by trees and plantings, the Seattle Airport Hilton manages to create a resort atmosphere along an airport-hotel strip. The 173 plush, larger-than-standard rooms (at posh prices) are set around a landscaped courtyard with pool and indoor/outdoor Jacuzzi; they feature desks and computer hookups, irons, ironing boards, and coffee-makers. An exercise room and numerous meeting and party rooms are available. So is a 24-hour business center, complete with fax, copy machine, computer, and laser printer. The Great American Grill serves breakfast, lunch, and dinner. ■ *17620 Pacific Hwy S; 244-4800 or (800)HILTONS; map:PP6; $$$; AE, DC, MC, V; checks OK.* ⟨

**Seattle Marriott at Sea-Tac** ★★ Business travelers (and folks who prefer to spend a night near the airport rather than fight traffic to catch an early-morning flight) will appreciate the swift, courteous service at this 451-room mega-motel about a block from the airport strip. The lobby, with its warm Northwest motif, opens up into an enormous, covered atrium complete with indoor pool and two Jacuzzis. There's also a sauna and a well-equipped exercise room. A casual dining room offers all the usual hotel fare—from sandwiches to steaks. Why bother with a standard room? For slightly higher rates, more spacious, handsomely appointed suites are available on the concierge floor. These include such amenities as higher-quality linens, robes, turn-down service, hairdryers, iron and board, and access to a lounge which serves continental breakfasts and nightly nibbles. ■ *3201 S 176th St; 241-2000 or (800)228-9290; map:PP6; $$$; AE, DC, MC, V; checks OK.* ⟨

▼

**Airport Area**

▲

**WestCoast Sea-Tac Hotel** ★ Meeting facilities at this WestCoast outpost accommodate up to 200; an outdoor pool, Jacuzzi, and sauna accommodate everyone who stays in the bright rooms. Terrycloth robes, hair dryers, and stocked honor bars are available in the 32 limited-edition suites. In-house guests are treated to free valet parking for seven days. (A slightly less upscale WestCoast hotel across the street caters handily to the business traveler; 18415 Pacific Highway S, 248-8200.). ■ *18220 Pacific Hwy S; 246-5535 or (800)426-0670; map:PP6; $$$; AE, DC, MC, V; checks OK.* ⟨

**Wyndham Garden Hotel** ★ You can't get much closer to the airport than this. Attractive styling inside, warm wood paneling in the lobby lounge, and an inviting library and fireplace make this a bit classier than your standard airport hotel. Accommodations include 180 guest rooms with writing desks, and 24 suites with coffee-makers and hair dryers. Room service (early evening only) and meeting space are available. ■ *18118 Pacific Hwy S; 244-6666; map:PP6; $$$; AE, DC, MC, V; checks OK.* ౹

## BAINBRIDGE ISLAND

**Beach Cottage B&B** ★ Right across Eagle Harbor from the ferry-stop town of Winslow is this charming, flower-bedecked four-cottage setup. Each cottage has a queen-size bed, a kitchen stocked with breakfast fixings, a fireplace with logs ready for use, and a stereo. All four cottages boast decks and a view of Eagle Harbor and its marina. Choose the Cabin if it's just you and your sweetie; the Pilot House is a two-bedroom cottage perfect for two couples traveling together. Smoking is allowed (pets and children under 16 are not). ■ *5831 Ward Ave NE, Bainbridge Island; 842-6081; $$$; no credit cards; checks OK.*

▼
**Bainbridge Island**
▲

**The Bombay House** ★★½ Set in a lavish flower garden with a rough-cedar gazebo overlooking scenic Rich Passage, this sprawling turn-of-the-century house with a widow's walk is just a sweet stroll from Fort Ward State Park. Offering a hearty dose of island-hideaway atmosphere, the Bombay House has five bedrooms done up in country antiques. Three have private baths, and the vast second-floor Captain's Suite has a parlor wood stove and a claw-footed tub. The living room has a large fireplace. Innkeepers Roger, Bunny, and their daughter, Cameron, are friendly hosts. In the morning, you'll have the good fortune of enjoying one of Bunny's feasts with freshly baked goodies. Children over 6 years are welcome. ■ *8490 Beck Rd NE, Bainbridge Island; 842-3926 or (800)598-3926; $$; AE, MC, V; checks OK.*

**West Blakely Inn** ★★ Sally Anderson and Sam Plaut's West Blakely Inn is a renovated Odd Fellows Hall (circa 1912). This three-bedroom B&B, located in one of the island's most picturesque neighborhoods, touts high-ceilinged rooms so spacious (one downstairs guest room with private entrance sleeps six) that the Odd Fellows could convene there comfortably today. Rooms have private baths and queen-size beds, and breakfast has received accolades from numerous guests. The beach and Fort Ward State Park are just a short stroll away—and it's just a few steps to the hot tub. ■ *8489 Odd Fellows Rd, Bainbridge Island; 842-1427 or (800)835-1427; $$; no credit cards; checks OK.*

**FERRY RIDES** *343*

**BAINBRIDGE ISLAND** *344*

**HOOD CANAL** *344*

**KITSAP PENINSULA** *347*

**MOUNT RAINIER** *351*

**OLYMPIA** *353*

**PORT TOWNSEND** *355*

**SKAGIT VALLEY** *357*

**SNOQUALMIE VALLEY** *358*

**TACOMA AND GIG HARBOR** *360*

**VASHON ISLAND** *363*

**VICTORIA** *365*

**WHIDBEY ISLAND** *368*

# Day Trips

## FERRY RIDES

No activity better captures the spirit of Seattle than a ferry ride—both for commuters who rely on ferries as transportation to their jobs and for sightseers who simply want to enjoy the sunset and the city skyline from an ideal vantage point.

Most of the ferries in Puget Sound (except Port Angeles to Victoria, Gooseberry Point to Lummi Island, and the *Victoria Clipper* fleet, as well as a handful of others which run seasonally) are run by the **Washington State Ferries** (464-6400 or (800)542-7052). This is the largest ferry system in the country. Ferries on 10 routes serve 20 terminal locations, transporting 23 million passengers a year. There are often more cars than space; as a walk-on passenger or bicyclist, your fare will be much cheaper, and you'll catch the ferry you want. (Cyclists pay slightly more than foot passengers.) Food service is available on almost all routes, beer and wine on some. However, you (and your wallet) will be happier dining at your destination rather than on the way to it.

Those interested in riding ferries from downtown Seattle should go to the Colman Dock at **Pier 52** (Alaskan Way and Marion Street; map:M9). From the main Seattle terminal, there are three ferry choices: a small, speedy walk-on ferry to Vashon Island or to the Navy town of Bremerton (used primarily by commuters), a ½-hour trip to Bainbridge Island on a jumbo ferry, or an hour-long excursion to Bremerton. If sightseeing is your mission, take the latter trip. It's a bit longer, but the scenic ride crosses the Sound and skirts the south end of Bainbridge Island, through narrow Rich Passage into the Kitsap Peninsula's land-enclosed Sinclair Inlet. The ferry to Bainbridge carries passengers across the Sound to the island's

Eagle Harbor. If you'd rather spend more of the day exploring a nearby island than riding a ferry, this is a better destination. (See the Bainbridge Island, Kitsap Peninsula, and Vashon Island sections in this chapter.)

More and more folks are commuting by ferry, so drive-on passengers should arrive early, especially when traveling during peak hours (mornings eastbound, evenings westbound; summer weekends: Fridays and Saturdays westbound, Sundays eastbound).

## BAINBRIDGE ISLAND

Riding a ferry is the best way to catch the sea breeze and Seattle's skyline and to get a feel for the accessibility and grandeur of Puget Sound. There's a ferry leaving roughly every hour from **Pier 52** (foot of Marion Street) to **Bainbridge Island** (see Ferries under Transportation in the Essentials chapter).

You can walk off the ferry and up Winslow Way to explore some interesting shops or stop by **Streamliner Diner** (397 Winslow Way E, 842-8595), whose steamed-up windows beckon you in for brunches of home-fried potatoes and salsa omelets (see Restaurants chapter). A little farther on, imbibers can head for the estimable home branch of **Pegasus Espresso** (131 Parfitt Way SW, 842-3113) for coffee, or the deck of **The Harbour Public House** (231 Parfitt Way, 842-0969) for a beer and British pasties (see Bars, Pubs, and Taverns in the Nightlife chapter).

Bainbridge is at once rural and suburban. One way to get a feel for the charming duality of the island is to take your car and drive to the island's highlights: **Fay Bainbridge State Park** on the island's northeast corner (see Parks and Beaches in the Exploring chapter); **Fort Ward State Park**, a prime spot for a picnic and a walk along the paved waterfront path; **Lynwood Center**, the island's lesser commercial enclave with Bainbridge's only movie theater and two excellent restaurants; the 150-acre **Bloedel Reserve** (be sure to make reservations at least a day in advance, 842-7631; see also Gardens in the Exploring chapter); and **[FREE] Bainbridge Island Winery** (682 State Highway 305, 842-WINE), whose wine grapes are grown in a 7-acre vineyard just a short walk from the ferry terminal (informal tours Sunday at 2pm, tastings Wednesday through Sunday, noon to 5pm).

## HOOD CANAL

This narrow fjord stretches about 60 miles southwesterly from Admiralty Inlet, then changes its mind and swerves northeast for 15 miles to terminate at Belfair. Its eastern shore is almost solidly packed with mansions and modest homes built over the decades as summer retreats by urbanites, drawn by Olympic views and calm, swimmable waters. The west shore (paralleled by Highway 101) still has long stretches of forested slopes and accessible beaches. Three wild rivers plunge down from the Olympics and flow sedately (most of the year) into the canal: the **Duckabush**, the **Hamma Hamma**, and the **Dosewallips**. The big peninsula bracketed by the canal's two arms is largely undeveloped and roadless, with a notable scattering of public parks.

Most of tiny **Seabeck** is taken up by the Seabeck Conference Center, which may be rented by nonprofit groups, (360)830-5010. Just to its west is **Scenic Beach State Park**, with a marvelous beach, campsites, and views of the Olympics. At the tip of the peninsula, overlooking the canal's Big Bend, sprawling **Tahuya State Park** is reached by the Belfair–Tahuya Road, or by Highway 300 which follows the shore. The park embraces beach and forest and is sought out by mountain bikers, hikers, and horseback riders. Much more accessible **Belfair State Park**, 3 miles south of Belfair on Highway 300, is the busiest. Campers must reserve in summer, (360)478-4625. Some swim here, some fish, and some dig clams. For drama in the woods, seek out **Mountaineers' Forest Theater**, on the road to Seabeck; (360)284-6310 for information and reservations.

**Twanoh State Park**, on the eastern arm, is popular with families. It has a big, safe, shallow pool and a fast-food concession. More elevated cuisine is available at **Victoria's** near Union; (360)898-4400. The atmosphere is intimate and cheery, the views are splendid, and the seafood can be exceptional.

The **Union Country Store** (E 5130 Highway 106, (360) 898-2461) offers wonderful carryout entrees (though servings may be heated up on the spot, to be devoured while casing this friendly store). There's a great variety of wines, and an interesting selection of groceries and produce.

The **west arm** of Hood Canal, from Hoodsport to Quilcene, provides access to many recreational areas in **Olympic National Forest and Park** and to a host of canalside diversions. **Potlatch State Park** is a good spot for a picnic or a dip, with plenty of shaded trestle tables and grassy stretches. At low tide oysters may be gathered on the beach. Other public oystering beaches along the west reach of the canal include Cushman Beach, Lilliwaup Recreational Tidelands, Pleasant Harbor State Park, Dosewallips State Park (a choice stop, with 425 acres of meadows, woodlands, and beach), and Seal Rock Campground. Most of these have clam beds, too. Check the state hotline for red tide warning, (800)562-5632. Shucked oysters may be purchased at **Hama Hama Oyster Company**, just before the Hamma Hamma River, (360)877-5811; **Triton Cove Oyster Farms** near Brinnon, (360)796-4360; and **Coast Oyster Company**, at the end of Linger Longer Road in Quilcene, (360)765-3474. Call ahead to make sure they're open.

**Hoodsport Winery**, about a mile south of its namesake town, will match its wine to your oysters, (360)877-9894. The tasting room looks right out over the canal, and the tastable selections include a cabernet sauvignon, several white varietals, and some half-dozen fruit wines.

**Hoodsport**, the largest town on the canal, is a good place to stop to investigate hikes into the Olympics. The Hoodsport Ranger Station, just off Lake Cushman Drive, has informational trail fact sheets, complete with maps, for short hikes or serious backpack trips. Drive up to **Lake Cushman**, a man-made lake created when a wide stretch of the Skokomish River was dammed in the 1920s to provide power for Tacoma. Drive past all the development along the shore to the end of the lake where Olympic National Park begins and there's a ranger station, campground, picnicking, and trailheads. A short walk along the Staircase Rapids trail beside the crystal-clear Skokomish is a pleasure for both novice and veteran hikers.

In rhody season the **Whitney Gardens** in Brinnon are blindingly beautiful, but a walk through the 6.8-acre gardens is delightful anytime, with azaleas, magnolias, evergreens and maples—brilliant in fall. There's a small fee. The gardens are open every day, except in December and January when it's by appointment only, (360) 796-4411.

Tuesday nights at **Halfway House** in Brinnon (55 miles from the Bainbridge Island ferry, (360) 796-4715), chef Joseph Day puts on an impressively orchestrated dinner, starting with champagne and continuing through seven courses, with appropriate wines (reservations required). The rest of the week, the restaurant serves very good meals (breakfast, lunch, and dinner) that are less of a splurge.

Five miles south of Quilcene, undiscernible from Highway 101, is one of the canal area's most sensational viewpoints: 2,750-foot **Mount Walker**, accessed by a 5-mile dirt road (summer only) that snakes around the mountain to a topside view of Seattle, Mount Rainier, the Cascades, and the Olympics. Bring a picnic. You can hike the 2-mile trail to the top if you prefer. Near the Mount Walker turnoff from Highway 101, the **Walker Mountain Trading Post** crams into a onetime pioneer home a variety of antiques, crafts, and locally made jewelry. Comestibles, too.

On the west side of Highway 101, north of the turnoff to Mount Walker, **Falls View Campground** is a short hike from a lovely waterfall. For sustenance, stop at the substantial **Timber House**, which specializes in local seafood and prime rib. Open for lunch and dinner, (360) 765-3339. A good place to grab a bite and buy some fresh seafood is **Hood Canal Seafood Marketplace and Brager's Barnacle Seafood & Chowder Bar**, 294963 Highway 101, (360) 765-4880. Enjoy soup, a sandwich, and coffee on the glassed-in porch.

**Quilcene** has the world's largest oyster hatchery and, in its bay, what's said to be the purest salt water in the West. Quilcene Ranger Station, just south of town, can help with advice on nearby hiking and shellfishing. Quilcene's venerable **Whistling Oyster Tavern** is where the sociable locals hang out. North of town, the **Olympic Music Festival** holds forth at 2pm, Saturdays and Sundays, June through Labor Day in a turn-of-the-century barn turned concert hall. Listeners sit inside on hay bales or church pews, or outside on the grass. Picnics may be assembled from the well-stocked deli on the premises. The music is sublime, performed by the Philadelphia String Quartet with guest artists from around the world, (360)527-8839.

## KITSAP PENINSULA

The 3-mile-wide sliver of land between Allyn and Hood Canal connects the Kitsap Peninsula to the larger Olympic Peninsula, with which it shares some insular qualities. The Kitsap Peninsula is a place of rolling, timbered mountains and long, wild, shorelines dotted with small towns and waterfront parks. It's surrounded by a trio of awesome military complexes that keep its economy perking: Puget Sound Naval Shipyard in Bremerton, the Naval Undersea Warfare Center in Keyport, and Bangor Naval Submarine Base. The Kitsap Peninsula has 236 miles of shoreline, and all its towns are on the water.

**Port Gamble** still looks like a company town; unfortunately, the company has left. The Pope & Talbot mill—long touted as North America's oldest continually operating lumber mill—has closed. But the town, a National Historic Site, remains, and the drive along its maple-shaded streets lined with immaculate, authentic Victorian-era homes continues to provide visual enchantment.

In the gem of a historical museum, relive Port Gamble's timber-nurtured past and see re-creations of a ship's cabin, a sawdusty mill room, the lushly decorated lobby of the late Hotel Puget, and an Indian longhouse. Sound effects add to the illusions. Open daily, 10am to 4pm, Memorial Day through Labor Day; closed in winter, (360)297-3341. The **Port Gamble General Store** (360)297-2623), just above the museum, is the place to stop for a galvanized washtub, a kerosene lantern, a sandwich, or a mile-high ice cream cone. Picnic tables on the town's grassy slopes command fine views of the old mill and the water.

**Hansville** still draws fishermen, though fishing has declined. Now they may drive up to Buck Lake for trout and bass instead of launching boats for salmon. And Hansville is a wonderful family destination, with long beaches and the lighthouse at the end of the sandy spit still flashing and available for tours. (Call for information, (360)638-2261.)

A drive along Twin Spits Road leads to the very tip of the Kitsap Peninsula, Foulweather Bluff. It takes some doing to find the Nature Conservancy's **Foulweather Bluff Preserve**.

Drive 3 miles west from Hansville on Twin Spits Road; just before the Skunk Bay Road intersection, watch on the left for an inconspicuous sign on a tree (it's the trail that's flanked by two big alders); when you arrive at a sign with the rules of the preserve (no clam digging, pets, smoking, fires, vehicles, bikes, or horses), you know you're on the right track. The trail wanders through groves of alder and cedar and leads to a marsh, separated from Hood Canal by a natural sand berm. This 93-acre preserve—a rare combination of four habitats: forest, marsh, beach, and sea—is an important nesting area and has something for every nature enthusiast. The preserve closes at dusk.

**Kitsap Memorial State Park**, 3 miles south of Hood Canal Floating Bridge, is well stocked with seesaws and slides, ballfields, picnic tables, restrooms, camping spots, and views of Hood Canal. **Thomas Kemper Brewery**, north of Highway 305, offers tours, tastings, and a simple lunch; 22381 Foss Road NE, (360)697-1446.

In **Poulsbo** (Norwegian as pickled herring and proud of it), **Sluys Bakery** is usually thronged with enthusiasts of its high-cholesterol Nordic pastries and dense, healthful breads. Buy a latte and wander out to browse the shops, such as **Boehm's Chocolates** (18864 Front Street NE, (360)697-3318), and at the same address, **Cargo Hold**, (360)697-1424, a hoard of nautical wares. Like everything in Poulsbo, the waterfront is tidy, compact, and visitor-friendly. Liberty Bay Park is nicely landscaped and generously furnished with picnic tables, restrooms, and big rocks for kids to scramble over. **[FREE]** The **Marine Science Center** (215 Third Avenue S, (360)779-5549) offers youngsters a good chance to shake fingers with a sea cucumber.

Poulsbo has several inviting places to eat, such as **Judith's Tearooms and Rose Cafe** (18820 Front Street NE, (360)697-3449) for good homemade food and delicious sandwiches; or **Gazebo Cafe** (18830 Front Street, (360)697-1447), where you can enjoy a bowl of soup perched on a stool at the open-air counter. Out of town, **Molly Ward's Gardens** (27462 Big Valley Road, (360)779-4471) serves breakfast, lunch, and weekend dinners. The chef makes wise use of produce and herbs from the organic gardens.

The handsome **Suquamish Museum and Tribal Center**, off Highway 305 just west of Agate Pass Bridge, evokes a vanished way of life with a haunting video, *Come Forth Laughing: Voices of the Suquamish People*. School tours are welcome and groups may arrange for salmon feasts, (360)598-3311. Nearby are **Chief Sealth's grave** and **Old Man House State Park**, site of a long-gone Suquamish longhouse. The park has a sandy beach, picnic tables, and an informational display. East across Agate Pass Bridge is **Bainbridge Island**, a pastoral bedroom community for Seattle with a small downtown shopping and cultural center. A ferry from Seattle to Bainbridge departs roughly every hour. Call 464-6400 for schedule. (See Bainbridge Island in this chapter.)

**Silverdale** is noted for the huge Kitsap Mall and the many shopping complexes it has spawned. But make your way through the commercial clutter down to Old Towne Silverdale, which has seen little need to change with the times. It is graced by a peaceful waterfront park at the end of Washington Street, with a rocky beach, a children's play area, and a capacious picnic shelter, among other amenities. Stop in at the **Waterfront Park Bakery & Cafe** (3472 Byron, across from the Old Town Pub; (360)698-2991) for lunch, to be eaten in the tiny cafe or taken to the park. Enchanting **Silver Bay Herb Farm** (9151 Tracyton Boulevard; (360)692-1340) offers views of the Olympics and more than 100 varieties of herbs in its gardens, as well as kindred items in its gift shop. The **Kitsap County Historical Museum**, housed in cramped quarters in Old Towne Silverdale (3343 N Byron Street; (360)692-1949), has plans to move to the former SeaFirst Bank Building on Fourth Street in Bremerton. See the model of the new facility in the current museum and watch a slide show of area history. Open Tuesday through Saturday.

Silverdale probably has more fast-food eateries per square mile than any other place on the peninsula, but there's hope for the serious foodie. Visit **Bahn Thai** (98881 Mickleberry Road, (360)698-3663) for a wide variety of the brightly flavored dishes of Thailand; or **Hakata** (10876 Myhre Place, #108, (360)698-0929), where chef Yoshiyuki Sugimoto offers sushi with a difference. Excellent seafood is found at **Yacht Club Broiler**, on the water at 9226 Bayshore Drive, (360)698-1601.

Nearby **Bangor Naval Submarine Base** occupies 7,000 securely fenced acres on the west shore of the peninsula. Bangor is homeport for the huge Trident submarines, each one as long as the Space Needle is tall. Tours are available on a limited, prescheduled basis (no drop-ins, all applicants are screened). For tour information, call the base, (360)396-6111.

**Bremerton**—a hundred-year-old naval city, with its ghostly mothballed fleet in the harbor, its retail core that thrives or fades as ships come or go—has taken some giant steps to upgrade the tourist area along Sinclair Inlet. The waterfront now boasts Overwater Park, with its concrete promenade, just north of the ferry terminal. The promenade leads to the destroyer *USS Turner Joy*, which still claims fame for its role in the Gulf of Tonkin off Vietnam. The ship is open for self-guided tours, from fantail to fo'c'sle; daily in summer, Thursday through Sunday in winter; (360)792-2457. The star of the harbor from 1955 to 1984, the battleship *Missouri*, site of the Japanese surrender in 1945, has returned to Bremerton, and the Navy is slated to decide the fate of her future homeport status (among San Francisco, Honolulu, and Bremerton). Meantime, the historic dreadnought is impressively visible, all 887 feet of her, from shore or from the *Admiral Jack*, which tours the harbor hourly, daily in summer and on weekends in winter; call Kitsap Harbor Tours, (360)377-8924. The **Bremerton Naval Museum** (near the ferry terminal at 130 Washington, (360)479-7447), with its nautical displays recalling swashbuckling days of sail and its minutely detailed ship models—including the 15-foot-long aircraft carrier *Admiral Nimitz*—fascinates landlubbers and retired seafarers alike. Open daily in summer, closed Mondays in winter, 10am to 5pm.

The **Amy Burnett Fine Art Gallery**, a couple of blocks up from the waterfront (412 Pacific Avenue, (360)373-3187), displays Burnett's and other contemporary and Northwest Coast artists' works in spacious, well-lit galleries. The adjoining frame shop–cum–wine shop is open for wine tasting every Saturday afternoon. Bremerton's **Kitsap Harbor Tours**, (360)377-8924, depart the Bremerton Boardwalk, and include a 45-minute cruise to **Blake Island** for a salmon dinner in the longhouse and a stage show by the Tillicum Village Dancers, and summer cruises up the sound to Keyport and Poulsbo. You could take the *Admiral Pete* to Keyport; stop off to visit the splendid **Naval Undersea Museum;** hop on the next boat to Poulsbo; have lunch; and get a boat back to Bremerton—all between 10am and 4pm. The museum (610 Dowell Street, Keyport, (360)396-4148), a few blocks from the boat dock, is free, and displays a remarkable collection of torpedos, submersibles, diving suits, and other mementos of our naval history. You may choose to drive to Keyport via Highway 308 from Highway 3.

▼

**Kitsap Peninsula**

▲

Enjoy a meal at the **Boat Shed** on the water across Manette Bridge; 101 Shore Drive, (360)377-2600. The clam chowder is wonderfully rich and pastas showcase the bounty of local waters. Have a pint of ale on the deck, while scaups and scooters entertain you.

It's some 7 miles by road from Bremerton to **Port Orchard**, but a foot-passenger ferry sails every half-hour between downtown Bremerton and Port Orchard year-round, (360)876-2300. Port Orchard's downtown sports wooden arcades along Bay Street's sidewalks, where cafes, taverns, delis, and antique emporiums flourish and shoppers meander, protected from the rain. Besides enjoying one of the best water-oriented locations on Puget Sound, Port Orchard claims the title of antique capital of the Kitsap Peninsula. You could spend hours in **Olde Central Antique Mall** (801 Bay Street, (360)895-1902). It occupies the former Central Hotel and accommodates some 70 shops. **Sidney Gallery** (202 Sidney Street, (360)876-3693) shows and sells fine art in a restored historic building, two blocks uphill from Bay Street. It's worth a walk up the creaky stairs to the small historical museum—with its life-size reproductions of a 1909 schoolroom and its shirtwaisted teacher and well-scrubbed students—and a period grocery store, with grocer and nostalgia- inspiring shelves of bygone products. All of this is within easy walking distance of the marina and the three-block-long waterfront park, where the **Port Orchard Farmers Market** takes place every Saturday, end of April through October. Wares are displayed under gaily colored canopies, and range from pottery to scones to fresh basil to Hood Canal oysters and clams. The pavilion at the east end of the park doubles as bandstand and picnic shelter. You'll find good Lebanese food at **Hadi's Restaurant**, 818 Bay Street, (360)895-0347. It's all in the best Mediterranean tradition, from hummus and tabbouleh to shish kabobs.

Take a stroll through **Elandan Gardens**, a 5-acre open-air gallery of bonsai and sculpture both man-made and natural (skeletal, fire-blackened driftwood spires and logs). Included in its displays are tiny junipers that were alive when King Alfred reigned. A gallery and gift shop offer choice antiques and bonsai. The gardens are in Gorst, between Port Orchard and Bremerton, just beyond milepost 28 on Highway 16, coming from Port Orchard, (360)373-8260. **Springhouse Dolls & Gifts** (1130 Bethel Avenue, (360)876-0529), a 5-minute drive from downtown Port Orchard, boasts the largest collection of modern dolls in the Northwest. You may take breakfast, lunch, and espresso in its pretty Victorian Rose Tearoom or on the terrace with a calming view of lawn, gardens, and woods. High Tea is served every other Wednesday and Saturday at 3pm, by reservation; but you may sip tea and eat scones at any time (except Sunday, when Springhouse is closed).

**Manchester State Park**, a couple of miles east of Port Orchard on Beach Drive, is a former fort; the huge old torpedo warehouse with its arched windows is now an impressive picnic shelter. There's a short interpretive nature trail and a beach that isn't great for swimming, though it's popular with divers.

## MOUNT RAINIER

Mount Rainier, above all other natural wonders of this region, has garnered through the years the most grandiose adjectives imaginable. Sufficient to say that for Washingtonians, this abiding symbol of natural grandeur serves as landmark, symbol, moody god, and reminder of the geological glory that surrounds them. It seems fitting that Northwesterners feel a certain possessiveness about it.

This healthy reverence for the volcano reaches back into history. Native Americans who once inhabited its subalpine meadows tell of the great goddess Tahoma, who took her child and fled her husband (Mount Baker) in a jealous rage, but stretched her neck and looked back so many times along the way that she grew enormously tall. She finally stopped where she is today, 100 miles southeast of Seattle, and planted a garden around her. Today that "garden" is the 378-square-mile **Mount Rainier National Park** (98 miles southeast of Seattle on Highway 706, (360) 569-2211), a lushly forested reserve with the 14,410-foot-high active volcano as its centerpiece. Her "child" is Little Tahoma, a strikingly pointed peak on Rainier's east side. From Seattle the view of Mount Rainier's peak is often obscured by clouds or haze (the mountain is so large it creates its own weather), so when it appears, it overwhelms the landscape and imparts to Seattleites a renewed sense of the dominance of nature in this region. If you hear Seattleites say "the mountain's out," you'll know what they mean.

There are now **four ways to experience the mountain**: tour it by car, see it by train, hike its flanks, or climb to the summit. By far the favorite choice is to drive the 2½ hours to the National Park (entrance fee, $5). The most popular—and populated—visitors center is the one at **Paradise**, (360) 569-2211) which, at 5,400 feet, features the most complete tourist services, including the circular Jackson Memorial Visitor Center with a 360-degree view of the park, and countrified accommodations (late May to early October) at the **Paradise Inn** (Highway 706, call (360) 569-2275 for reservations). Paradise also features a network of easy-to-moderate hiking trails that wind past waterfalls, massive glaciers, and, in summer, through wildflower-laden meadows. (The road to Paradise is open all winter, when the rest of the park is closed, so you can cross-country ski, snowshoe, or go inner-tubing, but be sure to carry tire chains in case road conditions require them.) The **Sunrise** visitor area, at 6,400 feet, offers another take on the peak, from the northeast side. It's the highest point in the park open to automobiles (though the road's closed when the snow falls, approximately early October through late June). Pack a picnic— the food at both visitors centers is mediocre at best. Diverse naturalist talks are available to enlighten your trip: everything from a 6-mile alpine ecology hike (Paradise) to a 2-mile geologic walk (Sunrise) to a half-hour slide show (Paradise). On the half-mile evening walk, you can watch lights dim on the mountain while senses of sound and smell become more acute. In winter, there's a guided snowshoe tromp from Paradise.

The **Mount Rainier Scenic Railroad** is a good way to view the Mountain (or you could opt to take the dinner train from Elbe for a four-hour round-trip tour), but it never gets as close to Mount Rainier as you'd like; call (360) 569-2588 for reservations (the trains run on a varying seasonal schedule).

Those in search of more tranquil communion with the mountain can choose from 305 miles of trails within the park. The best known of these is the spectacular **Wonderland Trail**,

▼

**Mount Rainier**

▲

which makes a 95-mile circle around the mountain, passing through meadows of wildflowers, across streams, and past glaciers and alpine lakes. Backcountry permits, available at the ranger stations and visitors centers, are required for overnight camping. The park also has several **campgrounds**: at Ohanapecosh, White River, Cougar Rock, Ipsut Creek, and Sunshine Point (the only one open year-round).

Finally, you can climb the mountain. There are two ways to do this: with the concessioned guide service, **Rainier Mountaineering** (summer: Paradise 98397, (360)569-2227; or winter: 201 St. Helens Avenue, Tacoma 98402, (206)627-6242); or in your own party after registering at one of the Mount Rainier National Park ranger stations, (360)569-2211); a fee of $15 per person or $25 for an annual pass is charged. Unless you're qualified to do it on your own—and this is a big, difficult, and dangerous mountain on which lives are lost every year—you certainly should climb with the guide service. In a one-day training session they will teach you everything you need to know to make the climb; all you need is a sound heart. The climb itself takes two days and can be done year round, but the period from late May to mid-September is the best climbing season.

One slightly less wild way to see the area is at **Northwest Trek**, a remarkable natural habitat 60 miles from the east entrance to the mountain (11610 Trek Drive E, Eatonville, (360)832-6116; 55 miles south of Seattle off Route 161). Bison, bighorn sheep, caribou, moose, elk, and deer roam "free" in pastures, peat bogs, ponds, and forests, while human visitors view (and photograph) them from trams. Naturalists narrate the hour-long, 5½-mile trip, which is exciting for both kids and adults. General admission $7.85, reduced rates for children and seniors, kids under 3 are free.

▼

**Olympia**

▲

## OLYMPIA

As the home of the state capitol and three colleges, Olympia is an interesting mix of bureaucrats, lawmakers, students, and professors. You can plan an entire afternoon visit around the capitol campus alone, but be forewarned that much of the town closes up shop over the summer; the best time to venture to this city, 60 miles south of Seattle, is in springtime, when the legislature, the universities, and the businesses are all in full swing.

Most stages of the lawmaking process are open to the public, and a carefully scheduled trip to Olympia can reward visitors with glimpses of debates, demonstrations, speeches, and hearings. The **Legislative Building**, with the fourth tallest dome in the world, is home to the Senate and House of Representatives chambers, as well as the Governor's office. Legislative debates can be critiqued from the fourth-floor visitors galleries. Stop by the **State Capitol Visitor Center** (14th Avenue and Capitol Way, (360)586-3460) for guidance about campus sights. The grounds themselves are beautifully strollable, with their well-manicured lawns, centerpiece sunken garden, and conservatory greenhouse. **[FREE]** Free tours of the Capitol buildings, including the Governor's Mansion, can be arranged by calling (360)586-TOUR. Drop by the **State Capitol Museum** (211 W 21st Avenue, (360)753-2580), a few blocks south of campus, which houses a permanent exhibit including an outstanding collection of Native American baskets and memorabilia from the state's founding and early days of government.

On the town, you'll find a surprising variety of galleries, offbeat shops, cafes, and restaurants. **Dancing Goats Espresso** (124 E Fourth Avenue, (360)754-8187) offers fine espresso, sweet treats, and a mellow and slightly upscale atmosphere. For all your herbal needs, check out environmentally friendly **Radiance** (113 E Fifth Avenue, (360)357-5250), with its entire wall of herbs, teas, and spices, a book section, and a variety of health products, gifts, and cards. The staff also take appointments for in-house massage and Jacuzzi sessions.

Meanwhile, some of the best coffee you'll find anywhere brews a block away. **Batdorf and Bronson Coffee Roasters** (513 S Capitol Way, (360)786-6717) have a large following of folks who don't care if there *is* a Starbucks across the street. A large blackboard artfully lists all their coffees, teas, and espresso drinks, and the smell of beans roasting just a few feet away is enough to make any coffee lover swoon.

Take your latte up the block to **Sylvester Park**, a quiet spot nestled between the rushed paces of downtown and the capitol. Once the legislative and college sessions get rolling, this otherwise peaceful lawn with gazebo becomes a choice venue for outdoor concerts, rallies, and demonstrations. Across the street is the classy and wholesome **Urban Onion** in the old Olympian Hotel (116 E Legion Way, (360)943-9242). Their most famous creation, the Haystack—sprouts, tomatoes, guacamole, olives, and melted cheese piled high on whole-grain bread—draws crowds for lunch and dinner.

The **Washington Center for the Performing Arts** (512 Washington Street SE, (360)753-8586) has brought new life to the downtown. The **Capitol Theatre** (206 E Fifth Avenue, (360)754-5378) is a showcase for locally produced plays, musicals, and Olympia Film Society–sponsored flicks.

Toward the harbor, at the corner of N Capitol Way and W Thurston Street, the lively **Olympia Farmers Market** displays produce, flowers, and crafts from all over the South Sound; open Thursday through Sunday during the growing season. At **Percival Landing** (corner of State and Water Streets), the city's waterfront park, the highlight of 1½ miles of boardwalk is a viewing tower where one can scan the horizon from the harbor to the Capitol dome to the snowy peaks of the Olympic Range.

**The Evergreen State College** (Evergreen Parkway, (360)866-6000), one of the top liberal-arts schools in the country, has a beautiful, woodsy campus including an organic farm and 3,100 feet of beachfront property, and is venue to a wide range of film, music, theater, and dance events throughout the year.

**[FREE]** The area surrounding Olympia is rich in side-trip options. In neighboring Tumwater, the **Olympia Brewing Company** (Schmidt Place and Custer Way, (360)754-5000) offers free tours daily, April through September. The educational **Wolf Haven** (3111 Offut Lake Road, Tenino, (800)GIV-WOLF) lies 8 miles south of Tumwater. This nationally renowned research facility, home to nearly 40 wolves, teaches wolf appreciation and invites the public to join the wolves in a summertime "howl-in" (Friday and Saturday nights, May through September, by reservation only). They operate hourly tours year-round (closed Tuesday). Admission is $5 for adults, $2.50 for kids; prices a bit higher for howl-ins. **[FREE]** In Littlerock, the mysterious **Mima Mounds** cover a 450-acre plot of public land, with a primitive trail and a few information signs. The curious geological features, which average 8 to 10 feet high, are thought by many to have been caused by rapid glacier recession.

Outdoor enthusiasts will be drawn to the **Nisqually National Wildlife Refuge** (100 Brown Farm Road, (360)753-9467), 10 miles north of Olympia. This wetlands sanctuary includes a spectacular 5.7-mile bird-watching hike and opportunities for canoeing and fishing (though you'll have to bring your own canoe). Brush up on bird identification at the small nature center at the boat launch. Southwest of Olympia lies the **Capitol State Forest**, with countless hiking and mountain-biking trails.

## PORT TOWNSEND

Riding high until the 1890s, Port Townsend (located on the northeastern corner of the Olympic Peninsula) fell flat when Union Pacific failed to hook up the town with its transcontinental rail system. Lucky city, for people's energies aimed in other directions, and dozens of Victorian houses and commercial structures were spared. These buildings are the pride of the region and in themselves a reason for a visit. The town's charm can be quickly taken in on a walking tour of Water Street, an agreeable stretch of ornate old brick-and-stone buildings mostly erected about the same time Seattle's Pioneer Square was being rebuilt after the fire of 1889. Notable among the town's **historic mansions** are the Daniel Logan House (Taylor and Lawrence), with an iron roof crest; Bartlett House (end of Polk Street on the bluff), with its famous mansard roof; and the Ann Starrett Mansion (Adams and Clay), with a bed and breakfast in its 1890 Stick-style architecture. Old homes can be toured during the first weekend in May and the third weekend in September.

Buildings open for public tours are the Jefferson County Courthouse (Washington and Jefferson), with its clock tower and fantasy-castle appearance; City Hall (Water and Madison), with a fine museum, a jail, a restored Victorian hearse, and every imaginable whatnot; Rothschild House (Jefferson and Taylor), with an antique rose garden and period rooms with breathtaking views; and the Commanding Officer's House at Fort Worden.

The charm of the town is due in part to its impressive surroundings. Take in the views from **Fort Worden**, a former military post that guards the entrance to Puget Sound. The massive gun mounts on the bluff have been stripped of their iron, but the beautifully situated fort has become a state park, a conference center, the site of the splendid Centrum arts festival, and an unusual place to stay. Another dramatic vista is from **Chetzemoka Park**, at the northeast corner of town, with a charming gazebo, picnic tables, tall Douglas firs, and a grassy slope down to the beach; you can gobble up blackberries here in late summer.

▼

**Port Townsend**

▲

On Water Street, you'll find colorful shops. **Earthenworks** deals in ceramic and graphic arts; **Captain's Gallery** has an amazing selection of pricey kaleidoscopes; **Imprint Book Store** is a superior bookshop, well stocked with classics, best sellers, regional books, and a great selection of contemporary verse; **Phoenix Rising** offers all angles of New Age culture, from self-help and astrology books to crystals and aromatic oils. The best ice cream cone can be had at **Elevated Ice Cream**, the best pastry at **Bread and Roses Bakery**, and the best antiques selection at **Port Townsend Antique Mall** (802 Washington Street), where numerous merchants convene under one roof. For a nip with the natives, head for **Back Alley Tavern** for live music and local color, or the historic **Town Tavern**, where the pool tables, the huge bar, and the owner's great taste in music draw an interesting assortment of people. Finally, check out the retail revitalization of uptown Port Townsend at Lawrence and Tyler, specifically **Aldrich's**, a general store which recently celebrated its 100th anniversary and is now up to date with quality wines, cheeses, and produce, a deli, and a superior meat and seafood market.

Throughout the year Port Townsend holds a number of festivals. **Centrum Summer Arts Festival**, (360)385-3102, presents one of the most successful cultural programs in the state, with dance, fiddle tunes, chamber music, a writers conference, jazz, theater performances, and the celebrated

Marrowstone Music Festival; at Fort Worden from June through September. **The Rhododendron Festival** in May, with a parade and crowning of the queen, is Port Townsend's oldest festival. The **Wooden Boat Festival,** (360)385-3628, second weekend in September, offers a charming bit of creative anachronism.

**Ferries.** Washington State ferries travel between Port Townsend and Keystone on Whidbey Island (464-6400).

## SKAGIT VALLEY

To travelers on I-5 it is little more than a blur, except during the spring when the lush farmlands are brilliantly swathed in daffodils (mid-March to mid-April) and tulips (early to late April). Those who slow down and turn off the concrete artery discover that the pastoral Skagit Valley is a colorful excursion even after the tulips have been cut. The fertile countryside is flat and ideal for bicyclists (except when gridlock occurs during the Tulip Festival in April). U-pickers harvest the local farms, starting with strawberries in June and continuing through raspberries, blueberries, sweet corn, and pumpkins come October.

Mount Vernon is a rare working town: it's really about fresh food and beautiful flowers, products of surrounding Skagit Valley farms. Here's a blue-collar town in which there are more good restaurants and bookstores than taverns and churches. It is the Big City to residents of surrounding Skagit and Island Counties, and a college town to a surprising number of local folk, even though Skagit Valley College is but a small community college on the eastern outskirts of town.

**Little Mountain Park** (take Blackburn east out of Mount Vernon; it's at the top of the hill) has a terrific picnic spot plus a knockout vista of the valley—look for migratory trumpeter swans in February.

Just off I-5, en route to La Conner, you'll pass through the tiny town of Conway, where locals congregate at the classic **Conway Tavern** for their charbroiled burgers and super onion rings; (360)445-4733. Head west about 5 miles to Fir Island and you'll come across **Snow Goose Produce**, an enormous roadside stand (open late-February till mid-October) that is almost worth a day trip in itself. Stop for a fresh waffle cone filled with locally made ice cream ($1.50), a pound or two of just-caught Hood Canal shrimp, an array of local produce, and specialty foods including cheeses, pastas, and fresh rustic breads.

La Conner was founded in 1867 by John Conner, a trading-post operator, who named the town after his wife, L(ouisa) A. Conner. Much of what you see today was originally built before the railroads arrived in the late 1880s, when the fishing and farming communities of Puget Sound traded almost entirely by water. During a later age of conformity and efficiency, the town became a literal backwater and something of a haven for nonconformists (Wobblies, WWII COs, McCarthy-era escapees, beatniks, hippies, and bikers), always with a fair smattering of artists, including Mark Tobey, Morris Graves, and Guy Anderson.

The long-standing "live and let live" attitude of the town has allowed the neighboring Swinomish tribe to contribute to the exceptional cultural richness of La Conner. Even the merchants here have created a unique atmosphere, an American bazaar: **Chez la Zoom, Cottons, Nasty Jacks, the Ginger Grater** and **Intimate Dwellings**. **Cafe Pojante** is the place to go for coffee and a pastry, and **O'Leary's Books** is where locals stop for a read or a chat with owner Sally Cram. Hungry? Try **Hungry Moon Deli** for soup and a sandwich.

**Tillinghast Seed Company**, at the entrance of town, is the oldest operating retail and mail-order seed store in the Northwest (since 1885); it has (in addition to seeds) a wonderful nursery, florist shop, and general store, (360)466-3329. **Go Outside** is a small but choice garden and garden-accessories store, (360)466-4836.

**Gaches Mansion**, on Second Street overlooking the main drag, is a wonderful example of American Victorian architecture, with a widow's walk that looks out on the entire Skagit Valley. It is filled with period furnishings, and a small museum of Northwest art occupies the second floor. Open weekends, (360)466-4288.

▼

**Skagit Valley**

▲

### *SNOQUALMIE VALLEY*

Snoqualmie Valley, a stretch of cow country nestled just this side of the Cascades only 40 minutes or so from Seattle, makes for a great Sunday drive or bike ride. No longer dotted with the sleepy farm hamlets of yesterday—thanks to the eastward ooze of Seattle suburbs—this rural valley still holds a haystack full of charm, complete with U-pick berry farms, roadside stands, and country cafes.

Highway 203 links Duvall, Carnation, and Fall City, then Highway 202 takes over through Snoqualmie and North Bend—both crisscrossed by a web of backroads leading the curious driver to dairy farms, quiet lakes, river beaches, and tree-lined drives. Cyclists should stick to the backroads to avoid weekend traffic. Better yet, mountain bikers, hikers, and horseback-riders can hook up with the **Snoqualmie Valley Trail**, an old railroad connecting Stillwater (between Duvall and Carnation) and Tokul (south of Fall City), then continuing north all the way to the Snohomish County border, and south to Snoqualmie.

Despite commercial growth, **Duvall** has managed to preserve its small-town storefronts, including that of **Duvall Books** (15635 Main Street NE, no phone), with a remarkable range of used books and a fascinating display of old photos and other collectibles. Be sure to visit the delightful **Main Street Gallery** (15611 Main Street NE, 788-9844), an indoor sanctuary of plants, chimes, fountains, sundials, and other garden goodies. **[KIDS]**Autumn visitors should stop at **Game Haven Greenery** (on Carnation Farm Road, 7110 310th Avenue NE, (206)333-4313) to select a jack-o'-lantern from the Two Brothers pumpkin patch.

In **Carnation** itself, a giant cinnamon roll from **The River Run Cafe** (4366 Tolt Avenue, (206)333-6100) is practically mandatory. If it's open (usually 11am to 5pm, but call ahead), visit **Northwest Basketry** (4603 Tolt Avenue, (206)333-6354), where Cathy Iacobazzi (who has been weaving baskets from local and tropical materials for nearly 20 years) sells and displays her creations. **Remlinger Farms** (32610 NE 32nd Street, (206)333-4135 or 451-8740) is one of the biggest and best produce markets around (closed in winter). They sell their own farm-grown fruits and vegetables, as well as baked goods, grains, gift items, and canned and frozen foods. The restaurant in back no longer serves its famous fresh-fruit shakes, but there's still a range of ice cream, pies, cookies, and candy to supplement the lunch menu.

**Tolt River John MacDonald Park** (31020 NE 40th Street, 296-2964), at the confluence of the Tolt and Snoqualmie Rivers, is a fine place for a barbecue in one of the reservable picnic shelters. Throw the Frisbee on the rolling grass, hike the network of trails, bodysurf where the Tolt empties into the Snoqualmie, camp overnight, or watch brave teenagers take the plunge from the Tolt Hill Road Bridge. The perfect end to a day of inner-tubing, fishing, or canoeing on the Snoqualmie is **Small Fryes** (4225 Preston–Fall City Road, (206)222-7688), a great burger stand with specially seasoned french fries and a large range of milk shakes (try the banana or a mocha malt).

**[KIDS][FREE]** **The Herbfarm** (32804 Issaquah–Fall City Road, 784-2222 or (800)866-4372) in Fall City is a destination in its own right as an herbal oasis for gardeners (see Gardens in the Exploring chapter), diners (see Restaurants chapter), children, and browsers. It also offers year-round tours, classes, and workshops.

**[FREE]** **Snoqualmie Falls**, the region's 268-foot-high natural highlight, thunders past diners at the **Salish Lodge** (37807 SE Fall City–Snoqualmie Road, (206)888-2556). Visitors can observe the falls from a cliffside gazebo, or hike to the bottom for a closer look.

**[KIDS]** Railroad artifacts and old engines are on display at the Snoqualmie Depot, where, on weekends from April through October, you can board the **Puget Sound Railway** for a scenic round-trip train tour through the upper Snoqualmie Valley. (Call (206)746-4025 for fares and schedules.)

Across Snoqualmie's main drag, **Isadora's** (8062 Railroad

Avenue SE, (206) 888-1345) is a funky little country collectibles shop with a cozy cafe. Nearby **Northwest Cellars** (8050 Railroad Avenue SE, (206) 888-6176) presents tastings of the Northwest's best wines and microbrews, and packages splendid gift baskets of the Northwest's finest specialty foodstuffs, while **Big Foot Donut Shop and Bakery** (8224 Railroad Avenue SE, 831-2244) is where Sasquatch stops to assuage his beastly sweet tooth. Though the *Twin Peaks* craze in North Bend is a distant memory, you can still get a nice slice of pie at the now famous **Mar-T Cafe** (137 W North Bend Way, (206) 888-1221). Factory-outlet malls seem to be springing up all over the suburban Northwest, including here in North Bend where **Factory Stores of America** (Exit 31 off I-90, (206) 888-4505) claims to offer discounts on items from clothing and books to kitchenware and sporting goods.

## TACOMA AND GIG HARBOR

Tacoma is no longer strictly a blue-collar mill town. Sided by Commencement Bay and the Tacoma Narrows and backed by Mount Rainier, the city is a growing urban center with a thriving cultural core.

Much of the heavy industry that once dominated Tacoma's waterfront has left, although the tideflats are still home to the second-largest port on the West Coast. From the observation deck at the **Port of Tacoma** (E 11th Street), you can watch as dozens of giant mechanical pincers drop like spiders from cranes overhead to pluck cargo from ships shuttling in and out of Commencement Bay throughout the day.

Tacoma has fervently embraced the idea of preservation. Historic buildings in the downtown warehouse district are being converted from industrial use to residential and commercial functions, while some of the old warehouses are slated for a University of Washington branch campus.

The stately homes and cobblestone streets of the north end are often used as sets by Hollywood's moviemakers, and students still fill the turreted chateau of Stadium High School. Old City Hall, with its newly coppered roof, Renaissance clock, and bell tower; the Romanesque First Presbyterian Church; the rococo Pythian Lodge; and the one-of-a-kind coppered Union Station, now the much praised Federal Courthouse, delight history and architecture buffs. The old Union Station rotunda is graced by some spectacular work by glass artist and Tacoma native Dale Chihuly. This common-area exhibit is also an annex of the Tacoma Art Museum, open to the public at no charge during business hours.

**Pantages Center** (901 Broadway Plaza, (206) 5915894) includes the restored 1,100-seat Pantages Theater—originally designed in 1918 by nationally known movie theater architect B. Marcus Priteca—and is now the focal point of the reviving

downtown cultural life with dance, music, and stage presentations. The nearby **Rialto Theatre** has been restored for smaller
performance groups. **Tacoma Actors Guild**, Tacoma's popular professional theater at the Commerce Street level atop the
park-covered transit center, (206)272-2145, offers an ambitious
and successful blend of American classics and Northwest premieres.

   **Tacoma Art Museum** (12th and Pacific, (206)2724258)
is housed in a former downtown bank. The small museum ($3
admission) has paintings by Renoir, Degas, and Pissarro, as
well as a collection of contemporary American prints. [KIDS]
**Tacoma Children's Museum** (925 Court C, (206)627-6031;
$3.25 admission) features hands-on exhibits focusing on sci-
ence and art, and always proves to be an entertaining, educational family outing. The **Washington State Historical
Museum**, (206)593-2830, left its previous home near Stadium
High School in 1996 to reopen just south of Union Station (1911
Pacific Avenue). The new facility has many times the previous
exhibit space and now offers a state-of-the-art museum experience, providing history and innovation under one roof. From
the outside, however, the museum has been carefully designed
to blend into its surroundings and complement the Union Station built in 1911.

   If sightseeing and museum-hopping pique your appetite,
grab a burger and shake at the local favorite, **Frisko Freeze**
(1201 Division, (206)272-6843). For a sit-down meal and a brew,
too, stop by **Engine House No. 9** (611 N Pine, (206)272-
3435), which features an assortment of many of Washington's
best microbrews.

   There's always something going on under the **Tacoma
Dome**, (206)272-3663, the world's largest *wooden* dome, located at the confluence of I-5 and I-705. On the other side of
town, the Tacoma Narrows Bridge connects the city to the Kitsap Peninsula via State Route 16. The 188-foot-high and 2,800-
foot-long bridge is the fourth-longest suspension bridge in the
United States. (Directly below, sitting on the bottom of the
Tacoma Narrows, is the old bridge—nicknamed "Galloping
Gertie" because it rippled and swayed in high winds—that collapsed in 1940. The remains of the bridge were recently designated on the National Registry of Historic Sites to ensure that
no one disturbs the structure in its watery grave.)

   **Point Defiance Park** (entrance at Pearl and N 51st) is situated at the west side of Tacoma, with 500 acres of untouched
forest jutting into Puget Sound. Aside from its many other attractions, this park is one of the most dramatically sited and
creatively planned city parks in the country. The wooded 5-
mile drive and hiking trails open up now and then for sweeping views of the water, Vashon Island, Gig Harbor, and
the Olympic Mountains beyond. There are gardens: rose,

rhododendron, Japanese, and Northwest native plants; a railroad village with a working steam engine; a reconstruction of Fort Nisqually (originally built in 1833); a museum; a swimming beach; and the much acclaimed zoo/aquarium. Watching from an underwater vantage point as seals, sea lions, and the white beluga whale almost continuously play is a rare treat, (206)591-5335. Afterward, head to **Antique Sandwich Company** (5102 N Pearl St, (206)752-4069), two blocks south of the main entrance to Point Defiance Park, where fresh-fruit milk shakes and peanut-butter-and-jelly sandwiches with bananas tempt the kids, while homemade soups, quiches, and a variety of sandwiches will surely suit the grown-ups.

For something off the beaten path, check out **Brown's Point** (Hyada Boulevard) across Commencement Bay for a great view of the city. A working lighthouse still guides ships around the point. No doubt you'll get a close view of tugs and tankers as they slip through the relatively narrow passage between Vashon Island and Brown's Point toward the Port of Tacoma.

Take a drive just south of Tacoma to **Steilacoom**, once an Indian village and later Washington Territory's first incorporated town (1854). Steilacoom today is a quiet village of old trees and houses, with no vestige of its heyday, when a trolley line ran from Bair's Drugstore to Tacoma. October's **Apple Squeeze Festival** and midsummer's **Salmon Bake**, with canoe and kayak races, are popular drawing cards. **Steilacoom Tribal Museum** is located in a turn-of-the-century church looking out upon the South Sound islands and the Olympic range. Ferries run to Anderson Island, with restricted runs to McNeil Island (a state penitentiary); call Pierce County Public Works Department for more information, (206)591-7250.

Just across the Tacoma Narrows is **Gig Harbor**. Once an almost undisturbed fishing village (and still homeport for an active commercial fleet), it's now part suburbia, part weekend destination. Boating is still important here, with good anchorage and various moorage docks attracting gunwale-to-gunwale pleasure craft. When the clouds break, Mount Rainier holds court for all.

A variety of interesting shops and galleries line Harborview Drive, the single street that almost encircles the harbor. It's a most picturesque spot for browsing and window-shopping.

Gig Harbor was planned for boat traffic, not automobiles (with resulting traffic congestion and limited parking), yet it is still a good place for celebrations. An arts festival in mid-July and a jazz festival in mid-August are two main events. May through October (on Saturdays), **Gig Harbor Farmers Market** features locally grown produce, flowers, plants, and Northwest arts and crafts (Pierce Transit Park and Ride, off Highway 16, (206)884-2665).

Nearby, **Kopachuck State Park** is a popular destination, as are **Penrose Point** and **RFK State Parks** on the Key Peninsula, all with numerous beaches for clam digging. (Purdy Spit and Maple Hollow Park are the most accessible spots.) At **Minter Creek State Hatchery**, the public can observe the different developmental stages of millions of salmon of various species. About 15 minutes from downtown Gig Harbor, the recently rebuilt facilities are open to the public every day, or for group visits by special arrangement. Call (206)857-5077 for directions or information.

**Performance Circle** (6615 38th Avenue NW, (206)851-7529), Gig Harbor's resident theater group, mounts eight enjoyable productions each year, with summer shows staged outside in the meadow at 9916 Peacock Hill Avenue NW. Theatergoers bring picnics and blankets, and watch the shows beneath the stars.

Stop by the **Tides Tavern** (2925 Harborview Drive, (206)858-3982), perched over the harbor, for a game of pool, a charbroiled burger, and a beer on the deck when the weather complies; or take the whole family to **Marco's Ristorante Italiano** (7707 Pioneer Way, (206)858-2899), which bustles at lunch and dinner with Italian specialties.

## VASHON ISLAND

[KIDS] This bucolic, faintly countercultural isle is a perfect example of an idyllic Washington community: not enough civilization to detract from the main attractions—the serene countryside, the Rainier-to-Baker views—but just enough to make it a rather pleasing day trip. Vashon is a short ferry ride from either Seattle, Fauntleroy, or Tacoma (the passenger-only ferry leaves from Seattle and the car ferry from Fauntleroy, just south of West Seattle; call (800)843-3779 for schedule info). It's a wonderful island for exploring by bicycle, though the first long hill up from the ferry dock is a killer. Bring your own bike, since there's nowhere on the island to rent one.

Few beaches are open to the public, but **Dockton County Park** (Stuckey Road and SW 260th Street) on Maury Island makes one nice pausing spot. There's a lonely beach at **Point Robinson** (SW 243rd Place and Skalberg Road) presided over by a Coast Guard–maintained lighthouse that dates from 1915 and looped by a beach trail. Hikers should hit the forest trail at **Jensen Point Park** (at the tip of an almost-islet east of Burton).

[KIDS] You could spend an entire day just visiting all the island-based companies that market their goods both locally and nationally. Some of these offer tours (call ahead to make arrangements): **Seattle's Best Coffee** (known as SBC), Island Highway, (206)463-3932; **Maury Island Farms**, with berries and preserves, at 99th and 204th on Island Highway, (206)463-9659. **Wax Orchards**, on 131st SW north of 232nd, is no longer open for tours, but you can stop by and pick up fresh preserves, fruit syrups, and apple cider, (206)463-9735.

Many of these island products are available at **The Country Store and Farm** (20211 Vashon Highway SW, south of Vashon Center, (206)463-3655), a wonderful, old-fashioned general store that also stocks potted herbs, gardening supplies, and natural-fiber apparel. Across the street is **Sound Food Restaurant** (20312 Vashon Highway SW at SW 204th Street, (206)463-3565), a mellow, wood-floored place with healthy soups, salads, sandwiches, and aromatic home-baked goods. Good espresso, too.

Stop by **Blue Heron Art Center** (19704 Vashon Highway SW, (206)463-5131), an art gallery displaying rotational exhibits that is also home to **Vashon Allied Arts**, offering live arts events—from literary, to dance, to folk music, to plays—on weekends from September through June (and sometimes in the summer). Wider recognition and help from grants are bringing better-known artists to the island. Kids' programs, classes, and works-in-progress are also found here. The new **Heron's Nest Gallery** in the center of town now houses the Blue Heron's former crafts gallery, featuring the crafts of many local artisans.

Vashon's biggest affair is the **Strawberry Festival** in mid-July, when a parade, music, and crafts celebrate the island's prolific berry. Some farms on Vashon have U-pick strawberries and raspberries, in case you miss the big day, and foragers will be pleased to note that wild raspberries abound, roadside and elsewhere in late summer: bring along a bucket.

Dining options on Vashon are more varied than you'd imagine, a sign of creeping civilization that even isolationist islanders don't really mind. **Dog Day Cafe and Juice Bar** (Vashon Highway SW and Bank Road SW, (206)463-6404), a streetside cafe dolled up in gothic 1990s, sports tête-à-tête tables, great espresso, and interesting lunch fixings (roasted eggplant sandwich with tapanade; chicken sandwich with chutney and apples; a chapati roll with black beans, brown rice, and sprouts). Some locals just saunter by for a tall glass of juice, squeezed-to-order. Islanders also favor **Turtle Island Cafe** (9924 SW Bank Road, (206)463-2125), where the menu features an eclectic array of such treats as angel hair pasta tossed with sun-dried tomatoes and roasted garlic, oyster stew with polenta, or a hoisin-roasted chicken. Vashon's most formal dining room is in the **Back Bay Inn** (24007 Vashon Highway SW, (206)463-5355), a renovated turn-of-the-century landmark serving Pacific Northwest cuisine. Four rooms upstairs are available should you be charmed into staying overnight.

Round out your day with a return ferry trip from Vashon's southern terminal at **Tahlequah** (Tahlequah Road, on the south end of the island) to Tacoma's magnificent **Point Defi-**

ance Park (Pearl Street off Highway 16). (See Tacoma and Gig Harbor in this chapter.)

## VICTORIA

Romantic as Victoria may be, with its delightful natural harbor and its panoramas of the Olympic Mountains of Washington State, the provincial capital of British Columbia is less a museum piece nowadays than a tourist mecca. Visitors pour in to gawk at huge sculptured gardens and London-style double-deck buses, to shop for Irish linens and Harris tweeds, to sip afternoon tea and soak up what they believe to be the last light of British imperialism to set on the Western hemisphere. Raves in the travel press have brought a new crop of younger residents to upset Victoria's reputation as a peaceful but dull sanctuary for retiring civil servants from eastern Canada. Restaurants are improving in quality and variety as a result, and no longer are Victoria's streets silent after 10pm.

**Getting There**. A ferry ride can be half the fun of a trip to Victoria. Fares run the gamut from as little as $6.50 to as much as $120 depending on the carrier, the season, your embarkation point, and whether you walk or drive aboard (hint: you won't *need* a car if Victoria is your only destination). Call ahead for definitive rates. The *Victoria Clipper*, a waterjet-propelled catamaran, carries foot passengers only between Seattle and Victoria, leaving four times a day from mid-May to mid-September ($89 round-trip in summer), and once or twice a day (depending on the season) the rest of the year. The good window seats for the 2½-hour voyage are on the upper deck and are filled quickly, so board early; (206)448-5000 from Seattle, (604)382-8100, from BC, or (800)888-2535, outside Seattle or BC. For those intent on an overnight stay, the *Royal Victorian*—the Victoria Line's cushy BC ferry—offers the only car-ferry service (from mid-May to mid-September only) between Seattle and Victoria, leaving Victoria at 7:30am daily for the 4½-hour trip to Seattle, then departing from Seattle at 1pm and arriving in Victoria at 5:30pm. $120 round-trip; (604)480-5544 in Victoria or (206)625-1880 in Seattle.

Other ferry services from Washington to the Victoria area leave from Anacortes (destination Sidney, 27 kilometers north of Victoria), one of the most scenic routes in the Pacific Northwest, (206)464-6400; and from Port Angeles (via the privately run Black Ball ferry), a 1½-hour voyage (year-round) on which cars are allowed but for which no reservations are taken (call a day in advance to find out how long the wait will be), (360)457-4491 for Port Angeles departures or (604)386-2202 for BC.

Ferries from British Columbia depart from Tsawwassen (destination Swartz Bay, 32 kilometers north of Victoria) every hour from 7am to 10pm in summer, following a scenic route through the Gulf Islands; call BC Ferries at (604)386-3431.

▼

**Victoria**

▲

**Air transportation.** The fastest link from Seattle (Lake Union) to Victoria (Inner Harbour) is provided several times daily for about $142 round-trip on Kenmore Air, 486-1257 or (800)543-9595. You can also fly from Vancouver via Air BC, (604)688-5515, or Helijet Airways, (604)273-1414.

**Attractions.** First stop should be **Tourism Victoria**, a well-staffed office dispensing useful information on the sights; 812 Wharf Street, (604)953-2033. Then hop aboard one of Talleyho's horsedrawn carriages for an insightful lesson in the history of the city. Two Belgian draft horses clop along to the cadence of the driver's hour-long, narrated tour (complete with humorous historical anecdotes) starting at the Parliament Building and winding through Beacon Hill Park to the waterfront, then through the residential community of James Bay.

The **Royal British Columbia Museum** is one of the finest of its kind in Canada, offering dramatic dioramas of natural landscapes and full-scale reconstructions of Victorian storefronts. Of particular interest is the Northwest Coast Indian exhibit, rich with spiritual and cultural artifacts. Open every day, Belleville and Government, (604)387-3701. The **Art Gallery of Greater Victoria** houses one of the world's finest collections of Asian art (including the only Shinto shrine in North America), with special historical and contemporary exhibits on display throughout the year. Open every day, 1040 Moss Street, (604)384-4101. **Macpherson Playhouse,** a former Pantages vaudeville house done up with baroque trappings, offers evening entertainment throughout the summer. The box office, (604)386-6121, also has information about plays and concerts at the Royal Theatre and other sites. The free *Monday Magazine* offers the city's best weekly calendar of events.

An extraordinary city park spreading out over 177 acres, **Beacon Hill Park** provides splendid views of the water, but the real interest here is in the landscaping (much of it left wild). [KIDS] Everyone will enjoy **Beacon Hill Children's Farm**, where a $1 donation is a small price to pay to visit this kid-friendly minizoo and its turtle house, aviary, duck pond, chicken yard, and petting corral; closed in winter. **Crystal Garden** is a turn-of-the-century swimming-pool building converted into a glass conservatory with a tropical theme (lush greenery, live flamingos and macaws) and a palm terrace tearoom that is preferable to its counterpart at the Empress. It's a fine place to spend a rainy day; admission is $6.50 for adults. (Open every day, 713 Douglas Street, (604)381-1213.) Just across the street is **Victoria Conference Centre**, linked to the Empress by a beautifully restored conservatory and accommodating as many as 1,500 delegates.

One of Victoria's most impressive sights is not in the city, but 21 kilometers to the north. **Butchart Gardens** is a miracle of modern horticulture, the creation of Jenny Butchart, wife of cement manufacturer Robert Butchart, who made it her life's work (with a small army of helpers) to re-landscape her husband's limestone quarry. Many decades later, the Butchart estate is an international mecca for gardening enthusiasts, with 50 acres of gardens and beautifully manicured displays (lighted after dark). In summer, it's best to go late in the afternoon, after the busloads of tourists have left. Concerts, fireworks (on Saturday nights in July and August), a surprisingly good afternoon tea, and light meals provide diversions. Open every day, (604) 652-5256.

**Craigdarroch Castle** takes you back into an era of unfettered wealth and ostentation. Vancouver Island coal tycoon Robert Dunsmuir built this 19th-century mansion to induce a Scottish wife to live in faraway Victoria. Open every day, 1050 Joan Crescent, (604) 592-5323.

You can visit five of the better restored **Victoria Heritage Homes** (with some seasonal closures; call (604) 387-4697 for information): Helmcken House, behind Thunderbird Park, east of BC Royal Museum; Point Ellice House, at Bay Street and Pleasant Street; Craigflower Manor, 110 Island Highway; Craigflower Schoolhouse (Admirals and Gorge Road West); and Carr House, at Government and Simcoe. Admission to each is $4.

The **Esquimalt and Nanaimo (E & N) Railway** leaves early in the morning from a mock-Victorian station near the Johnson Street bridge and heads up-island to towns with fine resorts. The trip is slow but scenic; no food service.

Victoria offers much for shoppers. British woolens, suits, and toiletries can be found in the area north of the Empress Hotel on Government Street. **Piccadilly Shopper British Woolens** specializes in good-quality women's clothes; **W & J Wilson Clothiers** sells English wool suits and women's clothes; **Sasquatch Trading Company, Ltd.** offers some of the best of the Cowichan sweaters; **E A Morris Tobacconist, Ltd.** carries a very proper, Victorian mix of fine pipes and tobaccos; **Munro's Books**, a monumental 19th-century bank-building-turned-bookstore, has a thoughtful selection; **Murchie's Teas and Coffee** offers the city's best selection of special blends; and don't forget **Roger's Chocolates** and the **English Sweet Shop** for, of course, chocolates, as well as almond brittle, black-currant pastilles, marzipan bars, Pontefract cakes, and more, or **Chocolaterie Bernard Callebaut** for picture-perfect Belgian chocolates.

**Market Square** is a restored 19th-century courtyard surrounded by a jumble of shops, restaurants, and offices on three floors. A few blocks farther on at Fisgard Street is **Chinatown**, marked by the Gate of Harmonious Interest and offering an odd mix of Chinese restaurants and encroached upon by a growing number of upscale boutiques and decidedly non-Chinese coffee bars and bistros. Walk through **Fan Tan Alley**, Canada's narrowest thoroughfare, and stop in at **La Paz Raku Studio Gallery** to see the ceramic work of owner Larry Sims and other local artists. On Fisgard Street, enjoy an espresso at the prettily appointed **Grace Bistro** or an unpretentious Chinese dinner at **Wah Lai Yuen**.

Antique hunters should head east of downtown, up Fort Street to **Antique Row**—block after block of shops, including **David Robinson, Ltd.**, with excellent 18th-century English pieces. Visit **Bastion Square** for sidewalk restaurants, galleries, the **Maritime Museum**, the alleged location of Victoria's old gallows, and a great gardeners' shop called **Dig This**.

## WHIDBEY ISLAND

[KIDS] Seekers of an island idyll needn't travel all the way to the San Juans when **Whidbey Island** is as close as a drive to Mukilteo, 20 miles north of Seattle (see Ferries under Transportation in the Essentials chapter). From there you take a short ferry ride to Clinton on Whidbey Island. Whidbey boasts pretty villages, viewpoint parks, sandy beaches, and some lovely rolling farmland. It makes for a particularly nice family outing, during which you can combine browsing, varied sightseeing, and sun. Whidbey's flat, relatively untrafficked roads make this very long island great for biking.

Ten minutes north of Clinton is **Langley**, where the main drag, First Street, is a browser's paradise of classy shops and galleries and home to the **Clyde Theater**, (360)221-5525, which hosts periodic local theater productions in addition to regularly scheduled films. Swap stories with John Hauser of **Moonraker Books**, (360)221-6962, and for singular shopping, try **The Cottage**, (360)221-4747, for heirloom lace and linens; **Virginia's Antiques**, (360)221-7797, a repository of Asian and American wares; and **Boomerang Books**, (360)221-5404, with selections in all genres. **JB's Ice Creamery and Espresso**, (360)221-3888, is the place for both java and ice cream. **Annie Steffen's**, (360)221-6535, offers fine women's clothing and accessories. The **Star Store**, (360)221-5222, is a genuine mercantile outpost where you'll find a grocery and deli, clothing, gifts, and kitchen gadgets galore. Upstairs, the **Star Bistro**, (360)221-2627, is a deco oasis in quaintsville with an outdoor deck, a snappy menu, and excellent margaritas.

If you're looking to spend the night in the heart of downtown Langley, where better than at Linda Lundgren's tucked-away retreat, the **Garden Path Inn**, (360)221-5121, with two suites handsomely furnished with interior designs that are also on display at her adjoining First Street shop, **Islandesign**. **Cafe Langley**, (360)221-3090, with its Middle Eastern bent, is a busy, garlicky eatery. Join native islanders for a microbrew, along with a burger and fries, at the charmingly dumpy **Dog**

**House Backdoor Restaurant and Tavern**, (360)221-9996. Or take a picnic to **Double Bluff Beach** southwest of Langley—just the place to fly a kite, spot a bald eagle, watch a Puget Sound sunset, or stroll the length of an unspoiled sandy beach. For overnight stays, numerous excellent B&Bs abound. Or you can try for a room at the idyllic **Inn at Langley** (400 First Street, (360)221-3033), which marries a little bit of Northwest ruggedness with Pacific Rim tranquility.

A number of fine galleries line Langley's main street, including the **Artist's Cooperative of Whidbey Island**, (360)221-7675, where 30 island artists and craftspeople sell their wares. **Museo Piccolo Gallery**, (360)221-7737, offers the work of local and regional glass artists as well as rotating exhibits from artists worldwide, while **Hellebore**, (360)221-2067, features glass-art in the making (stop to see glassblowers in action on the premises). Be sure to drive a mile south of town to **Blackfish Studio** (you can't miss it, just look for the huge mural of beluga whales) to see Kathleen Miller's hand-painted silk and wool clothing and enamel jewelry and husband Donald Miller's art photography (5075 Langley Road, (360)221-1274).

About halfway up the island, on the narrowest portion, stop by **Whidbeys Greenbank Farm**, known near and far for its loganberry products. After a short self-guided tour, sample the Loganberry Liqueur or Whidbeys Port. Lots of pretty picnicking spots. And don't miss the two-day **Loganberry Festival** in July, featuring food and crafts booths and entertainment (and a pie-eating contest, of course), (360)678-7700.

**Coupeville**, second-oldest incorporated town in the state, dates back to 1852 when farming commenced on the fertile isle. A fort was built in 1855 after some Indian scares, and part of it, the **Alexander Blockhouse** on Front Street, is open for touring. Amid the growing pressures of development, the town has set itself a strict agenda of historical preservation.

Coupeville's downtown consists of half a dozen souvenir and antique shops and several restaurants. A must-see gallery is the **Jan McGregor Studio**, (360)678-5015, open on weekends throughout the year and every day in summer. McGregor has studied pottery around the world and specialized in rare porcelain techniques. **Toby's 1890 Tavern**, (360)678-4222, is a good spot for burgers, beer, and a game of pool. Homemade breads, pies, soups, and salads make a memorable meal at **Knead & Feed**, (360)678-5431, and you can get a fine cup of coffee at **Great Times Espresso**, (360)678-5358. **Island County Historical Museum**, (360)678-3310, tells the story of Whidbey Island's early history. Annual community events include the **Coupeville Arts & Crafts Festival**, the second weekend in August, and the **Penn Cove Water Festival** in May; for information, (360)678-5434. **All Island Bicycles** (302 N Main, (360)678-3351) sells, rents, and repairs bikes and equipment. An extra bike lane follows Engle Road 3 miles south of Coupeville to **Fort Casey**, a decommissioned fort with splendid gun mounts, beaches, and commanding bluffs. The magnificent bluff and beach at the 17,000-acre **Ebey's Landing** and **Fort Ebey State Park** are good places to explore. The **Keystone Ferry**, connecting Whidbey to Port Townsend, leaves from Admiralty Head, just south of Fort Ebey.

**Oak Harbor**, Whidbey's largest city, is dominated by Whidbey Island Naval Air Station, a big air base for tactical electronic warfare squadrons. For the most part, Oak Harbor is engulfed in new military and retired military folk. An interesting stop is **Lavender Heart**, which manufactures floral gifts on a 122-acre former holly farm. From the Hendersons' gift store, you can peek at the impressive 1,000-square-foot production facility (4233 N DeGraff Road, (360)675-3987). For the kids at heart, visit **Blue Fox Dri-Vin Theatre and Brattland Go-Karts** (1403 Monroe Landing Road, (360)675-5667). Stop for good Mexican food at **Lucy's Mi Casita** (1380 W Pioneer Way, (360)675-4800), then head upstairs to the lounge for a 27-ounce Turbo Godzilla margarita.

**Deception Pass**. The beautiful, treacherous gorge has a lovely, if usually crowded, state park with 2,300 acres of prime camping land, forests, and beach.

# RECREATION

**OUTDOOR SPORTS** *373*

**Bicycling** *373*

**Fishing/Clamming** *376*

**Golfing** *377*

**Hiking** *379*

**Horseback Riding** *381*

**Kayaking/Canoeing** *381*

**Kite Flying** *383*

**Mountain Biking** *383*

**Mountaineering/Climbing** *384*

**River Rafting** *386*

**Rollerskating/Rollerblading** *386*

**Rowing** *387*

**Running** *388*

**Sailing** *389*

**Skiing: Cross-Country** *390*

**Skiing: Downhill** *392*

**Swimming** *394*

**Tennis: Public Courts** *394*

**Windsurfing** *395*

**SPECTATOR SPORTS** *396*

# Recreation

## OUTDOOR SPORTS

### BICYCLING

Despite the large amount of rainfall and fairly hilly terrain, cycling—from cruising to commuting to racing—is all the rage
in and around Seattle. **Cascade Bicycle Club** organizes group
rides nearly every day, ranging from a social pace to strenuous
workouts. Call their hotline (522-BIKE) for listings for the current week and information about upcoming cycling events such
as the legendary **Seattle-to-Portland Classic** (the STP), a
weekend odyssey in which approximately 10 thousand cyclists
pedal from the Kingdome to downtown Portland (usually the
third or fourth weekend in June), as well as the season-open-
ing **Chilly Hilly**. The name says it all about this 36-mile late-
February trek around the rolling terrain of Bainbridge Island.
And for those worried about testosterone-laden individuals
spoiling the pleasant atmosphere of their ride, there is **Womyn
on Wheels** (324-0861), a lesbian cycling club which welcomes
all women on their rides.

[FREE][KIDS] The Seattle Department of Parks and Recreation sponsors monthly **Bicycle Saturdays/Sundays** (the
third Sunday and second Saturday of each month, May through
September except August, when it's the first Saturday) along
Lake Washington Boulevard, which closes to auto traffic. Anyone with a bike is welcome to participate. This great family activity offers a look at the Boulevard as it ought to be: a quiet
promenade (684-7092).

If racing is more your speed, either as spectator or com-
petitor, the calendar is rife with opportunities. From May
through August there's racing every Tuesday night at the

Seattle International Raceway (631-1550) in Kent, and every Thursday evening at Seward Park. Summer weekends mean racing venues in locations throughout the state. Ask at local bicycle shops or pick up a copy of *The Bicycle Paper* or *Sports Etc.* for dates and locales.

The greater Seattle cycling community also boasts a national-quality bike-racing track located just across Lake Washington in Redmond, at Marymoor Park. The **Marymoor Velodrome** is a 400-meter concrete track with sharply banked corners. It was built in 1975 for the 1976 Olympic trials and is now home to twice-weekly races from mid-May to September. On Wednesdays the racing starts at 7pm and features entry-level and developing racers. Friday's action starts at 7:30pm with elite riders traveling from as far away as Oregon and British Columbia to compete in a variety of events. Admission is free on Wednesday and $3 on Friday (free for children under 10). The relaxed outdoor atmosphere, with a view of Mount Rainier on clear days, makes the Velodrome a perfect destination for those with kids or dogs. The **Marymoor Velodrome Association** (389-5825) offers classes which enable all levels of cyclists to get out on the track, improve their handling skills, and learn a little bit about the sport ($35 adults, $10 under 18). Bikes are provided.

Serious racers can also join any of the dozens of racing clubs in the area. Two of the biggest are the **Puget Sound Cycling Club** (523-1822), sponsored by Gregg's Greenlake Cycle, and **Avanti Racing Team** (324-8878).

Following are some of the area's favored rides; the city Engineering Department also publishes a biker's map of Seattle, available at most bike stores. (See also the trails listed under Running and Mountain Biking in this chapter.)

**Alki Strip** This 6-mile West Seattle route from the beach at Alki to Lincoln Park is along a road wide enough for both bikes and cars, and now that motorized cruising has been outlawed here, cycling is safer. Avoid the Alki beach area on sunny Sunday afternoons, when it is crowded and often littered with broken glass. ▪ *Alki Beach Park to Lincoln Park; map:II9–KK9.*

**Bainbridge Island Loop** A pleasant, hilly 30-mile getaway for Seattle cyclists, this signed bike route follows fairly low-traffic roads around the island. This is the approximate route of Chilly Hilly, a February bike ride that officially marks the opening day of Seattle biking. Take your own bike across on the ferry for 50 cents more than the walk-on fee. ▪ *Start on Ferncliff (heading north) at Winslow Ferry Terminal (avoid Highway 305) and work your way counterclockwise around the island (follow the signs).*

**Blue Ridge** The view of Puget Sound and the Olympic Mountains beyond is spectacular on this ride of less than 2 miles. Try making a big loop from Green Lake through the Greenwood district to Carkeek and Golden Gardens Parks, then back by way of the Ballard (Hiram M. Chittenden) Locks. ▪ *Carkeek Park to Golden Gardens Park; map:DD8–DD9.*

### Burke-Gilman Trail [KIDS] It looks like a trail, but in spirit it's

a park that provides a lush corridor of green from Gas Works Park on Lake Union to Kenmore's Logboom Park at the northern tip of Lake Washington. The 12½-mile path is built on an old railway bed and offers a scenic route through the leafy University of Washington, along Lake Washington, and past neighborhood parks such as the family-oriented **Matthews Beach** (map:DD5). It's crowded with cyclists, joggers, walkers, and roller skaters (speed limit, 15mph). Cyclists often continue on to the **Sammamish River Trail**, which connects with the Burke-Gilman after about 1 mile on quiet surface streets, and a crossing of Juanita Drive. You can rent wheels at **The Bicycle Center** (4529 Sand Point Way NE, 523-8300, map:EE6), about 1 mile northwest of UW, just off the trail. ▪ *Gas Works Park to Kenmore Logboom Park; map:FF7–BB5*

### Elliott Bay Bikeway [KIDS] You get a grand view on this brief

ride along Puget Sound. The trail, 1½ miles long, skirts along the waterfront, passes between the Grain Terminal and its loading dock, winds its way through a parking lot of cars right off the ship, and continues to the Elliott Bay Marina. Full of runners and roller bladers at noontime. ▪ *Pier 70 to Elliott Bay Marina; map:HH8–GG8.*

### Lake Washington Boulevard [KIDS] There are great views all

along this serene 5-mile stretch between Madrona and Seward Parks. The road is narrow part of the way, but bicycles do have a posted right-of-way. The southern portion (from Mount Baker Beach southward) has a separate asphalt path, safer for children. On Bicycle Saturdays and Sundays, this latter portion is closed to auto traffic. The in-shape rider can continue south, via S Juneau Street, Seward Park Avenue S, and Rainier Avenue to the Renton Municipal Airport and on around the south end of Lake Washington, then return via the protected bike lane of I-90. This makes for a pretty, 35-mile ride. Take a map with you. ▪ *Madrona Park to Seward Park; map:HH6–KK5.*

### Mercer Island Loop A bicycles-only tunnel leads to the I-90

bridge on the way to Mercer Island (the entrance is off Martin Luther King Jr. Way, through a park of concrete monoliths and artwork by Seattle's Dennis Evans). You'll ride over moderate rolling hills the whole length of this 14-mile loop. The roads are curving and narrow, so avoid rush hour. The most exhilarating portion of the ride is through the wooded S-curves on the eastern side of the island. This is a great route for perusing the varied residential architecture. ▪ *Along E Mercer Way and W Mercer Way; map:II4–KK4.*

**Sammamish River Valley Trail** [KIDS] This very flat, peacefully rural route follows the quietly flowing Sammamish River for 9½ miles. Stop for a picnic at the park-like Chateau Ste. Michelle Winery, just off the trail at NE 145th (bring your own lunch or buy one there). Bike rentals are available at **Sammamish Valley Cycle** (8451 164th Avenue NE, Redmond, 881-8442, map:EE2). ■ *Near Bothell Landing, Bothell to Marymoor Park, Redmond; map:BB3–FF1.*

**Seward Park** Take this paved and traffic-free 2½-mile road around wooded Seward Park, which juts out into Lake Washington. The ride is extremely peaceful and offers a look at what may be the only old-growth forest left on the shores of the lake. Eagles sometimes soar overhead, as a few still nest in the park. ■ *S Juneau St and Lake Washington Blvd S; map:JJ5.*

### FISHING/CLAMMING

Washington is famous for its **salmon fishing**. The salmon's battling cousin, the steelhead—a seagoing trout that spawns in fresh waters and is often mistakenly referred to as a salmon—is avidly pursued as well. In recent years, however, the regulations covering these fish have become byzantine. To begin to unravel them, consult the Washington Department of Fish and Wildlife (600 Capitol Way N, Olympia, (360)902-2267; Regional Office: 16018 Mill Creek Boulevard, Mill Creek, 775-1311) or local tackle shops and guides.

Fishing in Washington State requires a fishing license and a catch-record card for salmon, steelhead, sturgeon, and halibut. You can get a license at most tackle shops and charter-boat companies, as well as at chain stores such as Fred Meyer, Chubby & Tubby, and Big 5. While you're getting your license, pick up a "Sport Fishing Rules" pamphlet to clarify the often confusing rules on tackle, catch limits, boundaries, and closures. Another good resource is the local fishing journal, *Fishing and Hunting News* (624-3845). Although fishing is allowed off all public docks in the area (see Parks and Beaches in the Exploring chapter), certain species of fish can be off-limits.— **Steelhead** season is roughly June through mid-March—but again, consult an authority to be sure. Some of the best rivers for steelhead fishing are the Skykomish, between Monroe and Index; the Skagit, a beautiful stretch of water between Sedro Woolley and Rockport; the Kalama, Green, and Cowlitz Rivers to the south of Seattle; and the Hoh, Soleduck, Bogachiel, and Quillayute Rivers in the rain forest of the Olympic Peninsula. To make the most of your angling trips, hire a local guide (*Fishing and Hunting News* lists licensed guides).

**Salmon** fishing remains popular but is often severely restricted, especially on the coast. Hence coastal charter-boat operators have been promoting—in addition to whale watching—halibut, rockfish, and lingcod as bottom fish alternatives to salmon fishing. Towns from the northern tip of Neah Bay to Ilwaco at the mouth of the Columbia River (where sturgeon fishing has become very popular)—and especially Westport, the biggest fishing draw—are teeming with charter-boat operators who will take you out on the high seas for about $65 to $100 per person. (Reservations—and Dramamine—may be necessary.) Sekiu and Port Angeles on the Strait of Juan de Fuca are also charter hubs. **Charter fishing** operations closer to home include: A Spot Tail Salmon Guide, Shilshole Bay, 283-6680 (pager 918-0707); Sport Fishing of Seattle, Pier 55, Suite 201, 623-6364; Ballard Salmon Charters, 1811 N 95th Street, 789-6202; and All Star Charters, 1724 W Marine View Drive, Everett, (206) 252-4188. You'll also find good salmon fishing on the Skykomish, Snoqualmie, Hoh, Soleduck, and Green Rivers. The rules for freshwater and saltwater salmon fishing vary widely depending on whether lake, river, or sea, so consult the Fish and Wildlife Department for specifics.

**Shellfish** are buried gustatory treasures you can pirate away without ever leaving the shore. [KIDS] Digging for clams and harvesting oysters and mussels are also great family activities. All you need are a small shovel or long-tined rake, a bucket, and a low tide. Seattle's public beaches are open for clamming year-round (butter clams are the big draw), unless pollution alerts are posted. **Alki Beach Park** (Alki Avenue SW, map:II9) is the most popular in-city spot, but the digging is good at public beaches in Edmonds, Mukilteo, Everett, and on Whidbey Island as well. **Clamming** does, however, require a license. (Indeed, everything harvested from or near the water now requires a license—even seaweed.) And be warned: Clamming seasons are sometimes shortened or canceled altogether because of drastic decreases in the clam population, so you should consult the Fish and Wildlife Department before setting off. There is also an ongoing danger of paralytic shellfish poisoning (PSP) caused by a microscopic organism that can turn the ocean water red, thus "red tide." The organism is a tonic for bivalves but highly toxic to humans. Cooking does not reduce the toxicity. To learn which beaches are safe, always call the **Red Tide Hotline**, (800)562-5632), before going shellfishing.

### GOLFING

In addition to a number of fine public golf courses in Seattle and the surrounding area, many in wonderfully scenic surroundings, the region boasts two challenging destination courses: **Port Ludlow Golf Course** (9483 Oak Bay Road, Port Ludlow, (360)437-2222) on the Olympic Peninsula—rated among the best in the country—and **Semiahmoo Golf and Country Club** (8720 Semiahmoo Parkway, Blaine, (360)371-7005), the very popular Arnold Palmer–designed course up north near the Canadian border. Day golfers should call for reservations.

**Bellevue Municipal Golf Course** This course (5,535 yards), the busiest in the state, is fairly level and easy. Eighteen holes, PNGA 66.6. ■ *5500 140th Ave NE, Bellevue; 451-7250; map:FF2.*

**Green Lake Golf Course** Far from a full-fledged golf course (the nine holes run between about 60 and 100 yards), this conveniently located course skirting Green Lake might be just the ticket for beginners, families that putt together, or anyone who doesn't take the sport too seriously. ■ *5701 W Green Lake Way N; 632-2280; map:EE7.*

**Jackson Park Municipal Golf Course** An interesting course over lovely rolling hills, but very crowded. Eighteen holes, 6,592 yards, PNGA 68.2. Jackson Park does, however, have a huge, well-maintained putting green, a nicely secluded chipping green, and a great short nine, which is sparely played. ■ *1000 NE 135th St; 363-4747; map:CC7.*

**Jefferson Park Golf Course** A congenial, conveniently located course in the middle of the city, but very crowded. Has a driving range. Eighteen holes, 6,146 yards, PNGA 67.9. ■ *4101 Beacon Ave S; 762-4513; map:JJ6.*

**Tyee Valley Golf Course** Right at the foot of the Sea-Tac runway, this easy course is perfect for a fast game between planes, but very noisy. Eighteen holes, 5,926 yards, PNGA men: 66.0, women: 70.6. ■ *2401 S 192nd St; 878-3540; map:PP6.*

**West Seattle Municipal Golf Course** A good but forgiving course just over the Duwamish River and tucked into an undulating valley, which makes for some surprising lies. 6,285 yards, PNGA 68.6. Tee times are the easiest to come by in the city, views of which are spectacular on the back nine. ■ *4470 35th Ave SW; 935-5187; map:JJ8.*

About an hour's drive out of the city are a number of fine, challenging courses, each with its own distinctive charms. Among these are the **Snohomish Golf Club** (7806 147th Avenue SE, Snohomish, (360)568-2676 or (800)560-2676), a comfortable but very solid, rural course nestled among the horse farms and towering red cedars northeast of Snohomish; **Northshore** (5 miles west of Federal Way on Highway 18, (206)927-1375 or (800)447-1375), a bracing, salty-air 18 with first-rate practice facilites, restaurant, and pro shop; **Kayak Point** (15711 Marine Drive, Stanwood, (360)652-9676 or (800)562-3094), an exciting, visually dramatic course carved out of dense forest and featuring head-scratching, imaginative holes; and **McCormick Woods** (5155 McCormick Woods Drive SW, Port Orchard, (360)895-0130), a fascinating shotmaker's course, impeccably groomed and laid out over beautiful, sylvan terrain.

The hiking in Washington is superlative. Alpine lakes, rain forests, ocean cliffs, mountain meadows—all are within easy access of Seattle, and day hikers can count on reaching any of a score of trailheads within an hour or two. For this reason, the national parks, state parks, national forests, and wilderness areas nearby are heavily used, but conservation efforts have managed to stay a small step ahead of the abuse. Destinations like **Mount Rainier National Park**, where car campers generally stick to short, low-elevation hikes, offer paved trails for the tenderfoot. Forest Service wilderness staff often practice triage—that is, letting a few popular spots take a pounding while quietly applying their energy and money to preserving more remote areas. Their efforts are supported by a statewide community of hikers, who maintain a strict creed of wilderness ethics.

If you're unfamiliar with the region, a good place to start planning your hikes is at one of the four branches of **REI (Recreational Equipment Inc.)**, which will move its flagship Capitol Hill store into huge new quarters at 222 Yale Avenue N in the fall of 1996, (map:H2). REI has a generous stock of hiking guides and US Geological Survey maps, as well as equipment (see Outdoor Gear in the Shopping chapter). The **U.S. Forest Service/National Parks Service Outdoor Recreation Information Center** (Henry M. Jackson Building, 915 Second Avenue, Suite 442, 220-7450, map:H2) offers trail reports, maps, guidebooks, and weather information. Its staff can also direct you to a ranger station near your destination. The best hiking guides are published by **The Mountaineers** (300 Third Avenue W, 284-6310, map:A9), a venerable and prominent outdoors club whose bookstore—open to the public—has the largest collection of climbing, hiking, mountain biking and paddling books in the Pacific Northwest. A Mountaineers membership gives you access to skills courses, group hikes, and a variety of other membership privileges. Another reliable information tap to the outdoors is the Seattle branch of the **Sierra Club** (8511 15th Avenue NE, 523-2147, map:HH7). The **Washington Trails Association** (1305 Fourth Avenue, Suite 512, 625-1367, map:K6), a nonprofit outreach group, welcomes telephone inquiries about hiking.

As with any other outdoor activity, hiking requires a marriage of caution to the adventurous spirit. One serious hazard is contaminated water. Unless it comes directly from the very source of the spring, any water you drink in the mountains could contain Giardia, a parasite that can cause devastating intestinal problems. Lake water, stream water, and melted snow should be boiled at least 15 minutes or purified with an iodine treatment. Another real danger is hypothermia (loss of body heat). Always bring extra clothing (wool or synthetics like polypropylene, not cotton) and rain gear, even if it's 80 degrees and sunny and you

▼

Outdoor
Sports

*Hiking*

▲

only plan to hike for two hours. Permits may be required for hiking or camping. Check with the local ranger station before setting out.

The following are some popular nearby hiking areas, described broadly by region:

**Central Cascades** The best backpacking near Seattle is in this section of the Cascade Range, one or two hours east of the city off Highway 2 or I-90. The Central Cascades are mainly national forest and include a stretch of the **Alpine Lakes Wilderness**, a scenic marvel. A gorgeous section of the **Pacific Crest Trail** cuts through the wilderness along the mountain ridges. ▪ *Between Snoqualmie Pass and Stevens Pass.*

**Issaquah Alps** The most easily accessible from Seattle, these comely Cascade foothills have dozens of day trails, frequented by both hikers and horses. Every week the **[KIDS]** **Issaquah Alps Trails Club** (PO Box 351, Issaquah 98027, (206) 328-0480) organizes day hikes through the hills, ranging from short and easy to strenuous—a good way to introduce children to hiking. ▪ *20 miles E of Seattle off I-90.*

**North Cascades** The high trails in this area are richly rewarding, reaching glaciers and old lookout shelters, as well as offering majestic panoramas of this magnificent, brooding mountain range. Seekers of solitude will find it here. The alpine flowers are in their glory in early August; the fall colors blaze brightest in early October, with snow following soon after. ▪ *Between Stevens Pass and the Canadian border.*

**Olympic Mountains** Journeying to the Olympics takes a bit longer from Seattle (plan on over two hours to get there via ferries), but is well worth the extra effort. Take your pick of glaciers, waterfalls, mossy rain forests, and alpine lakes similar to the Cascade tarns. Wildlife is abundant—you'll probably spot goats, deer, marmots, grouse, and, if you're lucky, a cougar or a bear. At **Hurricane Ridge** (visitors center: 3002 Mount Angeles Road, Port Angeles 98362, (360) 452-0330), a high point and hiking hub of the range, you'll also spot plenty of tourists. Rainfall is plentiful over the Olympic Range, so go prepared. ▪ *Olympic National Park, Olympic Peninsula.*

**South Cascades** **Mount Rainier**, offering numerous trails, including a wonderful trek around the base of the mountain, is the most popular hiking area here (see Mount Rainier in the Day Trips chapter). The rest of the South Cascades is a stunning contrast to the sections farther north. The rugged, more arid landscapes are in many places reminiscent of Montana or the Southwest. Sadly, logging roads and clearcuts dominate the views, including those on the South Cascades segment of the Pacific Crest Trail. ▪ *Between Snoqualmie Pass and the Oregon border.*

## HORSEBACK RIDING

[KIDS] Stables and outfitters abound on the Eastside and in the Cascade foothills. For weekend or extended trips (camping, exploration, or cattle roundups) on both sides of the Cascades, call **High Country Outfitters** (3020 Issaquah–Pine Lake Road, Suite 554, Issaquah, 392-0111).

**Aqua Barn Ranch** One of the oldest ranches in the area, Aqua Barn (you can swim there too, though, we assume, not with the horses) offers easy, guided rides in the evenings and on weekends through 100 acres of pasture and foothills. The cost is $19.50 an hour, and reservations are required. Anyone over age 8 can ride. For advanced riders, Aqua Barn also offers a two-hour Ridge Ride for $39; children must be 10 years old. ■ *15227 SE Renton–Maple Valley Hwy, Renton; (206) 255-4618; map:OO1.*

**Horse Country** Horse Country offers lessons, horse leasing, picnics, and day camps, and features guided rides ($17.50 an hour; $25 for 1½ hours) up into the Cascades and then down to the Pilchuk River. Kids age 5 and up are welcome, riders over 200 lbs. are not. ■ *8507 Hwy 92, Granite Falls; (360) 691-7509.*

**Tiger Mountain Outfitters** Specializes in three-hour rides to a lookout on Tiger Mountain, often on horse celebrities. (No kidding—many were used on "Northern Exposure" and other TV shows. No autographs, please.) Most of the 10-mile round trip ($40 per person) is along logging roads, and the rest is in dense forest. No tykes under 10. ■ *24508 SE 133rd St, Issaquah; 392-5090.*

## KAYAKING/CANOEING

There are dozens of rivers suitable for kayaks and canoes, with names Walt Whitman would love, like the Skagit, the Nisqually, the Stillaguamish, the Hoh, and the Humptulips. There are also 10,000 or so lakes in the state (in your face, Garrison Keillor). These sports require a good deal of instruction and preparation, so it's best to go with experienced paddlers. One of the oldest kayaking clubs in the nation is the **Washington Kayak Club** (PO Box 24264, Seattle 98124, 433-1983), a safety- and conservation-oriented club that organizes swimming-pool practices, weekend trips, and sea- and whitewater-kayaking lessons in the spring. Dues are $20 per year, with an initiation fee of $15; you must have your own equipment.

Rental outfits are leery of renting whitewater kayaks to the public because of the obvious dangers (and resulting insurance problems); most flat-out won't do it. You may occasionally find a place that will rent you a demo kayak if you've taken a whitewater course or have some proof of your experience.

Around Seattle, several bodies of water provide more

relaxed recreational opportunities for paddling that require little or no experience.

**Duwamish River** [KIDS] From Tukwila (where the Green River becomes the Duwamish) to Boeing Field (map:JJ7–QQ5), this scenic waterway makes for a lovely paddle. Beyond Boeing, you pass industrial salvage ships, commercial shipping lanes, and industrial Harbor Island, until the river empties into Elliott Bay. Rent a canoe or kayak at **Pacific Water Sports** (16055 Pacific Highway S, 246-9385, map:OO6) near Sea-Tac Airport—the staff can direct you to one of several spots along the river where you can launch your craft. The current is strong at times, but not a serious hazard for moderately experienced paddlers.

**Green Lake** Green Lake's tame waters are a good place to learn the basics. The **Green Lake Small Craft Center** (5900 W Green Lake Way N, 684-4074, map:EE7) at the southwest corner of Green Lake offers year-round sailing, rowing, canoeing, and kayaking instruction, and special boating programs. The **Seattle Canoe Club** operates out of here, with canoes and kayaks for members ($70 a year, previous paddling experience and float test required). **Green Lake Boat Rentals** (7351 E Green Lake Drive N, 527-0171), a Parks Department concession on the northeast side of the lake, also rents kayaks, rowboats, paddleboats, canoes, sailboards, and sailboats (open every day, except in bad weather).

**Lake Union** Lake Union offers fine paddling, great city views, and a lot of boat traffic. If you don't mind that, you can rent sea kayaks at **Northwest Outdoor Center** (2100 Westlake Avenue N, 281-9694, map:GG7) for use on Lake Union and beyond, including Lake Washington, Shilshole Bay, and the Arboretum. (NWOC also offers classes and tours to the San Juan Islands and the Olympic Peninsula.)

**Lake Washington** This Brobdingnagian lake has many public launch sites in addition to the **University of Washington Waterfront Activities Center** by the Montlake Cut (see Montlake/Arboretum in this section).

**Montlake/Arboretum** [KIDS] A cruise through the marshlands of the Arboretum (map:G6) is the most popular, yet peaceful, in-city canoe excursion. You can rent a canoe or rowboat at low rates across the Montlake Cut at the **University of Washington Waterfront Activities Center** (543-9433, map:FF6) behind Husky Stadium. Here the mirrored waters are framed by a mosaic of green lily pads accented by white flowers. Closer to shore, vibrant yellow irises push through tall marsh grasses, while ducks cavort under weeping willows. Pack a picnic lunch and wander ashore to the **marsh walk**, a favorite bird-watching stroll that meanders from just below the

Museum of History and Industry to the lawn of Foster Island. Be sure to have the boat back by 8:30pm.

**Puget Sound** Seattle's proximity to the open waters and scenic island coves of Puget Sound makes for ideal sea kayaking. Bainbridge Island's **Eagle Harbor** is a leisurely paddle in protected waters. Tiny **Blake Island**, a state park, is a short trip from Vashon Island, Alki Point, or Fort Ward Park on Bainbridge Island (see Parks and Beaches in the Exploring chapter). Bird-watchers can head for the calm waters of the **Nisqually Flats** Nisqually Delta Wildlife Area and Nisqually National Wildlife Refuge south of Tacoma. And the **San Juan Islands** provide endless paddling opportunities, though the currents can be very strong and unguided kayaking here is generally not for novices.

**Sammamish River** [KIDS] The trip up the gently flowing Sammamish Slough (map:BB5–FF1) is quiet and scenic. Ambitious canoeists can follow the river all the way to Lake Sammamish, about 15 miles to the southeast, passing golf courses, the town of Woodinville, Chateau Ste. Michelle Winery, and Marymoor Park along the way.

### KITE FLYING

[KIDS] In Seattle there are almost as many good places for kite flying as there are parks (see Parks and Beaches in the Exploring chapter). For advice on kite-flying conditions, suggestions on where to find breezy areas, and grand selections of colorful wind vessels, wind socks, and kite parts, visit **Good Winds Kite Shop** (3333 Wallingford Avenue N, 633-4780, map:FF7); **City Kites** (1501 Western Avenue, 622-5349, map:J8); or **Great Winds** (402 Occidental Avenue S, 624-6886, map:P9).

[FREE] Thanks to its windswept location, **Gas Works Park**—and particularly the grassy hill to the west of the Works (check out the sun dial at the top)—is a very popular kite-flying spot, attracting stunt fliers and novices alike. On sunny weekends, the sky above Lake Union is an arabesque of whimsical and colorful Mylar and silk. ▪ *N Northlake Way and Meridian Ave N; map:FF7.*

**Magnuson Park** (Sand Point Way NE and NE 65th St; map:EE5) is another popular kite-flying spot.

### MOUNTAIN BIKING

The booming popularity of mountain biking in the past few years presents something of a dilemma to environmentalists as well as bikers. The very trails that provide an optimum off-road experience—quiet, remote, untouched—are those that often end up closed by the National Forest Service because of the damage caused by increasing numbers of bikers. Your best bet for staying abreast of trail closures is **TRIS** (Trail Users Information System), a computer program (updated weekly in prime outdoor sports months, less often in the winter) providing the latest trail information for mountain bikers, hikers, backpackers, and horseback riders. There are TRIS computers at all REI outposts, as well as at the U.S. Forest Service/National Parks Service Outdoor Recreation Information Center (Henry M. Jackson Federal Building, 915 Second Avenue, Suite 442, 220-7450). It's free. The **Backcountry Bicycle Trails Club** (283-2995) organizes local rides for all levels of experience and is adamant about teaching "soft-riding" techniques which protect trails from the roughing-up that can eventually cause their closure. **Wedgwood Cycle** (523-5572) also leads rides every Sunday.

### MOUNTAINEERING/CLIMBING

Washington offers climbers, from beginning level to advanced, a rugged, unique alpine experience. Indeed, the mountain climber's Chartres Cathedral is the **North Cascades** area, which includes **Mount Baker** (see listing in this section) and other spires such as **Liberty Bell Mountain, Mount Shuksan, Forbidden Peak,** and **Glacier Peak. The Mountaineers** (300 Third Avenue W, 284-6310, map:A9), the largest outdoor club in the region, is a superb resource, offering group climbs, climbing courses, and general information on these and other climbs, both in the Northwest and elsewhere. REI's **Mountain School** is the place to start for an introduction to wilderness climbing. **Swallows' Nest**, with its series of outdoor seminars, is another good resource both for wilderness information and technical instruction. REI and Swallows' Nest rent some climbing equipment, but no ropes or harnesses.

The Northwest is replete with rock slabs and towers that inspire technical climbers to pack their cars with sleeping bags, 40 pounds of climbing hardware, and short-order vittles for a couple days' escape. Two favorites are the cliffs near Index, and Mount Erie just west of Mount Vernon. Farther afield is the climbing smorgasbord of Leavenworth—ranging from the breathtaking granite monolith of Castle Rock to the sunny friction climbs of the Peshastin pinnacles east of town. A somewhat longer drive will transport you to Oregon's rock-jock oasis, Smith Rocks. In this dusty ponderosa landscape, dry canyon walls rise hundreds of feet above a thin, cold stream. Gorgeous. And great for observing mountain climbing at its best.

On the **indoor climbing** front, the Northwest boasts a number of venues, including the two very striking **Vertical Worlds** (formerly known as the Vertical Club). The Redmond location (15036-B NE 95th, Redmond, 881-8826, map:DD2) offers 7,000 square feet of textured climbing surface, while the newer Seattle club (755 N Northlake Way, Suite 100, 632-3031, map:FF7), which moved to Fremont from its original Elliott

Avenue spot in 1995, sports 35-foot-high ceilings and a whopping 11,000 square feet of surface in addition to climbing-specific exercise stations. At either club, beginners, both adults and children, can take introductory climbing classes, and the club will even rent you shoes and chalk. The man-made **University of Washington Climbing Rock** behind Husky Stadium (map:FF6), **Sherman Rock** at Camp Long (5200 35th Avenue SW, 684-7434, map:JJ8), and Wednesday night and Saturday morning open climbs at REI's Lynnwood store (4200 194th Street SW, Lynnwood, 774-1300) are other convenient practice spots. **Marymoor Climbing Structure** (map:FF1) otherwise known as Big Pointy, just south of the Velodrome in Marymoor Park, is a 45-foot, concrete, brick, and mortar "house of cards" designed by the Godfather of rock climbing, Don Robinson, and features climbing angles up to and over 90 degrees. **Orion Expeditions** (4739 Thackeray Place NE, 547-6715, (800)553-7466, map:EE7) offers weeklong camping and climbing trips in Washington and in Joshua Tree National Monument, California's climbing paradise.

The following are some of the major peaks of the Washington Cascades, all volcanoes and all within three hours of Seattle:

**Mount Adams** Mount Rainier's "little brother" is similar to Rainier in terrain, but lower (12,326 feet) and much safer—a good first day-climb. Many people scale Mount Adams as a practice run for Rainier; others, just to ski down. ▪ *Information: Mount Adams Ranger Station; 2455 Hwy 141, Trout Lake, 98650; (509)395-2501; 200 miles SE of Seattle.*

**Mount Baker** Like Rainier, Mount Baker (10,778 feet) offers well-traveled alpine routes as well as rugged, highly challenging ascents, including lengthy rock walls and ice faces. Baker's Coleman Headwall, at 2,500 vertical feet, is the longest ice face in the North Cascades. You can go with your own group, but registration is required at either the Forest Service and Park Service headquarters or the **Glacier Public Service Center** (Box C, Glacier 98244; (360)599-2714). This climb can be completed in one day. Many prefer to climb with **American Alpine Institute** (1515 12th Street, Bellingham 98225; (360)671-1505), which leads moderate to very difficult ascents of Mount Baker. Weekends are extremely crowded on the mountain—as many as 500 climbers could be climbing on any given day. ▪ *North Cascades Forest Service and Park Service Headquarters, 2105 Hwy 20, Sedro Woolley 98284; (360)856-5700; 100 miles NE of Seattle.*

**Mount Rainier** See Mount Rainier in the Day Trips chapter.

**Mount St. Helens** Viewing the devastation wrought by the May 18, 1980, eruption is still the most compelling reason to

▼

Outdoor
Sports

*Moun-
taineering/
Climbing*

▲

visit Mount St. Helens, which now rises to 8,363 feet—more than 1,300 feet shorter than it was the day before the famous blast. The mountain was reopened to climbers in May 1987. Permits are required, and only a limited number are given out each day (free). Most climbers take the Monitor Ridge Route up the south face to the rim of the volcano—a steep upward climb that can take seven hours round-trip. After June, when the snow has disappeared, it's a long, dusty hike. ▪ *Mount St. Helens National Volcanic Monument, 42218 NE Yale Bridge Rd, Amboy 98601; (360)247-5473; 200 miles south of Seattle.*

## RIVER RAFTING

The Pacific Northwest is webbed with rivers, so it's no wonder that rafting has become one of the premier outdoor adventure sports. Rafting companies are sprouting up all over the state, particularly west of the Cascades, and are ready to give you a taste of wild water for $50 to $80 a day. Trips are tailored differently at each company, though there are two basic types: peaceful float trips, often in protected and scenic wildlife areas, and trips through whitewater rapids, which vary in their degree of difficulty. Spring and early summer is the season for whitewater trips. Eagle-watching trips are scheduled between January and March. The following are among the more prominent rafting companies in the area:

▼

**Outdoor Sports**

*Moun- taineering/ Climbing*

▲

**Downstream River Runners** Downstream River Runners leads day trips on 12 Washington and Oregon rivers, including the Green, Grande Ronde, Methow, and Klickitat. The bald eagle float trips down the scenic Skagit in winter (hot homemade soup included) make a great family expedition. ▪ *3130 Hwy 530 NE, Arlington; (800)234-4644.*

**Northern Wilderness River Riders** A trip with the River Riders promises a day full of rapids. They provide everything you need—from wet suits to lunchtime guacamole—and feature trips for every member of the family at every level of experience. In the winter, an 8-mile float trip from Marblemount to Rockport offers a chance to watch squadrons of bald eagles feast on spawned-out salmon. ▪ *PO Box 2887, Woodinville 98072; 448-7238.*

**Orion Expeditions** The veteran guides at Orion Expeditions give lessons and lead rafting trips in Washington, Oregon, Costa Rica, and on the Rio Grande in Texas. ▪ *4739 Thackeray Pl NE; 547-6715; (800)553-7466; map:EE7.*

## ROLLER SKATING/ROLLER BLADING

Roller skaters—and their ubiquitous subset, the in-line skaters—compose an ever-widening wedge of the urban athletic pie. In fair weather, skaters are found anywhere the people-watching is good and the pavement smooth, including the tree-shaded **Burke-Gilman Trail, the downtown waterfront,**

and along **Lake Washington Boulevard**. Farther afield, fine
skating is found on the **Interurban Trail** south out of Renton,
and north on the **Sammamish River Valley Trail** to Redmond's Marymoor Park (see Bicycling and Running sections
in this chapter). Note: Skate-rental shops won't let you out the
door if the pavement is damp.

   **Green Lake** (E Green Lake Way N and W Green Lake
Way N, map:EE7) is the skate-and-be-seen-skating spot in
town, where hotdoggers in bright spandex weave and bob
through cyclists, joggers, racewalkers, and leashed dogs. The
2.8-mile path around the lake is crowded on weekends, but during the week it's a good place to try wheels for the first time.
When the wading pool on the north shore of the lake isn't filled
for kids or commandeered by roller-skating hockey enthusiasts, it makes a good spot to learn to skate backward or to re-
fine your coolest moves. You can rent or buy skates and elbow
and knee pads at **Gregg's Greenlake Cycle** (7007 Woodlawn
Avenue NE, 523-1822). Another urban skating site excellent for
practicing is the grounds of the **National Oceanic and Atmospheric Administration** (7600 Sand Point Way NE, next
to Magnuson Park, map:EE5). The facility can be reached via
the Burke-Gilman Trail, and offers a quiet workout along a
smooth 1-kilometer loop, with one low-grade hill and some exciting turns. NOAA is gracious in sharing its roads, even al-
lowing an informal group-skate every Wednesday evening
around 5pm.

*ROWING*

In a city graced with two major lakes, many people opt to exercise on the water instead of jogging through exhaust fumes
or skating through the crowds at Green Lake. They've discovered an affinity for the sleek, lightweight rowing shells, and relish slicing across the silver-black water of early morning. The
**Seattle Parks and Recreation Department** (684-4075) runs
two rowing facilities: one on Green Lake out of the **Green
Lake Small Crafts Center** (5900 W Green Lake Way N, 684-
4074, map:EE7), and another on Lake Washington through the
**Mount Baker Rowing and Sailing Center**, at Sayers Park
(3800 Lake Washington Boulevard S, 386-1913, map:II6). Both
operate year-around, offer all levels of instruction, host yearly
regattas, and send their top boats to the national championships. (The Green Lake center also rents canoes and kayaks;
Mount Baker does not.) **Moss Bay Rowing Club** (820-1429),
which operates in Kirkland, also oversees a club out of **Yale
Street Landing** on Lake Union (682-2031).

   The **Lake Washington Rowing Club** (PO Box 45117,
Seattle 98145-0117, 547-1583) is an excellent organization for
self-starters. A coach is available three days a week, but the
rest of the time you're on your own. Open to all levels, from

▼
Outdoor
Sports

*Rowing*

▲

beginners to elite rowers training for international competition, with a very reasonable yearly fee. Another club for all skill levels and also with very reasonable fees is the **Falcon Rowing Club** (281-2743), which launches out of the Seattle Pacific University gymnasium (Royal Brougham Pavilion) in Fremont. Numerous other women-only, men-only, or age-specific clubs thrive in the Northwest. For a full list, call Ann Day, regional coordinator, **Northwest Region of U.S. Rowing**, (206)625-9003.

*RUNNING*

Step out just about any door in the area and you're on a good running course. The mild climate and numerous parks make running solo appealing, yet there is also a large, well-organized running community to link up with for company or competition.

Club Northwest's *Northwest Runner* is a good source for information on organized runs, and has a complete road-race schedule. Racers, both casual and serious, can choose from a number of annual races (at least one every weekend in spring and summer). Some of the biggest are the **College Inn Stampede** in July, the **St. Patrick's Day 4-Mile**, the 6.7-mile **Seward-to-Madison Shore Run** in July, the 8-kilometer **Seafair Torchlight Run** through the city streets in August, and the **Seattle Marathon** in November. Outside of Seattle, runners can test their mettle in the 12K **Sound-to-Narrows Run** in Tacoma or Spokane's **Bloomsday Run**, which, with its 50,000 participants, is the world's largest timed road race. One of the finest running outfitters in town, **Super Jock 'N Jill** (7210 E Green Lake Drive N, 522-7711, map:EE7), maintains a racing hotline (524-RUNS).

Listed below are some popular routes for runners (see also Bicycling in this chapter).

**Arboretum** A favorite. You can stay on the winding main drive, Lake Washington Boulevard E, or run along any number of paths that wend through the trees and flowers. (Though the paved Arboretum Drive is an agreeable, hilly jaunt, the park's main unpaved thoroughfare, Azalea Way, is strictly off-limits to joggers.) Lake Washington Boulevard connects with scenic E Interlaken Boulevard at the Japanese Garden. It then winds east and south out of the Arboretum and down to the lake itself. The northern lakeside leg, from Madrona Drive south to Leschi, is popular for its wide sidewalks; farther south, from Mount Baker Park to Seward Park, the sweeping views make it one of the most pleasing runs you will ever experience. ■ *Arboretum Dr E and Lake Washington Blvd E; map:GG6.*

**Green Lake** The 2.8-mile path around the lake has two lanes, one for wheeled traffic, the other for everybody else. On sunny weekends, Green Lake becomes a recreational Grand Central—great for people-watching, but slow going. Early mornings or early evenings, it becomes a lovely idyll, with importuning ducks and geese, mountain views, and quick glimpses of scullers and wind surfers. The path connects with a bikeway along Ravenna Boulevard. A painted line establishes the cycling lane; runners can follow the boulevard's grassy median. ■ *Latona Ave NE and E Green Lake Way N; map:EE7.*

**Kelsey Creek Park** This pretty Eastside park has a main jogging trail with paths that branch off into the wooded hills. ■ *13204 SE 8th Pl, Bellevue; map:II2*

**Kirkland Waterfront** The Eastside's high-visibility running path stretches along the water from Houghton Beach Park to Marina Park—a little over a mile each way. ■ *Along Lake Washington Blvd, Kirkland; map:FF3–EE3.*

**Lincoln Park** Various paths and roads cut through this thickly wooded park overlooking Vashon Island and Puget Sound. ■ *Fauntleroy Way SW and SW Trenton St; map:KK9.*

**Magnolia Bluff–Discovery Park** A striking run in clear weather, this route offers vistas of the Olympic Mountains across Puget Sound. From the Magnolia Bluff parking lot, run 2.1 miles, encountering a few hills along the way, to the other end of Discovery Park. ■ *Along Magnolia Blvd; map:GG9–EE9.*

**Medina–Evergreen Point** A scenic run along nicely maintained roads offers views of Lake Washington and some of the area's most stunning homes. Two and a half miles each way. ■ *Along Overlake Dr and Evergreen Point Rd, Bellevue; map:FF4–HH4.*

**Ravenna Boulevard** Follow this course along the wide, grassy median strip beginning at Green Lake and dip into Ravenna Park's woodsy ravine at 25th Avenue NE, near the boulevard's end. ■ *Green Lake Way N and NE 71st St; map:EE7–EE6.*

**Warren Magnuson Park** Magnuson Park, formerly part of the Naval Air Station at Sand Point, has many congenial running areas, including wide, paved roads and flat, grassy terrain, all overlooking Lake Washington. On clear days, the view of Mount Rainier is superb. ■ *Sand Point Way NE and NE 65th St; map:EE5.*

## SAILING

Seattle has a great deal of water but, in the summer at least, precious little wind. Thus many sailors hereabouts reckon that the *real* sailing season runs from around Labor Day to May 1st; more credulous souls rely on the late afternoon summer winds. The sailing territory in these parts is vast and varied: there is, for instance, the Inside Passage, from Puget Sound to Alaska, taking in the San Juans, the Gulf Islands, Desolation Sound and the myriad ravine-channels between Vancouver Island and the BC mainland, the Queen Charlotte Islands, and beyond, all the way to Ketchikan. For the intrepid, the Pacific Ocean beckons via the Strait of Juan de Fuca and Cape Flattery.

For weekend salts, in addition to the sailing on south Puget Sound, there's some fine sailing in the inner city. We list these below. Some in-city boat renters are cited here as well. For more information, contact *Northwest Yachting*, 789-8116.

**Green Lake** No more than a mile across in any direction, Green Lake is safe, quiet, and free of the hazards of motor cruisers, cigarette boats, floatplanes, and barge traffic. It's a perfect spot to learn to sail, or reacquaint yourself with the art. The **Seattle Sailing Association** is headquartered at the **Green Lake Small Craft Center** (5900 W Green Lake Way N, 684-4074, map:EE7), at the southwest corner of the lake; they'll let you use their boats on Green Lake for a $20 annual membership fee and proof that you know a thing or two about sailing. The association also organizes its own classes and races.

**Lake Union** On Tuesday evenings, when the Duck Dodge race (high silliness) is held, Lake Union is likely to make you pine for the peace and solitude of an I-5 interchange. At other times, what with its fluky wind; banks lined with houseboats, marinas, shipyards, restaurants; and areas that double as airport waterways, Lake Union is no Walden Pond either. The most interesting maritime experience on the lake, with beautiful, vintage rental boats, lessons, and a museum is at **[FREE] The Center for Wooden Boats** (1010 Valley Street, 382-2628, map:D1). **Sailboat Rentals and Yacht Charters** (1301 N Northlake Way, 632-3302, map:GG7) is open year-round and has day-sailers, cruisers, and racers for rent by the hour, day, or week both on Lake Union and Lake Washington.

▼

**Outdoor Sports**

*Sailing*

▲

**Lake Washington** Lake Washington is long, relatively narrow, and acts as a wind funnel, with a breeze nearly always blowing either due north or due south. This means that on a good day you can zip from the top to the bottom (or vice versa) in around three hours; but be warned, you may take the best part of a week to get back. You can launch craft from just about any waterfront park. Sailing lessons are available at **Mount Baker Park** through the Seattle Parks Department's **Mount Baker Rowing and Sailing Center** (3800 Lake Washington Boulevard S, 386-1913, map:II6). For a more extensive course, Kirkland's **Island Sailing Club** at Carillon Point (822-2470, map:EE4) offers 18 hours of instruction on 20-foot sailboats; at the course's end, you'll receive an American Sailing Association (ASA) certification and your own logbook.

*SKIING: CROSS-COUNTRY*

Cross-country enthusiasts can find wonderful skiing in the nearby Cascades, the Hurricane Ridge area of the Olympics, or on the drier snow and gentler slopes in Eastern Washington.

Care must always be taken, however, for this seemingly care-free form of recreation can be perilous. There is constant danger of avalanche in the mountainous backcountry and conditions change daily (sometimes hourly), so before setting out, always call the Forest Service's **Northwest Avalanche Information Hotline** (526-6677).

Most plowed parking areas near trailheads and along state highways require a **Sno-Park Permit**, which costs $20 per vehicle for the winter season. One- and three-day Sno-Park permits are also available. These can be purchased at several local retail outlets such as REI and Swallows' Nest, which also have the necessary topographical maps and compasses to help skiers find their way around unmarked areas.

**Crystal Mountain Resort** Although this area is better known for its downhill runs, cross-country skiers come for the big, broad, open areas of Silver Basin (just off chair 4 to the southwest). The ski patrol here will monitor your whereabouts if you check in and out, and for 50 cents they supply topographical maps of the area. No groomed trails, but there are acres of backcountry beauty around Elizabeth and Miners Lakes. ■ *1 Crystal Mountain Blvd, Crystal Mountain 98022, (360) 663-2265; 76 miles SE of Seattle off Hwy 410.*

**Hurricane Ridge** This crest in the heart of the Olympic Range is enormously popular. The views are spectacular, and there are good treks for all skill levels among the several roads and trails. Ski and snowshoe rental equipment is available from the National Park concessionaires (no sleds for rent), and the visitors center has trail maps. In winter, the Hurricane Ridge Road is open only from 9am to 4pm on weekends and holidays. Snow tires are frequently required. ■ *Olympic National Park, 600 E Park Ave, Port Angeles 98362; (360) 452-4501, ext 230; 17 miles S of Port Angeles on the Olympic Peninsula.*

**Methow Valley** One of the top cross-country spots in the state, the Methow Valley offers the charm of Vermont, the snow conditions of Utah, and the big sky of Montana. Too far from the city for a day trip, its 175 kilometers of groomed trails make for a great weekend getaway. More, the valley towns of Mazama, Winthrop, and Twisp offer an ample number of lodges, guides, lessons, and rental shops. Call Central Reservations, (800) 422-3048, for hut-to-hut skiing or housing/rental reservations. ■ *Methow Valley Sport Trails Association, PO Box 147, Winthrop 98862; (800) 682-5787; 250 miles NE of Seattle off Hwy 20.*

**Mount Baker–Snoqualmie National Forest** The U.S. Forest Service offers a wide variety of marked cross-country trails here, with trailheads clustered along I-90 (Snoqualmie Pass) and Highway 2 (Stevens Pass). The Gold Creek, Cabin Creek and Bandera areas off I-90 are especially good for beginners. For more specifics, check with local outdoor retailers to find when various areas are at their best.

**Mount Rainier National Park** Several marked cross-country trails in the Paradise area (to Narada Falls, Nisqually Vista, and Reflection Lakes) have breathtaking views of the mountain but are hilly and tough for novices. [FREE] Park rangers lead snowshoe walks along the Nisqually Vista Trail from Paradise on winter weekends. They provide the snowshoes ($1 donation suggested), and guide those 10 years and older on two-hour treks. Rentals and instruction are available from Rainier Ski Touring, (360) 569-2412. **Mount Tahoma Scenic Ski Trails Association (MTSSTA)** cuts almost 90 miles of trails through a spectacular area south and west of Mount Rainier National Park. The trail system includes two 8-person overnight huts (in the South District) and one 12-person hut (in the Central District). For more information, call (360) 569-2451.

**Ski Acres Cross-Country Center** [KIDS] At this full-service cross-country center, you can rent equipment, take lessons, go on guided treks, and, with the addition of trails above the Hyak downhill area, have access to 55 kilometers of trails (3 kilometers are lit for night track- skiing). Particularly good for kids and other beginners. ■ *PO Box 134, Snoqualmie Pass 98068; (206) 434-6646; 47 miles E of Seattle off I-90.*

▼

**Outdoor Sports**

*Skiing: Cross-Country*

▲

**Wenatchee National Forest** This area, which encompasses a huge portion of the Cascades east of Seattle, offers good trails, especially in the areas of Lake Kachess (off I-90) and Lake Wenatchee (off Highway 2, with 290 kilometers of trails), and near the alpine town of Leavenworth (also off Highway 2).

*SKIING: DOWNHILL*

They call it "Seattle Cement"—the rain-thickened, heavy snow of Cascade skiing areas. Some say that if you can ski it, you can ski anything. Even so, the weekend parking lots are plenty crowded. And despite the unpredictable weather, you can luck into a perfect day of fresh, light snow. Several of the ski areas on this side of the Cascades have weekend shuttle buses leaving from Seattle. All of the areas offer rentals; prices for a day of skiing vary from $18 to $30 (weekdays and nights are cheaper). If you plan to drive, carry tire chains and a shovel, and inquire ahead about road conditions at (206) 649-4366.

On the eastern side of the Cascades, temperatures are considerably chillier, but the payoff is drier snow. Mission Ridge and White Pass ski resorts are the closest to Seattle. There are other areas at the eastern extremities of the state (including 49 Degrees North, Bluewood, and Mount Spokane). More remote ski areas include British Columbia's Whistler and Blackcomb Mountains, Oregon's Mount Bachelor and Mount

Hood Meadows, and Idaho's Schweitzer Basin. (Note: There is exceptional cross-country skiing at these areas, too.)

The following is a list of the best ski areas in Western Washington. For daily updates on skiing conditions in downhill areas, call the **Cascade Ski Report** (634-0200, winter only).

**Alpental/Ski Acres/Snoqualmie Summit/Hyak** Now consisting of four neighboring sections along I-90, this complex (23 chair lifts and 10 surface lifts) offers many options for skiers of all abilities. Linked by a free shuttle-bus service (three are linked by ski trails) on Friday evenings, weekends, and holidays, these skiing areas all honor the same lift ticket, but each has its own distinct appeal. Alpental, for instance, boasts some high-grade challenges, including the nationally recognized Internationale run. Ski Acres offers intermediate-to-expert runs (try the Triple 60 chair lift to the steepest night skiing around). Snoqualmie Summit's gentler slopes are ideal for children and beginners as well as intermediate-level skiers. And Hyak and Ski Acres, with two lifts and 55 kilometers of cross-country trails, run the gamut of cross-country skiing, from the classic 12.5-kilometer Mount Catherine loop to challenging 1,000-foot-gaining verticals. For up-to-date snow conditions, call 236-1600.
- *Information: 7900 SE 28th St, Suite 200, Mercer Island 98040; 232-8182; 47 miles E of Seattle off I-90.*

**Crystal Mountain Resort** Crystal Mountain is the best (and most diverse) ski resort in the state. On a clear day, the 7,002-foot vantage point at the top of Green Valley affords a tremendous view of Mount Rainier and Mount St. Helens. Ten chair lifts lead to extensive runs, beginner to expert, and there's weekend night skiing all winter long. Call 634-3771 for snow conditions. ■ *1 Crystal Mountain Blvd, Crystal Mountain 98022; (360)663-2265; 76 miles SE of Seattle on Hwy 410.*

**Mount Baker Ski Area** The first to open and the last to close during the ski season, Mount Baker—which gets more snow than any ski area in the U.S. or Canada—is a terrific weekend destination, though most of the lodging is in Glacier, about 17 miles away. Open seven days a week November through February (except for Christmas), Wednesday through Sunday in March, and Friday through Sunday in April. The view is remarkable; the runs varied but mostly intermediate, with one bowl, meadows, trails, and wooded areas. No night skiing. Snow conditions: (360)671-0211. ■ *1017 Iowa St, Bellingham 98226; (360)734-6771; 56 miles E of Bellingham off I-5 on Hwy 542.*

**Stevens Pass** Challenging and interesting terrain makes Stevens Pass a favorite for many skiers, with conditions that tend to be drier than at Crystal. Ten chair lifts lead to a variety of runs, and the Double Diamond and Southern Cross lifts take you to some daunting expert slopes on the back side. For winter conditions, call 634-1645. ■ *PO Box 98, Skykomish 98288; (360) 973-2441; 78 miles NE of Seattle on Hwy 2.*

### SWIMMING

See Parks and Beaches in the Exploring chapter.

### TENNIS: PUBLIC COURTS

Tennis is popular here, but not so much so that it is impossible to get a public court. There is only one indoor public tennis facility in Seattle: **Seattle Tennis Center** (2000 Martin Luther King Jr. Way S, 684-4764, map:II6), with 10 indoor courts and 4 (unlighted) outdoor courts. The rates for the indoor courts are $12 for singles and $16 for doubles for 1¼ hours of play. Purchase of a $25 reservation card entitles you to make reservations up to six days in advance. A similar facility in Bellevue is **Robinswood Tennis Center** (2400 151st Place SE, Bellevue, 455-7690, map:II2), which has four (lighted) outdoor and four indoor courts. The rates for the indoor courts are $13.50 for singles and $18 for doubles for 1½ hours.

▼

**Outdoor Sports**

*Tennis: Public Courts*

▲

Most public outdoor courts in the city are run by the Seattle Parks Department and are available either on a first-come, first-served basis or by reservation. Purchase of a one-year $15 reservation card enables players to make phone reservations up to two weeks in advance (684-4082). Otherwise, reservations must be made in person at the scheduling office of **Seattle Parks and Recreation** (5201 Green Lake Way N, map:EE7). Reservation fees are $3 per 1½ hours, $4 for two hours. If it rains, your money is refunded. Eastside outdoor public courts cannot be reserved in advance. The best time to play is early in the day; in spring and summer, the lineups start at around 3pm.

Here are the best outdoor courts in the area:
**Ballard:** 14th Avenue NW and NW 67th Street (map:EE8)
**Bryant:** 40th Avenue NE and NE 65th Street (map:EE5)
**Grass Lawn Park:** 7031 148th Avenue NE, Redmond (map:EE2)
**Hillaire Park:** 15731 NE 6th Street, Bellevue (map:HH1)
**Homestead Field:** 82nd Avenue SE and SE 40th Street, Mercer Island (map:II4)
**Killarney Glen Park:** 1933 104th Avenue SE, Bellevue (map:HH3)
**Lincoln Park:** Fauntleroy Avenue SW and SW Webster Street (map:KK9)
**Lower Woodland Park:** W Green Lake Way N (map:FF7)
**Luther Burbank Park:** 2040 84th Avenue SE, Mercer Island (map:II4)
**Magnolia Playfield:** 34th Avenue W and W Smith Street (map:GG9)
**Marymoor Park:** 6046 W Lake Sammamish Parkway NE, Redmond (map:FF1)

**Meadowbrook:** 30th Avenue NE and NE 107th Street (map:DD6)
**Montlake Park:** 1618 E Calhoun (map:GG7)
**Norwood Village:** 12309 SE 23rd Place, Bellevue (map:II2)
**Rainier Playfield:** Rainier Avenue S and S Alaska Street (map:JJ5)
**Riverview:** 12th Avenue SW and SW Othello Street (map:KK7)
**Volunteer Park:** 15th Avenue E and E Prospect Street (map:GG6)

## *WINDSURFING*

Definitely not for dilettantes, windsurfing takes athleticism, daring, and a lot of practice. The sport is big in this town, partly because the Northwest helped put it on the world map. The **Columbia River Gorge** (about 200 miles south of Seattle) is the top windsurfing area in the continental United States (second only to Maui in the U.S.), due to the strong winds that always blow in the direction opposite the river's current—ideal conditions for confident wind surfers. Closer to home, the windsurfing can be good on virtually any body of water. Here are some popular nearby locations:

**Green Lake** This is the best place for beginners—the water is warm and the winds are usually gentle. Experts may find it too crowded, but novices will probably appreciate the company. You can take lessons and rent equipment at **Green Lake Boat Rentals** (7351 E Green Lake Drive N, 527-0171) on the northeast side of the lake. ▪ *E Green Lake Dr N and W Green Lake Dr N; map:EE7.*

**Lake Union** Lake Union has fine winds in the summer, but you'll have to dodge sailboats, commercial boats, and seaplanes. You can rent equipment from **Urban Surf** (2100 N Northlake Way, 545-9463, map:FF7) and take your board to **Gas Works Park** (N Northlake Way and Meridian Avenue N, map:FF7), the only public launch area—but the walk from parking lot to shore is farther than at many Lake Washington beaches.

**Lake Washington** Most windsurfers prefer expansive Lake Washington. Head to any waterfront park—most have plenty of parking and rigging space.

**Magnuson Park** (Sand Point Way NE and 65th Avenue NE, map:EE5) is favored for its great winds. At **Mount Baker Park** (Lake Park Drive S and Lake Washington Boulevard S, map:II6), you can take lessons at **Mount Baker Rowing and Sailing Center** (3800 Lake Washington Boulevard S, 386-1913), a public concession.

Choice Eastside beaches include Renton's **Coulon Beach Park** (1201 Lake Washington Boulevard N, Renton, map:MM3), where you can also rent boards and get instruction; **Houghton Beach Park**(NE 59th Street and Lake Washington Boulevard NE, Kirkland, map:FF4), with rentals nearby at **O. O. Denny Park** (NE 124th Street and Holmes Point Drive NE, Juanita, map:DD5).

**Puget Sound** On Puget Sound, which is warmer than Lake Washington in the winter, windsurfers head for **Golden Gardens Park** (north end of Seaview Avenue NW, map:DD9) or **Duwamish Head** at **Alki Beach Park** (Alki Avenue SW, map:II9) in West Seattle. For rentals, and lessons, try one of America's oldest windsurfing dealers: Alpine Hut (2215 15th Avenue W, 284-3575, map:FF8).

## SPECTATOR SPORTS

*See also the Calendar chapter for specific events.*

**Everett AquaSox** [KIDS] Real grass, real fans, real hot dogs—the AquaSox have it all. Watching this Class A rookie league team in the Seattle Mariners' farm system is always worth the drive to Everett (30 miles north of Seattle on I-5, take exit 192 to Memorial Stadium), where the M's brightest future stars begin their careers. The AquaSox attract a loyal cadre of fans, who give equally enthusiastic support to the players and the endless between-innings promotional antics (ranging from a tuxedo-clad unicyclist to a giant, walking hot dog named Frank). Games start at 7pm weekdays, 6pm Saturday and Sunday. Tickets are usually available at the gate (the popular "Chicken Night" sells out very fast, however) or through Ticketmaster outlets or David Ishii, Bookseller (212 First Avenue S, 622-4719, map:O8). Tickets are $5 for adults, $4 for kids 14 and under; reserved seats are a bit more. ■ *39th and Broadway, Everett; (206)258-3673.*

▼

**Outdoor Sports**

*Windsurfing*

▲

**Husky Basketball** Around here, real women play hoops—and they play it very, very well. The University of Washington's young, strong Husky women's basketball team put on a considerably better show than their male counterparts, but both teams are enjoyable and affordable to watch. Both Dawg-teams start play in early November and continue through March (varying nights); tickets are $6 to $12. The Husky-Stanford women's games sell out early every year, so get 'em while they're hot. ■ *Hec Edmundson Pavilion, University of Washington; 543-2200; map:FF6.*

**Husky Football** Beginning in September, the UW's beloved "Bad-to-the-bone Dawgs" play top-drawer football in the 73,000-seat Husky Stadium. Tickets are tough to get, so plan ahead, especially for big games (prices range from $13 to $28); when the Huskies are home, the games are on Saturdays. Be sure to pack rain gear, car pool (just follow the cars with the Husky flags), and wear purple. Also, plan to watch game highlights later on TV, as the lovely lake views from the stadium will likely distract even die-hard fans from some of the gridiron action. ▪ *Husky Stadium, University of Washington; 543-2200; map:FF6.*

**Seattle Mariners** Until the team's foray into the playoffs in 1995, the Mariners' record for the first 18 years of their history was uniformly horrible. Now, who knows? Baseball's finances may force the ballclub to move on to greener pastures. In the meantime, the M's continue to ply their trade in the Kingdome, and teams in the coming seasons will be sure to take them more seriously than in years past. The season lasts from early April through the first week of October (game time is 7:05pm or 7:35pm weeknights, 1:35pm on Sundays and occasional weekdays). Kingdome food has improved, although it's pricey if you're traveling with a pack of hungry kids, so consider packing your own goodies. Tickets are reasonable ($6 to $15), but beware of the far seats under ledges where fans must rely on nearby TV monitors to see much of the action. ▪ *Kingdome; 628-3555; map:Q9.*

**Seattle Seahawks** Time was, Seahawk tickets were as hard to get your hands on as Microsoft stock. A series of bad seasons, though, along with charisma-free owners and a player roster with a rap sheet 100 yards long, have combined to drive fans away in droves. These days, you can walk up to the Kingdome and get a good ticket on the day of the game. Prices range from $19 to $38. The season starts in September (preseason games in August) and runs through December; games are Sundays at 1pm, except for the occasional Monday night game, which starts at 5pm. Best bet is to take a free bus from downtown—parking near the Kingdome is an expensive nightmare. ▪ *Kingdome; 827-9766; map:Q9.*

**Seattle SuperSonics** The Sonics have been an uneven team, and it's hard to tell how they'll perform in a very competitive division, but serious Sonics-watchers say they're on the rise. They tear up the courts from early November to late April, and tickets often sell out early ($20 to $63). Games are at 7pm. ▪ *KeyArena; 281-5850; map:B7.*

**Thunderbirds Hockey** Arguably the best ticket buy in local sports, the Western Hockey League's Seattle Thunderbirds take to the ice in September and play through March—or May if they make the playoffs. No one could mistake these young icemen for the NHL, but what they lack in finesse (and years) they make up for with sheer energy and some of the most vocal, loyal fans in the region. Games are mostly on weekends; tickets are $12. ▪ *KeyArena; 728-9121; map:B7.*

# ESSENTIALS

## TRANSPORTATION *401*

**Airplanes: Seattle-Tacoma International Airport** *401*

**Airplanes: Charter** *403*

**Airplanes: Seaplanes** *403*

**Buses: Metro Transit** *403*

**Buses: Out-of-Town and Charter** *404*

**Ferries** *404*

**Trains** *406*


## KEYS TO THE CITY *406*


## BUSINESS SERVICES *411*

**Computer Rentals** *411*

**Conferences, Meetings, and Receptions** *411*

**Copy Services** *415*

**Messenger and Delivery Services** *416*

**Secretarial Services** *416*

# Essentials

## TRANSPORTATION

### AIRPLANES: SEATTLE-TACOMA INTERNATIONAL AIRPORT

Sea-Tac Airport (map:OO6) is located 13 miles south of Seattle, barely a half-hour freeway ride from downtown. Successful expansion, multimillion-dollar renovations to concourses in the main terminal, and a new, easily accessible parking facility have helped turn Sea-Tac into one of the most convenient major airports in the country. It now serves more than 23 million passengers a year. A high-speed computer-controlled subway system links the main terminal to two adjoining satellite terminals; allow an extra 10 minutes to reach gates in those terminals.

[FREE] **Travelers Aid**, on the ticketing level, offers assistance weekdays from 9:30am to 9:30pm, and weekends from 10am to 6pm. Besides providing free information on getting around town, the organization will escort children, the elderly or infirm, and disabled travelers within the airport. Sea-Tac's **Operation Welcome** sends bilingual staff to meet incoming international flights and help foreign passengers with customs and immigration procedures. Stop by the **airport information desk**, near the baggage claim, for information about ground transportation services. The [KIDS] **airport nursery**, on the ticketing level of the main terminal near the **Northwest Gift Shop**, has space for changing and feeding children (complete with chairs, couches, and cribs), and there are infant changing tables located in both women's and *men's* restrooms throughout the airport.

For exhaustive information on airport services and operating conditions, call the **airport information line** (431-4444) from a touchtone phone. You can choose from a long list of recordings on everything from parking to paging to lost and found. The **Sea-Tac parking complex**, which houses up to 8,000 vehicles, is a short walk from the main terminal through enclosed walkways. Express, short-term metered parking (up to two hours) costs $1 for 20 minutes. Long-term parking costs $12 per day, with no limit on the number of days you may park. Valet parking is available for $15 per day. Major credit cards are accepted. The pedestrian plaza on the third floor of the parking garage offers load-and-unload facilities, and you can even grab an espresso-on-the-go from carts stationed there.

For less expensive **long-term parking**, try the numerous commercial parking lots in the vicinity of the airport. The following operate 24 hours a day and offer free shuttle service for their parking and car-rental patrons: **Budget Rent A Car** (17808 Pacific Highway S, 244-4008), **Thrifty Airport Parking** (20620 Pacific Highway S, 242-7275), **Park Shuttle and Fly** (17600 Pacific Highway S, 433-6767), and **Doug Fox Airport Parking** (2626 S 170th Street, 248-2956).

One of the easiest, least expensive ways of getting to Sea-Tac Airport from downtown, and vice versa, is on the **Gray Line Airport Express** (626-6088). Going to the airport, the shuttle stops at half-hour intervals at the Renaissance Madison Hotel, Holiday Inn Crowne Plaza, Four Seasons Olympic, Hilton, Sheraton, Roosevelt, Warwick, and Westin, in that order, from about 5am until about 11pm. It runs from about 6am to midnight, leaving at half-hour intervals from the north and south ends of the airport baggage area. Additional runs are added in the summer months. The ride is about 50 minutes from the Renaissance Madison to Sea-Tac. Cost is $13 round trip, $7.50 one way. Children (ages 2 to 12) pay $9 round trip, $5.50 one way.

**SuperShuttle** (622-1424 or (800)487-RIDE) provides convenient door-to-door van service to and from the airport, serving the entire greater Seattle area, from Everett to Tacoma. The cost ranges from $16 (from within the city) to $28 one way (from outlying suburbs). Couples traveling from a single pickup point pay reduced rates; you may share the ride with other passengers, so expect to stop elsewhere en route. To ensure availability, make reservations two to three days ahead for trips to the airport. The shuttle from Sea-Tac operates 24 hours and requires no advance notice.

**Metro Transit** (553-3000) offers the cheapest rides to the airport ($1.10 one way, $1.60 during rush hour), via two routes: the #174 (every half hour, seven days a week; can take up to an hour from downtown) and the #194 Express (a 30-minute ride that runs until midafternoon on weekdays, and infrequently on weekends; call for schedules). The #194 uses the bus tunnel; the #174 originates on Ninth Avenue at Stewart

Street near the Greyhound depot and makes several stops along Stewart and Second Avenue up to Pioneer Square. Both stop on the baggage level of the airport.

## AIRPLANES: CHARTER

Most airplane and helicopter charter companies are based at **Boeing Field/King County International Airport** (296-7380, map:KK6). Others are located north of the city at **Snohomish County Airport** (Paine Field (206)353-2110). Services include flying lessons and aircraft rentals. Call the **Seattle Automated Flight Service Station** (767-2726) from a touchtone phone for up-to-date weather reports and flight-related information.

## AIRPLANES: SEAPLANES

*See Air Tours in the Exploring chapter.*

## BUSES: METRO TRANSIT

It is exceptionally easy to get around downtown Seattle without a car. **Metro** (821 Second Avenue, 553-3000) operates more than 200 bus routes in Seattle and King County. Many of the coaches are wheelchair-accessible and all are equipped with bike racks (mounted on the front of the bus) for bike-and-bus commuters. Bus stops have small yellow signs designating route numbers, and many have schedules posted. The fare is 85 cents in the city ($1.10 during peak commuter hours), $1.10 if you cross the city line ($1.60 peak). Exact fare is required. Seniors, youths, and handicapped riders are eligible for discount cards. Printed schedules and information on discounts and monthly and all-day passes are available at Metro headquarters and numerous convenient locations in the greater Seattle area.

[FREE] One of Metro's most valued services is the **Ride Free Area** in downtown's commercial core. In the area bordered by the Waterfront, the freeway, Jackson Street to the south, and Battery Street (near Seattle Center) to the north, you can ride free on any Metro bus. The sleek, L-shaped tunnel within the Ride Free Area has five stations, from the Washington State Convention and Trade Center at Ninth Avenue and Pine Street, to the International District. The tunnel was designed to accommodate a future light-rail system, but frustrated commuters—who grind their teeth at the length of time it takes Metro to travel the short distance through the downtown core during rush hours—are still keeping their fingers crossed on that one.

Metro also operates the [KIDS] **Waterfront Streetcar**. The vintage 1927 Australian mahogany and white-ash trolleys run along Alaskan Way on the waterfront from **Myrtle Edwards Park** to **Pioneer Square** to Fifth and Jackson. They depart at 20-minute to half-hour intervals from 7am (weekdays) or 9:30am (weekends) until 6pm, with extended hours in the summer. The ride takes 20 minutes from one end to the other and costs 85 cents (exact change only), $1.10 during peak hours. Metro monthly passes and discount permits are good on the streetcar.

[KIDS] The **Monorail**, which connects Seattle Center to the downtown retail district, was a space-age innovation of the 1962 World's Fair. The 90-second, 1.2-mile ride is a great thrill for kids and remains the only stretch of rapid transit in town. A smart way to avoid the parking hassle at Seattle Center is to leave your car downtown and hop on the monorail at **Westlake Center** (400 Pine Street, map:J6). Adults pay 90 cents one way, and children (ages 5 to 12) pay 70 cents. Trains leave every 15 minutes from 9am to 11pm.

For trips from as far out as Darrington, **Community Transit** runs buses on a regular schedule. Fare is $1.50 to Seattle from any point outside the city; fare within Snohomish County is 80 cents. Call for schedule and information (778-2185 or (800) 562-1375).

## BUSES: OUT-OF-TOWN AND CHARTER

**Greyhound Bus Lines** (811 Stewart Street, 628-5508) has the greatest number of scheduled bus routes connecting Seattle to other cities. The station is within walking distance of the downtown retail core. For package service, call 628-5555. Seattle has a number of **charter bus companies** offering local and long-distance transportation. **Gray Line of Seattle** (624-5077) has the largest fleet and the most competitive prices.

## FERRIES

[KIDS] Listed below are some of the destinations from Seattle and environs, with peak-season prices for a car and driver. For complete **schedule and route information**, call Washington State Ferries (464-6400). Schedules vary from summer to winter (with much longer lines in summer); credit cards are not accepted. Passengers to Canada should bring a passport or other proof of United States citizenship.

**Seattle–Bainbridge Island (Winslow)** The handiest day trip from Seattle, this crossing takes 35 minutes and is often loaded with commuters. Jumbo ferries leave frequently from Pier 52 (map:M9) on the Seattle waterfront; cost is $7.10 one way for car and driver and $3.50 round trip for walk-on passengers. (See Bainbridge Island in the Day Trips chapter.)

**Seattle–Bremerton (Kitsap Peninsula)** This run, with its good views of the Navy Shipyard, also departs from Pier 52 (map:M9). The auto ferry takes 60 minutes (one way) and costs the same as the Bainbridge Island trip; the passenger-only ferry takes 50 minutes and costs $3.50 round trip.

**Edmonds–Kingston (Kitsap Peninsula)** Kingston, close to the northern tip of the Kitsap Peninsula, is reached from Edmonds (about 15 miles north of Seattle; take the Edmonds–Kingston Ferry exit from I-5 and head northwest on Highway 104). The crossing takes 30 minutes and costs $7.10 one way for car and driver and $3.30 round trip for walk-on passengers.

## Fauntleroy–Vashon Island–Southworth (Kitsap Peninsula)
Vashon, an idyllic retreat west of Seattle, can be reached from Pier 50 in downtown Seattle or from Fauntleroy in West Seattle. Pier 50 offers a passenger-only ferry that sails several times daily Monday through Saturday (cars must travel via Fauntleroy). The crossing takes about 25 minutes and costs $3.50 round trip. Vashon is the first stop on a trip from the Fauntleroy terminal in West Seattle (exit 163 off I-5, map:LL9) to Southworth on the Kitsap Peninsula. The trip to Vashon takes 15 minutes; Southworth is reached in another 20 minutes (cost for Vashon is $9.55 one way for car and driver, $2.30 for walk-on passengers; for Southworth it's $7.10 for car and driver, $3.50 for walk-ons). If you bring your vehicle along, you can drive south on Vashon to the **Tahlequah terminal**. A 15-minute ferry ride from here lies **Point Defiance Park**, on the outskirts of Tacoma ($9.55 one way for car and driver, $2.30 for walk-on passengers). (See Vashon Island in the Day Trips chapter.)

## Mukilteo–Clinton (Whidbey Island)
Mukilteo is 26 miles north of Seattle (take exit 189 from I-5). The 20-minute passage to pretty Whidbey Island costs $4.80 one way for car and driver, $2.30 for walk-on passengers.

## Keystone (Whidbey Island)–Port Townsend (Olympic Peninsula)
From Keystone, 25 miles up-island from Clinton, another ferry reaches Port Townsend, one of the most enchanting towns in the state (see Port Townsend in the Day Trips chapter). The crossing takes 30 minutes and costs $7.10 one way for car and driver and $1.75 each way for walk-on passengers.

## Anacortes–San Juan Islands–Sidney, BC (Vancouver Island)
The San Juan Islands are reached by ferry from Anacortes (82 miles northwest of Seattle, exit 230 off I-5). The boats stops at Lopez, Shaw, Orcas, and San Juan Islands for fares from $14.75 to $20.30 round trip for car and driver. Once a day (twice in summer), the ferry continues on to Sidney on British Columbia's Vancouver Island, just 15 minutes by car from Victoria. It returns in the early afternoon. During the summer, you can reserve space for your car on this crowded run. The tariff is $35.65 for the trip from Anacortes to Sidney (walk-on passenger fare is $6.50).

## Seattle–Victoria, BC (Vancouver Island)
The *Victoria Clipper* fleet (448-5000, (800)888-2535) offers the only year-round ferry service to Victoria from Seattle. The waterjet-propelled catamarans carry foot passengers only between Seattle and Victoria four times a day from mid-May to mid-September, and

once or twice a day the rest of the year. The 2½-hour trip costs $89 round trip in summer, $83 the rest of the year. Reservations are necessary, and if you make them two weeks in advance for travel Monday through Friday, you'll save $20 on a round-trip ticket (see Victoria in the Day Trips chapter). The BC ferry *Royal Victorian* offers the only car-ferry service between Seattle and Victoria, leaving Pier 48 in Seattle at 1pm daily from mid-May to mid-September for a 4½-hour trip, returning from Victoria at 7:30am daily ($120 round trip).

### Port Angeles (Olympic Peninsula)–Victoria, BC (Vancouver Island)  Black Ball Transport's *MV Coho* (206)457-4491 makes two runs daily in winter and spring and four runs daily in summer from Port Angeles to Victoria ($26 for car and driver one way, $6.50 for walk-on passengers). It is privately run, not part of the Washington State Ferries.

### *TRAINS*
Catch the train at King Street Station (Third and Jackson, map:P8) at the edge of the International District. For passenger information and reservations, call Amtrak at (800)872-7245. For baggage offices, package express, and lost and found, call 382-4128.

## KEYS TO THE CITY

### *CITY OF SEATTLE COMPLAINTS AND QUESTIONS*
**Citizen Service Bureau** (600 Fourth Avenue, Room 105, 684-8811, map:O7) hears complaints about the city, from potholes in the road to your humble opinion on the Metro Sewage Plant. It will refer you to the agency that can best handle the problem.

### *CONSULATES*
Major consulates are the **British Consulate** (First Interstate Center, eighth floor, 999 Third Avenue, 622-9255, map:M7); the **Canadian Consulate** (412 Plaza 600, Sixth Avenue and Stewart Street, 443-1777, map:I5); the **French Consulate** (801 Second Avenue, Suite 1500, 624-7855, map:M7); the **German Consulate** (One Union Square, 600 University Street, Suite 2500, 682-4312, map:L5); the **Japanese Consulate** (601 Union Street, Suite 500, 682-9107, map:K5); and the **Mexican Consulate** (2132 Third Avenue, 448-3526, map:G7).

### *FOREIGN EXCHANGE*
Money-changing facilities are available at almost every major bank. **Thomas Cook** (906 Third Avenue, 623-6203, map:M7; and 10630 NE Eighth Street, Bellevue, 462-8225, map:HH3; and various Sea-Tac Airport locations) is a foreign-exchange broker. Several foreign banks also have branches in Seattle: **Bank of Tokyo** (1201 Third Avenue, Suite 1100, 382-6000, map:L7), **Hokkaido Takushoku Bank** (1001 Fourth Avenue, Suite

3920, 624-0920, map:L6), **Hong Kong & Shanghai Banking**
**Corp.** (700 Fifth Avenue, Suite 4100, 233-0888, map:N7),
**Sakura Bank** (1420 Fifth Avenue, Suite 2000, 682-2312,
map:M6) and **Sumitomo Bank** (1201 Third Avenue, Suite
5320, 625-1010, map:L7).

## FOREIGN VISITORS

There is a multitude of services for the foreign visitor or resident who does not speak English as a first language. **The
American Cultural Exchange** (200 W Mercer Street, Suite
504, 217-9644, map:GG8) provides English-language classes
(Intensive English Language Institutes) for foreigners who
want to study here. The Exchange also runs the downtown
Language School (where English speakers can learn any of up
to 16 languages) and arranges for summertime exchanges and
visits by foreigners to American homes. Another American
Cultural Exchange service, the ACE Translation Center, provides both interpreters and written translations. The **Central
Seattle Community Health Centers** (105 14th Avenue, Suite
2-C, 461-6910) is an umbrella organization for two hospital
translation services: the **Community Health Interpretation
Service** (461-6904), which provides translators for all the major Indo-Chinese languages; and **Community Interpretation
Services** (461-6907), a 24-hour service providing translators for
hospital patients. The **Milmanco Corp.** (651 Strander Boulevard, Suite 100, 575-3808) can help those involved in international business who are in need of technical written translations
(from and into foreign languages). Rates vary. The **[FREE] Red
Cross Language Bank** (323-2345) provides on-call interpretive assistance at no charge in emergency or crisis situations.

## HANDICAPPED AID

**RCH Technical Institute** (20150 45th Avenue NE, 362-2273,
map:AA6) provides vocational training and placement services
for handicapped citizens.

## INFORMATION

Seattleites are known to be helpful to visitors; if that doesn't suf-
fice, stop by the **Seattle–King County Convention and Visitors Bureau** (461-5840), on the main floor at the Union Street
entrance to the Convention Center, from 8:30am to 5pm Monday through Friday. **Westlake Information Center**, on the
third level of Westlake Center, offers a wealth of information,
from where to eat cheaply to how to pronounce the word "geoduck." **Seattle Public Library Quick Information Line**
covers a larger territory; dial 386-INFO to find out the answer
to anything you could possibly think to ask. The *Seattle Survival Guide* (published by Sasquatch Books and available in
bookstores) is a thorough, reliable resource for anyone who
wants to get anything at all done in this maze of a city.

## LEGAL SERVICES

**Lawyer Referral Services** (623-2551) puts clients in touch with lawyers who are members of this association. The cost is $30 for the first half hour, with a **pro bono** program for low-income clients. **Evergreen Legal Services** (464-5911) is a federally funded program that provides free consultation for clients with very low incomes. **Northwest Women's Law Center** (621-7691) provides basic legal information and attorney referrals, as well as advice on self-help methods.

## LIBRARIES

[KIDS] In addition to lending books, video and audio recordings, and even artwork, the 24 branches of the Seattle Public Library system, located throughout the city, offer lectures, films, and many other activities. Call the individual branches for specific events or questions. The [FREE] **Main Branch** (1000 Fourth Avenue, 386-4636, map:M6) leads tours Wednesdays and Saturdays and has a Quick Information number, 386-INFO. For mobile library service, call 684-4713. The **King County Public Library** (General Information, 684-9000) has 37 branches countywide, as well as a traveling library service, a film library, and an answer line (684-9000).

## LOST CAR

Begin by calling 684-5444 to find out if your car is listed as towed and impounded in auto records. If there is no record, it may have been stolen; call 911.

## MEDICAL/DENTAL SERVICES

**Doctor's Inc.** (622-9933) can put you in touch with a doctor 24 hours a day. **Dentist Referral Service** (443-7607) will do just what the name implies. **Chec Medical Centers** (drop-in health clinics) have numerous locations around Puget Sound, including one downtown at Denny and Fairview (682-7418).

## NEWSPAPERS

Seattle's two daily papers have merged their business functions under a joint operating agreement, but maintain entirely separate editorial operations. The evening paper, *The Seattle Times* (1120 John Street, 464-2000, map:F2), maintains its editorial and administrative offices downtown, but has moved its production facilities to a Bothell location, where [FREE] free tours are offered Tuesday through Thursday (call 489-7015; reservations required). The waterside offices of the early-morning *Seattle Post-Intelligencer* (101 Elliott Avenue W, 448-8000, map:B9) are home to one of the city's most eye-catching landmarks: a rotating neon-enhanced globe high atop the building. The [FREE] *Seattle Weekly* and its Eastside counterpart *Eastsideweek* (1008 Western Avenue, Suite 300, 623-0500, map:L8) provide coverage of politics, the arts, and civic issues.

Another [FREE] alternative weekly, **The Stranger** (1202 E Pike Street, Suite 1225, 323-7107), offers irreverent editorial comment and concise day-by-day music and dance-scene listings. On the Eastside, the Bellevue *Journal American* (1705 132nd Avenue NE, Bellevue, 455-2222, map:GG2) provides a local voice and a hedge against the hegemony of *The Seattle Times*.

## PUBLIC RESTROOMS

These are difficult to find downtown, with a few exceptions: at the base of the ramp in the Main Arcade of **Pike Place Market** (Pike Street and Western Avenue, map:J8) and at **Freeway Park** (Sixth Avenue and Seneca Street, map:L5). Public buildings are another option (e.g., Seattle Public Library, King County Courthouse, the Federal Building) for accessible facilities. Many larger parks also have public facilities, too (although most are only open until dusk).

## TELEPHONE NUMBERS

| | |
|---|---|
| AAA of Washington | 448-5353 |
| AIDS Hotline | 296-4999 |
| Alcoholics Anonymous | 587-2838 |
| Ambulance | 911 |
| Amtrak | (800)872-7245 |
| Animal Control | 386-4254 |
| Auto Impound | 684-5444 |
| Better Business Bureau | 448-8888 |
| Birth and Death Records | 296-4769 |
| Blood Bank | 292-6500 |
| Chamber of Commerce | 389-7200 |
| Child Protective Services Crisis Hotline | 721-4306 |
| City Light | 625-3000 |
| City of Seattle Information | 386-1234 |
| City Parks Information and Scheduling Office | 684-4075 |
| Coast Guard | 286-5450 |
| Coast Guard 24-Hour Emergency | (800)286-5400 |
| Community Information Line | 461-3200 |
| Customs | 553-4676 |
| Dial-A-Story (Seattle Public Library) | 386-4656 |
| Directory Information | (206)555-1212 |
| | (25 cents per call) |
| Domestic Violence Hotline | (800)562-6025 |
| DWI (Drunk Drivers) Hotline | (800)223-7865 |
| Emergency Feeding Program | 723-0647 |
| Environmental Protection Agency | 553-1200 |
| FBI | 622-0460 |

▼

**Keys to the City**

▲

Fire . . . . . . . . . . . . . . . . . . . . . . . . . . . . . . . . . . . . 911
Housing Hotline . . . . . . . . . . . . . . . . . . . . . . . . . 296-7640
Immigration and Naturalization Service . . . . . . . . . . 553-5956
Internal Revenue Service . . . . . . . . . . . . . . . . . . . . 442-1040
Locksmith, 24-Hour AAA Locksmith . . . . . . . . . . . . 325-1515
Lost Pets . . . . . . . . . . . . . . . . . . . . . . . . . . . . . . . 386-7387
Marriage Licenses . . . . . . . . . . . . . . . . . . . . . . . . 296-3933
Metro Information . . . . . . . . . . . . . . . . . . . . . . . . . 553-3000
Missing Persons . . . . . . . . . . . . . . . . . . . . . . . . . . 684-5582
Northwest Ski Report . . . . . . . . . . . . . . . . . . . . . . . 634-0071
Passports . . . . . . . . . . . . . . . . . . . . . . . . . . . . . . . 553-7941
Planned Parenthood . . . . . . . . . . . . . . . . . . . . . . . 328-7700
Poison Center . . . . . . . . . . . . . . . . . . . . . . . . . . . . 526-2121
Post Office Information . . . . . . . . . . . . . . . . . . . . . . 285-1650
Rape Relief . . . . . . . . . . . . . . . . . . . . . . . . . . . . . . 632-7273
Red Cross . . . . . . . . . . . . . . . . . . . . . . . . . . . . . . 323-2345
Red Tide Hotline . . . . . . . . . . . . . . . . . . . . (800) 562-5632
Seattle–King County Convention and
   Visitors Bureau . . . . . . . . . . . . . . . . . . . . . . . . 461-5840

Seattle–King County Department of
Public Health . . . . . . . . . . . . . . . . . . . . . . . . . . . . . 296-4600
Self-Defense (Alternatives to Fear) . . . . . . . . . . . . . 328-5347
Senior Information Center . . . . . . . . . . . . . . . . . . . . 448-3110
Sexual Assault Clinic . . . . . . . . . . . . . . . . . . . . . . . 223-3047
Shelter for Battered Women (New Beginnings) . . . . 522-9472
Sports Organizations:
   Seattle International Raceway (cars) . . . . . . . . . . 631-1550
   Seattle Mariners (baseball) . . . . . . . . . . . . . . . . 628-3555
   Seattle Seahawks (football) . . . . . . . . . . . . . . . . 827-9777
   Seattle SuperSonics (basketball) . . . . . . . . . . . . . 281-5850
   Seattle Thunderbirds (hockey) . . . . . . . . . . . . . . 728-9121
   University of Washington . . . . . . . . . . . . . . . . . . . 543-2100
   University of Washington Huskies . . . . . . . . . . . . 543-2200
State Patrol . . . . . . . . . . . . . . . . . . . . . . . . . . . . . . 455-7700
Suicide Prevention . . . . . . . . . . . . . . . . . . . . . . . . . 461-3222
Ticketmaster . . . . . . . . . . . . . . . . . . . . . . . . . . . . . 628-0888
Travelers Aid Society . . . . . . . . . . . . . . . . . . . . . . . 461-3888
Voter Registration . . . . . . . . . . . . . . . . . . . . . . . . . 296-1600
Washington State Ferries . . . . . . . . . . . . . . . . . . . . 464-6400
Weather . . . . . . . . . . . . . . . . . . . . . . . . . . . . . . . . 526-6087
Zip Code Information . . . . . . . . . . . . . . . . . . . . . . . . 285-1650

The **University of Washington**, the largest of the Washington State public universities, has an Information Center (4014 University Way NE, 543-9198, map:FF6) and the second-largest university bookstore in the country (4326 University Way NE, 634-3400). **Seattle Pacific University** (3307 Third Avenue W, map:FF8) is a private college associated with the Free Methodist Church; their information line is 281-2000. **Seattle University**, a private Catholic school located at the corner of Broadway and Madison on Capitol Hill (map:N1), has a general information line at 296-6000.

## BUSINESS SERVICES

### COMPUTER RENTALS

**Bit-by-Bit Computers** Rentals by the day, week, or month, leasing options, and delivery to anywhere in the state. Apple Macintosh and IBM-compatibles, with both available in laptop models. A complete system, with printer, runs about $70 to $175 a week. Free on-site repair, no in-house rentals. Known for accommodating service. ▪ *2715 152nd Ave NE, Bldg 6, Redmond; 881-5353; map:GG1; Mon–Fri.*

**Business Computer Systems Rentals (BCSR)** BCSR rents IBM, Compaq, Apple Macintosh, Toshiba, and Zenith by the day, week, or month. One- to two-year leasing available. No in-house rentals, but they'll deliver to you and make on-site repairs. Pricier than most other computer rental places. ▪ *11335 NE 122nd Way, Suite 105, Kirkland; 823-1188; map:DD3; Mon–Fri.*

### CONFERENCES, MEETINGS, AND RECEPTIONS

Most hotels and inns and many restaurants have meeting rooms for rent. The following is a list of other rental facilities appropriate for business meetings, private parties, and receptions. Private functions can also be held at branches of the Seattle Public Library, most museums, the University of Washington (which has numerous halls, auditoriums, and meeting rooms), and other educational facilities.

**The Atrium** The Atrium holds up to 900 people (for a cocktail party–style gathering) in a skylit, three-story covered courtyard with plenty of tall greenery. A great place for corporate events, weddings, parties, and reunions. You must use their catering. Good PA system. ▪ *5701 6th Ave S; 763-0111; map:JJ7.*

**Battelle Seattle Conference Center** Battelle Memorial Institute, a nonprofit research organization, operates this fully equipped conference facility on its attractive, 18-acre wooded grounds not far from the University of Washington. Battelle has 25 guest rooms, and the 11 carpeted conference rooms can accommodate up to 110 people. Catering is provided by Battelle. Rental policies are geared toward conferences of one day or longer. No weddings, but business-sponsored receptions are OK. ■ *4000 NE 41st St; 525-3130; map:FF6.*

**Camp Long** See Parks and Beaches in the Exploring chapter. ■ *5200 35th Ave SW; 684-7434; map:JJ8.*

**Chateau Ste. Michelle** In the quaint, original early-1900s Manor House on the grounds of this Eastside winery you can hold a meeting or reception for up to 80 people. The house boasts hardwood floors, a cozy fireplace, and formal gardens on either side. The Barrel Room accommodates gatherings of up to 250. Both rooms include custom, in-house catering. ■ *14111 NE 145th St, Woodinville; 488-4633; map:BB2.*

**Chinese Room** Resembling a Chinese museum with its deep red carpets and hand-carved wooden furniture, this sky-level room in the classic 1914 Smith Tower is a stunningly elegant backdrop for a party. Other features include ceramic ceiling tiles, an outside wraparound balcony, and express elevator service (complete with tuxedo-clad elevator operator). The Chinese Room accommodates 99 for cocktail party–style receptions. Bring your own caterer. ■ *Smith Tower; 506 2nd Ave, 35th floor; 622-4004; map:O7.*

**Court in the Square** A glassed-in alley between two brick buildings, the Court in the Square has a classy French Quarter ambience. A retractable glass roof allows for dancing under the stars. It's available evenings and weekends for parties of up to 300; all catering is done by the very high-quality in-house restaurant. A favorite among wedding planners, who must book six months to a year in advance. ■ *401 2nd Ave S; 467-5533; map:P8.*

**Daughters of the American Revolution House** Weddings and dance parties are the main events in this classic Capitol Hill mansion, patterned after George Washington's Mount Vernon. Downstairs is Colonial and genteel; rent it by itself or along with the barny upstairs ballroom for a total capacity of 250 people. Bring your own caterer and sound system; they have two pianos. Midnight curfew. ■ *800 E Roy St; 323-0600; map:GG6.*

**Gold Creek Lodge** The wooded trails of Gold Creek Park surround this rustic, pine-paneled room. The place holds 100 people for a meeting or reception, and two huge lofts sleep 33 (bring your own sleeping bags). ■ *16020 148th Ave NE, Woodinville; 296-2976 (King County Recreation); map:BB2.*

**Kiana Lodge** The waterfront lodge and longhouse at Kiana on the Kitsap Peninsula have a genuine Northwest flavor—good for both weddings and corporate get-togethers. You can even dock your boat right in front. The specialty is alder-grilled salmon dinners for large groups (up to 1,000). Kiana is usually booked several months in advance for weekend weddings. No overnight accommodations. ▪ *14976 Sandy Hook Rd NE, Poulsbo; (360)598-4311.*

**Langston Hughes Cultural Center** A large multipurpose room, 287-seat theater, and restaurant-capacity kitchen are available for rent at this recently renovated Seattle Parks Department facility. Fees are reasonable and determined on a sliding scale. ▪ *104 17th Ave S; 684-4757; map:HH6.*

**Lutheran Bible Institute** Religious groups and nonprofit organizations can rent this comfortable Issaquah conference facility with rooms seating 12 to 400 people. The institute has dorm rooms and motel-style lodgings, dining rooms, a gym, an indoor swimming pool, and a 400-seat chapel. No smoking or alcohol consumption anywhere on the grounds, but you can eat (they provide catering). ▪ *Providence Heights, 4221 228th Ave SE, Issaquah; 392-0400.*

**The Meeting Place in the Market** Located in the Economy Market Building in Pike Place Market, the Meeting Place has two unprepossessing rooms (one with a bay view) for rent on an hourly or daily basis. They can be used separately or together, with a maximum capacity of 200. No in-house catering service, but the staff will assist you with planning. The facility has a small pantry with a microwave oven and a refrigerator. ▪ *93 Pike St, Suite 307; 447-9994; map:J8.*

**Museum of Flight** This museum (see Museums in the Arts chapter) houses an impressive cross-section of aviation history; you can hold a meeting for up to 2,500 people in the Great Gallery, where these great machines are hung. A stroll around the balcony above the gallery takes you to the view lounge (a view, that is, of Boeing Field to the east and Mount Rainier to the south), with its handsome chrome wet bar. Best atmosphere: the Red Barn, original home of Boeing, where a stripped-down Curtiss Jenny occupies center stage. Catering is courtesy of McCormick and Schmick's. ▪ *9404 E Marginal Way S; 764-5706; map:LL6.*

**Museum of History and Industry** Located on Union Bay just west of Foster Island and the Arboretum, the museum rents out a 392-seat theater/auditorium and a carpeted room that accommodate 200 people for a sit-down gathering, or up to 350 for a stand-up reception. The room has an adjoining kitchen. Meetings and parties only, no wedding receptions. Facilities are rented in eight-hour blocks. Plenty of parking in the museum lot. ▪ *2700 24th Ave E; 324-1126; map:FF6.*

**Robinswood House** A comfortable, furnished two-story house that holds up to 120 people for parties is part of a well-tended 60-acre park. Parts of the house can be rented for smaller gatherings on weekdays, but on weekends the entire facility is rented as a unit. An additional 75 guests can be accommodated outdoors (there's an English garden on the premises). Robinswood is a popular place for weddings, but is not well suited to live band music. Bring your own caterer. ▪ *2432 148th Ave SE, Bellevue; 455-7850; map:II2.*

**Seattle Aquarium** Several hundred people can party right in the exhibit area, amid the fish and octopi. The underwater dome is an especially atmospheric spot for wedding ceremonies. The Aquarium also has a 200-seat auditorium and a conference room that will hold 20 people. Available evenings only; the Aquarium has caterers if necessary. ▪ *Pier 59, Waterfront Park; 386-4300; map:J9.*

**Seattle Art Museum** In the downtown museum, a lecture room and a 300-seat, acoustically perfect auditorium lend themselves to lectures, films, music, and dramatic performances. Evening parties can be staged in the main entrance and flow up the Grand Stairway, graciously interrupted midway by a comfortable cafe. ▪ *100 University St; 654-3100 or 625-8900; map:K8.*

**Seattle Center** The largest and most varied meeting and conference center in the city, Seattle Center can handle just about any need, from roundtables for 8,000 to small monthly workshops. The center also can provide catering services, planning assistance, and support staff. ▪ *305 Harrison St; 684-7202; map:GG7.*

**Seattle International Trade Center** The Seattle Trade Center, with over 50,000 square feet of flexible space, rents out mostly for large trade fairs and exhibitions. It will also accommodate conferences, seminars, and banquets for 50 to 700 people. Use the Trade Center's catering or bring your own. ▪ *2601 Elliott Ave; 441-3000; map:E9.*

**Skansonia** Permanently docked on Lake Union not far from Gas Works Park, this retired Washington State ferry is available for groups of up to 400. Besides the romance of it all, there's a large dance area, dining room, parlor, two garden decks, grand piano, full stereo system, working fireplace, and a postcard view of the city. Weddings and corporate parties are its main business. Catering is available. Wheelchair-accessible. ▪ *2505 N Northlake Way; 545-9109; map:FF7.*

**Snoqualmie Winery** The keg-filled wine cellar dresses up well for special occasions, the retail shop has a nice fireplace, and the terraced lawn has a wonderful view and picnic tables. ▪ *1000 Winery Rd, Snoqualmie; (206)888-4000.*

**Space Needle** The rooms themselves aren't much, but they face outward for a spectacular 360-degree view from 100 feet up. There are three rooms with a total capacity for about 250 people with seating (or 350 for a reception-style gathering); the Space Needle provides all catering. ■ *Seattle Center; 443-9800; map:C6.*

**St. Thomas Conference Center** This former seminary sits on 50 wooded acres next to a large state park on the northeastern end of Lake Washington. It is available to nonprofit groups only. Six conference rooms hold up to 180, and there are overnight accommodations for up to 100 people. Buffet meals are served three times a day; reception catering available. ■ *14500 Juanita Dr NE, Bothell; 823-1300 or (800)841-6721; map:CC5.*

**Stimson-Green Mansion** Two of Seattle's prominent industrialist families—the Stimsons and the Greens—once called this stately turn-of-the-century brick Tudor mansion home. It is now a designated historical site. Since the early 1980s, the house has been open for public tours and used for meetings, parties, and weddings, with room for 48 with seating or up to 200 for a stand-up buffet. We like it best on wintry evenings, when the place is infused with a rich, cozy glow. It's pricey, but exudes opulence. ■ *1204 Minor Ave; 624-0474; map:L2.*

**Union Station** Entertain up to 1,500 of your closest friends in the enormous Great Hall of Union Station, once the Grand Central of the Northwest. Special Events Catering provides the food service and handles bookings. With its high ceilings, mosaic tile floor, and stately ambience, Union Station is a top-choice venue for political fund raisers, wedding receptions, and corporate parties. ■ *401 S Jackson St; 623-2434; map:Q7.*

**Washington State Convention and Trade Center** Draped artfully across I-5, this gargantuan facility has reception rooms that accommodate 50 to 4,000 people, exhibit halls, press facilities, conference rooms, ballrooms, indoor parking for 900 cars, and wheelchair accessibility. Catering is available. The center is within walking distance of all major downtown hotels. ■ *800 Convention Place; 447-5000; map:L5.*

### COPY SERVICES

**Kinko's** Kinko's, with myriad locations open 24 hours all over town, offers copying, in-house IBM and Macintosh computer rentals, desktop publishing facilities, and résumé and fax services, among many other business necessities. ■ *4125 University Way NE (and branches); 632-0374; map:FF6; every day.*

**Superior Reprographics** A complete graphics and copy center, with black-and-white and color copying, and offset and diazo printing. Delivery within city limits. Occasional weekend color copies. ■ *1933 5th Ave (and branches); 443-6900; map:I5; Mon–Sat.*

*MESSENGER AND DELIVERY SERVICES*

**Bucky's Messenger and Delivery Service** Speedy service from radio-dispatched bicycle couriers. Delivery of messages and packages up to 20 pounds throughout Seattle and to the Eastside. Vehicle delivery up to 400 pounds to Tacoma, Everett, and Bremerton. ▪ *448-9280; Mon–Fri.*

**Elliott Bay Messenger** Considered the best and fastest bicycle courier service downtown. Packages weighing over 20 pounds levy a $4 surcharge. Downtown rush deliveries within a half hour, regular delivery within an hour, and more economical rates available for lengthier services. Car deliveries to all of the Puget Sound area. ▪ *728-8505; Mon–Fri.*

**Federal Express** Worldwide delivery and next-day service within the continental United States and to parts of Alaska, Hawaii, and Puerto Rico. Six offices in greater Seattle, three of them downtown. No weight limit. The toll-free number is for 24-hour customer service. ▪ *282-9766 or (800)238-5355; Mon–Sat.*

**Fleetfoot Messenger Service** Quick-service radio-dispatched bicyclists will deliver up to 20 pounds downtown. Vehicle delivery of packages up to a few hundred pounds statewide. ▪ *728-7700; Mon–Fri.*

*SECRETARIAL SERVICES*

**Business Service Center** Provides a range of secretarial services, including word processing, answering service, mail service, telex, and fax. Also rental of office and conference space by the hour, day, or long-term. ▪ *1001 4th Ave Plaza, 32nd Floor; 624-9188; map:M6; Mon–Fri.*

**Olympic Suites** Geared toward business executives, this reputable outfit occupies the 12th floor of the Four Seasons Olympic Hotel. A full range of secretarial services, plus office and conference room rentals. ▪ *411 University St, Suite 1200; 467-9378; map:K6; Mon–Fri.*

# CALENDAR OF EVENTS

**CALENDAR OF EVENTS CONTENTS**

**JANUARY** *419*

**FEBRUARY** *419*

**MARCH** *419*

**APRIL** *420*

**MAY** *421*

**JUNE** *422*

**JULY** *424*

**AUGUST** *426*

**SEPTEMBER** *427*

**OCTOBER** *428*

**NOVEMBER** *429*

**DECEMBER** *429*

# Calendar of Events

*Average daily maximum and minimum temperatures: 45, 35*
*Average rainfall: 6.38 inches*

**Chinese New Year** [FREE]  In January or February (depending on the lunar calendar), the International District greets the Chinese and Vietnamese New Year with a fanfare of festivals, displays, and a lively parade complete with lion dancers. ▪ *International District; 623-5124; map:R6.*

## FEBRUARY

*Average daily maximum and minimum temperatures: 49, 37*
*Average rainfall: 4.12 inches*

**Chilly Hilly Bike Ride**  Held at the end of February, this 30-plus-mile family ride sponsored by the Cascade Bicycle Club has come to be recognized as the opening day of bike season. As many as 4,000 cyclists fill the morning ferries to Winslow. Don't expect the ride to be warm or flat. ▪ *Bainbridge Island; 522-BIKE.*

**Fat Tuesday**  Seattle's weeklong Mardi Gras celebration brings a colorful parade and the beat of Cajun, jazz, and R&B to the streets and clubs of Pioneer Square. Nightclubs levy a joint cover charge, and proceeds from several events benefit Northwest Harvest, a local food bank. Held the week before Lent. ▪ *Pioneer Square; 622-2563; map:N8.*

**Northwest Flower and Garden Show**  For five days in mid-February, this enormous horticultural happening occupies almost 5 acres at the Convention Center. Landscapers, nurseries, and noncommercial gardeners outdo themselves with over 300 demonstration gardens and booths. Shuttle bus service is available from Northgate and Longacres. General admission is $9 (evenings $8). ▪ *Washington State Convention and Trade Center; 224-1700; map:K4.*

**Seattle International Raceway**  SIR's season begins in February and continues with a busy schedule of races through the good-weather months. Though the dirt track for motorcycles is not much, the nine-turn, 2¼-mile road-racing track (originally built in 1959 for sports-car racing) is a very good facility. Open February through October. ▪ *31001 144th Ave SE, Kent; take exit 142A east off I-5; 631-1550; map:RR2.*

## MARCH

*Average daily maximum and minimum temperatures: 52, 38*
*Average rainfall: 3.54 inches*

**Imagination Celebration/Arts Festival for Kids** [FREE][KIDS]  Free activities and workshops in the visual and performing arts are features of this weekend-long, fun-filled, child-centric event. Kids and their parents can participate in hands-on learning activities, including arts, crafts, and music. Call for dates and schedule. ▪ *Center House, Seattle Center; 684-7200; map:C6.*

**NW Buddy Werner Ski Racing Championships** [KIDS] An alpine ski event designed just for the younger members of your family. About 300 kids from ages 7 to 12 compete in the frosty event. Come out and watch Olympic hopefuls give it their all. Races are held in Washington, Oregon, or Idaho. ▪ *Call for location; 392-4220.*

**Saint Patrick's Day Dash** In a festive atmosphere, the greatest number of participants of any local run follow the easy 4-mile course along the Alaskan Way viaduct. ▪ *At Larry's Market, 100 Mercer St, to the Kingdome; 522-7711 or 865-1934; map:A7–Q9.*

**Saint Patrick's Day Parade** Faith 'n' begorra this downtown parade features bagpipes, singing, dancing, and the laying of a green stripe down the center of Fourth Avenue. ▪ *City Hall to Westlake Center; 329-7224; map:N7–J6.*

**Whale Migration** From March to May, after wintering and calving in Baja, the gray whales return to Alaska. Along the Washington coast are a number of excellent whale-watching spots; some towns, such as Westport, offer charters specially for whale seekers. The southward migration occurs from October to December, less favorable for whale-watching due to the weather. ▪ *For information, call Westport Chamber of Commerce; (360)268-9422.*

**Whirligig** [KIDS][FREE] From late March through early April, this indoor winter carnival fetes the coming of spring with rides, music, and games just for kids. The entertainment is free; rides cost 25 cents to 50 cents apiece. ▪ *Center House, Seattle Center; 684-7200; map:C6.*

## APRIL

*Average daily maximum and minimum temperatures: 57, 41*
*Average rainfall: 2.33 inches*

**Daffodil Festival Grand Floral Parade** The Daffodil Festival, a springtime tradition for 60 years, celebrates the fields of gold in the Puyallup Valley. One of the largest floral parades in the nation visits downtown Tacoma, Puyallup, Sumner, and Orting—all in one day. ▪ *Tacoma; (206)627-6176.*

**Seattle Mariners Baseball** The crowd is predictably loyal, and in 1995 that loyalty finally paid off when Ken Griffey Jr. and company led the team to an unprecedented winning season and a playoff extravaganza. The season lasts from early April through the first week of October. Bring your own peanuts (Kingdome food is too expensive) and prepare to do the Wave. Tickets are cheap ($6 to $16). ▪ *Kingdome; 628-3555; map:Q9.*

**Skagit Valley Tulip Festival** [FREE] When the 1,500 acres of tulip fields burst into brilliant color in early April, Mount Vernon seizes the moment and entertains visitors with a street fair and parades. Makes a nice—and flat—bicycle trip. ▪ *Mount Vernon; 60 miles north of Seattle via I-5; (360)428-5959.*

---

**Yakima Spring Barrel Tasting** [FREE] Over the last weekend in April, 20-some wineries from Union Gap to Kiona hold special open houses in order to educate the public on the finer points of winemaking. Both owners and winemakers are on hand to explain the process, and wines from the barrel—some two or three years away from maturity—are available for tasting. Individual wineries add entertainment and food. ▪ *Various wineries, Yakima (call for map); (509) 786-2163.*

## MAY

*Average daily maximum and minimum temperatures: 64, 46*
*Average rainfall: 1.70 inches*

**Bicycle Saturdays/Sundays** [FREE][KIDS] Every third Sunday and second Saturday of the month, May through September (except August, when it's the first Saturday), winding, tree-lined Lake Washington Boulevard is closed to autos from Mount Baker Beach to Seward Park (from 10am to 6pm) when cyclists truly own the road. Wonderful for families. ▪ *Lake Washington Blvd; 684-4075; map:II5–KK5.*

**Bike Racing at the Velodrome** Track racing is a much more watchable sport than road racing, and many nights at this lovely course include national-caliber racers. The season runs from mid–May through mid–September. (See Bicycling under Outdoor Sports in the Sports chapter.) ▪ *Marymoor Park, Redmond; 389-5825; map:FF1.*

**International Children's Festival** [KIDS] Professional children's performers come from all over the world for this popular event. Crafts, storytelling, puppet shows, and musical and theater performances (some free) entertain kids and their parents for six days in early May. ▪ *Seattle Center; 684-7338; map:C6.*

**Nordstrom Beat-the-Bridge Run** Hordes of local athletes participate in this late-May favorite, a 2-mile fun run, a 4-mile walk-along, and an 8K race along a winding U District area course. If you don't "beat" the University Bridge (the drawbridge opens to signal the end of the race), you won't take the prize. Registration begins in April; proceeds benefit the Juvenile Diabetes Foundation. ▪ *Husky Stadium, University of Washington; 546-1510; map:FF6.*

**Northwest Folklife Festival** [FREE] The largest folk fest in the nation runs throughout Memorial Day weekend, and brings ethnic groups and their folk-art traditions (dance, music, crafts, and food) to stages all around Seattle Center. A must. ▪ *Seattle Center; 684-7300; map:C6.*

**Opening Day of Yachting Season** [FREE] Boat owners from all over the Northwest come to participate in this festive ceremonial regatta, which officially kicks off the nautical summer. Arrive early to watch the world-class University of Washington rowing team race other nationally ranked teams through the Montlake Cut. Parade registration for watercraft is free. ▪ *Lake Washington/Lake Union; Seattle Yacht Club, 1807 E Hamlin St; 325-1000; map:GG7.*

**Pike Place Market Festival** [KIDS][FREE] The Pike Place Market Merchant Association sponsors a free celebration of the Market on Memorial Day weekend: food, drink, and crafts aplenty, as well as clowns, some of the city's finest jazz musicians, and an entire Kids' Alley chock-full of activities. ▪ *Pike Place Market; 624-3961; map:J8.*

**Poulsbo Viking Fest** [FREE] In mid-May, Puget Sound's "Little Norway" celebrates Scandinavian independence with a weekend of folk dancing, live music, a carnival and parade, and a lutefisk-eating contest. ▪ *Poulsbo; 12 miles northwest of Winslow on Hwy 305; (360) 779-4848.*

**Rhododendron Festival** The Rhody Festival has been a cherished tradition in Port Townsend for a long time, and it improves every year. Highlights of the two-week-long mid-May event include a Rover Run (dog and owner), beard contest (scruffiest, longest), adult tricycle race, carnival, senior citizen coronation and dance, and more. The "Grand Finale" is a classic parade; the "Anti-Climax Grand Finale" is the 12K Rhody Run. See all of the Rhododendron Queens' handprints in cement in downtown Port Townsend. ▪ *Port Townsend, northeast tip of Olympic Peninsula; take Hwy 20 off US Hwy 101; (360)385-2722.*

**Seattle International Film Festival** Founded in 1976 by Darryl MacDonald and Dan Ireland, the 3½-week Seattle International Film Festival brings films for every taste—art house to slapstick—to Seattle theaters every May and June. Fans of the obscure will appreciate the SIFF's archival treasures and independent films. Series tickets (full and partial) go on sale in January. ▪ *Citywide; 324-9996.*

**Ski-to-Sea Festival** A Bellingham civic festival over Memorial Day weekend that revolves around an 80-plus–mile seven-event relay race, including skiing, running, cycling, canoeing, and sailing. ▪ *Mount Baker to Bellingham's Marine Park; 90 miles north of Seattle on I-5; (360) 734-1330.*

**University District Street Fair** [FREE] On the third—and usually the hottest—weekend in May, this juried festival features over 400 artists' booths in a 10-block area. Street mimes and clowns hold court in the crowd, which is as rich in variety as the selection of crafts. ▪ *University Way NE; 527-2567; map:FF6.*

## JUNE

*Average daily maximum and minimum temperatures: 70, 52*
*Average rainfall: 1.50 inches*

**AquaSox Baseball** The Seattle Mariners' farm team plays real baseball on real grass in real sunshine from mid-June through August—just up the road in Everett. Tickets are $7 for adults, $5 for kids 12 and under. Call for season schedule. ▪ *Everett Memorial Stadium, Everett; (206)258-3673.*

**Centrum Summer Arts Festival** From June through September, one of the most successful cultural programs in the state enlightens thousands, with a multitude of workshops held by the nation's leading artists and musicians. For fiddlers, there's the Festival of American Fiddle Tunes. Jazz musicians can hone their skills at the Bud Shank Jazz Workshop or listen to the music at Jazz Port Townsend, one of the West Coast's foremost mainstream jazz festivals. Workshops are held at Fort Worden State Park; performances are on the park grounds or in various locations around town. During the Marrowstone Music Festivals, young virtuoso musicians perform in two symphony orchestras. There are also a writers conference and theater performances. ■ *Port Townsend, northeast tip of Olympic Peninsula; take Hwy 20 off US Hwy 101; (360)385-3102.*

**Fremont Fair** [FREE] Fremont celebrates the beginning of summer with a solstice parade, music, crafts booths, food, and dance. This event gets bigger, better, and crazier every year. Along the Fremont Ship Canal. ■ *N 34th St; 548-8376; map:FF7.*

**Gay Pride Week** A week of sporting events, dances, forums, and a pride festival, culminating on the last Sunday of June with the all-in-good-fun parade down Broadway (attracting over 70,000 revelers and gawkers) and a rally at Volunteer Park. ■ *Broadway and other Capitol Hill locations; 323-1229 (Freedom Day Committee); map:HH6–GG6.*

**Mercer Island Summer Arts Festival** [FREE] Mercer Island's artists-at-work festival, sponsored by the local Visual Arts League, is usually held on the second weekend of July in the island's downtown. Displays in over 150 crafts booths include handmade toys, jewelry, pottery, and stained glass. ■ *8236 SE 24th Ave, Mercer Island; 232-6354; map:JJ4.*

**Northwest Microbrewery Festival** Nearly 50 microbrewers convene at the Herbfarm for this outdoor fun fest held on Father's Day. Live music, food, beer tasting, and forums highlight the event. A $12.50 admission fee ($10 in advance) buys six taste tickets, a beer glass, and the chance to wander around the herb gardens. ■ *The Herbfarm, 32804 Issaquah–Fall City Rd, Fall City; 784-2222.*

**Out to Lunch** [FREE] From mid-June to early September, the Downtown Seattle Association brings local musicians to various (outdoor) venues to entertain brown baggers. Between 60 and 75 concerts feature jazz, classical music, and show tunes, modern dance, and calypso. Just the thing to break up stir-crazy summer days in the office. ■ *Various downtown locations; 623-0340.*

**Seattle International Music Festival** The former Santa Fe Chamber Music Festival (under artistic director Dmitry Sitkovetsky) has expanded the format to include vocal and orchestral music as well as chamber music. ■ *Various locations, Seattle and Bellevue; 233-0993.*

**Seattle-to-Portland Bicycle Ride (STP)** There is a 10,000-rider limit for this 200-mile bike ride from Seattle to Portland sponsored by the Cascade Bike Club. Complete the course in one or two days (overnight facilities are provided at the halfway point). Registration is first come, first served. ■ *522-BIKE.*

**Shore Run** Held sometime from the end of June through early July, this popular 6.7-mile run benefiting the Fred Hutchinson Cancer Research Center attracts 3,000 walkers and runners—as much for the run as for the T-shirt, always an artful status symbol among Seattleites. ▪ *Seward Park to Madison Park along Lake Washington Blvd; 667-5096; map:JJ5–GG5.*

**Special Olympics** In 1968, an act of Congress created the organization known today as the Special Olympics. It has since grown to be the largest single sports training and competition program in the world for the mentally and physically handicapped. The June event is the biggest competition in the state. ▪ *Fort Lewis, Tacoma; (206)362-4949.*

**Summer Nights on the Pier** A former working pier transformed into a 3,000-seat concert grounds has become a perfect place to spend a summer evening—listening to the sounds of acts such as the Indigo Girls, Hootie and the Blowfish, or Ringo Starr against the backdrop of sailboats and the setting sun. This concert series extends through the summer. ▪ *Piers 62/63 on Alaskan Way; 622-5123 ; map:I9.*

## JULY

*Average daily maximum and minimum temperatures: 75, 55*
*Average rainfall: .76 inch*

**Bite of Seattle** A chomp fest that brings cheap nibbles from over 60 restaurants to Seattle Center in mid-July. All tastes are under $5. Admission is free. ▪ *Seattle Center; 232-2982; map:C6.*

**Caribbean Festival—A Taste of Soul** Be transported to the islands during one of Seattle's most temperate months. Let yourself be tempted by luscious Caribbean and African foods while calypso, soca, gospel, and reggae music soothe your soul. There's a limbo contest if you're feeling flexible; otherwise, you can just pretend the winds off the Sound are the gentle breezes of Montego Bay. Mid-July. ▪ *Myrtle Edwards Park; 329-8818; map:DD5.*

**Chinatown International District Summer Festival** [KIDS][FREE] The International District's mid-July extravaganza celebrates the richness and diversity of Asian culture with dancing, instrumental and martial arts performances, food booths, and arts and crafts. A children's corner features puppetry, storytelling, and magic shows; various craft demonstrations (classical ikebana, a Japanese tea ceremony, basket weaving, calligraphy, and Hawaiian lei-making) take place in the cultural corner. ▪ *Hing Hay Park, International District; 382-1197; map:Q6.*

**Darrington Bluegrass Festival** Every summer during the third weekend in July, bluegrass fans from all over the country turn their attention to the tiny town of Darrington, nestled in the Cascade foothills. Terrific, foot-stomping, thigh-slapping bluegrass is played outdoors by the country's best musicians. A convenient ticket package includes three nights of camping and three days of music: $60 for couples, $35 single. ▪ *Darrington; 80 miles north of Seattle off I-5; (360)436-1077.*

**Emerald City Flight Festival (Flightfest)** [KIDS] More than just an air show, Flightfest encourages families to look, listen, and eat. There's always an aircraft in the sky—with occasional aerobatics—and entertainment on the ground. Headliners in past years have included the Apollo-Soyuz mission cosmonauts and the Golden Knights Parachute Team. General admission $10 (kids under six free). ■ *Boeing Field, near the Museum of Flight; 764-5703; map:NN6.*

**Fourth of July Fireworks** [KIDS][FREE] Dueling fireworks: the Lake Union version, sponsored by Cellular One, explodes to the sound of the Seattle Symphony at Gas Works Park, while Ivar's Elliott Bay show is best viewed from Myrtle Edwards Park. A lucky few who think to make reservations for a late dinner at the Space Needle can view them both. The pyrotechnics start just after dark. ■ *Ivar's: Myrtle Edwards Park; 587-6500; map:HH8.* ■ *Cellular One: Lake Union; 622-5123; map:FF7–GG7.*

**Good Vibrations World Music and Jazz Festival** A re-creation of the old Bellevue Jazz Festival, Good Vibrations now offers a day of outdoor concerts featuring world music and jazz. Tickets are $10 (general admission), $8 teens and seniors. Dates vary. ■ *Bellevue Community College, 3000 Landerholm Circle SE, Bellevue; 455-6207; map:HH3.*

**King County Fair** [KIDS] The oldest county fair in the state is also its best, featuring live music with country headline acts, a rodeo, 4H and FAA exhibits, a loggers show (remember ax-throwing contests?), crafts, and food. Begins the third Wednesday in July. ■ *King County Fairgrounds, Enumclaw; take I-5 south to Auburn exit, Hwy 104; (360)825-7777.*

**Lake Union Wooden Boat Festival** For three days, around the Fourth, the Center for Wooden Boats lures the nautically minded with rowing, sailing, and team boat-building competitions, plus workshops, food, and crafts. Spectators can board various wooden boats (including the *Wawona*, a schooner built in 1897). Water taxis shuttle people from events to demonstrations during the day. Donations of $3 per person or $5 per family are suggested. ■ *1010 Valley St, south end of Lake Union; 382-2628; map:GG7.*

**Marymoor Heritage Festival** [KIDS][FREE] The rich ethnic heritage of the Puget Sound area comes to life over the Fourth of July, with food, crafts, and music in the pastoral setting of Marymoor Park. There's plenty to fascinate kids; admission is free, though parking on the grounds sets you back $5. ■ *Marymoor Park, Redmond; 296-2964; map:FF1.*

**McChord Air Show** Come see pilots in action as the F-16s do their thing. Afterward watch military demonstrations—from an all-services attack demo to antique aircraft—and get your picture taken in the cockpit of a jet. In July or August; call for dates. ■ *McChord Air Force Base, Tacoma; (206)984-2350.*

**Nordstrom Anniversary Sale** A bonafide Northwest event—folks actually line up for this annual sale (which usually begins July 21st) at Seattle's favorite store. Prices on upcoming fall apparel are excellent. Happens for two weeks in late July. ■ *5th Ave and Pine St (and branches); 628-1690; map:J6.*

**Northwest AIDS Foundation International Croquet Tournament**  Since 1984, Gary Manuel Salon has sponsored this way-too-fun event—where participants dress in their whitest whites or in "theme" garb (Viva Las Vegas! brought out a world of Elvis and Wayne Newton impersonators) and strut their stuff on the croquet lawn. Entry fees are $25 per person ($150 for teams of six—gawking is free) and all proceeds benefit Northwest AIDS. Last Sunday in July. ▪ *Volunteer Park; 728-1234; map:GG6.*

**Olympic Music Festival**  The Philadelphia String Quartet opens its season with one of Puget Sound's premier music festivals, held in a turn-of-the-century barn nestled on 40 acres of pastoral farmland near Quilcene on the Olympic Peninsula. Sit in the barn on hay bales ($20) or spread a picnic on the lawn ($9). The festival runs from June through Labor Day weekend. Bring a blanket. ▪ *Quilcene; 11 miles west of Hood Canal Bridge on Hwy 104, take Quilcene exit; 527-8839.*

**Pacific Northwest Arts and Crafts Fair**  [FREE] The Northwest's largest arts and crafts fair covers Bellevue Square with an excellent juried selection of West Coast arts and crafts and a juried exhibition in the Bellevue Art Museum, the last weekend in July. ▪ *Bellevue Square, Bellevue; 454-4900; map:HH3.*

**Pacific Northwest Scottish Highland Games**  Kilts are not the only thing you'll find here. Scottish piping, drumming, dancing, Parade of the Clans, and games are the major attractions, not to mention a chance to sample authentic Scottish food and drink. Seven dollars gets you in for the day. ▪ *King County Fairgrounds, Enumclaw; take I-5 south to Auburn exit, Highway 104; (360)522-2541.*

**San Juan Island Dixieland Jazz Festival**  A three-day festival, $45 for all three days, sponsored by the San Juan Island Goodtime Classic Jazz Association, brings fans out to enjoy the jazz of yesteryear, mid- to late July. ▪ *Friday Harbor, San Juan Island; (360)378-5509.*

**Seafair**  [KIDS][FREE] Seattle's frenzied summer fete has been around since 1950 and—to the chagrin of many locals—isn't likely to go away. The hoopla begins on the third weekend of July with the milk-carton races at Green Lake and ends on the first Sunday in August when the hydroplanes tear up the waters of Lake Washington. Bright spots include a couple of triathlons; some excellent ethnic festivals: Bon Odori, late July; Chinatown International District Summer Festival, mid-July; Hispanic Seafair Festival, late July; Black Mardi Gras (mid-July); and the Torchlight Parade (Friday before the hydroplane races), which is a full-scale march through the downtown area and a kids' delight. Practically all Seafair events are free. ▪ *Citywide; 728-0123.*

## AUGUST

*Average daily maximum and minimum temperatures: 74, 54*
*Average rainfall: 1.27 inches*

**Evergreen State Fair**  [KIDS] For 11 days, late August through Labor Day, the Monroe fair features country-music headliners, roping and riding, stock-car races, a lumberjack show, and a carnival. Great fun. ▪ *Monroe; take I-405 north from Bellevue to Hwy 522, then northeast to Monroe; (360) 794-7832.*

**Gig Harbor Jazz Festival** The grassy natural amphitheater makes a great setting for this two-day festival that draws national jazz artists. Boat owners can sail up to the site. ▪ *Celebrations Meadow, Gig Harbor; south on I-5 to Tacoma, west on Hwy 16 over Tacoma Narrows Bridge; (206) 627-1504.*

**RSVP (Ride from Seattle to Vancouver, BC, and Party)** It's two days and 185 miles from Seattle to Vancouver, BC, and the Cascade Bicycle Club makes the trip worth the sweat with a reception and buffet at the end. On the third day, the Vancouver Bicycle Club offers optional rides around their beautiful city. Register early; there's a 700-rider limit. ▪ *From UW to UBC; 522-BIKE.*

**Washington State Open Tennis Tournament** The top players in Washington and the men's western pro circuit compete side by side during the first week in August at the exclusive Seattle Tennis Club. Tickets range from $1 to $5, and it's worth the admission just to stroll the idyllic grounds. ▪ *922 McGilvra Blvd E (Seattle Tennis Club); 324-3200; map:GG6.*

## SEPTEMBER

*Average daily maximum and minimum temperatures: 69, 52*
*Average rainfall: 1.88 inches*

**Bumbershoot** The longest multi-arts festival north of San Francisco is a splendid, eclectic celebration. Select craftspeople, writers, poets, and performing artists entertain the hordes on stages throughout Seattle Center over the long Labor Day weekend. A $10 daily pass ($9 if you buy in advance) is all you need to stay thoroughly entertained. ▪ *Seattle Center; 622-5123 or 682-4FUN; map:C6.*

**Ellensburg Rodeo** The biggest rodeo in these parts brings riders in from far and wide for four days of Wild West events over Labor Day weekend. Cost of admission for the big, colorful event is $9 to $18, depending on your seat. ▪ *Ellensburg, 115 miles east of Seattle on I-90; (800) 637-2444 or (509) 962-7831.*

**Leavenworth Autumn Leaf Festival** [FREE] The last weekend of September and first weekend in October are grand times for a drive over the Cascades to Leavenworth, a mountain town gussied up Tyrolean style for a festival celebrating the fall glory of deciduous trees. A parade, arts and crafts, and Bavarian music are all part of the festivities. Most events are free. ▪ *Leavenworth; 120 miles east of Seattle via 405 north to Hwy 522, then east on Hwy 2; (509) 548-5807.*

**Northwest AIDS Walk** Begun in 1986, this annual event just keeps growing— in number of participants, and in the amount of money raised. In 1995, over 15,000 walkers raised more than $1.3 million for AIDS care and education agencies statewide. ▪ *Starts and finishes at Seattle Center; 323-WALK (July–Sept) or 329-6923; map:C6.*

---

**The Puyallup Fair (Western Washington State Fair)** [KIDS] Everybody "does the Puyallup." This 17-day extravaganza begins in early September, and it's the rural county fair you remember from your childhood—only bigger. Rodeo, music, barnyard animals, carnival rides, exhibits, and vast amounts of food (including the legendary scones). ■ *35 miles south of Seattle via I-5; (206)841-5045.*

**Greek Festival** For three days in late September (or early October, depending on Husky football games), enjoy traditional Greek food and festivities galore at this noble Byzantine church. Church tours, folk-dancing performances, music, arts and crafts, and wonderful baklava make this a favorite neighborhood and Grecophile event. ■ *St. Demetrios Church, 2100 Boyer Ave E; 325-4347; map:GG6.*

**Seattle Seahawks Football** The Seahawks may play conservative ball (and may have seen better seasons in years past), but the fans' loyalty is steadfast. Consequently, it's nearly impossible to get tickets ($19 fo $38), and Kingdome-area parking is a crunch, so take a free bus from downtown. The season starts in September (preseason games in August) and runs through December; games are usually Sundays at 1pm. ■ *Kingdome; 628-0888; map:Q9.*

## OCTOBER

*Average daily maximum and minimum temperatures: 60, 46*
*Average rainfall: 3.23 inches*

**Arboretum Bulb Sale** It's a wonderful sale of specialized bulbs and imports from Holland. Loyal customers go year after year, the first weekend in October, for expert advice from folks who know their stuff. ■ *Visitor Center parking lot, Seattle Arboretum; 543-8800; map:GG6.*

**Issaquah Salmon Days** [KIDS] Issaquah celebrates the return of the salmon the first weekend of October, with a parade, food, crafts, music, dancing, displays, shows, and 5- and 10K runs. A Kids' Fair keeps the tykes entertained with pony rides and face painting, and the hydro races at Lake Sammamish are fun for kids of all ages. At the state hatchery you can get excellent views of chinook and coho thrashing up the fish ladder. ■ *Issaquah; 15 miles east of Seattle on I-90; 392-7024.*

**Mushroom Show** Sponsored by the Puget Sound Mycological Society, this mid-October fest celebrates the height of the mushroom foraging season in the Northwest, featuring 150 to 300 different mushroom species. ■ *Center for Urban Horticulture, University of Washington; 522-6031; map:FF6.*

**Northwest Bookfest** Seattle's first book festival debuted in 1995 with a wide range of programs, including author appearances and signings, bookseller and publisher exhibits, multimedia demonstrations, children's activities, panel discussions, writing workshops, and more. ■ *Pier 48; 789-9868; map:N9.*

## NOVEMBER

*Average daily maximum and minimum temperatures: 50, 40*
*Average rainfall: 5.83 inches*

**Model Railroad Show** [KIDS] A slew of model train setups and clinics on how to make whistles and scenery bring out the kid in all of us ($6.50, with reduced prices for kids) over Thanksgiving weekend. ▪ *Pacific Science Center; 443-2001; map:C7.*

**Seattle SuperSonics Basketball** From early November to late April, Seattle's home team tears up the court. The Sonics play smart, competitive, entertaining, and somewhat uneven basketball, and the fans love 'em. Tickets cost $7 to $65; games are at 7pm. ▪ *KeyArena; 281-5850; map:B7.*

## DECEMBER

*Average daily maximum and minimum temperatures: 45, 36*
*Average rainfall: 5.91 inches*

**A Christmas Carol** [KIDS] Based on an original adaptation written for ACT, this festive production has become a holiday tradition for many families, and sells out every year. Runs from Thanksgiving to Christmas Eve. ▪ *ACT; 100 W Roy St; 285-5110; map:GG7.*

**Christmas Ship** [FREE] One of Seattle's cherished Christmas traditions comes to life every December, as area musical groups serenade folks gathered at various shores. Call for a schedule. ▪ *Beaches citywide; 623-1445.*

**Community Hanukkah Celebration** [KIDS] The largest community Hanukkah celebration around offers arts and crafts, holiday wares, children's games, food, and music. Everyone is welcome to take part when members of the area's Jewish community gather for the Festival of Lights—complete with the traditional symbolic candle-lighting ceremony. ▪ *Stroum Jewish Community Center, 3801 Mercer Way, Mercer Island; 232-7115; map:JJ4.*

**Leavenworth Christmas Lighting** Crafts, music, and food are part of Leavenworth's ceremony kicking off the Christmas season. Around dusk (usually on the first and second Saturdays of the month), the Bavarian village square is officially lit up for the season. In addition, you'll find all the ingredients for a traditional holiday: roasted chestnuts, sleigh rides, Santa and Mrs. Claus, and Scrooge. All's free except the sleigh rides and evening concerts after the ceremony. ▪ *Leavenworth; 120 miles east of Seattle via 405 north to Hwy 522, then east on Hwy 2; (509)548-5807.*

**The Nutcracker** [KIDS] Pacific Northwest Ballet's annual production is a Northwest tradition noted for the spectacular set designs of Maurice Sendak. A good introduction to the ballet for children. Early December through the end of the month; tickets go on sale in mid-October. ▪ *Pacific Northwest Ballet, Seattle Center Opera House; 441-2424; map:C6.*

# Index

## A

A & J Meats, 293
A Contemporary Theatre (ACT), 157, 180
A Cook's Tour, 291
A Grand Affair, 234
A La Francaise, 241
A Little Bit of Saigon, 175
A Piece of Cake, 174, 241
Abercrombie & Fitch, 234
Abodio, 276
Adriatica, 13, 13, 103
AHA! Theater, 157
Air tours, 218
Airplane charters, 182
AKA Eddie Bauer, 234
Al Boccalino, 13, 169
Aldrich's, 356
Alexandra's, 261
Alexis Hotel, 164, 323
Alfalfa's, 283
ALFI News, 201
Alhambra, 287
Alice B. Theater, 157
Alki Beach Park, 377, 396
The Alki Tavern, 103
All for Kids, 246
All Wrapped Up, 308
Allegro! Dance Festival, 150
Almost Antiques, 231
Alpine Hut, 294
Alvin Goldfarb Jeweler, 289
American Eagles, 310
Anglomania, 288
Ann Marie Lingerie, 292
Ann Taylor, 235
Annex Theater, 157
Anthony's HomePort, 14, 103, 201
Antique Importers, 231
Antique Liquidators, 232
Archie McPhee, 310
Argosy Tours, 201, 218, 221
Armadillo Barbecue, 14
Arnie's Northshore, 103
Artworks Gallery, 141
Asia Gallery, 288
Assaggio Ristorante, 15
Athenian Inn, 103, 167
The Atrium, 411
The Attic, 104
Ayutthaya, 15
Azaleas, 16, 198

## B

B & O Espresso, 129, 177
Baby & Co., 235
Backstage, 120
Backtrack Video, 314
Bacon Mansion, 333
Bagel Oasis, 241
Bahn Thai, 16, 349
Bailey/Coy Books, 177, 247
Bainbridge Bakers, 241
Bainbridge Gardens, 272
Bainbridge Island, 222, 344, 348, 374
Bakeman's, 16
Ballard, 184
Ballard Baking Company, 241
Ballard Blossoms, 272
Ballard Firehouse, 121, 185
Bally of Switzerland, 305
Bamboo Gardens of Washington, 272
Banana Republic, 235
Barnes & Noble Books, 247
Barneys New York, 235
Bathhouse Theatre, 158
Battelle Seattle Conference Center, 411
Bauhaus, 129
Bavarian Meats, 293
Bay Hay and Feed, 272
Beach Cottage B&B, 340
Beacon Market, 265
Beatnix, 121
Beatty Bookstore, 247
Beeliner Diner, 16
Beks Bookstore, 247
Belle Arte Concerts, 153
Belle Provence, 278
Bellevue, 196, 229
Bellevue Art Museum, 145, 197
Bellevue Club Hotel, 336
Bellevue Downtown Central Park, 202
The Bellevue Hilton, 336
Belltown Billiards, 104
Belltown Pub, 104
Ben Bridge, 289
Benjamin's, 104
Bergman Luggage, 230
The Best of All Worlds, 285
Best Western Executive Inn, 323

Betsey Johnson, 235
Beyond the Closet, 247
Bicycling, 373
Big Time Brewery and Alehouse, 104, 190, 192
Big Time Pizza, 17
Bistro Provencal, 17, 201
Bitters Co., 278
Bizzaro Italian Cafe, 18
Blackbird, 247
Blacksheep Cafe and Catering, 18
Blake Island, 202, 350, 383
Bloedel Reserve, 211, 222, 344
The Blue Moon Tavern, 104, 190
Blue Ridge, 374
Boat Street Cafe, 130
Boat tours, 218
Boca, 18
Boehm's Chocolates, 348
Bohemian Cafe, 121
The Boiserie, 130
The Bombay House, 340
The Bon Marché, 164, 264
Bonneville's, 235
The Book Store, 104
Bop Street Records, 301
Borders, 248, 314
Borracchini's, 241, 265
Boston Street, 257
Bothell Landing, 203
Boulangerie, 242
Boulevard Espresso, 130
Bowie & Company Booksellers, 170, 248
Bread and Roses Bakery, 356
Bremerton, 349
Brenner Brothers Bakery, 242
Brewery hopping, 191
Bridle Trails State Park, 198, 203
Brie and Bordeaux, 317
Bright Coffee, 130
British Pantry Ltd., 265
Broadway Guest House, 333
Broadway New American Grill, 19
The Brooklyn, 105
Brooks Brothers, 235
Bud's Jazz Records, 301

Bulldog News and Fast Espresso, 190, 248
Bumbershoot, 427
Burberrys, 236
Burk's Cafe, 19, 185
Burke Museum, 145, 189
Burke Museum Store, 278
Burke-Gilman Trail, 183, 203, 222, 375, 386
Burrito Loco, 20
Bush Garden, 20
Bushell's Auctions, 240
Business services, 411
Butch Blum, 236
Byrnie Utz, 230

**C**

C.C. Filson Co., 171, 296
C.P. Shades, 236
Cabaret de Paris, 158
Cactus, 21
Cafe Allegro, 131, 190
Cafe Campagne, 24, 167, 220
Cafe Counter Intelligence, 131, 168
Café Dilettante, 131, 177, 256
Cafe Flora, 21
Cafe Illiterati, 21
Cafe Juanita, 22
Cafe Lago, 22
Cafe Nola, 23
Cafe Paradiso, 131
Cafe Septième, 23
Cafe Veloce, 24
Cafe Vizcaya, 24
Caffe Ladro, 132
Caffe Vita, 132
Calendar of events, 417
Calico Corners, 270
The Camera Show, 254
Cameras West, 255
CameraTech, 254
Camp Long 203, 412
Campagne, 24, 105
Canlis, 25, 105
Cape Cod Comfys, 276
Capitol Hill, 175, 228
Capitol Hill Inn, 334
Captain Cook's Pub, 121
Car Toys, 310
Carillon Point, 201
Carkeek Park, 203
Carnation, 359
Carolyn Staley Fine Prints, 141
Carolyn's Cakes, 242

Carroll's, 289
Casa U-Betcha, 105
CasCioppo Brothers, 293
Catfish Corner, 26
Caveman Kitchens, 26
Cellophane Square, 190, 301
Center for Wooden Boats, 145, 182, 390
Center on Contemporary Art (COCA), 141
Central, 121
Central Co-op Grocery, 284
Chambered Nautilus, 332
Chameleon, 248
Chandler's Crabhouse, 26
Chanterelle Specialty Foods, 27
Charlotte Martin Theatre, 178
Charter airplanes, 403
Charter buses, 404
Chases Downtown Florist, 272
Chetzemoka Park, 222, 356
Chez Shea, 27, 168,
Chicago's, 122
The Children's Museum, 146
The Chile Pepper, 27
Chinatown Discovery, 219
Chinese Room, 412
Chinook's at Salmon Bay, 28
Chism Beach Park, 203
Chocolaterie Bernard C, 256
Chubby & Tubby, 282
Church's English Shoes, 305
Chutney's, 28
Ciao Bella Ristorante, 29
Ciao Italia, 29
Cibol, 288
Cinema Books, 248
Cinema Video, 152
City Cellars Fine Wines & Foods, 317
City Fish, 304
City Flowers Inc., 273
City Kitchens, 291
City Kites/City Toys, 311, 383
City People's Garden Store, 273
City People's Mercantile, 177, 282
Claremont Hotel, 324
Clothes Connection, 261
Cloud Room, 105
The Coach Store, 230

Coastal Kitchen, 30, 177
College Inn, 106, 332
Colman Park, 206
Colourbox, 122
Comedy Underground, 122
Comet Tavern, 106
The Computer Store, 260
The Confectionery, 256
Conor Byrne's Public House, 106, 185
Consulates, 406
Contintental Restaurant and Pastry Shop, 30
Continental Store, 265
Cooper's Northwest Ale House, 106
Copacabana, 30
Copy services, 415
Cottage Creek Nursery, 273
Cottontail Corner, 288
Coulon Park, 204, 395
Country Village, 228
Coupeville, 369
Court in the Square, 412
Cowen Park, 208
Crackerjack Contemporary Crafts, 279
The Crane Gallery, 232
Crpe de Paris, 31
Crissey Flowers, 273
Critics' Choice, 314
Crocodile Cafe, 122, 221
Crossings, 294
The Crow's Nest, 294
Crowne Plaza Hotel, 324
The Crumpet Shop, 242
Crystallia, 285
Cucina Fresca, 167, 265
Cucina! Cucina!, 31, 106
Cunningham Gallery, 142
Current, 276
Cutters Bayhouse, 32, 106
Cyclops, 32, 106

**D**

Dahlia Lounge, 32
The Daily Planet (Bellevue), 198
The Daily Planet (Seattle), 183, 232
Dakota, 236
Dakota Art Store, 200, 308
Dance, 149
Daniel Smith, 308
Daniel's Broiler, 107, 223
Darbury Stenderu, 236
Dark Horse Boutique, 261

David Ishii, Bookseller, 248
David Morgan, 294
David Weatherford, 232
Davidson Galleries, 142
DaVinci's, 33, 200
de Medici/Ming Fine Paper
  Company, 308
Deception Pass, 370
Definitive Audio, 310
Del-Teet Furniture, 276
DeLaurenti, 166, 266, 318
Delivery services, 416
Deluxe Bar and Grill, 107,
  176
Deluxe Junk, 183, 315
Design Concern, 285
Design Products Clothing,
  236
Designers' Fabrics, 270
Dessert Works, 242
Detour Tavern, 122
Dimitriou's Jazz Alley, 122
Discovery Park, 204
The Disney Store, 311
Dita Boutique, 237
Ditto Tavern, 107
Dixie's BBQ, 33
Doc Maynard's, 123
Domus, 285
Don & Joe's, 293
Don's Hobbies, 311
Donald Young Gallery, 142
Doppler Computer, 260
Doubletree Suites/Inn, 338
The Down Factory, 261
Dreamland, 177
Dubliner Pub, 123
The Duchess Tavern, 107
Duke's Bar and Grill, 107
Duncan and Sons Boots and
  Saddles, 171, 306
Duvall, 358
DV8, 123

**E**
Eagle Harbor, 383
Ear Wax, 301
Early Music Guild, 153
East West Book Shop, 249
Eastlake Zoo, 107
Eastside Trains, 311
Easy Rider, 295
The Easy, 107
Eddie Bauer, 295
The Edgewater, 324
Edmonds Harbor Inn, 332
Egbert's, 286

Egghead Software, 260
The Egyptian, 152, 177
Eileen of China, 174, 232
El Greco, 34
El Lobo Loco, 123
El Mercado Latino, 266
El Puerco Lloron, 34
Elements Gallery, 280
Elliott Bay Bicycles, 295
Elliott Bay Book Company,
  170, 249
Elliott Bay Cafe, 132
Elliott Bay Park, 172
Elliott Bay Stationery Store,
  309
Elliott Brown, 142
Emmett Watson's Oyster
  Bar, 34, 167
Empty Space Theatre, 158
Enzo Angiolini, 306
Ernie's Bar and Grill, 108
The Erotic Bakery, 242
Espresso Roma, 132
Espresso to Go (ETG), 132
Esquin Wine Merchants,
  318
Etta's Seafood, 35, 220
European Vine Selections of
  Washington, 318
Exotique Imports, 302
Explore More Store, 279
Expressions Furniture, 277
Ezell's Fried Chicken, 35

**F**
F.X. McRory's, 108, 171
Fabulous Buckaroo, 108
Facere Jewelry Art, 289
Fallout Records, 302
The Famous Pacific Dessert
  Company, 133
Fantastic Games and Toys,
  311
FAO Schwartz, 311
Fast Forward, 231
Fast Lady Sports, 295
Fay Bainbridge State Park,
  204, 344
Feathered Friends, 295
Fenix, 123
Fiddler's Inn, 108
Fifth Avenue Theater
  Company, 158
Filiberto's, 36
Fillipi Book and Record
  Shop, 249

Fine Threads, 257
Firenze, 36
The Fireside Room, 108
FireWorks Gallery, 170, 279
Fischer Meats and
  Seafoods, 293
Fishermen's Terminal, 183
Fishing/Clamming, 376
Five Point Cafe, 108
5 Spot Cafe, 37
Flora and Fauna, 249
Flying Fish, 37
Flying Shuttle, 279
Folk Art Gallery/La Tienda,
  190, 288
The Forum Menswear, 237
Foster/White, 142, 200
Four Seasons Olympic
  Hotel, 164, 325
The Four Swallows, 38
Fox Paw, 279
Fox's Gem Shop, 290
Fran's Chocolates, 256
Francine Seders Gallery,
  142
Franco's Hidden Harbor,
  109
Frank and Dunya, 286
Fremont, 183, 221, 229
Fremont Antique Mall, 315
Fremont Classic Pizza, 38
Fremont Noodle House, 38
Fremont Place Book
  Company, 249
Friedlander Jewelers, 290
Frontier Room, 109, 221
Frye Art Museum, 146
Fullers, 39
Funk You, 315
Furney's Nursery, 273
Fury, 261
The Future Shop, 260

**G**
G. Gibson Gallery, 143
Galleries, 141
Galway Traders, 288
The Gap, 237
Garden Botanika, 245
Gardens, 210
Gargoyles, 279
Gas Works Park, 183, 204,
  383, 395
Gaslight Inn, 334
Gem Design Jewelers, 290
Gene's Ristorante, 39

Gentlemen's Consignment, 262
George's Sausage and Delicatessen, 266
Georgian Room, 40
Gerard's Relais de Lyon, 40
Gibson's Bar & Grill, 123
Gig Harbor, 360, 362
Giggles, 123
GlamOrama, 183
Glazer's, 255
The Globe Books, 250
Godiva Chocolatier, 256
Gold & Silver Shop, 290
Gold Creek Lodge, 412
Golden Gardens Park, 186, 205, 396
Golden Oldies, 302
Goldman's Jewelers, 290
Golfing, 377
Gordo's, 41
Grady's Montlake Pub, 109
The Grainery, 284
Grand Central Baking Company, 242
Grand Central Mercantile, 170, 291
Grand Illusion, 133, 152
Gravity Bar, 41, 177
The Great Northwest, 277
The Great Wind-Up, 312
Great Winds Kite Shop, 312, 383
Greek Active, 157
Green Cat Cafe, 133
Green Lake, 205, 221, 382, 387, 388, 390, 395
Greenwood Bakery, 243
Greenwood Hardware, 282
Greg Davidson Antique Lighting, 232
Greg Kucera Gallery, 143
Gregg's Greenlake Cycle, 222, 296, 387
The Group Theatre Company, 158, 178
Guess Where, 316

**H**
Half-Price Books, 250
Hands of the World, 288
Hansville, 347
Harbor City Barbecue, 41
Harbor Video, 314
Harbour Public House, 109, 222, 344
Hardwick's Swap Shop, 282

Hart Brewery and Pub, 109, 192
Harvard Espresso, 133, 177
The Harvard Exit, 151, 177
Hattie's Hat, 110, 185
HD Hotspurs, 124
Helen's (Of Course), 237
Henry Art Gallery, 146
The Herbalist, 245
The Herbfarm, 42, 212, 222, 359
Hi-Spot Cafe, 42
High & Mighty Store, 307
Higo, 175, 289
Hiking, 379
Hilltop Alehouse, 110
Hing Hay Park, 205
Hiram M. Chittenden Locks, 185
Hoffman's Fine Pastries, 200, 243
Hold Everything, 286
Holiday Inn of Renton, 338
Honey Bear Bakery, 133, 243
Honeychurch Antiques, 233
Hood Canal, 344
Hoodsport, 346
Hopvine Pub, 110
Horizon Books, 250
Horseback riding, 381
Hotel Vintage Park, 325
Houghton Beach Park, 199, 396
Houseboat Hideaway, 325
Howard Mandeville Gallery, 200
The Hunt Club, 43
Huong Binh, 43, 175
Husky Deli, 266
Hyatt Regency, 336

**I**
I Love Sushi, 43
Iguana Cantina, 124
Il Bacio, 44
Il Bistro, 44, 110, 168
Il Paesano, 45, 191
Il Terrazzo Carmine, 45, 110, 170
Il Vecchio, 296
Imagination Toys, 312
IMAX Theater, 179
In the Beginning Fabrics, 270
The Incredible Link, 293

Inn at the Market, 167, 220, 326
Inn at Virginia Mason, 326
International Chamber Music Series, 154
International District, 173
International Music Festival of Seattle, 154
Intiman Playhouse, 179
Intiman Theatre Company, 159
Intimate Dwellings, 358
Isabella Ristorante, 45
Isadora's, 316,
Issaquah Brewhouse, 110
Italianissimo, 46
Itineraries, 220
Ivar's, 46
Ivey Seright, 255.
Izumi, 47, 201

**J**
J & M Cafe, 110
J. Crew, 237
J.F. Henry Shop, 286
Jack's Fish Spot, 168, 304
Jean Williams Antiques, 233
Jehlor Fantasy Fabrics, 270
Jessica McClintock, 237
Joan & David Shoes, 306
John Fluevog Shoes, 306
John Nielsen Pastry, 244
Juanita Bay Park, 199
Juanita Beach Park, 199
Judkins Barbecue, 47

**K**
Kabul, 47
Kaizuka, 48
The Kaleenka, 48
Kamalco, 48
Kasala, 277
Kaspar's, 49, 111
Kathy's Kloset, 262
Kayaking/Canoeing, 381
Keeg's, 286
Kells, 49, 111, 167
Kelsey Creek Park, 198, 206, 389
Kenmore Air, 218
Kerryman Pub, 124
Kiana Lodge, 412
The Kids Club, 257
Kids in the Park, 258
Kids on 45th, 262
Kikuya, 50
Kilimanjaro, 124
Kilimanjaro Market, 266

---

Kimura Nursery, 273
King County Public Library, 408
Kinokuniya, 174, 250
Kirkland, 199
Kirkland Arts Center, 143, 200
Kirkland Roaster, 50, 111
Kirkland True Value Hardware, 282
Kitchen 'n Things, 291
Kitchen Kitchen, 291
Kitsap Peninsula, 222, 347
Klondike Gold Rush Museum, 168
Kokeb, 124
Koryo Restaurant, 50
Kosher Delight, 267
Kym's Kiddy Corner, 258

**L**

La Cantina, 318
La Conner, 357
La Dolce Vita, 73
La Panzanella, 243
La Residence Suite, 336
Lake Sammamish State Park, 206
Lake Union, 181, 382, 390, 395
Lake Union B&B, 333
Lake Union Pub, 124
Lake Washington, 206, 382, 390, 395
Lampreia, 51
Langley, 368
Langston Hughes Cultural Center, 413
Larry's Greenfront, 124
Larry's Markets, 180, 267, 284, 318
Larsen's Danish Bakery, 243
Latona by Green Lake, 111
Laura Ashley, 238
Le Frock, 316
Le Gourmand, 51
Le Panier, 167, 220, 243
Learning World, 312
Left Bank Books, 168, 250
The Legacy, 143
Legal services, 408
Leo Melina, 111
Leschi Lakecafe, 111
Leschi Park, 206
Li'l People, 258
Lighthouse Roasters, 134
Lillian's Pearl Shop, 290

Lincoln Park, 207, 389
Linda Cannon Gallery, 143
Linda Hodges Gallery, 143
Linda's Tavern, 111
Local Brilliance, 238
Lockstock, 125
Loehmann's, 262
The Loft, 270
Lombardi's Cucina, 52
London's Bakehouse, 244
Lord's, 238
Louie's Cuisine of China, 112
Luna Park Cafe, 52
Luther Burbank Park, 207

**M**

M Coy Books, 251
M. J. Feet's, 306
M. L. Mallard, 271
Macrina, 244
Madame & Company, 316
Maddox Grill, 53
Made in Washington, 167, 280
Madison Park, 206, 223, 229
Madison Park Bakery, 244
Madison Park Books, 251
Madison Park Cafe, 53
Madison Park Hardware, 282
Madison Valley, 229
Madison's Cafe, 125
Madrona Park, 206
Mae's Phinney Ridge Cafe, 53, 221
Maggie Bluffs, 61
Maggie's Shoes, 306
Magic Mouse, 312
The Magic Spoke, 296
Magnano Foods, 284
Magnolia Hi-Fi, 310
Magnuson Park, 207, 383, 395
Magus Bookstore, 251
Maltby Cafe, 54
Maltese Falcon, 314
Manca's, 54
Mandarin Garden, 54
Maple Leaf Grill, 55
Mar-T Cafe, 222, 360
Marco's Supperclub, 55, 221
Mario's of Seattle, 238
Market Graphics, 286
Market House Corned Beef, 294
Market Theater, 168

MarketSpice, 258
Marlee, 238
Marlene's Market and Deli, 284
Marley's Snowboards and Skateboards, 296
Marmot Mountain Works, 297
Marriott Residence Inn (Bellevue), 337
Marriott Residence Inn (Lake Union), 326
Marshalls, 262
Martha E. Harris, 274
Marvel on Madison, 233
Marymoor County Park, 207
Marymoor Velodrome, 374, 421
Masins, 277
Maximilien in the Market, 55
Maxine's Pickity Patch, 274
Maya's, 56
Mayflower Park Hotel, 326
McCarthy and Schiering, 318
McCormick & Schmick's, 56, 112
McCormick's Fish House and Bar, 112
McGraw Street Bakery, 244
McHale & Co., 297
McLendon's, 282
McMenamins, 112, 192, 193
Me 'N Mom's, 258
Meany Tower Hotel, 333
Mecca Cafe, 112
Medical/Dental Services, 408
Medina Grocery and Deli, 267
Mediterranean Kitchen, 57
Megan Mary Olander, 274
Mephisto, 306
Mercer Island Ski and Cycle, 297
Metro Man, 231
Metro Transit, 402, 403
Metropolis, 125, 309
Metropolitan Grill, 57
Metsker Maps, 170
The Mexican Grocery, 267
MIA Gallery, 143
Michael Farrell, 290
Miller-Pollard Interiors, 287
Milmanco Corp., 407
MisterE Books, 251

Modele's, 277
Moe's Mo'roc'n Cafe, 125
Moghul Palace, 57
Molbak's, 196, 274
Mona's, 58
Monorail, 178, 404
Monsoon, 289
Moonphoto, 255
Morgan's Lakeplace Bistro, 112
Motherhood Maternity, 307
Motor tours, 219
Mount Baker, 384, 385
Mount Baker Park, 206, 390, 391, 395
Mount Rainier, 223, 351, 379, 392
Mount St. Helens, 385
Mountain Bike Specialists, 298
Mountain biking, 383
Mountaineering/Climbing, 384
Movies, 151
Mr. "J" Kitchen Gourmet, 291
Mr. Peepers, 312
The Mrs. Cooks, 292
Munro's Books, 367
Murphy's Pub, 113
Musashi's Sushi & Grill, 58
Museum of Flight, 147, 413
Museum of History and Industry, 147, 413
Music series, 153
Mutual Fish Company, 304
MV Challenger, 327
Myrtle Edwards Park, 208, 403

N
N.B. Nichols and Son, 233
Nancy Meyer, 292
NOAA, 182, 207, 387
The Nature Company, 280
Nature's Pantry, 284
NBN Outlet, 297
Neelam's, 58
Neighbours, 125
Nelly Stallion, 238
New City Theatre, 159
New Jake O'Shaughnessey's, 59, 113
New Mikado, 59, 175
New Orleans Restaurant, 125

New World Restaurant and Lounge, 125
Newcastle Beach Park, 208
Newcastle's, 126
Newport House, 238
Nickerson St. Saloon, 113
Nicolino, 59
Nido, 280
Nikko, 60, 113
911 Media Arts Center, 144, 152
Noble Court, 60
Nordic Heritage Museum, 148, 185
Nordstrom, 164, 245, 264, 425
Nordstrom Rack, 262
North Bend, 222
The North Face, 297
Northshore, 378
Northwest Asian American Theater, 157
Northwest Chamber Orchestra, 154
Northwest Craft Center, 144
Northwest Discovery, 280
Northwest Gallery of Fine Woodworking, 144, 170
Northwest Outdoor Center, 221, 382
Nubia's, 239

O
O.O. Denny Park, 199, 396
Oak Harbor, 370
Oasis Water Gardens, 274
Off Ramp, 126
Office Max, 261
OK Hotel, 126
Old Milltown, 228
The Old Pequliar, 113
Old Timer's Cafe, 126
Old Town Alehouse, 113, 222
Olsen's Scandinavian Foods, 267
Olympia, 353
Olympic Mountains, 380
Olympic Music Festival, 222, 347, 426
Olympic National Forest and Park, 345
Olympic Peninsula, 222
On the Boards, 150, 159
110 Espresso, 134
Open Books, 251
Opera, 156

Optechs, 255
Opus, 177, 239
Organized tours, 217
Oriental Mart, 267
Orpheum, 302
The Other Place, 263
Owl 'N Thistle, 113, 126

P
Pacific Food Importers, 268
Pacific Galleries, 240
Pacific Guest Suites, 327
Pacific Inn, 114
Pacific Iron and Building Materials, 283
Pacific Northwest Ballet, 150
Pacific Northwest Brewing Company, 114, 170, 192
Pacific Plaza Hotel, 327
Pacific Science Center, 178, 179
Pacific Water Sports, 298, 382
The Painted Table, 60
Palisade, 61
Palomino, 114
PANACA Gallery, 280
Pandasia, 61
Paper Cat, 309
The Paper Tree, 309
Paragon, 114, 127
Paramount Theater, 159
Parfumerie Elizabeth George, 246
Parfumerie Nasreen, 246
Parkplace Books, 201, 251
Parks and Beaches, 201
Partners in Time, 233
Pasta & Co., 62
Patagonia, 298
Patisserie Alinea, 244
Patrick's Fly Shop, 298
PCC Natural Markets, 285
Pegasus Coffee, 258, 344
Pegasus Pizza and Pasta, 62
Pelayo's, 233
Pendleton, 239
Pennsylvania Woodworks, 196, 278
Penny University, 134
Pensione Nichols, 328
Perennial Tea Room, 259
Pescatore, 114
Pete's Supermarket, 319
Peter Kirk Park, 200
Peter Miller Books, 252

Phad Thai, 62
Philadelphia Fevre, 63
Philip Monroe Jeweler, 291
Pho Bac, 63, 175
Phoenecia at Alki, 63
Phoenix Rising, 280
Photo-tronics, 255
Photographic Center
Northwest, 255
Piecora's, 64
Pike & Western Wine
Merchants, 319
Pike Place Fish, 304
Pike Place Flowers, 275
Pike Place Market, 165, 227
Pike Place Market
Creamery, 168, 268
Pin-Down Girl, 316
The Pink Door, 64, 114
Pinocchio, 312
Pioneer Square, 168, 220,
227, 403
Pioneer Square Hotel, 328
Pioneer Square Saloon, 115
Pirosmani, 64
Pizzeria Pagliacci, 65
Pizzuto's Italian Cafe, 65
Place Pigalle, 66, 115
Platters, 302
Play It Again Toys, 313
Pleasant Beach Grill, 66, 115
Pogacha, 66
Pon Proem, 67
Ponti Seafood Grill, 67
Port Chatham Packing
Company, 304
Port Gamble, 222, 347
Port Orchard, 350
Port Townsend, 222, 355
Portage Bay Goods, 281
Pottery Barn, 287
Poulsbo, 222, 348
President's Piano Series,
155
Price Costco, 263
Prima Mexico, 289
Procopio Gelateria, 134
ProLab, 256
Provinces, 67
Public access, 215
Public art, 139
Public restrooms, 409
Puget Sound, 383, 396
The Pumphouse, 115
Puyallup Fair, 428

**Q**
Quality Cheese, 268
Queen Anne, 179, 229
Queen Anne Avenue Books,
252
Queen Anne Thriftway, 181,
304, 319
Queen City Grill, 68, 115
Queen Mary Teahouse, 134
Quilcene, 346

**R**
R & E Cycles, 298
R & L Home of Good
Barbeque No. 1, 68
Ragamoffyn, 263
Rainbow Grocery, 285
Rainier Photographic
Supply, 256
Ravenna Park, 208
Ray's Boathouse, 69, 222
Ray's Cafe, 115
Re-Bar, 127
Re-Dress Consignment
Shop, 263
Read All About It, 166, 252
Recycled Cycles, 299
Red and Black Books, 177,
252
Red Door Alehouse, 116
Red Mill Burgers, 69
The Red Onion Tavern, 116
Red Robin, 116
Redhook Brewery, 183, 191
REI, 379
Renaissance Madison, 328
Rendezvous, 127
Restaurant Shilla, 69
Retro Viva, 177, 316
Retrospect Records, 302
RetroViva, 177
Rhinestone Rosie, 317
Ricky Young Surfboards,
299
Rikki Rikki, 70
Ring of Fire Gallery, 289
Ristorante Buongusto, 70
Ristorante Machiavelli, 71
Ristorante Paradiso, 71, 200
River rafting, 386
The River Run Cafe, 359
Riverside Inn, 127
RKCNDY, 127
Roadrunner Coffeehouse
and Coyote Comics, 135
Roanoke Inn, 116

Roanoke Park Place Tavern,
116
Roberta's, 334
Robinswood House, 413
Roche Bobois, 278
Roller skating/Roller
blading, 386
Romper Room, 127
The Roost, 71, 117
Rooz Market, 268
The Rose Bakery and
Bistro, 72
Rover's, 72
Rowing, 387
RR Hardware, 283
Rubato Records, 303
Ruby Montana's, 317
Ruby's on Bainbridge, 72
Running, 388

**S**
Saigon Bistro, 73
Sailing, 389
Saleh al Lago, 73
Salisbury House, 335
Saltwater State Park, 208
Salty's, 117
Salute, 73
Salvatore, 74
Sammamish Valley Cycle,
376
San Juan Islands, 383
San Marco, 307
Sanctuary Theatre, 152
Santa Fe Cafe, 74
Satori Fine Art Auction, 240
Sawatdy Thai Cuisine, 75
Scandinavian Specialty
Products, 268
Scarecrow Video, 314
Scarlet Tree, 128
Schmitz Park, 209
Schober Chocolates, 257
Sea Garden, 75, 174
Sea-Tac Dahlia Gardens, 275
Sea-Tac Red Lion Inn, 338
Seabeck, 345
Seafair, 388, 426
Seafirst Gallery, 144
Seattle Airport Hilton, 339
Seattle Aquarium, 172, 414
Seattle Art, 309
Seattle Art Museum (SAM),
148, 152, 165, 217, 220, 414
Seattle Asian Art Museum,
148, 209

Seattle Athletic and Exercise, 299
Seattle Bagel Bakery, 75, 245
Seattle Caviar Company, 305
Seattle Center, 178, 220, 414
Seattle Chamber Music Festival, 155
Seattle Children's Museum, 178
Seattle Children's Theatre, 159
Seattle Fabric, 271
Seattle Garden Center, 167, 274
Seattle Gilbert and Sullivan Society, 159
Seattle International Film Festival, 152, 422
Seattle International Raceway, 374, 419
Seattle International Trade Center, 414
Seattle Mariners, 397, 420
Seattle Marriott at Sea-Tac, 339
Seattle Men's Chorus, 155
Seattle Mystery Bookshop, 252
Seattle Opera, 156
Seattle Parks and Recreation Department, 394, 387
Seattle Pen, 309
Seattle Public Library, 408
Seattle Repertory Theatre, 160
Seattle Seaplanes, 218
Seattle Sheraton, 329
Seattle Super Smoke, 294
Seattle SuperSonics, 397, 429
Seattle Symphony, 155
Seattle Youth Symphony, 156
Seattle's Best Coffee (SBC), 167, 259, 363
Seattle-Tacoma International Airport, 401
Second Story Books, 252
The Secret Garden Children's Bookshop, 252
Seoul Olympic, 76
Serafina, 76
Seven Gables, 151
74th Street Alehouse, 76, 117
Seward Park, 208, 376

Shamek's Button Shop, 271
Shamiana, 77, 201
Shamshiri, 77
Shanghai Garden, 78, 174
Shark Club, 128
Sharky's, 128
Shea's Lounge, 27, 117, 220
Shiro's, 78
The Shoe Zoo, 258
Shorey Bookstore, 253
Showbox, 128
Shuckers, 78, 117
Shumway Mansion, 337
Si Senor, 79
Siam on Broadway, 79, 176
Silberman/Brown, 309
Silver Platters, 303
Silverdale, 349
Simply Desserts, 135, 245
Sisters, 80
Sit and Spin, 135
Six Arms, 193
Sixth Avenue Inn, 329
60th Street Desserts, 245
Skagit Valley, 357, 420
Skansonia, 414
Skiing: cross-country, 390
Skiing: downhill, 392
The Sloop, 117
Smokie Jo's Tavern, 118
Snappy Dragon, 80
Sneakers, 118
Snoqualmie Falls, 222, 359
Snoqualmie Valley, 358
Snow Goose Associates, 144
Snowboard Connection, 299
The Soap Box, 246
Sorrento Hotel, 329
Sostanza, 80, 223
The Souk, 269
Sound Flight, 218
Space Needle, 118, 178, 220, 414
Spazzo, 81
Speakeasy Cafe, 135
Speakerlab, 310
Spot Bagel Bakery, 245
Spud Fish and Chips, 81
St. Thomas Conference Center, 415
Stage Right Cafe, 82
Stampola, 309
Starbucks, 177, 220, 259
Steilacoom, 362
Stephenson Ace Hardware, 283

Steve's Broadway News, 177, 253
Still Life in Fremont, 82
Stimson-Green Mansion, 415
Stone Way Cafe, 82
Stoneway Hardware, 283
Streamliner Diner, 83, 222, 344
Stuteville Antiques, 233
Sub Pop Mega Mart, 303
Sunlight Cafe, 83
Sunshine Kitchen Company, 292
Super Jock 'N Jill, 299, 388
Sur La Table, 168, 292
Surrogate Hostess, 84
Sushi-Ten, 84
Swallows' Nest, 300, 384
Swanson's, 275
The Sweet Addition, 257
Swiftwater, 300
Swingside Cafe, 84
Szmania's, 84

T
Tacoma, 360
Take 2 Consignment, 263
Talbots, 239
Tandoor, 85, 191
Taqueria Guaymas, 85
Targy's Tavern, 118
Tashiro's, 283
The Tea Cup, 259
Teahouse Kuan Yin, 136, 259
Temple Billiards, 118
Temptations, 257
Tennis: public courts, 394
Tenzing Momo & Co., 246
Teri's Toybox, 313
TestaRossa, 86, 176
Thai Restaurant, 86, 221
Thai Terrace, 86
That's Amore, 87
Theater, 156
Thinker Toys, 313
Third Floor Fish Cafe, 87, 201
Thirteen Coins, 87
Thompson's Point of View, 88
Three Furies, 281
Three Girls Bakery, 88, 168
Thumpers, 118
Tilden, 281
The Timberline, 128

Tokyo Japanese Restaurant, 89
Tommy Thai's, 89
Top Ten Toys, 313
Torino Sausage Company, 294
Torrefazione Italia, 170, 259
Tosoni's, 89
Totally Michael's, 239
Totem Smokehouse, 167
Tower Books, 253
Tower Records, 303
Tower Video, 314
Tractor Tavern, 128
Trader Joe's, 269
Trains, 406
Trattoria Mitchelli, 90, 169
Tree Top Toys, 313
Triangle Tavern, 90, 118
Tricoter, 271
Trolleyman Pub, 119, 191
Tsue Chong, 269
The Tudor Choir, 156
Tulio, 90
Tully's Coffee, 260
Turgeon Raine Jewelers, 291
Tweedy and Popp, 283
Twice Sold Tales, 253
Two Angels Antiques, 234
Two Bells Tavern, 91, 119
211 Club, 119

**U**

Ultima, 307
Un Deux Trois, 91
Under the Rail, 128
Underground Tours, 169, 219
Union Bay Cafe, 91
Union Square Grill, 92, 119
Union Station, 415
University Book Store, 190, 198, 253
University District, 188, 228
University Inn, 333
University of Washington, 188, 411
University of Washington School of Drama, 160
University of Washington Waterfront Activities Center, 215, 382
University Seafood & Poultry, 305
Uno/Duo, 239
Uptown Bakery, 136
Uptown Cinemas, 180
Uptown Espresso Bar, 136

The Urban Bakery, 136
Urban Outfitters, 240
Uwajimaya, 174, 269

**V**

Varsity, 152
Vashon Island, 363
Velvet Elvis, 157
Veneto's, 136
Victor Steinbrueck Park, 167, 209
Victor's, 129
Victoria's Secret, 293
Victoria, BC, 221, 365
Video Isle, 315
Videophile Inc., 315
Viet My, 92
Viet Wah, 175, 269
Villa Heidelberg, 335
Village Green Perennial Nursery, 275
Village Maternity, 307
Vintage Voola, 317
The Virginia Inn, 119
Virginia's Antiques, 368
Vito's, 119
Vogue, 129
Volunteer Park, 178, 209
Vox Populi, 145

**W**

Waldo's, 129
Walking tours, 219
Wall of Sound, 303
Wallaby Station, 308
Warren Magnuson Park, 389
Warshal's, 256, 300
Warwick Hotel, 330
Washington Park Arboretum, 209, 214, 382, 388
Washington State Convention and Trade Center, 164, 415
Washington State Ferries, 343, 404
Waterfall Gardens, 171, 209
Waterfront, 171, 227
Waterfront Park, 210
Waters, 93
Waverly Park, 199
WE Hats, 231
Weathered Wall, 129
The Weaving Works, 271
Wedgwood Alehouse, 119
Wedgwood Cycle, 300, 384
The Weed Lady, 281
Welcome Supermarket, 270
The Well Made Bed, 287

Wells-Medina Nursery, 275
Wessel and Lieberman Booksellers, 254
West Blakely Inn, 340
West Marine Products, 300
West Seattle Nursery, 275
WestCoast Bellevue, 337
WestCoast Camlin, 330
WestCoast Plaza Park Suites, 330
WestCoast Roosevelt, 331
WestCoast Sea-Tac, 339
WestCoast Vance, 331
Westin Hotel, 331
Westlake Center, 164, 404
What's That?, 240
Whidbey Island, 368
Wicker Design Antiques, 234
Wide World Books and Maps, 254
Wild Ginger, 93, 120, 223
Wild Rose Tavern, 120
Wiley's Waterski Shop, 301
William Traver Gallery, 145
The Williams House, 335
Williams-Sonoma, 292
Windsurfing, 395
Winery tours, 193
Wing Luke Asian Museum, 149, 174
Wood Shop Toys, 170, 313
Woodinville, 195, 222
Woodland Park, 210
Woodland Park Zoo, 186, 221
Woodmark Hotel, 338
Woodside/Braseth Galleries, 145
The Woolly Mammoth, 307
World Dance, 151
Wright Brothers Cycle Works, 301
Wrinkled Bohemia, 317
Wyndham Garden, 340

**XYZ**

Yanni's Lakeside Cafe, 94
Yarn Shop in Old Bellevue, 271
Yarrow Bay Grill and Beach Cafe, 94, 201
Ye Olde Curiosity Shop, 281
Young Flowers, 276
Your Hidden Closet, 308
Zanadia, 287
Zeek's Pizza, 94
Zula, 95

# Seattle Best Places

## REPORT FORM

Based on my personal experience, I wish to nominate the following restaurant, place of lodging, shop, nightspot, sight, or other as a "Best Place"; or confirm/correct/disagree with the current review.

_____

_____

_____

_____

_____

Please include address and telephone number of establishment, if convenient.

## REPORT:

Please describe food, service, style, comfort, value, date of visit, and other aspects of your experience; continue on the other side if necessary.

_____

_____

_____

_____

_____

_____

_____

I am not concerned, directly or indirectly, with the management or ownership of this establishment.

Signed _____

Address _____

_____

_____

Phone Number _____

Date _____

Send to: *Seattle Best Places*
615 Second Avenue, Suite 260
Seattle, WA 98104

# We Stand by Our Reviews

Sasquatch Books is proud of Seattle Best Places. Our editors and contributors go to great lengths and expense to ensure that all of the reviews are accurate, up-to-date, and as honest as possible. If we have disappointed you, please accept our apologies; however, if the seventh edition of Seattle Best Places has seriously misled you, Sasquatch Books would like to refund your purchase price. To receive your refund:

1) Tell us where you purchased your book and return the book to: Satisfaction Guaranteed, Sasquatch Books, 615 Second Avenue, Suite 260, Seattle, WA 98104.

2) Enclose the original restaurant or hotel receipt from the establishment in question, including date of visit.

3) Write a full explanation of your stay or meal and how *Seattle Best Places* misled you.

4) Include your name, address, and phone number.

Refund is valid only while the seventh edition of *Seattle Best Places* is in print. If the ownership of the establishment has changed since publication, Sasquatch Books cannot be held responsible. Postage and tax on the returned book is your responsibility. Please allow four weeks for processing.